hRac

D1552271

MAY - - 2018

Ghosts, Spirits, and Psychics

Ghosts, Spirits, and Psychics

The Paranormal from Alchemy to Zombies

MATT CARDIN, EDITOR

ABC-CLIO™

An Imprint of ABC-CLIO, LLC
Santa Barbara, California • Denver, Colorado

Library of Congress Cataloging-in-Publication Data

Ghosts, spirits, and psychics : the paranormal from alchemy to zombies / Matt Cardin, editor.—First Edition.
    pages cm
 Includes bibliographical references and index.
  ISBN 978-1-61069-683-8 (hardback : alk. paper)—ISBN 978-1-61069-684-5 (ebook)
 1. Parapsychology—Dictionaries. 2. Occultism—Dictionaries. I. Cardin, Matt, editor.
 BF1025.G46 2015
 130.3—dc23   2015010867

ISBN: 978-1-61069-683-8
EISBN: 978-1-61069-684-5

19 18 17 16 15   1 2 3 4 5

This book is also available on the World Wide Web as an eBook.
Visit www.abc-clio.com for details.

ABC-CLIO, LLC
130 Cremona Drive, P.O. Box 1911
Santa Barbara, California 93116–1911

This book is printed on acid-free paper ∞

Manufactured in the United States of America

Contents

Guide to Related Topics

PARAPSYCHOLOGY AND PSYCHICAL RESEARCH

Extrasensory Perception (ESP)
Ganzfeld Technique, The
Paranormal
Parapsychology

Pseudoscience
Psychical Research
Sheep-Goat Effect

PSI, HEALING, AND OTHER PARANORMAL POWERS

Clairvoyance
Healing, Psychic and Spiritual
Precognition
Prophecy
Psi
Psychic Archaeology

Psychokinesis (PK)
Remote Viewing
Siddhis
Telepathic Hypnosis
Telepathy
Thoughtography

SPIRITUALISM, MEDIUMSHIP, SÉANCES, AND CHANNELING

Automatic Writing
Channeling
Ectoplasm
Mediumship

Séance
Spiritism
Spiritualism

GHOSTS, POLTERGEISTS, APPARITIONS, AND HAUNTINGS

Apparitions
Discarnate Entity
Enfield Poltergeist
Ghosts

Haunting
Poltergeist
Vampires and Poltergeists
Witches and Poltergeists

STRANGE PHENOMENA AND EXTRAORDINARY EXPERIENCES

Abduction Experience
Animals and the Paranormal
Bilocation
Doppelgänger
Electronic Voice Phenomenon (EVP)
Fortean Phenomena
Near-Death Experience (NDE)

Out-of-Body Experience (OBE)
Past-Life Readings
Past-Life Regression
Sleep Paralysis
Synchronicity
UFO

RELIGION, MYSTICISM, AND THE PARANORMAL

Angels
Exorcism
Imaginal
Miracles
Mystical Experience
Possession

Reincarnation
Religion and the Paranormal
Science of Mysticism
Shamanism
Survival after Death

PSYCHOLOGY, NEUROLOGY, AND THE PARANORMAL

Anomalistic Psychology
Consciousness
Drugs and the Paranormal
Hallucinations
Hypnagogic State

Lucid Dreams
Mesmerism
Paranormal Dreams
Transpersonal Psychology
Unconscious Mind

MAGIC, DIVINATION, AND OCCULTISM

Akashic Records
Alchemy
Astral Plane
Astrology
Aura
Demonology
Divination
New Age

Occultism
Ouija Board
Ritual Magic
Scrying
Tarot
Theosophy
Witchcraft
Zombies

PARANORMAL ART, LITERATURE, AND MEDIA

Art, Creativity, and the Paranormal
Fate Magazine
Kirlian Photography
Paranormal in Literature

Paranormal in Movies
Paranormal on Television
Spirit Photography

BIOGRAPHIES

ORGANIZATIONS AND INSTITUTIONS

Preface

This book is a sweeping compendium of information about the paranormal—including information about the very history and meaning of "paranormal" itself as a word and a concept. In more than 120 entries written by leading experts from various backgrounds (scientists, psychologists, historians, religion scholars, literary scholars, and more), *Ghosts, Spirits, and Psychics* presents a wealth of knowledge on such topics as:

- psychic and paranormal powers (telepathy, psychokinesis, precognition, clairvoyance, remote viewing, and more)
- ghosts, poltergeists, apparitions, and hauntings
- Spiritualism, mediumship, séances, and channeling
- anomalous and extraordinary experiences (near-death experiences, out-of-body experiences, abduction experiences, and more)
- psychology, neurology, and the paranormal (mesmerism, hallucinations, dreams, drugs and the paranormal, and more)
- religion and the paranormal (miracles, mystical experiences, reincarnation, possession, exorcism, shamanism, and more)
- strange phenomena (UFOs, Fortean phenomena, etc.)
- magic, alchemy, divination, and the occult
- the fields of formal parapsychological and psychical research, including important institutions, organizations, publications, and schools of thought
- important scientists, scholars, authors, philosophers, psychologists, mystics, and others who have contributed to the history and study of the paranormal
- skeptical critiques of paranormal beliefs and claims
- the evolution of cultural attitudes toward the paranormal
- the history of the paranormal in literature, movies, and television

The presentation is designed to be helpful and useful to both casual and more serious readers, including those who want to read the book in its entirety and those who just want to look up specific entries of interest. Both approaches are aided by various features, including:

- Two tables of contents, one alphabetical and the other topical
- A master timeline of the paranormal—one of the most comprehensive ever created, extending from prehistory to the present—that chronologically organizes and illuminates the information in the entries as well as presenting additional facts and dates of significance
- Nearly 50 sidebars, including several subject-specific minitimelines and several excerpts from significant books and texts in the history of the paranormal
- A general bibliography and guide to further valuable reading, grouped by topics for extra usefulness
- A comprehensive index to general subjects covered in the book

Aimed at high school students, college students, and general readers, *Ghosts, Spirits, and Psychics* provides reliable information on the various phenomena, experiences, encounters, and ideas that make up the fascinating and controversial field of the paranormal, as well as the people, institutions, and organizations that have devoted themselves to studying it, promoting it, attacking it, debunking it, and—sometimes—being transformed by it.

Acknowledgments

A complex project like this one doesn't come to fruition without substantial help and input from many different people. During the writing and creation of *Ghosts, Spirits, and Psychics*, several individuals provided substantial help with the massive amount of networking that was required to assemble such an excellent group of contributors. Others helped by suggesting entries to ensure breadth of coverage. Still others reviewed written content (such as the Master Timeline and the Introduction) and offered valuable advice and feedback. The editor would like to acknowledge and thank the following people for their efforts in these areas:

Jeffrey Kripal, Christopher Laursen, George Hansen, Stephan Schwartz, Darryl Caterine, Roger Luckhurst, David Luke, B. D. Mitchell, James Matlock, Philip Deslippe, Joel Gruber, Kevin Whitesides, Jack Hunter, Vikas Malhotra, Matt Staggs, Gary Baddeley, Michael Kinsella, Gordon Melton, Ryan Hurd, Tom Ruffles, Angela Voss, Cal Cooper, Simon Sherwood, Shannon Taggart, Richard Broughton, Caroline Watt, Imants Baruss, and Russell Targ.

Additional thanks go out to each and all of the contributors for their investment of time and effort and for their generosity in sharing their expertise and insight.

Introduction

As this book goes to press, the idea of the paranormal is ubiquitous and inescapable in American culture. It is entrenched in Britain, Europe, and most other parts of the world as well. From one point of view this is hardly an earth-shattering observation, since, depending on how one frames the parameters of the term "paranormal," the subject has occupied a central place in every culture throughout history, with religious, spiritual, magical, and occult beliefs and practices playing a key role in shaping the evolution of peoples and nations.

That said, the particulars of the present situation are striking. One of the most immediate areas where the current paranormal fixation can be seen is popular entertainment, which, in an age of accelerated evolution in communication forms and technologies, has begun to appear positively haunted. In the early 21st century, screens and store shelves everywhere are teeming with movies, novels, games, and television shows about ghosts and ghost hunters, hauntings, demons, vampires, zombies, exorcisms, psychic powers, and more. One finds it ever more difficult to disagree with Victoria Nelson's thesis in *The Secret Life of Puppets* that some kind of Platonic transcendental longing for the mystical, the esoteric, and the occult is using the vehicle of pop culture, and especially the genres of horror, science fiction, and fantasy, as a kind of "back door" to sneak in and subvert or counterbalance the ideals of a culture and a civilization that is committed on a conscious level to pursuing and embodying the Aristotelian ideals of logic, order, and scientific rationality. In short, weird things speak loudly through our popular culture.

But entertainment is hardly the only area where this phenomenon is visible. It affects intellectual culture as well, and in this realm the presence of paranormal ideas is far more controversial. To summarize just one notable recent development, in April and May 2013 a controversy erupted over the decision by TED, the globally prominent ideas conference, to delete two TEDx talks from its main repository, one of them by British author Graham Hancock and the other by British author and biologist Rupert Sheldrake. Both talks focused on questions about the limits of scientific materialism, the possible nonlocal nature of consciousness, and the possible reality of paranormal or paranormal-like phenomena. TED also pulled its license from a long-planned TEDx conference in Hollywood in April 2013 because of the conference's focus on paranormal phenomena such as remote viewing. The resulting row over both decisions, which saw a flood of online reactions both attacking and defending TED's actions, became a kind of lightning rod for questions about the boundaries drawn around what is considered to be legitimate science and the possibility that the cultural dominance of scientific materialism may be undergoing an evolutionary shift.

Around the same time, Wikipedia became an ideological battleground as a group founded in 2010 and calling itself Guerrilla Skeptics pursued its avowed mission to "improve skeptical content" on the reference website through a sustained campaign of monitoring and editing articles to make them reflect the skeptical point of view. These involved articles on parapsychology and the paranormal (including, significantly, Sheldrake's biography), which became a collective case study in the so-called "edit wars" that afflict Wikipedia. In 2013 the University of Oxford and three other institutions conducted a formal study of Wikipedia articles on 10 different language versions of the site to discover which ones are most subject to these kinds of conflicting editorial interventions. Among the top 10 controversial topics hailing from those different versions, along with a predictable roster of articles on various hot-button religious, political, and historical matters were entries on telepathy, UFOs, and psychotronics (i.e., psychic warfare).

Meanwhile, the paranormal aspects of religion—or, to use the descriptor that was more common in an earlier era, the *supernatural* aspects of religion—have likewise come to the fore in an ongoing development that not only flies in the face of centuries' worth of secularist claims about the supposedly inevitable decline of religious belief, but also embarrasses the exponents and adherents of many first-world religions that have sought to accommodate themselves to a largely secular cultural environment by, among other things, jettisoning, downplaying, or watering down the supernatural aspects of their theologies and traditions. For example, in the past two decades the Roman Catholic Church has conspicuously revived and reinforced its program of training and placing exorcists around the world, with Pope Benedict XVI and Pope Francis both publicly emphasizing the need to combat what they describe as a very real presence of demonic evil in the world. A Protestant counterpart to this trend is highly visible in the continued popularity of exorcism and the general belief in miracles among the Pentecostal, Charismatic, and even evangelical subcultures. These mainstream religious engagements with the paranormal are paralleled by the ongoing prominence of Scientology—the most overtly paranormal of all religions—in Western media and the dramatic penetration of formerly marginal spiritual and religious ideas and practices into mainstream consciousness, as in, for example, the rise of neo-shamanism with its focus on altered states of consciousness accompanied by entity encounters and the acquisition of paranormal knowledge and powers. And all the while, repeated polls and surveys show that huge proportions of Americans and Britons continue to express a belief in God, angels, demons, heaven, hell, ghosts, hauntings, ESP, UFOs, and the like.

In all of these areas and more, matters that should have been consigned long ago to the disreputable dustbin of superstition and pseudoscience according to the dominant establishment narrative of Western cultural progress have, in fact, gained a new cultural currency. For anyone who really pays attention, this represents a fascinating opportunity to ask questions and come to terms with a resurgent fact of human thought and experience.

It also presents an interesting object lesson in the persistence of the paranormal. From a historical perspective the upshot of this development is that in recent years the paranormal has begun to assume a cultural prominence in the West that recalls the explosion of popular interest in psychic powers, mystical religion, and altered states of consciousness that occurred during the counterculture years of the 1960s and 1970s, and before that, the similarly expansive interest in ghosts, hauntings, séances, psychical research, and spirit communication that characterized American, British, and European cultures in the late 19th and early 20th centuries. As in those periods, the current resurgence of interest in paranormal matters has spawned a cultural conversation that involves questions about the boundaries of science, the nature of mind and personality, the clash between materialism and supernaturalism, the relationship between religion and the paranormal, and the validity of what passes for mainstream, conventional, or orthodox opinion in all of these areas.

To make sense of it all, it is necessary to recognize that deeply thoughtful and highly trained people—scientists, philosophers, psychologists, cultural historians, literary scholars, authors, journalists, filmmakers, and more—have contributed to this conversation in a multitude of ways. Their ideas have met with varying receptions, and this shifting cultural status of the paranormal is one of the subject's most interesting and important aspects. People everywhere have witnessed and experienced strange phenomena throughout history, but it was not until the 19th century that the study of these things became a formal subject of academic and scientific investigation on a large scale. In those early days, such studies went under the name of *psychical research* and were often carried out by eminent mainstream scientists and scholars who investigated reports of ghosts, hauntings, precognitive dreams, the purported powers of spirit mediums, and so on. The field also attracted important artists and authors, and for a time during the heyday of psychical research the idea of the paranormal carried a tentative air of seriousness and semi-respectability ("tentative" because it never fully transcended its status as nonsense and pseudoscience in the eyes of vocal establishment figures who criticized it).

Psychical research, although it used some quantitative method—for instance, by performing statistical analyses of reports of paranormal phenomena—was not a hard science, and it was not until the 1930s that J. B. Rhine did his pioneering work at Duke University that transformed paranormal studies into a laboratory science under the name of parapsychology. All through the middle decades of the 20th century, parapsychology and its associated practices and paraphernalia—most famously, experiments that involved people staring at cards bearing images of squares, circles, crosses, stars, and wavy lines while others tried to "see" those symbols telepathically—provided the dominant image of the paranormal in the popular imagination. Meanwhile, the more "traditional" subfields of ghost studies and related approaches continued as well (along with, notably, the broader field of Fortean studies as advanced in the works of John Keel and Jacques Vallée, for example). The Israeli-born psychic Uri Geller became a celebrity on American and European television for his spectacular demonstrations of apparent psychic powers. Rumors swirled and books were published about investigations into psychic abilities being funded by the U.S. and Soviet governments for use in warfare and espionage. Culturally speaking, this stage of modern paranormal history may have reached its climax in 1984 when the movie *Ghostbusters*, with its giddy comedic fusion of ghost hunting and lab-based parapsychology, became an international hit and popularized more widely than ever before Zener cards, the term "ectoplasm," and other items from the repertoire of paranormal research.

During the final decade of the 20th century and the early decades of the 21st, yet another evolutionary mutation in paranormal studies became evident, and that is where the field stands as this book is published. Psychical research and the institutions associated with it—most prominently the Society for Psychical Research in England—still exist, but their status is much diminished since the glory days of a century ago. Parapsychology still exists and maintains a limited academic and cultural presence, with the Parapsychological Association, a professional association founded in 1957, remaining active. But parapsychology's presence began to diminish significantly in the 1990s, especially in America, while a new era of paranormal studies was heralded by the work of a number of individuals whose views represent a novel direction.

Among the most prominent of these is religions scholar Jeffrey Kripal, chair of the religious studies department at Rice University. From this position of mainstream respectability, Kripal has spoken and written voluminously about paranormal matters not merely in a cautiously or detachedly scholarly manner free of personal commitment, but in a way that makes clear his personal position that paranormal and anomalous events and experiences are *real* in some sense. In his 2010 book *Authors of the Impossible: The Paranormal and the Sacred*—published by University of Chicago Press—he established the paranormal as a viable category within religious studies. In 2011's *Mutants and Mystics: Science Fiction Comics, Superheroes and the Paranormal*, from the same press, he interpreted American pop culture's long-running science fiction and superhero tropes as cultural myths referencing authentic intuitions of possible paranormal powers. In 2014's *Comparing Religions*, from the academic publisher Wiley-Blackwell, he created the first academic textbook of comparative religion to include an entire chapter on the paranormal, thus placing the paranormal in its various manifestations on a level equal with the more traditionally conceived and classified world religious traditions.

Kripal's basic position on the paranormal is that the laboratory approach of parapsychology, while interesting and valuable in some ways, may actually miss—systematically, as a built-in outcome of its basic outlook and method—the subject's most salient aspects. The paranormal, he argues, presents itself not as objective

effects or outcomes to be measured instrumentally and subjected to statistical analysis, but as something intimately and intrinsically bound up with our subjectivity. Paranormal things have undeniably intense, and even personally or culturally
transformative, meanings. They enable us to address metaphysical and existential
questions. They demonstrate that there is more to our world and universe than
can be revealed through materialism. They signify all kinds of speculative possibilities and potentials. They are phenomena that are both objective and subjective
in nature; they occur somewhere between these poles. In other words, Kripal approaches the paranormal as a realm of living narrative, where the key to understanding is not measurement but meaning.

Nor is he alone in this. A new focus that brings cultural studies to bear on the
paranormal has emerged on many fronts, and this is combined with an attitude that
rejects both sides of the unproductive skepticism versus believerism standoff. This
multidisciplinary approach deeply considers the subjectively situated role and position of the observers of paranormal phenomena. George Hansen, for instance, in his
2002 book *The Trickster and the Paranormal* draws on anthropology, literary criticism,
psychology, sociology, folklore studies, semiotics, religious studies, and other interpretive fields and frameworks to complement his personal experiences as a laboratory parapsychologist in laying out a vision of the paranormal as elusive, slippery, and
tricky—much like the archetypal trickster figure of folklore and mythology—that
inherently evades and dissolves the boundaries of the social, psychological, scientific, cultural, linguistic, and other structures by which we try to impose a rational and
logical order upon the world and our experience of it. A related approach shows up
in *Paranthropology: Journal of Anthropological Approaches to the Paranormal*, founded
in 2010, which has an impressive cross-disciplinary group of scholars on its editorial
board and is "devoted to the promotion of social-scientific approaches to the study of
paranormal experiences, beliefs, and phenomena in all of their varied guises." Many
more people and publications—far too many to be covered in a brief space—could
be noted besides these, all of them working out this new direction that moves away
from parapsychology's focus on the search for scientifically measurable and replicable results in favor of taking a more humanistic and multidisciplinary approach
to understanding the paranormal. They refuse the skeptic/believer dichotomy, remaining open to the possibility of the paranormal in a way that is antithetical to the
dominant intellectual culture, which continues to relegate the whole subject *en masse*
to the gutter status of what some are fond of calling "woo": an intellectual dumping
ground of silliness, gullibility, and pseudoscience, where cranks and hoaxers try to
convince people to buy into false beliefs that more serious and respectable thinkers
reject as absurd.

According to the emerging new paradigm, this conventional skeptical position
is ideologically motivated and epistemologically blinkered by its (mostly implicit
and unexamined) commitment to scientific materialism. Theorists in this new vein
argue that, far from being a revealed result or demonstrated reality about the way
things really are, scientific materialism is the result of applying a specific mental

and philosophical filter to the totality of experience. This filter is made up of methodological naturalism, the scientific method in its various iterations, and an assortment of highly inflected sociocultural motivations, biases, and assumptions stemming from the late Renaissance and, especially, the Enlightenment. Nor is this filter applied to some existing field of phenomena that presents itself spontaneously as "evidence," since what counts as "evidence" in the first place is determined by the filter itself. Everything else is screened out and effectively hidden from awareness by those who choose to construct their view of reality based on the results of, and from within the bubble of, this single philosophical filter. With this or something like it in mind, the proponents of the new multidisciplinary paradigm advocate bringing various aspects of cultural studies to bear on the matter of anomalous and paranormal experiences as a way of acknowledging, engaging with, and perhaps transcending what they view as an arbitrary and destructive presuppositional bias that accompanies not only the dogmatic skeptical position but perhaps the practice of laboratory parapsychology as well. The sciences, as they stand, have accomplished much. They could advance further by coming to terms with controversial, misunderstood things that occur between objective and subjective realities.

That is where things stand today. If the reader takes away only a single idea from *Ghosts, Spirits, and Psychics*, it should be that the paranormal—far from being just a trivial or peripheral subject associated mainly with gullible "true believers" and adolescent entertainment (although much of it is indeed associated with these)—is a major force in the world that has inspired art, literature, and religion; aroused fascination and fear; driven the evolution of science; and shaped entire cultures and societies. Nor is this purely a matter of the past; the paranormal remains active today. This is the broad and deep context within which the current wave of interest in the subject is unfolding. Through the background presented in these pages, we can work towards an intelligent understanding of how we can better regard the paranormal in our collective and individual lives and discover what it means, in pluralistic ways, to all of us. This book represents an attempt to contribute something toward opening rather than narrowing perspectives on the paranormal so that we can locate ourselves on the map between where we have been and where we are heading.

Chronology

ca. 3000–2000 BCE	The earliest written records of ghosts are produced in Sumer.
ca. 1000 BCE	The first written mention of a lucid dream appears in the Upanishads.
ca. 440 BCE	Herodotus offers the first written description of what sounds like remote viewing in Book I of his *Histories*.
400 BCE	Lucid dreaming is mentioned in the yoga sutras of Patanjali.
ca. 380 BCE	Plato offers what may be the first written description of a near-death experience in *The Republic*.
44 BCE	The Roman orator Cicero writes *On Divination*, a two-volume dialogue on the subject in which he ultimately expresses skepticism and judges divinatory practices to be based on superstition.
480	Constance de Lyon writes one of the earliest poltergeist accounts.
1127	The earliest English account of a black dog apparition is written, beginning a trend of similar testimonials that continues into the present day.
ca. 1400	Tarot cards are invented in northern Italy.
1484	Pope Innocent VIII condemns witchcraft and authorizes its persecution.
1500–1700	Various European publications attempt to categorize and classify ghosts.
1521	Martin Luther becomes one of the first to use the term "poltergeist" in a written account of strange paranormal disturbances.
1531	A Marian apparition appears to Juan Diego on a hill in Tepeyac near Mexico City, prompting the construction of the Basilica of Our Lady of Guadalupe.

1584	Reginald Scot publishes *The Discoverie of Witchcraft*, putting forth a skeptical and disapproving position on both medieval witchcraft and those who prosecute it.
1597	King James publishes his demonology and witch-hunting manual *Daemonologie*.
1603	The ghost of Hamlet's father is unleashed on world stages by Shakespeare.
1668	Joseph Glanvill publishes *A Blow at Modern Sadducism*, followed in 1681 by *Saducismus Triumphatus*, on witchcraft and ghosts, including the Drummer of Tedworth poltergeist from 1662–1663.
1692–1693	The Salem Witch Trials lead to 20 executions in colonial Massachusetts. The French stonemason Jacques Aymar-Vernay rises to fame for his skills as a dowser; when invited by the Prince de Condé to submit his skills to the test, he fails.
1693	Cotton Mather publishes *Wonders of the Invisible World*, laying out a vision of the world as menaced by demons and witches.
1735	The passing of the Witchcraft Act in Britain makes it a crime to claim that anyone is a witch or has magical powers.
1743	Emanuel Swedenborg begins to experience trance visions filled with divine communications, giving rise to his influential spiritual-paranormal theology.
1748	Scottish philosopher David Hume argues against belief in miracles in "On Miracles," a section of his *An Enquiry Concerning Understanding*.
1759	While visiting Gothenburg, Swedenborg accurately describes a fire that had broken out several hundred miles away in Stockholm.
1762–1764	The Cock Lane ghost in London attracts mass publicity and a defamation scandal.
1770s	Franz Anton Mesmer develops animal magnetism, later renamed mesmerism, in Vienna and Paris.
1784	King Louis XVI commissions the French Academy of Sciences to investigate Mesmer and animal magnetism; they appoint a committee that includes Antoine Lavoisier, Paris mayor Jean Bailly, Dr. Joseph Guillotin, and

	Benjamin Franklin; the committee's report is negative and destroys Mesmer's reputation in France.
1785	Mesmer's student, the Marquis de Puységur, records the first observations of supernatural phenomena associated with mesmeric trance.
1796	Historian James Petit Andrew introduces the term "pseudoscience," applying it to alchemy.
1804	Thomas Jefferson completes an early version of the so-called "Jefferson Bible," an abridgement of the four New Testament gospels that brings them into line with Enlightenment ideas of scientific reality and reasonableness by removing all references to miracles and the supernatural.
1817–1820	The controversial Bell Witch haunting takes place in Tennessee, ending with the deal of John Bell.
1832	Scottish physicist Sir David Brewster publishes *Letters on Natural Magic*, an attack on magic and superstition in the name of science.
ca. 1836	Charles Poyen Saint Sauveur brings mesmerism to America.
1838	The practice of mesmerism in the wards of University College Hospital in London leads to the resignation of Professor John Elliotson. The first published reference to a zombie in the United States appears in the short story "The Unknown Painter."
1840	In England, James Braid modifies mesmerism to lay the foundations of modern hypnotism.
1843	The first issue of *Zoist*, the leading journal of mesmerism, is published. Charles Dickens publishes the ghost story *A Christmas Carol*.
1848	Modern Spiritualism is launched from the preternatural rappings experienced by Kate and Maggie Fox in Hydesville, New York, on March 31. Catherine Crowe introduces the word "poltergeist" into English with her book *The Night-Side of Nature*.
1849	Margaret Fox gives the first public demonstration of mediumship in Rochester, New York.
1850s–1860s	Professional mediums spread across America, Britain, and Europe. American newspapers are filled with stories of séances and spirit communications.

1851	The first meeting of the New York Circle, a group of prominent men and women interested in spiritualistic phenomena, is convened in November. The Ghost Club Society is formed at Cambridge University.
1852	A number of Harvard faculty members give their signature to a manifesto titled "A Modern Wonder," attesting to the veracity of the physical mediumship of the celebrated medium Daniel Dunglas Home.
1853	Michael Faraday publishes the results of his experiments to prove that "table turning" at séances is caused by the participants' ideomotor (unconscious) action. Hippolyte Léon Denizard Rivail, better known by the pen name Allen Kardec, introduces the planchette as a device for taking dictation from spirits.
1855	Leading Spiritualist medium Daniel Dunglas Home leaps to fame in Europe with his séances; he becomes a highly respected figure, although he is mocked by Robert Browning in his long 1864 poem, "Mr. Sludge, The Medium."
1856	Eliphas Levi, the French ritual magician, publishes his key work *Transcendental Magic: Its Doctrine and Ritual* in Paris.
1860	Robert Dale Owen, a leading radical and Spiritualist convert in America, publishes *Footfalls on the Boundary of Another World*.
1861	Eliphas Levi visits Lord Bulwer-Lytton in London and conducts magical workings, helping to establish a revival of magic in England.
1857	Kardec publishes *The Spirits' Book*, one of the founding texts of Spiritism.
1858	Bernadette Soubirous sees a Marian apparition in a grotto at Lourdes, France, which leads to her canonization as a Catholic saint and mass pilgrimages to the site.
1862	In London, The Ghost Club is founded, making it the longest standing paranormal investigative organization in the world, counting among its members writer Charles Dickens and actor Peter Cushing.
1867	The Marquis d'Hervey de Saint-Denys becomes the first to use the term "lucid dream" (French: *rêve lucide*) in *Dreams and the Ways to Direct Them: Practical Observations*.

1871	William Crookes, a leading chemist, announces the discovery of a new form of energy, "psychic force," which he measures in experiments with women mediums.
1872	Victoria Woodhull—stockbroker, suffragette, free love advocate, and spiritual medium—runs as the first female candidate for President of the United States.
1873	The British National Association of Spiritualists is founded in London.
1874	Alfred Russel Wallace, co-founder of evolutionary theory with Charles Darwin, publicly announces his conversion to Spiritualism in his two-part essay "A Defence of Spiritualism."
1875	The Theosophical Society is founded. The Psychological Society of Great Britain is founded, representing the first attempt to shift the language of Spiritualism into a language of psychology. William Mumler publishes *The Personal Experiences of William H. Mumler in Spirit Photography*.
1876	Biologist Edwin Ray Lankester and medical doctor Horatio Donkin prosecute leading Spiritualist Henry Slade in the staging of a "science vs. religion" case.
1879	The Cassadaga Lake Free Association—the original name for today's Lily Dale Assembly—is founded as a Spiritualist camp in New York.
1880	After years of producing materialized spirits that convinced many people, including William Crookes, medium Florence Cook is caught committing fraud.
1882	The Society for Psychical Research (SPR) is founded in London, with Cambridge philosopher Henry Sidgwick as its first president. The London Ghost Club, a gentleman's private club devoted to relating "real" ghost stories, is founded by leading Spiritualist Rev. Stainton Moses and occultist A. A. Watts as a revitalization of the 1862 club (although this is not initially acknowledged). Frederic Myers introduces the term "telepathy."
1884	The SPR publishes the first issue of the *Journal of the Society for Psychical Research*. A schism develops between the SPR and Spiritualism over the former's neutral scientific stance toward psychical matters. The College of Psychic Studies is founded in London. Sarah Winchester purchases a house in California and continually

	adds a series of rooms to it over 38 years, today known as the Winchester Mystery House.
1884–1885	The SPR investigates the mediumship of Leonora Piper.
1885	The American Society for Psychical Research (ASPR) is founded as a sister organization to the Society for Psychical Research. The SPR investigates the Theosophical Society and concludes that it is based on fraud.
1886	The SPR publishes *Phantasms of the Living*.
1888	Kate and Maggie Fox confess that the 1848 rappings were fraudulent; Kate later recants. The Hermetic Order of the Golden Dawn is founded. Madame Blavatsky publishes *The Secret Doctrine*.
1889	The SPR sends Richard Hodgson to Boston to revive the struggling ASPR.
1889	The word "parapsychologie" is coined by German philosopher Max Dessoir. Europe's preeminent neurologist, Jean-Martin Charcot, delivers a lecture titled "Spiritualism and Hysteria" in which he ascribes belief in spirits to degenerative mental illness.
1890	The Ouija board is patented. Russian psychical researcher Alexander D. Aksakof introduces the term "telekinesis."
1891	Florence Maryat publishes *There Is No Death*, which becomes one of the bestselling books on Spiritualism. Controversial atheist Annie Besant announces she has converted to Theosophy. Madame Blavatsky dies in London; Besant becomes the leading advocate of the Theosophical Society.
1893	The National Spiritualists' Association is founded in America. Celebrated journalist and newspaper proprietor W. T. Stead begins publishing the quarterly occult journal *Borderland* after his conversion to Spiritualism. In Romania the writer Bogdan Petriceicu Hasdeu and Dr. Constantin Istrati conduct one of the earliest documented telepathic photography experiments.
1894	The SPR publishes its pioneering Census of Hallucinations. Frederic Myers introduces the term "precognition." French physiologist and future Nobel Prize winner Charles Richet coins the term "ectoplasm."

1895	The SPR investigates the Eusapia Palladino, resulting in a highly critical report that attributes her apparent mediumistic powers to clever trickery.
1898	Ada Goodrich Freer and the Marquis of Bute publish *The Haunting of B—House*, a "psychical research" investigation of a Scottish haunting; there is a controversy in *The Times* over the evidence, and the book later forms the basis for Shirley Jackson's celebrated ghost novel *The Haunting of Hill House*. Henry James publishes the ghost story *The Turn of the Screw*.
1899	Sigmund Freud publishes *The Interpretation of Dreams*.
1900	French astronomer Camille Flammarion begins publishing on his psychical research, including works on life after death and haunted houses.
1901	The Society for Psychical Research begins the cross-correspondences, a three-decade-long experiment with mediums to seek proof of survival after death.
ca. 1901–1910	The birth of Pentecostal Christianity with its emphasis on miraculous manifestations reignites an old Christian debate about the "cessation of charismata"—the position that the age of miracles has now ended.
1902	William James publishes *The Varieties of Religious Experience*.
1903	Frederic Myers's *Human Personality and Its Survival of Bodily Death* is posthumously published.
1905	Richard Hodgson dies unexpectedly, essentially shutting down the ASPR in Boston.
1907	The ASPR is reformed in New York under James Hyslop and begins publication of the *Journal of the American Society for Psychical Research*. W. T. Stead sets up "Julia's Bureau," a Spiritualist contact service for the grieving to contact their deceased loved ones. American psychical researcher Hereward Carrington begins a long writing career with his book *The Physical Phenomena of Spiritualism*.
1909	The Waite tarot deck with paintings by Pamela Colman-Smith is published, becoming the most popular modern deck.
1910	Psychology professor Tomokichi Fukurai at the Imperial University in Tokyo introduces the term "Thoughtography."

1912	Carl Jung publishes *Psychology of the Unconsciousness*, which soon results in the schism between him and his teacher, Sigmund Freud. American housewife Pearl Curran begins communicating with the spirit "Patience Worth" through a Ouija board, resulting in the writing of many novels, stories, and poems. W. T. Stead dies on the *Titanic*; Spiritualists claim that his spirit communicates the news of the ship's sinking faster than the telegraphs.
1913	Fukurai publishes *Clairvoyance and Photography*.
1914	German psychiatrist Albert von Schrenck-Notzing documents physical mediumship in his book *The Phenomena of Materialization*. American writer, publisher, and psychical researcher Henry Holt suggests the term "psychokinesis" as a replacement for "telekinesis." American psychical researcher James Hyslop investigates the Doris Fischer possession case. The legend of the angel of Mons, a protective apparition army seen on the front line during the First World War, is circulated through the press.
1915	The term "paranormal" is introduced by psychical researchers to replace the term "supernormal."
1916	Physicist and psychical researcher Sir Oliver Lodge writes *Raymond, or Life and Death*, detailing spirit communications with his son killed in the First World War; it becomes a bestseller and part of a major expansion of Spiritualism.
1917	On October 13 the "Miracle of the Sun" at Fatima, Portugal, is witnessed by between 30,000 and 100,000 people—the climax to a series of Marian apparitions that had begun the previous year.
1918	Frederick Bligh Bond, respected English architect and archaeologist, publishes *The Gate of Remembrance*, about his use of psychical methods to aid in the excavation of Glastonbury Abbey. The French psychical research organization Institut Metaphysique International is formed in Paris, with physician Gustave Geley as its first director.
1919	Albert von Schrenck-Notzing begins studying the mediumistic brothers Rudy and Willi Schneider. Charles Fort publishes *The Book of the Damned*. Sigmund Freud publishes his essay "The Uncanny."

1920	Scottish journalist Lewis Spence publishes *An Encyclopaedia of Occultism*.
1922	Sir Arthur Conan Doyle publishes *The Coming of the Fairies* on the Cottingly Fairies, which years after Doyle's death are admitted to have been fraudulent. Occultist and mystic Dion Fortune sets up the magical group The Fraternity of the Inner Light; her work on magic, Kabbalah, and Christian mysticism exerts a major influence on the later development of Wicca.
1923	The International Spiritualists' Federation is formed. Charles Fort publishes *New Lands*. French physician and psychical researcher Eugene Osty publishes *Supernormal Faculties in Man*. Latvian-American Edward Leedskalnin begins constructing the mysterious structure Coral Castle in Florida, purportedly using psychokinetic abilities.
1924	The American physical medium Mina "Margery" Crandon is investigated by *Scientific American* with a team that includes Harvard psychology professor William McDougall and magician Harry Houdini; a writer for *Scientific American* initially publishes a positive report, but subsequent investigation discredits Margery's mediumistic claims. Gustave Geley publishes *Clairvoyance and Materialization*.
1925	Walter Franklin Prince, the ASPR's Research Officer, leaves the ASPR because of its controversial association with the medium Margery and joins the Boston Society for Psychic Research.
1926	Psychical researcher Harry Price sets up National Laboratory for Psychical Research in London. Sir Arthur Conan Doyle publishes *A History of Spiritualism*.
1929	Aleister Crowley publishes *Magick in Theory and Practice*. French writer Alexandra David-Neel writes on Mahayana Buddhism in *Magic and Mystery in Tibet*, in which she details the concept of the tulpa (thoughtform). William Seabrook publishes *The Magic Island*, whose influential account of "dead men walking in cane fields" popularizes the idea of the zombie in America.
1930	At Duke University, J. B. Rhine begins experiments on ESP using a set of cards with special symbols designed by psychologist Karl Zener. Sir Arthur Conan Doyle publishes *The Edge of the Unknown*, his last published work, surveying various paranormal and psychical

themes. American astrologer Evangeline Adams publishes *Astrology: Your Place among the Stars* and launches a popular radio show about astrology (the first of its kind).

1931   Charles Fort publishes *Lo!* The Fortean Society is founded; Fort himself refuses to join. Edgar Cayce founds the Association for Research and Enlightenment. The Irving family is haunted by a clever, psychic talking mongoose named Gef on the Isle of Man through the early 1930s.

1932   Charles Fort publishes *Wild Talents* (his final book).

1933   Nandor Fodor publishes *An Encyclopaedia of Psychic Science*.

1934   J. B. Rhine publishes *Extra-Sensory Perception*, an account of his research with the Zener cards.

1935   J. B. Rhine founds the Parapsychology Laboratory within the psychology department at Duke University, the first major scientific lab devoted to parapsychology.

1936   Dane Rudhyar publishes *The Astrology of Personality*. A photographer for *Country Life* magazine takes a picture of a ghostly figure on the staircase at Raynham Hall, Norfolk, England. The haunted ocean liner *Queen Mary*, currently docked in Long Beach, California, makes its maiden voyage from New York to France.

1937   The first manufactured ESP cards are produced, allowing Rhine's research to be replicated in other places. The Parapsychology Laboratory publishes the first issue of *The Journal of Parapsychology*. Harry Price takes out a year-long lease to investigate Borley Rectory, making the controversial claim that it is the most haunted house in England.

1938   Zora Neale Hurston publishes *Tell My Horse*, about voodoo in Haiti, which includes the first photograph of a "real" zombie.

1939   Kirlian photography is born from the work of Russian scientists Semyon and Valentina Kirlian. Gerald Gardner and his "New Forest Coven" found the modern-day Wicca religion in series of rituals.

1940   Harry Price publishes *The Most Haunted House in England: Ten Years' Investigation of Borley Rectory*, documenting his stay in Borley Rectory; it arouses considerable controversy and is later debunked and decried as fraudulent by members of the SPR.

1941   The Margery crisis abates, and the Boston Society merges with the ASPR.

1942   Austrian physiologist Bertold Wiesner and British psychologist Robert Thouless introduce the term "psi" to serve as a neutral word for talking about paranormal phenomena. Psychology professor Gertrude Schmeidler becomes the first to demonstrate the "sheep-goat effect" in an apparent psi performance.

1943   The term "out-of-body experience" is introduced by G. N. M. Tyrrell in his book *Apparitions*.

1944   Scottish medium Helen Duncan becomes the last person to be tried and imprisoned under England's Witchcraft Act of 1735; her séances are said to have breached national security via sensitive messages coming from dead military personnel.

1946   The Stanford Research Institute (SRI) is founded by Stanford University.

1947   Rhine's Parapsychology Laboratory is moved out of the Duke psychology department and becomes the Parapsychology Laboratory at Duke University.

1947   On June 24, pilot Kenneth Arnold witnesses nine unknown objects flying in formation near Mount Ranier, Washington; his description of them gives birth to the term "flying saucer." On July 8, the Roswell Army Air Field in New Mexico announces that they recently recovered a crashed "flying disc."

1948   The first issue of *Fate* magazine is published. The United States Air Force launches Project Sign to investigate UFOs. The Edgar Cayce Foundation is established.

1949   *The Washington Post* publishes a story about a real-life exorcism in Mount Ranier, Maryland; it will later inspire William Peter Blatty in his writing of *The Exorcist*. English astrologer Charles Carter founds the Faculty of Astrological Studies in London.

1950   United States Marine Corps pilot Donald Keyhoe publishes *Flying Saucers Are Real*. Parapsychologist Hans Bender founds the Institute for Frontier Areas of Psychology and

Mental Health, Institut für Grenzgebiete der Psychologie und Psychohygiene (IGPP), at Freiburg University in Germany.

1951 Irish-American medium Eileen J. Garrett and American congresswoman Frances Payne Bolton found the Parapsychology Foundation (PF) in New York City.

1952 Carl Jung publishes *Synchronicity: An Acausal Connecting Principle.* Martin Gardner publishes *In the Name of Science,* offering a wide-ranging critique of pseudoscience, superstition, and paranormal beliefs that helps to establish modern scientific skepticism.

1953 The Church of Scientology is founded, becoming the most successful religion promoting paranormal abilities.

1954 A UFO wave is reported over France, later documented in Aimé Michel's influential book *Flying Saucers and the Straight-Line Mystery* (1958).

1956 Morey Bernstein publishes *The Search for Bridey Murphy,* which creates a worldwide sensation with its story of an American housewife who recalls verified details from a past life. Bob Monroe commences studies on enhancing human consciousness that lead to the founding of the Monroe Institute in Virginia.

1957 The Parapsychological Association, an international professional association, is established under the auspices of the Parapsychology Laboratory at Duke. The Mind Science Foundation is founded in San Antonio, Texas, to study consciousness, parapsychology, and more. The story of Brazilian farmer Antônio Vilas-Boas becomes the first widely known account of "alien abduction." The first account of the Marfa lights in Texas is published in *Coronet* magazine. Carl Jung publishes *Flying Saucers: A Myth of Things Seen in the Sky.*

1958 After investigating a case in Seaford, New York, William G. Roll and J. Gaither Pratt of J. B. Rhine's Parapsychology Laboratory coin the term "recurrent spontaneous psychokinesis" (RSPK) to describe potential psychological mechanisms behind the poltergeist phenomenon. The Astrological Association of Great Britain (AA) is established in London.

1959 Shirley Jackson publishes *The Haunting of Hill House.*

1960	The Psychical Research Foundation spins off from the Parapsychology Laboratory at Duke University with William G. Roll as director. Ian Stevenson publishes a review article in which he reports having found 44 cases of people, mostly children, who gave evidence of remembering a previous life, inaugurating the first systematic program of research on reincarnation.
1960s–1970s	Unexplained livestock mutilations take place around the United States, leading to an FBI investigation and widespread popular theories about alien experiments, occult sacrifices, and government conspiracies. Stanley Krippner and Montague Ullman conduct dream telepathy research in the Division of Parapsychology and Psychophysics at Maimonides Medical Center in Brooklyn, New York.
1961	The Psychical Research Foundation is established at Duke University. Betty and Barney Hill claim to have been abducted by aliens in New Hampshire, establishing the model of modern abduction cases. Michael Whiteman publishes his first book, *The Mystical Life: An Outline of Its Nature and Teachings from the Evidence of Direct Experience.*
1962	In Big Sur, California, Michael Murphy and Dick Price found the Esalen Institute, the birthplace of the human potential movement. British ghost hunter Peter Underwood begins a 31-year term as the president of the Ghost Club.
1963	American medium Jane Roberts begins receiving channeled information from a purported male spirit calling itself Seth; the resulting books profoundly affect the New Age movement.
1964	J. B. Rhine retires from Duke. Religion scholar Mircae Eliade publishes *Shamanism.*
1964–1967	Psychiatrist Jule Eisenbud studies Ted Serios and his apparent ability to produce Thoughtography.
1965	J. B. Rhine moves the Parapsychology Laboratory to the newly established Foundation for the Research on the Nature of Man, which gives birth to the Institute for Parapsychology.
1965–1973	American psychologist Helen Schucman transcribes the words of an "inner voice," resulting in the popular spiritual self-help manual *A Course in Miracles.*

1966	The American game company Parker Brother acquires the Ouija board, which soon becomes popular all across America as a game for young people. Ian Stevenson publishes *Twenty Suggestive Cases of Reincarnation.*
1967	Jule Eisenbud publishes *The World of Ted Serios: "Thoughtographic" Studies of an Extraordinary Mind.* Hans Bender investigates the Rosenheim poltergeist in Bavaria.
1968	Celia Green publishes *Lucid Dreams*, a groundbreaking book about the subject. Parapsychologist Alan Gauld publishes *The Founders of Psychical Research*. A Marian apparition repeatedly appears at the St. Mary Coptic Church in the El-Zeitoun suburb of Cairo, Egypt. Director George Romero's *Night of the Living Dead* establishes the infectious, flesh-eating zombie that will come to dominate American, British, and European popular culture.
1969	The Parapsychological Association becomes an affiliated organization of the American Association for the Advancement of Science. The academic, peer-reviewed *Journal of Transpersonal Psychology* is inaugurated. After 21 years the United States Air Force shuts down its UFO investigation program, now titled Project Blue Book. The Mutual UFO Network (MUFON) is founded. Jacques Vallée publishes *Passport to Magonia*. Charles Tart publishes *Altered States of Consciousness*, which helps to establish the title subject in modern psychology. Dutch painter and poet Johan Borgman establishes an educational foundation on energy healing and parapsychology. The International Society for Astrological Research (ISAR) is established. Secular humanist Paul Kurtz founds the skeptical press Prometheus Books.
1970	Sheila Ostrander and Lynn Shroeder publish *Psychic Discoveries behind the Iron Curtain.* Louisa Rhine publishes an overview of Duke University's psychokinesis experiments, *Mind over Matter*. Psychiatrist and medical historian Henri F. Ellenberger publishes his monumental study *The Discovery of the Unconscious*, which connects psychiatry's roots to mesmerism and spiritual rituals.
1970s	Uri Geller rises to prominence in Europe and America by giving spectacular demonstrations of psychic powers (most famously, spoon bending) on television. Dr. Thelma Moss experiments with Kirlian photography in

UCLA's parapsychology lab. British mathematician and psychical researcher A.R.G. (George) Owen starts the New Horizons Research Foundation in Toronto, which tests a psychokinetic hypothesis of alleged spirit communication in the Philip experiment.

1971   Colin Wilson publishes *The Occult*. Konstantins Raudive publishes his study on electronic voice phenomena, *Breakthrough*. Clinical neuropsychologist Michael Persinger begins work at Laurentian University in Canada on geophysical relationships to paranormal experiences.

1972   SRI becomes the initial site of remote viewing experiments sponsored by the U.S. government and later to be included as part of the Stargate Project; the research is funded by the CIA and led by physicists Russell Targ and Harold Puthoff. William Roll publishes *The Poltergeist*. American astronomer J. Allen Hynek publishes *The UFO Experience: A Scientific Inquiry*, in which he establishes his now-standard classification system for "close encounters." Eastern Airlines Flight 401 crashes into the Florida Everglades; in the following year, apparitions of the deceased pilot are reportedly seen on aircraft that use salvageable parts from the crashed plane.

1973   The film version of *The Exorcist*, adapted by William Peter Blatty from his 1971 novel, incites new popular interest in possession and exorcism. In an appearance on *The Tonight Show* in America, Uri Geller is unable to bend the spoons supplied by host Johnny Carson, lending further weight to the charges of Geller's many skeptical critics. The Institute of Noetic Sciences is founded by Apollo 14 astronaut Edgar Mitchell. Bob Rickard founds *The News*, which becomes the magazine *Fortean Times* in 1976. Ronald Pearsall publishes his historical study *Table-Rappers*, a semi-affectionate exposé of Spiritualist fraud and trickery.

1974   The American science fiction writer Philip K. Dick experiences a series of paranormal experiences that "reprogram" him by an entity that he terms VALIS (vast active living intelligence system). The American physicist William Corliss begins publishing his multivolume *Sourcebook Project*, collecting a vast amount of data on anomalous phenomena. Parapsychology researchers begin conducting experiments using the ganzfeld technique. Targ and Puthoff publish the results of Uri

Geller's remote viewing experiments at SRI in *Nature*. Young British psychic Matthew Manning publishes *The Link*, his memoir of poltergeist disturbances and psychic phenomena affecting him and his family. Stephen King publishes his debut novel about psychokinetic vengeance, *Carrie*.

1975

The *European Journal of Parapsychology*, a peer-reviewed journal, is founded at the University of Utrecht. John Keel publishes *The Mothman Prophecies*. Jacques Vallée publishes *The Invisible College*. Raymond Moody publishes *Life after Life*, in which he coins the term "near-death experience." The Institute of Transpersonal Psychology is founded.

1976

The Committee for the Scientific Investigation of Claims of the Paranormal (CSICOP), later to be renamed the Committee for Skeptical Inquiry, is founded at a meeting of the American Humanist Association. It launches an official journal, *The Zetetic*, later to be retitled and relaunched as *Skeptical Inquirer*. German teenager Anneliese Michel dies from malnutrition after intensive exorcisms in Klingenberg am Main; two Catholic priests are subsequently found guilty of manslaughter. In England, "The Spectre Inspector" Andrew Green publishes *Ghost Hunting: A Practical Guide*.

1977

Targ and Puthoff publish *Mind-Reach*, detailing the results of their remote viewing research at SRI. The remote viewing research at SRI is taken over by the U.S. Army. Stanley Krippner launches a new series of anthologies, *Advances in Parapsychological Research*. Erlendur Haraldsson and Karlis Osis publish *At the Hour of Death* on deathbed visions in the United States and India. The Australian Institute of Parapsychological Research is founded. John F. Kennedy University launches a master's degree program in parapsychology. Steven Spielberg's *Close Encounters of the Third Kind* (named after J. Allen Hynek's classification of UFO encounters) becomes a big-screen sensation. The weekly television series *In Search Of …* premieres; hosted by Leonard Nimoy, it airs for six seasons. Jay Anson publishes *The Amityville Horror*, which becomes one of the bestselling accounts of a "true" haunting in America and spawns a highly successful horror film; the case is widely argued to be a hoax.

1977–1978	The Enfield poltergeist occurs at a house in Enfield, North London, causing a media sensation and drawing an investigation by the SPR. Benjamin Wolman edits *Handbook of Parapsychology*.
1978	The International Transpersonal Association is founded. Parapsychologist Keith Hearne conclusively proves the existence of lucid dreams by asking a lucid dreamer to send eye-movement signals. British psychologist Stan Gooch publishes *The Paranormal*. Stephen Schwartz publishes *The Secret Vaults of Time*, on psychic archaeology.
1979	The Princeton Engineering Anomalies (PEAR) laboratory is established in Princeton University's School of Engineering and Applied Science. Psychophysical Research Laboratories is established in Princeton, New Jersey, by personnel from the Maimonides laboratory after the latter closes. American philosopher Stephen Braude publishes his first book on parapsychology, *ESP and Psychokinesis: A Philosophical Examination*. Parapsychologists Alan Gauld and Tony Cornell publish *Poltergeists*. Parapsychology writers D. Scott Rogo and Raymond Bayless publish *Phone Calls from the Dead*.
1979–1983	James Randi engineers the Project Alpha hoax, planting fake psychics in parapsychology research laboratories to expose parapsychology as "junk science."
1980	Historians Seymour Mauskopf and Michael McVaugh publish a study of the early years of J. B. Rhine's Parapsychology Laboratory, *The Elusive Science*.
1981	The International Association for Near-Death Studies (IANDS) is founded. The Association for the Scientific Study of Anomalous Phenomena (ASSAP) is formed in England. Psychophysiologist Stephen LaBerge duplicates Hearne's 1978 lucid dreaming confirmation and publishes the result in a peer-reviewed journal. Marian apparitions appear to children in a mountain village in the former Yugoslavia.
1982	The Society for Scientific Exploration (SSE) is founded in the United States as a professional organization for scientists and scholars to study unusual and unexplained "fringe" phenomena. Dale Kaczmarek establishes the Ghost Research Society in Chicago. David Hufford publishes *The Terror That Comes in the Night: An Experience-Centered*

Study of Supernatural Assault Traditions. Leonard Zusne and Warren Jones publish *Anomalistic Psychology*. Alan Gauld publishes *Mediumship and Survival*. Sociologist Charles Emmons publishes his study *Chinese Ghosts and ESP*. Pollster George Gallup publishes his survey on American beliefs in the afterlife, *Adventures in Immortality*. Steven Spielberg's *E.T.: The Extra-Terrestrial* becomes one of the top grossing films of all time.

1983	Ruth Brandon publishes her historical study *The Spiritualists*. Susan Hill publishes the novella *The Woman in Black*, which goes on to become a popular motion picture in 2012.
1984	William Roll investigates a major poltergeist case in Columbus, Ohio; a photograph of a telephone flying across 14-year-old Tina Resch's lap is published in the Columbus *Dispatch*. Historian R. C. Finucane publishes *Appearances of the Dead*, the first cultural history of ghosts. Sociologist James McClenon publishes a study of the challenges faced by parapsychologists, *The Deviant Science*. *Ghostbusters* becomes a hit movie and popularizes the vocabulary of parapsychology and psychical research, such as the word "ectoplasm."
1985	The Koestler Parapsychology Unit (KPU) is established in the psychology department at the University of Edinburgh. Science Unlimited Research Foundation (SURF) is established in San Antonio, Texas, to study parapsychology and other matters. Psychotherapist Adam Crabtree publishes *Multiple Man: Explorations in Possession and Multiple Personality*. Historian Janet Oppenheim publishes a study on Spiritualism and psychical research, *The Other World*. Anthropologist Wade Davis publishes *The Serpent and the Rainbow*, which offers a biological theory for Haitian zombies.
1987	Whitley Strieber publishes *Communion*; it becomes the single most popular book to influence public conceptions of the alien abduction phenomenon. Erlendur Haraldsson publishes *Modern Miracles*, on the Indian guru Sai Baba. Toni Morrison publishes her haunting novel *Beloved*, which goes on to win the Pulitzer Prize for Fiction. The SSE launched *The Journal of Scientific Exploration*. The television program *Unsolved Mysteries* begins and runs for 14 seasons, often featuring paranormal case studies.

1988	Colin Wilson publishes *Beyond the Occult*. Tim Burton's movie *Beetlejuice* depicts the afterlife in a comical way.
1989	A two-year-long UFO wave commences in Belgium and is openly investigated by the military and police. The first edition of Harvey Irwin's textbook *An Introduction to Parapsychology* is published. Historian Alex Owen publishes her study of women, power, and Spiritualism, *The Darkened Room*, and Ann Braude publishes *Radical Spirits*, on Spiritualist connections to women's emancipation.
1990	The romantic movie *Ghost* becomes a huge hit.
1991	The Survival Research Institute of Canada is founded to study life after death. Anthropologist David Hess publishes his study of Brazilian Spiritism, *Spirits and Scientists*.
1992	MIT hosts a conference on alien abduction experiences; it is attended by a host of prominent scientists, scholars, psychologists, and others. The Skeptics Society is founded by science writer Michael Shermer to promote scientific skepticism; it launches *Skeptic* magazine as its official publication.
1993	The television series *The X-Files* launches and enraptures audiences with ideas about alien abductions and assorted paranormal phenomena for nine seasons.
1995	The Foundation for Research on the Nature of Man is renamed the Rhine Research Center. In rural Norfolk, England, the five-year-long Scole Experiment begins, inviting many observers to see advanced displays of physical mediumship. The U.S. government determines there is no value in continuing remote viewing research: it terminates the remote viewing-oriented Stargate Project and declassifies many associated documents.
1996	The Transpersonal Psychology Section is formed as an official part of the British Psychological Society. Historian Paul Heelas publishes *The New Age Movement*.
1997	Dean Radin publishes a meta-analysis of scientific studies of psi, *The Conscious Universe*.
1998	The Global Consciousness Project is launched at Princeton University. Historian Alison Winter publishes *Mesmerized*, on mesmerism's status as a mainstream science in Victorian Britain.

1999	*The Sixth Sense* and the mock "found footage" movie *The Blair Witch Project* become box office smashes. Controversial medium John Edward's television show *Crossing Over* premieres.
2000	Psychologist Christopher French establishes the Anomalistic Psychology Research Unit (APRU) at Goldsmiths at the University of London.
2001	Magician and former parapsychology researcher George Hansen publishes *The Trickster and the Paranormal*, offering a sweepingly comprehensive theory of paranormal phenomena.
2002	In Britain, the reality ghost-hunting television series *Most Haunted* premieres.
2004	Historian Alex Owen's *The Place of Enchantment* evaluates British occultism at the turn of the 20th century. Corinna Treitel publishes *A Science for the Soul*, which looks at occultism during the Wilhelmine, Weimar, and Nazi regimes in Germany. The reality television series *Ghost Hunters*, hosted by The Atlantic Paranormal Society (TAPS), premieres, inspiring many similar programs. British psychological illusionist Derren Brown recreates Spiritualist phenomena in his television special *Séance*.
2005	"The Perfect Medium: Photography and the Occult" exhibition is held at the Metropolitan Museum of Art in New York City. The American television drama *Medium*, based on the real-life medium Alison DuBois, starts a seven-season run, while the popular program *Supernatural* continues to air.
2006	CSICOP shortens its name to CSI, the Committee for Skeptical Inquiry.
2001	American medium and author Susy Smith dies, leaving an "afterlife code" to be deciphered in hopes of proving her survival of physical death.
2007	The PEAR lab at Princeton closes; the nonprofit International Consciousness Research Laboratories (ICRL) is established in its place.
2008	The *GHost* Project is launched in London to examine ghosts and hauntings in artistic and cultural contexts.
2010	Religion scholar Jeffrey Kripal publishes *Authors of the Impossible: The Paranormal and the Sacred*; the publisher

is a reputable university press, and the book establishes the paranormal as a critical category within the history of religion. *Paranthropology: Journal of Anthropological Approaches to the Paranormal* is launched.

2011   American psychologist Daryl Bem publishes experimental results in the *Journal of Personality and Social Psychology* that appear to provide statistical evidence for the existence of precognition; other researchers fail to replicate his results; a later review appears to support Bem's initial findings. Jeffrey Kripal publishes *Mutants and Mystics: Science Fiction, Superhero Comics, and the Paranormal*.

2012   Parapsychologist James Carpenter publishes *First Sight: ESP and Parapsychology in Everyday Life*. American neurosurgeon Eben Alexander publishes *Proof of Heaven: A Neurosurgeon's Journey into the Afterlife*, detailing his personal experience. British screenwriter Philippa Langley helps archaeologists successfully locate the lost body of Richard III based on an apparent psychic/intuitive perception.

2013   A major poll finds that 42 percent of Americans say they believe in ghosts. TED, the global idea conference, revokes the license of a planned TEDx event in West Hollywood on the grounds that some of its speakers, including Russell Targ, promote pseudoscience with their psychic and/or mystical themes. The *Journal of Exceptional Experiences and Psychology* (JEEP) is launched as an international, peer-reviewed journal exploring anomalous and paranormal experiences.

2014   Jeffrey Kripal publishes *Comparing Religions*, the first academic textbook of comparative religion to include an entire chapter on the paranormal.

A

ABDUCTION EXPERIENCE

Abductions of humans by non-human entities are recorded in folklore and myths throughout human history. Reports of kidnappings by extraterrestrial beings constitute the most common form of contemporary abduction experience narratives. Such experiences are typically considered to be subjectively real events or memories of events in which individuals recall being taken aboard a spacecraft and subjected to various psychological and/or medical procedures by nonhuman entities. These experiences are oftentimes traumatic, but some reports of abduction experiences are marked by a more positive emotional tone. People who recall abduction experiences are usually referred to as "alien abductees" or simply as "experiencers." While the majority of abduction experiences seem to be recalled with the assistance of hypnosis, other alien abductees have conscious recall of part or all of their experiences.

The first contemporary alien abduction account to receive widespread attention originated in Brazil in 1957. A farmer named Antônio Vilas-Boas claimed that one night a strange craft landed in a field while he was on his tractor. He tried to flee, but his tractor's engine died and he was kidnapped by strange entities. They carried him into their craft, where he had sexual intercourse with an alien, leading to what he believed was an alien pregnancy. Vilas-Boas died in 1991, having always claimed that the encounter really occurred.

The first well-known alien abduction reported in the United States came from Betty and Barney Hill. While traveling on a rural road in New Hampshire in 1961, the Hills spotted an unidentifiable flying disc that seemed to follow them for some time. They arrived home that night feeling rather odd, and they both were unable to account for a period of about four hours. The Hills experienced growing anxiety and felt that the events of that night were somehow responsible. Betty and Barney eventually underwent hypnosis to retrieve their period of missing time, which led to their remembering an abduction experience.

Since that time, thousands of people have reported memories of being been taken by alien beings. One of the most famous abductees is Whitley Strieber, who has written several books about his numerous encounters with nonhuman entities that he refers to as "the Visitors." The cover painting of Strieber's 1987 book *Communion* depicted one of these visitors and is among the most popular images of a particular kind of reported alien being known as a "Gray."

Many, but not all, self-identified abductees have little or no conscious memory of abduction episodes without the assistance of hypnosis. It is largely hypothesized by

A Brief Chronology of Notable "Alien Abductions"

The experience of being abducted by nonhuman entities has been reported throughout human history, but in modern technological societies it is primarily associated with the idea of "alien abduction."

1957 Brazilian farmer Antônio Vilas-Boas reports being abducted by beings from a flying craft. The story becomes the first widely known "alien abduction" account.

1961 Betty and Barney Hill experience an episode of "missing time" after seeing a mysterious flying disc while driving on a rural New Hampshire road. Later, under hypnosis, they recall details of an alien abduction.

1975 American logger Travis Walton experiences an abduction in Arizona, with accompanying aerial phenomena corroborated by eyewitnesses. In 1978 he publishes his account of what happened under the title *The Walton Experience*. The book is later adapted as the 1993 American movie *Fire in the Sky*.

1987 Whitley Strieber's book *Communion* is published. It details his personal experiences with alien abductions. Both the story and the book's cover painting of an alien "gray" lodge in the public mind as the phenomenon's iconic representation.

1992 In June the Massachusetts Institute of Technology hosts a conference on the alien abduction experience, co-chaired by David Pritchard, a physics professor at MIT, and John Mack, a professor of psychiatry at Harvard Medical School.

UFOlogists and others who believe in the objective reality of the phenomenon that abductees are forced to forget their ordeal by their kidnappers through some kind of technology or procedure, and that hypnosis is required to unlock or otherwise recover most abduction memories. Several of the most prolific alien abduction researchers, including the artist Budd Hopkins, the Harvard psychiatrist John Mack, and retired Temple history professor David M. Jacobs, have used hypnosis. However, this is generally considered to be an unreliable tool for recovering accurate memories of past trauma events, and many within the UFO community have increasingly moved away from its use. One argument for its continued application, though, is that the abduction experience occurs during an altered state of consciousness, and therefore hypnosis might offer a means with which to recollect events occurring during altered awareness by inducing another altered state of awareness. Regardless, there is substantial evidence that hypnosis can lead to fabrication.

Abduction experience reports often sound incredibly bizarre and surreal, although folklorist Thomas E. Bullard has written that the majority of reports do contain a series of underlying common features, including: capture of the abduct-ee, the conducting of a scientific or medical examination upon the abductee, a conference or meeting with the captors, a tour of the space craft, missing periods of time, the return of the abductee, a mystical experience that accompanies the abduction, and multiple aftereffects of the experience. Many abductees report ex-periencing a variety of aftereffects, including ongoing experiences of paranormal phenomena, which have led psychologists and psychiatrists to speculate that ab-ductees often demonstrate personality traits that make them particularly prone to report unusual experiences. But this position assumes that the abduction experi-ence is itself an effect of a personality trait, whereas it might be that the experience, whether subjectively real or otherwise, transforms the personality of the experienc-er. Still, mainstream science generally views abduction accounts as hallucinatory in nature, or as the results of confabulation or faulty memory.

Reports of abduction experiences have played a significant role in the develop-ment of the modern UFO myth, including descriptions of different races of alien beings and where they come from. While the stories told by abductees are usually viewed as being either "true" or "false," some researchers into the phenomenon, such as Jacques Vallée and the late John Mack, have argued that the abduction experience might occur, either in part or in whole, within a domain of reality gen-erally considered to be imaginal—that is, residing in a kind of "third space" where the psychical and physical meet in ways that defy conventional logic. Viewed this way, abduction narratives are stories depicting actions and events that have oc-curred in a hyper-dimensional reality that transcends three-dimensional thought. Some abduction researchers point to the psychedelic qualities of many abduction narratives and hypothesize that many abduction experiences are the results of nat-urally occurring psychedelic compounds produced in the brains of experiencers.

Regardless of the objective reality of the abduction experience, these events can traumatize those who recall them. Some abductees view their ordeals with disdain, while others eventually come to embrace what they believe to be a spiritually trans-formative event.

Michael Kinsella

See also: Imaginal; Strieber, Whitley; UFO; Vallée, Jacques

Further Reading

Clancy, Susan. 2007. *Abducted: How People Come to Believe They Were Kidnapped by Aliens* Cambridge, MA: Harvard University Press.

Hopkins, Budd. 1988. *Missing Time*. New York: Ballantine Books.

Mack, John. 1999. *Passport to the Cosmos: Human Transformation and Alien Encounters*. New York: Crown Publishing.

AKASHIC RECORDS

The akashic records are a Western metaphysical concept that refers to a cosmic storehouse of the entirety of human experience. They are said to exist on a subtle plane of material reality and can be accessed by ascended beings and clairvoyants. The term itself derives from the Sanskrit word *akasha*, which was adopted and transformed by members of the Theosophical movement during the late 19th century. Charles W. Leadbeater (1854–1934), who first popularized the term within Theosophical discourse, defines it as "the memory of nature" and "the only really reliable history of the world" (Leadbeater 1896, 26). The concept became prominent within Theosophical doctrine and trickled down into derivative movements such as Rudolf Steiner's Anthroposophy and the occult works of Alice A. Bailey before dispersing throughout the New Age Movement of the late-20th century.

Akasha signifies "space," "atmosphere," or "sky" in the Sanskrit language and appears in the complex system of Indian metaphysics known as Samkhya as one of the five elements making up gross material nature (alongside air, fire, water, and earth). Early Indologists associated *akasha* with the concept of ether, due to its apparent similarity to the latter's status as the fifth element of the ancient Greeks. When Helena Blavatsky (1831–1891) drew on both Eastern and Western metaphysics in codifying the foundations of Theosophical doctrine, she cemented the occult association between the two terms. Blavatsky herself never used the term "akashic records," but spoke of an etheric, astral, or akashic (all of which she uses synonymously) level of reality, which exists just beyond the ordinary gross sphere of material nature. Her contemporary, Alfred P. Sinnett (1840–1921), referenced the idea of "permanent records in the Akasa" in his Esoteric Buddhism (1883) when discussing the spiritual progression of the Buddha's many births. The concept has obvious parallels within Indian thought, specifically where dealing with the metaphysics of *karma* and the transmigrating self, and it appears that later Theosophists drew primarily on these ideas when they eventually introduced the term into their discussion of subtle materiality. The particular term was first used by Leadbeater in his *Theosophical Manual No. 6* (1896), derived from his earlier treatment of the "Records of the Astral Light," which he described as a "photographic representation" of everything that has ever happened. Leadbeater also canonized the idea that a spiritual adept or a clairvoyant may be capable of accessing the akashic records for the purpose of gaining knowledge of lost histories and subtle truths.

Subsequent to their explication by Leadbeater, the akashic records were referenced by multiple Theosophist authors (Annie Besant, Bertram Keightley, Rudolph Steiner, and Alice A. Bailey, among others), who employed the term with various degrees of abstraction. At times the akashic records appear to be described as holographic imprints in an actual universal substrate of energy (i.e. the luminiferous ether), while, in other contexts, they are characterized as a sort of Neoplatonic ideal realm. In the second half of the 20th century, the term was taken up by the diverse strains of metaphysical spirituality generally referred to as the New Age

Movement and related schools of thought such as Wicca and the UFO Contactee Movement. The akashic records became a particularly useful concept in explaining the mechanics of New Age channeling.

Anna Pokazanyeva

See also: Astral Plane; Cayce, Edgar; Channeling; Clairvoyance; New Age; Theosophy

Further Reading

Leadbeater, C. W. 1896. *Theosophical Manual No. 6: The Devachanic Plane, Its Characteristics and Inhabitants.* London: Theosophical Publishing Society.
Washington, Peter. 1995. *Madame Blavatsky's Baboon: A History of the Mystics, Mediums, and Misfits Who Brought Spiritualism to America.* New York: Schocken Books.

ALCHEMY

Although often assumed to be a form of proto-chemistry, alchemy is better understood as a devotional and philosophical art that uses empirical investigation of matter for unveiling the deepest levels of reality to the practitioner. In this description, the term "art" is used to denote the qualitative and experiential use of empirical methodology, as opposed to the quantitative and inferential use that became popular during the 18th century Enlightenment and continued on into the material sciences, as they are known today. Rooted within the holistic worldview of the ancient and classical periods, alchemy's procedures developed from the practical utilization of material processes, such as the alloying of gold, distilling of tinctures, calcination of salts, and other familiar chemical processes, with the understanding that each of these manipulations was but a focused application of wider universal principles. The alchemist in turn sought to experience these principles to open and reveal the inner workings of the natural world such that the very root act of creation and transmutation of matter became possible within the alchemist's laboratory. It is this direct application and understanding of the dynamic interconnected ratios of microcosm and macrocosm that differentiates alchemical practice from scientific methods that were developed later through specialization and deconstruction of earlier holistic empirical arts of investigation.

Contemporary historians have provided valuable insight into the wide range of understandings that have worn the label "alchemy" over the past few centuries. This information allows current inquiries into the "Royal Art" to forego much of the mystification that has distracted from the core principles of the field in the past. Alchemical scholar Aaron Cheak, in his introduction to the *Alchemical Traditions* anthology, explains that "the classical applications of alchemy have always been twofold: chrysopoeia and apotheosis (gold-making and god-making)—the perfection of metals and mortals" (Cheak 2013, 18). It is the simplification and specialization of techniques utilized in the first application that has led many scholars to characterize alchemy as an early form of the material sciences, just as the simplification of the second has led to psychological motifs being applied to alchemy, as well as supernatural and occult interpretations. Any limited view of the alchemical art fails to see the full spectrum of devotional practice that allows it to act as a gateway to a unified vision encompassing the essential nature of the unbroken phenomenal continuum.

Similar practices that locate material practices alongside more spiritual concerns can be found in traditions around the globe. Central Asian Tantric practices, Chinese Taoism, certain Islamic mystical practices, European alchemy, and earlier forms found in Greco-Roman and Hellenic-Egyptian contexts all share correspondences in their mutual drawing on the idea that it is possible to access relationships within the natural order that allow for movement between levels of purity. This entails an understanding of the world that can be seen in the classical conception of reality as a whole being divided into a hierarchy of interpenetrating layers or parts. Those practices that find themselves grouped under the term "alchemy" form arts that seek to allow free movement throughout this structure, most often from a state of impurity to purity—although statements such as "you must have gold to make gold" offer insight into the essential purity that exists even before the transmutation occurs. The outward movement towards purity, in which some form of change is seen in the phenomenal body of the transmuted material, was seen in the European alchemical process as the art of "perfecting nature."

Though the exact details of the alchemical process vary depending on the source and tradition of instruction, there are many shared commonalities. Within European and Islamic alchemy these consist of concepts such as the classic elemental quaternity of earth, air, fire, and water, which makes up the material world, as well as the trinity of fundamental essentials: salt, sulfur, and mercury, or body, soul and spirit, which define the qualities through which the unified and singular first matter, *prima material*, manifests in multiple forms as the intelligible world. Alchemical forms stemming from Tantric, Taoist, and other Asian traditions follow similar expressions, and as still-living traditions they allow us to better understand some of the less explicit areas left unrevealed in the European traditions of alchemical practice.

The well-known alchemical notion of turning lead into gold provides a good starting point for examining the basic structure of the alchemical worldview. Once we understand that within alchemical practice, lead is representative of the most impure or base metal, and gold the most perfect or pure metal, and that metal itself was seen as a specific phenomenal state of a more rarified "first" element, we can see how this process becomes not merely a transmutation of one metal into another, but a way in which to understand the nature of metals as a holistic category within the natural order. Moreover, the movement from one state to another provides a microcosmic relationship through which to observe, by ratio, the larger macroscopic processes. Here again we find that this category reflects an accompanying complexity within the whole, and that these procedures in themselves become a sort of "lead" that can be worked with to move into more rarefied, perhaps even spiritual, transmutations.

When alchemy as an applicable form of material investigation fell fully into disrepute during the 18th and 19th centuries, and the philosophical aspects had become equally misunderstood, the mytho-poetic and symbolical veils that had elucidated the art became grounds upon which supernaturalist and paranormal claims became more prevalent in describing the fruit of alchemical practice. During this time figures such as Raymond Lull, a Christian missionary and mystic; Albertus Magnus, a Christian naturalist and theologian; Paracelsus, a naturalist mystic and medical theorist; and others who during their lifetimes wrote and worked prominently within their historical milieu began to take on popular personae as alchemystical adepts capable of the most astounding feats of transmutation. Alongside this tendency to impute occult aptitude to historical personages, writings from figures such as Basil Valentine, Nicolas Flamel, and others with a less solid historical basis became popular sources for understanding the alchemical art, further provoking the curiosity of the credulous and inflaming critics who saw alchemy as little more than charlatanism and superstition.

While it may seem easy to dismiss such dalliances with fictitious sources, the conscious use of hoaxes, blinds, and pseudonymous publications provides yet another example of the integral relationship between the practice of alchemy and the idea of microcosmic and macrocosmic interaction. As nature hides her secrets, so too with the secrets of those who investigate within the deeper veils and interactions of fact and fiction. Moreover, it is through these pseudonymous and false faces that alchemy moved into more political and sociological concerns during the 17th and 18th centuries.

Coinciding with the publication of the anonymous Rosicrucian Manifestos in the 17th century, the symbolism of alchemy began to be applied not just the individual alchemist or the immediate substances being worked on, but to reformation of the world itself. Although the manifestos in themselves were not immediately identifiable with the practical manuals of the art, those who propagated their ideology, such as Michael Maier, Robert Fludd, Francis Bacon, and others within their circles, both practiced practical alchemy and held ideas of social reforms that can be seen to apply alchemical ideologies to a wider realm of understanding. References to Paracelsus also served to tie the manifestos to alchemical ideologies. Within this milieu the "invisible" Rosicrucians were seen as adept masters of nature's secrets, capable of restoring or transmuting European society into a new golden age. Through the mystification of this "hidden order" of adepts, the idea of alchemy attained a broader and more supernaturalist or occult veil than it had previously assumed.

Though the manifestos represented an ideal fraternity of secret artisans and healers, they served as a means to support a vision of rational reformation that utilized the power of the millennial and apocalyptic fears common to the Catholic, Protestant, Judaic, and Islamic groups, which dominated the political structure of Europe, North Africa, and the Near East at the time, while focusing on cross-cultural and secularist goals of social integration and renewal. In a certain sense they can be seen as a means to apply the Platonic idea of the "noble lie," a fiction that serves the purpose of truth, to the ideological infrastructure of society. In another sense we can see how the tensions of the time were utilized as the catalytic fire that sparked the transmutation of the social infrastructure. Acting on the subtle image of society through the early Renaissance equivalent of a transmedia game, the Manifestos represent an important turning point in the way alchemy was conceived by those who took up its practice.

During the 18th century this process was further elaborated by the use of alchemical symbolism as a core component within the development of Haute Grade Masonic initiations, as well as independent fraternal orders such as the Gold und Rosenkreuz, which utilized alchemical symbols to represent stages of initiatory development for their members. The key position of these groups within the political life of Europe provided support for the development of a more specifically spiritualized understanding of alchemy that would ultimately find its full expression in the 19th century with works such as those of Ethan Allen Hitchcock, an administrator in the War Department of the United States during the Civil War, who in his *Remarks upon Alchemy and the Alchemists* (1855) stressed the end of the art as moral perfection; and Mary Anne Atwood's *A Suggestive Inquiry into the Hermetic Mystery*, which presented an ideal of alchemy as a spiritual quest almost completely divorced from material practice. For Atwood and others who proceeded with a spiritualized, occult-oriented idea of alchemy, it was the advanced spiritual states attained by the adepts that led to their being able to manipulate the more impure aspects of reality, such as matter. In this the original concept of ascending the ladder of creation from material to Creator is almost completely reversed, requiring the attainment of a spiritual state divorced from material concerns before effects are able to be attained in practice.

This view can be seen as a radical example of the significant changes that occurred in the perception of scientific inquiry in the preceding centuries. With the popularity of Spiritualism in the 19th century and the continued influence of late 18th century Romanticism, diverse areas of discarded theory, such as Mesmer's ideas of animal magnetism, Swedenborg's theories of spiritual agency, and the legendary powers of Rosicrucian adepts, began to intermix in opposition to the rapid specialization of more materialist scientific orthodoxy. Although many early pioneers of the scientific method, such as Robert Boyle, Isaac Newton, and Robert Starkey, had successfully combined alchemical work with the emergent fields of modern chemistry and physics, by the 19th century these areas were radically separated by polemical arguments against superstition, supernaturalism, and charlatanism. Those who continued to write and discuss alchemy found support in occult and theosophical organizations, rather than in the mainstream scientific societies, and

Although frequently dismissed today as a mixture of superstition and pseudoscience, alchemy was the precursor to modern chemistry. Many of the early pioneers of the scientific method, including Robert Boyle ("the father of chemistry"), Isaac Newton, and Robert Starkey, were practicing alchemists who viewed their pursuit not merely as a means of interrogating the natural world but as a spiritual practice intended to purify and elevate their souls.

thus the alchemical worldview became further isolated from the popular scientific discussions of the day. However, due to the popularity of occult societies, especially among the social elite, alchemical ideas, while not openly discussed as such, remained influential within the field of experimental inquiry.

Although the materialist focus of the popular scientific orthodoxy of the late 19th and early 20th centuries disavowed the holistic worldview necessary to fully understand alchemy, its symbol system became central to the ideas of psychologist Carl Jung, who saw in this holism a perfect model for developing a healthy psyche. Using imagery from alchemical texts, he outlined what he saw as the stages of development of a unified and functional mental life. Jung's archetypal theory of consciousness remains one of the most popular approaches to alchemy today, although it relies on a subjective and limited reading of the original material.

According to Dennis William Hauck, a contemporary practical alchemist and author of numerous books on the subject, some of the giants of 20th century science, mathematics, and philosophy, such as Max Planck, Kurt Gödel, and Ludwig Wittgenstein, rather than dispelling the alchemical worldview have actually helped bring contemporary theory in line with the ancient art in its exposition as a practical outgrowth of Neoplatonic and Hermetic cosmology. This is backed up by statements by Lord Martin Rees, former Astronomer Royal and past president of the Royal Society, that the ouroboros (the ancient image of a snake or dragon swallowing its own tail) represents the perfect symbol for the contemporary understanding of cosmology.

Even Einstein's famous equation, $E = mc^2$, can be viewed as a verification of the truth behind the alchemical worldview. In an article published in *The Rose Croix Journal*, Hauck points out that "Einstein proved an ancient tenet of alchemy that was previously unknown in physics: the fundamental idea of 'All Is One' and the equivalence between energy and matter. His revolutionary equation of the universe is $E=mc^2$, where E is energy, m is mass, and c is the speed of light. This theorem is a restatement of the Three Essentials concept of the alchemists in which Sulfur is energy, Salt is mass or matter, and Mercury represents light" (Hauck 2011, 82). Lest it seem that the critics are right in charging such arguments as ahistorical reworkings that were not in the original tradition of alchemy, we need only look at the fact that Isaac Newton was able, through alchemical speculation, to discover the dual nature of light as both particle and wave, and only held back publication of his theory due to fears that the scientific orthodoxy of the time was not ready to accept such a radical theory. Contemporary physics is no longer so sheepish, and Newton's alchemically based insight provides a cornerstone of our present understanding of the nature of the universe.

Newton in particular was inspired by one of the oldest examples of alchemical writings, the Tabula Smaragdina, or the Emerald Tablet. From this text comes the oft-quoted statement, "As above, so below," which provides the key to how the alchemists' *prima material*, the primal chaos or first matter, relates ultimately to the pure, essential unity of all reality. That one of Europe's most original and formative scientific thinkers held alchemy in such a central place in his investigations is striking, and amid mounting evidence that contemporary science's understanding is returning to the philosophical core of this ancient art, it remains to be seen what the future holds for those bold enough to peer beyond nature's veil in search of the gold within.

David Metcalfe

See also: Jung, Carl; Occultism; Pseudoscience; Ritual Magic

Further Reading
Albertus, Frater. (1960) 1987. *The Alchemist's Handbook*. Revised expanded edition. York Beach, ME: Weiser Books.
Cheak, Aaron. 2013. "Circulambulating the Alchemical Mysterium." In *Alchemical Traditions: From Antiquity to the Avant Garde*, edited by Aaron Cheak, 18–43. Melbourne, AU: Numen Books.
Cottnoir, Brian. 2006. *The Weiser Concise Guide to Alchemy*. York Beach, ME: Weiser Books.
Hauck, Dennis William. 2008. *The Complete Idiot's Guide to Alchemy*. New York: Alpha Books.
Hauck, Dennis William. 2011. "*Materia Prima:* The Nature of the First Matter in the Esoteric and Scientific Traditions." *Rose Croix Journal* 8: 72–88. http://www.rosecroixjournal. org/issues/2011/articles/v018_72_88_hauck.pdf.
Newman, William R., and Anthony Grafton, eds. 2006. *Secrets of Nature: Astrology and Alchemy in Early Modern Europe*. Transformations: Studies in the History of Science and Technology. Cambridge, MA: The MIT Press.

AMERICAN SOCIETY FOR PSYCHICAL RESEARCH

The American Society for Psychical Research (ASPR) was officially founded in January of 1885 as a sibling society of the British Society for Psychical Research (SPR), which was founded by Frederick Myers, Edmund Gurney, and others in London, England in 1882. Plans had been underway for the establishment of the ASPR as early as the fall of 1884, when William Barrett, then vice president of the SPR, was invited to Boston by William James in order to give an account of the SPR's goals and research projects. Barrett's goal, in turn, was to get Americans on board with psychical research, and he succeeded. After Barrett's talk on September 23, 1884, a committee was formed to discuss the creation of the ASPR, and, after subsequent meetings in the following weeks, the organization was officially born on January 8, 1885, as reported in the periodical *Science*.

Founding ASPR members included Simon Newcomb, the society's first president; G. Stanley Hall, psychologist and Harvard graduate; and Hall's Harvard mentor, William James. James and Myers were friends, based in no small part on James's interest in Myers's research and investigations into the psychic phenomena associated with spiritualism. In fact, James's interest in mystical and psychical phenomena greatly influenced his famous lectures on religion and mysticism, *The Varieties of Religious Experience* (1902), still a seminal work in the study of religion.

The ASPR and the SPR were originally created for the same purpose: to investigate spiritualist phenomena and the paranormal possibility that something—call it spirit, mind, or consciousness—could survive after a person physically died. Indeed, the mass spiritualism that was popular at that time involved the belief in the existence of human spirits after bodily death. One of the central rituals of the spiritualist faith, the séance, involved communicating with spirits through human mediums, many of whom were women. During these séances, the mediums would usually come under the psychic control of a spirit—that is, they would be under a kind of spirit possession. The spirit would then communicate, or prophesy, through the medium.

In addition to this kind of mental mediumship, there were often claims of physical mediumship, where spirits would either materialize in the physical world or would in some way make things happen in it, such as moving objects or making knocking sounds. Many cases of physical mediumship were readily discredited, which meant that one of the main issues psychical research had to address was how much of spiritualist mediumship was real and how much was fake.

After its formation, the ASPR underwent many hardships. As early as 1887 the society showed signs of crumbling. But as James was struggling to keep the ASPR together, the SPR's Richard Hodgson came to Boston to help reorganize it. In 1889, the ASPR merged with the SPR in order to alleviate some financial troubles but continued to function under the research auspices of Hodgson. Hodgson was famous for debunking many spiritualist frauds, including Helena Petrovna Blavatsky, cofounder of the Theosophical Society, against whom he found considerable evidence of fraudulent behavior. But not even Hodgson could debunk the powers of the American medium Leonora Piper, who became one of the most famous case studies of the ASPR.

Hodgson died in 1905, and the ASPR essentially dissolved. It was given new life in 1906 when it became the psychical research wing of James Harvey Hyslop's American Institute for Scientific Research. Hyslop eventually restructured the ASPR as an independent organization, and he continued to lead it until his death in 1920. Although somewhat autocratic, Hyslop was a respected scientist who was open to the belief in spirit communication while being critical of the spiritualist frauds who gave both spiritualism and, by association, psychical research a bad name.

After Hyslop's death, Walter Franklin Prince took charge of the ASPR and its research. A schism emerged within the society, however, over the reputed psychical powers of the medium Mina S. Crandon, or "Margery," whom Prince considered a fraud. When one of Margery's staunchest supporters was elected to a high-ranking research position within the ASPR, Prince and many of his supporters left and founded the Boston Society for Psychic Research (BSPR) in 1925. The BSPR famously published J. B. Rhine's parapsychological tract Extrasensory Perception (1934), and in 1941 the BSPR re-merged with the ASPR under the leadership of James Hyslop's son, George. Ties between the ASPR and the parapsychologists got stronger in 1957 with the establishment of the Parapsychological Association. The ASPR remains active today as a tax-exempt non-profit organization based in New York City (www.aspr.com).

Albert C. Silva

See also: Ectoplasm; James, William; Mediumship; Myers, Frederick W. H.; Parapsychology; Possession; Séance; Society for Psychical Research; Spiritualism; Survival after Death; Telepathy

Further Reading

Blum, Deborah. 2006. *Ghost Hunters: William James and the Search for Scientific Proof of Life after Death*. New York: Penguin Press.
Gauld, Alan. 1968. *The Founders of Psychical Research*. New York: Schocken Books.
Hess, David J. 1993. *Science in the New Age: The Paranormal, Its Defenders and Debunkers, and American Culture*. Madison, WI: University of Wisconsin Press.
Moore, R. Laurence. 1977. *In Search of White Crows*. New York: Oxford University Press.

ANGELS

The word "angel" comes from the Latin word *angelus*, meaning "messenger of God." The Latin word was in turn borrowed from Greek *ángelos*. Angels exist in monotheistic religions as intermediaries between the omnipotent God and the people who require guidance, education, protection, or punishment in line with the Deity's plans. Belief in angels is one of the six articles of faith in Islam, and in Judaism angles are known as *malakim* or *mal'akh*, also "messengers." Saints are said to have one or more guardian angels with them at all times. In addition to these traditional religious functions, in paranormal lore angels have often provided special knowledge to magicians and diviners and have been involved in stories of miraculous divine appearances and manifestations, including in the modern world, where a veritable "angel craze" has been long-lived among certain segments of America's alternative spiritual tradition, including the New Age movement.

Early Biblical references to angels describe the "angels of the Lord," such as in Genesis 18:2 and Joshua 5:13–15. Impersonal agents, such as pestilence in 2 Samuel 24:16–17 and the wind in Psalm 104:4, are also described as messengers of God and are therefore angels. Angels are enforcers and powerful warriors, as in Isaiah 37:36. Angels are invisible but can dramatically make themselves visible. The traditional depiction of an angel shows a beatific human with vast wings sprouting from his or her back. The cherubim have generally been depicted since the Renaissance as small, winged, toddler-aged children. There are pre-Christian precedents for each of these; the Greek goddess of victory *Nike* was depicted as a winged woman, and the traditional Italian motif of the *putti* had the appearance of winged young boys and could—as with the Roman Cupid—control human emotions. In Ezekiel the angels were multi-winged creatures with the four faces: lion, eagle, and bull, as well as human. In other instances, Genesis in particular, angels were mistaken for ordinary humans.

Various extracanonical and deuterocanonical scriptures have also added important elements to angel lore. In fact, the lives and identities of angels more often exist in Apocrypha, in Hebrew occultism such as the Kabbalah, and in grimoires. For example, the Hebrew Book of Enoch tells of rebellious angels who disobeyed God by breeding with human women. Occultists have long attempted to use angelic power for their own gains; the most famous was Elizabethan alchemist John Dee, who claimed that he had learned the angelic language *Enochian*. In his *A Dictionary of Angels*, Gustav Davidson points out that although he originally went to the Bible alone in search of the many named angels so familiar from angelic lore, "I soon learned that, on the contrary, the Bible was the last place to look for them" (Davidson ix).

Angels continued their warlike interventions in human history once the biblical period had closed. During the Battle of Lepanto in 1571 CE, an army of angels reportedly joined Christ, Saint Peter, and Saint Paul to assist in a naval victory over a Muslim fleet. But Islam has its battle angels, too: during the Battle of Bedr in 624 CE, the angel Gabriel led 300 Muslims to a victory over a Koreishite army of 1,000. The most famous case of angels on the battlefield was the angels reported during the British retreat from Mons at the start of the First World War. This and other stories of modern battlefield angels have often been attributed to the influence of the fictional story "The Bowman" by Arthur Machen.

Angelic interactions with humans became more banal in the later 20th century, as in, for example, the domestic encounters described in Hope Price's 1994 book *Angels: True Stories of How They Touch Our Lives*. This has not, however, extinguished an ongoing popular interest in these supernatural beings and their paranormal interventions in human affairs.

Scott Wood

See also: Astral Plane; Demonology; Discarnate Entity; Miracles; New Age; Occultism; Religion and the Paranormal; Swedenborg, Emanuel; Synchronicity

Further Reading
Brewer, E. 1884. *A Dictionary of Miracles: Imitative, Realistic and Dogmatic.* Philadelphia: J. B. Lippincott. https://archive.org/details/adictionarymira00brewgoog.
Cardin, Matt. 2007. "The Angel and the Demon." In *Icons of Horror and the Supernatural: An Encyclopedia of Our Worst Nightmares*, edited by S. T. Joshi, 31–64. Greenwood Icons. Westport, CT: Greenwood Press.
Clarke, David. 2004. *The Angels of Mons: Phantom Soldiers and Ghostly Guardians.* Chichester, UK: Wiley.
Davidson, Gustav. 1971. *A Dictionary of Angels, Including the Fallen Angels.* New York: The Free Press.
Guiley, Rosemary Ellen. 2004. *The Encyclopedia of Angels.* 2nd ed. New York: Checkmark Books

ANIMALS AND THE PARANORMAL

Animals occupy many supernatural cosmologies and experiences. How are animals symbolically entangled in myths and folklore, and how does that translate into strange real-world encounters? What evidence is there that animals have an afterlife or roam about as spirits? What studies have been done on animal psi, and how have animals displayed fantastical talents?

In many world cultures, specific animals have a particular spiritual or supernatural status. Japanese legends contain one of the most colorfulvarieties of animal: *y kai*, literally meaning a bewitching apparition or mystery. They include the octopus-like *akkorokamui* of Hokkaid; *kama-itachi*, weasels that ride on whirlwinds; and the mind-reading apes *satori*. Some, including *Kitsune* (foxes) and *tanuki* (a relative of the North American raccoon), have shape-shifting abilities and trickster personas. *Tanuki* can magically transform landscapes and hypnotize humans, as depicted in Studio Ghibli's animated film, the environmentalist parable *Pom Poko* (1994). Animal *y kai* have become popular worldwide via traditional art, manga, and anime, as well as films such as Akira Kurosawa's *Dreams* (1990), Hayao Miyazaki's *Princess Mononoke* (1997), and Takashi Miike's *The Great Yokai War* (2005).

Shape-shifting from human to animal and vice-versa is common across world cultures, such as werewolves in Europe (lycanthropes), seals that transform into women (selkies) in Gaelic and Faeroese lore, and skin-walkers among indigenous Americans. Half-human, half-animal creatures are common in mythology, such as the Greek minotaur (part bull), the Egyptian sphinx (part lion), the deity Ganesha (part elephant) in Hinduism and Buddhism, and the Chinese P'an Hu (part dog).

Strange animal encounters have been reported in contemporary life. For example, in 1985, soon-to-be Nobel laureate biochemist Kary Mullis reported seeing a glowing raccoon that spoke to him one night outside of his rural northern California cabin. The next thing he knew, he was walking along a road near his cabin the following morning. A friend of Mullis's who didn't know about this incident encountered the same glowing raccoon in 1993. He decided not to stick around but then encountered a small glowing man who transformed into a full-sized one and promised, "I'll see you tomorrow." The following night, returning to Mullis's cabin, the friend encountered the "glowing" man again on the road and left frightened. It turned out the man on the road was Mullis's neighbor, but the neighbor had not been at Mullis's cabin the previous night. Such strange animal sightings, shape-shifting, and missing time events have been reported in the literature on alien abductions.

At times, multiple paranormal events involving animals intersect. Over the past several decades in Clapham Woods, England, various anomalous phenomena from apparitions to unidentified flying objects have been reported. Psychical researcher Peter A. McCue has noted that several pet dogs mysteriously disappeared, became ill, or showed great distress in these woodlands. There is a lack of wildlife, but anomalous animals, such as a black panther-like big cat and a lynx, have been sighted in the area. Black magic rituals in the woods reportedly involved the occasional sacrifice of domestic and farm animals. McCue has called such places as Clapham Woods "zones of strangeness" because of the many unusual things that people have encountered there.

Animals have been harmed or killed under allegedly paranormal circumstances. Most famous have been livestock mutilations in the United States since the 1960s, in which animal parts and organs were removed with apparently surgical precision. An FBI inquiry into these mutilations in the mid-1970s found that most animals had been killed by natural predators, but a number of the cases they investigated remained unexplained. Hypotheses ranging from alien experiments to occult sacrifices to government conspiracies have been circulated. Other mutilations have been attributed to a mysterious, monstrous dog in the Americas known as *chupacabra*. The elusiveness of such creatures, known as cryptids, suggests paranormality. Famous cryptids also include the Loch Ness monster in Scotland; the Mothman in Point Pleasant, West Virginia; and a variety of large, bipedal, ape-like creatures known in North America as Bigfoot or Sasquatch, in the Himalayas as Yeti, and in Australia as Yowie. The bones of dragons in China have been shown to be dinosaur fossils.

Animals' spiritual significance may serve a political purpose, such as the veneration of cows and their protection in Hindu India that furthered Mahatma Gandhi's goal of national unity. Religious and shamanic systems may impart mystical status to animals as powerful spirit guides or signs. Funerary traditions may also intersect with animals as well, such as the mass sacrifice of cattle in animist Christian Torajan ceremonies in southern Sulawesi, or the placing of human remains inside of a sarcophagus shaped like a bull for cremation among contemporary Hindu Balinese royals. Animal sacrifices may be done as spiritual or magical offerings—for example, to heal people or to appease spirits as in Santería and Haitian Vodou.

Metaphysical questions have persisted concerning whether or not animals possess consciousness as humans do. Animal lovers usually respond in the affirmative. Buddhism has long valued animals as sentient beings. But only recently did Western scientists reach a crucial consensus, at the Francis Crick Memorial Conference, to include animals in the Cambridge Declaration on Consciousness in 2012. Some people claim to have special abilities in communicating with animals, from the American horse whisperer Buck Brannaman to "pet psychic" Joan Ranquet.

Questions also emerge concerning the possibility of animal personalities surviving physical death. Mediums have regularly reported encountering deceased pets in their spiritual consultations. A large variety of books have come on the market in which people share personal anecdotes about encountering apparitions of their deceased dogs and cats. In other situations, animals seem to synchronously connect to people who have died. In 1996, American grief counselor Louis E. LaGrand reported on a letter he had received from a widow who, when she was visiting her husband's grave one day, was surprised by a bird landing on her shoulder. This incident, for her, seemed related to the small ceramic birds her husband had given her as gifts. In cases of hauntings, pets are at times reported to be sensitive to the alleged paranormal presence, while in other cases they show no reaction at all. Often, cats stare at what seems to be an invisible entity but turns out to be a spider or insect sitting on the wall.

In the 1920s, the Polish physical medium Franek Kluski was photographed at séances with animal-like manifestations—one like a bird of prey, another like a large ape or hairy caveman. These materializations were verified by the other people who were present. People who attended the séances of another Polish medium, Jan Guzik, reported being touched, bitten, licked, or clawed by animal-type manifestations resembling dogs, cats, and squirrels. Both mediums were investigated by the French physician and psychical researcher Gustave Geley.

Ghost-like animals have been historically reported. Apparitions of black dogs recurrently reported in England are among the best known—a tradition going all the way back to the first report of such a thing in 1127 CE. The British parapsychologist Simon Sherwood's interest in them stemmed from a personal experience he had at the age of four when a "massive black animal" with eyes that were "bright yellow and big as saucers" galloped into his bedroom and then vanished. Starting in the 1990s, he collected many accounts from across the country of similar ghostly dogs going back nearly a millennium. At times, the eerie dog transforms into another shape, such as another animal or even a human.

There are scientists who study animal psi (also known as anpsi). In the early 19th century, Russian neurophysiologist Vladimir Bekhterev claimed success in testing dogs' abilities to respond to non-verbal mental suggestions. In the 1990s, biologist Rupert Sheldrake conducted experiments with dogs, arguing there was evidence that they knew when their owners were coming home through telepathy. Such research has been inspired by the many anecdotes that suggest animal psi, such as the dog or cat that covers hundreds of miles of unfamiliar territory to find its owner. A famous case is that of the cat Puss, which crossed a thousand miles from Australia's Gold Coast back to her home in Adelaide in a 12-month journey in 1977–1978. In 2013 in Stoney Creek, Ontario, a dog halted during its routine morning walk and led its owner to the home of a neighborhood resident who was inside her home and nearly dead from suffocating on a mucous plug, thus saving her life. Other animal anomalies have included animals that have fled impending natural disasters such as the Indian Ocean tsunami in 2004; talking animals such as Gef the mongoose (Isle of Man, 1930s) and Whitey the cat (Florida, 1960s); animals that deliver profound messages and portents (referred to as auguries); horses that solve math problems (Counting Hans in Germany in the early 19th century); children who were raised by wild animals; and mutations such as cats with wings.

Christopher Laursen

See also: Apparitions; Fortean Phenomena; Psi

Further Reading
Sheldrake, Rupert. 1999. *Dogs That Know When Their Owners Are Coming Home and Other Unexplained Powers of Animals.* London: Hutchinson.
Sherwood, Simon. 2012. "Apparitions of Black Dogs." Last modified September 2012. http://www.simonsherwood.co.uk/blackdog.htm.

ANOMALISTIC PSYCHOLOGY

Anomalistic psychology is a subdiscipline of psychology that is primarily focused upon explaining paranormal and related beliefs and ostensibly paranormal experiences in terms of known (or knowable) psychological and/or physical factors. It adopts as a working hypothesis the assumption that paranormal forces (i.e., forces that defy explanation in terms of currently understood conventional scientific concepts) do not exist. Within anomalistic psychology there is an emphasis upon the need to produce, wherever possible, empirical evidence in support of such nonparanormal explanations. It should also be noted that the assumption that paranormal forces do not exist is a working hypothesis only. In general, most anomalistic psychologists would accept that it is theoretically possible that at some future date parapsychologists may prove that paranormal forces really do exist. They would generally not accept, however, that such proof has been forthcoming to date.

Even in ancient times, there were those who proposed nonparanormal explanations for ostensibly paranormal phenomena. To give but one example, Hippocrates argued around 400 BCE that the symptoms of epilepsy were nothing to do with possession by demons but instead were caused by brain malfunction. Two centuries ago, Dr. John Ferrier argued that ghosts were nothing more than optical illusions, and famous names in the history of psychiatry, such as Karl Jaspers and Henry Maudsley, argued that paranormal experiences were best explained in psychological, not supernatural, terms. Other examples could be cited, but they are few and far between. Until relatively recently, with a few very notable exceptions, psychologists and psychiatrists showed little interest in understanding ostensibly paranormal experiences despite high levels of belief in the paranormal across all societies, both historically and geographically. It was not until 1982 that the term "anomalistic psychology" was first used. It was the title of a textbook by Leonard Zusne and Warren H. Jones (with a second edition in 1989). From that time on, interest in the area has grown.

Anomalistic psychology is sometimes viewed as being in opposition to parapsychology, but it would be more accurate to view the two areas as complementary. As stated, anomalistic psychologists adopt as a working hypothesis the position that paranormal forces do not exist but are open to the possibility that parapsychologists may one day produce a robust, reliable, and replicable demonstration that proves that assumption wrong. If so, anomalistic psychologists would have provided a valuable service to parapsychologists by helping them to distinguish between that which is genuinely paranormal and that which only looks as if it is paranormal. If such proof is never forthcoming, we can still learn a great deal about human psychology by studying ostensibly paranormal experiences. To ignore such experiences would be to ignore an important part of what it means to be human.

It should be noted that parapsychologists and anomalistic psychologists typically adopt somewhat different definitions of the term *paranormal*. Most parapsychologists restrict their subject matter to three key areas: extrasensory perception (that is, telepathy, clairvoyance, and precognition), psychokinesis, and evidence relating to life-after-death. Anomalistic psychologists, on the other hand, tend to adopt a much looser definition of the paranormal that more or less equates to anything "weird and wonderful," including topics such as astrology, alien abduction, UFOs, and the Loch Ness monster. The reason for this is that it is often the case that a topic that falls within the strict definition of the paranormal may be explained in psychological terms that also apply to a related topic that does not fit that strict definition.

An example of such a pair would be mediumship compared to astrology. Whereas the former allegedly involves communication with the dead, the latter does not fall within the strict definition favored by parapsychologists. However, it is clear that a reading from a medium and a reading from an astrologer can be very similar, both allegedly giving the client personal information relating to their past, present, and future. The psychological factors involved in the two situations are likely to be very similar if not identical. A further example would be hypnotic past-life regression compared to alien abduction claims. Whereas the former allegedly involves survival after death, the latter is clearly not included within the strict definition of paranormal. However, a strong case can be made that both types of claims are often best explained in terms of false memories.

Anomalistic psychologists draw on cognitive psychology, neuropsychology, clinical psychology, social psychology, and other subdisciplines within the field of psychology as a whole to explain purported paranormal phenomena in terms of known psychological and/or physical factors. They adopt the working hypothesis that paranormal phenomena do not actually exist—although they are open to the possibility that such phenomena may someday be proved real.

Anomalistic psychology is able to draw upon each of the other major subdisciplines of psychology in terms of what each has to offer by way of insights into understanding the psychology of ostensibly paranormal experiences. For example, cognitive psychology shows us that the processes that underlie perception, memory, reasoning, and so on, are all prone to biases of various kinds. Both perception and memory are constructive processes in which, although we are not aware of it, we automatically "fill in the gaps" without even realizing that we are doing so. The role of so-called "top-down processing" is emphasized within anomalistic psychology. This refers to the ways in which our prior beliefs, knowledge, and expectations about the world around us can affect both perception and memory of events. The effects of such biases have been demonstrated, for example, by having people take part in staged séances where all of the spooky effects are achieved by deliberate trickery. Those taking part are very likely to misperceive and misremember the events that take place during the séance and believers in the paranormal are particularly susceptible to the misleading suggestions from the fake medium.

Neuropsychology can also provide insights into many ostensibly paranormal experiences. For example, direct electrical stimulation of certain areas of the cortex of the brain can produce out-of-body experiences at the flick of a switch, supporting the claim that such experiences are hallucinations generated within the brain. As another example, our understanding of the psychophysiology of the sleep cycle provides insight into the nature of sleep paralysis, another hallucinatory experience that accounts for many claimed encounters with ghosts, demons, and aliens.

Further insights are provided by the perspectives of other subdisciplines of psychology. Findings from clinical psychology indicate that although some ostensibly paranormal experiences are indeed the result of psychopathology, the majority are not. There are, however, certain personality measures that are consistently found to be higher in paranormal believers compared to skeptics including fantasy proneness and magical thinking. If we turn to developmental psychology, we can consider the relationship between children's beliefs in the power of wishing and magical beings (such as fairies, Santa Claus, and the Easter Bunny) and adult paranormal beliefs. Such research demonstrates that both children and adults are capable of magical thinking in some contexts as well as nonmagical thinking in others.

Although personal experience of ostensibly paranormal events is a major factor in accounting for belief in the paranormal, many people believe on the basis of second-hand accounts from trusted others and the media. Social psychology casts light upon the psychological processes involved in either accepting or rejecting such communications from others.

There are many reasons for the growing popularity of anomalistic psychology. The subject matter of anomalistic psychology is inherently fascinating for most people, whether they believe in the paranormal or not. Topics covered range from the techniques used by psychic fraudsters and conjurors to perform feats that apparently defy explanation to the most profound issues facing us, such as the nature of consciousness and whether or not consciousness survives beyond physical death. In critically assessing the nature of evidence put forward in support of paranormal claims, we must consider the possible role played by the various biases that characterize human cognition including those which might lead us to perceive things that are not really there (e.g., hallucinations), to misremember events that we have witnessed or even to apparently remember events that never happened at all (false memories), to misinterpret evidence as a consequence of poor reasoning, and so on. Thus familiarity with anomalistic psychology implicitly provides an excellent grounding in critical thinking.

Since the 1980s anomalistic psychology has seen steady growth in terms of the number of relevant scientific papers and books published each year, the number of conferences held, media coverage, and so on. The number of universities offering courses that cover anomalistic psychology either as part of psychology degree programs or in courses on critical thinking has also grown steadily over this period. There is every indication that anomalistic psychology has a very bright future.

Christopher C. French

See also: Abduction Experience; Astrology; Clairvoyance; Consciousness; Demonology; Extrasensory Perception (ESP); Ghosts; Hallucinations; Mediumship; Out-of-Body Experience (OBE); Paranormal; Parapsychology; Past-Life Regression; Possession; Precognition; Psychokinesis (PK); Reincarnation; Séance; Sleep Paralysis; Survival after Death; Telepathy; UFO

Further Reading

French, Christopher C., and Anna Stone. 2014. *Anomalistic Psychology: Exploring Paranormal Belief and Experience*. Basingstoke, UK: Palgrave Macmillan.
Holt, Nicola, Christine Simmonds-Moore, David Luke, and Christopher C. French. 2012. *Anomalistic Psychology*. Basingstoke, UK: Palgrave Macmillan.

APPARITIONS

To many people an apparition is another word for a ghost and suggests the appearance of a person (or an animal) that could not have been physically present at the time. Traditionally, apparitions have been taken as possible evidence for survival of bodily death. However, apparitions can be of the living as well as the dead, and their appearance does not necessarily need to be associated with a particular location; sometimes apparitions can also be of inanimate objects, such as cars, boats, and planes. It is difficult to give a comprehensive and precise definition of an apparition that everyone would agree with. Apparitional experiences tend to be primarily visual and can be very vivid and realistic. Witnesses often do not realize that anything out of the ordinary is happening until the apparition does something unexpected and inexplicable, such as fading away, suddenly vanishing, or walking through a wall. An ongoing issue is whether apparitions are subjective or objective; in others words, are they a hallucinatory mental phenomenon or is there something actually present in the environment that is being perceived via the normal senses? This issue is complicated by the fact that some apparitions demonstrate properties that suggest they are objective, such as being seen by more than one person simultaneously or being reflected in a mirror, while others demonstrate properties that suggest that they are subjective, such as moving through solid objects or not leaving any physical trace. Recent theories and research have suggested that apparitional experiences may depend partly upon the characteristics of the witnesses and partly on those of the context and the environment. This might explain why not everyone present will necessarily share the same experience. The possible effects of environmental variables, such as electromagnetic and geomagnetic fields and infrasound, which might induce certain features of apparitional experiences, are currently receiving a lot of attention. Given the diversity of different kinds of apparitional experiences, there may be different explanations for different experiences.

Most apparitional experiences seem to be spontaneous and unpredictable. Many involve people who are emotionally close to us and who are suffering some kind of crisis at the time (crisis apparitions), or else they have died recently (post-mortem apparitions). Other kinds of apparition include deathbed or takeaway apparitions where people on their deathbed report visits from deceased relatives who have come to collect them. Haunting apparitions are associated with a specific location. Interestingly, apparitions are rare in poltergeist cases. Some apparitions seem to be aware of their surroundings, behave accordingly, and might attempt to communicate with witnesses; in other cases they seem completely unaware and behave in a predetermined fashion—for example, they might walk through a wall. There are a few cases of so-called experimental apparitions where a person has apparently successfully projected an apparition of himself or herself at a remote location that has been witnessed by someone else; such experiences overlap with out-of-body experiences (OBEs). Of particular interest are collective

Types of Apparitions

Crisis apparition: An apparition involving someone who is emotionally close and suffering a crisis.

Post-mortem apparition: An apparition of someone who has recently died.

Deathbed apparition (a.k.a. takeaway apparition): An apparition experienced when someone who is dying perceives a visit from deceased relatives who have come to take him or her away.

Haunting apparition: An apparition that is associated with a specific location.

Experimental apparition: An apparition that occurs when someone apparently successfully projects an apparition of him- or herself to a remote location, where it is witnessed by another person.

Collective apparition: An apparition witnessed simultaneously by more than one person.

apparitions that are witnessed simultaneously by more than one person, though not everyone present will necessarily share the experience.

Apparitions have tended to be investigated via surveys and the collection of spontaneous case reports, but fieldwork has also been carried out at allegedly haunted locations. There have also been experimental attempts to facilitate apparitional experiences using techniques, such as psychomanteum chambers, where participants gaze into a mirror in a dimly lit room while thinking about a particular deceased person that they would like to have a reunion with. It is difficult to get a precise figure on the prevalence of apparitional experiences, given the different wording of the questions and the different samples used, but some estimates suggest that between 10 and 32 percent of respondents have had some kind of experience of this kind. In England in 1894, the Society for Psychical Research published a classic study titled *Census of Hallucinations*. Of the 17,000 respondents, 9.9 percent had had some kind of apparitional-type experience; most of these apparitions were of people (74.7 percent) and almost a third (31.7 percent) of the visual experiences were impressions of the living. The experiences were mainly visual (69 percent), auditory (24 percent), or tactile (7 percent) in nature. The visual experiences occurred both indoors and outdoors, with a sizeable proportion occurring while the witness was in bed. Some researchers would also include a sense of presence as an apparitional experience.

There are a variety of possible normal and paranormal explanations that have been proposed for apparitional experiences, but none of them can, as yet, fully explain all of the features of all types of apparitional experience. Normal explanations include deliberate fraud and misinterpretation, hallucinations (such as hypnagogic or hypnopompic imagery), and the effects of environmental variables on the brain. Paranormal explanations include extrasensory perception (ESP) of current or past events on the part of the witnesses, psychokinesis (PK) that has somehow created the apparition, or the ability of consciousness or the spirit or soul to exist independently of the physical body. One of the challenges of the evidence for survival of bodily death is to overcome the super-psi hypothesis, which claims that exceptional ESP and/or PK are a more likely alternative explanation. In order to support the survival hypothesis, the apparition really needs to demonstrate intelligent consciousness and show awareness of the environment, be able to interact with witnesses, and demonstrate the personality, abilities, and memories that would be expected of that individual.

Simon Sherwood

See also: Animals and the Paranormal; Bilocation; Discarnate Entity; Extrasensory Perception (ESP); Ghosts; Haunting; Hypnagogic State; Out-of-Body Experience (OBE); Psi; Psychokinesis (PK); Religion and the Paranormal; Society for Psychical Research; Survival after Death

Further Reading

Green, Celia, and Charles McCreery. (1975) 1989. *Apparitions.* London: Hamish Hamilton.
Haraldsson, Erlendur. 2012. *The Departed among the Living: An Investigative Study of Afterlife Encounters.* Guildford, UK: White Crow Books.
MacKenzie, Andrew. 1982. *Hauntings and Apparitions.* London: Heinemann.
Sidgwick, Henry, Alice Johnson, Frederic W.H. Myers, Frank Podmore, and Eleanor Sidgwick. 1894. "Report on the Census of Hallucinations." *Proceedings of the Society for Psychical Research* 10: 25–422.
Tyrrell, George N. M. (1943) 1973. *Apparitions.* London: The Society for Psychical Research.

ART, CREATIVITY, AND THE PARANORMAL

The paranormal has long and widely been associated with the arts, and not only as fodder for artistic productions. Perhaps more profoundly, paranormal experiences have parallels with the creative process itself. The paranormal has provided material for artistic genres, including film (e.g., *Red Lights*, *The Others*), fiction (e.g., the classic ghost stories of M. R. James or Edith Nesbit) and the visual arts (e.g., the video installations of Susan MacWilliam, such as *Remote Viewing*, or the photography of Clare Strand). Historically, Spiritualism and Theosophy have influenced movements in Modern Art, such as abstract expressionism (e.g., through the works of Piet Mondrian, Paul Klee, and Wassily Kandinsky) and Surrealism (e.g., André Breton and Remedios Varo), influencing both forms of abstraction such as representations of "spiritual constants" through color and form and methods of obtaining inspiration

through automatic writing or drawing. Further, the arts in various forms have pu-
tatively facilitated the expression or communication of the occult or paranormal
through spirit photography, psychic photography, and psychic art. Consider, for example, the "thoughtography" of Ted Serios, who purported to use psychokinesis to
produce images on film, or the music of Rosemary Brown, who claimed to channel
the work of dead composers such as Igor Stravinsky and Sergei Rachmaninoff. In
some cultures, art and the "paranormal" are intertwined, so that art making per se
involves connection with spirits or the divine in the process of image making (e.g.,
Balinese sacred art). Indeed, various Western artists have attributed artistic inspiration to paranormal sources or have reported paranormal experiences, including
writers such as W. B. Yeats, Mark Twain, Sylvia Plath, and Ted Hughes; visual artists
such as William Blake, Alex Grey, and Cecil Collins; and musicians such as Robert
Schumann and Alexander Scriabin.

The mathematician John Nash is reputed to have said that "the ideas I had
about supernatural beings came to me the same way that my mathematical ideas
did. So I took them seriously" (Nasar 1998, 11). Phenomenological parallels have
been drawn between experiences of inspiration in the creative process and paranormal experiences, both being described as being spontaneous and difficult to
control, and as involving altered states of consciousness, flashes of visual imagery,
increased access to "unconscious material," and a sense of noesis, a profound sense
of having "received knowledge." Creative inspiration typically occurs after a long
period of struggle with a particular problem, spontaneously arising as a potential
solution, sometimes in a dream or hallucination, during a time of exhaustion or
relaxation, as famously reported by scientists such as August Kekulé and Henri
Poincaré. However, in some cases inspiration is reported as arising as a complete
product, ready to be communicated to others (e.g., the thirty lines of Coleridge's
poem "Kubla Khan"). In such cases inspiration can be accompanied by the feeling
that it came from beyond the self and may be attributed to an "autonomous other,"
akin to the Greek Muses. Carl Jung described this as "visionary creativity." For example, William Blake described his poems as being dictated to him by angels and
himself as surrendering his conscious "will" in the process. Robert Louis Stevenson
described his dreams, or "Brownies" in the night, as dictating his stories. There are
clear parallels between these experiences and descriptions of channeling spirits in
mediumship, exemplified by the psychic art of Pearl Curran, who attributed her
novels to a channeled identity, Patience Worth. Hence, paranormal-like experiences that occur in the creative process have been described as being of two types:
hallucinatory-like moments of inspiration and experiences of "the muse."

Psychological research bears out the apparent connection between art, creativity,
and the paranormal. Among the general population, low to moderate correlations
have been found between measures of creativity and the holding of paranormal beliefs. In an early review of the characteristics of creative people, Gary Davis and colleagues described them as attracted to the mysterious, showing an unusually strong
interest and belief in ESP (extrasensory perception), flying saucers, and ghosts.

Frederic Myers and the "Subliminal Uprush"

Psychologist and psychical researcher Frederic Myers wrote at length about what he called the "subliminal uprush" of unconscious materials into consciousness, which he viewed as central to both creative inspiration and paranormal experiences:

> I shall suggest . . . that Genius—if that vaguely used word is to receive anything like a psychological definition—should rather be regarded as a power of utilising a wider range than other men can utilise of faculties in some degree innate in all;—a power of appropriating the results of subliminal mentation to subserve the supraliminal stream of thought;—so that an "inspiration of Genius" will be in truth a *subliminal uprush*, an emergence into the current of ideas which the man is consciously manipulating of other ideas which he has not consciously originated, but which have shaped themselves beyond his will, in profounder regions of his being. I shall urge that there is here no real departure from normality; no abnormality, at least in the sense of degeneration; but rather a fulfilment of the true norm of man, with suggestions, it may be, of something *supernormal*;—of something which transcends existing normality as an advanced stage of evolutionary progress transcends an earlier stage.

—Frederic W. H. Myers, *Human Personality and Its Survival of Bodily Death* (1903)

Further, both involvement with the arts and the ability to make remote cognitive associations, thought to be indicative of creative cognition (e.g., responding "soldier" to the word "foot," rather than "shoe"), predict the reporting of paranormal and other anomalous experiences such as mystical experiences and hallucinations.

Several explanations have been proffered to explain these links. The Victorian scholar Frederic Myers theorized that a "subliminal uprush" of ideas into conscious awareness was central to both creative and paranormal experiences, mediated in imagistic form. This idea of increased permeability between "subliminal" and "supraliminal" awareness has been developed in recent years by Michael Thalbourne with the concept of transliminality. Transliminality is thought to be a personality trait that involves a "hypersensitivity" to psychological (e.g., subconscious) and environmental (e.g., subliminal) stimuli. However, research correlating scores on a transliminality questionnaire with cognitive measures of creativity, such as divergent thinking—the making of numerous original responses to visual or verbal stimuli—has obtained mixed results. As such, no firm conclusions can be made regarding the transliminality hypothesis. Other researchers, noting the significant correlations in some studies between the making of remote associations and paranormal beliefs and experiences have postulated a continuum of associative processing to explain both. Along this continuum, cognitive associations range from commonplace stereotypical associations to creative associations, which are remote but accurate, through to paranormal ideation in healthy individuals, and finally to psychopathological delusion. Associations along this continuum become increasingly remote until any links are thought to be illusory or apophenic, the experience of abnormal meaningfulness. However, other explanations could explain the associations found between involvement with artistic hobbies or professions and paranormal beliefs and experiences, such as reporting artifacts. For example, artists may be more likely to share unusual, potentially taboo, experiences in surveys, or they may pay more attention to such experiences and thus be more likely to remember them. Alternatively, artists may have more open belief systems—artists tend to score highly on the personality trait of openness-to-experience, which involves seeking out novel ideas and experiences—which may lead to higher scores on measures of paranormal belief and experience. As such, although creativity and paranormal beliefs and experiences do appear to be connected, further research is required to explain why and in what way.

It is worth noting that some psychological models link both creative and paranormal cognition with poor mental health. However, Frederic Myers argued that genius, both creative and psychic, depended upon an increased ability to control access to potentially "supernormal" realms of consciousness, which he thought was associated with superior mental health. Indeed, the ability to adaptively shift between focused and unfocused cognitive states is required by two-factor models of creativity, in which creativity involves both unusual ideation and the evaluation of ideas thus produced in order to meet a goal. Furthermore, research suggests that creative individuals score highly on measures of both cognitive eccentricity and psychological resilience, leading the humanistic psychologist Frank Barron to refer to creative people as exhibiting "controllable oddness," a variant of healthiness.

Such are the links between art, creativity, and the paranormal that J. B. Rhine, the father of modern parapsychology, suggested the "parapsycho-artistic" as an area of special study. Parapsychological research has examined whether creativity is associated with ESP performance in the laboratory. If creative inspiration and paranormal experiences share, at least in part, a common cognitive microgenesis, then creative individuals might be expected to perform better on ESP tasks. Numerous experimental studies have tested this hypothesis. For example, in the 1960s Thelma Moss observed that artists performed better than nonartists on an ESP test. Further research, employing the ganzfeld technique, consistently reports significant outcomes in support of the ESP hypothesis in studies with artistic populations, although these studies have no nonartistic controls, making it difficult to rule out the influence of other features, such as experimenter effects. Nevertheless, these studies have been taken to suggest that there is something about being an artist that is associated with ESP-performance. However, it is not clear what this factor is. Psychological indices of creativity have met with limited success as indicators of ESP-performance in the laboratory. Other factors could include belief in the paranormal or the ability to shift into altered states, which have both been associated with ESP-performance and artistic involvement.

Despite the numerous interconnections between creativity, art, and the paranormal, much has yet to be learned about them. This topic has implications for our understanding of the creative process and the potentially adaptive role of anomalous experiences within it. Competing models suggest either that creativity and the paranormal are connected by aberrant cognition (clinical perspectives) or the parapsychological hypothesis that artists might have genuine paranormal abilities. Future research might enable the drawing of firmer conclusions on such issues and a better understanding of why creativity and paranormal experiences often co-occur.

Nicola Holt

See also: Automatic Writing; Extrasensory Perception (ESP); Ganzfeld Technique, The; Hallucinations; Myers, Frederic W. H.; Rhine Research Center; Sheep-Goat Effect

Further Reading

Cardeña, Etzel, Ana Iribas, and Sophie Reijman. 2012. "Art and Psi." *Journal of Parapsychology* 76: 3–23.

Carpenter, James C. 2012. *First Sight: ESP and Parapsychology in Everyday Life*. Lanham, MD: Rowman & Littlefield Publishing Group.

Holt, Nicola. 2012. "The Muse in the Machine: Creativity, Anomalous Experiences and Mental Health." In *Exceptional Experience and Health*, edited by Christine Simmonds-Moore, 131–170. Jefferson, North Carolina: McFarland.

Nasar, Sylvia. 1998. *A Beautiful Mind*. London: Faber and Faber.

ASTRAL PLANE

The astral plane is an ambiguous term representing a variety of claims that there exists a level of being beyond the observable world, in which various entities are located, such as ghosts and other discarnate spirits, which can be contacted by individuals who claim various psychic, mediumistic, or clairvoyant abilities.

The idea of a plane or planes of being that exist beyond the material dates back at least to Plato. Through the Middle Ages and into the modern world the idea of existence beyond the physical persisted, although these planes were represented in a variety of ways. These planes also became the home of a variety of entities such as gods, angels, demons, ghosts, and many other kinds of non-material entities. Beginning in the early modern period, natural philosophers began to postulate that there was an aspect of the material world that connected directly with the spiritual world, as well as with the bodies in the heavens, such as stars and planets. They called this connection the astral, and claimed that this astral level of existence was located between the material world and the realm of the divine. By the late 19th century, these ideas of the astral became represented not as something beyond the material world, but instead as consisting of a different kind of materiality, one that was composed of a finer material than the normal world, one which people could interact with on a day-to-day basis. This extension of the astral plane into the material world also imbued the human body with an astral body or bodies.

These notions of the astral plane having at least some level of materiality resulted in claims that the astral plane was open to scientific experimentation and that it operated in similar ways to the known material universe. One of the leading groups to posit the existence of the astral plane was the Theosophical Society, which was founded in 1875 in New York City. Theosophists claimed that a human being has not only an astral body but numerous astral components to it, and that all extend into various planes of existence, which are all composed of finer levels of matter. The difficulty is that these levels of being are hidden from the majority of humanity, and a person must have clairvoyant abilities to see and interact with them. This area of religious belief and practice was therefore called occultism, coming from the word "occult," meaning hidden.

Theosophists made a variety of claims about the astral plane, astral bodies, and the way matter operates in these astral planes. For instance, in the beginning of the 20th century, Theosophical leaders claimed all elements and molecules have an astral component. They began to describe and diagram this reality, calling it "occult chemistry." Similarly, Theosophists and other occultists claimed that the astral body in people can separate from the physical body and travel in the astral plane, leaving the physical body temporarily behind. This kind of movement was called astral travel or astral projection. Some claimed that when freed from the physical body, the astral body can travel anywhere in the physical universe, travel backward or forward in time, and travel to symbolic realms that exist in universes separate from the one in which people live.

Within the history of the astral plane, a number of figures, organizations, and literary works have had a substantial influence on its development and how it is understood.

Emanuel Swedenborg (1688–1772)

Emanuel Swedenborg was a Swedish scientist, philosopher, theologian, and mystic. While he never used the term astral plane, he described various visions and dreams in which he was allowed by God to travel freely in heaven and hell. Additionally, he also communicated with the angels, demons, and various deceased people he encountered. He described these visions and conversations in a variety of books, the most famous being *Heaven and Hell* (1758). In these books, the places he visits, including the various planes of hell and the different planets of the solar system, and the beings he encounters, including angels and demons, are all very human, and the environment he describes appears similar to the material world. For many who read Swedenborg, the afterlife began to look like an extension of the life lived in this world.

Modern Spiritualism

In 1848, in upstate New York, two sisters, Margaret and Kate Fox, began to communicate with the spirit of a peddler who claimed to have been murdered and buried under the basement floor of their home. Initially the communication came as a series of knocks based on a code. As word spread of the Fox sisters' communication with the dead, other people found that they, too, had the ability to communicate with the dead. These spirits of the dead claimed to live in the spirit world, which was just like the material one. Those who could communicate with the dead were called mediums. This movement of spirit communication came to be called Modern Spiritualism. Spiritualists asserted that they could communicate with the dead in a variety of ways, including through knocks, trance writing, speaking, and drawing. Sometimes spirits would play musical instruments, write, and move objects. Later in the movement, spirits began to materialize for spectators. Andrew Jackson Davis wrote a series of books explaining how spirit communication works. He claimed that when people die, they continue to have the same personality and physical traits that they had in life. Between 1850 and 1861, Davis published a six-volume series called *The Great Harmonia*, in which he claimed that people would retain their race, gender, and appearance after death. Moreover, those who passed continued to grow and evolve spiritually or religiously. Other Spiritualists claimed that even babies and children, who died while young, would grow up in the spirit world and would even attend school.

The Theosophical Society

Initially the founders of the Theosophical Society, Helena Petrovna Blavatsky (also known as Madame Blavatsky) and Henry Steel Olcott, had roots in the Spiritualist movement. However, they were critical of the claims made by spiritualists and, in particular, their understanding of the spirit world. Theosophists claimed that, instead of communicating with the realm of the dead, mediums were connecting with the astral remnants of people who had died. They claimed that after death, the spirit or soul of a person moves on to higher planes of existence or is reincarnated. Left behind are "shells" of the person, temporarily existing in the astral plane but eventually dissolving. Later Theosophists expanded on these ideas and began to systematize the various aspects of the astral world. In 1895, Charles Webster Leadbeater published *The Astral Plane*, in which he claimed that a large variety of mythological beings actually exist, in some form or another, on the astral plane. Included in his list were vampires, werewolves, shells of the dead, astral bodies of animals, elementals, angels, ghosts, fairies, and various nature-spirits. Later he and other Theosophists, such as Annie Besant, began to explain the complex, seven-part composition of the human body and its aura; the way astral matter coalesces into various shapes and with various colors based on human thoughts and emotions, called Thought-Forms; and how the astral plane fits into the spiritual evolution of humanity.

The Hermetic Order of the Golden Dawn

In England, in 1888, a new magical group emerged that built on the teachings of the Theosophical Society. However, it claimed that astral travel also allows people to visit symbolic realms based on ideas related to universal systems of correspondence. This opened up opportunities for astral travelers to interact with imaginative worlds. Moreover, it also asserted that progression through these symbolic worlds was a practice called "Rising in the Planes," which would assist in spiritual growth and help develop various psychic or clairvoyant abilities. Conceptually, these practices of rising in the planes were not unlike practices originating from the Neoplatonists.

New Age Religion

Beginning in the early and mid-20th century, various spiritual leaders, such as Alice Bailey, Guy Ballard, Paul Foster Case, Edgar Cayce, Dion Fortune, Max Heindel, and Elizabeth Claire Prophet, began to build on the previous ideas of the astral plane, giving it new descriptions and devising new practices relating to it. These were brought to the forefront in the counterculture movement of the 1960s and 1970s and continued well into the 1980s. By then the New Age movement was making various claims about the astral plane and frequently focusing on issues relating to it, including astral projection, the aura, and spiritual evolution to higher states of being.

Today the astral plane is a broad term used in relation to a variety of claims of planes of existence lying beyond the physical and inhabited by all kinds of imaginable entities, including angels, ghosts, and aliens. It is also related to the body, the aura, and myriad other spiritual phenomena.

John L. Crow

See also: Akashic Records; Aura; Discarnate Entity; Ghosts; Imaginal; New Age; Occultism; Spiritualism; Theosophy

Further Reading

Denning, Melita, and Osborne Phillips. 1979. *The Llewellyn Practical Guide to Astral Projection: The Out-of-Body Experience*. Woodbury, MN: Llewellyn Publishing.

Leadbeater, C. W. 1895. *The Astral Plane: Its Scenery, Inhabitants and Phenomena*. London: Theosophical Publishing Society. http://www.gutenberg.org/ebooks/21080.

Leadbeater, C. W. 1903. *Clairvoyance*. London: Theosophical Publishing Society. http://www.gutenberg.org/ebooks/29399.

LeLand, Kurt. 2010. *The Multidimensional Human: Practices for Psychic Development* and *Astral Projection*. Boston: Spiritual Orienteering Press.

Shirley, Ralph. (1938) 2004. *The Mystery of the Human Double: The Case for Astral Projection*. Whitefish, MT: Kessinger Books.

ASTROLOGY

Astrology is the practice of consulting, reading, and interpreting the relative positions and motions of the sun, moon, stars, and planets for the purpose of predicting the future, telling fortunes, revealing the likely outcomes of various possible courses of action, and/or gaining insight into personal relationships and life meanings. It is one of the most ancient forms of divination and also one of the most universal, having been practiced in various forms by virtually every people and culture throughout history, including, notably, the Chaldeans, Babylonians, Chinese, Indians, Mayans, Romans, Greeks, Egyptians, and early Islamic cultures, with roots extending well into Neolithic prehistory. In some ways the historical and cultural trajectory of astrology parallels that of alchemy (although astrology's lifespan has been vastly longer), in that, just as alchemy gave way to chemistry, belief in astrology was nearly universal until the practice was recast as pseudoscience during the scientific revolution, after which it was primarily viewed by mainstream intellectual culture as a precursor to the more scientifically respectable science of astronomy. Also like alchemy, astrology has continued to have its champions and has persisted as a subcultural subject of serious reflection. Unlike alchemy, on a popular level astrology has maintained considerable prominence, with the "daily horoscope" remaining a staple of American newspapers, and with an ever-proliferating number of books on astrology continuing to populate the metaphysical or New Age section of mainstream bookstores.

Astrology is founded on the notion that the celestial bodies influence events on planet earth and in human life, and/or that their motions and positions reveal meaningful information and insight about human affairs. In its earliest organized forms it was used primarily by kings and other high political rulers in relation to matters of government and commerce. Many of the Roman emperors, for example, retained royal astrologers as standard members of their court. The philosophical component was also present from the beginning; Plato and Aristotle both affirmed the influence of the stars, and this belief was echoed by virtually all other philosophers and early scientists. In the West the proto-systems of the Babylonians were codified by the Chaldeans around the fifth century BCE to produce a system of natal astrology—the use of astrology for interpreting a person's life and fate based on astrological conditions at the time of his or her birth—that exerted an enormous influence. Even more important was Ptolemy's *Tetrabiblos*, a four-part treatise written in the second century CE that went on to serve as the basis for nearly all subsequent Western astrological thought.

The rise of Christianity led to a general condemnation and suppression of astrology in the West, with Saint Augustine, for instance, condemning the practice as incompatible with Christian teachings, although others among the Church fathers disagreed with this assessment. At the Council of Laodicea in the fourth century, the Church formally banned priests from practicing astrology, not long after Constantine the Great, having converted to Christianity, banned astrology in the Roman Empire and threatened its practitioners with death. Astrology effectively went underground in the West for nearly a millennium, even as it flourished and remained vital elsewhere—for example, in the Byzantine Empire and the burgeoning Islamic civilization. Eventually, the translation of various Arab astrological texts into Latin in the 11th century, in tandem with the channeling of ancient Platonic and Aristotelian astrological ideas into European culture via the rise of Medieval Christianity, produced a Western rebirth of astrology. This carried forward into the age of the Italian Renaissance with its widespread ferment of esoteric and occult ideas. However, astrology was soon checked yet again by the rise of the new material science in the 16th century. At the century's outset the most renowned scientists—Galileo, Kepler, and so on—all held astrology in high regard, but by 1700 this had completely reversed, and scientists had definitively turned against astrology, a notable exception being Isaac Newton, who remained ardently interested in astrology, as well as in other mystical and esoteric matters, throughout his life. Astrology retreated again to the cultural margins, where it found a particularly welcoming environment among Rosicrucians and other occult secret societies.

This ousting from mainstream scientific respectability remains in effect to the present day, when astrology is officially labeled a pseudoscience by the scientific establishment. At the same time, it has persisted as both a subject of popular interest, especially in relation to the New Age movement, and a matter of serious study and practice on the margins of mainstream intellectual culture. This can be seen, for example, in several developments in the mid-20th century. In 1930 the American astrologer Evangeline Adams published a bestselling book titled *Astrology: Your Place among the Stars*. She also launched the first astrology-themed radio show, which achieved considerable popularity. The 1940s through the 1960s saw the founding of several astrological organizations in Europe and America: the English astrologer Charles Carter founded the Faculty of Astrology Studies in London in 1949, the Astrological Association of Great Britain was founded in London in 1958, and the International Society for Astrological Research was founded in 1969. The French psychologist and statistician Michel Gauquelin caused a stir in 1955 when he published *L'influence de Astres* (The influence of the Stars), in which he offered apparent statistical evidence for an astrological correlation between cases of noted athletic excellence and the position of Mars at the time of the athlete's birth. The so-called "Mars Effect" became a magnet for controversy, attracting both supporters and debunkers.

One of the more interesting and influential evolutionary transformations of astrology in the modern period has been the rise of so-called psychological astrology, which fuses astrological concepts and symbols with depth psychology, humanistic psychology, and transpersonal psychology. The field draws heavily on the work of Carl Jung, who, as he also did with alchemy, regarded astrology as a system of archetypal symbols that could be fruitfully mined for depth psychological purposes. His work in this area influenced, among others, the French-born modernist composer Dane Rudhyar, who in 1936 published *The Astrology of Personality*, followed by many additional books. In a slightly different but deeply related vein, in 2006 Richard Tarnas, author of the bestselling 1991 intellectual history *The Passion of the Western Mind*, published a book titled *Cosmos and Psyche: Intimations of a New World View*, in which he presented a critique of scientific materialism and argued for an astrological interpretation of humanity's place in the cosmos based on the correlations between astrological phenomena and significant events in human history, especially in relation to the lives of major historical figures.

In general, it appears likely that astrology will continue to dwell on the margins of scientific and intellectual culture for the indefinite future. At the same time, it also appears likely that astrology will continue to thrive in that marginal space. Given the crisis of legitimacy that has come to afflict science, religion, and most other mainstream cultural institutions in the early 21st century, it is conceivable that this ancient practice and worldview will, at some point, cycle yet again into a position of conventional respectability.

Matt Cardin

See also: Alchemy; Committee for Skeptical Inquiry; Divination; Jung, Carl; New Age; Tarot

Further Reading

Bobrick, Benson. 2005. *The Fated Sky: Astrology in History*. New York: Simon & Schuster.

Campion, Nicholas. 2009. *A History of Western Astrology, Volume I: The Ancient World*. London: Bloomsbury Academic.

Campion, Nicholas. 2009. *A History of Western Astrology, Volume II: The Medieval and Modern Worlds*. London: Bloomsbury Academic.

Newman, William R., and Anthony Grafton, eds. 2006. *Secrets of Nature: Astrology and Alchemy in Early Modern Europe*. Cambridge, MA: The MIT Press.

Tarnas, Richard. 2006. *Cosmos and Psyche: Intimations of a New World View*. New York: Viking.

Whitfield, Peter. 2004. *Astrology: A History*. London: British Library.

AURA

The word "aura" etymologically derives from the Greek word αὔρα, meaning "breath" or "breeze." Over time, it also has come to refer to a subtle emanation coming from any substance or thing (e.g., the smell of flowers or essential oils). When used in reference to human beings and living creatures, aura refers to an energetic emanation—almost like a field or pattern of spiritual energy—coming from and enveloping them. Some people believe that everything with an atomic structure—that is, anything that is made up of the stuff of our universe, including a nonliving entity such as a rock—has an aura. Auras have a mystical and paranormal quality to them because, quite simply, not everybody can see them; they are the kind of phenomena that require a special human ability in order to be detected. The ability to see auras is often considered to be a kind of clairvoyance and/or spiritual intuition and can therefore be classified as a form of extrasensory perception (ESP). Auras, therefore, are observable phenomena (though not by everybody) that not only exist in the physical world but that point to a spiritual realm as well. Put differently, they are the observable energetic radiation of each person's spiritual essence. In this way, when it comes to human beings, the aura is sometimes seen as a representation of the soul.

The modern usage of the word "aura" emerges from the history of Western metaphysical religious traditions whose theologies, doctrines, and/or rituals involved a blending of both religious and scientific themes and concerns. Within these traditions, the central theological concept that connects religion and science is "energy." Metaphysical religions typically involve (1) an emphasis on the power and importance of the mind; (2) a belief in the theory of correspondence between the universe (or spiritual realm) and the material world; (3) an understanding of healing (of the body and the mind) as a sign of spiritual salvation; and (4) a preoccupation with energy as the ultimate spiritual essence, that is, as the "stuff" of which the entire universe, including all of humanity, is made.

A central tenet of metaphysical religiosity is "as above, so below," which means that there is an equivalence between macrocosm and microcosm, or between the universe/spiritual realm and the human world/material realm. Since both macrocosm and microcosm are made of energy, metaphysicians would argue, then the correspondence between them must occur through the movement or transfer of that energy. In this way, spiritual energy is understood by many as flowing into human bodies from the higher spiritual realm, radiating from human bodies during life and exiting the body upon death. This belief is central to many popular forms of alternative medicine, including various forms of energy or auric healing. Many people seek the help of energy healers in order to address a variety of health concerns. Energy healers usually work by observing—usually within some sort of trance or deeply introspective state—human auras and removing any energetic blockages found within them.

The development of the current understanding of auras originates in the 19th century with the metaphysical religious traditions of Spiritualism and Theosophy. Both of these traditions also shared a preoccupation with promoting health and healing in human beings, and they addressed this preoccupation in and through the language of energy.

Spiritualism began as a Quaker offshoot movement, and it took on mass appeal around the 1870s when séances and Spiritualist mediums became ubiquitous in popular and religious culture. Its development was especially tied to the work of the American trance physician Andrew Jackson Davis (1826–1910), who provided it with the closest thing to a doctrinal text, *The Principles of Nature* (1847). Davis's work combined many Swedenborgian and mesmeric themes, including emphases on mind and magnetism, but he also once described the process of death itself in ways that inform the current understanding of auras. In *The Great Harmonia: Being a Philosophical Revelation of the Natural, Spiritual, and Celestial Universe* (1850), Davis described witnessing the death of one of his patients. He said he saw a light-filled atmosphere around her head, and, as her body and soul began to separate, he eventually saw two bodies, one spiritual and one physical, connected by "a stream or current of vital electricity" (Albanese 2000, 41).

Theosophy, for its part, provided the energetic, spiritual body that Davis saw luminously radiating from and then leaving his patient's human body with a discernible anatomy. The Theosophist Charles Leadbeater (1854–1934) popularized the notion of the chakras in Western culture with the publication of his book *The Chakras* (1927), and the understanding of this term as referring to energy centers within the human body that serve as sites for energetic exchange between human individuals and the greater universe comes from the theosophical tradition. Despite the fact that the language of the chakras comes from eastern (Hindu) roots, ever since it was taken up by the Theosophists it has become part of a Western spiritual vernacular that generally refers to divine energy. In fact, in many combinative forms of metaphysical religion, the chakras are fused with everything from the meridian lines and acupuncture points of traditional Chinese medicine to the Christian sacraments (see Albanese 2000; Myss 1996).

Modern energy healers such as Rosalyn Bruyere, Barbara Ann Brennan, and Caroline Myss all consider the chakras to be the spiritual anatomy of human beings. Auras, then, can be read in order to diagnose and treat spiritual ailments associated with each chakra. There are typically seven chakras, ranging from the base of the spine through the crown of the head. Energy healers intuitively attempt to figure out which chakras are not functioning properly in a patient by sensing where energy is either blocked or leaking from a person and then either directly manipulating the auric energy itself, working with the physical body, assessing the person's psychological and emotional history, or usually a combination of the above.

Authors of popular paranormal literature, especially comic books, have been greatly influenced by metaphysical notions of energy, chakras, and auras. For example, Alan Moore featured detailed discussions and descriptions of such energetic phenomena in his comic book series *Promethea*, especially in issue number 10, wherein the heroine participates in tantric sex, which systematically unlocks the energy potentials of her seven chakras (Kripal, 13–15). Another interesting connection between comics and auras involves Alvin Schwartz, author of several *Batman* and *Superman* comic strips in the 1940s and 1950s. Once, while eating at a sandwich shop in New York, Schwartz recalled "all the ordinary 'super' powers he had encountered in his life," which included an encounter with a lithographer who could intuitively read people's auras and help them heal themselves (Kripal, 238). That epiphany happened in 1944, almost a half-century before intuitive energy healers such as Brennan and Myss became popular.

Scientific attempts to investigate the nature of auras usually receive little notice within conventional scientific communities, but they do garner a good amount of attention from parapsychologists and metaphysical religious practitioners. Aside from the mesmeric trances of the 19th century, which allowed people like Andrew Jackson Davis to see aura-like apparitions, some of the earliest modern scientific research into auras was conducted by Dr. Walter J. Kilner in London at the turn of the 20th century. According to his book, *The Human Atmosphere* (1911), Kilner was able to see auras with the naked eye. Like the mesmerists before him, Kilner noticed that auras responded to magnetic and electrical forces and were also affected by the powers of the human mind. Weak mental capacities led to weak auric fields. He also noted that auras seem to leave the body after death. In the 1970s, another scientifically informed yet metaphysically inclined technology, Kirlian photography, supposedly allowed people to see auras, but after more rigorously controlled experiments were performed, the auric effects vanished.

Albert C. Silva

See also: Clairvoyance; Extrasensory Perception (ESP); Healing, Psychic and Spiritual; Kirlian Photography; Mesmerism; New Age; Spiritualism; Theosophy

Further Reading

Albanese, Catherine L. 1999. "The Subtle Energies of Spirit: Explorations in Metaphysical and New Age Spirituality." *Journal of the American Academy of Religion* 67 (2): 305–25.

Albanese, Catherine L. 2000. "The Aura of Wellness: Subtle Energy Healing and New Age Religion." *Religion and American Culture: A Journal of Interpretation* 10 (1): 29–55.

Andrews, Ted. 1995. *How to See and Read the Aura*. St. Paul, MN: Llewellyn Publications.

Brennan, Barbara Ann. 1988. *Hands of Light: A Guide to Healing Through the Human Energy Field*. New York: Bantam.

Hunt, Valerie V. 1996. *Infinite Mind: Science the Human Vibrations of Consciousness*. Malibu, CA: Malibu Publishing.

Kripal, Jeffrey J. 2013. *Mutants and Mystics: Science Fiction, Superhero Comics, and the Paranormal*. Chicago: University of Chicago Press.

Myss, Caroline. 1996. *Anatomy of the Spirit: The Seven Stages of Power and Healing*. New York: Harmony Books.

AUTOMATIC WRITING

Automatic writing is the production of graphic marks—images, words, short messages or full-scale narratives—that emerge when the conscious mind, will, or intent is disabled, as when focal attention is distracted, or in states of mental dissociation, or in waking dream, fever, or trance states. Such "ecstatic" conditions have a long cross-cultural and religious history, associated with access to transcendent knowledge and experience, from ancient oracular devices in Greece and Rome to John Dee's magical "scrying" and transcription of angelic messages in the 16th century. Automatism only became the name for these states in disputes between the authority of natural and supernatural explanations in the 19th century.

The objective existence of automatic phenomena was only belatedly accepted by Victorian medical men because it threatened the model of the willed and unitary self. The meaning and mechanism of automatism was much disputed. These arguments were fueled by the emergence of mesmerism, which often claimed to reveal heightened sensitivity and supernatural powers during induced trance. In the 1840s, "table turning" became the new fashionable form of "automatic" action, when groups moved objects without exerting conscious muscular effort. From the 1850s, it was automatic writing that became one of the principle avenues of "communication" in the dissociated trance states often favored by Spiritualist mediums. The Spiritualist movement consistently claimed that such messages originated from the surviving spirits of the dead. The production of automatic writing was aided by new technologies. Initially spirits at séances laboriously knocked and rapped their answers, like inefficient telegraph operators, but in 1853 the French occultist Allan Kardec introduced the *planchette*, a device that mounted a pen on a rolling platform that could then take fluent dictation from the spirits. The planchette was taken to America by the Spiritualist leader Robert Dale Owen in 1858. In 1890, entrepreneur Elijah Bond patented the Ouija board, although it did not become a popular device for spelling out messages from spirits until the medium Pearl Curran used it during the First World War. It has remained the most popular device associated with occult automatic messages ever since.

Prominent automatic writers in the Victorian period included the Reverend William Stainton Moses, a prime mover in respectable, middle-class Christian Spiritualism in England, who appeared to be a reluctant automatist, surprised by his own mysterious talent. This was the same for the William and Mary Howitt family circle, who produced much admired automatic art and writing in an atmosphere of sober religious inquiry. In America, Mrs. Leonora Piper was a retiring Bostonian woman whose trance states were investigated for over 40 years by Harvard professors; psychologist William James was fascinated by her case. Mediums often confounded professional psychologists with the inventiveness of their automatic writings. The Swiss professor, Théodore Flournoy, studied the medium Hélène Smith in the 1890s, who in trance state wrote not only in apparently authentic historical styles, but also produced Indian languages and even a transcription of what she claimed was the Martian language. The most famous automatic writer of the era was the editor and yellow journalist, William T. Stead. Stead, a passionate early advocate of typewriters, telephones, and transcription devices, started to receive automatic messages from the spirit of the recently deceased Julia Ames in 1892. He published *Letters from Julia* and incorporated automatic writing entirely into his journalism. He ran the journal *Borderland* (1893–1897), co-edited with Ada Goodrich-Freer, also an automatic medium. The Spiritualist movement produced a vast library of "inspirational" automatic writings that depicted "Summerland," the Spiritualist afterlife.

In contrast, experimental psychologists used the same evidence to suggest that automatism proved only the fact of "unconscious cerebration," the residual action of lower brain centers that produced "ideomotor effects" beyond the willed mind. The idea that consciousness could be unconscious to parts of itself was counterintuitive yet increasingly accepted with the experimental confirmation of the ability to induce trance artificially through hypnosis. For physiological psychologists this provided entirely material explanations for "supernatural" automatism. The physicist Michael Faraday first explained table turning in this way in the 1840s. It was then picked up by physiologist William B. Carpenter, who used the idea of "unconscious cere-bration" in his tireless public campaigns against Spiritualistic and other supernatu-ral claims. After 1880, the emergence of dynamic psychology began to offer more complex models of mind and dissociation, using automatic writing as evidence of the split self or "multiplex" personality. The leading figure of the English Society for Psychical Research, Frederic Myers, attended séances in the 1870s and began to use new dynamic psychology from France and Germany to explore automatic writing in the 1880s. Automatic writing was a key evidential strand of psychical research, perhaps because writing left a documentary trace, on which tests of "proof" could be conducted. Indeed, written messages from the "dead" Myers through a variety of automatic mediums obsessed psychical researchers for many years after he died in 1901. Theorists of new ideas about the "subliminal mind," the "subconscious" or the "unconscious," such as Carl Jung and Sigmund Freud, often hovered, like Myers, uncertainly between·natural and supernatural explanations of these phenomena.

Automatic writing crossed into the arts relatively early. Robert Louis Stevenson and Arthur Conan Doyle were explicit about allowing states of fever, dream, or dissociation to open them to inspiration. Rudyard Kipling talked of the "daemon" that flashed ideas. All were familiar with the blurred realm between the natural and supernatural. In the 1920s automatic writing became a part of the aesthetics of Modernist artistic movements. In "What is Surrealism?" André Breton declared that Surrealism was "pure psychic automatism" as the group experimented with dream and trance states. Writer Gertrude Stein worked with psychologists, explor-ing dissociated states. Writers William B. Yeats, Hilda Doolittle, and James Merrill used automatic writing and Ouija boards. Occult written messages remain a key trope in Gothic fiction and film to the present day.

Roger Luckhurst

See also: Art, Creativity, and the Paranormal; Mesmerism; Myers, Frederic W. H.; Ouija Board; Possession; Psychical Research; Spiritualism; Unconscious Mind

Further Reading

Flournoy, Théodore. (1899) 1994. *From India to Planet Mars.* Princeton, NJ: Princeton University Press.
Myers, Frederic. 1885. "Automatic Writing." *Proceedings of the Society for Psychical Research* 3: 1–65.

B

BILOCATION

Bilocation has been described as the act or condition of having a simultaneous presence in two differet locations at the same time, as corroborated by eyewitnesses. Essentially, bilocation is said to have occurred when someone reports seeing or interacting with a person's *double* (or living apparition), when that person is verified to have been located somewhere else at the time. Psychical research may explain this second appearance as the *astral counterpart* of the physical body, which at certain times, through altered states of consciousness, may temporarily separate from the body, travel, and be seen by others in states displaying varying degrees of density (i.e., a solid human form, an unidentifiable mist).

Bilocation has frequently been considered a religious phenomenon due to the early Roman Catholic recognition of the bilocation of several saints, including St Anthony of Padua in 1226. According to the story, on Holy Thursday Anthony realized he was due to give a service at the other side of town at that very hour. He drew his hood over his head and knelt down for several minutes in a form of meditative state while his congregation waited. Suddenly, the saint was seen by the congregation to step forth from his stall in the monastery chapel. He read the appointed passage and instantly disappeared.

The projection of the astral body is often also classified as an out-of-body experience, and more so when the percipient has a conscious awareness of this projection and of where he or she ended up traveling while in the out-of-body state. *Phantasms of the Living* (1886), one of the most classic pieces of literature in the history of psychical research, documents several instances of people experiencing a bilocation. To the early psychical researchers, this demonstrated that it is just as common for people to experience apparitions of the living as it is for them to experience apparitions of the dead.

Dr. Robert Crookall was a major contributor to the literature on astral projection and the author of a number of books on the subject around the mid-20th century. It was also around this time that the use of the term "out-of-body experience," or OBE, became more commonly used. Dr. Crookall's books contain details on hundreds of cases of apparent astral projection that he collated and classified. A number of parapsychologists in modern research have also conducted studies of the out-of-body state, including Dr. John Palmer, Dr. Charles T. Tart, Dr. Karlis Osis, Dr. Nancy Zingrone, and Dr. Carlos Alvarado.

Dr. Osis is well known within the field of parapsychology for having worked with the scholar and psychic Dr. Alex Tanous, who claimed he could consciously control his out-of-body state, which he described as an astral body and named "Alex 2." His abilities were tested by Dr. Osis at the American Society for Psychical Research. Dr. Tanous was placed in one room while four rooms away was an optical illusion device showing different images on a spinning disc that would stop during each trial to display a target image. The aim was for Dr. Tanous to go out-of-body and say what was on the disc. Additionally, the room containing the device had a strain-gauge wired up to test for physical changes around the device where Dr. Tanous claimed his double was standing. At periods during the experiment when he gave several correct answers in a row, the strain-gauge became highly active, which may suggest that it was being activated by something that was in the room demonstrating a physical presence. This could be argued as one of the most unique laboratory studies to test bilocation.

These experiences also occurred spontaneously for Dr. Tanous. In one such instance, as reported by Loyd Auerbach in the book *ESP, Hauntings, and Poltergeists*, Dr. Tanous was asleep in New York while a friend in Canada reported having tea with him in his living room at that same moment. The friend's wife heard the conversation from another room. Both Dr. Tanous and the friend in Canada wrote up their accounts of where they were at the time to be verified and confirmed by Dr. Osis.

Callum E. Cooper

See also: Astral Plane; Out-of-Body Experience (OBE); Psychical Research

Further Reading

Auerbach, Loyd. 1986. *ESP, Hauntings and Poltergeists: A Parapsychologist's Handbook*. New York: Warner Books.

Crookall, Robert. 1966. *The Study and Practice of Astral Projection*. New York: University Books.

Greenhouse, Herbert B. 1975. *The Astral Journey*. New York: Doubleday.

Gurney, Edmund, Frederic W. H. Myers, and Frank Podmore. (1886) 2011. *Phantasms of the Living*. 2 vols. Cambridge Library Collection: Spiritualism and Esoteric Knowledge. Cambridge: Cambridge University Press.

Tanous, Alex, and Harvey Ardman. 1976. *Beyond Coincidence*. New York: Doubleday & Co.

Tanous, Alex, and Callum E. Cooper. 2013. *Conversations with Ghosts*. Guildford, UK: White Crow Books.

C

CAYCE, EDGAR

Edgar Cayce (1877–1945), often called the "sleeping prophet," was arguably the most documented psychic of the 20th century. Cayce's placing of spiritualist and Theosophical material into a Christian framework helped make him a significant influence on the development of the New Age, particularly the popularity of crystals. He has also had a considerable influence on alternative therapies and "alternative archaeology."

Cayce was born in Hopkinsville, Kentucky, to small landowners Leslie and Carrie Cayce. The young Edgar was quiet and withdrawn, and according to an oft-repeated story, had read the Bible a dozen times by the age of 13. Most biographical material on Cayce is hagiographical in nature and includes fantastical elements such as his having invisible friends called the "Little Folk" who entertained him with tales of ancient Egypt and having been visited by an angel who told him to use his abilities charitably. The Cayce family were Congregationalist Protestants and members of the Disciples of Christ (Christian) Church, and his biographers have tended to portray him as an ideal Christian. However, Cayce's religious curiosity as a child was stymied because the family did not own a Bible, and the teenaged Cayce worked with his father selling insurance to Freemasons through the Fraternal Insurance Company.

This career stalled when Cayce fell gradually mute between 1898 and 1900. Concerned that the malady might be mental rather than physical, the 24-year-old Cayce was hypnotized by a local bookkeeper. While under, he was able both to speak in a confident voice which identified itself as "The Source" and which was apparently able to diagnose the waking Cayce's condition as being caused by "nerve strain." He gradually recovered and thus was launched his career as a medical clairvoyant, which was to be his occupation for the remainder of his life.

He began to offer readings for others with physical ailments. He would induce a trance, and "The Source" would speak through him, diagnosing the ailment, prescribing a remedy, and also often giving general lifestyle advice. The latter tended to stress the importance of integrating physical, mental, and spiritual well-being, prefiguring the "holistic" approach of much alternative healthcare in the later 20th century. He was successful enough that *The New York Times* carried a story on him on October 9th, 1910 entitled "Illiterate Man Becomes a Doctor When Hypnotised." In 1920, Cayce moved his family to Texas to become an oil prospector. This venture was unsuccessful, however, and by 1922 he refocused his efforts on clairvoyance and undertook a lengthy lecture tour.

1877	Edgar Cayce is born in rural Kentucky.
1898–1900	He gradually falls mute until being hypnotized at age 24, when under hypnosis he speaks in a confident voice calling itself "The Source," which can apparently diagnose illnesses.
1910	Cayce's success as a medical clairvoyant earns him a mention in the *New York Times*, which runs a story titled "ILLITERATE MAN BECOMES A DOCTOR WHEN HYPNOTIZED."
1920	He goes on a lengthy lecture tour.
1931	He founds the Association for Research and Enlightenment (A.R.E.) to disseminate his ideas.
1945	Cayce dies, having previously prophesied that he might return in 1998.
1960s–2000s	The A.R.E. becomes a significant philosophical and cultural nexus for the American counterculture and the New Age movement.

In this latter period, his readings began to diversify into distinctly esoteric areas not typical of his waking self. Although never formally a Theosophist, Cayce was certainly influenced by Blavatsky's ideas. Encouraged by Arthur Lammers, a printer and keen Theosophist from Dayton, Ohio, and later Morton Blumenthal, a New York stockbroker, Cayce began to give readings that included material on Atlantis, astrology, and, particularly, reincarnation. Beginning with the unsolicited observation, given in a trance, that Lammers "once was a monk," Cayce recounted a long series of previous incarnations of himself and his associates, who were claimed to have also been his associates in past incarnations. Cayce saw reincarnation as part of a process of "co-creation": individual souls, through their choices, moved toward their fullest potential, enabling other beings and ultimately all of creation to do the same.

Cayce's descriptions of Atlantis elaborate on the ones famously given by Blavatsky: Atlanteans are described as having a life-span of a thousand years and practicing the "[t]ransmission of thought through ether" (Cayce 1968, 22). Their power source was a crystal, which would ultimately be instrumental in the destruction of the island continent. Cayce also reported incarnations in the time of Jesus, whom he portrayed as a mystically minded Essene, echoing later New Age constructions.

However, the largest proportion of Cayce's past-life reading concerned Egypt. Cayce alleged to have incarnated around 10,500 BCE as a Caucasian priest named Ra-Ta, who helped design the Sphinx and the Great Pyramid and eventually became High Priest of Egypt. He also alleged that there was a "Hall of Records" beneath the Sphinx that contained records from Atlantis. These are recurrent ideas in later "alternative archaeology" publications, particularly Graham Hancock and Robert Bauval's *The Message of the Sphinx* (1996), although Hancock and Bauval do not make it clear that this information comes entirely from channelled sources. In recent decades, Cayce's followers have invested in archaeological research in Egypt.

Cayce did not limit himself to the past, however. He predicted that "earth changes" (a term with continued usage in environmentalism) would occur in 1998, ushering in the "Aquarian Age" and the emergence of the "fifth root race" (Johnson 1998, 9). Furthermore, Cayce also prophesied his own possible return in 1998. He founded the Association for Research and Enlightenment (A.R.E.) in 1931 to disseminate his ideas in order to—as currently stated at the organization's official website at www.edgarcayce.org—promote research into "spirituality, holistic health, intuition, dream interpretation, psychic development, reincarnation, and ancient mysteries." The A.R.E. also "promotes the purposefulness of life, the oneness of God, the spiritual nature of humankind, and the connection of body, mind, and spirit." Based in Virginia Beach, Virginia, it became a significant nexus for the New Age in the United States, particularly through the popular thematically edited volumes produced by Cayce's son and secretary Hugh Lynn, which achieved a large countercultural readership in the late 1960s and 1970s. This was the result of Lynn's organizing and cataloguing of his father's readings, totaling some 14,000 over his career. The entire archive is now available online.

David G. Robertson

See also: Channeling; Healing, Psychic and Spiritual; New Age; Past-Life Regression; Prophecy; Theosophy

Further Reading

Cayce, Edgar. 1968. *Edgar Cayce on Atlantis.* New York: Warner Communications.

Johnson, K. Paul. 1998. *Edgar Cayce in Context: The Readings, Truth and Fiction.* Albany, NY: State University of New York Press.

Schorey, Shannon Trosper. 2012. "Sleeping Prophet: The Life and Legacy of Edgar Cayce." In *Brill Handbook on the Theosophical Current,* edited by Olav Hammer, and Mikael Rothstein, 135–149. Brill Handbooks on Contemporary Religion. Leiden, NL: Brill.

Sugrue, Thomas. 1945. *There Is a River: The Story of Edgar Cayce.* New York: H. Holt and Company.

CHANNELING

Channeling is an altered state of consciousness in which a human being, known as a "channel," accesses and expresses spiritual information from a source located in an alternate realm of reality. In this sense, channeling is a more contemporary form of the practice of Spiritualist mediumship, wherein human mediums communicated with the spirits of deceased human beings in rituals called séances. Whereas Spiritualist mediums primarily contacted the spirits of the dead, channels usually contact, communicate with, and act as conduits for ascended masters that are not necessarily human in origin. The kinds of spirit guides and ascended masters that appear in channeling phenomena range from real historical figures (i.e., known human beings) who are dead to former inhabitants of lost civilizations, such as the famous channel JZ Knight's master, Ramtha, who is purportedly from the lost continent of Lemuria; to extraterrestrial masters from other parts of the universe or other dimensions. There are also many cases of people who claim to channel collective beings such as the group soul "Abraham," who is channeled by Esther Hicks.

Many channels, like the famous Jane Roberts (1929–1984), enter trance-like states of consciousness while they channel their masters. The level and depth of the trance state usually dictates how consciously present the channel is during these sessions. Some channels remain present throughout the entire session and even engage their sources/spirit masters in conversation. Other conscious channels do not even enter into a trance state, acting instead as intuitive or clairvoyant healers or spiritual guides. In other cases the channels enter such a deep trance state that they have no recollection of what happens during the channeling session. In most cases where the master (i.e., the spiritual source) verbally communicates through the channel, the channel's voice and mannerisms change when the master takes control. Also noteworthy is the connection between channeling and healing. The early 20th century trance physician Edgar Cayce (1877–1945) intuitively read people in order to diagnose their health problems and was sometimes even said to channel the contents of a spiritual source from another dimension.

In theory, human channels function in ways that are very similar to radio and television channels: they receive energy waves and frequencies from great distances (both in time and space), and they are attuned to and can therefore "tune in" to and transmit those energies to others in meaningful ways. This use of scientific and technological language in order to describe paranormal phenomena is not uncommon. See, for example, the writings of Frederick W. H. Myers, founder of the Society for Psychical Research, who coined the term "telepathy" at a time when the telegram and telegraph were the cutting edge of telecommunication technology. Interestingly, the mode of transmission through which human channels receive their messages often takes the form of telepathy, which refers to the transmission of thoughts from one being to another via a process that exists beyond the normal sensory and cognitive processes.

More recently, there has been yet another shift in the language that describes these kinds of spiritual/paranormal phenomena, this time from "channeling" to "downloading." In the early years of the 21st century, when the technological vernacular is heavily influenced by advances in Internet technology and social media, it became commonplace to hear spiritual people say they had "received a download"—often a *spiritual* download—from a source in a higher, more divine realm. Put differently, spiritual downloads are another form of channeled information.

The change in language from "mediums" to "channels" indicates a preoccupation with science and technology that is common to many forms of metaphysical religion. Part of the language of channeling emerged from the UFO contactee culture of the mid-to-late-20th century, coinciding with the public success and popularity of Jane Roberts, one of the first and most famous American channels. Roberts channeled "Seth," a "personality without a physical body," for many years, producing 16 books until her death in 1984. Around the same time, Helen Schucman, a renowned psychologist, created the 1,200 page *A Course in Miracles*, one of the most popular books of the New Age and beyond. From 1965 until 1973, Schucman transcribed the words of an inner voice that told her at the outset, "This is a course in miracles. Take notes." She did, and 1,200+ pages later the *Course* was fully downloaded.

While channeling is a relatively recent phenomenon, there are many significantly older religious phenomena that appear to be quite similar to it. Some people see the mystical qualities of channels and Spiritualist mediums, including the trance-like states of many channels, as being similar to those of the ancient Greek oracles and various other "seers" or "prophets" in previous times. There also appear to be some similarities between the information channels receive and the kinds of religious revelations common to more conventional religions. But despite the universal comparisons that can be made between channeling and other religious traditions and practices, it is important to note the direct historical lineage of metaphysical religions that led directly to the channeling phenomenon as we know it today.

The roots of channeling can be traced back to the 19th century, specifically to Spiritualism and Theosophy. The historical roots of those two traditions, however, go much farther back in time. Both Spiritualism and Theosophy were heavily influenced by Hermetic philosophy, which flourished in Europe in the 15th century when the *Corpus Hermeticum*, a mysterious text supposedly written by an ancient Egyptian known as Hermes Trismegistus, made its way into European culture. The philosophy found in the *Corpus* includes an emphasis on the Divine Mind whose Intelligence could "flow" into the human mind (Albanese 2007, 26). These notions of the divine nature of Mind and, therefore, the divine infusion of humanity, are central metaphysical tenets that later appeared in the theology of Emmanuel Swedenborg (1688–1772). In 1743 and 1744, Swedenborg began having visions that would put him into a trance state. He claimed that in this state he traveled to worlds and realms other than this earthly one. Like the most adept channels of the New Age, he was able to master these altered states of consciousness, and he began building his own theology based on his first-person paranormal experiences of receiving divine intelligence.

Swedenborg's teachings would eventually influence the American trance physician and mesmerist Andrew Jackson Davis (1826–1910), the "Seer of Poughkeepsie" and father of Spiritualist philosophy. One night in March 1844, after a particularly intense mesmeric/hypnagogic experience, Davis claimed to have met Swedenborg's spirit, who described his terrestrial and extraterrestrial travels.

Swedenborg also supposedly called Davis "an appropriate vessel for the influx and perception of truth and wisdom" (quoted in Albanese 2007, 208). In the language of the New Age, Swedenborg essentially called Davis an appropriate channel.

The Theosophists eventually took the mass spiritualism that arose from Davis's philosophy and reformed it. They claimed to correspond with ascended spiritual masters in a manner almost identical to channeling. The "ascended masters" of Theosophy eventually turned into the space brothers and collective spiritual beings that spoke through New Age channels. Also, it was through the work of Alice Bailey, a prominent early Theosophist, that the notion of "rays" entered into spiritual vocabulary. Rays, according to Bailey, were units of consciousness that emanated from the divine universe. These rays, in turn, constituted human beings, therefore making different kinds of people the expressions of different rays.

This understanding of rays was prominent in 20th century spirituality, and it found a slightly altered, yet highly influential expression in the life and work of the science fiction author Philip K. Dick. In 1974, Dick experienced a series of paranormal events in which, as he described it, he was reprogrammed by pink beams (or rays) of light emanating from a kind of overmind that he termed VALIS (vast active living intelligence system). Like Bailey's "rays," VALIS's pink beams were noetic energies—streams of consciousness that transmitted vital information. After one of his experiences of being zapped by VALIS's pink beams, Dick had a vision that his young son had a bad internal hernia. Dick took his son to the doctor, who confirmed the diagnosis and operated on the child, essentially saving his life. Dick, in this telling case, essentially channeled his ascended master's (VALIS's) information—a message he received through ray-like transmissions of noetic energy—and then acted as an intuitive healer.

Albert C. Silva

See also: Aura; Cayce, Edgar; Healing, Psychic and Spiritual; Hypnagogic State; Mediumship; Mesmerism; Myers, Frederick W. H.; New Age; Spiritualism; Swedenborg, Emanuel; Telepathy; UFO

Further Reading

Albanese, Catherine L. 2007. *A Republic of Mind and Spirit: A Cultural History of American Metaphysical Religion.* New Haven, CT: Yale University Press.

Albanese, Catherine L. 1999. "The Subtle Energies of Spirit: Explorations in Metaphysical and New Age Spirituality." *Journal of the American Academy of Religion* 67 (2): 305–25.

Brown, Michael F. 1997. *The Channeling Zone: American Spirituality in an Anxious Age.* Cambridge, MA: Harvard University Press.

Kripal, Jeffrey J. 2013. *Mutants and Mystics: Science Fiction, Superhero Comics, and the Paranormal.* Chicago: University of Chicago Press.

Melton, J. Gordon, Jerome Clark, and Aidan A. Kelly. 1991. *New Age Almanac.* New York: Visible Ink Press.

CLAIRVOYANCE

"Clairvoyance"—the French term for "clear seeing"—and the associated term "clairvoyant" acquired their supernatural associations with the ability to sense beyond the limits of ordinary human capacities for perception only once these words were transferred to English in the late 18th century. Although the idea of such a paranormal power is ancient, with written descriptions of it going as far back as the fifth century BCE, when Herodotus described an apparent instance of supernatural seeing-at-a-distance in Book I of his *Histories*, the term "clairvoyance" itself was first associated with mesmerism in the 1780s and was swiftly adopted by the Spiritualist movement as another term for "mediumship" in the 1840s. The foreign word helped emphasize the exotic, alien nature of the mediumistic state. It was also a key idea in psychical research, although as a nascent science the field of psychical research soon proliferated new technical terms for this alleged ability, either displacing it entirely with words like "hyperaesthesia" (heightened perceptual sensitivity) or developing parallel terms such as clairaudience (hearing), clairsentience (touch), clairalience (smell), and clairgustance (tasting). Perhaps because the term "clairvoyance" remains associated with the musty world of the Victorian séance, many ideas carried by the term have been replaced since the 1970s by the neutral, descriptive, but equally controversial "remote viewing."

Clairvoyance was an unexpected side effect of mesmeric treatments in the 1780s. Franz Mesmer was a sensation in Paris with his theory and practice of "animal magnetism." One of those he allegedly cured by putting into trance state and restoring their "magnetic" balance was from the eminent Puységur family. The Marquis de Puységur (1751–1824) became interested in the technique and was soon an accomplished magnetizer himself. In May 1784, he treated Victor Race and discovered that there were peculiar side effects of the trance state. The *rapport* between the patient and the magnetizer appeared to create a mental link between them and enhance certain perceptual and cognitive abilities. De Puységur could silently command Race through their invisible bond and could apparently be understood and obeyed. Race suddenly became an eloquent speaker and could see where the illness in his body was located. In the trance state, he was also able to diagnose the illness of others. De Puységur published a series of case studies and claims in 1784 (translated into English in 1786). This in part prompted an investigation of these claims by the French Royal Commission, which discredited them and refused mesmerism the status of orthodox medicine or science. However, mesmerism remained a popular and democratic form of marginal science for the next 60 years. Clairvoyance was at the core of its many contested wonders, and peculiar and uncanny effects of trance states shadowed the emergence of hypnotism in the 1880s as well.

Clairvoyance had entered English usage by the 1840s. "Mediumship" in the Spiritualist movement after 1848 was a capacious term that included many supernatural abilities that shaded into clairvoyance. The trance condition of the medium was a crucial part of the séance, as it also was for inspired writers or platform speakers who claimed to receive dictation from higher beings or the spirits of the departed. A typical book title from the mid-century comes from the American inspirational writer Andrew Jackson Davis, who published *Memoranda of Persons, Places, and Events; Embracing Authentic Facts, Visions, Impressions, Discoveries in Magnetism, Clairvoyance, and Spiritualism* in 1868. It suggests the rich cross-fertilization of different occult strands at the time.

Psychical research took interest in the term "clairvoyance" because it was merely descriptive of a disputed, fugitive phenomenon and presumed no "spirit hypothesis" as an explanation. Consequently, clairvoyance was considered a form of supernormal psychology, to be explained by heightened perceptions as a result of certain mental conditions, including altered states of consciousness such as trance or dream. These were natural rather than supernatural conditions, which could be experimentally tested and eventually, they hoped, proved to exist. The lead theorist of the Society for Psychical Research, Frederic Myers, was an enthusiastic coiner of terms that aimed to scientize these states. Telepathy was his most successful term, and since Myers, clairvoyance has often been associated with the "distant touch" of telepathy. The 1911 edition of the *Encyclopedia Britannica* defined clairvoyance as "a technical term in psychical research" for "a supernormal power of obtaining knowledge in which no part is played by (a) the ordinary processes of sense-perception or (b) supernormal communication with other intelligences, incarnate or discarnate." This paved the way for clairvoyance to be subsumed into the new language of "extrasensory perception" in the 1930s.

In 1972, Harold Puthoff and Russell Targ conducted a series of experiments at the Stanford Research Institute that they claimed proved the existence of "remote viewing," yet another reiteration of the central idea of clairvoyance. The proliferation of such quasi-scientific terms has meant that clairvoyance is now largely associated with more supernatural explanations of fortune-telling, Spiritualism, or Theosophy.

Roger Luckhurst

See also: Extrasensory Perception (ESP); Mediumship; Mesmerism; Myers, Frederic W. H.; Psychical Research; Remote Viewing; Séance; Spiritualism; Telepathy; Theosophy

Further Reading

Crabtree, Adam. 1993. *From Mesmer to Freud: Magnetic Sleep and the Roots of Psychological Healing*. New Haven, CT: Yale University Press.
Gauld, Alan. 1992. *A History of Hypnotism*. Cambridge, MA: Cambridge University Press.
Winter, Alison. 1998. *Mesmerized: The Powers of Mind in Victorian Britain*. Chicago: University of Chicago Press.

COMMITTEE FOR SKEPTICAL INQUIRY

The Committee for Skeptical Inquiry (CSI), previously known as the Committee for the Scientific Investigation of Claims of the Paranormal (CSICOP), publicizes scientific investigations of paranormal and pseudoscientific phenomena. Its mission is to promote scientific inquiry, critical investigation, and the use of reason in examining controversial and extraordinary claims.

CSICOP was founded in 1976 at a conference on "The New Irrationalisms: Antiscience and Pseudoscience" held in conjunction with an annual meeting of the American Humanist Association at the State University of New York at Buffalo. Organizer Paul Kurtz, a philosophy professor at SUNY-Buffalo and a renowned secular humanist, brought together philosophers, scientists, psychologists, and paranormal investigators such as Lee Nisbet, Carl Sagan, Isaac Asimov, Martin Gardner, Ray Hyman, James Randi, and Philip Klass. Their goal was to counteract the increasing social and media acceptance of paranormal and pseudoscientific phenomena, such as psychics, astrology, parapsychology, extrasensory perception (ESP), hauntings, UFOs, faith healings, alternative medicine, and creation science. For Kurtz, paranormal phenomena are illusions of people's own making, reflecting their desires for the impossible.

An early disagreement within the group centered on whether to grant equal time to pro-paranormal researchers. Marcello Truzzi, a sociology professor and editor of the organization's first journal, *The Zetetic*, launched in 1976, argued for their inclusion in conferences and publications. However, the rest of the executive committee maintained that the pro-paranormal view already received great publicity in pseudoscientific journals and mass media, and thus CSICOP should be devoted to promoting scientific skepticism only. Truzzi left the organization that year and CSICOP began a new journal in 1977, the *Skeptical Inquirer*, edited by science journalist Kendrick Frazier. The goals of the journal and of CSICOP were to criticize paranormal and pseudoscientific claims, use rigorous scientific methods in investigating such claims, present a scientific view of these claims to the media, and promote science education and knowledge of scientific methodology.

Members maintain that they are not trying to debunk paranormal assertions but rather to investigate them rationally and scientifically. According to CSICOP, its paranormal investigators have an open mind and seek to test the uncanny with experimental rigor and scientific integrity. Their three basic principles are that the burden of proof is on the claimant, that extraordinary claims require extraordinary proof, and that the simplest plausible explanation is mostly likely correct. Investigators insist that they do not dismiss paranormal claims out-of-hand, but when empirical results find in the negative, then they must declare so and disseminate such findings widely. For these researchers, scientific skepticism means to examine only those phenomena for which there are empirical or experimental means for evaluation; thus theological or moral claims are excluded from research.

In the late 1970s, CSICOP was embroiled in a scientific controversy surrounding the so-called Mars Effect, a theory by French psychologist and statistician

Michel Gauquelin that claimed that sports champions are often born when Mars is rising. This theory seemed to support aspects of astrology. CSICOP members Kurtz, George Abell, Marvin Zelen, and Dennis Rawlins investigated the Mars Effect, determining that the dataset was insufficient and nonrandom, and that the statistics were therefore skewed. A comparative study of U.S. athletes confirmed that Mars's position has no relationship to athletes' abilities. However, an internal dispute about statistical and scientific methodologies within CSICOP's investigation resulted in Rawlins quitting the group. CSICOP formally adopted a policy in 1981 that it would not conduct original scientific research but rather would publicize others' research like other scientific societies do.

In the late 1980s to early 2000s, CSICOP faced several lawsuits brought by Uri Geller, a self-declared psychic who claimed that be had been libeled by Randi, Kurtz, and CSICOP itself. These suits were primarily prompted by Randi's writings about Geller as well as statements made by Randi in the media. While Geller lost his cases and was ordered to pay court costs, the expense and long duration of the lawsuits threatened CSICOP's finances. It also resulted in CSICOP separating itself from Randi for a time. Despite these troubles, in the 1990s CSICOP expanded the *Skeptical Inquirer's* frequency and added more explanatory articles about cutting-edge scientific discoveries. In 1991, it became an affiliate of the newly created Center for Inquiry, led by Kurtz, which seeks to foster a secular society based on science, reason, freedom of inquiry, and humanist values.

CSICOP shifted its mission and changed its name to CSI in 2006. While the organization had been mostly concerned with examining paranormal and related phenomena, the chief goal was to provide scientific examinations of such claims, so that reliable, fact-based, and verified information could be used to determine their empirical validity. The focus was on promoting science and reason all along. Nonetheless, the word "paranormal" in CSICOP's name kept away some scientists who agreed with the central aim of promoting scientific inquiry and the public understanding of science but who wanted to broaden the group's focus beyond the paranormal and into wider issues at the intersection of scientific and public concern, such as climate change, intelligent design, and polygraph testing. The organization revised the end of its mission statement from "investigation of paranormal and fringe-science claims" to "investigation of controversial and extraordinary claims," and emphasized science education more prominently. Additionally, the executive council wanted a shorter name because the original name was too long for most media to print, thus hindering their publicity and educational ambitions.

Today, CSI is a global organization with local affiliates and paranormal investigators located around the world, including Russia, China, Mexico, Italy, and The Netherlands. It continues to hold annual conferences and to shape public debate about paranormal and pseudoscientific phenomena. As envisioned by Kurtz, who died in 2012, CSI is part of the modern skeptical and humanist movement that seeks to create a world of reason and compassion.

Dusty Hoesly

See also: Geller, Uri; Pseudoscience; Randi, James

Further Reading
Frazier, Kendrick, ed. 1986. *Science Confronts the Paranormal*. Amherst, NY: Prometheus Books.
Gardner, Martin. 2001. *Did Adam and Eve Have Navels?: Debunking Pseudoscience*. New York: W. W. Norton.
Kurtz, Paul, ed. 2001. *Skeptical Odysseys: Personal Accounts by the World's Leading Paranormal Inquirers*. Amherst, NY: Prometheus Books.

CONSCIOUSNESS

"*Cogito ergo sum.*" Though René Descartes (1596–1650) first pronounced "I think, therefore, I am" in the 17th century (and set the framework for much of Western philosophy), to understand consciousness—both what it is and why we have it—is one of the fundamental questions of existence. What does it mean to be alive? Do we survive death? Why do we sleep? Why do we dream? All of these questions are the result of the acknowledgement that consciousness exists, and that we possess it. *What it is* and *why we have it*, as well as *how it works* and *where it comes from*, are questions that humanity has tried to answer since the dawn of time. They are the basis of philosophy, religion, spiritual traditions, biology (an attempt to define and understand life), psychology, and more. They are also central to the fields of parapsychology and the paranormal, since the possible existence and nature of paranormal realities, abilities, and phenomena is fundamentally linked to questions about the nature of consciousness and how it may characterize, reveal, and/or interact with matter in ways that contradict, overturn, transcend, or reframe the reigning paradigm of mainstream science, where skepticism about paranormal phenomena is the norm.

While there are no concrete answers to the questions "What is consciousness?" and "Why do we have it?" and "How does it work?" and "Where does it come from?" there are many theories that attempt to provide answers—some of which propose that consciousness does not even exist. As a full accounting of each would be unwieldy in a short space, this entry will instead offer a broad survey of the field, including major theories and current opinions. Readers are highly encouraged to refer to the Further Reading list, which will provide a number of introductory resources that can be used as a starting point for conducting their own research.

Though historically Sigmund Freud is commonly considered the father of modern psychology, having published *The Interpretation of Dreams* in 1899, it was actually William James who set the foundation for modern consciousness studies in 1890, with his landmark two-volume work, *The Principles of Psychology*. Here and in his later work, *The Varieties of Religious Experience*, James set about understanding the mind and how it works. James is credited with popularizing the phrase "stream of consciousness," which describes the continual flow of thoughts that pass through the mind (both verbal and nonverbal). For James consciousness is a process, is personal, is usually conscious *of* something, and has both agency and the ability to discriminate. As one's awareness is constantly shifting, evolving, and drawing on new sensations as well as previous experience, James echoes the observations of Heraclitus (d. 475 BCE), who observed that one "can never step into the same stream twice." In essence, any moment of conscious awareness is influenced by previous experience and immediate context.

To paint the quest for consciousness in broad strokes, there are four central approaches. *Dualism* (as articulated by Descartes) maintains that mind and matter are separate, yet interact with each other "somehow." *Monism* counters that mind and matter are either intrinsically linked or are both aspects of a deeper "something." *Materialism*, by contrast, argues that consciousness has its basis in matter, and that it "emerges" either from complex systems or relationships, or is somehow generated by the brain, or may not even exist. Finally, *mysterianism* takes an agnostic approach, arguing that we can never really know the ultimate nature of consciousness.

In broad terms, dualism proposes that consciousness (mind) and matter (body) are two separate and distinct things. This school of thought is credited to René Descartes and is oftentimes referred to as Cartesian Dualism. At first, it might seem that consciousness and matter are obviously separate and distinct things. Descartes called these two things *res cogitans* (the mind / soul / consciousness), and *res extensa* (physical substance). What dualism has a difficult time addressing is the issue of how these two substances interact. How can the nonphysical *res cogitans* affect the physical *res extensa?* Or, practically speaking, how does one's decision to move one's arm lead to one's arm moving?

Descartes believed the pineal gland, located deep within the brain, was the most likely point of interaction. He went so far as to call this gland "the seat of the soul." But even so, the pineal gland is still *physical*, and a method of interaction between the nonmaterial and the corporeal still requires a mechanism or method of interaction. *That* they interact is obvious, as seen in, for example, the reality of the placebo effect, or the decreased cognitive function that comes with sleep deprivation, or the impact on consciousness when drugs are taken to affect the body, or the impact on the body when meditation is practiced to affect the mind. *How* they interact still remains unexplained. There is still a gap that must be bridged even if the pineal gland is involved. Thus, some philosophers and scientists have looked for alternative frameworks to understand the nature of consciousness.

Many Eastern and some Western philosophers advocate for monism as an alternative explanation for the problem of consciousness. Again, and broadly speaking, monism proposes that mind and matter are actually properties of a single "thing." This underlying thing may be either purely material or purely psychic. Often this line of inquiry leads down some interesting philosophical paths.

The Nature of Consciousness

The question of what consciousness ultimately is and does is central to the study of the paranormal, including parapsychology, which explores the possibility that consciousness may have properties and powers that transcend the boundaries of conventional science. There are presently four basic approaches to the question of consciousness:

Dualism holds that mind and matter are separate but somehow interact.

Monism holds that mind and matter are intrinsically linked, and/or that they are both aspects of some deeper reality.

Materialism holds that consciousness is based in matter and somehow emerges from it or is generated by it—or that consciousness may not even truly exist.

Mysterianism adopts an agnostic approach by arguing that the ultimate nature of consciousness is unknowable.

One notable flavor of monism is *panpsychism*: the belief that all matter is inherently capable of interior experience or possesses a form of consciousness. In this view, there is no barrier or dualistic gap that needs bridging.

Panpsychism is not without its critics. If one posits that "all matter is capable of interiority," then what are the interior lives of, for instance, tables and chairs? What is "table consciousness" or "chair consciousness"? To answer these questions, panpsychists usually refer to philosophical concepts such as "heaps" or "aggregates" in order to differentiate between "piles" of matter (such as rocks) and organisms (borrowing heavily from the works of Alfred North Whitehead). An organism's identity (or whole) influences its constituent parts. Protons, neutrons, electrons, will possess consciousness appropriate to them. These are then subsumed by atomic consciousness when they come together as atoms. Atomic consciousness is then subsumed by molecular consciousness, and so on, all the way up the chain into organisms. A rock is a rock, and it will possess interiority up to a molecular level. A person, animal, plant, and so on is different in the way its constituent parts relate to each other. Unfortunately, since a body continuously replaces its constituent matter, even in instances as simple as weight loss or gain, it is unclear how or why this does not affect the unified sense of self that people experience. In some respects, the discussions of complexity and relationships within panpsychism can be viewed in terms of "systems theory." Systems theory places stronger emphasis on the interactions and relationships of constituent components rather than on the components of the system itself. For example, a stadium full of sports fans "doing the wave" is an example of a complex behavioral system. Group consciousness supersedes the consciousness of the individual sports fan who participates. Panpsychism, in terms of heaps versus organisms, can be viewed as embracing a type of systems theory—though, as stated above, panpsychists tend toward looking at the whole as it influences its constituent parts.

Materialist systems theories of consciousness (again, broadly speaking) tend to work from the bottom up, with consciousness either emerging from or as an epiphenomenon (by-product) of a significantly complex system of matter. The brain, for instance, is one such complex system. Thus, proponents of AI (artificial intelligence) believe that one need only build a sufficiently complex computer in order to create consciousness. Other systems theorists view consciousness as merely an epiphenomenal by-product or property of complex arrangements of matter, much like "wetness" is a property of water. This is slightly different than panpsychism, in that the matter involved in these systems does not already possess consciousness or interiority.

Among notable brain-based materialist theories of consciousness is the controversial Orchestrated Objective Reduction (Orch-OR) model of consciousness. Orch-OR is the creation of physicist Sir Roger Penrose and anesthesiologist Stuart Hameroff, a founder of the Center for Consciousness Studies in Arizona. For Penrose and Hameroff, communications between neurons in the brain do not offer sufficient complexity to allow for the generation of consciousness. Instead, they propose that consciousness is to be found in quantum interactions of hypothetical condensates in the microtubules found in the cytoplasm of the individual neurons. These quantum interactions are subject to what Penrose terms "objective reduction," which relies on the curvature of space-time to collapse quantum wave functions. In Orch-OR, this objective reduction is further *orchestrated* by proteins within the microtubules. This process, per Penrose and Hameroff, is what gives rise to consciousness and conscious experience. At this time, Orch-OR is still under review, and experimental results have been mixed. As the finer nuances of Orch-OR are beyond the scope of this article, readers are encouraged to research it further through the suggested readings below.

Rather than attempting to theorize whether the brain produces consciousness or consciousness utilizes the brain, some have chosen to deny the existence of a unified consciousness altogether. In his book *Consciousness Explained* philosopher Daniel Dennett looks to information processing to create what he calls his "multiple drafts" model. Per Dennett, any moment or event that we experience is presented to the brain via multiple sensory inputs. The perceptions of these sensory inputs each arrive at the brain separately and within varying amounts of time and are processed by the brain independently of each other. As each perception is processed, the information perceived by the brain can be used to discern the contents of the next input's information. Each sensory input presents a narrative "draft" describing the event to the brain. Finally, the "multiple drafts" are reconciled by the brain, and an appropriate response to the event is generated and enacted. Within Dennett's model, there is no unitary consciousness, and the sense of such a thing is only an illusion generated by the multiple drafts.

If Dennett's model might be akin to atheism in its denial of the existence of consciousness, Colin McGinn's approach to understanding consciousness might be likened to agnosticism. Per McGinn's mysterianism, there may be a perfectly reasonable and natural explanation or explanations for *what consciousness is* and *how it works*. Unfortunately, McGinn argues, we may simply be incapable of comprehending what these explanations are. To understand these mysteries may be beyond the range of what our brains can perceive or what our cognitive abilities can process. Both brain and mind have their limits. The interaction mechanism missing in Cartesian dualism may not be missing at all; it may merely be beyond our comprehension.

What is consciousness? Why do we have it? How does it work? Where does it come from? Is it dependent on the body? How does it interact with matter? Does it even exist? Can we ever know? The answers to all of these questions still remain to be determined. At the time of this writing, there are graduate degrees in consciousness studies, an academic *Journal of Consciousness Studies*, a Center for Consciousness Studies at the University of Arizona in Tucson, and an annual conference (Toward a Science of Consciousness) devoted to these questions. The field of parapsychology also continues to be active, with the annual conference of the Parapsychological Association, for instance, drawing large numbers of scientists and scholars who continue to explore the possibility that consciousness may possess properties and powers that extend well beyond the boundaries imputed to it by the materialistic stance of conventional scientific opinion.

Kevin Kovelant

See also: Anomalistic Psychology; James, William; Meditation; Myers, Frederic W. H.; Parapsychology; Princeton Engineering Anomalies Research; Synchronicity; Unconscious Mind; Zombie

Further Reading

Chalmers, David. 1996. *The Conscious Mind: In Search of a Fundamental Theory*. New York: Oxford University Press.

Dennet, Daniel. 1991. *Consciousness Explained*. New York: Back Bay Books.

De Quincey, Christian. 2002. *Radical Nature: Rediscovering the Soul of Matter*. Montpelier, VT: Invisible Cities Press.

James, William. 1950. *The Principles of Psychology*. New York: Dover Press.

James, William. 1994. *The Varieties of Religious Experience*. New York: The Modern Library

Lancaster, Brian L. 2004. *Approaches to Consciousness: The Marriage of Science & Mysticism*. New York: Palgrave Macmillan.

Ornstein, Robert, ed. 1974. *The Nature of Human Consciousness: A Book of Readings*. New York: Viking Press.

Solms, Mark, and Oliver Turnbull. 2002. *The Brain and the Inner World: An Introduction to the Neuroscience of Subjective Experience*. New York: Other Press.

Tart, Charles T. 1975. *States of Consciousness*. New York: E.P. Dutton.

D

DEMONOLOGY

Demonology, or the study of demons, can be understood in its most simple form as the identification, classification, and study of evil spirits. Each of the Abrahamic religions has developed its own unique relationship to the invisible world of subcelestial spirits, with specific systems of demonology emerging out of theological considerations particular to that tradition. Without the metaphysical reflections common to the Abrahamic faiths, including the direct importance of a linear, eschatological understanding of history, in other traditions negative spirits become more central to everyday considerations of health and well-being, but dealing with them lacks the weight associated with damnation and eternal punishment. Customs relating to demonology within the Abrahamic faiths are rarely fully orthodox as the core texts of the Torah, Tanakh, New Testament, and Quran do not contain detailed lists of demons, and much of what falls under the label demonology requires accessing alternate, often heterodox, sources such as the folk traditions and polytheistic and animistic belief systems. The subject of demons is related to the paranormal by way of possession and exorcism phenomena and also through the paranormal and supernatural phenomena that are sometimes attributed to demonic activity.

One of the more interesting etymological possibilities for the origin of the word "demon," and one that would please some skeptics of the subtle influence of spirits, comes from the original Greek term *daimon*, which can be translated as "shadow"—making demonology the study of shadows. To the ancient Greeks, and also in the wider Hellenistic cultural milieu, a daimon was a spirit that influenced events and people, including, according to some traditions, by serving as a person's divinely appointed spirit companion throughout life.

Moving beyond the specific Greco-Roman origins of the word demon, we find that systems for classifying negative spirits reach back into the earliest annals of recorded history as a central part of medical practice. Since disease in the ancient and classical world was often associated with the influence of malignant spirits, the study and analysis of these spirits became central to the medical systems of most ancient civilizations.

Although early Christian figures dealt with the influence of demons in the context of spiritual development, in the European context what we would today consider demonology begins with the grimoire tradition, which includes classifications suitable to the evocation, invocation, and exorcism of specific spiritual agencies. Late Medieval and early Renaissance works dealing with natural magic, from figures such as Agrippa and Paracelsus, also include classifications of spirits as part of the hierarchical structure of natural correspondences. It is during the 15th century, however, that we find systematic attempts to classify specifically evil spirits attendant to the persecution of supposed sorcerers and witches. As witchcraft trials became more prevalent in the 16th and 17th centuries, works such as King James the First's *Daemonologie* and Cotton Mather's *Wonders of the Invisible World* were influential in codifying the supposed influence of demons on the material world.

Current views of demonology owe much to the comparative mythography and folklore studies that developed in the 19th and early 20th centuries. Orthodox Evangelical and Catholic researchers in the 19th century often classified their findings under the domain of demonology, and the popularization of the occult late in the same century was accompanied by a tendency toward the sensational to tantalize audiences eager for diabolic secrets. One of the stranger examples from the 1800s is a translation of a purported 17th-century Latin manuscript by the "Rev. Sinistrari of Ameno," that is, the Reverend Left-Handed, titled *Demoniality*. In the form of a demonological study, this text gives instructions for sexual union with incubi and succubi as well as detailed instructions for satanic pacts.

A century later, in the 1970s with the popularity of movies such as *The Exorcist* and with cover stories in *Time* magazine featuring lurid stories about Satanism, media figures such as the anomaly investigators Ed and Lorraine Warren emerged to define demonology as a companion study to field investigations into anomalous experiences. The fact that they self-identified as Catholic lay workers is harmonious with this focus; despite the connotation that has developed for the word "demon" to denote a supernatural entity beyond human origin, in the context of the New Testament usage of the word, as well as its development in the early church, demons were often connected to the influence of the spirits of deceased persons. While many parapsychologists and anomalists balk at the use of demonology in contemporary paranormal investigations, in some ways this trend reflects a return to the original usage of the term.

David Metcalfe

See also: Angels; Discarnate Entity; Exorcism; Occultism; Possession; Ritual Magic

Further Reading

Bonzol, Judith. 2009. "The Medical Diagnosis of Demonic Possession in an Early Modern English Community." *Parergon* 26 (1): 115–139. http://www.academia.edu/772481/ The_Medical_Diagnosis_of_Demonic_Possession_in_an_Early_Modern_English_ Community.

Brown, Robert. 1889. *Demonology and Witchcraft: With Especial Reference to Modern Spiritualism, "So-Called"; and the "Doctrines of Demons."* London: John F. Shaw and Co. http://babel.hathitrust.org/cgi/pt?id=inu.39000005582957;view=1up;seq=3.

Cardin, Matt. 2007. "The Angel and the Demon." In *Icons of Horror and the Supernatural: An Encyclopedia of Our Worst Nightmares*, edited by S. T. Joshi, 31–64. Greenwood Icons. Westport, CT: Greenwood Press.

Conway, Moncure Daniel. 1879. *Daniel, Demonology and Devil-Lore*. New York: Henry Holt and Company. https://archive.org/details/demonologyandde04conwgoog.

Greer, John Michael. 2011. "Demons." In *Monsters: An Investigator's Guide to Magical Beings*, by John Michael Greer, 175–188. Revised and expanded edition. Woodbury, MN: Llewellyn Publications.

Mather, Cotton. (1693) 1998. *The Wonders of the Invisible World. Observations as Well Historical as Theological, upon the Nature, the Number, and the Operations of the Devils.* Edited by Reiner Smolinski. Electronic Texts in American Studies. Libraries at University of Nebraska-Lincoln. http://digitalcommons.unl.edu/etas/19.

Nevius, John L. 1894. *Demon Possession and Allied Themes.* 7th ed. Chicago: Fleming H. Revell Company. https://archive.org/details/demonpossessiona00neviiala.

Osterreich, T. K. 1920. *Possession Demoniacal and Other Among Primitive Races, in Antiquity, the Middle Ages, and Modern Times.* London: Kegan Paul, Trench, Trubner and Co., Ltd. https://archive.org/details/possessiondemoni031669mbp.

Rogo, D. Scott. 1974. "Demonic Possession and Parapsychology." *Parapsychology Review* 5 (6): 18–24. https://archive.org/details/DemonicPossessionAndParapsychology.

DISCARNATE ENTITY

The term "discarnate entity" refers to any nonphysical being without a material body. It is, therefore, a broad term encompassing a variety of different spiritual and nonphysical beings, from spirits of deceased humans to incorporeal deities who never occupied a physical body, malignant demons, and interdimensional extraterrestrial intelligences. Discarnate entities may be encountered in a variety of different ways: in dreams, in hypnagogic and hypnopompic states, via shamanic journeys and spirit mediumship, or through the ingestion of psychoactive substances, among numerous others. In his pioneering experimental work with the highly psychoactive compound DMT, for example, Rick Strassman was surprised to find that at least half of his participants claimed to have made contact with entities while under the drug's influence. Strassman's participants reported encounters with a range of entities, including beings that resembled clowns, reptiles, mantises, bees, spiders, cacti, and stick figures. Discarnate entities may also take on a variety of other forms, from ghostly apparitions and shadow-like figures to fairies, angels, and luminous entities of light. They may also have no discernible form at all. They may be recognized as the spirits of deceased relatives or friends, or appear as hideous hag-like creatures, as frequently occurs during sleep paralysis. They can make themselves known by interacting with physical objects, as occurs in alleged poltergeist cases; through natural phenomena, such as the wind or lightning; through uncanny coincidences; or through direct mind-to-mind communication with sensitive individuals, shamans, or mediums. They may even make themselves known through moments of inspiration, as in the tradition of the daimonic muse. Discarnate entities may also be summoned or invoked to carry out tasks, usually through the performance of specific rituals, incantations, and spells.

Discarnate entities are thought to inhabit invisible worlds, sometimes conceived of as parallel dimensions. Traditional Celtic fairy lore, for example, describes a land known as Tir-Na-Nog, or the "Otherworld," which is inhabited by the fairy-folk and other supernatural beings. Many traditional belief systems posit the existence of some form of "spirit world" that is co-existent with the physical world. Among the Campa people of Peru, for example, the world is conceived as consisting of a series of layers arranged one above the other, with each layer inhabited by its own class of beings, generally visible only to the shamans. However, not all discarnates necessarily originate in parallel worlds; the paranormal investigator John Keel, for example, coined the term "ultraterrestrial" to refer to supernatural entities native to the planet earth.

There have been many scholarly attempts at explaining the widespread belief in discarnate entities. The pioneering anthropologist Sir E. B. Tylor (1832–1917), for example, coined the term "animism" to refer to this belief, which he held to be the most basic form of religion. Tylor reasoned that the belief in supernatural beings arose from the misinterpretation of experiences such as dreaming and trance states. He argued that early humans might have mistaken their meetings with deceased acquaintances in dreams for real encounters with real people. From such experiences early humans posited the existence of a nonphysical component of the person that could continue to exist after the death of the physical body. Tylor further reasoned that primitive humans expanded this idea out to other aspects of the world, attributing spirits, or souls to animals, plants, and other natural phenomena such as the wind, lightning, mountains, rivers, and the sun, among many others, which often seem to possess a consciousness of their own. Sociological explanations, following the work of the French sociologist Emile Durkheim, suggest that spirits, gods, and other discarnate entities are socially constructed and represent little more than focal points for collective worship and belief. Through worshiping or believing in the same spiritual beings, a social group is able to develop its own sense of identity, and so the solidarity of the group is reinforced. Psychological explanations are very similar in that they suggest that belief in discarnate entities arises out of a psychological need for stability in a transient and unpredictable world. Supernatural beings provide psychologically satisfying explanations for natural events, illnesses, fortune, and misfortune. Cognitive explanations suggest that belief in the existence of discarnate entities is the product of misinterpreted or misunderstood normal cognitive processes. A good example would be the human propensity to see faces in clouds. Cognitive anthropologist Stewart Guthrie has suggested that belief in supernatural beings arises from a failure to understand that such cognitive processes are hardwired into our brains (perhaps as by-products of natural selection) and that such observations do not necessarily mean that there are actual entities out there in objective reality. More recently cognitive anthropologist Justin Barrett has coined the term "Hyperactive Agency Detection Device" (HADD) to refer to these innate cognitive processes, which, he suggests, give rise to beliefs about disembodied intelligences.

This, of course, flies in the face of the traditional beliefs of a very wide proportion of human cultures, which hold that discarnate entities are real and play a significant role in everyday life. In considering whether these ideas are simply to be brushed aside as "primitive" and "irrational," or whether they might instead hint at a deeper ontological truth, it is important to note that there is also a body of parapsychological literature that suggests the possibility that discarnate entities may be ontologically real. In particular, some of the most recent experimental work on spirit mediumship appears to point toward the possibility that mediums may actually be in touch with the spirits of the dead, and if this is indeed the case then it opens up the possibility that there may be other forms of nonphysical, discarnate intelligence.

Jack Hunter

See also: Angels; Apparitions; Demonology; Ghosts; Mediumship; Spiritualism

Further Reading
Evans, Hilary. 1987. *Gods, Spirits, Cosmic Guardians: A Comparative Study of the Encounter Experience.* Wellingborough, UK: The Aquarian Press.
Hunter, Jack. 2012. *Why People Believe in Spirits, Gods, and Magic.* Newton Abbott, UK: David & Charles.
Strassman, Rick. 2001. *DMT: The Spirit Molecule: A Doctor's Revolutionary Research into the Biology of Near-Death and Mystical Experiences.* Rochester, VT: Park Street Press.
Turner, Edith. 1993. "The Reality of Spirits: A Tabooed or Permitted Field of Study?" *Anthropology of Consciousness* 4 (1): 9–12.
Voss, Angela, and William Rowlandson, eds. 2013. *Daimonic Imagination: Uncanny Intelligence.* Newcastle Upon Tyne, UK: Cambridge Scholars Press.

DIVINATION

Divination is the attempt to elicit from some higher power, or supernatural being, or synchronicity, or the collective unconscious, or our personal subconscious, the answers to questions beyond the range of ordinary human understanding: future, past, things hidden in space, right conduct, time and mode of religious worship, or choice of persons for a particular task. Most methods of divination are ancient and used widely in all cultures. For example, Tibetans use divination for arranging marriages, at the birth, when undertaking journeys, for affairs of business, to site a house, in the treatment of disease, to determine the outcome of legal disputes, for finding lost objects, and in a variety of social relationships. The Romans had a College of *augurs* and State controlled divination practices. The Japanese had a ministry of religious affairs responsible for festivals, rites, and ceremonies, which used divination.

Dowsing

A common form of divination is dowsing: finding water for a well, or a lost object (archaeology), or metal ores. Water divination was traditionally done with a forked hazel twig, but most dowsers today use metal rods. A sudden movement indicates

Divination is an age-old human practice by which people try to get information that exceeds the conventional range of human understanding. It can take many different forms, including:

- Dowsing
- Tarot cards
- The I Ching
- Runes
- Tibetan Mo divination
- Scrying
- Astrology
- The use of oracles (that is, divination through mediums)

that the object has been detected. A medieval woodcut shows dowsers in Germany searching for mineral ores. Some people search by dowsing a map using a pendulum. In this method the type of swing of the pendulum gives the answer, and psi is paramount.

People nowadays also use dowsing for healing, such as diagnosing disease and determining the remedy. Spiritual dowsing in sacred sites has also become extremely popular. Geomancy, which has been popularized in the West as *Feng Shui*, is traditionally concerned with selecting some land whose qualities will be favorable for a particular purpose. Modern Westerners use it to harmonize the layout of their homes. It is based on the idea that the energy of the earth is either life bringing (*chi*) or destructive (*sha*).

Research suggests that the dowser is using body responses to reveal to the conscious mind what the subconscious already knows, possibly acquired through—for example, in the case of water and mineral ores—changes in the geomagnetic field.

Tarot, *I Ching*, and Runes

Most fortune telling in the West is done either by tarot cards, the I Ching, or runes. These methods use chance, such as the fall of dice or the shuffle of cards. This random process enables psychokinesis or synchronicity to work, together with archetypal symbolism.

The Tarot traditionally used Egyptian symbolism, mixed with the Jewish Kabbalah and the tree of life. Nowadays there are many modern packs with a huge variety of archetypal symbolism, such as Native American, Celtic, or New Age. There are many different ways of using the cards, from picking one at random to complex layouts, with specific meanings related to the placing of the card within the layout. The interpretation can be direct from the cards—or the cards can be used as a focus for psi or intuition.

The *I Ching* is said to be 4,000 years old. The symbolism and philosophy is a mixture of Taoism and Confucianism. One can think of it as a "wise old sage." Two methods are used: throwing three coins for a quick reading; or yarrow sticks, which are randomly divided into two piles and counted out in groups of four, which makes for a slow, meditational process. The advice given is in the form of 64 different hexagrams, which correspond to different situations in life. This advice must be taken as given, but there is a learned skill in interpretation.

Tibetans use the *Mo* divination, normally with a *mala* of 108 beads which is grasped by both hands at random. Then the beads between the hands are counted in groups of four until between one and four remain; this is repeated three times. Sometimes dice are used instead of the *mala*. There is a special book for interpretation of the outcome. Most monasteries have a lama who does the *Mo*, and most villages have "wise women" who do *Mo* divination.

The traditional Norse method uses 23 runes. These are made from stone, clay, or wood with a symbol marked on each piece. There are two versions, the symbols being either Norse or Germanic in origin.

Scrying

Scrying is where a gifted seer gazes into a crystal ball, a pool of water, or a dark mirror in order to become psychically aware of information through a vision. The Mayans used polished obsidian to make a dark mirror; the Delphic oracle gazed into a bowl of water; and traditional Celtic practitioners used water, typically in wells, while gypsies used a crystal ball. Tibetans use a wide variety of methods, scrying in sacred lakes, the sky, stones, a bronze mirror, or even the thumb. In palmistry, the traditional gypsy method of divination, the lines of the hand are read in order to determine the questioner's future.

Astrology

This system is far more complex since it uses the movements of the planets within the ecliptic constellations to predict what is going to occur. English words reflect the belief that we are affected by the stars, as in dis—aster (astro = star) and cat—astrophe. Every year Tibetan astrologers make a calendar where each day will have its specifics delineated, such as a good day to start a business or a bad day to get married. This is a general prediction for everyone. Most Western astrologers use a system that originated 4,000 years ago, when Aries was the constellation rising in the east at sunrise at the spring equinox. Westerners concentrate more on personal predictions.

Oracles

Oracular divination is through mediums who have a vision while entranced or receive the information through dreams, especially at a sacred site, or through inspection of the entrails of a sacrificed animal, or the flight of birds in the sky, or the outcome of throwing of bones or dice, or by roasting animal bones or turtle shells, thus creating cracks upon their surface, which are then interpreted. In some of these cases the oracle both receives and translates the vision for the questioner. In Greece this person is called the *sophos*, which means a knower and a healer. The function of the *sophos* was to produce good order and harmony in society.

The most famous Greek oracle was the *pythia*—a woman past childbearing who sat on a tripod to go into trance in the *sanctum* at Delphi. Originally this was done on only the seventh day of the month in spring. In the case of the *pythia*, she received the vision while another person, the *mantis*, interpreted it for the questioner. The *hiereus* was a priest who made sacrifices for divinatory purposes, and the *oneiropolos* was the interpreter of dreams.

In Tibet, oracular divination is performed by reincarnated lamas embodying a deity, such as the Nechen oracle, who is consulted by the Dalai Lama and the Tibetan parliament. Most monasteries used to have their own oracle. A similar tradition exists in Japan. In both cultures, the deity is summoned into the body of the medium by chanting and drumming.

Another common form of oracle is using natural phenomena (omens, or portents) such as bird behavior, comets, and earthquakes, to warn of coming events. Across the world crows are recognized as sacred messengers from the gods.

All cultures recognize sacred places, such as a mountain, a well, or a grove of oak trees, which are visited for divination or healing. The Greeks induced dreams at specific temples, such as at Olympia. The Japanese also induct oracular dreams at specific Shinto or Buddhist shrines. In Greece a figure emerges from the inner sanctum and speaks to the sleeper. Commonly, for the healing to occur, one has to undertake abstinence, or make specific vows, or offer prayer to the shrine.

Theories of Divination

Anthropologist Michael Winkelman advances the hypothesis that simple societies primarily use intuitive methods of divination, often in an altered state of consciousness, while complex societies use randomization techniques. Dowsing is an intermediate method.

Divination is an expression of an underlying world order. As one works with the symbolism and penetrates deeply into its meaning, one learns to arrive at an integrated view of the world, to see the one in the many. It is used as a means of communication with sacred powers that lie beyond the senses and is seen as a manifestation of universal truths that transcend the mundane purposes of daily life. Divination also demonstrates and explains the regular cycles of birth, decay, and rebirth. Omens are signs of cosmic upset that reverberate throughout the universe. This is a magical philosophy where everything in the universe is interdependent and interconnected.

Even in our modern Western scientific materialist culture, divination is still widely used and very popular.

Serena M. Roney-Dougal

See also: Astrology; Ghosts; Mediumship; Ouija Board; Possession; Precognition; Prophecy; Psi; Psychokinesis (PK); Ritual Magic; Scrying; Synchronicity; Tarot; Unconscious Mind

Further Reading
Gauquelin, Michel. 1974. *Cosmic Influences on Human Behaviour*. London: Garnstone Press.
Graves, Tom. 1990. *The Diviners Handbook*. Rochester, VT: Destiny Books.
Loewe, Michael and Carmen Blacker, eds. 1981. *Divination and Oracles*. London, UK: Allen & Unwin.
Willhelm, Richard, ed. 1968. *The I Ching or Book of Changes*. 3rd ed. Translated by Cary F. Baynes. London, UK: Routledge & Kegan Paul.
Willis, Tony. 1986. *Discover Runes: Understanding and Using the Power of Runes*. London: Aquarian/Thorsons.
Winkelman, Michael J. 1983. "The Anthropology of Magic and Parapsychological Research." *Parapsychology Review* 14 (2): 13–19.

DOPPELGÄNGER

"Doppelgänger" is a German word signifying double, literally "double-walker." In Germanic traditions where the term originated, the doppelgänger is a spirit double. The word was first used in English in 1851.

The Doppelgänger in Gothic Literature

The English doppelgänger theme was largely forged in 19th century literature, where the phenomenon of the double was used to discuss the mysteries of consciousness, selfhood, and often madness. In general, the doppelgänger device in Western literature explores the psychological paradox of a "second self" that is capable of reflecting one's most intimate thoughts and spurring on unexpected behavior and yet is simultaneously hidden and unknowable. Sometimes the double is uncontrollable and even diabolical. The concept is central to Gothic horror classics such as Mary Shelley's *Frankenstein* and Bram Stoker's *Dracula*, which reflect the frustrating duality of human nature as well as the Greco-Roman theme of Prometheus as trickster: the "disobeying" aspect of human psychology that erupts from the dangerous pursuit of higher knowledge. This theme, of course, parallels biblical traditions of the forbidden fruit and Goethe's *Faust*.

Edgar Allan Poe often used alter egos as plot devices in works. Most notably, Poe's 1839 story "William Wilson" depicts the psychological struggle between a man and his double, ending in a murder-suicide. Similarly, Fyodor Dostoevsky's 1846 novel *The Double* details the relationship of a government clerk and his double, who attempts to take over the man's life. The novel ends with the clerk being locked away in an insane asylum. Another variant of the doppelgänger theme involves a shadow self that arises in diametrical opposition to the primary self, most famously explored in Robert Louis Stevenson's 1886 novella *Strange Case of Dr. Jekyll and Mr. Hyde*.

Folklore and Traditions

Folkloric examples of the doppelgänger theme are readily found in European and early American sourcebooks. The core concept of the physical spirit double is extremely common historically and cross-culturally. European myths consider the seeing of one's own doppelgänger as a bad omen, often interpreted as imminent death. Doppelgängers could also be seen by friends and relatives and have also been reported to arrive somewhere without individuals' knowledge and acting in their stead. Unlike most apparitions, doppelgängers are not ephemeral presences but are often described as physically interacting with the material world in the same way that living people do.

French scholar Claude Lecouteux points out that the doppelgänger theme known today is derived from early Germanic notions of spirits and the afterlife. In the Middle Ages, Celtic and Norse traditions highlight the double as a phenomenal reality that seers and healers set loose from the body. The Double is seen in these traditions as an intermediary between the material world and the spirit world through which humans could communicate with all sorts of supernatural forces. In this sense, the Double is a tether to the entire cosmos, including the land of the dead. The double in Christian and Pagan literature could take a diversity of forms and is connected with witchcraft, fairies, animal transformation, and nightmare or "pressing spirit" cursing traditions (what we today call *sleep paralysis*). While many of these traditions were later forcibly put down by the Church, they survive in fairy tales and literature, which are still read with interest due to fresh experiences by ordinary people.

The Doppelgänger Today

In modern usage, the term has lost much of its ominous tone and become synonymous with seeing someone who closely resembles another individual. For example, Chad Smith, drummer for the Red Hot Chili Peppers, and actor Will Ferrell have been described as each other's doppelgänger, and the two men report that they are often mistaken in public for one another. However, the uncanny themes of the "alter ego" or hidden self remain popular in mass media and largely carry on the dark themes first explored in Gothic horror. For example, the film *Fight Club* chillingly depicts a psychotic alter ego, and *Invasion of the Body Snatchers*—the 1954 novel plus its multiple film adaptations spanning the 1950s through the 2000s—is a veritable phenomenon of a cult sci-fi story in which extraterrestrials make perfect replicas of their human hosts and proceed to take over their lives. More recently, this theme of doubles as replacements is cleverly spun in the 2009 British film *Moon*, in which human clones fight for identity and basic rights in a dystopian industrial future.

Thousands of ordinary people continue to report doppelgänger experiences. In contemporary ethnographies around the world, the doppelgänger is still related to the experience of soul flight, which, along with other dissociative somatic effects, is induced at will for ritual and information-gathering purposes. In general, modern psychiatry has long recognized the splitting or dissociation of the self from the perception of the body as a signal of worsening mental illness. Clinically, hostile interactions between the viewer and the double are more common than friendly interactions. Peter Brugger of Zurich University Hospital, Switzerland, coined the "Doppelgänger Syndrome," suggesting a similarity to the "phantom limb" effect known by amputees. Sufferers of this syndrome experience a phantom self or "felt presence" by projecting the self-construct into the world. "Heautoscopy" is the medical term for seeing the complete duplication of the body. This effect may be due to activity in the temporo-parietal junction of the brain, which has also been associated with out-of-body experiences and other body distortion effects. Oliver Sacks, MD, has recently reviewed many sources of benign hallucinations—including the doubling of consciousness—that are not associated with mental illness in his book *Hallucinations* (2012). Another neurological interpretation, especially for encounters that take place at night or related to sleep, includes sleep paralysis and hypnagogic hallucinations, in which the experiencer comes face to face with an unsettling self-like "Other" while lying in bed and unable to move.

These scientific explanations are helpful for identifying and treating maladaptive forms of the doppelgänger experience, but of course the scientific worldview does not make room for the uncanny clairvoyant content that is often central to historical accounts of doppelgängers. The philosophical mystery will never be solved as well but should be appreciated as an open question: what happens when I experience myself as someone else? Or as the question is phrased in the film *I Heart Huckabees*, "How am I not myself?"

Ryan Hurd

See also: Apparitions; Ghosts; Out-of-Body Experience (OBE); Unconscious Mind

Further Reading
Lecouteux, Claude. 2003. *Witches, Werewolves and Fairies: Shapeshifters and Astral Doubles in the Middle Ages*. Rochester, VT: Inner Traditions.
Sacks, Oliver. 2012. *Hallucinations*. New York: Knopf.

DRUGS AND THE PARANORMAL

The studies of parapsychology and psychedelic research are relatively recent academic endeavors, going back approximately 120 years and 70 years respectively. Despite the disparate nature of these two fields now, the first discoverers and popularizers of psychedelics all developed an interest in the apparently paranormal dimensions these substances induced. The discoverer of LSD, Albert Hofmann, reported an out-of-body and near-death-like experience on his very first trip and thereafter attended parapsychology conferences. The discoverer of psilocybin-containing mushrooms, R. Gordon Wasson, witnessed a shaman demonstrate ostensible psychic abilities in his first mushroom ritual. The man who coined the term "psychedelic," Dr. Humphrey Osmond, reported demonstrating frighteningly good extrasensory perception (ESP) in a test with a colleague after consuming mescaline, so much so that their research assistant began to panic. The list goes on.

A review of the literature on psychedelics and parapsychology indicates that there are multitudinous accounts of drug-induced paranormal experiences occurring in recreational, clinical, and experimental settings. The typical clinical observations, rather than coming from psychiatric reports, stem from the psychotherapeutic context, primarily from the 1960s when such psychedelic-assisted therapy was at its peak. Estimates indicate that ESP, with good supporting evidence, occurred in about two percent of such psychedelic-assisted therapy sessions, a figure that is much higher than the reported occurrence of well-supported ESP within ordinary psychotherapy.

Regardless of the source of drug-induced paranormal experience, it is clear that of all substances, those termed psychedelic are the only ones to reliably and repeatedly induce paranormal experiences, and the occurrence of such paranormal experiences is far greater than the occurrence of these experiences without such substances. Furthermore, such psychedelically induced experiences from within the Western academy also match reports from explorers, ethnobotanists, and anthropologists concerning the occurrence of such apparently paranormal experiences among the indigenous tribes that are known to use these substances for magico-religious purposes, especially shamanism. Surveys with recreational users typically indicate that those who report paranormal experiences are more likely than those who do not to have tried psychedelic substances and, vice-versa, those that do imbibe psychedelics are also more likely to report paranormal experiences.

The most common experience reported by survey respondents was telepathy, which occurred in up to 83 percent of those under the influence (of cannabis in this particular case), with reports of psi experiences in general (i.e., telepathy, precognition, clairvoyance, or psychokinesis) under the influence of psychedelics more generally at 18 percent of substance users at the lowest. Psychokinesis was typically the rarest form of psi reported, whereas out-of-body experiences (OBEs) were common with psychedelics and tended to occur with most every substance of this kind, but especially with dissociative anesthetics such as ketamine. Paranormal beliefs also tend to increase with the number of consumed psychedelic substances, as do fears of the paranormal, whereas such beliefs are typically not related to nonpsychedelic drugs, as with cocaine, heroin, and alcohol, where the relationships are reversed. Such trends also reflect the folklore around such substances, as only psychedelic plants are traditionally used in shamanic practices for transcending time and space and for accessing apparent latent psychic abilities.

Nevertheless, such accounts are based merely on subjective experience, and while such reports can indicate trends in the kinds of experiences that are forthcoming with particular types of substances, they do nothing to verify the genuine occurrence of apparently paranormal phenomena. Furthermore, most of the surveys do

Paranormal experiences have long been associated with the effects of psychedelics on consciousness, beginning with the traditional use of entheogens for divinatory and shamanic purposes. The most common of these experiences include:

• Extrasensory perception such as telepathy

• Precognition

• Out-of-body experiences

• Encounters with ghosts, spirits, and other entities

not report the specific substances being used and typically lump together all classes of drugs, such as psychedelics or mind-altering drugs, making specific psychopharmacological insights difficult.

The results of a recent survey that was specifically devised to attempt to classify paranormal experiences by drug show that, while there is a degree of overlap between drugs and these experiences in general, certain substances are more prone to producing or being associated with certain experiences. Cannabis was particularly associated with telepathic experiences, ketamine with OBEs, N,N-dimethyltryptamine (DMT) with entity encounters, and a host of psychedelic plants (as opposed to synthetic chemicals) with plant-spirit encounters. Additionally, the survey showed some small correlations between the frequency of drug use and the frequency of experiences associated with certain types of commonly paired drugs and experiences, particularly in regard to experiences that are termed mystical.

While surveys are useful in identifying trends in subjective experience, no real evaluation of the genuine nature or not of these experiences is possible without exploring the apparently paranormal effects of these substances under experimentally controlled conditions. In this regard there have only been 23 published experiments that have been conducted, primarily with LSD and psilocybin (the active principle in so-called magic mushrooms), but also with ayahuasca (an Amazonian psychedelic jungle decoction), mescaline (derived from psychedelic cacti), cannabis, and *Amanita muscaria* (a different type of psychedelic mushroom from those containing psilocybin). Most of these studies were also conducted in the golden age of psychedelic research between the late 1950s and the late 1960s.

The degree of success of the experiments in inducing genuine clairvoyance or telepathy (the only type of ESP tasks attempted) varied in relationship to the type of test employed, with rigid "forced choice" tasks requiring repeated guessing of a few basic symbols (as with the five simple designs of the Zener cards) returning poor results and those tasks utilizing more dynamic "free response" targets, whereby the participant just gave a description of his or her internal mental landscape, tending to produce positive results more often than not. There is also some indication that the experiments using participants who were more experienced with psychedelics tended to do better than those using drug naïve participants, as might be expected, because first-timers tended to become lost in the seminal mystical rapture of the experience. One participant taking their first psychedelic during such an experiment was reported to say that it was "psychedelically immoral" to get them to do boring and repeated tasks on their first trip, and others said they preferred to engage with their visionary experience rather than do the meaningless tests.

Overall the results of those initial "psi-chedelic" experiments remain promising, despite the problems involved in working with the psychedelically inexperienced. Nevertheless, these seminal experiments cannot be considered as evidential in any meaningful way because of poor reporting and the lack of the sophisticated control procedures to ensure against sensory leakage that would be expected by today's standards in parapsychological research. Some further advances might also be made through developing new methodologies for testing psychedelically induced ESP, such that the important factors of set and setting found in shamanic practices are integrated into experiments, or field research might be conducted within shamanic ceremonies. Furthermore, other techniques might also be considered, such as the hypnotic reinduction of psychedelic states; the use of emotionally bonded pairs, such as twins, for going on simultaneous voyages; or the use of skilled participant-experimenters in procedurally tight precognition protocols that fuse the best of the subjective and the objective to create optimum conditions for maximizing ESP effects under the influence of psychedelics.

The advantage of psychedelic parapsychology to that of ordinary ESP research is that the psychologically amplifying nature of these psychoactive substances can help magnify both the beneficial and detrimental dimensions of ordinary psi research. Furthermore, the psychedelic experience can help researchers get a better first-hand grasp and clearer notion of the psi experience, and this also allows psychedelic researchers to identify the possible limitations of ordinary psychological research.

Weaving together the many investigative stands of this research, it is clear that in exploring the rich tapestry of human potential, parapsychological research and psychedelic research have much to share. There are also obvious implications for aligned fields, and it should never be assumed that subjective paranormal experiences are delusional (although this may sometimes be the case) when informing psychiatric and psychotherapeutic professionals of the capacity of these drugs to induce them. Going beyond any preexisting prejudices against the exceptional, it may be valuable to see paranormal experiences, especially ones that are chemically induced, as producing meaningful insights into the experient's personal growth. At the transpersonal juncture between what may be regarded as medicine, magic, or madness, perhaps it is best to consider such "psi-chedelic" experiences holistically in relation to the concepts of spiritual emergence and holotropic states, within the framework of the "psychology of the future" expounded by Stanislav Grof.

David Luke

See also: Extrasensory Perception (ESP); Near-Death Experience (NDE); Out-of-Body Experience (OBE); Precognition; Psi; Psychokinesis (PK); Shamanism; Telepathy

Further Reading

Grof, Stanislav. 2000. *Psychology of the Future: Lessons from Modern Consciousness Research.* Albany, NY: State University of New York Press.

Heaven, Ross, ed. 2012. *Cactus of Mystery: The Shamanic Powers of the Peruvian San Pedro Cactus.* Rochester, VT: Inner Traditions.

Luke, David P. 2012. "Psychoactive Substances and Paranormal Phenomena: A Comprehensive Review." *International Journal of Transpersonal Studies* 31: 97–156. http://www.transpersonalstudies.org/ImagesRepository/ijts/Downloads/Luke%20 IJTS%2031(1)-2012.pdf.

ECTOPLASM

Ectoplasm is a mysterious, semi-physical substance ostensibly produced by physical mediums of the Spiritualist tradition and is the substance from which spirits
are said to materialize during séances. The term "ectoplasm" itself is borrowed
from cellular biology and was first used by Charles Richet in the late 19th century
to refer to phenomena produced by the Italian physical medium Eusapia Palladino
(1854–1918). Other names for the substance include Teleplasm and Ideoplasm,
both of which suggest that the substance may be molded or shaped by thought
and intention.

Ectoplasm is said to take the form of hands, limbs, and rods (referred to in the
literature as pseudopods) as well as animate heads and full-body materializations.
It is reportedly secreted from the mouth, nose, pores, and other bodily orifices
while the medium is in a deep state of trance. Ectoplasm is said to be particularly sensitive to light; hence, many physical séances are conducted in blackout
conditions or, with certain mediums, in red light. It is also said to be sensitive to
touch, which is one of the reasons why séances are so heavily controlled; if a sitter
reaches out to touch a materialized form without the permission of the medium or
their spirit controls, the ectoplasm is said to violently snap back into the medium,
causing bruising and pain. When sitters are allowed to touch materializations,
their reports of the texture of the substance vary considerably, ranging from cold
and damp to the texture and temperature of human skin. Descriptions of its appearance also range from a white, viscous fluid to a smoke-like emanation that
coalesces into solid forms. Witnesses frequently report that the substance builds
up from the floor before taking on human form, which then collapses back down
to the floor again before the ectoplasm is reabsorbed into the body of the medium.
Fake ectoplasm has sometimes been found to consist of cheesecloth or muslin and
is thought to be swallowed by the medium beforehand and then regurgitated during the séance. In the case of the American medium Mina Crandon (1888–1941),
her ectoplasmic secretions were found to be composed of animal intestines.

Despite the apparent outlandishness of ectoplasmic phenomena and the abun-
dant exposures of fraud, many eminent researchers were convinced of the reality
of the substance. Nobel Prize winner Charles Richet (1850–1935), for example,
once remarked, "It is prodigiously strange, prodigiously unusual, and it would
seem so unlikely as to be incredible; but we must give in to the facts. Yes, it is
absurd; but no matter—it is true" (Richet 1923, 618). By the late 1950s physical
mediumship had all but died out in Euro-American culture, owing primarily to

Ectoplasm is a form of materialization: the sudden creation of matter from a supernatural or paranormal source. It has reportedly taken the form of hands, limbs, rods ("pseudopods"), and even animate heads and full-body materializations that are secreted from the mouth, nose, pores, and other bodily orifices of a trance medium. Two of the most accurate cinematic depictions of it—"accurate" according to traditional accounts from, for example, Victorian Spiritualism (where it was often faked)—can be found in *The Legend of Hell House* (1973) and *The Haunting in Connecticut* (2009).

the unwillingness of mediums to associate themselves with an activity considered fraudulent. In the 1990s, however, a renewed interest in physical mediumship, including the production of ectoplasm, emerged, and now in the 21st century the so-called "New Age of Physical Mediumship" is in full swing, with groups such as the Felix Experimental Group in Germany claiming to produce a range of ectoplasmic phenomena. Researchers are still undecided as to whether the phenomena are genuine or not.

Although ectoplasm as a distinct phenomenon is primarily a product of the 19th- and early 20th-century Spiritualist movement, it does appear to have some cross-cultural parallels that resemble the substance in a number of ways. One such example is a phlegm-like substance produced by ayahuasqueros in the Amazon, from which magical darts are said to be extracted and which is also used in healing rituals. Another similar substance is found in traditional Australian Aboriginal accounts of a "magic cord" produced by "clever men." The magic cord was said to move around independently, like a snake slithering across the floor and was extruded from the mouth. Anthropologist Edith Turner, in her account of her experiences during a healing ceremony amongst the Ndembu in Zambia, also records witnessing a substance, which she describes as a large gray blob of plasma, being extracted from the back of a patient afflicted by the Ihamba spirit. Although not conclusive, these cross-cultural parallels are at least suggestive of the possibility that ectoplasm is not solely limited to the Euro-American Spiritualist tradition.

Jack Hunter

See also: Psychical Research; Séance; Spiritualism

Further Reading

Braude, Stephen E. 1997. *The Limits of Influence: Psychokinesis and the Philosophy of Science.* New York: University Press of America.

Haule, John Ryan. 2011. *Jung in the 21st Century, Vol. II: Synchronicity and Science.* London: Routledge.

Richet, Charles Robert. 1923. *Thirty Years of Psychical Research*. London: The Macmillan Company.

Turner, Edith. 1994. "A Visible Spirit Form in Zambia." In *Being Changed by Cross-Cultural Encounters: The Anthropology of Extraordinary Experience*, edited by David E. Young and Jean-Guy Goulet, 71–96. Ontario, CA: Broadview Press.

ELECTRONIC VOICE PHENOMENON (EVP)

Electronic voice phenomenon (EVP) is the occurrence of voices, utterances, raps, and taps that appear on audio recording devices without the operator being aware of them at the time the recording was taking place. In many cases, the voices heard on playback can be very distinct, yet most are barely coherent at all. People have also reported hearing spontaneous voices "live" through radios and televisions, a phenomenon known as Instrumental Trans-communication or ITC. Still others claim to have had contact with the dead via the telephone. There are numerous conventional explanations for EVP and related electronic voices, but some instances have yet to be explained in this way.

Through practical research and investigation, EVP was first discovered in 1956 by a California-based psychical researcher named Raymond Bayless. In a rented studio in Hollywood, Bayless began the experiments with a psychic and astral projector by the name of Atilla von Szalay, who claimed he could produce direct voice phenomena. Bayless aimed to see if he could record these independent voices. Within the studio, a large wooden cabinet was built in which a microphone was placed (leading to a tape recorder outside of the cabinet), and von Szalay would sit inside the cabinet at first to try and produce the voices. Once they began to occur, he would leave the cabinet in an attempt to have them continue in his absence and subsequently be recorded. The first experiments began in November of 1956, and they continued for several years until Bayless published a report on the findings. On many occasions, after von Szalay had left the cabinet, or while he and Bayless were sitting in the studio in silence, the tape recorder on playback produced scratching noises, bangs, taps, raps, voices, and utterances that could not be accounted for by any person present. This report was published in 1959 as a correspondence in the *Journal of the American Society for Psychical Research*. Although the report went unnoticed within the parapsychological community, Bayless's research continued until the mid-1970s, with the help of a young D. Scott Rogo who joined him in the late 1960s.

Only three months after Bayless published his report in 1959, the Swedish filmmaker Friedrich Jürgenson announced that he had discovered anomalous voices and raps while recording birdsongs. These recordings also included what sounded like the anomalous voices darting into normal recorded conversation. Jürgenson is often described as the discoverer of EVP, and although this is incorrect, he did play a part in the field's progression because it was through his accidental discovery of EVP that the phenomenon began to gain further recognition. The subject was picked up by one of Jürgenson's experimenters, Dr. Konstantin Raudive, a Latvian savant living in Germany, who announced that he had also managed to replicate EVP and had found an electronic method for contacting the dead. These EVPs were reported to be similar to that of Jürgenson's recordings. They featured additional voices that would appear on playback of normal conversations and that would sometimes apparently comment on the conversations.

Dr. Raudive's claims were not well known in the UK or United States until 1971, when his book about his research was translated and published in English under the title *Breakthrough*. It came with an accompanying LP record featuring examples of his recordings. This brought EVP into current mainstream thought for parapsychology. It also put an end to von Szalay's research for several years; EVP was often referred to during that period as "Raudive Voices." However, Raudive's recordings were highly questionable, and some have said that his best EVPs, which consist of unclear speech and utterances, are comparable to von Szalay's worst. As Raudive spoke several languages, his analysis of the sounds attributed multiple languages to them, leading to a wide range of possible interpretations and opening him and his claims to much criticism. Although no one undertook first-hand testing of his claims, there were many valid criticisms and alternative explanations for the voices on his recordings.

Around the same time (1970–1972), Cambridge University gave its Perrot-Warrick Studentship to David Ellis, who at the time had no previous background in psychical research. His two-year research project set out to test some of the claims of Raudive and EVP in general in an attempt to gain an understanding of the recordings and their possible causes. D. Scott Rogo found Ellis's work to be generally negative in its assessment of EVP, and Rogo questioned whether Ellis had really demonstrated anything at all. At the very least, Ellis highlighted some of the conventional explanations for EVP, such as the claims that they are really fragments of radio transmissions, mechanical noises, and unnoticed remarks, aided by "imaginative guess work and wishful thinking." With these latter comments, Ellis highlighted an interesting psychological component of EVPs known as the pareidolia effect. This is a natural psychological phenomenon whereby people "make sense" of unclear images or sounds with little or no conscious effort or intention and attribute a humanly relatable reality of meaning to them.

Following a lifetime of interest in the paranormal, George Meek became fascinated with EVP. He was convinced that for electronic communication with the dead to become truly effective, more sophisticated techniques and equipment would be needed. He claimed to enlist the help of "departed scientists and engineers" in order to develop such a device. In 1977 he and a colleague named Bill O'Neil developed a machine they called the Spiricom, by which many alleged live recordings of EVP were produced. The history of the Spiricom continues to generate much interest today and also a great deal of skepticism.

The study of EVP has expanded rapidly since the field's inception in the mid-20th century, and there are currently many active researchers pursuing it. One of these, Dr. Anabela Cardoso, established the *ITC Journal* in 1999 to encourage such research. Steve Parsons and Ann Winsper, who founded the organization Para. Science, UK, have presented new EVP research in recent years, and Winsper has focused her doctoral research on the field.

Callum E. Cooper

See also: Parapsychology; Spirit Photography

Further Reading

Bayless, Raymond. 1959. Correspondence. *Journal of the American Society for Psychical Research* 53: 35–39.

Cooper, Callum E. 2012. *Telephone Calls from the Dead*. Old Portsmouth, UK: Tricorn Books.

Ellis, David J. 1978. *The Mediumship of the Tape Recorder*. Pulborough, UK: D.J. Ellis.

ITC Journal. http://www.itcjournal.org.

Para.Science. http://www.parascience.org.uk.

Parsons, Steve T., and Callum E. Cooper, eds. 2014. *Paracoustics*. Guildford, UK: White Crow Books.

Raudive, Konstantin. 1971. *Breakthrough: An Amazing Experiment in Electronic Communication with the Dead*. Gerrards Cross, UK: Colin Smythe.

Rogo, D. Scott. 1976. *In Search of the Unknown: The Odyssey of a Psychical Investigator*. New York: Taplinger. Republished by Anomalist Books, 2005.

Rogo, D. Scott, and Raymond Bayless. 1979. *Phone Calls from the Dead*. Englewood Cliffs, NJ: Guild Publishing.

ENFIELD POLTERGEIST

The Enfield poltergeist is considered the most important British poltergeist case of the 20th century. The events took place in a semidetached council house in Enfield, North London, from 1977 to 1978. The case is the subject of a best-selling book and extensive documentation, with a major film version due to be released in 2015.

The occupants of the house were Mrs. Peggy Harper and her two sons and two daughters, all in their teen or preteen years. The first incidents occurred on August 31, 1977, when furniture began to move by itself. Things rapidly escalated, and the Harpers sought help from neighbors. The police were called as well, with two officers witnessing phenomena. The matter soon came to the attention of the press, and following an article in the *Daily Mirror*, the case was brought to the attention of the Society for Psychical Research (SPR).

Two investigators from the SPR, Maurice Grosse and Guy Playfair, spent many months, along with other researchers, observing events at the house. Spiritualists, mediums, and journalists also attended at various stages. In many respects it appeared to the investigators that this was a classic poltergeist case centered on adolescent girls, principally 11-year-old Janet and, to a lesser extent, her older sister Margaret, aged 13. But notably, a very wide variety of effects were reported, including fires, object movements, breakdowns in equipment, noises, levitations, and strange trance-like states in the girls that resembled accounts of possession. In all, the phenomena lasted some 14 months.

The documentation and evidence surrounding the Enfield case is extensive, comprising over 1,000 hours of observations gathered from approximately 180 visits (including 25 all-night vigils) between September 5, 1977, and June 1978. Over 140 hours of tape recordings were made, and transcripts of events run to over 500 pages, with a number of the recordings still not transcribed. In addition, the Society for Psychical Research conducted a follow-up investigation, which concluded that genuinely paranormal incidents occurred. In addition to its presentation of a wide range of well-attested and recorded poltergeist incidents, many detailed in Guy Playfair's book *This House Is Haunted* (1980), the Enfield case was remarkable for the phenomenon of a strange voice, resembling that of an old man, which emerged from Janet and, on occasions, her sister Margaret, and which has never been satisfactorily explained. Analysis suggested it was produced by the girls' false vocal cords, but its sustained nature and the content of certain aspects of what it declared have never been fully explained. Like many alleged poltergeist voices and séance communications, much of what the voice said was banal, but on occasions it seemed to generate startlingly accurate information that was not known consciously to anyone present.

The Enfield case has been subjected to various skeptical analyses, but these have not advanced since the original outbreak, because of the failure to examine any of the primary data or interview either the investigators or the primary witnesses. As of 2014, only one skeptic on the case, Dr. Melvyn Willin, archivist for the SPR, has examined any quantity of the Enfield data, principally the audio recordings. His opinion, given in an e-mail, is interesting: "Yes, having listened to all the tapes (over 100) and sifted through Maurice's letters etc I changed my mind from being dismissive ('It's kids mucking about') to believing that there was far more to this case than simple tomfoolery" (Melvyn Willin, e-mail message to the author, February 14, 2012).

One interesting discovery with respect to the Enfield recordings is that rapping sounds obtained at Enfield in 1977 and 1978 contain an anomalous acoustic signature found in other poltergeist recordings. This effect was identified in 2010 by Dr. Barrie Colvin and is detectable only by an instrumental analysis. It shows up on samples of the raps at Enfield attributed to the poltergeist but not with raps deliberately made by the contemporary investigators in response, trying to encourage the phenomena. If the Enfield raps were a trick, how were they accomplished? This poses an explanatory puzzle for those who claim the manifestations were faked, as any postulated hoaxer would have to possess the advanced knowledge to devise and create an effect detectable only by instrumental analysis and only identified some 33 years later.

Alan Murdie

See also: Haunting; Poltergeist

Further Reading

Colvin, Barrie. 2010. "The Acoustic Properties of Unexplained Rapping Sounds." *The Journal of the Society for Psychical Research* 73.2 (899): 65–93.

Nickell, Joe. 2012. "Enfield Poltergeist: Investigative Files." *The Skeptical Inquirer* 36 (4), July/August: 12–14. Accessed October 29, 2014. http://www.csicop.org/si/show/enfield_poltergeist.

Playfair, Guy Lyon. 2011. *This House Is Haunted: The Amazing Inside Story of the Enfield Poltergeist* (originally subtitled *The True Story of a Poltergeist*). 3rd ed. Guildford, UK: White Crow Books.

EXORCISM

Exorcism refers to the banishment of unwanted spirits, either from a place or a person in a state of possession. Most cultures believe in spirit possession. From 1963 to 1968, anthropologist Erika Bourguignon directed "The Cross-cultural Study of Dissociational States" with support from National Institute for Mental Health. The study examined ethnographies of 488 cultures around the world and found that some form of spirit possession occurred in 77 percent of them. However, many cultures regard possession as a positive experience in which shamans or other figures voluntarily enter a trance-state allowing spirits and gods to speak through them. Belief in involuntary possession that requires exorcism—usually by demons or spirits of the dead—is more rare.

Anthropologists regard possession as a form of interpretation in which certain symptoms and behaviors are regarded as evidence of possessing spirits. For cultures that practice exorcism, possession may manifest as a normal illness with only physical symptoms. In the New Testament, some people in need of exorcism are described as blind and mute (Matthew 12:22) or crippled (Luke 13:10–13). Historian Moshe Sluhovsky suggests that in medieval Europe exorcism was primarily a means of curing the body and that it was only in the early modern period that possession came to be understood as a disease of the soul.

The three Western religions of Judaism, Christianity, and Islam all have traditions of exorcism and, with some exceptions, regard spirit possession as involuntary and negative. In Jewish tradition, exorcism appears in the apocryphal Book of Tobit. This book, written between the third and second centuries BCE, describes how an Israelite named Tobias banishes the demon Asmodeus with the help of the angel Raphael. Belief in the *dybbuk* emerged among the Jewish communities of early modern Europe. The *dybbuk* (literally "cleaving") is a spirit of the dead that attaches to the living. Skilled rabbis are required to exorcize the *dybbuk*. Muslim culture has a tradition of *jinn*, spirits that possess people causing madness. Various techniques for exorcizing *jinn* can be found throughout the Muslim world. However, exorcism plays the greatest role in Christianity. In the gospels, the power of

Jesus and his disciples to cast out demons is evidence of their spiritual authority. Exorcism remains important in many modern Christian churches. For instance, in the 2007 Baylor Religion Survey, 48 percent of American respondents either agreed or strongly agreed with the statement "It is possible for people to be possessed by the Devil/demons."

Western notions of exorcism have been transformed but not eliminated by the cultural authority of science. Prior to the Protestant Reformation, European Christians used many local techniques of exorcism. Unregulated practices led Protestant critics to accuse Catholics of superstition and sorcery. In response, the *Rituale Romanum*, promulgated in 1614, effectively banned folk practices of exorcism by establishing the official version of the ritual and restricting who could perform it. Despite skeptical attitudes toward exorcism among some educated circles, the 17th century was a "golden age" of demonic possession. Mass possessions involving entire convents of nuns and even entire towns were reported throughout Europe and in colonies in the New World.

Following the scientific revolution, medical interpretations of abnormal behavior gained increasing authority over supernatural ones. Many of the founders of psychiatry, including Jean Martin Charcot and Sigmund Freud, were fascinated by accounts of possession, which they reinterpreted as a mental illness they called "hysteria." William James was also interested in demonic possession, which he regarded as an altered state of consciousness distinct from hysteria. By the 20th century, many Christian denominations deferred to medical experts to assess alleged cases of possession. Most Catholic bishops will only approve an exorcism after a medical expert has been consulted and if truly inexplicable phenomena have been observed, such as levitation or the ability to speak in languages the person has not studied (xenoglossy).

Some medical experts arrived at less reductionistic interpretations of exorcism. Carl Jung theorized that possession occurred when an individual came to identify with an archetype from the collective unconscious. In a series of interviews in the 1930s, Jung described Hitler as "possessed" by the collective archetype of the Aryan unconscious. He believed that psychotherapy could be used to cure such people by adjusting their relationship with the archetype. Carl Wickland (1861–1945), an American psychiatrist trained at Durham Medical College, concluded that some mental illnesses result from a form of possession in which spirits of the dead attach themselves to sensitive individuals. To dislodge these spirits, he created an electrical generator called a Wimhurst machine that provided a mild shock to the patient in order to jolt the spirit out of their body. The spirit would then be guided into the body of a psychic medium who attended the treatment. Through the medium, the doctor could communicate with the spirit and persuade it pass on. Wickland's wife Anna was a medium and played an integral role in the treatment of his patients.

In 1949 an article appeared in *The Washington Post* about a boy (now believed to have been Ronald E. Hunkeler) in Mount Rainier, Maryland, who had undergone a Catholic exorcism. When the boy's symptoms began, the family first turned to Luther Miles Schulze, a Lutheran pastor. Schulze was persuaded that something inexplicable really was occurring and wrote to J. B. Rhine, then Director of the Parapsychology Laboratory at Duke University. Rhine continued a correspondence with Schulze but only met him some time after the events had ceased and at no time had contact with the boy or his family. Rhine was probably responsible for an account that appeared in the *Parapsychology Bulletin* (August 1949). Newspaper accounts inspired the writer William Peter Blatty, then a student at Georgetown University, to write his novel *The Exorcist* (1971). The film adaptation of this novel is widely credited with starting a revival of popular interest in possession and exorcism. Another wave of popular interest was ignited in the early 21st century by the confluence of trends in religion and popular entertainment as the Roman Catholic Church began to reestablish and reinforce its focus on and practice of exorcism, even as a spate of new horror films focused on the subject, often employing a highly sensationalistic approach. Among the most subtle and substantial of these was director Scott Derrickson's *The Exorcism of Emily Rose* (2004), inspired by a real-life case in which two priests were convicted of manslaughter for the 1976 death of the German college student Annaliese Michel, who died of malnutrition after undergoing multiple and intensive exorcisms.

Joseph Laycock

See also: Haunting; James, William; Jung, Carl; Possession; Unconscious Mind

Further Reading
Bourguignon, Erika. 1976. *Possession*. San Francisco: Chandler and Sharp.
Sluhovsky, Moshe. 2009. *Believe Not Every Spirit: Possession, Mysticism, & Discernment in Early Modern Catholicism*. Chicago: University of Chicago Press.

EXTRASENSORY PERCEPTION (ESP)

Extrasensory perception refers to the awareness of information that is unavailable to the perceiver using the normal sensory processes, *as they are currently understood to function*. Experiences are labeled as "extrasensory" when people appear to have received information when that information is not physically available to them. Extrasensory perception has been studied qualitatively, with a focus on subjective experiences, and quantitatively, where researchers focus on exploring whether (or not) ESP has occurred. Research on ESP experiences can be divided into three main categories: exploring what ESP experiences are like ("phenomenology"); exploring whether ESP actually occurs (so-called "proof-oriented" research); and exploring which factors are associated with ESP (so-called "process-oriented" research). The majority of research on ESP has been proof-oriented. Here, researchers test the hypothesis that an "anomaly" has occurred against what one would expect to have occurred through chance (guessing), using probability theory and statistics. Such experiments are designed to occlude the identity of target information from a person who then attempts to guess the identity of that target.

There are several subcategories of ESP. Experiences labeled as "telepathy" describe the anomalous acquisition of information from the mind (or physical experiences) of another person. An example of a telepathic experience might be when a twin reports that she experienced pains at the same time that her twin went into early labor in a distant location but without any normal reason for the pains in the experiencer or normal means of communication between the two. Other ESP experiences occur when there is anomalous awareness of events or information present at a distant location. Such information may be experienced visually as "clairvoyance," in auditory form as "clairaudience," and in embodied or felt experience as "clairsentience." An example of a clairvoyant experience might be if a person had a visual impression of a fire taking place at his home while he was at work, and it was later discovered that a fire did occur at the time of the experience. Experiences labeled as "precognition" include the anomalous awareness of information that will take place in the future. Many such experiences are reported prior to traumatic events. For example, many precognitive experiences were reported surrounding September 11, 2001. "Premonitions registries" enable experiencers to record experiences that seem compelling, and it is then possible to "timestamp" them and look back at the features of the experience after a matching event has taken place. "Retrocognitive" experiences are a fourth category of ESP experiences and describe the anomalous acquisition of information that appears to come from the past. An example of this type of experience might be visiting a particular location and having awareness of information about something that happened at that location in the past. Much experimental research has ignored retrocognition, since it is difficult to rule out normal explanations that at some point an experiencer had in fact been exposed to the information about events that occurred at the given location.

ESP experiences are reported by a significant proportion of the population. They are often highly meaningful and are frequently associated with other people. Many are associated with positive mental health, although some may be felt to be more negative. Factors that impact health include having a sense of control over experiences, organization and assimilation of experiences, having a meaningful (organizing) context for experiences, having a useful application for experiences, and being able to share experiences with others.

Louisa Rhine's case collection found that ESP experiences fall into four main categories: realistic dreams, unrealistic dreams, hallucinations, and intuitive impressions. Realistic dreams are those in which the apparent ESP information seems to be directly represented. In contrast, a symbolic dream is one in which the information appears to be symbolically represented—for example, a black crow may represent death, or a dove may represent peace. Interestingly, precognitive experiences are extremely likely to occur in the form of a realistic dream, while symbolic dreams are more likely to refer to events that are occurring in real time. ESP experiences are also reported during the waking state. Hallucinatory experiences are those in which there is a sensory experience occurring in the absence of any local stimulus; for example, a person may perceive the voice of a person asking for help, but that person is not there. This may be labeled as extrasensory if it is later discovered that the person asking for help was experiencing a problem or being hurt. Intuitive experiences refer to ESP experiences that are feelings or a desire or compulsion to perform a certain action in the absence of any normally derived information. For example, a person may feel compelled to drive a different way home from work one day and later discover that she avoided an accident by following this feeling. These patterns have also been found by other researchers who have adopted a similar case study approach. Louisa Rhine noticed that ESP experiences have different levels of completeness of information associated with the various forms of ESP that are reported. In fact, realistic images provide the most complete information, followed by unrealistic imagery, intuitions, and finally hallucinations. There are also individual differences in how convinced the experiencer is that he or she has experienced ESP. Interestingly, *conviction* is usually higher in experiences that provide *less* information to the experiencer. As such, intuitive experiences are often associated with higher levels of conviction.

Case studies are limited in terms of demonstrating that ESP has actually occurred. In fact, there are a number of ways in which experiences can *seem* to be psychic but actually have a more mundane explanation. Such explanations include chance or coincidence; for example, a person just *happens* to dream about a plane crash the night before a plane crash actually occurred. There are other cognitive and perceptual biases that can explain many of these real world experiences. For example, eyewitness testimony for any event is actually very unreliable. In addition, human memories are highly malleable, and it is possible to alter and even implant memories of events that *never* actually occurred. In addition, prior beliefs can work as organizational "schemas" for events that are observed and/or remembered. In contrast, Louisa Rhine felt that case studies might provide *clues* as to how, if genuine, ESP might actually work, and that these clues might be explored systematically under laboratory conditions.

The term ESP was popularized by J. B. Rhine in the 1930s following the publication of the results of a series of card-guessing experiments that claimed to show evidence for "above chance" awareness of the order of cards in a deck. Rhine used specially designed cards, which are known as ESP or "Zener cards" (after Paul Zener who designed them). There are five symbols that each appear five times in a standard deck of cards. Participants, who were mainly students at Duke University, would attempt to guess the order of cards in a series of "runs" of 25 cards. Each card that was correctly guessed was deemed a "hit," while those guessed incorrectly were labeled "misses." Such card-guessing studies used probability theory and compared guess rates to what would be expected by chance, here 5 cards correct out of 25. This type of design is labeled "forced choice." Rhine undertook research into telepathy, clairvoyance, and precognition using this approach. His research found several ESP "stars" among the students he tested, such as Adam Linzmayer and Hubert Pearce, who were consistently able to guess the identity of targets better than would be expected by chance. Card-guessing research identified several interesting patterns in the data, including "psi missing," where the guess rate is statistically *lower* than expected by chance. Other studies have found that missing may be associated with anxiety and negative emotional states, while hitting is associated with openness and relaxation. In "free response" methodologies the target is one of many possibilities in an overall "pool" of possible targets.

The Maimonides dream telepathy studies explored whether ESP can actually occur in dreams. To do this, a series of dreamers who were each wired up to an EEG (electroencephalogram, measuring brain wave activity) were monitored while they slept in the laboratory. At the same time a sender (or senders, including a famous group sending during a Grateful Dead concert) attempted to influence the dreamer with target information (art prints). The dreamer was then awoken during REM sleep, when dreaming is most likely, to see to what extent dreams included the target information. Results were supportive of the ESP hypothesis.

Other methods that have been used to explore ESP include the "ganzfeld" and "remote viewing" methods. The ganzfeld uses partial sensory deprivation procedures to induce a mild altered state of consciousness among receivers. Like the dream studies, a sender then attempts to influence the thoughts of the receiver, who verbalizes his or her impressions during the sending period. At the end of the sending and receiving period, the receiver is usually shown four possible targets and asked to rate how similar his or her imagery is to each, and to select the one that is most similar. Results are compared to what would be expected by chance. The remote viewing method asks viewers to psychically view the location of someone who is actually visiting a geographical location or the identity of an object or the details at a given coordinate on a map. Interestingly, the U.S. government funded this research for over 20 years, and the findings were declassified in the 1990s. Both databases have been the focus of much controversy and debate but are generally considered to demonstrate above chance outcomes. In the ganzfeld, "hitting" is more likely when certain types of participants take part. For example, those who practice a mental discipline (e.g., meditation), who have had prior ESP experiences, and who are highly creative (e.g., students at the performing arts school Juilliard) tend to score higher. Some researchers have suggested that there is a "recipe" for ESP success and note that there are several factors that interact in so-called successful ESP studies. These include the beliefs, personality, state of consciousness, and attitudes of the receiver alongside the beliefs and attitudes of the experimenter. For example, the sheep-goat effect, where believers perform better at ESP tasks than do disbelievers, is an intriguing finding. Interestingly, ESP also appears to work better when the earth's geomagnetism is low.

Recent experiments have focused on unconscious measures of ESP, including psychophysiology and neural correlates. Others have explored implicit ESP, where the ESP task is hidden, or where the person does not have to try consciously to be psychic. ESP may well be better measured unconsciously or implicitly than explicitly (as conscious guessing). When a person is exposed to an arousing stimulus, the body responds to prepare for action. Presentiment effects refer to the observation that physiological systems begin to respond to arousing stimuli *before* the person has been exposed to such stimuli. Psychologist Daryl Bem's "feeling the future" studies have famously run psychological experiments backward and found evidence that cognition runs both forward and backward in time, thus lending support to the existence of precognition.

Several theories have attempted to explain ESP phenomena. These include theories—many based in the domain of physics—to explain how information may register in the system in the first place and how the mind might be processing ESP once it arrives there. One recent influential psychological theory is Jim Carpenter's First Sight Model, where ESP is considered to be occurring all the time and unconsciously biasing the way in which our cognitive-perceptual system functions.

Christine Simmonds-Moore

See also: Anomalistic Psychology; Art, Creativity, and the Paranormal; Clairvoyance; Ganzfeld Technique, The; Hallucinations; Paranormal Dreams; Parapsychology; Precognition; Psi; Psychokinesis (PK); Remote Viewing; Rhine Research Center; Sheep-Goat Effect; Telepathy

Further Reading

Cardeña, Etzel, Stephen J. Lynn, and Stanley Krippner, eds. 2013. *Varieties of Anomalous Experience: Examining the Scientific Evidence.* 2nd ed. Washington, DC: American Psychological Association.

Carpenter, James C. 2012. *First Sight: ESP and Parapsychology in Everyday Life.* Lanham, MD: Rowman & Littlefield Publishing Group.

Irwin, Harvey J., and Caroline Watt. 2007. *An Introduction to Parapsychology.* 5th ed. Jefferson, NC: McFarland.

Radin, Dean. 2006. *Entangled Minds: Extrasensory Experiences in a Quantum Reality.* New York: Paraview.

Rhine-Feather, Sally, and Michael Schmicker. 2005. *The Gift: ESP, the Extraordinary Experiences of Ordinary People.* New York: Macmillan.

FATE MAGAZINE

Fate magazine is an American magazine dedicated to the paranormal. It is the longest running periodical of its kind and has published more than 700 issues over its remarkably durable six-decade-long existence. It currently exists as both a print and electronic publication with a website and radio program. Despite having a limited niche audience, *Fate* has been enormously influential as it helped introduce flying saucers and Scientology to a wider audience, created a known composite audience for those interested in disparate supernatural topics, and connected its readers to a wide array of emerging metaphysical and occult groups through its advertisement pages.

Curtis and Mary Fuller cofounded *Fate* in 1948 with Raymond Palmer, who had been a prolific author and the editor of the science-fiction magazine *Amazing Stories* for the preceding decade. Palmer's time at the helm of *Amazing Stories* was marked by exciting, fast-paced stories and the long running "Shaver Mystery," stories by a man named Richard Shaver who claimed that the world was controlled by sinister robot-like descendants of prehistoric races who lived inside the hollow earth. Palmer presented Shaver's tales as fact, which led to both an increase in circulation and ridicule of *Amazing Stories*.

With *Fate*, Palmer and the Fullers cast a wider net that included almost everything that could be described as paranormal or supernatural. Vivid full-color covers promised readers "True Stories of the Strange, the Unusual, the Unknown," and articles regularly included topics such as psychic and Fortean phenomena, mystical experiences, ghosts, superhuman abilities, dreams, hypnotism, cryptozoology, and extraterrestrials. While decidedly modern and American at its core, *Fate* was also global and historical in its coverage, and it routinely dedicated articles and covers to African and Asian religions, lost civilizations in South America, and ancient Egyptian deities.

Fate appealed to its audience on many levels. On one hand, it presented the paranormal within a scientific and rational frame that cited research and experimental evidence, offered its content as fact and truth, and even debunked claims to the paranormal at certain times. On the other hand, particularly in its formative years, *Fate* appealed to a popular audience, as did other pulp magazines, through lurid cover art and sensational topics designed to stand out on crowded newsstands. It also was democratic in its direct addressing of readers in editorials, its letters section, and the space regularly used for readers' submissions of their own paranormal experiences. In fact, many of the articles in *Fate*'s early years were explicitly instructional and promised its readers ways to see into the future and read minds.

The most significant moment in the magazine's history most likely came with *Fate's* very first issue when Palmer solicited a piece by Kenneth Arnold, a pilot who had witnessed nine flying discs near Mount Rainier in Washington State the previous year. Arnold, an Eagle Scout who worked for the Red Cross, was an impeccable witness, and his earlier eyewitness account was reused and titled "I Did See the Flying Disks" for the cover story of the inaugural issue of *Fate*. Arnold's piece not only gave a massive amount of attention to the nascent *Fate*, but it is also seen by many as marking the beginning of the modern UFO period as it propelled "flyer saucers" into the national spotlight.

In 1955 Palmer sold his interest in *Fate*, and the magazine was left under the control of Fuller and his wife, who broadened the scope of its coverage. By the mid-1970s the monthly readership of *Fate* had swelled to nearly 150,000 readers, up from 60,000 at the dawn of the 1960s. In the 1980s it featured a regular column by John Keel of *The Mothman Prophecies* fame. In 1988 the Fullers sold *Fate* to Lewellyn Publications, which in turn sold it to Phyllis Galde of Galde Press in 2001. Today *Fate* is bi-monthly, and while it is online, it still keeps itself anchored in its history with retro-looking cover art, digest-sized magazine, and continuations of columns such as the reader-submitted "True Mystic Experiences."

Philip Deslippe

See also: Fortean Phenomena; Keel, John A.; Paranormal; Society for Psychical Research; UFO

Further Reading

Nadis, Fred. 2013. *The Man from Mars: Ray Palmer's Amazing Pulp Journey*. New York: Tarcher/Penguin.
Steiger, Brad. 1976. "Chicago's Fate—Magazine, That Is." In *Psychic City: Chicago*, by Brad Steiger, 11–22. Garden City, NY: Doubleday & Company.

FORT, CHARLES

The American writer Charles Fort (1874–1932) was the author of four extremely influential books on anomalous phenomena: *The Book of the Damned*, *New Lands*, *Lo!*, and *Wild Talents*. These works cover many of the areas of interest to students of the paranormal, such as ghosts, poltergeists, psi phenomena, UFOs, and witchcraft. Fort has been referred to as the man who invented the supernatural. He has also frequently been accused of being blindly opposed to science, and a bald summary of his works may indeed do nothing to dispel this impression. It must be borne in mind, however, that his books are in fact radically skeptical and refuse

I believe nothing. I have shut myself away from the rocks and wisdoms of ages, and from the so-called great teachers of all time, and perhaps because of that isolation I am given to bizarre hospitalities. I shut the front door upon Christ and Einstein, and at the back door hold out a welcoming hand to little frogs and periwinkles. I believe nothing of my own that I have ever written. I cannot accept that the products of minds are subject-matter for beliefs. But I accept, with reservations that give me freedom to ridicule the statement at any other time, that showers of an edible substance that has not been traced to an origin upon this earth, have fallen from the sky, in Asia Minor.

—Charles Fort, *Lo!* (1941)

to invest belief in any particular form of explanation, including his own: he once wrote, "I believe nothing of my own that I have ever written. I cannot accept that the products of minds are subject-matter for beliefs" (Fort 1974, 555–56). In Fort's view the cosmos is organically interconnected, ever-shifting, and fundamentally indescribable: in the final analysis paranormal phenomena are perhaps no more and no less anomalous than any other types of phenomena.

Charles Hoy Fort was born on August 6, 1874, in Albany, New York. By his own account he had an unhappy childhood, suffering at the hands of his brutal father. At the age of 16 he started working as a reporter, but he gave up this profession to lead an itinerant life, traveling through the United States, Britain, and South Africa. By 1896 he was in New York City, where he married Anna Filing, who was to be his constant companion throughout his life. They lived in some poverty in New York, where Fort began to write short stories. In 1909 he published a novel called *The Outcast Manufacturers*. In or around 1912 he took to visiting the New York Public Library every day, where he gathered anomalous data of all kinds from newspapers and from scientific and technical journals, making notes on small scraps of paper. These were to form the raw materials for his major works.

His first attempt at writing up the data was completed in 1915, but it remained unpublished, and he later destroyed the manuscript. The work, called simply *X*, argued, according to Fort's latest biographer, that all world history is controlled by a mysterious evil force, apparently emanating from Mars.

In 1916 an inheritance gave Fort some measure of financial security, and in 1919 he published *The Book of the Damned*. The "damned" of the title refers to data excluded by established science from its picture of reality. In the book he writes, for example, of showers of objects from the heavens, such as stones, fish, lizards, snakes, blood, ice, and—most notoriously—frogs. He claims that these objects originate in what he calls the Super-Sargasso Sea in the skies. Among many other subjects Fort also looks at poltergeist phenomena, fairy lore, and what would now be referred to as UFOs. His declaration that the earth was visited and colonized by extraterrestrials in the distant past and that we remain their property inspired writers of speculative fiction such as H. P. Lovecraft and Arthur C. Clarke.

In 1920 he burned his entire collection of notes, which by then totaled some 40,000 references. In November of the same year he left New York for London. There he once more devoted himself to research, now collecting data in the round Reading Room of the British Museum. The result was his next book, *New Lands* (1923), published after he had returned to New York. In this work Fort describes strange things seen in the sky, but now he abandons his Super-Sargasso Sea idea as an explanation of their origin and posits instead the existence of lands in the skies up above us. In the first part of the book he ridicules the alleged errors of astronomy. The second part then presents things that have apparently actually been witnessed in the sky. The latter phenomena include such anomalies as angels and soldiers, artificial structures on the moon, lights on the surface of planets, and successive waves of mystery airships (Fort was perhaps the first person to collect the airship reports of 1896–1897 and to interpret the vehicles as extraterrestrial craft). He further maintains that beings from other planets have been misidentified as spiritual entities by theologians and psychic researchers.

Fort returned once more to London in 1923 and this time stayed until 1928. There he worked on what were to be his final two books. *Lo!* appeared in 1931 and is the book in which he coined the term "teleportation" to explain the appearance of unusual and out-of-place phenomena (including psychic phenomena). Fort conceives of teleportation as a kind of reordering force manifested throughout the cosmos and sometimes wielded by human beings.

The *Wild Talents* that form the title of his final work (published in 1932) are anomalous gifts or powers, which may be used to—among many other things— cause fires or photograph thoughts. Notably, Fort suspects that poltergeist phenomena are often unconsciously produced by the young: he was possibly one of the first to put forward this now widely recognized view. He uses the term "witchcraft" to describe all of these powers, arguing that the only drawback the concept has in relation to more modern scientific explanations is that it is unfashionable.

In his final years Fort suffered from considerable ill health. His failing eyesight meant that after 1929 he was unable to conduct research in libraries. He began to lose weight (he had always been a large man), was in constant pain, and appears to have been diagnosed with leukemia. He always refused medical attention, but on May 2, 1932, he was taken to the Royal Hospital in the Bronx. He died there the next day, aged 57. His work went on to exert a powerful influence over many other writers and theorizers about the paranormal.

Simon Wilson

See also: Fortean Phenomena; Paranormal; Poltergeist; Pseudoscience; Psi; Religion and the Paranormal; UFO

Further Reading
Fort, Charles. 1974. *The Complete Books of Charles Fort*. Mineola, NY: Dover Publications.
Steinmeyer, Jim. 2008. *Charles Fort: The Man Who Invented the Supernatural*. London: William Heinemann.

FORTEAN PHENOMENA

The term "Fortean phenomena" is usually taken to refer to any phenomena generally regarded as paranormal or somehow anomalous or out of place. It was coined in honor of Charles Fort, who wrote widely on such topics. Typical examples include UFOs, psi phenomena, and showers of strange objects from the sky. It would be wrong, however, to believe that "Fortean" is simply a synonym for "paranormal," since it denotes, at least in its purest form, a particular attitude or approach that rejects all systems of classification as arbitrary, including those of the present encyclopedia (or of any other sort of reference work). It is neither skeptical nor credulous but rather both at the same time and promotes a humorous tolerance of universal eccentricity.

The word "Fortean" was first used in 1920 by the prominent writer Ben Hecht in a review praising Fort's *The Book of the Damned*. When, however, a group calling itself The Fortean Society was founded in 1931, Fort refused to join: he did not want his name to become associated with any new form of dogma, least of all the dogma of the strange.

Fort himself did not regard the phenomena bearing his name as being in any way out of the ordinary: "All books written by me are of quite ordinary occurrences" (Fort 1974, 863). He was only interested, he wrote, in things that had appeared repeatedly over many years and were not therefore unusual. But neither did he believe that repetition could prove that what we call Fortean phenomena actually existed: "nothing ever has been proved" because "there is nothing to prove" (Fort 1974, 11). All things are continuous, merge into each other and everything else, and are in constant flux, meaning that no definition or classification describes any actual phenomenon but, on the contrary, is the product of the assumptions structuring the thought of the investigator (who themselves are the product of other assumptions, and so on). Science, for instance, can only define its objects of investigation by imposing demarcation lines that serve to arbitrarily exclude other data, which it then must "damn" by denying their existence. By this analysis, then, Fortean phenomena such as vampires, poltergeists, or fairies are no more or less anomalous than anything else in the world, but also no more (or less) real.

The Fortean approach, by definition, can never be a school, and people have interpreted it in various ways. Fort's view of science, for example, was quickly reinterpreted in terms of conspiracy. Tiffany Thayer often used his position as editor of *The Fortean Society Magazine* (renamed *Doubt* from its 11th issue onwards) from 1937 to 1959 to assert the existence of various conspiracies. He claimed the conventional views regarding World War II, the atom bomb, fluoride in the water, and vaccination were all somehow the work of powerful conspirators. UFOlogy, which from its very beginnings at the end of the 1940s often drew on Fort's research, has seemed especially prone to conspiracy theorizing: countless books argue that high-level politicians, scientists, and members of the armed forces know the truth about UFOs but keep it hidden (see, for example, the works of Donald E. Keyhoe or Timothy Good). Some alternative historians see in ancient monuments and archaeological finds evidence, otherwise covered up by scientists, for extraterrestrial intervention in human evolution. Erich von Däniken's books, especially *Chariots of the Gods?*, are probably the best known examples of such thinking.

Other Fort-influenced writers argue that Fortean phenomena are themselves the means by which a kind of paranormal conspiracy of cosmic proportions is perpetrated against human beings. Such authors seem to share Fort's view that reality is a construct, but they rarely apply that insight to their own theories. John Keel, for example, drew on Fort's assertion that humans are the property of superior beings to argue in books such as *The Mothman Prophecies* (1975) and *Disneyland of the Gods* (1988) that phenomena such as UFOs, sea serpents, poltergeists, and fairies are all generated by the ancient rulers of the Earth to manipulate our belief systems, with the ultimate aim of enslaving us. Keel frequently called himself a Fortean. The other leading representative of this branch of Fortean research is Jacques Vallée, who argues along lines similar to Keel's but in somewhat less specific terms. In books such as *The Invisible College* (1975) and *Messengers of Deception* (1979) he describes how UFOs and other phenomena such as fairies are manifestations of a nonhuman consciousness that has responded to and in turn shaped human beliefs and society throughout history. The exact aims and nature of this consciousness are left unclear, but Vallée believes that humans sometimes collaborate with it for their own purposes.

Perhaps the closest approach to Fort's in contemporary thinking on anomalous phenomena is that taken by George P. Hansen, who argues that the paranormal cannot be accommodated within the structures of modern science because it is inherently unstable, liminal, and ambiguous. Hansen, however, does not take the step of concluding that these are characteristics shared by all phenomena.

A contrasting approach to Fortean phenomena concentrates on amassing the anomalous data but does not place it within an explicitly philosophical framework. William Corliss epitomized this method. Partly inspired by Fort, he scoured scientific journals for references to anomalies, allowing them to speak for themselves in the multi-volume *Sourcebook Project*, which he published from 1974 onwards.

Today's Forteans tend to tread a middle ground between cataloguing phenomena and theorizing about them. They practice "a cool, wry, open-minded analysis of . . . mysteries" (Steinmeyer 2008, xiv). This certainly characterizes *Fortean Times*. Founded by Bob Rickard in 1973, it is probably the leading journal of Fortean phenomena.

Simon Wilson

See also: Animals and the Paranormal; Fort, Charles; Keel, John A.; Paranormal; UFO; Vallée, Jacques

Further Reading
Fort, Charles. 1974. *The Complete Books of Charles Fort*. Mineola, NY: Dover Publications.
Hansen, George P. 2001. *The Trickster and the Paranormal*. Bloomington, IN: Xlibris.
Rickard, Bob, and John Michell. 2007. *The Rough Guide to Unexplained Phenomena*. 2nd ed. London: Rough Guides.
Steinmeyer, Jim. 2008. *Charles Fort: The Man Who Invented the Supernatural*. London: William Heinemann.

FOX SISTERS, THE

Catherine (Kate) and Margaret (Margaretta or Maggie) Fox were two of the daughters of a farmer, John Fox, and his wife, who lived in Rochester, New York, having moved there in December 1847. In 1848, at ages 12 and 14, the two Fox sisters became renowned for various physical phenomena (primarily knocks and raps) that were claimed to occur in their presence, and that were interpreted as communications from a peddler who had been murdered in the house four or five years earlier. Word of these phenomena reached a number of religious reformers, whose involvement led to the Fox sisters' becoming public demonstrators of spirit communication, or mediumship. The public interest prompted by the activities of the Fox sisters and their supporters were central elements in the early development of the movement known as Spiritualism. Many Spiritualists date Spiritualism to 1848 because of the prominence of the Fox sisters within the movement.

At first it was thought that the phenomena were connected with the house, and Kate and Maggie Fox were sent to stay with their married older sister Leah Fox Fish, who had three children of her own; there was also a married brother, David, who lived nearby. Early attempts to deal with the phenomena included exorcisms conducted in the family home. Quaker friends of the family who had taken an interest found that the communications continued, initially keeping to the form of a number of knocks indicating "yes" or "no" in response to questions. It was found that the older sister Leah also had mediumistic abilities when entranced by Isaac Post, a family friend interested in magnetism, or mesmerism. The verbal mediumship enabled by Leah and Isaac's activities enabled a wider range of communications to be explored.

The traditional account is that, from 1849, the spirit communicators instructed the Fox sisters to give public demonstrations of mediumship, and by 1850 the first demonstrations were given in the Barnum Hotel in New York; invited and paying guests included a number of prominent figures from the publishing and newspaper industries, and the resulting publicity soon made the Fox family famous. Leah Fox Fish maintained a séance room in New York, while her two younger sisters travelled widely to major cities in the eastern United States.

1848	Kate and Maggie Fox, ages 12 and 14, become famous for the various knocks, raps, and other physical phenomena from a supposedly supernatural force that occurs in their presence.
1849	The spirit communicators purportedly begin telling the sisters to give public demonstrations of mediumship. They are joined by their older sister, Leah, who has also shown mediumistic abilities.
1850	The Fox sisters hold public séances in New York. These are attended by prominent figures from the publishing and newspaper industries.
1850–1860	Interest in the sisters declines.
1888	Kate and Maggie confess that the rappings they produced many years earlier were fraudulent. Kate later recants the confession.

During the 1850s, the activities of the Fox sisters, by demonstrating that there was sufficient interest in mediumship for a public and professional career to be possible, inspired and encouraged a number of other mediums to develop their own abilities. Many admirers began their own private groups, leading to the establishment of Spiritualist development or learning groups (known as circles) and subsequently churches. Many people were inspired to become Spiritualists by seeing the demonstrations given by the Fox sisters.

As the 1850s progressed and other mediums demonstrated more sophisticated forms of mediumship than simple rappings, interest in the two younger sisters waned. Leah's second marriage to Daniel Underhill, a wealthy insurance salesman and Spiritualist, meant that she no longer needed to use her mediumship to support herself, and she came to demonstrate less often. The explorer Elisha Kent Kane sponsored Maggie Fox, paying for her education; after his death in 1857, Maggie claimed that they had been married in secret, but she was unsuccessful in seeking support from his family, and she converted to Roman Catholicism. By the end of the decade, only the youngest sister, Kate, was still giving public demonstrations of mediumship, but her career was in decline. Both Kate and Maggie struggled with alcoholism, blaming the pressures of public mediumship; in Rochester in 1888, Kate was arrested for drunkenness, subsequently losing custody of her two sons. In the same year, both Kate and Maggie confessed that the rappings they had produced many years earlier were fraudulent, although Kate's confession was later recanted. Whatever the Fox sisters knew or thought privately, it is almost certainly the case that their lives were made much more difficult by their mediumistic careers than they might otherwise have been. Kate died on July 1, 1892, and was followed by Maggie on March 8, 1893, by which time neither had any public presence or involvement in the Spiritualist movement.

Although the Fox sisters are given a special place in the history of Spiritualism, their fame was initially based on a new example of the haunted house familiar from European tradition. The Fox sisters did not participate significantly in the establishment and development of Spiritualism as a new religious movement and cannot therefore be regarded as its founders: Spiritualism was founded by others who were impressed by, and who interpreted, their mediumship.

The Fox sisters have remained prominent because of the publicity (and later notoriety) surrounding them, but it had already been possible for mediums such as Andrew Jackson Davis to establish professional careers in the mid-1840s; indeed, Davis remains significant for Spiritualism as its first example of a medium who produced a large body of inspired spiritual and philosophical writings. The Spiritualist habit of dating the movement from 1848 is understandable and convenient but also somewhat arbitrary. Mediumship is an activity that was already familiar; the publicity prompted by the activities of the Fox sisters paved the way for a new religious tradition to be established around the practice of mediumship in the absence of any formal doctrine or single founder.

The careers of the Fox sisters are also relevant to understanding the long-standing Western characterization of mediumship as an archetypally female activity, despite the prominence of many male mediums. Many academics have identified Spiritualism as a tradition that is particularly revealing of gender issues in Anglo-American society. Public mediumship certainly offered women an escape route from traditional female roles but arguably did so in ways that indirectly reinforced existing stereotypes. In Spiritualism, the authority of a medium remains attributable to spirit rather than to the medium personally, offering women a liminal status that remains highly vulnerable. The careers of the Fox sisters also demonstrate that communal recognition as a proficient medium can never be assumed and must be maintained on an ongoing basis.

David Gordon Wilson

See also: Haunting; Mediumship; Mesmerism; Séance; Spiritualism

Further Reading

Braude, Ann. (1989) 2001. *Radical Spirits: Spiritualism and Women's Rights in Nineteenth-Century America.* 2nd ed. Bloomington & Indianapolis: Indiana University Press.
Nelson, Geoffrey K. 1969. *Spiritualism and Society.* London: Routledge & Kegan Paul.
Weisberg, Barbara. 2004. *Talking to the Dead: Kate and Maggie Fox and the Rise of Spiritualism.* New York: HarperCollins.

G

GANZFELD TECHNIQUE, THE

The ganzfeld technique, German for "whole field," is an experimental technique used within psychology, introduced by the German psychologist Wolfgang Metzger during the 1930s. While investigating human perception Metzger discovered that an individual provided with repetitive and unpatterned sensory stimulation experienced an effect similar to sensory deprivation, in which people reported various kinds of spontaneous imagery (mild hallucinations and dreamlike experiences) that were internally generated rather than derived from sensory input. In Metzger's original approach participants would sit in front of a blank, uniformly lit wall in silence and describe the inwardly generated images they began to see. This early technique was subsequently adapted by parapsychologists in order to test for the existence of psi processes such as telepathy and other forms of extrasensory perception (ESP).

Two key developments within parapsychology led to the adoption of the ganzfeld technique. First, in a review of spontaneous accounts of ESP, Louisa Rhine found that over half of her large case collection happened when respondents were relaxing, dreaming, or engaged in simple tasks that required little conscious attention. Accounts of ESP experiences while actively awake in a task were fewer and, by comparison, less detailed—findings that were consistently replicated across other studies with a range of nationalities. Charles Honorton theorized that this evidence may indicate that ESP is not something we need to make happen but something that is occurring all the time, functioning much in the same way that other human senses do. Ordinarily ESP may be outcompeted by these other modalities or filtered out unconsciously; as the information provided is not relevant to our current concerns at the time, it does not reach consciousness. In this way ESP would be encoded, processed, and consciously experienced in ways that reflect information gained by our other senses and would be subject to the same processing limitations and biases as any other sensory stimulus. However, while dreaming or in a relaxed and unengaged state, there is less competing background "noise" as information incoming from other senses is reduced, and this may lead to the ESP "signal" coming through more clearly into awareness. This hypothesis would explain the high proportion of ESP experiences occurring during dreams and the comparative clarity of those experiences when compared to wide-awake ESP reports.

Second, as dreams were considered the most psi-receptive state, the only way to perform controlled research on dreamers was with a sleep laboratory, which required state-of-the-art physiological monitoring equipment, an overnight staff, and a requirement that participants spend either a sleepless or a frequently disturbed night at the lab during trials. The research responsible for this method was conducted at the Maimonides Medical Center in Brooklyn, New York. Although the findings were very impressive, true replications proved difficult due to the fact that few researchers had access to the necessary facilities.

A method was required that allowed for easy replication, while also providing a valid simulation of the subjective experience of drifting off to sleep without the necessity for expensive, time-consuming overnight research. This ultimately led to parapsychology's adoption and adaptation of the ganzfeld procedure by three groups of researchers in 1974 and 1975.

The ganzfeld procedure generally uses pairs of participants, one taking the role of sender, the other of receiver. In order to drown out as much sensory noise as possible and give the weak psi signal its boost, receivers in the ganzfeld procedure lie back in a reclined chair, located within a soundproofed room. In order to present a homogenous visual field, ping-pong ball halves are laid over the receiver's eyes and taped in place, and a red light is shone on the face. With the participant's eyes open, this gives the experience of an unchanging, unpatterned red glow to which one habituates. A similar auditory effect is achieved by placing headphones over the ears and playing white noise (an electronically produced drone of varying frequencies). Due to the nature of the procedure, it is not uncommon for receivers to feel a degree of nervousness when being readied for their initial trial. This could result in internal somatic noise affecting the psi signal, and therefore receivers are led through a series of relaxation techniques at the beginning of a trial. Once the receiver has had time to habituate, the sender, seated in another room, concentrates on a randomly selected target to send telepathically to the receiver, who is asked to describe everything that appears in their mind's eye. This is recorded and transcribed. After the trial, transcripts are sent to blinded independent judges, who match up the content of the transcript to a series of possible targets. If the correct target is chosen, this is considered a hit. Alternatively, a quicker method involves the receiver's being presented with the target image alongside three alternate images. The identity of the true target is blind to both researcher and receiver. The received is asked to rate which image most reflects his or her thoughts. Using this method, it would be expected for receivers to be correct 25 percent of the time by guesswork alone.

Early ganzfeld research (independently conducted by three separate labs) was exceptionally successful and led to a large number of replications throughout the 1970s and 1980s. The results were summarized in a mathematical review in 1985 by Honorton, who concluded that the number of significant ganzfeld experiments ranged between 50 and 58 percent, whereas only 5 percent would be expected by chance if there was no evidence demonstrated for ESP. In response to this, Ray Hyman, a psychologist and critic of parapsychology, conducted his own meta-analysis of 42 ganzfeld studies and concluded that the evidence was insufficient to support the existence of ESP due to research flaws. The three areas Hyman suggested for

The ganzfeld technique uses sensory deprivation to produce an altered state of consciousness that is, according to some, especially receptive to extrasensory perception such as telepathy. It rose to prominence in the parapsychology community in the 1970s and 1980s when a large number of experiments appeared to replicate the initially positive results. These were later challenged on various grounds.

flaws were methodological procedure, statistical analysis, and security. In the same year Charles Honorton published his own meta-analysis of a range of the studies included in Hyman's paper and demonstrated that, when accounting for the issues highlighted by Hyman, evidence of psi was still found. This led to a lengthy discourse between both authors with several other contributors, famously known as the Honorton-Hyman debate, culminating in the publication of a joint communiqué from both authors in 1986 in which they concluded, "There is an overall significant effect in this database that cannot reasonably be explained by selective reporting or multiple analysis. We continue to differ over the degree to which the effect constitutes evidence for psi, but we agree that the final verdict awaits the outcome of future experiments conducted by a broader range of investigators and according to more stringent standards."

Honorton and his team took up the challenge and developed a new ganzfeld procedure meeting the criteria specified within the communiqué. This method became known as the "autoganzfeld method," as much of the procedure, such as random selection of the target, is under automated computer control in order to avoid potential human error. In 1990 Honorton and colleagues published a review of 11 autoganzfeld studies including 355 sessions. The results demonstrated an overall hit rate of 34.4 percent, with 25 percent expected by chance. Although this may not seem a large difference, due to the number of trials, this is statistically highly significant. With associated odds of one in a million billion of the effect occurring by chance alone, this is strongly indicative of the existence of psi.

These findings were criticized again by Hyman. Although these later studies addressed his initial critiques, he argued that the data were made up predominantly of Honorton's research. Hyman stressed what was needed were truly independent replications in order to support the findings presented. In the years that followed a range of independent replications were conducted. Two separate reviews of these studies were published several years apart and came to differing conclusions, fuelling the discussion around the relevance of the ganzfeld findings as evidence for the existence of ESP and the selective reporting of skeptics. A review conducted in 2010 compared ganzfeld ESP studies against other forms of free-response methodology such as dream and meditation ESP studies. It found that the ganzfeld was the most effective method for eliciting performance above chance level in ESP trials, but so far an effect as large as that demonstrated in Honorton's 1990 review has not been replicated. Recent research has questioned the effectiveness of the ganzfeld method in inducing an experience reflective of an altered state of consciousness, demonstrating that brain scans of participants during the ganzfeld show neural activity closer to a waking state than a dreamlike one. In answer to this criticism, Professor Chris Roe has argued that the ganzfeld cannot be expected to create the same subjective experience in all participants, since certain characteristics such as low hypnotic suggestibility may make individuals more resistant to an induced altered state of consciousness.

Presently, more research is needed to refute the ganzfeld technique's effectiveness at inducing an altered state that is psi-receptive, and debate continues regarding the strength of evidence for ESP demonstrated via this technique. The ganzfeld technique has also inspired popular culture, as seen in the release of a horror movie in 2014 titled *The Ganzfeld Haunting*.

David Saunders

See also: Art, Creativity, and the Paranormal; Extrasensory Perception (ESP); Hallucinations; Hypnagogic State; Krippner, Stanley; Parapsychology; Psychical Research; Telepathy

Further Reading

Irwin, Harvey, and Caroline Watt. 2007. *An Introduction to Parapsychology*. 5th ed. Jefferson, NC: McFarland & Co.
Ramakrishna, Rao. 2001. *Basic Research in Parapsychology*. 2nd ed. Jefferson, NC: McFarland & Co.

GELLER, URI

Uri Geller is world famous as a psychic, an entertainer, and a celebrity whom many believe to possess remarkable telepathic and psychokinetic abilities. Great controversy has surrounded his performances, with a large number of "believers" standing ready and even eager to accept almost everything and defending him as a genuine source of paranormal phenomena, backed by positive results, particularly obtained during extensive testing by parapsychologists in Europe and North America during the 1970s. Equally, there are many who dispute these findings and dismiss his performances as attributable to the work of a skilled illusionist adept at deception. A huge body of literature exists concerning his abilities, his imitators, and the many controversies surrounding them, with scientists and magicians ranged on both sides. Ultimately these arguments have become a sociological topic in their own right.

Uri Geller was born on December 20, 1946 in Tel Aviv, Israel. His family moved to Cyprus when he was 11, and he attended high school there. After graduating from school he served as a paratrooper in the Israeli army and fought in the Six-Day

War. In his twenties he began performing in nightclubs in Israel, and by the 1970s he had become famous in both Europe and America, where he appeared on numerous television shows (giving many spectacular demonstrations of apparently paranormal powers) and was the subject of a slew of journalism, much of it scathingly skeptical even as he attracted many prominent supporters and endorsers.

Among the most impressive evidence for telepathy that Geller has produced are the results obtained from experiments in the remote sensing of drawings conducted at Stanford Research Institute, California, in the course of a five-week investigation. The results were subsequently published in 1974 by Drs. Russell Targ and Harold Puthoff in a paper in the scientific journal *Nature*. It was accompanied by an editorial stating that the purpose of publishing the paper was to stimulate and advance the controversy over Geller's alleged abilities. However, a critical comment on the SRI tests was published simultaneously by *New Scientist* following investigation by Dr. Joseph Hanlon.

Of particular note are Geller's apparent metal-bending powers, typically demonstrated with cutlery. Stories of Geller's ability to distort spoons and forks without touch are legion, and to some extent his powers have been endorsed under experimental conditions by a number of scientists such as the late Professor John Hasted, a renowned physicist. At the same time, other scientists have moved from acceptance of his abilities to positions of skepticism. For example, Professor John Taylor of King's College London initially endorsed Geller's powers in his book *Superminds* (1976) but later changed his mind after deciding that the effects were nonexistent since no force in nature could realistically explain the claimed effects (see *Science and the Supernatural*, 1980). A difficulty in gaining scientific acceptance was the fact that in the experimental situation, Geller needed to have physical contact with the spoon or any other object that he was asked to bend. It was not clear whether the spoon was being bent because he had extraordinarily strong fingers and good control of micro-manipulatory movements, or whether the spoon in fact "turns to plastic"—as he claimed—as a result of psychokinesis.

His demonstrations of PK abilities on television in the 1970s triggered a spate of claims of psychokinetic events occurring simultaneously in the homes of viewers. Consequently, Geller was able to convince many people that his PK was genuine and that he could demonstrate effects in their own homes through what he called "mass experiments." Thousands of people in Europe spontaneously communicated with newspapers and television stations to claim that similar PK phenomena occurred in their homes when Geller was active. Geller's public reputation even inspired the appearance of a considerable number of teenager imitators (dubbed "mini-Gellers") who claimed to have similar powers. It also drew many ongoing skeptical attacks and debunking attempts, most notably by James "The Amazing" Randi.

In recent years Geller has adorned a 1976 Cadillac with examples of bent and distorted cutlery, which he uses in charitable and campaigning activities. He has also been employed by mineral prospecting companies to discover deposits of oil and metals and has become very wealthy as a result, one feat his critics have not been able to emulate. In the second decade of the 21st century he continues to lead a prominent life in the media—for example, by hosting and being featured on many recent television programs in Europe. In 2013 the British documentary film *The Secret Life of Uri Geller—Psychic Spy?* publicized Geller's claim to have worked with U.S. intelligence agencies during the Cold War as part of a "psychic arms race." In 2014 he returned to Israel and became the official face of the country's disaster-readiness campaign, appearing in television and Internet advertisements sponsored by the Israeli army and showing viewers how to take shelter from earthquakes and missile attacks.

Ultimately, if viewed in isolation, Geller is likely to remain an enigma like the 19th-century physical medium Daniel Dunglas Home, who was never detected in trickery but remains controversial simply on account of the extraordinary phenomena that he apparently produced with such regularity, and that strained the credulity of many.

Alan Murdie

See also: Psychokinesis (PK); Randi, James; Stanford Research Institute; Telepathy

Further Reading

Collins, H. M., and T. J. Pinch. 1982. *Frames of Meaning: The Social Construction of Extraordinary Science*. London and New York: Routledge, 2009.

Geller, Uri. 1975. *My Story*. New York: Praeger. http://www.uri-geller.com/books/my-story/ms.htm.

Hasted, John. 1981. *The Metal Benders*. London: Routledge. http://www.uri-geller.com/books/metal-benders/h.htm.

The Secret Life of Uri Geller—Psychic Spy? 2013. Directed by Vikram Jayanti. http://vimeo.com/98253565.

GHost

GHost is a visual arts and creative research project that explores the phenomena of ghosts and their various manifestations within society. The *GHost* project is comprised of two central research strands. First, *GHost* organizes a program of interdisciplinary seminars that consider the significance of ghosts across different cultures and branches of knowledge. Second, the project curates a program of contemporary art exhibitions, film screenings, and performances designed to examine the aesthetics of ghosts and haunted spaces. The curation of *GHost's* visual arts program is largely informed by the findings from the research seminars.

The project was initiated in London, United Kingdom, in 2008 by artist, curator, and lecturer Sarah Sparkes (University of the Arts London) and curator and lecturer in Visual Cultures Dr. Ricarda Vidal (Kings College London). From October 2008 to September 2011, Sparkes and Vidal ran the project together; since October 2011 Sarah Sparkes has been *GHost's* sole director. The project's name is, in part, a homage to the title of an art work by influential French artist Marcel Duchamp, "A GUEST + A HOST = A GHOST" (1953). *GHost* has adopted Duchamp's ghost formula insomuch as the project acts as a host for guest researchers to manifest and interrogate the idea of the ghost. In addition, the capital H in *GHost* visually makes "host" a guest inside "ghost."

To date, *GHost* has organized 14 interdisciplinary research seminars known as the *Hostings*—an allusion to a medium hosting spirits. From 2009 to 2012 the *Hostings* were based at Senate House, University of London, where they were awarded research funding as part of the School of Advanced Study's knowledge transfer program. The *Hostings* have covered wide-ranging ghost topics that have been grouped under the following subject areas: *Haunted Houses, Ghost Voices, Ghost-hunters, Haunted Landscapes, Manifesting Ghosts* and *Ghosts as a Force for Cultural and Political Movement.* Since 2013, and to date, the *Hostings* have been held at Central Saint Martins College of Arts and Design, where they are supported by the Drama and Performance Programme. Speakers from wide-ranging research fields and from around the world have presented at the *Hostings*, which have been referenced in both academic and nonacademic publications.

GHost's visual arts exhibitions feature the work of established and emerging UK and international artists and demonstrate the ways in which ghosts can be created sensorially. *GHost I* (2008), *GHost II* (2009), *GHost III* (2010), and *GHost IV* (2012) were large-scale exhibitions of moving images, audio installations, performances, and film screenings at the historic church of St. John Bethnal Green in London, UK. In 2011 *GHost* was awarded a three-month curatorial residency at *Folkestone Triennial*, an international art festival in the UK. Other curatorial projects include a show reel of artists' films for the London Art Fair, 2011 and two film nights and exhibitions for the *London Free Film Festivals* in 2014.

The *GHost* project's seminars and exhibitions continue to develop in parallel, and further publications discussing the project are due to be released in 2016.

Sarah Sparkes

See also: Art, Creativity, and the Paranormal; Ghosts; Haunting; Mediumship; Séance

Further Reading

GHost (official website). http://www.ghosthostings.co.uk.

GHost (official blog). http://www.host-a-ghost.blogspot.co.uk.

Sconce, Jeffery. 2000. *Haunted Media: Electronic Presence from Telegraphy to Television.* London: Duke University Press.

Sparkes, Sarah. 2013. "The *GHost* Project: Manifesting Ghosts through Visual Art and Creative Research." In *The Ashgate Research Companion to Paranormal Cultures*, edited by Olu Jenzen and Sally R. Munt. Surrey: Ashgate Publishing Limited.

Warner, Marina. 2006. *Phantasmagoria: Spirit Visions, Metaphors, and Media into the Twenty-first Century.* Oxford: Oxford University Press.

GHOSTS

A ghost is the incorporeal part of a human being (or sometimes an animal or, more rarely, an object) manifesting after death to the living. This concept of the ghost as an immaterial presence of the deceased haunting the living exists around the world and throughout recorded history.

A number of characteristics have been assigned to ghosts. They have been described as intangible, translucent, shadowy, cloudy, or misty forms that are able to pass through solid matter. In other reports they appear as a substantial presence physically interacting with the living and with material objects. Generally ghosts are clothed, sometimes in the shrouds or garments in which they were buried. They may look just as in life, or they may appear in a state of decomposition, sometimes appearing fair and other times appearing frightful. They can be invisible and can be perceived through unexplained noises, moving objects, smells, changes in temperature, and breezes. They may have no obvious sensorial presence but rather manifest as a perception that "something" is there. Ghosts range from benevolent to malevolent in intention. Some ghosts have such distinctive characteristics that they have been recognized with their own names, such as the poltergeist, a malevolent ghost well documented throughout history. Generally, ghosts are described as solitary and human in appearance, although there have been legends and accounts of ghost armies and ghost animals. Ghost objects have also been reported, and in particular ghost vehicles such as carriages, ships, trains, and, more recently, cars.

The locations that ghosts frequent are referred to as haunted. Ghosts' haunts may be restricted to a specific dwelling or a landscape; often this is a place they were associated with in life or their final resting place. However, they may also haunt a particular person. Ghosts may haunt an object that they were emotionally attached to in life; examples include dolls and mirrors. In the past two centuries they have been reported to haunt technological apparatuses, particularly those used to communicate or transmit information such as the television and telephone.

The word "ghost" originates from the old English word *gast*, meaning spirit, soul, breath, or life, with the latter two here having connotations of something immaterial. Specter, phantom, apparition, and spirit, all from French and Latin etymological roots, are some of the other words used to refer to a ghost in English-speaking countries. Each word has a different nuance deriving from its original meaning and the evolution of this over time. "Specter" suggests a visual manifestation of a menacing ghost; both "phantom" and "apparition" give the impression of something immaterial or illusory in appearance. "Spirit" has religious connotations; the word has been translated as "holy ghost" in English versions of the Bible. Languages around the world contain words to describe the spirit or immaterial part of a deceased person. Often these words, like the type of ghost they describe, have traversed national borders and been assimilated across cultures.

For the greater part of their history, ghosts have been associated with religious belief and practice; it is only in more recent times that the ghost has evolved into a secular phenomenon. Ghosts are said to have originated from animism, the belief

The word "ghost" originates from the old English word *gast*, meaning spirit, soul, breath, or life. Various English words have been used to refer to ghosts, each with its own particular shade of meaning:

Specter suggests a visual manifestation of a threatening ghost.

Phantom and **apparition** both imply something immaterial or illusory.

Spirit suggests something with a religious significance.

that everything in the material world contains an immaterial spirit. The earliest ghosts were closely linked to ancestor worship, with its belief that spirits of the dead must be appeased with ritual or offerings to prevent them from haunting the living. To date, the earliest written records of ghosts are from ancient Sumer, from around 3000 to 2000 BCE, where *gidim*, a spirit double of the deceased, could inflict illness and misfortune on the living. The ancient Egyptians believed more than one immaterial aspect was released from the material body at death. One of these was a ghost-double, the *ka*, which haunted the tomb of the deceased. Inscriptions on papyrus and tomb paintings are evidence of the elaborate rituals performed to ensure spirits of the dead had comfortable afterlives and so did not trouble the living. Chinese philosopher and writer Confucius (551–479 BCE) warned people to respect and stay away from ghosts. Mo Tzu (470–391 BCE), another Chinese philosopher, observed that hauntings have been reported since the dawn of time.

In classical Greek narratives ghosts give advice and deliver prophecy. In Virgil's epic poem *Aeneid*, generally dated to between 70 and 19 BCE, as well as in the *Iliad* and *Odyssey*, both of which are attributed to Greek poet Homer in the eighth century BCE, there are several references to portentous ghosts. Accounts of how ghosts look and sound also exist from classical antiquity. Homer's ghosts are vapor-like in appearance and emit a wailing sound. The Romans referred to ghosts as "shades" and described them as shadowy presences. The now-stereotyped image of a ghost rattling chains is first found in the writing of Roman lawyer Pliny the Younger in 2 BCE.

Throughout history types of ghost characteristics have traveled from country to country. The "hungry ghost" is one such example. Originating in the Indian subcontinent, hungry ghosts or *preta* are found in the Hindu religious texts. The *preta* were assimilated into the Buddhist faith in approximately 6–4 BCE. Via Buddhism they made their way to China as *egui* around the first century CE, and from there to Japan around 250–500 CE, where they are called *gaki*.

From the medieval Christian phase of Europe, and up to the present day, the subject of ghosts, including what they may do and whether they exist, has been much debated. By the later Middle Ages the Roman Catholic doctrine of purgatory was widely established; ghosts were seen as a warning that one should observe the teaching of the Church to avoid punishment after death. A 15th century Cistercian monk at Byland Abbey, Yorkshire, reported numerous penitent ghost stories. The European Reformation of the 1500s saw Protestant reformers reject the idea of ghosts as souls of the dead. Successful reformist publications of the period, such as Lewes Lavatar's *Of Ghosts and Spirits Walking by Night* (1570), categorizes ghosts as hallucinations of the insane, superstitions of the ignorant, or corpses under demonic or angelic possession.

During the European and American Enlightenment of the late 17th and 18th centuries, leading intellectuals questioned traditional faith-based interpretations of the world as they sought to reform and advance society through scientific methods. Enlightenment philosophies and theological movements added to the debate on ghost belief, and the existence of ghosts was disputed in texts and public debates. English physician and chemist Peter Shaw, writing in 1750, noted that, in a time of increased rationality, ghosts were becoming scarce. Still, it was only 12 years later, in 1762, that the story of "Scratching Fanny," the so-called Cock Lane ghost in London, attracted enormous attention and became a media sensation.

Although ghosts are often considered to be best avoided, throughout recorded history there have been those who have sought to raise and communicate with spirits of the dead. The practice of necromancy (summoning the dead, generally for divination) was prevalent in Western antiquity, with records of its practice existing in Egypt, Babylon, Greece, and Rome. The ancient Babylonian *Epic of Gilgamesh* depicts a holy woman raising a ghost through necromancy. In ancient Greece, *nekyia* was a rite by which ghosts were called up and questioned. There are also references to necromancy in the Hebrew Old Testament and in Europe's Norse mythology. With the spread of Christianity, necromancy was condemned as a demonic practice. In Islam also, the practice of consulting spirits was prohibited. During the Enlightenment era many scientists experimented with the technique of mesmerism, some claiming to have used it to contact spirits. However, it was one 19th-century movement, Spiritualism, that was to turn the practice of communicating with ghosts into a popular activity in the Western world. Offering the potential for anyone to make contact with ghosts of loved ones or strangers, Spiritualism promoted equality in the spirit world; one might speak with the ghost of a relative or a president at the same sitting. The latter part of the 19th century also saw the rise of psychical research, with the establishment of professional organizations intending to investigate ghosts and other phenomena by scientific means. Early psychical investigators tried to avoid the term ghost, preferring phantasms or apparitions instead because "ghost" carried too much historical baggage. Pioneering psychologists of the late 19th and early 20th centuries, such as Freud, emphasized the role of the unconscious mind on human perception. For some, the power of the unconscious mind strengthened the argument that a ghost is no more than a projection of a disturbed imagination, an example of this being hallucinations of a dead loved one, which is a recognized experience of the recently bereaved. For others, it supported the idea that ghosts represent human mental energy projected beyond the material body.

Ghosts continue to play an important role in the cultural life of the living. Throughout history there is evidence of ghost festivals being an important part of the cultural calendar. Both the ancient Greeks and Romans had ghost festivals, and hungry ghost festivals are an important part of the cultural calendar in many Asian countries to this day. The Mexican Day of the Dead (*Dia de los Muertos*) is famous throughout the world and attracts huge crowds of tourists every year. This festival combines pre-Columbian beliefs with the Christian festival of All Souls Day, from which the popular Western festival of Halloween evolved. Ghosts have also had a great impact on literature through the genre of the ghost story, which made the successful transition to ghost films and ghost television shows during the last century. Ghost faking has also been a popular form of cultural entertainment over the past centuries. From the days of the phantasmagoria or ghost shows of the 18th century, to the haunted house ride at the funfair, paying to be frightened by fake ghosts has been considered a great thrill by many.

In an increasingly secular era when masses of people are freed from religious doctrines, ghosts are often vague in their intentions, with many ghosts having no message to impart and no recognizable identity. Their manifestations often mimic anomalies occurring in the technologies we use in our everyday lives, such as the orb anomaly found in digital photography and the "noise" that interrupts recorded or transmitted sound. Today the debate on the existence of ghosts continues among academics, independent researchers, and others. Ghost belief is on the increase in the West, with a 2013 Harris poll finding that 42 percent of Americans said that they believe in ghosts. In the UK, opinion polls have shown a consistent rise in ghost belief since the 1950s. The ghost narrative is still a popular genre in film, television, and literature. The rise of computer (or video) gaming means that dynamic interactions with ghosts can be played out in a virtual world. Through the media of television and the Internet, the ghost hunter has also become an international phenomenon in the world of popular culture. Ghost hunting today has become both a popular hobby and a lucrative moneymaking enterprise. The increasing availability of the Internet enables an international community to share its ghost experiences, opinions, and documentation.

Around the world, the ghost still has many cultural functions. It may be a signifier of respect for ancestors. It may serve as a warning, moral, religious, or otherwise. It may represent a level of existence beyond material life. In an age of scientific explanation, the ghost is a testament to the endurance of the unexplained.

Sarah Sparkes

See also: Apparitions; Automatic Writing; Channeling; Ectoplasm; Electronic Voice Phenomenon (EVP); Enfield Poltergeist; Fox Sisters, The; *GHost*; Haunting; Mediumship; Mesmerism; Myers, Frederic W. H.; Ouija Board; Poltergeist; Séance; Society for Psychical Research; Spiritualism; Spirit Photography

Further Reading

Finucane, R. C. 1996. *Ghosts: Appearances of the Dead and Cultural Transformation*. Amherst, NY: Prometheus Press.

Warner, Marina. 2006. *Phantasmagoria: Spirit Visions, Metaphors, and Media into the Twenty-first Century*. Oxford: Oxford University Press, 2006.

GOOCH, STAN

The English psychologist Stan Gooch (1932–2010) was the author of several books about the paranormal, consciousness, and human evolution, specifically focused on the biological, psychological, and cultural legacy that, he argued, modern man has inherited from his Neanderthal ancestors. Although receiving high acclaim from readers such as Colin Wilson and Stanley Krippner, Gooch spent his last years in isolation, living in poverty in a run-down trailer camp in Swansea, Wales, embittered by the lack of recognition his work received. His early championing of a "hybrid-theory" of human evolution, arguing for cross-breeding between Neanderthal and Cro-Magnon man, was ridiculed in the 1970s and 1980s, yet recent research has vindicated much of Gooch's thinking. In 2011 *Nature* published research findings establishing that up to four percent of modern human DNA comes from Neanderthal. This development came too late for Gooch to appreciate, and he would no doubt have been unsurprised that his name is not mentioned in relation to these and other recent discoveries about Neanderthal that Gooch advanced decades earlier.

Stanley Albert Gooch was born in Lewisham, south London, to a working class family. After earning a scholarship to Colfe's Grammar School, he later took a degree in Modern Languages at King's College, London. Following a year spent in the scrap metal business, Gooch earned a degree in psychology from Birbeck College, London University. He then joined the National Children's Bureau, where he became a senior research fellow; at this time he also underwent Jungian analysis. During this period Gooch published several papers on child psychology and co-authored important studies, most notably *Four Years On* (1970), with M. L. Kellmer-Pringle. Gooch was offered the directorship of the National Children's Bureau and a professorship in psychology at Brunel University, but he turned both positions down in order to focus exclusively on his independent research and writing.

An experience Gooch had in 1958 at the age of 26 influenced this decision. While working as a school teacher, Gooch attended a séance, invited by a friend. Gooch admits that he accepted the invitation because he had nothing else to do. Soon into it, however, he felt light-headed and then heard a roaring wind and the sound of rushing water before losing consciousness. Gooch then "woke up" to learn that he had been "speaking in voices," one of which was that of a cousin who had been killed in World War II. That evening Gooch discovered that he was psychic. Gooch continued to attend séances and other spiritualist meetings, and his experience with the paranormal informed his life's work. During one séance he believed he saw a figure of a "cave man" crouching in a corner—a sign, he later believed, of developments to come.

Gooch's first book, *Total Man: Notes Toward an Evolutionary Theory of Personality* (1972), argued that human psychology is dual, consisting of a "light," logical, masculine Ego and a "dark," intuitive, feminine Self. This dark Self is the seat of dreams, intuitions, and the imagination and is the root of myths of vampires, troglodytes, and other strange creatures. It is also responsible for paranormal faculties. Gooch's division of the human psyche into two systems—logical and magical—informed his later work, *The Paranormal* (1978), in which he writes about his own psychic experiences, yet is also sharply critical of much paranormal and "occult" literature. In *Personality and Evolution* (1973) and *The Neanderthal Question* (1977) Gooch developed his theme that modern humans are the result of cross-breeding between the logical, sun-worshipping Cro-Magnons and the magical, moon-worshipping Neanderthals and that our paranormal faculties—Gooch's "System B"—are part of our Neanderthal legacy. Gooch rooted paranormal faculties in the cerebellum, an older part of the brain that preceded the development of the more modern cerebrum, and which was more pronounced in Neanderthals. In *The Double Helix of the Mind* (1980) Gooch took issue with the split-brain theory of consciousness, developed by Roger Sperry and others, and which anchored paranormal faculties in the right cerebral hemisphere, in favor of his cerebrum/cerebellum divide.

In other books, such as *Guardians of the Ancient Wisdom* (1979) and *Cities of Dreams: When Women Ruled the Earth* (1989), Gooch argued that, unlike the clichéd image of an unintelligent "cave man," Neanderthals instead possessed a highly developed culture that included religion and a belief in an afterlife. Neanderthals, he said, indeed had a civilization of their own, and the remnants of this can be found today in our myths, fairy tales, and the esoteric philosophies—Kabbalah, Rosicrucianism, Freemasonry—that make up much of contemporary occultism.

Gary Lachman

See also: Mediumship; Séance; Unconscious Mind

Further Reading

Callaway, Ewen. 2011. "Ancient DNA Reveals Secrets of Human History." *Nature* 476: 136–137. http://www.nature.com/news/2011/110809/full/476136a.html.

Gooch, Stan. (1989) 1995. *Cities of Dreams: When Women Ruled the Earth*. London: Aulis Books.

Gooch, Stan. 1980. *The Double Helix of the Mind*. London: Wildwood House.

Gooch, Stan. 1978. *The Paranormal*. London: Fontana.

Gooch, Stan. 1972. *Total Man: Notes Toward an Evolutionary Theory of Personality*. London: Allen Lane.

H

HALLUCINATIONS

Hallucinations are vivid and autonomous perceptual experiences that occur without an appropriate external stimulus, such as hearing a voice when nobody in the environment has spoken. Hallucinations differ from illusions, in which real perceptual cues are distorted, and from delusions, where beliefs about reality are erroneous. The study of them has been significant in the history of the paranormal. For instance, they were among the subjects studied in depth by the psychologists Frederic Myers and Edmund Gurney, both early and significant members of the Society for Psychical Research, and parallels have been drawn between hallucinations and paranormal experiences; the parapsychologist Louisa Rhine, for instance, classified some reports of extrasensory perception as being experienced as a waking hallucination.

Hallucinations may take place in one or more of the sensory modalities (visual, auditory, olfactory, gustatory, tactile, proprioceptive), although the most common forms are auditory (and then visual). These can range from simple experiences, such as whistles or flashes, to more complex, organized, and meaningful experiences, such as voices talking, music, or lifelike scenes. Hallucinations have a number of triggers, including sensory and sleep deprivation, the inducement of altered states of consciousness (e.g., through psychotropic drugs), expectation effects, stress, dramatic life events, and the onset of mental illness. For example, hallucinations of deceased partners are commonly reported by the recently bereaved and are referred to as "grief hallucinations."

Hallucinations have mostly been studied in the context of schizophrenia, for which they are one of Kurt Schneider's first rank symptoms. These typically take the form of auditory hallucinations consisting of a voice, or voices, commenting on one's behavior or making persecutory statements (although, positive, encouraging voices have also been reported). However, in surveys of the nonclinical general population, approximately 10 percent report having had at least one, non-drug-induced hallucinatory experience. This incidence is higher than those who receive diagnoses of schizophrenia or psychosis (0.5–3 percent), suggesting that hallucinations occur outside of mental illness. One of the first investigations of the occurrence of hallucinations in non-psychiatric patients (7,717 men and 7,599 women) was conducted in the UK in 1894 by Henry Sidgwick, of the Society for Psychical Research. Excluding individuals with clear symptoms of mental or physical illness, the experience of at least one vivid hallucinatory experience was reported by 7.8 percent of the men and 12 percent of the women. Indeed, given the right expectations, hallucinations can be induced in members of the general population. For example, in their classic *White Christmas* study, conducted in 1964, Theodore Barber and David Calverey found that when listening to white noise, more than half of a sample of healthy participants reported that they clearly heard this Bing Crosby song when in fact it was never played. Participants were asked to imagine hearing the song beforehand, illustrating the role of suggestion in hallucinations.

Most theorizing on hallucinations comes from researchers in clinical psychology and medical researchers seeking to understand hearing voices in the context of schizophrenia and related disorders. Explanatory models typically involve perception and attribution. For example, inner speech might be perceived and mistakenly attributed to an external source. Neuroscientific research suggests that hallucinations involve the same mechanisms as ordinary perceptions; for example, the same cerebral structures are involved in both the perception of speech and hearing voices. This supports the perceptual part of these models. Further research on source monitoring supports the role of attribution. Voice hearers tend to perform less well on tasks that involve correctly identifying material that was self- versus other-generated, such as responses to a previous word task, being more likely to misattribute the source of self-generated words as being generated by others. The implication is that such individuals are less able to monitor the source of mental content, being more likely to confuse imagination and reality.

More broadly conceived, hallucinations vary in intensity and may be placed on a continuum with other, more common, perceptual experiences, such as hypnagogia and vivid daydreams, for which the psychologist Anthony Morrison suggests a common inhibitory mechanism, perhaps related to rapid eye movement sleep, that enables "dreaming awake." Indeed, it has been proposed that individuals vary along a continuum that reflects a predisposition towards having such experiences, variously termed transliminality, positive schizotypy, or hallucination proneness. Other anomalous experiences that commonly reported in the general population (sometimes reported as occurring on the cusp of sleep) may also have hallucinatory-like components, including out-of-body experiences, apparitions, and sleep paralysis. However, beyond the medical model of hallucinations, the ontological nature of these experiences, and thus the role of misattribution, is disputed. For example, regarding out-of-body experiences, it is disputed whether the perception of leaving one's body is hallucinatory or veridical; and work on apparitions questions whether these are hallucinatory or indicative of survival after death, thus offering competing interpretations on the nature of reality itself.

Nicola Holt

See also: Apparitions; Hypnagogic State; Out-of-Body Experience (OBE); Sleep Paralysis

Further Reading

Bentall, Richard. 2014. "Hallucinatory Experiences." In *Varieties of Anomalous Experience*, edited by Etzel Cardeña, Steven J. Lynn, and Stanley Krippner, 109–143. Washington, DC: American Psychological Association.

Sacks, Oliver. 2012. *Hallucinations*. London: Pan Macmillan.

HARALDSSON, ERLENDUR

Erlendur Haraldsson (b. 1931), Professor Emeritus at the University of Iceland, is one of the most experienced field workers in parapsychology today. He has studied and written on Icelandic mediums and apparitions, the Indian holy man Sathya Sai Baba, and children with past-life memories in Sri Lanka and Lebanon, among other topics.

The name "Haraldsson" is a patronymic and not properly a surname, although it is used that way in academic writing. Erlendur was born on November 3, 1931, near Reykjavik, Iceland. He studied philosophy at the graduate level at the Universities of Copenhagen (Denmark), Edinburgh (Scotland), and Freiburg (Germany) and then travelled in Asia for two years, supporting himself as a journalist. In 1963 he returned to the University of Freiburg to begin studies in psychology under Hans Bender. He spent the 1969–1970 academic year with J. B. Rhine at the Institute for Parapsychology of the Foundation for Research on the Nature of Man, the precursor of the Rhine Research Center, in Durham, North Carolina. There he conducted the experiments that formed the basis of his doctoral dissertation, which he wrote up the following year at the University of Virginia, where he did an internship in clinical psychology and met Ian Stevenson. He received his PhD from the University of Freiburg in February 1972.

Immediately upon completing his dissertation, Erlendur was asked by Karlis Osis, research director of the American Society for Psychical Research, to assist him on a survey of observations by physicians and nurses of persons near death in India as a complement to a study Osis had already conducted in the United States. This groundbreaking research led to the book *At the Hour of Death*, first published in 1977 and still in print in its third edition. Erlendur visited India nine more times over the next several years to interview Sai Baba and collect accounts of his many exploits before writing his book about him, *Miracles Are My Visiting Cards* (called *Modern Miracles* in its American edition), reprinted with twelve new chapters in 2013 as *Modern Miracles: Sathya Sai Baba: The Story of a Modern Day Prophet*. In Iceland he made extensive studies of historical and modern physical and mental mediums and conducted a major survey with follow-up investigations of apparitions, the subject of his most recent book, *The Departed Among the Living*. He has also performed parapsychological experiments and researched the relation of personality variables to paranormal beliefs.

In 1988 Erlendur accepted Stevenson's offer to participate in a project to replicate his findings regarding children who remember previous lives. Erlendur began his studies of children with past-life memories in Sri Lanka, later following these up with similar studies among the Lebanese Druze. To date he has investigated more than 90 such cases, one of them in Iceland, and written several journal papers about them. He conducted important research comparing children with past-life memories with their peers on psychological tests in both Sri Lanka and Lebanon, showing that children with past-life memories were no more fantasy prone than children without them. Children with past-life memories often were judged better adjusted socially than their peers were, and they often did better in school than their peers did. In follow-up studies with older subjects who had claimed past-life memories as children, Erlendur found that many more of them than previously believed retained some of their memories into adulthood.

Erlendur retired from teaching at the University of Iceland in 1999, but he continues to research, write, and lecture on the topics in which he has specialized. Three major documentaries have been produced in the United States and United Kingdom about his work. He received the Outstanding Career Award from the Parapsychological Association in 1997 and the Myers Memorial Medal from the Society for Psychical Research in 2010.

James G. Matlock

See also: Apparition; Mediumship; Reincarnation; Rhine Research Center; Survival after Death

Further Reading

Haraldsson, Erlendur. 2013. "The Question of Appearance and Reality." In *Men and Women of Parapsychology: Personal Reflections*, ESPRIT vol. 2, edited by Rosemarie Pilkington, 162–173. San Antonio, TX: Anomalist Books.

Matlock, James G. 2013. "The Principal Reincarnation Researchers: Erlendur Haraldsson." In *Signs of Reincarnation*, by James G. Matlock. http://jamesgmatlock.net/resources/researchers/haraldsson (accessed October 6, 2014).

Osis, Karlis, and Erlendur Haraldsson. 1997. *At the Hour of Death*. 3rd ed. Norwalk, CT: Hastings House.

HAUNTING

A haunting can be described as the unwelcomed incursion of an unseen other into a human habitation, which persists over time. Hauntings of various kinds have been reported across cultures and throughout history, but in the modern Western world, perhaps the most common image associated with haunting is that of the haunted house. Indeed, the Society for Psychical Research, founded in London in 1882 as the world's first organized parapsychological association, included "apparitions and haunted houses" as one of the six kinds of paranormal activity that it investigated, due to their widespread reports in Victorian-era England. But the topic of haunting is much broader. The unseen other may be human or other-than-human, and the "habitation" that it haunts includes a wide range of sites: from the body of an individual to an entire settlement or region.

The word "haunt" comes from the medieval French verb, *hanter*, which means to practice (an action) or to visit (a place) habitually. The notion of haunting carries over both of these meanings: a haunted site is one at which an invisible presence manifests over time—with the qualification that it does so uninvited. It is easy to forget in the modern context that for most of human history, the visitation of disincarnate souls and other-than-human beings was an expected and regular feature of human life. For example, the Aztec-derived Mexican festival *Dia de los Muertos* (Day of the Dead) is a yearly celebration in which the living make prayers and offerings to their ancestors. In the ceremony of the *bembe* in the Afro-Cuban religion of Santería, practitioners hold festivals of dancing and drumming to invite the ever-present *orishas*—other-than-human manifestations of the life force—into their midst. In both of these examples, members of the human community take care to observe the boundaries between the living and the dead, or between the human and more-than-human worlds.

Hauntings occur when these boundaries have been violated or neglected. Unwelcomed visitations of the dead thus occur most often when a soul has not been able to cross completely from this world to the next, usually as the result of a traumatic death. In medieval Christianity, for example, the ghosts who came to haunt the living were the souls of those in purgatory who had died before having a chance to repent for their sins. In Santería, *orishas* are said sometimes to create misfortune for the human beings who are meant to serve them; bad luck discontinues when the afflicted person identifies the particular *orisha* and promises to work with it.

In the modern Western world, interest in haunting mushroomed during the 19th century, as the new religion of Spiritualism swept through the United States and Europe. This movement began with a classic example of haunting and its resolution. As the legend is recounted in Spiritualist literature, the first mediums of the tradition were two young girls—Katherine and Margaret Fox—daughters of a family in Hydesville, New York, who in 1848 entered into communication with a poltergeist who had been tormenting their home. It was soon discovered that the spirit haunted not the house but the Fox sisters themselves, as disturbances followed them after they moved out of the home. Further, it was soon learned that the girls had a rapport not only with the original Hydesville poltergeist but also with a wide array of spirit beings, who came to communicate through them a variety of personal, theological, and political messages. As news of the Fox sisters spread throughout the nation, the practice of mediumship spread rapidly, and the religion of Spiritualism was born.

What started as the tale of a single family's haunting by a poltergeist, however, became a chapter in modern history for an entire generation tormented by the possibility of a meaningless death. In the decades leading up to the events of Hydesville, scientific discoveries had threatened to destroy the foundations of American Protestant Christianity, including its belief in an afterlife. However, the culture-wide craze for communing with the dead prevented this outcome, at least for a time. Although Spiritualism broke in important ways from Protestant teachings, it succeeded in reviving Americans' Christian faith in personal immortality.

Today, the religious significance of ghosts is often overlooked. Since the mid-19th century, two other movements have emerged to reframe the way that contemporary people think about hauntings. The first of these is the field of parapsychology, set in motion by the aforementioned Society of Psychical Research (SPR) in 1882. By the time the SPR was founded, mediumship had become rife with fraud. The founders of the SPR hoped to find scientific evidence supporting claims of mediumship, as well as apparitions and haunted houses, by moving the study of ghosts into a more controlled setting. On the one hand, their controlled studies suggested to them that there was scientific evidence for haunting. On the other hand, their break from the Spiritualist movement meant that they had to find new ways of making sense of the facts. SPR member Frederic Myers hypothesized that at the deepest levels of the mind, human consciousness was free from the constraints of the body and the physical world. This subliminal self was capable, Myers thought, of communicating with other minds, as recorded in both experiences of telepathy and experiences of mediumship. Fellow SPR member William Fletcher Barrett further hypothesized that some place-specific hauntings resulted from the psychic imprints left by the energy of consciousness on material structures or locales. In either case, haunting was imagined as a property of the natural world and was explored without reference to any explicit religious framework.

The second modern movement that has reframed the way modern people think about haunting is the field of psychoanalysis. Inaugurated by Sigmund Freud, psychoanalytic theory explains haunting as the projection onto the external world of some forgotten, traumatic event. While Freud was receptive to Myers's hypothesis of telepathy, nothing of the SPR theories appears in his writings. Rather, for Freud and his heirs, hauntings are explained as a return of repressed memories projected onto all-too-human situations.

This psychoanalytical interpretation has reappeared in academic studies of "ghosts" for the last two decades. Beginning with Jacques Derrida's 1993 essay, *The Specters of Marx*, scholars have revived the idea of the "ghost" as a symbol for people or events that have been passed over or marginalized in modern narratives of history. Derrida predicted that Karl Marx's hopes for the end of capitalism would continue to haunt the world long after the experiments of the Soviet Union had been written out of history. Other academic writers have likewise written about the haunting power of marginalized groups like Native and African Americans who have been passed over in national histories of the modern age.

Despite their different interpretations, Spiritualism, parapsychology, and psychoanalysis all assume that haunting is a phenomenon created in some way by human beings. In Spiritualism, human spirits haunt the living; in parapsychology, the consciousness of one human being affects another, either directly or through its energetic traces; and in psychoanalysis, repressed memories of another individual or individuals return to disturb people's experience of the world.

In popular culture, however, alternative explanations for hauntings have come from two other sources. The first is conservative Christianity, which suggests that at least some hauntings stem from demonic interferences. This belief has a very old history within the Christian tradition. In medieval Catholic ghost stories, the living always took care to address the specter in the name of Jesus; only authentic, human ghosts remained after the mention of God's name. Another alternate explanation for haunting comes from the religion of Theosophy, whose founder, Helena Blavatsky, was once a 19th-century medium. Blavatsky broke with Spiritualism in teaching that most of the phenomena observed in séances were the product of mischievous elementals, a class of spiritually unenlightened beings.

Academic culture has also offered an alternate explanation of haunting in drawing attention to the many technological metaphors in Spiritualism. The Fox sisters, for example, were widely perceived as human telegraph machines, while subsequent mediums have been compared to radios and even quantum computers. Some scholars suggest that the real causes of haunting in the Spiritualist movement are the various machines of our modern world, which alter our experience of the body and mind in ways that are only partly noticed. Similarly, some scientific theories suggest that ghosts result from invisible interactions between the physical world and the human body (e.g., electromagnetically induced hallucinations). While these naturalistic interpretations might seem to explain away ghosts, their break from Christian or Christian-derived theories—that hauntings are always caused by human agents—opens up new ways of thinking about the subject. Haunting is an unwelcome transgression of boundaries separating the world of unseen others from a human community. Uninvited visitations from human sprits may represent the most common form of haunting in the modern West, but they do not exhaust the range of hauntings reported across cultures and throughout time.

Darryl V. Caterine

See also: Discarnate Entity; Enfield Poltergeist; Fox Sisters, The; Ghosts; Myers, Frederic W. H.; Parapsychology; Poltergeist; Psychical Research; Society for Psychical Research; Spiritualism; Survival after Death; Unconscious Mind

Further Reading
Bergland, Renee. 2000. *The National Uncanny: Indian Ghosts and American Subjects (Reencounters with Colonialism: New Perspectives on the Americas)*. Hanover, NH: University of New England Press.

Gauld, Alan. 1968. *The Founders of Psychical Research*. New York: Schocken Books.

Gordon, Avery. 2008. *Ghostly Matters: Haunting and the Sociological Imagination*. Minneapolis: University of Minnesota Press.

Hansen, George. 2001. *The Trickster and the Paranormal*. Bloomington, IN: Xlibris Press.

Richardson, Judith. 2005. *Possessions: The History and Uses of Haunting in the Hudson Valley*. Cambridge, MA: Harvard University Press.

Schmidt, Jean-Claude. 1999. *Ghosts in the Middle Ages: The Living and the Dead in Medieval Society*. Chicago: The University of Chicago Press.

HEALING, PSYCHIC AND SPIRITUAL

Miraculous or seemingly inexplicable healings or cures have long been a feature of religious and folk traditions, whether they be the healings of the Christian New Testament or accounts given by travelers or anthropologists of the activities of shamans or witchdoctors. In some cases, healings no longer appear remarkable because the mechanisms involved have been identified so that they now form part of conventional Western medicine. In some cases, herbal lore has come to form the basis of modern medicines; in many other cases, it continues to sit alongside more conventional approaches, often being referred to as complementary or herbal medicine. Many accounts of healings continue to go unexplained, and there are many complementary therapies whose usefulness remains contested. Among paranormal researchers, a hypothesis frequently explored is that there is some form of energy transfer between practitioner and client (or patient) involved that can give rise to healing of psychological and physical ailments. This is commonly referred to spiritual or psychic healing, but this also covers a wide range of understandings and practices.

The suggestion that an energy transfer can take place between human beings relies upon the understanding that we are, at some level, beings of energy rather than only physical matter. Spiritual and psychic healing are therefore commonly found in traditions that entertain the perception of humans as souls or spirits with a physical form. Among the Christian (and Christian-derived) traditions, spiritual healing is discussed across the spectrum, from the Eastern and Russian Orthodox churches, through Roman Catholicism, various Protestant traditions (especially Pentecostal ones), through to Spiritualism and (in South America) Kardec's Spiritism. In fact, healing narratives can be found in most of the widespread religious traditions and also in more localized shamanic traditions in which healing is often a noted feature. Further, healing traditions need not be an adjunct of a religious tradition; for example, the relatively modern tradition of Reiki could be argued to stand alone as a healing tradition that does not embody a particular cosmology or moral code beyond those rules directly relevant to the healing practice.

Underlying cosmologies can be relevant, as they can provide tools for understanding and exploring what happens when a healer heals a client or patient.

Common to most understandings of healing is the concept of an energy field surrounding the human form, often referred to as an auric field or aura; opinion can differ as to whether this aura is generated by the physical form or by the soul.

In most traditions, the healer is an individual who is either naturally able or has learned how to have a beneficial effect on other people, whether by focusing on them mentally or by placing his or her hands on them so as to make a physical contact enabling some form of energy transfer; in many traditions mental focus and physical contact are employed together.

Psychic and spiritual healing might seem to be alternate terms for the same phenomena, but they can indicate a major difference of understanding. In Spiritualism and Reiki, for example, healers are generally taught that although they are a conduit for healing energy, they are not the source. In this understanding, the source of healing energy is said to be God or some other universal source, with the practitioner acting or being used as a channel for the transmission of that energy; when sharing personal energy, a healer is said to be acting at a psychic level (which may or may not be to the benefit of the client), but when acting as a channel or medium of transmission, the healer is said to be acting at a spiritual level. In traditions based upon the idea of continuing souls or spirits, healers may be assisted by healing guides, as with other forms of mediumship. Opinion may also vary as to whether the universal energy or spirit is an energy humans are naturally part of or whether it is an energy that healers, whether by natural ability or training, are able to connect with in a way or to an extent that others are not.

Within traditions that hold to the understanding that healers learn to connect when working, the state of mind the healer works in is naturally considered relevant. Some degree of mental focus is generally mentioned, but in some traditions this can extend to the understanding that healers work in some form of trance state or altered state of consciousness and in some cases extend even to controlled forms of overshadowing or possession by a benevolent spirit. The healer's awareness (or lack of it) can raise issues of healer responsibility, which is in turn relevant to the formulation of relevant ethical codes for the conduct of healing.

As mentioned, not all healing traditions require the healer and patient to be touching or even to be in close proximity; in Spiritualism, for example, distinctions are drawn between contact, distance, and absent healing. Contact healing involves some degree of touch of the patient by the healer, although some healers maintain that it is not necessary to touch the point of injury or ailment directly, and that it is enough that there is some physical contact between healer and patient. Distance healing obviously implies some distance between the physical forms of healer and patient, although the distance may not be great. Rather than touching the patient, some healers may describe themselves as working with energies directed at the patient or directly with the aura so that they remain at a short physical distance but close enough for the auras of healer and patient to connect. Absent healing is where the healer is entirely absent from the vicinity of the patient and may even be in a different country but is nevertheless directing appropriate energies towards the patient, possibly by maintaining a mental image of the patient.

There is much discussion among healers as to whether the state of mind of the patient is relevant, and if so, why. The possibility being explored here is that certain states of mind (including as to particular beliefs) may render the patient more susceptible to the beneficial effect of the healing or, alternatively, act as a block or form of resistance. It has been suggested that the mediumistic role of the healer involves connecting not only with spirit or other energy but also with the patient; accordingly, many healing codes of practice contain protocols for managing patient expectations and putting him or her at ease.

The ailments said to be capable of benefitting from healing are wide ranging as are the possible diagnoses and healing practices found in different traditions. Some shamanic traditions hold that the human soul has a number of different parts and that some physical ailments can be caused by the patient having suffered some degree of soul loss. In such cases, the expectation is that the shaman will travel to the spirit world(s) to retrieve the lost part of the patient's soul and reunite it so that the patient is whole again; some researchers have drawn comparisons here with Western forms of psychotherapy. In shamanic traditions, there is also the possibility that the patient is being affected, injured, or possibly even possessed by an unhelpful or aggressive spirit, so that the shaman's role is to break a connection or attachment and thereafter ensure that it does not recur. A similar context exists for the Christian tradition of exorcism. An important point here is that in some traditions, especially in non-Western societies, an important aspect of the healer's role is as the one who diagnoses the nature of the illness or malady; without an appropriate diagnosis, an appropriate remedy will not be apparent. In traditionally shamanic societies, the shaman would be expected to deal with maladies regardless of whether the cause is physical, psychological, or spiritual; indeed, it is the shaman's task to determine which it is.

In many traditions, the possibility of effecting physical healings is also admitted; in such cases, there is a physical change or transformation to the body of the patient that is in some way beneficial. It is important to note that such healings need not be immediate; in some accounts, dramatic healings are achieved but as a result of repeated healings over periods of weeks, months, or even over a year.

Some traditions offer accounts of healing processes that involve the excretion of unwanted matter from the body (including by vomiting). Such accounts can also extend to traditions that involve a form of healing that has become known as psychic surgery, something that has been a feature of some shamanic traditions, and of healings within Spiritist traditions in South America; a number of such accounts can also be found in the literature of Western Spiritualism. Rather than the healing giving rise to the excretion of matter from the body, psychic surgery is described as involving the active intention of the healer to undertake a form of surgery upon the patient's body. In the available accounts, this may either take the form of actual surgery that apparently causes no pain to the patient so that no form of anesthetic is required, or alternatively, the surgery itself is psychic, so that an operation is undertaken upon the patient's body without causing any visible wound. The surgery is undertaken for the usual range of reasons, whether to correct an injury or abnormality or to extract a diseased organ, parasite, or physical item causing the illness.

One final distinction that can be discerned in the literature is that between healing and cure. Many healers maintain that the curative effects of their practice can be expected to be permanent, but it is sometimes accepted that a condition that has been healed may recur if it is caused by, for example, lifestyle factors that the patient refuses or is unable to change. In such cases, a patient may be said to have been healed but not cured.

Accounts of unusual healings are heavily contested but have never entirely lost legitimacy in Western culture simply because examples of such healings have retained religious acceptance. A significant difficulty remains that of verifying the effects (if any) of particular instances of healing or of particular healing practices, or of exploring the possible mechanisms involved. Accounts of unusual or miraculous healing accumulate, but it is difficult to make progress in testing or comprehending such phenomena in the absence of an appropriate methodology. A small number of scholars have undertaken the process of apprenticeship involved in some healing traditions, but the difficulty with such research is that it leads to the accumulation of personal knowledge and experience that cannot readily be demonstrated to others who have not been through a similar process; it is difficult to have such research regarded as anything other than an additional set of insider claims.

Most Western scholars who have taken an interest in spiritual healing have undertaken analyses of social attitudes towards such practices, with increasing recognition that the degree of acceptance of spiritual healing is often much greater than has always been recognized.

David Gordon Wilson

See also: Aura; Exorcism; Shamanism; Spiritualism; Unconscious Mind

Further Reading

Duffin, Jacalyn. 2009. *Medical Miracles: Doctors, Saints, and Healing in the Modern World.* New York: Oxford University Press.

Klassen, Pamela E. 2011. *Spirits of Protestantism: Medicine, Healing, and Liberal Christianity.* Berkeley, CA: University of California Press.

Solomon, Grant. 1997. *Stephen Turoff: Psychic Surgeon.* London: Thorsons.

Stutley, Margaret. 2003. *Shamanism: An Introduction.* London: Routledge.

Young, Alan. 1981. *Spiritual Healing: Miracle or Mirage?* Marina del Rey, CA: DeVorss & Co.

HYPNAGOGIC STATE

Drifting off to sleep each night, people often find themselves subjected to a bizarre assortment of hallucinatory phenomena even before they begin to dream. The term "hypnagogia" (from the Greek, meaning "leading toward sleep") is commonly used to describe the transitional state of consciousness that comes with the onset of sleep. It is a state that has been the source of creativity and inspiration for some and problem solving for others. It plays an important role in a variety of spiritual practices and is believed to have psychological benefits. Some believe that the hypnagogic states may either favor or account for paranormal experiences.

The term "hypnagogic" was first coined in 1848 by Alfred Maury (1817–1892), a French physician, scholar, and dream researcher. One of Maury's own dreams provided material for Salvador Dali's painting *Dream Caused by the Flight of a Bee around a Pomegranate a Second before Waking* (1944). Subsequent to Maury, early psychical researcher Frederic Myers created the term "hypnopompic" to describe the state between sleeping and waking. Phenomenologically, the two states of consciousness are very much alike. There is some debate as to whether they are identical or merely similar. "Hypnagogia," as its own separate term (as opposed to Maury's "hypnagogic") came into favor with the 1983 doctoral dissertation (and later 1987 book) on the subject by Andreas Mavromatis.

Even though the term is not used, references to hypnagogia can be found throughout history and across cultures. Aristotle mentions the hypnagogic state in his treatise *On Sleep* (350 BCE). Iamblichus (d. 325 CE) also makes mention, and later, Christian mystic Emmanuel Swedenborg (1688–1772) wrote extensively of his hypnagogic experiences. Hypnagogic states are also described in Tibetan Buddhism, most noticeably in the practice of dream yoga, where practitioners are trained to remain aware during hypnagogia as training for discerning the various layers of reality encountered during the dying process. The value of hypnagogic awareness was also acknowledged by P. D. Ouspensky, who advocated for it as useful for inducing lucid dreaming. Some researchers, such as Herbert Silberer, believe that the strangeness of alchemical symbolism may have had its roots in hypnagogic hallucinations as well.

What is the phenomenological experience of hypnagogic hallucinations? What are they like? Mavromatis notes that hypnagogic hallucinations can be experienced across the full spectrum of sense. They can include visual, auditory, tactile, olfactory, and gustatory hallucinations, as well as somasthetic (perception of the body's position in space), thermal, and kinesthetic hallucinations. Dream researcher Harry T. Hunt likens these hallucinations to psychedelic drug experiences, schizophrenic episodes, and spiritual experiences and suggests that they might be responsible for some reports of out-of-body experiences.

In the hypnagogic state, visual hallucinations can range from shifting colors, bursts of light, and geometric patterns up to coherent images of people, places, and things. Auditory hallucinations can include words (including neologisms), sentences, dialogue, music, environmental sounds, hearing one's name, and loud

The hypnagogic state, also known as *hypnagogia*, is the transitional state of consciousness that is encountered on the way from waking to sleep. Its complement is the hypnopompic state, which is encountered on the way from sleep to waking. Many painters, writers, and artists have used these states for creative inspiration, and both states have been associated with the possible production of psi phenomena, such as telepathy and precognition, and also paranormal phenomena, such as visits from apparitions and entities.

crashes. Olfactory hallucinations can be both pleasant and unpleasant, and physical sensations can include variations in temperature, body distortions, and sensations of falling (called "hypnic jerk"). Sleep paralysis has also been noted in the hypnagogic state.

Rather than grouping all hypnagogic activity together, Mavromatis breaks hypnagogia into four separate and distinct stages. Stage one is the experience of colors and flashes of light. These sorts of flashes were documented by Hervey de Saint-Denis in 1867. Although de Saint-Denis believed that dreams were based in memory, he attributed these phenomena to retinal stimulation. The second stage, according to Mavromatis, is more somatic in nature, including sound and body sensations. This stage is home to auditory hallucinations, the aforementioned "hypnic jerk," and sleep paralysis. It can also include static visual imagery (faces, objects, etc.) merging into one another, randomly or in a related manner. These images may or may not be related to any thoughts the person is having. The third stage involves "autosymbolic" phenomena, which were described by Silberer as representing the thoughts and state of mind of the person undergoing hypnagogia. Finally, in stage four, hypnagogic dreams arise, which, for Mavromatis, are indistinguishable from regular dreams.

Beyond this overview of the subjective experience of hypnagogia, what is happening in the brain during this time? What occurs biochemically? Early research into hypnagogic phenomena was largely based on self-reporting. As such, it was difficult to determine whether the hypnagogic reports were a result of a relaxed waking state or sleep onset. Later studies with EEG devices were able to provide a method for differentiating between the two. A 1964 study by Wolfgang Kuhlo and Dietrich Lehmann correlated sleep onset with slower brain waves. Although their methodology also involved controlled waking (where research participants were repeatedly awoken and asked about their experiences), test subjects were also requested to push a button when hypnagogic phenomena appeared.

Modern sleep research has identified four distinct stages of sleep that each person experiences several times per night. Sleep Stage 1 is the very onset of sleep. Activity may be reduced, and eyes may be closed. One can be easily awakened, however, and upon so, may not even feel as if they have been asleep. This stage generally lasts for 5 to 10 minutes. Stage 2 is generally associated with light sleep. Heart rate decreases as does body temperature, and two types of brain waves begin to appear that are related to sleep: "sleep spindles" and "K-complexes." Stages 3 and 4 are increasingly deeper stages of sleep. Generally, all four stages happen prior to REM (rapid eye movement) sleep, which is the stage associated with dreaming (though dreams have been reported from non-REM stages). After a period of REM sleep (which is not as deep as stages 3 and 4), one's sleep returns to Stage 1, beginning the descent to Stage 4 again. This entire cycle happens several times throughout the night within increasing amounts of REM and decreasing amounts of deep sleep as the night progresses.

J. Allan Hobson, another dream researcher, who studies the biochemistry of dreams, believes that the strangeness of hypnagogia may be the result of neurotransmitter depletion due to fatigue in animergic neurons in the brain stem. Animergic neurons use monoamines as neurotransmitters and generally keep Pontic-geniculo-occipital (PGO) waves in the brain low during wakefulness. PGO waves are usually found in the brain just prior to REM sleep. As the animergic neurons become tired, their firing rate decreases at the onset of sleep and continues to slow down as one approaches REM.

Though it might be tempting to write off hypnagogic hallucinations as the meaningless byproducts of a tired brain, hypnagogia does seem to have many uses and benefits. As mentioned above, Salvador Dali based a painting on Alfred Maury's hypnagogic imagery. Dali also regularly induced his own hypnagogic states for inspiration. Other artists have also utilized hypnagogic states for inspiration as well, including Gordon Onslow Ford (1912–2003), whose paintings consist of what he terms the three foundational elements of art (lines, circles, and dots), and his student, John Anderson (1932–2011). Both painters drew heavily from hypnagogic trance states, and their paintings are reminiscent of the visual patterns and flashes of light that come with early sleep onset. Aside from painters, composers such as Brahms, Puccini, and Wagner, as well as authors including Poe, Goethe, Tolstoy, Twain, and poets such as Coleridge, Keats, and more are also said to have used hypnagogia for inspiration.

The creativity of hypnagogia has also proven useful for problem solving. The oft-told tale of chemist Friedrich August Kekule dreaming of an ouroboros (the snake eating its own tail) and being able to "discover" the structure of benzene rings as a result may have actually described a hypnagogic vision. Thomas Edison, too, drew inspiration from hypnagogia, creating elaborate systems of waking himself up before becoming too involved with his naps. Nikola Tesla and Isaac Newton are also reported to have utilized hypnagogia for inspiration.

Finally, there is some discussion as to whether hypnagogia as a state of consciousness might facilitate psi phenomena such as telepathy or precognition or explain or facilitate paranormal experiences such as visits from apparitions. A number of articles in *The Journal of Parapsychology* have appeared in recent years that show there may at least be a possibility of hypnagogic and hypnopompic states being fertile for both. Caution is also urged, however, in that the nebulous nature of hypnagogia and hypnopompia make it difficult to always accurately interpret the phenomena one encounters.

Kevin Kovelant

See also: Hallucinations; Imaginal; Paranormal Dreams; Sleep Paralysis

Further Reading

Dement, William C., and Christopher Vaughan. 1999. *The Promise of Sleep*. New York: Dell Publishing.

Hobson, James A. 1988. *The Dreaming Brain: How the Brain Creates Both the Sense and the Nonsense of Dreams*. New York: Basic Books.

Hunt, Harry T. 1989. *The Multiplicity of Dreams: Memory, Imagination and Consciousness*. New Haven, CT: Yale University Press.

Mavromatis, Andreas. 1987. *Hypnagogia: The Unique State of Consciousness between Wakefulness and Sleep*. New York: Routledge.

Silberer, Herbert. 1971. *Hidden Symbolism of Alchemy and the Occult Arts*. New York: Dover.

IMAGINAL

The term "imaginal" is often used to describe a hypothetical realm where dreams take place, where the deceased reside post-mortem, or where communications from the deceased are facilitated in dreams. The imaginal realm is described as an ontological reality that exists outside of space and time, yet has influence on our world. Though this concept of the imaginal can be viewed as a descendent of both Platonic and Neoplatonic schools of thought, it also figures prominently in Sufi cosmology and philosophy, having been further developed and refined by notable Sufi sages Shihabuddin Yahya al-Suhrawardi (1151–1191 CE) and Ibn al-'Arabi (1165–1240 CE). Variations of the theme of "imaginal" can also be found in some contemporary Western philosophical circles as well.

To fully understand "the imaginal" and how this layer of reality works, it is important to clarify the difference between "imaginal" and "imaginary." "Imaginal" in this context refers to "as pertaining to images." This is different from "imaginary," which is associated with fantasy and make-believe. The imaginal realm is accessed through the mental faculty of imagination. There is a subtle difference between this use of imagination and the modern vernacular that equates it with the imaginary.

To understand the development of the idea of an imaginal realm, one must first revisit the Greek philosopher Plato and his concept of forms. For Plato, a "form" is an idealized metaphysical proto-version of an object. For instance, the term "chair" may refer to a recliner, a stool, a desk chair, a white chair, a blue chair, a metal chair, a wooden chair, and so on. They are all "chairs," however, and it is this classification of "chair" that informs each of them. Without the concept, or form, of "chair," and its inherent "chair-ness," none of these actual chairs could exist. The idea of "chair" must exist prior to any actual chairs. For Plato the forms reside separate from and outside of time and space, and are nonphysical. They are ultimate ideal concepts that manifest in a variety of ways in the physical and temporal world. This notion of "ideals" forms the basis of the philosophy known as idealism.

Idealism is essential to understanding the imaginal. There are many flavors of idealism, but the term can be broadly used to describe a worldview that emphasizes and places primary importance in an ideal (or at times spiritual) realm that informs the physical realm. Plotinus (204–270 CE), a Neoplatonist philosopher ("neo" meaning "new" and "platonist" as "follower of Plato"), in his major work *The Enneads*, places the soul as outside of time and space, and in a similar setting to Plato's forms. One could argue that the soul (or psyche, or higher self, or consciousness) is the ideal form of the individual.

It is in the Middle East where the concept of the imaginal realm became further refined and articulated. As European thought stagnated during the Dark Ages—the Church having purged its libraries of anything that might be even remotely "heretical," such as the works of Socrates, Aristotle, and the like—science, math, philosophy, and the arts flourished in the Arab world. Greek and Roman texts that had been burned in Europe were fuelling a complex society and culture, as well as providing fertile source material for Muslim and Sufi scholarship. It is within this environment that two Sufi philosophers, Shihabuddin Yahya al-Suhrawardi and Muhyiddin Ibn al-'Arabi, formulated their conceptions of the universe.

Drawing on both Zoroastrianism and Plato, Suhrawardi outlined his cosmology in his work *The Philosophy of Illumination*, earning him the name "Shaykh al-Ishraq" ("Master of Illumination"). In this book, written in 1186, Suhrawardi's model of the universe is based in light, which is considered to be the "true" reality and the foundation of this world. This light emanates from the Divine, gradually losing intensity as it reaches the material level of reality. Suhrawardi proposes a layer of reality called *alam al-mithal*, or The World of Images. This is a separate ontological level where immaterial images exist. A prime example of an "immaterial image" is a reflection in a mirror. It is not the actual item one sees in the mirror, but its imaginal form. The mirror image looks exactly like the object but contains no actual physical characteristics associated with the object.

The work Ibn al-'Arabi, a contemporary of Suhrawardi, is also essential to the continued development of the concept of the imaginal. Central to Ibn al-'Arabi's cosmology is the concept of *barzakh*, or "bridge" (literally, "isthmus"). If Suhrawardi gives the imaginal realm its own ontological reality, Ibn al-'Arabi goes one step further, placing it as a state "between." It is a bridge, a reality that resides between two worlds (this world, and the next), and it contains features of both. In joining two landmasses together, a bridge or isthmus (*barzakh*) ultimately belongs to neither, yet may contain features of both. To return to the example of a mirror image, the image contains features of the object it is reflecting. It also contains features of the mirror. Ultimately, however, the image is neither the object nor the mirror.

Ibn al-'Arabi also uses dreams as evidence of the imaginal realm. People, places, and objects that appear in dreams are by their very nature imaginal. They appear *as* these things but lack the physicality of them. God, suggests Ibn al-'Arabi, created dreams so that we can bear witness to the power of imagination and know that there are similar, yet distinct worlds to this one. The imagination is the key to perceiving the imaginal, which, again, should not be confused with the imaginary. This association with dreams is also based in the Qur'an (Surah 39:42), which indicates the potential for the dream realm also being the place where the living can converse and interact with the dead. Visitation dreams are regularly facilitated by the imaginal realm and are recorded extensively in both Muslim and Sufi literature.

After studying the works of Surhawardi and Ibn al-'Arabi extensively, French philosopher Henri Corbin (1903–1978) brought the concepts of *alam al-mithal* and the imaginal realm—or, in his terms, *Mundus Imaginalis*, the world of the imaginal—to modern Westerners, presenting it first in his paper *Mundus Imaginalis* in Paris in 1964, and later in several books on Sufism, and Shi'ite mysticism in particular. Like Suhrawardi and Ibn al-'Arabi, Corbin identifies the imaginal realm as ontologically real and something perceived by (not created by) imagination, coupled with cognition. It is higher and more immaterial than the sensory world but lower and less immaterial than the intelligible world. For Corbin, not only is it the realm of dreams and visionary experience, but it is also the realm of the archetypes. To travel to this realm requires cognitive imagination, independent of physicality. This frames the imaginal realm as a prime candidate for an afterlife realm.

Though he makes no mention of Corbin, Ibn al-'Arabi, Suhrawardi, Sufism, or Islam, philosopher and parapsychologist H. H. Price, known for his contributions to the philosophy of perception, arrives at a similar hypothesis about what the afterlife might be like. In his essay *Survival and the Idea of "Another World"* (1965), Price argues that the next world, as he terms the realm of the deceased, could be much like the dream world, composed of mental images. Price also emphasizes the need to differentiate "imaginal" (using his term, "imagy") from "imaginary." Price's next world has no spatial location, and as it is similar to the dream world, sensory input and cognition would be handled in a manner akin to that in dreaming. Corbin and Price both presented these topics in 1964, and while it is unclear how familiar Price was with Corbin's work or the Sufi philosophers, their descriptions are almost identical.

The imaginal realm presents an attractive model for envisioning how dreams might work or what happens when we die. Unfortunately, the unanswered questions that attend this model are also notable. In dreams, for instance, how does one travel between worlds? Do we visit the dead, or do they visit us? Either way, how? These questions do not discount the idea of an imaginal realm; they only offer opportunities for further refinement of the model.

Kevin Kovelant

See also: Abduction Experience; Apparitions; Astral Plane; Hypnagogic State; Paranormal Dreams; Survival after Death

Further Reading

Chittick, William C. 1994. *Imaginal Worlds: Ibn al-'Arabi and the Problems of Religious Diversity.* New York: SUNY Press.

Corbin, Henri. 1994. *The Man of Light in Iranian Sufism.* New Lebanon, NY: Omega Publications.

Nasr, Seyyed H. 1993. *An Introduction to Islamic Cosmological Doctrines.* New York: SUNY Press.

Price, H. H. 1965. "Survival and the Idea of 'Another World.'" In *Brain and Mind: Modern Concepts of the Nature of Mind*, edited by John R. Smythies, 1–33. London: Routledge & Kegan Paul.

Smith, Jane I., and Yvonne Y. Haddad. 2002. *The Islamic Understanding of Death and Resurrection*. New York: Oxford University Press.

Suhrawardi, Shihabuddin. 2000. *The Philosophy of Illumination*. Translated by John Walbridge and Hossein Ziai. Provo, UT: Brigham Young University Press.

J

JAMES, WILLIAM

The American psychologist William James (1842–1910) was one of the most influential intellectuals of the 19th century, and as the decades following his death increased in number, his influence increased as well. By the 21st century, he was considered the "father of American psychology," and his famous cross-cultural study on religious experience had become a fixture on the syllabi of college courses throughout the United States. Yet when the weightiness of James's legacy is considered, his specific impact on the study of religion is incommensurately difficult to evaluate. Most scholars agree that he is a foundational figure, but few have continued his research, even fewer utilize his methodology, and almost none would publically recognize the validity of several of his conclusions.

Compared to his contemporaries, including Edward Burnett Tylor (1832–1917), James George Frazer (1854–1941), and Sigmund Freud (1856–1939), James's approach to studying religion is unique; he was one of the few who did not believe scientific knowledge would, or should, become a replacement for the religious truths that shaped the values of the 19th century. Though James maintained that modern science was better equipped to address questions regarding the evolution of man and the creation of the universe, answers previously deemed the intellectual property of religion, he also believed that science needed to do more to account for mankind's spiritual evolution. Moreover, James maintained that each academic discipline and/or intellectual tradition's approach to analyzing the physical and metaphysical components of life was based on fallible methods of inquiry, and thus no matter how thorough each believed its methodology to be, each was limited in terms of the scope of data that it could effectively account for. Therefore, James insisted that scholars supplement their findings with those of other fields, and rather than treating religion and science as wholly separate objects of study, or as being at odds with another, he believed a more comparative approach would be beneficial to all.

The impact of James's legacy is seemingly evident in the field's movement toward a more scientific study of religion, yet each of the figures previously mentioned—Tylor, Freud, and Frazer (among others)—also claimed to favor a scientific approach. Religious studies scholars have, like James, attempted to avoid exclusionary Christo-centric religious jargon in an effort to better analyze the social function of various religious traditions, yet as the field moved in this direction, religious studies also became increasingly specialized. As of today, many focus on one aspect of a single culture's religion during one historical epoch, and few engage in comparison across traditions.

No matter where you open [history's] pages, you find things recorded under the name of divinations, inspirations, demoniacal possessions, apparitions, trances, ecstasies, miraculous healings and productions of disease, and occult powers possessed by peculiar individuals over persons and things in their neighborhood. We suppose that "mediumship" originated in Rochester, N.Y., and animal magnetism with Mesmer; but once you look behind the pages of official history, in personal memoirs, legal documents, and popular narratives and books of anecdote, and you will find that there never was a time when these things were not reported just as abundantly as now.

—William James, "What Psychical Research Has Accomplished" (1902)

In contrast to the specialization of most contemporary scholars, James' seminal contribution to the field, *The Varieties of Religious Experience*, is, as one might expect, an analysis of a variety of religious experiences. Although the "variety" among the experiences he studied is debatable, the work is a paradigmatic example of James's interdisciplinary approach. By incorporating observations drawn from the physical sciences, the social sciences, and multiple religious traditions, James analyzes the more exceptional experiences of the world's great religious geniuses, arguing that through these more extreme cases, we can better understand the unique features of experiences deemed religious, and we can better understand the function of religion in terms of the individual and his or her communities.

As evident in his studies of psychical phenomena, including extrasensory perception (ESP) and mediumship, and in his co-founding of the American Society of Psychical Research, James maintained that there was a deeper level of consciousness beyond the ever-present and recognizable waking thoughts of most individuals, a subconscious that connected them to a hidden world, but unlike many psychologists of his time (or since), James believed that the subconscious provided an opportunity to access a far greater reality that extended well beyond the individual's suppressed or hidden memories, thoughts, and emotions. He hypothesized that spiritually gifted persons throughout history possessed an enhanced ability to access their subconscious, or subliminal self. To James, this readily available access to the subconscious also came with a dark side, and he believed that the intense suffering many revered religious figures experienced prior to religious conversion was the product of a "divided self," a psychological state indicative of an ongoing internal battle with this subliminal self. He believed that a divided self often drove persons with exceptional religious abilities to madness and even suicide, and he hypothesized that the religious geniuses of history avoided such a fate by eventually giving in to this subliminal consciousness, effecting a life-altering connection with divinity, which he maintained was another term for the "greater reality" accessible through the subconscious. As a result of this religious conversion experience, James argued, the saintly figure achieved the lasting peace and happiness that eludes most of us.

Despite the field's admiration of James, contemporary religious studies scholars have since favored approaches that recognize the socially constructed nature of religious experiences, steering well clear of James's interest in paranormal phenomena and his claim that distinctly religious experiences signify a contact with a greater reality that can alter the reality of individuals and communities. A contemporary scholar who made such a claim regarding religious experiences would be widely criticized on the grounds that (1) the nature of religious experience is relative, differing from culture to culture, and thus (2) claiming that a religious experience is universally "X" or "Y" would indicate bias or ethnocentrism. Moreover, (3) to argue that religious experiences possess any distinctive features would be to ignore (1) and be guilty of (2) and to naively engage in apologetics or crypto-theology, both of which are unwelcome in a field that has undergone significant reform since the late 19th century.

Though James would undoubtedly approve of criticisms ostensibly aimed at removing the remaining vestiges of colonialist Christian-centric biases, he might argue that, in the process, scholars of religion have stopped studying religious experience; he might also argue that those interested in studying the psychological effect of profound religious and paranormal experiences on the individual must now search for comparable studies and replicable methodologies within parapsychology, a discipline where his legacy is a bit easier to understand.

Joel Gruber

See also: American Society for Psychical Research; Myers, Frederic W. H.; Mystical Experience; Parapsychology; Religion and the Paranormal; Unconscious Mind

Further Reading

Blum, Deborah. 2007. *Ghost Hunters: William James and the Search for Scientific Proof of Life after Death*. New York: Penguin Books.

James, William. 2012. *The Heart of William James*. Edited by Robert D. Richardson. Cambridge, MA: Harvard University Press.

JUNG, CARL

The Swiss-born Carl Jung (1875–1961) was, after Sigmund Freud, the most famous psychologist of the 20th century. Although, unlike Freud, his work never received mainstream intellectual acceptance, Jung's influence on popular consciousness has perhaps been greater and continues to this day. His contributions to our vocabulary include terms such as "complex," "archetype," "psychological type," "collective unconscious," "introvert," and "extrovert." But Jung's influence reaches beyond popular psychology. More than anyone else he is responsible for the widespread grassroots inner-directed spirituality that has characterized Western religious sensibilities since the 1960s. This is true in no small part because of Jung's interest in the occult. Yet throughout most of his career, Jung voiced an often confusing ambivalence toward the occult, insisting that he was not a mystic, nor an occultist, but a scientist. This desire to maintain scientific credibility while speaking of phenomena science regularly dismisses can account for some obscurities in Jung's style. Yet Jung's links to the occult were strong, and his public attitude toward the supernatural softened in 1944 after a near-death experience following a myocardial infarction. He found himself floating in space and was only brought back to earth by the spirit of his doctor, in his archetypal form, who convinced him that his work was not yet done. Jung's prediction that his doctor sacrificed his own life for Jung's was seemingly proven true when his doctor died from septicemia a few days after Jung awoke from his coma.

Carl Gustav Jung was born to a poor family in 1875 in the village of Kesswil, on the shore of Lake Constance in the Swiss canton of Thurgau. Jung's father was a Protestant clergyman riddled with religious doubts. There were clergymen on both sides of Jung's family, the most famous being Jung's maternal grandfather, Samuel Preiswerk, who believed in the reality of spirits. In her late teens, Jung's mother, Emilie, developed mediumistic powers, entering trances, speaking in tongues, and prophesizing. She was also a "split personality," a trait Jung developed at the age of twelve, when he became aware of another personality he called "the Other," a commanding, domineering figure of the 18th century, much unlike his shy adolescent self. Jung was also from an early age given to powerful dreams, waking visionary states, and a curiosity about the dead.

Jung's mother figured in two psychic episodes that were central to his development. Once while studying in his room, Jung heard a loud crack and discovered that the walnut dining table had split from side to center. Nothing could account for it, and when Jung thought, "There certainly are curious accidents" his mother read his thoughts and replied, "Yes, this means something." Another time Jung returned home to find his mother and sister upset. A loud report had come from the sideboard, and they couldn't understand it. Jung discovered that the bread knife had been broken into several neat pieces. A cutler told him that natural causes could not account for it; the knife would have to have been broken on purpose. Years later Jung sent a photograph of the broken knife to the psychic researcher J.B. Rhine.

Jung had a deep interest in spiritualism and took part in séances organized by his mother; these centered around his cousin, Helly Preiswerk. Helly spoke in different voices (including those of Samuel Preiswerk and Carl Jung Sr., Jung's paternal grandfather) and made accurate predictions. She also spoke in a more mature, developed voice named Ivenes, who called herself the "real" Helly, and who seemed buried beneath her less mature, undeveloped self, an early example of what Jung would later call "individuation." Jung based his dissertation, *On the Psychology and Pathology of So-Called Occult Phenomena* (1903), on these séances, yet failed to mention his own participation or that Helly, their focus, was his cousin and most likely in love with him, an early sign of his ambivalence toward the occult.

In 1900 Jung joined the faculty of the Burghölzli Mental Clinic in Zürich, where he devised word association tests and developed his notion of "complexes." He also discovered the work of Freud. From 1906, when they started corresponding, to 1912, when their friendship ended, Jung was a staunch supporter of Freud's work. Yet Jung rejected Freud's dismissal of psychic phenomena as superstition. While he was visiting Freud in 1909, they argued about this, and Jung felt a strange glowing sensation in his chest. When a sudden banging noise exploded in the room, he suggested it was psychically caused. Freud rejected this, and Jung said that another, similar noise would soon follow. Freud laughed, but when another report did sound in the room, he was shocked and suspected Jung of somehow causing it.

Jung's break with Freud sent him into a psychological and spiritual crisis, what he called his "descent into the unconscious." As recorded in his *Red Book* (2009) and *Memories, Dreams and Reflections* (1963), between 1913 and 1919 Jung was subject to visions, waking dreams, precognitive experiences, trance states, and several other strange phenomena, some of which involved the dead. Jung discovered that he shared his inner world with "other intelligences" that had a life of their own and nothing to do with him. He later said that all of his psychology of the archetypes and collective unconscious emerged from this time. It was also then that he developed his technique of "active imagination," a kind of conscious dialogue with the unconscious mind.

In the 1920s Jung began his researches into alchemy; more than anyone else, he is responsible for salvaging alchemy as a discipline worthy of serious study, and his writings on it include the difficult *Mysterium Coniunctionis* (1963), his last major work. He also began to experiment with the *I Ching*, the Chinese divination technique, although he did not openly speak of his interest in it until the late 1940s. Jung's interest in astrology became clear in his strange work *Aion* (1951), although, again, he had already been casting horoscopes for his patients for some time, and in 1952 he published, with the physicist Wolfgang Pauli, *Synchronicity: An Acausal Connecting Principle*, his study of "meaningful coincidences," Jung's most important contribution to parapsychology. More occult-informed works followed. In *Flying Saucers: A Modern Myth of Things Seen in The Sky* (1957), Jung presents the theory that UFOs are "mandalas from outer space," projections of psychic wholeness emitted by the collective unconscious to mitigate the schizoid global split during the early years of the Cold War. During his crisis of 1913 to 1919, the image of the mandala or Tibetan "magic circle" had come to Jung as a symbol of psychic integration, and in the post-War era it seemed to him that the planetary crisis of immanent nuclear war had prompted the collective mind to produce a similar result on a wider and collective scale. Another theme of the book was the idea of a coming astrological "Age of Aquarius," a notion that by the mid-1960s was central to the burgeoning counterculture movement with its occult and esoteric spiritual orientation. Jung was also responsible for the popular spread of Eastern wisdom, in the form of the introductions or commentaries he wrote for *The Tibetan Book of the Dead*, *The Secret of the Golden Flower*, and books on Zen and other Eastern traditions.

Jung died in 1961, just on the cusp of the modern occult revival that he had done much to bring about. His canonization by the counterculture took place in 1967 when the Beatles put his face on the cover of their album *Sgt. Pepper's Lonely Hearts Club Band*, along with that of the dark magician Aleister Crowley and several Hindu gurus. Today Jungian ideas are at the heart of much of the New Age (although Jung himself would have found the New Age rather naïve), and they inform a wide variety of developments in psychology, literature, the arts, and spirituality.

Gary Lachman

See also: Alchemy; Astrology; Divination; Exorcism; Imaginal; New Age; Occultism; Spiritualism; Synchronicity; UFO; Unconscious Mind

Further Reading
Jung, Carl Gustav. (1963) 1989. *Memories Dreams Reflections*. London: Vintage Press.
Jung, Carl. 2009. *The Red Book*. London: W.W. Norton & Co.
Lachman, Gary. 2010. *Jung the Mystic: The Esoteric Dimensions of Carl Jung's Life and Teachings*. New York: Tarcher/Penguin.

K

KEEL, JOHN A.

John Alva Keel, born Alva John Kiehle (March 25, 1930–July 3, 2009), was an American journalist, humorist, and paranormal investigator. In addition to numerous articles and screenplays, he produced several widely read books on the paranormal. Keel is most famous for his work *The Mothman Prophecies* (1975), which describes his investigation of paranormal events in Point Pleasant, West Virginia, from 1966–1967. He popularized the concept of "Men in Black," whom he claimed shadowed some his investigations. He was also an early proponent of the theory of a unified phenomenon behind all paranormal encounters, which witnesses variously experience as UFOs, monsters, ghosts, angels, or other entities. Keel described these entities as "ultra-terrestrials," suggesting that they came from another dimension that he sometimes referred to as "the super-spectrum." He hypothesized that the ultra-terrestrials are tricksters who manipulate humankind and appear in different forms depending on what their human audience expects to see. Keel theorized that ultra-terrestrials could induce hallucinations in people or even manifest temporarily as material entities that could interact with the world before dissolving. His theory explained the apparent connections between such topics as fairy lore and modern reports of UFOs. It also explained phenomena such as Bigfoot, which produces eyewitnesses but leaves no material evidence.

Keel was born in Hornell, New York. He was raised by his grandparents after his parents separated. He was interested in stage magic from an early age and published his first story in a magician's magazine at age 12. He was also interested in the writings of Charles Fort and *Amazing Stories*. At 14, he became a columnist for the local paper and produced several columns on reports of strange phenomena.

At 16 he left school, having lost interest after completing all of the science courses, and pursued a career as a writer. At 17 he moved to New York City, where he initially had to sleep on park benches for lack of money. Keel eventually found work writing newspaper articles and scripts for local radio and television outlets. He was drafted into the army during the Korean War and served in Frankfurt, Germany, on the staff of the American Forces' Network. After leaving the military he worked as a foreign radio correspondent in Paris, Berlin, Rome, and Egypt. At 24, he resigned and spent his savings on a four-year journey through the Middle East and Southeast Asia. This resulted in his travel memoir *Jadoo* (1957), which describes his investigations into stories of magic and the Himalayan Yeti. He promoted the book by performing with cobras in the window of the Midtown Aquarium at Times Square.

Following *Jadoo*, Keel edited the magazine *Echo* and worked as the science and geography editor for Funk and Wagnall's encyclopedias. In the 1960s he joined the Screenwriters Guild and produced numerous television scripts. He also wrote his novel *The Fickle Finger of Fate* (1966), a parody of the spy novel genre. *Playboy* commissioned him to write an article on UFOs in 1966. Although the piece Keel wrote was ultimately rejected, this began his career of travelling the country to speak with UFO witnesses.

He began contributing articles to *Flying Saucer Review* and started his own newsletter *Anomaly*. In 1966, he made repeated visits to Point Pleasant, West Virginia, to investigate sightings of UFOs and a winged humanoid dubbed "the Mothman." During this research he experienced strange phone calls, and witnesses described threatening encounters with mysterious men in black. It has been theorized that at least some of these phone calls were pranks played by Gray Barker and other UFOlogists. However, Keel concluded that investigating the paranormal draws unwanted attention from sinister and paranormal forces. In 1967, Keel popularized the term "Men in Black" in an article for the men's adventure magazine *Saga*, entitled "UFO Agents of Terror."

His third book *UFOs: Operation Trojan Horse*, introduced the concept of ultraterrestrials. Keel abandoned his hypothesis that UFOs are extraterrestrial visitors and instead declared that UFOlogy should be considered a branch of psychical research. He hypothesized a larger phenomenon in which seemingly intelligent forces sought to communicate with and possibly manipulate humankind. This hypothesis caused him to become interested in religious phenomena, particularly the "Miracle of the Sun" reported in Fatima, Portugal, in 1914. He hypothesized that when these forces attempt to communicate with a single person, the entire community may experience collateral encounters with the paranormal, resulting in "flaps" like the phenomena he encountered in Point Pleasant. Keel's ideas about the nature and motivations of ultraterrestirals were expanded in *Our Haunted Planet* (1971), *The Eighth Tower* (1975), and *Disneyland of the Gods* (1988).

Keel made several friends in Point Pleasant, including reporter Mary Hyre. He also maintained an ongoing correspondence with Linda Scarberry, one of the first four witnesses to report seeing the Mothman. On December 15, 1967, Point Pleasant's Silver Bridge collapsed, killing 46 people. Keel discussed his investigation of the sightings and the collapse in *The Mothman Prophecies* (1975). This work was adapted into a 2002 film of the same name starring Richard Gere.

Keel remained a bachelor and lived for many years in the Upper West Side of New York City. In the 1980s, he attempted several plays and novels, none of which were published. However, he revived the New York Fortean Society and wrote a regular column for *Fate* magazine called "Beyond the Known." In his later years, he suffered from diabetes and its complications. He also had cataracts, and the resultant eye surgery made writing difficult.

Keel's ideas influenced a number of contemporary writers on the paranormal, including Loren Coleman, Jerome Clark, Rosemary Ellen Guiley, and Jacques Vallée.

Joseph Laycock

See also: *Fate* Magazine; Fortean Phenomena; UFO; Vallée, Jacques

Further Reading

Keel, John A. 2013. *The Mothman Prophecies*. New York: Tor.

Sherwood, John C. 2002. "Gray Barker's Book of Bunk: Mothman, Saucers, and MIB." *The Skeptical Inquirer* 26 (3). Accessed March 28, 2014. http://www.csicop.org/si/show/gray_barkers_book_of_bunk_mothman_saucers_and_mib.

Skinner, Doug. "John Keel: Not an Authority on Anything." Accessed March 27, 2014. http://www.johnkeel.com.

KIRLIAN PHOTOGRAPHY

The Kirlian process is a cameraless photographic technique used to capture electrical discharges. It applies a high voltage, high frequency electrical current across a grounded object in order to record electrical patterns onto photographic material. Although this method became popularly known as Kirlian in the 1970s, it has been in existence since the 1880s and has been referred to by a variety of names including the Electrograph, Electronograph, and Effluviograph. Its emergence occurred in an era of faith in technology's ability to conquer the invisible. Disembodied communication was happening with the telegraph, telephone, and phonograph, the power of radiation was revealed, germ theory was discovered, and the X-ray first appeared at this time. Kirlian photographic experimentation preceded the discovery of the X-ray, so its revelation of the body's interior inspired confidence in the potential of the Kirlian electrical process. Simultaneously, there was also a fear and curiosity about electricity, especially in relation to the human body. Electricity's power to seemingly stir dead tissue to life through Galvanism suggested its ability to release mysterious life forces.

From roughly 1880–1898, the Kirlian process was used in attempts to prove the existence of a universal life force, to diagnose disease, and to make psychological states visible. Experimenters such as Hippolyte Baraduc and Jacob von Narkiewicz-Jodko were getting results they interpreted as effective, and they assigned scientific conclusions to the electrical patterns they recorded. Photography itself was relatively new at the time, and these experiments were soon debunked as results caused by the chemical processes of photography. Scientists such as Adrien Guebhard and Emil Jacobsen claimed these patterns were made simply by photographic reactions to heat or moisture, not disease, mesmeric fluid, or feelings

ca. 1880–1898	Prior to being named as such, the Kirlian photographic process is used in attempts to prove the existence of a universal life force, to diagnose disease, and to make psychological states visible. It is rejected by mainstream science.
1939	The process reappears in 1939 when Russian scientists Semyon and Valentina Kirlian, inspired by the work of Nikola Tesla, unknowingly rename and reinvent it.
1958	The Kirlians publicize their results for the first time. The popularity of Kirlian photography spreads through Eastern Europe.
1970	Kirlian photography in first recognized in the United States with the publication of *Psychic Discoveries behind the Iron Curtain*.
ca. 1971	Dr. Thelma Moss begins experimenting with Kirlian photography in the parapsychology lab at UCLA's Neuropsychiatric Institute.
1975	The International Kirlian Research Association is founded in New York City.
1976	Thelma Moss appears on *The Dinah Shore Show* to talk about Kirlian photography.
1979	Dr. Moss's funding at UCLA is pulled after her work is attacked by other scientists.

emerging from the body. One of Jacobsen's debunkings demonstrated that the Kirlian process could just as easily illustrate the "antipathy" between two sausages purchased from rival butchers, suggesting that the revelation of a life force through the Kirlian process was false. The technique was soon abandoned by science and forgotten.

The Kirlian process reappeared in 1939 when Russian scientists Semyon and Valentina Kirlian, inspired by the work of Nikola Tesla, unknowingly renamed and reinvented the process. They publicized their results for the first time in 1958, and the method spread through Eastern Europe. It became most popular in Romania, where the government dedicated a multi-million-dollar program to Kirlian research. These Romanian investigations focused on using X-ray material in combination with the Kirlian process in order to make Chinese acupuncture points visible for medical diagnosis.

Kirlian photography was first recognized in the United States with the publication of *Psychic Discoveries behind the Iron Curtain* (1970) by researchers Sheila

Ostrander and Lynn Schroeder. Popular interest created by this book led to the formation of the International Kirlian Research Association in New York City in 1975. The Kirlian experiments described in *Psychic Discoveries behind the Iron Curtain* also piqued the interest of Dr. Thelma Moss at the University of California, Los Angeles (UCLA). Moss had experienced successful electric shock treatment for debilitating depression and became curious about electricity in relation to the body after her doctors could not explain exactly how or why electric shock therapy worked. As a professor at the Neuropsychiatric Institute at UCLA, she built a lab and began Kirlian research in the early 1970s. Her experimentation was wide-ranging and imaginative. She used Kirlian photography to compare the paw of a cat with and without acupuncture needles, and she experimented with dead hands, broken limbs, and rats with sliced tails. Moss also worked with psychics and sensitives, including the faith healer Olga Worrall and the illusionist Uri Geller. Interested in the effects of certain substances on the body, Moss conducted experiments with people who were under the influence of coffee, cigarettes, and alcohol. She gave David Bowie his own Kirlian device to use at the height of his cocaine addiction. They appeared together on the *Dinah Shore Show* in 1976.

Moss also used the Kirlian process in attempts to document interpersonal relationships, eye contact, and emotional states. Years into her research, Thelma Moss was surprised to discover that she was replicating work already done in the late 19th century when one of her critics within the parapsychology community sent her the work of Baraduc and Narkiewicz-Jodko. History fully repeated itself when other scientists debunked her work, arriving at the same conclusions as Adrien Guebhard and Emil Jacobsen. Her funding at UCLA was pulled in 1979. Thelma Moss always defended her work as not the result of heat, moisture, or other artifacts of the photographic process. She believed there *was* something profound about the energy field produced by the Kirlian process.

The "phantom leaf effect," where the Kirlian corona traces the full outline of a healthy leaf from one that has been cut, is considered the ultimate proof of Kirlian's efficacy. Although there are striking visual examples of this phenomena by Guy Lyon Playfair and H. G. Andrade, it is considered to be unsubstantiated as it has not been repeated under controlled conditions by other experimenters. The mystery of the Kirlian process remains.

Shannon Taggart

See also: Aura; Spirit Photography; Thoughtography

Further Reading

Iovine, John. 1993. *Kirlian Photography: A Hands-on Guide*. New York: McGraw Hill.
Ostrander, Sheila, and Lynn Shroeder. 1977. *Psychic Discoveries behind the Iron Curtain*. London: Abacus.

KOESTLER PARAPSYCHOLOGY UNIT

The Koestler Parapsychology Unit is one of the few endowed parapsychological research centers worldwide. It is a research group within the Department of Psychology at the University of Edinburgh in Scotland that is supported by a bequest from the author and journalist Arthur Koestler.

The Koestler bequest began amid some controversy when the terminally ill Arthur and his healthy wife Cynthia died in a suicide pact in 1983. Koestler had a long-standing interest in the paranormal, and his will provided support to establish a chair in parapsychology at a British university. The bequest came to Edinburgh principally because a member of the University's Psychology Department named Dr. John Beloff was already conducting parapsychological research there. Beloff had joined Edinburgh University in 1962 and for many years supervised undergraduate and postgraduate students on parapsychological research projects. The university therefore was accustomed to the idea that parapsychology could be studied in a careful and rigorously scientific fashion under its auspices. Beloff was an executor for Koestler, and he played an important role in the selection panel that appointed Robert Morris as the first Koestler Chair of Parapsychology. An American who had worked in J. B. Rhine's parapsychology laboratory at Duke University in North Carolina, Morris took up the Koestler Chair in December 1985. He was chosen, in part, because of his balanced approach to parapsychological research.

Morris's attitude aligned well with the definition of parapsychology that the University adopted to set the Koestler Chair's remit: "the scientific study of paranormal phenomena, in particular, the capacity *attributed to* some individuals to interact with their environment by means other than the recognised sensory or motor channels." Importantly, the italicized text indicates that it is not assumed that paranormal abilities or phenomena really exist. Rather, the question concerns what lies behind people's attributions of paranormality. Seemingly paranormal experiences may sometimes be due to normal psychological or physical factors, whereas "psi" is the term that parapsychologists use to denote a postulated paranormal process. In order to test the psi hypothesis, Morris argued, one also has to be well acquainted with how psychic effects might be simulated or artifactually produced.

Over almost two decades, Morris supervised students and collaborated with researchers from a wide variety of backgrounds, including some like Richard Wiseman, who had expertise in conjuring and who studied the psychology of deception; others like Charles Honorton, who had experience in laboratory psi research; and some like the present author, who had a training in psychology or related disciplines such as philosophy and social history. This small group became known as the Koestler Parapsychology Unit (KPU). Beloff retired just before Morris took up the Koestler Chair, but continued his association with parapsychology and the KPU until his death in 2006.

Probably the defining feature of the KPU's work was—and is—that it takes a broad definition of parapsychology, studying pseudo-psi and the psychology of paranormal experiences as well as conducting psi research. Furthermore, it regards parapsychology as an interdisciplinary problem area. Under Morris's supervision, many students obtained psychology PhDs specializing in parapsychological topics. They went on to obtain lectureships at other universities, so an important function of the KPU has been developing the skills of new researchers and seeding these well trained scholars out into other universities.

After Morris's death in 2004, Edinburgh University used the Koestler bequest to appoint two permanent lecturers who conduct and publish parapsychological research, teach undergraduate psychology students, supervise PhD students, and provide public information about parapsychology through books, talks, websites, and an open access online course. Parapsychologists have always been particularly aware of methodological issues, and one of the KPU's recent endeavors is the first registry for parapsychological research studies. Through its trial registry, the Koestler Parapsychology Unit continues the tradition of methodological excellence in parapsychology established by John Beloff and Robert Morris.

Caroline Watt

See also: Anomalistic Psychology; Parapsychology; Princeton Engineering Anomalies Research; Pseudoscience; Psi; Rhine Research Center; Stanford Research Institute

Further Reading

An Introduction to Parapsychology. Online course taught by Caroline Watt. 2014. http://www.koestler-parapsychology.psy.ed.ac.uk/teachingDistanceLearning.html (accessed October 10, 2014).

Irwin, Harvey. 2013. *Education in Parapsychology: Student and Instructor Perspectives*. Monograph No. 2 in the AIPR Monograph Series in Parapsychology. Edited by Dr. Lance Storm and Dr. Adam J. Rock. Gladesville: Australian Institute of Parapsychological Research Incorporated.

Koestler Parapsychology Unit (official website). 2014. http://www.koestler-parapsychology.psy.ed.ac.uk (accessed October 10, 2014).

KPU Registry for Parapsychological Experiments. 2014. http://www.koestler-parapsychology.psy.ed.ac.uk/TrialRegistry.html (accessed October 10, 2014).

KRIPPNER, STANLEY

Stanley Krippner (b. 1932) is an American psychologist and parapsychologist who has made contributions on topics as diverse as learning disabilities, human sexuality, post-traumatic stress disorder, and dream telepathy. Much of his work has centered on altered states of consciousness, especially dreaming, dissociation, hypnosis, hallucinogens, mediumistic trance, and shamanic healing. Since 1972 he has been associated with Saybrook University in San Francisco. He has been

Alan Watts Professor of Psychology in the College of Psychology and Humanistic Studies there since 1991.

Krippner was born in Edgerton, Wisconsin, on October 4, 1932. He graduated from the University of Wisconsin in Madison with a major in speech education in 1954 and spent the next two years working as a speech therapist for public school systems in Warren, Illinois, and Richmond, Virginia. He received an MA in counseling and guidance from Northwestern University in 1957 and a PhD in educational psychology from the same institution in 1961. From 1961 to 1963 he served as Director of the Kent State University Child Study Center in Kent, Ohio, and from 1964 to 1973, as Director of the Maimonides Medical Center's Dream Research Laboratory in Brooklyn, New York. In this last capacity, he helped to design a highly successful and influential series of experiments on the telepathic reception of images in dreams. These experiments are reported in one of his best-known books, *Dream Telepathy*, coauthored with psychiatrist Montague Ullman and psychic Alan Vaughn. They inspired what has turned out to be one of the most productive experimental paradigms in parapsychology, the ganzfeld sensory-restriction technique.

Krippner's interest in paranormal events was piqued as a teenager when he became aware that an uncle had died moments before his family received a telephone call with the news. His time in Richmond gave him the opportunity to visit J. B. Rhine at Duke University in Durham, North Carolina, and this led to his first field investigation, of alleged poltergeist disturbances in the home of an elderly couple who were being cared for by their grandson. Krippner and fellow graduate student Arthur Hastings determined that the grandson had been responsible for the flying and falling objects, motivated by a desire to scare his grandparents out of the house so that he could resume his playboy lifestyle. During these early years, Krippner also investigated the famous talking horse Lady and noticed that she responded with certain letters when whipped in certain places, suggesting that she had been well conditioned. In subsequent years, he has traveled widely, studying shamans and other psychic practitioners on six continents. His most extensive overseas work has been in Brazil, where he has observed psychic healing, apports, stigmata, and mediumistic painting, among other phenomena. In 2002 he published the first article on shamanism to appear in *The American Psychologist*, the flagship journal of the American Psychological Association (APA). He pointed out that shamans perform many psychological and medical functions in their communities and argued that these are deserving of scientific scrutiny.

Krippner's work has helped to bridge psychology, parapsychology, and anthropology, and to promote cross-cultural understanding in these fields. He is the coeditor of *Varieties of Anomalous Experience*, a bestselling volume from the APA, now in its second edition, and of *Debating Psychic Experience: Human Potential or Human Illusion?* The latter book, published in 2010, pitted parapsychologists against their critics. It proved so successful that its debate was repeated in person at the APA annual meetings the following year. In all, Krippner has authored or coauthored, edited or coedited, over 40 books and many hundred research papers or book chapters. He has lectured and presented papers in many national and international venues. He served or now serves on a great variety of institutional boards, from the Association for Humanistic Psychology to the Parapsychological Association, and has received numerous awards, including the Award for Distinguished Contributions to the International Advancement of Psychology from the APA and the Outstanding Career Award from the Parapsychological Association.

James G. Matlock

See also: Ganzfeld Technique, The; Healing, Psychic and Spiritual; Paranormal Dreams; Parapsychology; Poltergeist; Shamanism

Further Reading

Krippner, Stanley. 2013. "My Parapsychological Odyssey." In *Men and Women of Parapsychology, Personal Reflections*, ESPRIT vol. 2, edited by Rosemary Pilkington, 200–224. San Antonio, TX: Anomalist Books.

Ullman, Montague, Stanley Krippner, and Alan Vaughan. 2003. *Dream Telepathy: Experiments in Nocturnal Extrasensory Perception*. 3rd ed. Charlottesville, VA: Hampton Roads Publishing Company.

LILY DALE ASSEMBLY

Lily Dale Assembly is a Spiritualist community and hamlet located within the town of Pomfret, New York. Established in 1879, it has operated continuously as a Spiritualist summer camp since that time. Today, "the Dale" also houses the main headquarters of the National Spiritualist Association of Churches (NSAC), the oldest, continuously running denomination of American Spiritualism, founded in 1893. Each year, an estimated 25,000 visitors come to the camp to immerse themselves in explorations of mediumship, or communication with the dead. They also come to study the metaphysics of Spiritualism, which conceives of divinity as an Infinite Intelligence giving rise to all natural and spiritual phenomena.

Spiritualist camps like Lily Dale proliferated throughout the United States in the decades following the Civil War. Originating in Upstate New York in the 1840s, Spiritualism had earlier spread throughout America and Europe as a spontaneous movement focused on attempts to contact the dead. In the pre-Civil-War era, mediumship was most commonly practiced in home séances or performed in the lyceum circuit by trance speakers delivering messages from the spirits on politically progressive issues. Beginning in the Victorian era, Spiritualists became increasingly interested in "physical mediumship," demonstrations of such visual phenomena as spirit photography and full-body apparitions of the dead. As exposés of fraudulent physical mediums came to tarnish the reputation of Spiritualism, camps emerged as private centers where Americans could come to judge for themselves the veracity of its phenomena.

The idea for Lily Dale began as a directive from the spirit world. In 1877, Jeremiah Carter, a self-identified Free Thinker and a native of Laona, New York, was told by spirits to build a camp on a tract of land along Lake Cassadaga. The camp opened in 1881, and by 1900, thanks to the donations of wealthy patrons, it had swelled to a permanent settlement. In 1906, the camp named itself the "Lily Dale Assembly." Throughout the 19th century, the camp continued earlier forms of Spiritualism, inviting both trance mediums and progressive leaders—including Susan B. Anthony and Elizabeth Cady Stanton—to speak. It also offered various kinds of physical mediumship—most famously its "precipitated spirit paintings," allegedly created by the deceased—but discontinued all of them in the 1940s.

The constant feature of the Dale has always been its public message services, which are offered several times a day and free of charge. Some of these are performed today as part of formal worship services in various on-site churches representing both NSAC and other Spiritualist denominations. Others are held in

1877	Jeremiah Carter of Laona, New York, is purportedly told by spirits to build a camp on a tract of land along Lake Cassadaga.
1879	Members of the Spiritualist church in Laona buy the land and found the Cassadaga Lake Free Association.
1906	The camp renames itself Lily Dale Assembly.
2000–2015	A growing popular interest in mediumship brings renewed public interest in Lily Dale Assembly, now one of the last surviving Spiritualist camps in America.

outdoor venues, where observers are free to determine the meaning of mediumship on their own terms. Since the 1980s, many mediums have blended elements of New Age spirituality with the traditional teachings of Spiritualism, and today both self-identified Spiritualists and metaphysical seekers are among the camp's regular guests. One of the last remaining Spiritualist camps in America, Lily Dale Assembly has recently begun attracting public interest once again, as popular interest in mediumship has risen in 21st-century America.

Darryl V. Caterine

See also: Mediumship; New Age; Spiritualism

Further Reading

Caterine, Darryl. 2011. *Haunted Ground: Journeys through a Paranormal America.* Santa Barbara, CA: ABC-CLIO/Praeger Press.

Lily Dale Assembly. 2014. http://www.lilydaleassembly.com.

Wicker, Christine. 2003. *Lily Dale: The True Story of the Town that Talks to the Dead.* New York: HarperCollins.

LUCID DREAMS

A lucid dream is an exceptional dream experience, broadly defined as knowing that one is dreaming within the dream. It is considered a rare phenomenon, regularly experienced only by a small minority of people. However, surveys have indicated as many as 56 percent of people have reported experiencing a lucid dream at least once during their lifetime. Disagreement exists over how best to define a lucid dream, as some lucid dreamers report considerable control over the dream environment and therefore advocate possessing this control, alongside complete access to waking memories and full cognitive faculties, to be the criteria necessary to determine a dream as lucid. Alternatively, many leading scholars advocate a simpler definition in which lucid dreaming exists on a continuum where only awareness of one's state is fundamental, with other characteristics recognized as additional aspects of lucidity but not deemed required for a dream to be determined lucid.

Despite being the topic of sustained Western research for over 40 years, knowledge of the experience itself is considerably older. The first written mention of lucid dreams appears in 1000 BCE within the Upanishads, a collection of Vedic texts. In the ancient East lucid dreaming had a strong association with religious practice, especially within the Buddhist Yogic traditions, which utilized it as tool for helping achieve enlightenment. Lucid dreaming is further mentioned in 400 BCE within the Yoga sutras of Patanjali, highlighting lucidity as a central element of the Tibetan dream yogic tradition.

In the West it wasn't until many centuries later that an interest in exploring lucid dreaming developed. The Marquis d'Hervey de Saint-Denys published *Dreams and the Ways to Direct Them: Practical Observations* in 1867. Within its pages Saint-Denys systematically documented over 20 years of his own lucid dreams in which he conducted countless experiments. Saint-Denys describes how he developed his ability to lucid dream, making him the first Westerner to demonstrate it as a learnable skill and to use the term lucid dream or *rêve lucide* to describe the experience's visual sharpness. This term was later refined by Society for Psychical Research (SPR) member Frederik Van Eeden in the society's 1913 proceedings to describe the entire experience.

Decades later, in 1968, English SPR member Celia Green published her influential work on lucid dreams, which placed them in a model of human experience alongside out-of-the-body experiences, false-awakenings, and apparitional experiences. Initially, mainstream psychology was not affected by Green's work; the dominant explanation of lucid dreaming viewed them as the result of "micro-awakenings," brief periods of arousal during the night. This explanation was rejected by researchers inspired by Green's work. Keith Hearne in 1978 and Stephen LaBerge in 1981 used the knowledge that during dreaming atony occurs to the body, paralyzing the muscles, during which only the eyes can move freely. Thus, asking a lucid dreamer to send predetermined eye signals when they had become lucid within their dream was attempted. These signals were successfully picked up in the sleep lab by an electrooculogram (eye sensor) and thus the existence of lucid dreams was conclusively proven.

Evidence suggests that more people than ever before are now aware of lucid dreaming. The success of movies such as *Inception* and the development of lucid dreaming-related iPhone apps and induction gadgets such as the Remee demonstrate that people are interested in the experience. Current research into lucid dreaming is becoming one of the busiest areas of scientific dream inquiry, and it tackles three main questions: what causes lucid dreams' occurrence? How can lucid dreams best be induced? And what are the benefits of experiencing them? Researchers have recently induced lucid dreams by applying a tiny 40Hz electrical current to the frontal lobe of dreamers, kick-starting the area of the brain believed responsible for higher-order consciousness. Lucid dreaming has also been linked to frequently playing video games, with a positive correlation between hours played and frequency of lucidity. It has been practically applied to help cure nightmare sufferers by helping them face and overcome their nightly fears, and research investigating the use of lucid dreaming to improve people's waking motor-skills for sports and dance is ongoing.

David Saunders

See also: Hypnagogic State; Meditation; Out-of-Body Experience (OBE); Paranormal Dreams; Sleep Paralysis; Society for Psychical Research

Further Reading

LaBerge, Stephen, and Howard Rheingold. 1990. *Exploring the World of Lucid Dreaming.* New York: Ballantine Books.
Waggoner, Robert. 2008. *Lucid Dreaming: Gateway to the Inner Self.* Needham, MA: Moment Point Press.

M

MEDITATION

The majority of religious traditions contain practices that could rightly fall under the rubric of meditation. In addition to their more practical applications in cultivating a particular mode of ethical behavior or generating and maintaining a particular philosophical worldview, meditation practices are also practical methods for eliciting the experience of altered states of consciousness, a mystical perception of or union with the divine, realization of the nature of reality, and the ability both to bend the natural elements to one's will and to transcend the limitations of physical embodiment altogether. Meditation is a tool that can be applied toward the attainment of a diverse spectrum of goals. It is thus much better to speak of various styles of meditation, each reflecting various practices and goals, than to combine all of these together into a single thing called "meditation." Here, those aspects of meditation that result in the attainment of altered or enhanced states of consciousness, mystical revelations, and the attainment of gnostic states will take precedent.

Prayer, often either a verbal or internal recitation or contemplation of a particular liturgy or a silent contemplation directed toward interaction with some supernatural being, is the most fundamental, accessible, and universal form of meditation. Most forms of prayer assume the individual's ability to communicate with a power beyond the physical senses, the physical body, and the physical world, that is able both to interact with and to intervene on behalf of the subject. Prayer belongs to the first type of meditation examined here, best categorized as "cataphatic," or a meditation technique that employs positive terminology in its description of the absolute, usually a supernatural deity identified with a transcendent or ultimate reality, as well as in its description of the relationship between the supernatural and the natural world. This style of meditation affirms the power of language and conceptual thought to express a divine or ultimate truth. It often relies upon the recitation of entire texts or shortened liturgies and the visualization of various deities designed to bring about a mystical revelation of a divine being or a direct realization of the gnostic fabric of reality itself. Prayer, in nearly all of its forms, can be characterized as a kind of meditation that the subject directs at some manner of supernatural being or principle toward a wide variety of ends, ranging from the mundane to the transcendent.

The second general type meditation practice consists of meditation techniques that employ a language of negation to the mind's cognitive and sensual experience that elicits some form of mystical revelation or transcendent realization. Perhaps one of the best examples of this approach to meditation practice in Christian traditions is found in the medieval work *The Cloud of Unknowing*, in which the contemplative experience leads to a state beyond thought in which one is no longer bound by the conventions of time, space, and the physical body. This category of meditation is generally referred to as "apophatic" and is characterized by the employment of a meditation technique that primarily relies upon a language of negation.

Many meditation traditions employ a combination of these two approaches. For example, in Hindu devotional traditions, the meditation practitioner may employ visualizations, mantras, and offerings, in which the expression of devotion clearly takes place between a subject and some form of transcendent deity. A single meditation tradition may initially employ a technique that focuses on a deity that is "endowed with characteristics" (*saguṇa*), meaning it has a host of physical attributes that may appear to the senses, yet ultimately be directed toward the realization of a deity that, in its universal aspect, is considered to "lack all characteristics" (*nirguṇa*) and thus be beyond the realm of conceptual thought and the senses. In the meditation tradition of the *Yogasūtras* (second century BCE), this process is reversed. Here the practitioner first withdraws the mind from contact with the external sense faculties, external objects, and conceptual thought, yet ultimately attains the power of "yogic-direct perception" (*yogapratyakṣa*), which, when directed outward, is able to perceive the entire cosmos accurately and directly.

Buddhism is perhaps the tradition that is most often directly associated with meditation. Meditation constitutes one of the most important aspects of this tradition, as is evident in the integral role that meditation plays in the story of the Buddha's enlightenment. It is safe to say that without meditation, there would be no Buddhism. The meditative techniques found throughout the Buddhist world are extremely diverse. *The Path of Purification* (*Visuddhimagga*), an encyclopedic work compiled in the fifth century CE by the Buddhist scholar Buddhaghoṣa, lists forty different objects of meditation. The object of one's meditation often determines the kind of realization or supernatural ability one is able to attain. For instance, through practicing a meditation on the earth element, one gains mastery over this element. As a result, the meditation practitioner is said to gain the ability to superimpose the obstructing, solid characteristics of the earth element onto other elements, allowing him to, for example, walk across a body of water. Advanced Buddhist and Hindu meditation practitioners are also said to leave hand and footprints in the solid rock surrounding their meditation caves as signs of their high level of realization. In both cases, it is clear that meditation is believed to be one way in which an individual gains mastery over the physical elements, resulting in a number of supernatural powers that are most often understood as signs that the practitioner is advancing in his practice.

Buddhist meditation techniques often fall under two general headings: those that calm the mind and allow for increased concentration and attention (*śamatha*), and those that apply some mode of analysis to a given object of meditation, producing a greater awareness of the nature of reality (*vipaśyanā*). Whereas calming

Although meditation is commonly viewed by many people today as a means of achieving relaxation, peace of mind, and increased physical health, throughout history it has been associated with religious concerns and mystical states of consciousness and has often been accompanied by reported paranormal phenomena. People have meditated to receive knowledge from spiritual sources, achieve supernatural powers, and transcend the normal limitations of material reality.

meditation allows the meditator to attain profound levels of concentration, analytical awareness meditation allows the meditator to apply that profound level of concentration to an object of analysis in order to reveal its true nature. Both practices are directly associated with the experience of altered states of consciousness in the practitioner and the arising of intense bliss.

Meditation constitutes one of the five paths in the Mahāyāna Buddhist tradition, or the Buddhism of the "Great Vehicle." In this system, a meditation practitioner who has already attained insight into the nature of reality traverses the path of meditation through integrating this insight with his experience of the phenomenal world. As the practitioner passes through each of ten stages on the path of meditation, he is able to emanate more and more bodies throughout multiple universes, gaining a greater understanding of the nature of reality with each increased level of emanation, and actualizing the goal of a bodhisattva, or one whose actions in the world are directed toward abating the suffering of all living beings and leading them to awakening. In the Tibetan Buddhist tradition, meditators who reach these levels in their practice are believed to gain the ability to choose their own rebirth and continually return in human form in order to be of benefit to human beings. Here, meditation not only leads to mastery over the physical elements and a transcendence of the limitations of the physical body in this lifetime, it results in mastery over death itself.

Traditionally, meditation practices are oriented toward experiences such as the attainment of mystical union with a divine being or omniscient understanding of some gnostic principle, the cultivation of supernatural powers, the experience of altered states of consciousness, and the transcendence of physical limitations of both the internal world of the body and external world of the elements. The presentation of meditation in the modern scientific community and the popular media represents a dramatic divergence from this traditional understanding and application of meditation. The meditation practices currently receiving the most media attention are generally those developed and promoted by the Transcendental Meditation (TM) and Mindfulness Based Stress Reduction (MBSR) movements. These movements limit their meditation instruction to a few practice techniques and largely ignore the traditional association of these techniques with paranormal experiences.

Both the scientific study and popular practice of the meditation techniques that have come to dominate popular media in the late 20th and early 21st centuries represent a process of reimagining meditation within a specifically modern context. The reimagination of meditation in the modern world reflects a set of contemporary beliefs regarding the power of the mind that has largely rejected the traditional association between meditation and the experience of paranormal phenomena.

Adam Krug

See also: Mystical Experience; Reincarnation; Religion and the Paranormal; Siddhis

Further Reading

Conze, Edward. 1956. *Buddhist Meditation*. London: George Allen and Unwin LTD.
Merton, Thomas. 1969. *Contemplative Prayer*. New York: Random House.
Underhill, Evelyn, ed. 1922. *The Cloud of Unknowing*. 2nd ed. London: John M. Watkins.
Wallace, B. Alan. 1999. *The Four Immeasurables: Cultivating a Boundless Heart*. Edited by Zara Houshmand. Ithaca, NY: Snow Lion Publications.

MEDIUMSHIP

Broadly speaking the term "mediumship" refers to the belief that certain individuals are able to interact with spiritual entities and to mediate between the world of spirits and the world of the living. According to anthropologist Erika Bourguignon, belief in some form of spirit mediumship is near-universal, occurring, in one form or another in approximately 77 percent of human societies. There is, therefore, a wide spectrum of different cultural variations of mediumship practices from the relatively tame clairvoyant mediumship of Euro-American Spiritualist platform mediums, to extremes of self-mortification in traditional Taiwanese spirit mediumship, and to elaborate theatricality in South Indian Theyyam performances. Despite differences in the cultural expression of mediumship, however, there remain key underlying core similarities, chief among which is the near-ubiquitous use of some form of altered state of consciousness, ranging from light trances to deep dissociative states, during which the spirit communication takes place.

In the Euro-American Spiritualist tradition, mediums most frequently claim to communicate with the spirits of deceased human beings, but in other cultures and subcultures nature spirits, deities, or even extraterrestrials are just as likely to be invoked. In Candomblé, an Afro-Brazilian mediumship tradition, for example, mediums incorporate deities known as *Orixas*, a pantheon of gods originally worshipped by the Yoruba in Africa. Each *Orixa* is recognized during the mediumistic performance by distinctive rhythms, gestures, and dances. The South Indian Nayaka incorporate nature spirits known as *devaru* during mediumship performances. The *evaru* may be spirits of animals, stones, rocks, rivers, or hills, among others.

Western New Age channelers often claim to incorporate interdimensional extraterrestrial intelligences.

In Euro-American Spiritualism, mediumship is often split into two categories: "mental mediumship" and "physical mediumship." Mental mediumship, by far the most popular form of mediumship in contemporary Spiritualism, usually involves clairvoyant, clairaudient, or clairsentient modes of communication with spirits, who generally communicate using personally significant symbolic images. Mental mediumship also includes automatic writing, a practice whereby spirits apparently assume control of the medium's hand in order to communicate through the written word. The Brazilian Spiritist medium Chico Xavier (1910–2002), for example, wrote over four hundred books ostensibly under the influence of discarnate spirits. Deceased painters and musicians have also ostensibly produced new works of art through the bodies of entranced mediums.

Physical mediumship, on the other hand, involves the manifestation of physical phenomena to demonstrate the presence of spirits. Such manifestations may include bangs, knocks, cold drafts, movement, levitation and dematerialization of objects, and the production of ectoplasmic materializations. The mediumship of the Fox sisters in 1848, which initiated the Spiritualist movement, was a form of physical mediumship involving communication with spirits through physical raps and knocks.

Trance mediumship involves the voluntary incorporation of spirits, who take over the body of the medium for the duration of the medium's trance state. Trance mediumship séances usually involve communications with a regular group of distinctive spirit personalities, often referred to as a "spirit team." Trance mediums will usually work with a "control spirit" or "gatekeeper," a discarnate entity whose role is to assist other spirit personalities to communicate through the medium, and to help the medium in and out of his or her trance state. The control spirit is often the most fully developed personality in the medium's spirit team.

The terms "trance mediumship" and "channeling" are frequently used interchangeably, though a distinction is often made between the two on the grounds that spirit mediumship predominantly involves communication with the spirits of the dead, while channeling may involve communication with other entities, including extraterrestrial beings. Spirit mediumship and spirit possession are also frequently used interchangeably, especially in academic anthropology. Among practitioners and experiencers, however, a distinction is usually made whereby spirit mediumship refers to the *voluntary* incorporation of spirits, while spirit possession refers to the *involuntary* incorporation of spirits—usually of a malignant or demonic nature.

Spirit mediumship has classically been distinguished from shamanism on the grounds that following trance mediumship demonstrations, the medium often claims complete, or near-complete, amnesia of what took place during the trance state, while for the shaman the conscious recollection of journeys into the spirit world is essential for their role within the social group. Control, then, is often taken as the defining difference between mediumship and shamanism: while the medium surrenders control of his/her body to the spirits, the shaman remains in control and may even have control over the spirits themselves, sending them on errands in the spirit world. However, although there are clear differences between shamanistic and mediumistic traditions, there are also a number of commonalities, and spirit mediumship may also be a tool in the wider spiritual repertoire of the shaman.

The careers of mediums begin in several different ways. In some instances mediumship appears to be a natural gift, with children discovering their ability to communicate with spirits at a young age and then going on to develop this ability over the course of their practicing career. For others mediumship develops following spontaneous experiences of spirit possession or other anomalous phenomena that eventually come to make sense when interpreted through the framework of spirit mediumship. For others, mediumship, like the shamanic vocation, emerges following some form of trauma or illness, after which mediumistic experiences begin to manifest. Mediumship may also be more or less developed in certain individuals; in other words, some are better at it than others.

Scientific investigations of spirit mediumship in the Western world have generally tended towards attempts to experimentally verify whether or not mediums are genuinely making contact with the dead. Over the past 130 years, countless Spiritualist mediums have been subjected to stringent experimental testing. Over the course of this testing, many mediums, and particularly physical ones, have been found to be fraudulent, employing a wide range of tricks such as cold reading in the case of mental mediumship or the simulation of ectoplasm with white muslin in physical mediumship. However, there still remain well-documented cases that are, at the very least, suggestive of the possibility of survival of consciousness after death and of the unusual abilities of certain mediums. A particularly interesting case can be seen in the Scole Experiment, in which a diverse team of highly credentialed investigators observed a group of people in the village of Scole in Norfolk, England, who used séances to try to manifest a new form of spiritual mediumship over a span of years in the 1990s. The outcome remains contested, and aspects of the experiment's design and execution have been subjected to skeptical critiques, but by some accounts the project as a whole produced some impressive results.

In parapsychological experiments, once all normal and fraudulent means have been theoretically ruled out, there remain two competing hypotheses regarding the way in which mediums are able to access accurate information about their sitters. One, of course, is the "survival hypothesis," which suggests that mediums are actually making contact with deceased spirits. The other is the "psi" or "super-psi" hypothesis, which suggests that mediums are employing a heightened form of psi (ESP, remote viewing, psychokinesis, etc.) to access information either directly from the mind of the sitter or from some form of universal information repository, often referred to as the Akashic field or Akashic records. The task for contemporary parapsychological mediumship researchers, then, is to distinguish between evidence for psi and evidence for survival of consciousness. One method currently being employed adopts a phenomenological approach by analyzing accounts of the subjective experiences of mediums while giving readings in order to see whether mediums have different sensations when using psi to give a reading compared to when they are ostensibly communicating with discarnate entities. Preliminary research suggests that the experience is indeed different, which lends credence to the possibility of two distinctive processes.

Academic approaches to spirit mediumship have tended toward a set of dominant explanatory frameworks, which include the notion that mediumship is essentially a pathological phenomenon, owing to similarities with pathological conditions such as dissociative identity disorder (DID), schizophrenia, and temporal lobe epilepsy. Recent neuroimaging work, however, seems to suggest that spirit mediumship represents a separate phenomenon with its own characteristic neurological activity that is distinct from that associated with pathological disorders. Spirit mediums also tend to have very good mental health, perhaps suggestive of mediumship's therapeutic potential. Another dominant framework, especially within anthropology, has been the social-functionalist approach, which suggests that spirit mediumship serves the social function of allowing socially repressed individuals (usually women) to protest against their repression in the context of mediumship performances. While mediums are possessed by spirits, their actions are not their own, thus allowing them to do things that would normally be frowned upon. This model, however, fails to explain the anomalous experiences reported by mediums, which appear to be consistent across cultures and suggestive of an underlying core experience.

Despite more than a century of investigation, then, mediumship is still something of a mystery. Investigations have uncovered fraud in certain cases, but experiments have also found evidence suggestive of genuine mediumistic abilities. Similarly, despite a plethora of social and psychological theories, no single model seems able to provide a completely satisfactory explanation. Further serious study is most certainly required.

Jack Hunter

See also: Akashic Records; Automatic Writing; Channeling; Discarnate Entity; Ectoplasm; Fox Sisters, The; Possession; Séance; Shamanism; Spiritualism; Survival after Death

Further Reading

Beischel, Julie, and Adam J. Rock. 2009. "Addressing the Survival vs. Psi Debate through Process-focused Mediumship Research." *Journal of Parapsychology* 73: 71–90.
Gauld, Alan. 1982. *Mediumship and Survival: A Century of Investigations.* London: Palladin.
Hunter, Jack, and David Luke, eds. 2014. *Talking with the Spirits: Ethnographies from Between the Worlds.* Brisbane, AU: Daily Grail Publishing.
Klimo, Jon. 1987. *Channeling: Investigations on Receiving Information from Paranormal Sources.* Los Angeles: Jeremy P. Tarcher.

Krippner, Stanley, and Harris L. Friedman, eds. 2010. *Mysterious Minds: The Neurobiology of Psychics, Mediums and Other Extraordinary People*. Oxford: Praeger.
Lewis, I. M. 1971. *Ecstatic Religion: An Anthropological Study of Spirit Possession and Shamanism*. London: Penguin Books.

MESMERISM

Originally known as "Animal Magnetism," mesmerism is a term that denotes a variety of medical treatments based on the belief that an invisible, universal magnetic fluid permeates the universe and that through influencing this fluid, an individual can put people into trance and heal their health problems. Mesmerism evolved into a variety of theories and practices, the most well-known today being modern hypnosis.

Animal Magnetism was originally developed in the early 1770s by the German theologian and doctor, Franz Anton Mesmer (1734–1815). Born in Germany, Mesmer practiced medicine in Vienna where he developed the theory that the entire universe was connected by the flowing of a universal fluid. His theory originated, in part, through earlier theories that claimed planets influence the health of individuals. However, Mesmer concluded that it was not just planets that could influence health, but also the doctor, who could manipulate this universal fluid by simply using his will. Mesmer claimed that simply by a few passes of his hand he could cure illness. He also used a variety of apparatuses, such as magnets, or a *baquet*, Mesmer's invention that consisted of a tub-like object constructed of oak and was assembled with lengths of woven rope with eight iron rods, evenly spaced around the tub, emerging out of a wooden lid and curving down the side. Patients would stand around the outside of the *baquet* and push their bodies against the metal bars while holding hands to complete the magnetic circuit.

By 1777 Mesmer's reputation in Vienna became blemished. Some claimed he was a talented healer, but to others he was a charlatan and fraud. Mesmer relocated to Paris where his practice became successful with the upper classes, which led to wealth and a large student following. However, like in Vienna, many Parisians were skeptical of Mesmer's claims and complained to the King of France. In 1784 the king ordered a committee of well-known scientists to investigate Animal Magnetism and its effectiveness. The committee included famous French scientists such as Antoine Laurent de Lavoisier, a chemist, and Jean-Sylvain Bailly, an astronomer, as well as Benjamin Franklin, the American ambassador to France from 1776–1785. The committee's report both supported and repudiated Mesmer's claims. While the report acknowledged that many individuals claimed medical cures, the committee found the assertion of a universal fluid dubious and explained the perceived medical benefits as being derived from individuals wanting to be healed, as well as from their imagination, rather than from any direct influence by Mesmer. Modern scientists today call this the placebo effect. By 1785 the unfavorable com-

The Far-Reaching Influence of Mesmerism: A Brief Timeline

Early 1770s   Franz Anton Mesmer develops Animal Magnetism in Vienna.

1777   Mesmer moves to Paris to continue his practice after accusations of fraud in Vienna.

1784   The King of France orders a committee of scientists (including Lavoisier and Benjamin Franklin) to investigate Animal Magnetism. The resulting report is mixed and leads to the collapse of Mesmer's practice.

1789–1815   Mesmer's practices continue in France through the Revolution and the reign of Napoleon, sustained by his student Puységur and others.

ca. 1836   Mesmerism arrives and begins spreading in America.

1837   Another French committee discredits mesmerism as a medical practice in France.

1838   Phineas Parkhurst Quimby of Maine becomes a student of mesmerism and eventually opens his own practice. He becomes one of the founders of the "New Thought" and "mind cure" movements.

1840s   Scottish surgeon James Braid adapts and modifies mesmeric practices in England to become a pioneer in hypnotism and hypnotherapy.

1875   Quimby's student Mary Baker Eddy publishes *Science and Health with Key to the Scriptures*, the central text of Christian Science.

20th–21st centuries   Mesmeric influences proliferate in Spiritualism, Theosophy, New Thought, the New Age, occultism, hypnosis, Orgone therapy, neurolinguistic programming, and more.

mittee report caused the collapse of Mesmer's medical practice, and he fled Paris, living in seclusion until his death in 1815.

Despite the discrediting of Mesmer, many of his students adopted and transformed his theories, creating new and influential medical practices. Mesmer's most successful student was Armand Marie Jacques Chastenet, Marquis de Puységur (1751–1825). Puységur, as he was generally called, found that he could induce patients into trance-like states by which their health and, frequently, personalities were changed. He called these states "magnetic" or "artificial" somnambulism, which is known today by the term "sleepwalking." During the French Revolution (1789–1799) and the reign of Napoleon Bonaparte (1799–1815), Puységur and other mesmerists continued to practice, but only after the restoration of the monarchy in 1815 did the practices of Puységur and others emerge as viable, once again igniting debate. In 1837 another committee investigated mesmeric practices, concluding the claims were imagination or fraud. Such a conclusion resulted in the complete discrediting of mesmerism as a medical practice in France. However, the practice continued as a cultural phenomenon and was connected to many other esoteric and occult phenomena, including Spiritualism, or Spiritism, as it is called in France, and clairvoyance.

Around 1836, a French student of Puységur, Charles Poyen Saint Sauveur (?–1844), arrived in America spreading the teachings of mesmerism. He initially traveled throughout New England, giving lectures and demonstrations. In 1838, a watchmaker from Maine, Phineas Parkhurst Quimby (1802–1866), attended a Poyen lecture and became a follower, quitting his job and accompanying Poyen on lecture tours from 1838–1840. After parting with Poyen, Quimby opened his own successful medical practice, eventually concluding that all illness was from error in understanding the world and that it could be cured by changing how people think. This theory eventually came to be called "mind cure" or "mental healing," and by 1900 there were schools teaching mental healing, such as Leander Edmund Whipple's (1848–1916) American School of Metaphysics located in New York City. In contrast, Mary Baker Eddy (1821–1910), a patient of Quimby's, claimed that she had a divine revelation that illness was in the mind and that all matter was an illusion. To receive correct understanding and healing, one should pray to God and reject conventional medical cures. These revelations were published in 1875 as *Science and Health with Key to the Scriptures*, which remains the central text of the Christian Science religion that Eddy founded.

In England, Mesmer's ideas were adapted by James Braid (1795–1860), a medical surgeon. Around 1840, Braid sought to replace supernatural elements of mesmerism with conventional medical and psychological explanations. He explained the effects of mesmerism by appealing to the neurological aspects of the patients. He initially called his theory, "Neurohypnology." Others built on his ideas and adopted the term "hypnosis," although Braid rejected it. Nevertheless, his ideas began to spread throughout Europe and into America. Some doctors even experimented with hypnosis in place of anesthesia.

By the end of the 19th century, mesmerism had evolved along two different tracks, one theological, the other secular. The theological developments had Mesmer's ideas influencing a number of religious traditions, including Spiritualism, Theosophy, New Thought, the New Age, and various forms of occultism. The secular developments of Mesmer's ideas continue today within the practices of hypnosis, Wilhelm Reich's Orgone therapy, various psychological therapies, and neuro-linguistic programming (NLP). While the derivatives of Mesmer's ideas flourish in various religious traditions, they are universally rejected by the scientific community, which labels them pseudoscience.

John L. Crow

See also: Imaginal; New Age; Occultism; Spiritualism; Theosophy

Further Reading

Darnton, Robert. 2009. *Mesmerism and the End of the Enlightenment in France.* Cambridge, MA: Harvard University Press.

Eddy, Mary Baker. 1875. *Science and Health with Key to the Scriptures.* Boston. http://books.google.com/books?id=eBE9AAAAIAAJ

Mesmer, Franz Anton. 1980. *Mesmerism: a Translation of the Original Scientific and Medical Writings of F.A. Mesmer, M.D.* Translated by George Block. Los Altos, CA: William Kaufmann.

Waterfield, Robin. 2002. *Hidden Depths: The Story of Hypnosis.* London: Pan Books.

Whipple, Leander E. 1893. *The Philosophy of Mental Healing: A Practical Exposition of Natural Restorative Power.* New York: The Metaphysical Publishing Company. http://books.google.com/books?id=vrQRAAAAYAAJ

Winter, Alison. 1998. *Mesmerized: Powers of Mind in Victorian Britain.* Chicago: University of Chicago Press.

MIRACLES

The term "miracle" is commonly used in the English language in both a general and in a more specifically religious context. At its broadest, the term can be applied to any unexpected event that seems to defy the laws of nature. If someone emerges unscathed from a terrible accident, for example, or against all odds passes their exams, these might be described as miraculous occurrences. When used in a religious narrative, particularly in the three Semitic or Abrahamic religions (Judaism, Christianity, and Islam), a miracle refers to the intentional intervention of a benevolent supernatural being for a beneficial end. To defy, control, or supersede the laws of nature necessitates some agreement as to what these laws might be. In practice there is little cultural uniformity in notions of what constitutes the laws of nature, nor the circumstances in which these norms might be breached.

Miracles can be ambiguous, with the dividing line between supernatural and demonic intervention hard to determine. Whether something is regarded as a miracle depends more on an interpretation of events than the events themselves. Miracles are contested and affirmed within and between religions. In both ancient and modern times some people have ridiculed the notion of miracle in the name of science and rationality. One reason for this is that proponents of religion and rationalism, as a philosophical position, are often at cross-purposes. R. G. Collingwood posited the conundrum as follows. Religions err when they mistake what they say for what they mean. Rationalism attacks what is said, rather than what is meant, and fails to see that such an attack is too easy to be sound. Dismissing the logical plausibility of God's creating the world in seven days, for instance, or turning Lot's wife into a pillar of salt (Genesis 19:26) is for the rationalist tantamount to dismissing the claims of religion per se. For those who believe in miracles, however, they can point to the interrelationship between human and supernatural activity and assert the possibility of a personalized moral universe.

The British reformed rabbi, author, and broadcaster Lionel Blue tells the story of a man stuck on the roof of his house as the water rises around him. He prays to God to save him, fervently believing in a miracle. A boat comes past and offers to rescue him, but the man refuses, stating that God will come to his rescue. The waters continue to rise and a second boat turns up, again offering to take him to safety. Once more the man refuses as he has put his faith in God. Finally a helicopter hovers overhead to winch him to dry land. Again the man refuses to leave. As the water finally reaches his head the man calls out to God, "Why didn't you save me?" To which a voice replies, "I sent two boats and a helicopter, but you turned them away." This story illustrates some of the different understandings in Semitic religions of the ways in which God might act. For the Christian theologian Thomas Aquinas (1225–1274), as with the drowning man, a miracle is understood as an act of God working against nature—although as nature is God's creation, miracles could be viewed as perfecting rather than violating the natural order. For others however, such as the Dutch Jewish philosopher Baruch Spinoza (1632–1677), God and nature are one and the same. What is contrary to nature is contrary to reason and therefore absurd. If God acts at all, he does so through his creation, not in opposition to it.

Jesus of Nazareth, as presented in the Christian New Testament, is often referred to as a miracle worker. Jesus started his adult ministry with a miracle, turning water into wine at a wedding feast at Cana in Galilee (John 2:1–11). He went on to heal the sick, drive out demons, multiply food, and even walk on water and restore the dead to life. After rising from the dead, leaving an empty tomb, Jesus appeared to his followers by moving through solid walls, appearing and disappearing at will. He could walk and talk, make a charcoal fire, and cook and eat a meal of fish and bread with his disciples (John 21:1–14). Not all of Jesus' nature-defying actions are regarded as miraculous, but only those with a positive outcome. Cursing a fig tree for failing to bear fruit out of season and its subsequent withering (Mark 11:12–25) is not normally counted among Jesus' miracles. Although the precise meaning of the biblical texts is disputed, most Christians also regard Jesus's birth as miraculous. In both Christianity and Judaism attitudes toward miracles are ambiguous, and enthusiasm for them has waxed and waned in different places and periods of history. Apart from the philosophical questions as to whether the need for divine intervention undermines the concept of a divinely created natural order, there are issues of status and control.

If miracles break through ordinary reality, asserting the power of the divine and legitimizing the recipients of divine grace, they can destabilize the power of church hierarchies. Social anthropologist John Eade, discussing Christian pilgrimages to the Roman Catholic shrine of Lourdes in southern France (1991), pointed to the tension between a discourse based on suffering and a discourse based on miracles. Thousands of sick pilgrims visit the shrine each year to bathe in its healing waters in the hope of a miraculous cure. The intermediaries in this transaction are female: the peasant girl Bernadette Soubirous, to whom the Virgin Mary appeared, having told her where to dig to discover the healing spring and the Virgin herself. The Church hierarchy, by contrast, through its male priests and shrine guardians emphasizes the value of imitating Christ's suffering. The Church wishes to stress the value of suffering and of spiritual healing and downplay the role of the miraculous cure.

The ancient pagan practice of making a pact with God is seen at Lourdes as well as at numerous other holy wells, trees, and shrines throughout the world. In return for a miraculous intervention, the recipient promises to undertake a pilgrimage and to place a sign or symbol of thanksgiving at the shrine as a mark of gratitude. This in turn acts as a witness and encouragement to others. Thus one can find shrines like Lourdes full of crutches and other symbols of miraculous cures and trees and wells decorated with flowers, colored rags, or tokens to represent a prayer answered. The hope and piety involved in the search for a miracle, whether those concerned are Western Christian pilgrims, Pagans, or members of other traditions in various parts of the world, is often balanced by a lack of faith that such things are rationally possible, skepticism regarding the claims of miracle workers, and guilt at not being found worthy of healing.

The Prophet Muhammad was a miracle worker. Like Jesus, he is credited with miraculous healings and feedings and is said to have produced water from his fingertips to quench the thirst of his army. Both Jesus and Muhammad exhibited the ability to foretell the future, although clairvoyant and premonitory powers, commonly attributed to holy men and women, are not in themselves usually regarded as miraculous. Debates between rationalists and mystics are also found within Islam. Some Sunni Muslim theologians emphasize the power of Allah working through human beings, using them as channels of his grace. No intermediaries are needed in this process. Within the mystical Sufi tradition, with its saints and shrines, the power of Allah is manifest in the person and miraculous activities of the holy man. The cults that grow up around these saints attract Muslims and non-Muslims alike. Their tombs continue to exert an influence, becoming places of pilgrimage and objects of devotion.

Hinduism and Buddhism also have their holy men and women capable of performing miracles. Here, however, a miracle is not a disruption or break in the natural law but displays the power of the developed mind of the yogi to master it and thus change the laws of causation. In Tibetan Buddhism meditation is related to the development of psychic powers. The discipline of *shamatha*, or pointed concentration meditation, brings about enlightenment, psychic awareness, and miraculous abilities; these attributes cannot be separated from one another. Sathya Sai Baba (1926–2011) is one of India's most famous 20th century miracle workers, a Swami (religious teacher) accepted by millions of his followers world-wide as an avatar, a deity or "descent" or manifestation in human form of the Divine Being. Sai Baba was probably best known to the wider public for his apports, that is, the ability to materialize objects out of thin air, make objects disappear, or transform baser objects into something precious. His particular signature was the production of *vibuti*, a form of sacramental ash, which would be given as a form of blessing to his followers. In common with some Christian saints, Sai Baba was sometimes associated with a "divine fragrance," both around his person and around pictures of him at a distance. When asked how he performed these feats, Sai Baba is reputed to have said he just thought of them, and the objects appeared. Erlendur Haraldsson investigated Sai Baba over a number of years and was able to dismiss various forms of fraud as an explanation for his miraculous gifts. Among disaffected followers the main area of tension appears not to have been whether Sai Baba possessed such gifts, but whether they were genuinely associated with divine status. Was it possible for someone to display psychic powers and perform such miracles without also being enlightened?

For the majority of non-Western people practicing a so-called traditional or indigenous religion (often alongside a "world" religion), the term "miracle" has little meaning, as the boundaries between the natural and supernatural, material and immaterial worlds are drawn rather differently. In very general terms the human moral universe encompasses various seen and unseen forces that can be manipulated for good or evil, to serve oneself or one's community or to harm others—sometimes simultaneously. In sub-Saharan Africa, witchcraft beliefs and practices are based on the notion that psychic powers are common and often dangerous. A thought or emotion can have real effects in the physical world. In the hands of skilled practitioners, various natural substances ("medicines"), accompanied by appropriate words and actions, can heal, protect, or attack others. Ritual practitioners are often trained to travel to unseen worlds to perform cures—as in shamanic soul-retrieval, for example—or to control the behavior of animals, the weather, spirits, or people. Although such ideas are not mainstream in the West, there are parallels with many of these practices. The availability and popularity of Western shamanism and growth in the number of spirit-release practitioners in the United Kingdom and North America, for instance, attests to the universal appeal of such practices.

There is no single standard definition of the term "miracle," and its use tends to imply a religious context and to draw on notions of faith. Similar phenomena, invoking the use of psychic powers or gifts, when looked at from the perspective of parapsychology, transpersonal, or anomalistic psychology, become the object of scientific research and measurement. Someone like the American psychic, mystic, and healer Edgar Cayce (1877–1945) was a Christian who saw his powers as a gift from God, albeit not a gift he sought. For those he cured his powers might seem miraculous, and for those who investigated him, his powers might seem to be examples of anomalistic phenomena. The Spiritist healers described by Sidney Greenfield in Brazil perform extraordinary feats of diagnosis and healing, ostensibly with the help of discarnate healers, often described as German doctors. Some of the most famous, like José Carlos Ribeiro from Fortaleza on the north coast of Brazil, would perform surgery without the use of anesthetics, and apparently without his patients suffering from infection, despite the unsterile conditions in which the surgery was performed. Among Brazilian Spiritist healers surgery generally involves actual cutting of the patient's body. In Africa and the Philippines, removal of objects from a patient's body by healers is often without the use of incisions.

Skeptics, who often include those within these healing traditions, are on the lookout for fraud, either because they do not believe such phenomena are possible per se or because they distrust a particular individual or instance of faith or spirit healing. In a famous case described by Belgian anthropologist Claude Lévi-Strauss, taken from a fragment of an autobiography gathered by German-born anthropologist Franz Boas (1858–1942), a Kwakiutl Indian named Quesalid from the Vancouver region of Canada, described his initiation as a shaman. Like any good modern skeptic, Quesalid had embarked on the process out of curiosity, with a desire to learn about the shamans' tricks and expose them. He eventually did discover a great deal of theatre and some outright trickery but also forms of healing that, much to his surprise, appeared to work. Quesalid's own reputation as a shaman increased with each success, even when he used techniques such as the concealment of objects that can later be produced by sleight of hand. Edith Turner, in her study of African healing, speaks about a world of ritual objects that are effective in their own right, spirits, and specialists who know how to operate a ritual process that can be sensed. This world is not confined to Africa. It is universal, even if not universally recognized. Its processes will be defined as anomalous or miraculous only when and where the symbolic classifications of a society draw the boundaries of the normal in such a way as to exclude their intrusions.

Fiona Bowie

See also: Angels; Cayce, Edgar; Haraldsson, Erlendur; Healing, Psychic and Spiritual; Meditation; Paranormal; Religion and the Paranormal; Shamanism; Siddhis; Spiritism

Further Reading

Bowie, Fiona. 2011. "Miracles in Traditional Religions." In *The Cambridge Companion to Miracles*, edited by Graham H. Twelftree, 167–83. Cambridge, UK: Cambridge University Press.

Collingwood, R. G. 1924. *Speculum Mentis or the Map of Knowledge*. Oxford, UK: Clarendon Press.

Duffin, Jacalyn. 2009. *Medical Miracles: Doctors, Saints, and Healing in the Modern World.* Oxford, UK and New York: Oxford University Press.

Eade, John, and Michael J. Sallnow. 1991. *Contesting the Sacred: The Anthropology of Christian Pilgrimage.* London and New York: Routledge.

French, Christopher C., and Anna Stone. 2014. *Anomalistic Psychology: Exploring Paranormal Belief and Experience.* Houndmills, Hampshire, UK: Palgrave Macmillan.

Greenfield, Sidney M. 2008. *Spirits with Scalpels: The Cultural Biology of Religious Healing in Brazil.* Walnut Creek, CA: Left Coast Press.

Haraldsson, Erlendur. 2013. *Modern Miracles: The Story of Sathya Sai Baba: A Modern Day Prophet.* Hove, Sussex, UK: White Crow Books.

Lévy-Strauss, Claude. 1963. "The Sorcerer and His Magic." In *Structural Anthropology* by Claude Lévy-Strauss, 167–85. Harmondsworth, Middlesex, UK: Penguin.

Roney-Dougal, S. M. 2012. "Tibetan Psychic Traditions." Psi Research Centre. Accessed November 6, 2014. http://www.psi-researchcentre.co.uk/article_5.htm.

Sugrue, Thomas. 1997. *There Is a River: The Story of Edgar Cayce.* Virginia Beach, VA: ARE Publishing.

Turner, Edith. 1992. *Experiencing Ritual: A New Interpretation of African Healing.* Philadelphia: University of Pennsylvania Press.

Twelftree, Graham H., ed. 2011. *The Cambridge Companion to Miracles.* Cambridge, UK: Cambridge University Press.

Woodward, Kenneth L. 2000. *The Book of Miracles: The Meaning of the Miracle Stories in Christianity, Judaism, Buddhism, Hinduism and Islam.* New York: Simon & Schuster.

MYERS, FREDERIC W. H.

Frederic Myers was one of the founders of the Society for Psychical Research in London in 1882. Myers's primary objective was to pursue scientific evidence that humans have a soul and that the conscious personality survives bodily death. The results of his work with the SPR, spanning a period of over twenty years, are condensed into his *Human Personality and Its Survival of Bodily Death*, which was published in 1903, two years after his own death in Rome in 1901.

Born in Keswick, England, in 1843, Frederic William Henry Myers was initially a Cambridge scholar of the classics and earned his livelihood as an appointed inspector of schools. In 1882 he co-founded the Society for Psychical Research (SPR) in London together with other academics, scientists, and intellectuals who all had their respective interests in a wide variety of psychic phenomena. Myers introduced the term "telepathy" in 1882.

Myers is widely acknowledged for his contribution to psychology and to the scientific investigation of a wide range of psychic phenomena including the possibility of life after death, spiritualism, animal magnetism, telepathy, hypnosis, creative inspiration, apparitions and hallucinations, automatic writing, and multiple personality. However, his discovery of the objective reality of spirit possession is still not acknowledged by mainstream science and parapsychology. He argued that because 19th-century science was unable to accommodate such concepts, it needed to expand its conceptual framework, and he advocated an "expanded

The question of man's survival of death stands in a position uniquely intermediate between matters capable and matters incapable of proof. It is in itself a definite problem, admitting of conceivable proof which, even if not technically rigorous, might amply satisfy the scientific mind. And at the same time the conception which it involves is in itself a kind of avenue and inlet into infinity. Could a proof of our survival be obtained, it would carry us deeper into the true nature of the universe than we should be carried by an even perfect knowledge of the material scheme of things. It would carry us deeper both by achievement and by promise. The discovery that there was a life in man independent of blood and brain would be a cardinal, a dominating fact in all science and in all philosophy. And the prospect thus opened to human knowledge, in this or in other worlds, would be limitless indeed.

—Frederic W. H. Myers, *Human Personality and Its Survival of Bodily Death* (1903)

naturalism" that regards *all* human experience as normal. Myers maintained that the term "supernatural" was meaningless because everything that could be observed or experienced was part of the natural world and was therefore open to scientific scrutiny.

Myers's contribution to psychology in formulating a model of mind that he called the "Subliminal Self" was a far greater contribution to our modern understanding of the mind than is generally recognized. Myers was a pioneer in identifying what we now term the "unconscious" or "subconscious." His theories had a significant influence on the ideas of the American psychologist and philosopher William James, who often referred to Myers in his classic text *The Varieties of Religious Experience*. Myers is also credited with providing Swiss psychiatrist Carl Gustav Jung, who founded analytical psychology, with a precursor to his theory of the "collective unconscious," and Jung is known to have referenced the work of Myers in his own doctoral thesis.

Myers also influenced the French psychiatrist Pierre Janet in the formulation of his theory of "dissociation" in hysterics. Janet made use of Myers' radical approach to "subliminal tendencies" to explain "automatisms" (involuntary acts and behaviors) and the existence of hidden states of consciousness that were unknown to the hysteric's ordinary conscious awareness. The application of Janet's theory of dissociation has become known in modern psychiatry as dissociative identity disorder (DID), which has evolved from what was previously known as multiple personality disorder (MPD). Although Myers and Janet agreed on the formation of dissociated personality states, Myers disagreed with Janet's assertion that all such states are pathological, which implies that all people who hear voices or go into trance must be mentally ill. Myers argued that dissociation from normal conscious awareness was experienced by healthy-minded people who were spiritualist mediums.

Phantasms of the Living, published in 1886, was written by Myers in collaboration with Frank Podmore and Edmund Gurney and was the first comprehensive scientific study undertaken by the Society for Psychical Research on telepathy, apparitions, astral traveling, and altered states of consciousness. Myers's preferred method of investigating such phenomena was by the use of an artificially induced alternate state of consciousness that has become known as "hypnosis," and he hypothesized that the power of suggestion was not a sufficient explanation for all hypnotic phenomena, including clairvoyance and automatic writing. He therefore sought experimental methods that bypassed any influence of the power of suggestion, and this led him to conduct experiments in "telepathic hypnosis" whereby the beliefs and expectations of the subject could be excluded.

Myers and Janet successfully conducted experiments with telepathic hypnosis, and these led to further experiments by a long line of distinguished international scientists, including the Russian neurologist Leonid Vasiliev, who investigated this phenomenon long after Myers's death and well into the 20th century.

Myers linked the quality of genius with the classical notion of "inspiration," saying that an inspiration of genius is a "subliminal uprush," an emergence into conscious awareness of ideas that a person has not consciously originated but which have shaped themselves beyond the individual will, in profounder regions of one's being. Myers also suggested that in some people genius was possibly inspired by discarnate spirits, and much of his work involved testing this theory by application of his expanded scientific framework.

Although Myers is becoming acknowledged by a growing number of modern researchers, such as the authors of the 2007 book *Irreducible Mind*, which tries to reclaim Myers's memory and legacy while mounting a challenge to contemporary neuroscientific reductionism, his scientific explanation for psychic phenomena and his methods of researching them are largely dismissed by today's mainstream psychology. However, those scientists who agree with Myers argue that the constraints of the physical sciences are being loosened by quantum theory and that his vision of a scientific "expanded naturalism" is coming to fruition. Myers's methods are being applied in the modern clinical practice of Spirit Release Therapy, which is a practical alternative to traditional religious exorcism in the treatment of people who are negatively affected by discarnate spirit entities and the earthbound souls of the deceased.

Terence Palmer

See also: Discarnate Entity; Exorcism; James, William; Jung, Carl; Possession; Society for Psychical Research; Telepathic Hypnosis; Unconscious Mind; Vasiliev, Leonid Leonidovich

Further Reading

Gurney, Edmund, Frederic W. H. Myers, and Frank Podmore. (1886) 2011. *Phantasms of the Living*. 2 vols. Cambridge Library Collection: Spiritualism and Esoteric Knowledge. Cambridge, UK: Cambridge University Press.

Janet, Pierre. 1976. *Psychological Healing: A Historical and Clinical Study*. New York: Arno Press.

Kelly, Edward F., Emily Williams Kelly, Adam Crabtree, Alan Gauld, Michael Grosso, and Bruce Greyson. 2007. *Irreducible Mind: Toward a Psychology for the 21st Century*. New York: Rowman & Littlefield.

Myers, Frederic W. H. (1903) 2011. *Human Personality and Its Survival of Bodily Death*. 2 vols. Cambridge Library Collection: Spiritualism and Esoteric Knowledge. Cambridge, UK: Cambridge University Press.

Palmer, Terence. 2013. *The Science of Spirit Possession*. Saarbrucken, DE: Lambert Academic Publishing.

MYSTICAL EXPERIENCE

Defining religious experience in general and mystical experience in particular is inherently difficult, especially because experience varies from individual to individual. Moreover, the term "experience" suggests that there is a division between the person who is experiencing something and that which he or she experiences, a division that runs counter to the ways in which mystics write of their experiences. In the broadest sense, however, mystical experience can be defined as any human experience in which an individual is brought into union with something greater or more than him- or herself. In this broad sense, the mystic may be deeply encountering a personal deity like those believed in by a number of the world's major religions. However, this need not be the case according to the definition given above, which is broad enough to include experiences of union with the natural world, with the absolute or infinite, with the emptiness of existence (as in Buddhism), and/or with "reality" itself. Additionally, mystical experience, like religion in general, intersects with concepts and phenomena commonly described in other contexts as paranormal. Thus, it is not surprising that a number of important figures in the history of the paranormal, including Emanuel Swedenborg and William James (regarding both of whom, see below) have also been important figures in the history of mysticism and mystical experience.

Although mystical experience is now a category used to describe phenomena in a wide variety of religions and cultures, the origin of the terms "mystic," "mysticism," and "mystical experience" is decidedly Christian. These English terms derive from the ancient Greek word *mystikos*, which means "secret" or "hidden." The mystic is therefore one who has been initiated into or has encountered that which lies secret or hidden to many. The word "mystical" was first used to describe Christian theology by Pseudo-Dionysius the Areopagite (late fifth-century CE) in his treatise *The Mystical Theology*, a text that describes how the Christian can attain union *with* God only by laying aside rational thought *about* God. While Dionysius is the first to explicitly call his theology "mystical" and link it directly to union with the divine, he is drawing from earlier Christian thinkers, including Gregory of Nyssa (c.330–390 CE), as well as New Testament sources (see, for example, Ephesians 3:19 and 2 Peter 1:4) that speak of union with God.

Pseudo-Dionysian theology was greatly influential in both Eastern and Western Christianity (Dionysius was believed to have been a companion of the Apostle Paul) and has thereby deeply shaped the mystical traditions of both Roman Catholicism and Eastern Orthodoxy. In the East, Maximus the Confessor (580–662) and Gregory Palamas (1296–1359) are among the most influential expositors of mysticism, and it is with Palamas that the Eastern Church understands mystical experience in terms of the believer's union with the "energies" of God. That is, one does not come into union with God's essence, which is unknowable and unattainable, but one does become deified by taking on all of the energies or properties of the divinity (e.g., love, peace, joy, goodness). In Roman Catholicism, some of the most influential mystics include Bernard of Clairvaux (1090–1153), Bonaventure (1221–1274), Teresa of Avila (1515–1582), and John of the Cross (1542–1591). While these figures do not use the Palamite language of divine energy, as their Eastern counterparts do, the understanding of mystical experience is arguably similar in that it maintains that one can become united with God without losing personal identity and becoming identical with God. In both East and West, the Christian generally exercises spiritual disciplines of fasting, prayer, meditation, and so on in order to strip the ego away and experience union with God, becoming a vessel of the divine will.

Although the term "mysticism" derives from these Christian origins, it has been frequently applied to thinking about experiential phenomena in other monotheistic religions. Sufism is often referred to as Islamic mysticism, while Jewish mysticism is most widely associated with Kabbalah. In Sufism, practitioners often describe states and paths of self-discipline very similar to those of the Christian mystics, especially in the "sober" mysticism taught by figures such as Junayd of Baghdad (830–910). According to these Sufis, one achieves union with God and takes on the characteristics of God (as with Christian mysticism) while retaining one's own personal identity. In "intoxicated" Sufism, however, such as that espoused by Bayazid Bistami (804–874) and Mansur al-Hallaj (858–922), there is a marked tendency to identify so thoroughly with the deity that the identities of each party collapse into each other. Accordingly, Bistami is reported to have exclaimed, "Glory be to me!" and Hallaj to have declared, "I am the truth!" Each of these utterances appears to have a more radical sense of union, and each has been considered controversial within Islam more broadly, as well as in more "sober" forms of Sufism. Jewish mysticism, or ecstatic Kabbalah, also employs ascetic practices to achieve states of divine union, including a strong focus on practiced meditation on the names of God.

Thinking of mysticism in non-Western and non-monotheistic traditions, however, means moving beyond notions of union with a sole personal divinity; hence the expansive definition of mystical experience given above. In the polytheistic traditions often grouped together under the term Hinduism, for example, disciplines like yoga are employed in order to achieve union with various deities, rather than the sole personal deity of monotheism. In Buddhist traditions, which grew out of Hinduism and are generally nontheistic, mystical experiences of union with a deity are not the goal. Instead, the practitioner aims to achieve enlightenment through his or her ascetic practices. This enlightenment grants one insight into the emptiness of the self and of reality, frees one from suffering, and allows one to become a vessel of compassion. Though one does not become united to a divinity (since there is none to unite with), one does become enlightened in the same manner as the Buddha and possesses the same characteristic of compassion. For this reason, Buddhist experiences of enlightenment have often been considered forms of nontheistic mystical experience. Still another example of non-Western mystical experience can be found in Daoism. In Daoist practice, one does not attempt to come into union with a deity as such but rather with reality itself. In so doing, one comes into harmony with and harnesses the force of life (or *Qi*) so as to exist in unison with reality instead of living in a state that is out of sync with it.

Mystical experience may also be associated with individual figures who did not stand firmly within any major religious tradition. Emanuel Swedenborg (1688–1772), William Blake (1757–1827), Ralph Waldo Emerson (1803–1882), and Henry David Thoreau (1817–1862) are all examples of individuals who have been considered mystics while standing outside the mainstream of Christianity. Swedenborg placed a high value on visionary experiences that brought one into union with God and disclosed his will. Blake, Emerson, and Thoreau were each in their own way influenced by Swedenborg, and each emphasized communion with the natural world as a path to communion with the divine.

Mystical experience continues to be a generally accepted category today, although there is ongoing debate as to how it should be understood. Is it something foundational to human existence that merely expresses itself in different terms depending on the cultural context? Or do particular cultural frameworks themselves construct mystical experiences? William James (1842–1910), one of the first thinkers to explore the idea of religious experience in general, held that mystical experience is founded upon an essential and foundational category that is found in every religion and culture. This approach is often called "essentialism" (or "perennialism") and maintains that there is a common core, either theological or psychological, to the experiences often called "mystical." Other scholars, notably Steven Katz, espouse what is known as constructivism. From the constructivist perspective, mystical experiences do not derive from a common core but are rather always conditioned by the theological and philosophical beliefs of a particular religious and cultural milieu.

Recently, a third way of thinking about mystical experience has become increasingly popular. This line of thinking argues for a middle way between the constructivist and essentialist approaches to mystical experience. Frederick Streng, for example, has argued that both the essentialist and constructivist perspectives fail to do justice to the writings of mystics themselves and express a binary or dualistic viewpoint that is foreign to them. That is, previous approaches have separated the core of experience from the mediating context and have proceeded to ask which is more important than the other in accounting for mystical experiences. Streng points out that mystics consistently write of their core experiences *and* their contextual beliefs as a complete whole and that the one cannot be separated from the other as an object of study. In this way, mystical experiences might be most successfully understood as simultaneously core to human existence and situated within a particular cultural context.

Rico G. Monge

See also: Art, Creativity, and the Paranormal; Imaginal; James, William; Meditation; Near-Death Experience (NDE); Religion and the Paranormal; Spiritualism; Swedenborg, Emanuel; Theosophy; Whiteman, Michael

Further Reading

James, William. (1902) 1982. *The Varieties of Religious Experience*. New York: Penguin Paperbacks.

Katz, Steven T., ed. 1983. *Mysticism and Religious Traditions*. New York: Oxford University Press.

Streng, Frederick. 1978. "Language and Mystical Awareness." In *Mysticism and Philosophical Analysis*, edited by Steven T. Katz, 141–169. London: Sheldon.

NEAR-DEATH EXPERIENCE (NDE)

Near-death experiences, or NDEs, are close brushes with death that incite altered states of awareness typically accompanied by any of the following sensations and perceptions: feeling detached from one's body (and often visually perceiving one's own body from a distance), feelings of ineffability, a sense of entering some kind of tunnel, encountering a brilliant light, meeting deceased loved ones or mystical beings, undergoing some kind of life review (an event in which people see or relive past life events—sometimes people report reviewing past events not from their own perspective, but from the perspective of those with whom they interacted), feeling overwhelming love and joy, a sense of transcending time and space, apprehending that one has approached a border or limit of some sort, feelings of cosmic unity, and sensing that one has access to special or sacred information. Many people who report having had a near-death experience also claim to experience a number of persistent aftereffects, including heightened intuition and/or psychic abilities, reduced fear of death, a greater sense of purpose in life, strengthened belief in an afterlife, a new or enhanced spirituality that is often universalistic, being less materialistic, feeling more compassionate, and developing an increased desire for knowledge. While the majority of NDEs reported are positive or benign, some reports depict the experience as distressful and frightening.

Throughout recorded history, people have reported visiting the otherworldly domains of the afterlife. Arguably, the earliest account of a near-death experience was recorded by Plato in *The Republic* in which he writes of a soldier named Er who returned from death to report on the afterlife. But the actual term "near-death experience" was coined in 1975 by Raymond A. Moody in his book *Life After Life* to identify the varieties of anomalous experiences reported by over fifty persons who had been close to death. Shortly after the publication of this book, a community of researchers interested in quantitatively verifying near-death experiences founded the International Association for Near-Death Studies (IANDS). Research conducted by these individuals eventually revealed that there was a distinct phenomenon consisting of a range of features quite similar to those recorded by Moody.

Since its beginning, IANDS has been responsible for disseminating NDE-related literature, encouraging the development of local special-interest and support groups, bringing experiencers into contact with researchers, and educating people about near-death experiences. IANDS defines a near-death experience as "a profound psychological event" that includes "transcendental and mystical elements" and categorizes the experience as a "spiritually transformative event." Since IANDS

Various pleasant and positive sensations and perceptions can accompany a near-death experience, according to those who have had one. These include:

• Feeling detached from the physical body

• Entering or traveling through a tunnel

• Seeing a bright light

• Meeting deceased loved ones or mystical/supernatural beings

• Reviewing past life events

• Being overwhelmed by love and joy

• Experiencing a sense of cosmic unity

• Experiencing heightened intuition or psychic abilities afterward

However, NDEs may also be unpleasant and distressing.

---

is largely responsible for putting near-death researchers and experiencers of the phenomenon into contact with one another, the organization has played a vital role in the public perception of near-death experiences.

About 15 to 20 percent of people who have been resuscitated from cardiac arrest report having had NDEs. A near-death experience can happen to anyone, and so far research has demonstrated that there are no key individual factors that make one particularly predisposed to having an NDE or experiencing any of the particular characteristics associated with the experience. The most commonly used measure among researchers for determining whether someone has had a near-death experience is Bruce Greyson's NDE Scale. This scale uses a threshold score of seven or higher, meaning that if an individual reports fewer than seven out of sixteen characteristics, then that individual is said not to have had an actual NDE. There is some disagreement on this point because individuals may have life-changing experiences while being close to death, but these experiences may only consist of one or two remarkable features (and would thus not be considered by researchers as a genuine near-death experience).

Some consider various aspects of near-death experience reports to be supernatural or paranormal, including extra-sensory perception, communicating with the dead, and out-of-body experiences. This has led some experiencers and researchers to consider that NDEs might not only demonstrate that consciousness is capable of functioning apart from the body, but that consciousness is capable of continuing after death. Veridical NDEs are those experiences in which people report having found themselves out of their bodies and witnessing events that occurred while they were physically unconsciousness that were later verified as accurate by others;

veridical NDEs also include those in which blind people were able to see during their experience. Veridical NDE accounts are commonly used to support the after-life hypothesis. Although such accounts have not been validated under scientific observation, they contribute to the belief that near-death experiences have some basis in objective reality, and as such they are often referred to by others in order to validate other aspects of NDEs, such as visions of the future, meeting deceased loved ones, and encountering divine beings.

NDE reports that include miraculous healing or premonitions later found to be factually correct are also used to promote certain paranormal interpretation of NDEs. Within the community of near-death studies, conversion stories that depict medical doctors and scientists as having their worldviews altered by a near-death experience are also quite popular. For instance, the 2012 best-selling book *Proof of Heaven* was written by Eben Alexander, a neuroscientist claiming that his materialistic worldview was forever altered by his NDE, which included veridical perceptions and a miraculous recovery from bacterial meningitis.

Some researchers promote the idea that not only do NDEs result in transforming the lives of experiencers, but stories about NDEs have the ability to transform the lives of nonexperiencers, and that the more people there are who learn about near-death experiences, the more human consciousness will evolve. One of the earliest proponents of this position, Kenneth Ring, believes that knowledge about near-death experiences acts as a kind of "benign virus" and is contagious. In seeming support of this, people who immerse themselves in NDE-related literature tend to report being more spiritually focused, less materialistic, and less fearful of death. In his 1998 book *Lessons from the Light*, Ring prescribes meditating upon the spiritual teachings of near-death experiences to cultivate personal change. Other researchers have also focused on the fact that various positive effects are associated with learning about near-death experiences, including increased well-being and the lessening of grief.

Not all NDEs are positive, however. Up to 20 percent of people who report near-death experiences say that they were frightened or distressed by the experience (and this percentage might not be accurate, as the fear, shame, and anxiety arising from these kinds of experiences might prevent people from talking about them). Researchers have identified three particular types of distressing NDEs. The first and most common type of distressing NDE is one wherein features usually reported as being pleasurable, such as finding oneself out of the body, are viewed instead as being terrifying to the experiencer. The second type of distressing NDE includes being in a void or empty space and having an accompanying, overwhelming sense of despair and abandonment. The third—and rarest—kind of distressing NDE includes imagery typically associated with Hell, such as terrifying landscapes, macabre otherworldly beings, and tortured souls. While the field of near-death studies and the IANDS community have been slow to acknowledge these negative experiences, this is changing. However, in keeping with a focus on the overall positive, spiritually transformative nature of near-death experiences, IANDS and other researchers view typically distressing experiences as events that present opportunities for spiritual growth.

NDE reports have decidedly influenced contemporary ideas about spirituality, death, and dying, although cultural teachings about death and afterlife beliefs also influence people's interpretations as to what near-death experiences actually are. For example, some Christian fundamentalists take the position that NDEs must be the work of the devil since atheists and non-Christians report visits to heaven and encounters with loving being of light. A variety of New Age and alternative spiritualities, however, point to near-death experiences as evidence that life extends beyond death and that a spiritual dimension infuses everyday reality. And there are a number of scientists and others who remain convinced that NDEs are nothing more than subjective experiences resulting from psychophysiological stress.

The near-death experience is a phenomenon that has been recorded throughout history, but with advances in medicine, particularly with the development of cardiopulmonary resuscitation (CPR), these experiences have become much more frequently reported by greater numbers of people. Never before have so many come so close to death and been able to recount stories of their experiences to others. Speculation as to what these experiences actually are will undoubtedly remain open to ongoing discussion and debate.

Michael Kinsella

See also: Survival after Death

Further Reading

Fox, Mark. 2003. *Religion, Spirituality and the Near-Death Experience.* New York: Routledge.
Holden, Janice Miner, Bruce Greyson, and Debbie James, eds. 2009. *The Handbook of Near-Death Experiences: Thirty Years of Investigation.* Santa Barbara, CA: ABC-CLIO, LLC.
Moody, Raymond A. 1975. *Life after Life.* Atlanta: Mockingbird Books.

NEW AGE

The New Age movement is difficult to place within a simple and concise definition, since it has been known for its amorphous structure, the vast array of spiritual practices and philosophies that it includes, and the personalized autonomy that marks its individual adherents. In general, most agree that the New Age movement is marked by two emphases—transformation of the individual and large-scale transformation on a global or cosmic scale—as well as the use, in different combinations and to varying degrees, of an eclectic assortment of traditions including, but not limited to channeling, astrology, self-help, transpersonal psychology, meditation, shamanism, biofeedback, the deep environmentalism of the Gaia hypothesis, and elements of nearly every major religious tradition.

Some observers, particularly critics, see the New Age movement as a unique phenomenon unto itself, with common aims and shared language underlying its diversity. Others see the term "New Age" as being not much more than a place-holder that is applied out of convenience to a broad cluster of movements that are as dissimilar as often as they are alike. In her work *A Republic of Mind and Spirit*, Catherine Albanese describes the New Age movement as "a late-20th-century re-configuration of the metaphysical [tradition]" (Albanese 2007, 10). On this count, that the New Age movement did not appear *sui generis* but had clear forerunners and influences, there is near universal agreement although some trace it to move-ments of the 19th century, and others see it as far back as Late Antiquity.

The teachings of the Theosophical Society were incredibly influential on the New Age movement, especially as it advanced the idea of the perennial philosophy, which states that all religious traditions are based in a single, universal truth. The American Edgar Cayce, who was able to answer questions and diagnose illness while in a trace state, is seen as another powerful influence on the New Age move-ment, particularly its emphasis on channeling as a source of wisdom and guidance. The specific term "New Age" can also be found among some of these predecessors. Warren Felt Evans, an early proponent of Mind Cure, published a work titled *The New Age and Its Message*.

Beyond the phrase, the main concept of the New Age movement—that human-ity is moving toward a major shift in consciousness or development—was most commonly associated with the Age of Aquarius, the movement from the astrolog-ical house of Pisces to Aquarius that would also entail a parallel shift in human civilization. The Theosophical Society also fed into this concept with the earlier predictions of several messiah-like figures, or world teachers, in the 20th cen-tury, as did Benjamin Crème, who predicted the appearance of the world savior Maitreya in the early 1980s. Others have noted the UFO religions in the decades preceding the New Age movement, which often revolved around extraterrestrial "space brothers" who promised a new era for humanity. Although often at odds with the New Age movement, there was also a strong apocalyptic sense among Christians that existed concurrently with New Age expectations of a radically new time in human history, punctuated by books such as *The Late Great Planet Earth* (1970). True to its nature, the New Age movement pulled from a host of sources, from Buddhism to Christianity to the Mayan calendar, to support the general idea of a coming new era.

There is little consensus as to an exact beginning of the New Age movement. Some have cited books such as Ram Dass's *Be Here Now* (1971), Helen Schucman's *A Course in Miracles* (1975), or *Revelation: The Birth of a New Age* (1976) by David Spangler of the Findhorn Foundation. Others have pointed to particular events as moments that defined and established the New Age, such as the Harmonic Con-vergence in August of 1987, in which meditation events were coordinated across the globe as the sun, moon, and six planets were in alignment. There is more agreement that as the mass social and political movements of the Counterculture began to wane in the early 1970s, the New Age movement, with its dual emphasis on personal development and large-scale transformation, began to grow as a response or replacement to them.

Rather than a traditional denominational religious group that met regularly in churches and whose beliefs and practices could be clearly explained by its leadership, the New Age movement was defined by its flexible, nonhierarchical structure, in which individuals were led by their own needs and experiences and would often move from one aspect of the New Age to another or include multiple strands. This flexibility was one of the reasons the New Age movement grew and sustained itself, but it also made it difficult to study and be understood by observers who have estimated the New Age movement as including from tens of thousands to tens of millions of members. In line with Rodney Stark and William Sim Bainbridge's idea of "audience cults" (as laid out in their 1985 book *The Future of Religion: Secularization, Revival, and Cult Formation*), many New Age adherents were simply readers of books who had little if any contact with one another. The organizational nodes of the New Age were often bookstores, dyadic relationships with teachers and healers, or large-scale festival-like events such as the Rainbow Gatherings.

Individuals within the New Age movement were usually concerned with healing and personal development and not organizational affiliation or dogma. As a result they typically combined practices and moved from one to another as they wanted. Studies of New Age individuals found them most likely to be well-educated, middle-class, and female. The involvement of those within the New Age movement ran along a spectrum from those who were dedicated to it completely to those who occasionally used aspects of it, raising questions as to whether the New Age could be understood as a social movement, type of religion, or lifestyle.

The New Age movement was not without its critics. Popular critiques saw the New Age as a type of dilettante faith that was pursued by adherents for little more than their own satisfaction and well-being. Others took issue with the tendency of the New Age movement to engage in exploitive cultural appropriation by adopting elements of Asian and Native American traditions and misrepresenting them and making money at the expense of these sources.

In 2003, the Roman Catholic Church concluded a six-year study and published a ninety-page document titled *A Christian Reflection on the New Age*, which was sharply critical of the New Age movement and described it as irreconcilable with Christianity, even when taken in part. Evangelical Christians in the United States and Britain were in agreement with the Catholic Church. For much of the 1980s, they had attacked the New Age as antithetical to Biblical teaching, even going so far as to see a sinister conspiracy in the New Age movement to supplant Christianity and become the dominant and singular worldwide religion.

Within popular culture and mass media the term "New Age" quickly moved from being used as a descriptive term to a pejorative and derogatory one that expressed a critique of New Age practices, adherents, and beliefs. By the late 1980s, the term was employed as a punchline on the cover of *Time* magazine with Shirley MacLaine, signaling the marginal and credulous beliefs associated with the New Age. It is no wonder, then, that it has become an archaic term, and many who were once within the New Age movement have stopped referring to themselves as such in recent years, preferring to adopt a wide array of other progressive and neutral terms such as evolutionary, integral, holistic, or transformational.

While many observers think of the New Age movement as something that has largely come and gone with its highpoint in the early 1990s, as with many of its metaphysical forbears such as New Thought the imagined death of the New Age may actually be a mark of its greater success and lasting impact on culture at large. Many of the particular practices and beliefs that were once largely the provenance of the New Age, such as yoga and alternative medicine, are now so accepted and popular that they are unrecognizable as the inheritance of the New Age movement.

The same could be said for the unstructured nature of the New Age movement itself. The most common critiques of the New Age made several decades ago—that its members felt free to pick and choose from various traditions and practices, and considered themselves and not institutions to be authorities in matters of faith and practice—are now the hallmark of the so-called "spiritual but not religious," one of the largest and most rapidly expanding groups in America's spiritual landscape.

Philip Deslippe

See also: Akashic Records; Angels; Astral Plane; Aura; Cayce, Edgar; Channeling; Jung, Carl; Lily Dale Assembly; Mediumship; Mesmerism; Miracles; Near-Death Experience (NDE); Prophecy; Religion and the Paranormal; Scrying; Shamanism; Spiritualism; Synchronicity; Theosophy; Transpersonal Psychology; UFO; Unconscious Mind

Further Reading

Albanese, Catherine. 2013. "Fundamentals of the New Age: Present-Time Pluralism and Postpluralism." In *America: Religions and Religion*, 5th ed., by Catharine Albanese, 237–272. Boston: Wadsworth.

Albanese, Catherine. 2007. *A Republic of Mind and Spirit: A Cultural History of American Metaphysical Religion*. New Haven, CT: Yale University Press.

Hanegraaff, Wouter. 1996. *New Age Religion and Western Culture: Esotericism in the Mirror of Secular Thought*. New York: Suny Press.

Lewis, James R., and J. Gordon Melton, eds. 1992. *Perspectives on the New Age*. New York: Suny Press.

0

OCCULTISM

In the most general of terms, Occult organizations are considered "occult" in large part because they each claim to be in possession of secret religio-philosophical knowledge. There is, however, some variance in regards to each organization's explanation of the relationship between "secret" and "knowledge." For some, occult knowledge is considered to be secret because it contains information that would endanger the uninitiated and thus must be guarded to protect the well-being of others. For others, the potency of this knowledge is derived from it being a secret, and thus it would lose its power if it were to become public domain. Still others maintain that occult wisdom is "self-secret," which is to say that even if those outside of the tradition were provided access to the teachings, they would appear meaningless to the unstudied and uninitiated. Or, similarly, others believe that occult knowledge is secretive in nature because it only becomes comprehensible through some sort of ritual empowerment. Regardless of the chosen interpretation, each Occult organization privileges knowledge considered to be secret (esoteric) and beyond ordinary (paranormal).

The most recognizable predecessors of Occultism include Western esoteric traditions such as Gnosticism, Hermeticism, Alchemy, Kabbalah, and Neoplatonism, many of which claimed to offer a path to gnosis capable of transforming a devotee's consciousness into wisdom and/or transforming their corporeal form into divinity. Occultism is a more recent subset, unique for its role in reviving and modernizing 15th through 18th-century Western esoteric traditions. It is distinct from these earlier groups in that it emerged following the European Enlightenment as part of a larger religio-philosophical reaction against the perceived strictures of rationalism and materialism. As the self-proclaimed heir of ancient practices that purportedly enabled access to secretive celestial realms, hidden energies, and otherwise guarded powers, Occult lineages offered an alternative to a scientism some believed had abandoned the spiritual wisdom vital to humanity's well-being; through more heterodox ritualistic practice, physical postures, meditations, magic, alchemy, astrology, or divination, Occult organizations offered practices and teachings that its proponents believed to be superior to those of dogmatic Abrahamic orthodox traditions. Those groups most commonly associated with early Occultism include the Hermetic Order of the Golden Dawn, the Rosicrucians (Order of the Rose Cross), the Ordo Templi Orientis (O.T.O.), Spiritualism, the Society of the Inner Light, and the Theosophical Society.

As modern science studied the anatomy of the body, Occult science claimed to study an individual's life principle, soul, and/or vital force, and as scientists analyzed the physical universe, Occult scientists studied the physical laws of the universe, as well as the metaphysical principles of the cosmos (which Occultists claimed remained beyond modern science's purview). Although most Occult groups self-identified as being Christian-based in origin, several also claimed that true Christianity was rooted in the ancient wisdom of the Hermetic and Pagan schools that had been suppressed by the Orthodox Church for centuries. According to these interpretations, the life story of Jesus was not actually the history of one man, but instead was more of an allegory providing a secret template for the quest for spiritual perfection. Based on similar assumptions, Occult sects provided alternative readings of the life of Jesus, heterodox explanations regarding the nature of the divine, and doctrine purporting to profess the true teachings of Christianity.

By 1910, the loose conglomerate of sects constituting the broader Occult movement had splintered into different groups, with each attempting to address the interests of Westerners in search of more heterodox "religious" practices. For example, the Hermetic Order of the Golden Dawn focused on a Rosicrucian magical tradition that emphasized a more practical occultism, that is, ritual magic. The Fraternity of the Inner Light emerged as a splinter from Alpha et Omega (the successor group to the Golden Dawn), and its founder, Dion Fortune, combined magic, Kabbalah, and Christian mysticism into a syncretic mixture that proved influential on contemporary and later movements. Others, such as the Ecclesia Gnostica Catholica (E.G.C.), traced their roots to a Gnostic form of Catholicism and focused on the more metaphysical aspects of Occultism, including the Law of Thelema, which emphasized the divinity in humanity. Others, including the Theosophical Society, the most popular Occult movement of the time, emerged with a focus on the Eastern traditions of Buddhists and Hindus, claiming that the East that was the true source of ancient and secret occult wisdom.

Beyond the Theosophical Society, most Occult practices were rooted in Judeo-Christian heterodox traditions, which in retrospect seems somewhat surprising due to Occultism's frequent association with the "darker arts," including witchcraft and Satanism. Within modern-day popular culture, including horror/crime-noir/science fiction movies, television shows, and novels, Occultism is often portrayed as a sinister secret set of practices conjured by a more supernatural variety of villains, each of whom utilized the occult to manipulate unseen, yet extraordinary, malevolent forces and spirits. To better understand how Occultism became associated with Satanism, it is important to consider four broader historical trajectories. First, Orthodox Christian traditions often rebuked the teachings of their more popular heterodox competition by claiming that these groups were preaching a false doctrine, and in their more extreme condemnations, they labeled them as being a form of Satanism. In this way, alternative interpretations of Jesus's teachings were said to be concocted by the devil to win over the souls of devout Christians. Second, throughout much of history, miraculous events or occurrences that were not deemed miracles by orthodoxy, but which otherwise lacked rational or scientific explanation, were instead designated as belonging to the occult. Because these phenomena were not considered the work of God, the assumption was that they were the work of some malevolent but powerful entity, and in Christianity, none was more malevolent and powerful than Satan. Third, prominent members of Occultist groups such as the Theosophical Society maintained that Lucifer (also known as Satan) had in actuality taught a form of Gnosticism that was unknown to orthodoxy but which represented the true teachings of God. Among the proliferation of periodicals and academic journals devoted to different aspects of occultism, the Theosophical Society boasted the largest list of subscribers, publishing several journals including the *Theosophist*, *Theosophical Sings*, and most provocative of all, *Lucifer*. At the same time, two of the most influential Occultists of the era, Theosophy's enigmatic leader, Madame Blavatsky, along with the novelist Edward Sinnett, championed their own unique brand of Eastern esotericism, and in the process, each of their publications included the occasional anti-Christian polemic. Last, but certainly not the least, arguably the most vocal antagonist of Christianity in recent history (who lived to tell his story) was a self-identified Occult practitioner, and although he was not a Satanist, he is widely considered to be one of the Church of Satan's most influential forefathers. In the end, few did more to ensure that Occultism was associated with Satanism than Aleister Crowley (1875–1947).

Crowley was a member of the Ordo Templi Orientis (O.T.O.), an organization that also had an ecclesiastic branch, the aforementioned Ecclesia Gnostica Catholica. Even though Crowley was largely disliked (and even despised) by Occultists and Christians alike, he was neither Satan (as had been alleged) nor a worshipper of the devil. These misrecognitions are, however, understandable, for it was the self-proclaimed "most dangerous man alive" himself who did the most to cultivate the image of Crowley, Satanist Extraordinaire. Crowley seemed to revel in the negative attention and did his best to personify the Christian tradition's greatest fears regarding occult and heterodox traditions. He boasted of sacrificing babies (he did not) and called himself the "Great Beast" from the Book of Revelation, whom many Christians associate with Satan. The impact of Crowley's persistent antagonism cannot be overestimated, and no single figure did more to strengthen the connection between Occultism and the darker arts during the 20th century, particularly once groups such as the Church of Satan, founded by Anton LaVey in 1966, emerged in the late 20th century and claimed Crowley as a founding forefather.

As a result of Occultism's association with practices deemed "evil" by orthodoxy, despite practicing within traditions firmly rooted in Occultism, some 21st-century Occultists attempted to distance themselves from the word "occult." As part of an effort to dissociate themselves, some even criticized rivals by calling them "Occult practitioners." Other groups, such as the Church of Satan and the Temple of the Set, embraced the darker side of Occult history and exaggerated its connections with Satanism, even utilizing much of the ritual and imagery preferred by Crowley. Once other late 20th-century groups such as Wicca called their magical practices witchcraft, the darker associations of Occultism's legacy were all but set in stone. In the process, the relationship between Occultism and the teachings and practices of heterodox Christianity and Western Gnosticism became hidden knowledge, a casualty of history. Instead, most assumed that Occult knowledge was secret for an entirely different reason. Within contemporary popular culture, Occult knowledge is not seen as being secretive because it has remained hidden to protect the uninitiated, or because Occultists have guarded their practices to ensure they retain potency, or because the Occult tradition is so complex and ritualistic that its knowledge is self-secret; rather Occult knowledge is now considered secret because of its association with Satan.

Joel Gruber

See also: Demonology; Paranormal in Movies; Ritual Magic; Spiritualism; Theosophy; Witchcraft

Further Reading

Lachman, Gary. 2005. *A Dark Muse: A History of the Occult.* New York: Thunder's Mouth Press.
Owen, Alex. 2004. *The Place of Enchantment: British Occultism and the Culture of the Modern.* Chicago: University of Chicago Press.

OUIJA BOARD

The Ouija board is a divination tool used to communicate with disembodied spirits. It is most often comprised of a flat, usually wooden, board printed with the letters of the alphabet, the digits zero to nine, the words "yes" and "no," and often the word "goodbye." Users of the Ouija board place their fingers on a planchette, a small cursor of wood or plastic that will move to parts of the Ouija board to spell out words or answer binary questions. The Ouija board has had a remarkable lifespan over the last century and a half: from Spiritualist aid and divination tool to parlor game and finally to staple of both popular and paranormal culture.

Precursors to the Ouija board have been claimed by some to have existed in a wide array of cultures for millennia, ranging from Egypt to Pythagoras, but most of these are specious. There was a well-documented tradition of automatic planchette writing in 12th century China known as *fuji* in which the gods communicated through two persons holding a stick and sieve over sand who produced characters. Clearer forerunners began to appear in the mid-19th century as planchettes, dial plates, and alphabet boards appeared in Europe in the United States and were often used by Spiritualists who previously would have to go tediously through the entire alphabet for the spirits to "knock" at a single letter.

The patent for the Ouija board was filed in Baltimore, Maryland, in 1890 by a group of businessmen who manufactured it through the city's Kennard Novelty Company. While the board's name "Ouija" is often thought to be a combination of two words meaning "yes," the French "oui" and German "ja," the sister-in-law

From its origins as a parlor game, Spiritualist aid, and divination tool in the late 19th century to its emergence as a Parker Brothers board game and a staple of popular and paranormal culture in the 20th and 21st centuries, the Ouija board has had a remarkable lifespan over the past century and a half.

of one of the founding Baltimore business men allegedly came up with the name through the board itself and said it was an Egyptian phrase meaning "good luck." The more likely source may have been a women's rights activist named "Ouida" whose portrait she wore in a locket.

One of the young employees of the Kennard Novelty Company, William Fuld, soon filed a rival patent, began manufacturing his own boards, and then became synonymous with Ouija as he connected his name to the product. Over the next three decades, Fuld's success would be shadowed by a host of competing boards and lawsuits. In 1927 Fuld met an untimely and freakish end when he fell six stories to his death from the roof of his factory.

Ouija's popularity soared during the two World Wars, as the uncertainty of war and massive causalities gave large numbers of people a deep desire to know the future or contact recently deceased loved ones. Another aspect of the board's popularity in the early 20th century was that as a parlor game, it was not only amusing and mysterious but allowed pairs of people to be in close physical proximity to one another.

The Fuld era ended in the late 1960s when Parker Brothers, the giant toy and game manufacturer, bought the rights to the Ouija board at the same time that America was experiencing an occult revival and there was a growing popularity of channeling, a similar way of receiving messages from the beyond. Its popularity soared to the point that its sales were on par with the board game Monopoly, and it became a staple of suburban homes and the late-night slumber parties of teenagers.

Over the last several decades Ouija boards have been attacked by Christian critics who see it as a gateway to the occult that leaves users open and susceptible to the demonic. This perception is shared in popular culture through numerous stories and urban legends that depict the harmless game as not only being supernaturally accurate, but opening up unsuspecting users to dangerous forces far beyond their control.

The most accepted scientific explanation of the Ouija board is that the planchette moves through the ideomotor effect or unconscious motions, and the messages are crafted by the participants who are unaware of their role. Sociologists and psychologists have posited that use of the Ouija board is a way for groups of people to work out fears and shared anxieties. The use of the Ouija board is also tied into what folklorists would call "legend tripping" or "ostention." Users who are familiar with stories about the board look to recreate them or test their veracity, while the legends create the context in which they use the Ouija board and interpret their experiences with it.

The Ouija board has also had a long history as a subject of culture and, occasionally, its creative source. Bill Wilson, the founder of Alcoholics Anonymous, was a user of the Ouija board, as was a young G. K. Chesterton. Dozens of horror movies from the 1960s onward have featured Ouija boards. The American poet James Merrill wrote an epic poem titled "The Book of Ephraim" that recounted his use of the Ouija board for nearly two decades, and it won the Pulitzer Prize in 1976. The most prolific artistic use of the Ouija board came from Pearl Curran, an American Spiritualist who began to communication with a spirit known as "Patience Worth" through a Ouija board in 1912. Curran eventually grew past needing the Ouija board to receive messages from Patience Worth, and the earthly and spiritual partnership ended up producing a host of novels, short stories, and poems, many of which received critical praise.

With its long history and fixed position in culture and myth, the Ouija board will doubtlessly be used and feared for a long time to come.

Philip Deslippe

See also: Art, Creativity, and the Paranormal; Automatic Writing; Divination; Mediumship; Paranormal in Literature; Scrying; Séance; Unconscious Mind

Further Reading

Horowitz, Mitch. 2009. "Don't Try This at Home: Ouija and the Selling of Spiritualism." In *Occult America: The Secret History of How Mysticism Shaped Our Nation*, by Mitch Horowitz, 66–79. New York: Bantam Books.
McRobbie, Linda Rodriguez. 2013. "The Strange and Mysterious History of the Ouija Board." *Smithsonian Magazine*, October 27. Accessed October 15, 2014. http://www.smithsonianmag.com/history/the-strange-and-mysterious-history-of-the-ouija-board-5860627/?no-ist.

OUT-OF-BODY EXPERIENCE (OBE)

The core feature of an out-of-body experience (OBE) is the realistic sensation of moving outside the physical body. The sensation is multi-sensory, including felt shifts of gravity, visual effects corresponding to a shift in POV, and strange noises and vibrations. An OBE also can have a distinct tactile sensation of slipping out of the perceptual body, rather similar to breaking through the surface tension of water when exiting a pool. Sometimes, after exiting, an individual also sees his or her body from a distance, an uncanny experience in itself known as "autoscopy," which is probably one of the neurological causes of the doppelgänger phenomenon. Imagery in OBEs can range from precise impressions of one's environment to less accurate representations that are more similar to dream imagery. Although dreamlike in setting, mentally the experience usually occurs with a high degree of clarity that is described as similar to a waking cognition style and also lucid dreaming. Beyond these core features, the OBE varies wildly in its timing, its circumstances, and its cultural traditions and applications.

Circumstances of Entry

The OBE is often noted in clinical psychiatric settings and is considered by modern medicine to be a hallucination. Over 40 percent of schizophrenics report having OBEs. However, OBEs are common in mentally healthy individuals as well. About 10 percent of the general population has an OBE once in their lives, and close to 25 percent in student populations has one. Primarily, OBEs in the healthy occur when falling asleep or coming out of sleep. Second, OBEs are associated with general anesthesia during surgery or other medical treatments. Third, OBEs can be triggered by trauma and sudden death anxiety.

Spontaneous OBEs are especially linked with sleep, trance, and relaxation. They are also reported during times of intense physical activity, such as rock climbing or long-distance running. Remarkably, OBEs have also been reliably induced clinically by a variety of triggers, including the use of mirrors and virtual reality glasses. Scientists have also discovered that the OBE can be triggered through transcranial stimulation, in which a low power current is directly applied to an area in the brain known as the temporo-parietal junction (TPJ).

Neurology

The TPJ is part of the brain stem or inner ear, and mediates the body's sense of balance and proprioception, locating and positioning the body in relationship to the environment. When the right angular gyrus of the TPJ area is stimulated, the brain temporarily loses its ability to integrate all the information of the senses, resulting in feelings of floating, spinning, and shifting gravity. For this reason, a popular neuroscientific theory of OBE suggests that the transient disintegration of sensory and vestibular information, for whatever reason, is a prerequisite for the OBE to occur.

Traditions and Variations

Out-of-body experiences became of scientific interest in the Victorian era, especially due to the popularity of the Spiritualism movement in which OBEs were celebrated and cultivated as a way to soul travel and commune with the dead, an ability called "traveling clairvoyance." Earlier works by mystics, such as those by Emanuel Swedenborg, were reread with interest for clues to navigating the strange dream-like realms of this visionary landscape. Theosophists in the early 20th century later postulated a "subtle body" theory, which has been further popularized by modern writers. This tradition continues today, and the out-of-body experience is known by many as astral projection.

In indigenous cultures, the cluster of OBE phenomena generally translates to "soul flight." The OBE is described by influential religion scholar Mircea Eliade as an intended result of applying techniques of ecstasy in ritual social settings. Many cultures around the world are known to use drumming, dance, sleep deprivation, fasting, and psychedelics to bring about OBEs and other dissociative states. In many cultures, the OBE is a shamanic tool for gathering information for the purpose of healing. It is important to keep in mind that, given the large role of culture on the modulation of the brain, scientists still do not have a clear understanding of how these trances are related to clinically determined stages of sleep or Western-classified altered states of consciousness.

OBEs and Remote Viewing

The OBE is not the same experience as remote viewing, which has been popularized in, for example, the films *Suspect Zero* and *The Men Who Stare at Goats*. During remote viewing, the individual enters a light trance state and focuses on lost objects or specific environments in order to receive information. Both the OBE and remote viewing are techniques used by individuals to ostensibly gather information beyond the limits of physical body. However, in remote viewing, the experiencer never loses contact with the body or awareness of position in space, while the OBE is a fully immersive journey of perception: visually, kinesthetically, and mentally.

OBEs and Sleep Paralysis

OBEs are commonly experienced as a side-effect of sleep paralysis, the strange but brief occurrence of awareness during REM paralysis. Typically, sufferers of sleep paralysis feel a weight on the throat or chest and become alarmed when they try to move and are in fact paralyzed due to the normal muscle atonia that accompanies REM sleep. Some people also experience dream-like visions, known as hypnagogia, as well as bizarre kinesthetic effects like gravity rolling over or the body image stretching or compacting. These sensations can culminate in a complete OBE.

OBEs and Lucid Dreaming

Lucid dreaming is the experience of knowing that one is dreaming while dreaming. People who experience both OBEs and lucid dreams often differentiate the two by an internal feeling and a corresponding belief that the OBE environment is not malleable as in a lucid dream. Many scholars insist that this differentiation is a naive realism or a folk phenomenology, reinforced by expectation, and argue that the OBE is a dream in all respects, except the dreamer thinks they are really out-of-body. The association between lucid dreams and OBEs cannot be easily dismissed, as OBE-type experience in sleep often start with the classic moving out of body sensations and then grade into dream settings. In the sleep laboratory, OBEs have been show to occur in REM sleep, also known as "dreaming sleep," the stage of sleep most often associated with lucid dreaming.

Neuroscientist Kevin Nelson has written that the OBE is one possible experience occurring when REM sleep intrudes into waking life, creating "borderlands of consciousness" that blend dreaming and waking styles of cognition. Out-of-body experiences and lucid dreams are interrelated not only on a phenomenological level but also in regard to the experiencers themselves: those who experience lucid dreams are more likely to report OBEs, and vice versa.

Veridical OBEs and Near-Death Experiences

While it is tempting to hastily conclude that OBEs are simply realistic dreams, medically validated accounts of OBEs occurring in hospital settings include many instances of the experiencer bringing back valid, or "veridical," information. In many of these cases, the individual is in a medically induced coma, cardiac arrest, and in some cases, legally dead. Near-death experiences or NDEs often include the out-of-body dimension, but go on to include other uncanny experiences, such as meetings with ancestors and religious figures. Although these narratives are more than "just anecdotes" as they are recorded and verified by medical specialists, they still cannot be explained by the current scientific paradigm in which consciousness exists solely within the brain. Only a handful of these reports have been made, and numerous research problems plague this study, so it is too early to declare one thing or another regarding veridical information in OBEs.

Theories and Applications

One popular REM hypothesis for out-of-body experiences and near-death experiences posits an original evolutionary advantage. REM paralysis may be a vestige of an "opossum effect," in which under times of extreme stress, the body goes limp, and the mind disassociates from pain, creating a separate locus of self, or a distinct self-model, that allows for high levels of metacognition without strong emotion. This could be useful not only for avoiding being eaten, but also for staying calm during high-stress situations. Anthropologist Michael Winkelman suggests another evolutionary theory, in which OBEs and other altered states of consciousness were originally incorporated into early hominid rituals that facilitated social cohesion and emotional bonding. These tendencies, when later combined with language sharing, would serve the community by providing powerful, emotional shared journeys that simultaneously give meaning and primacy—and status—to the bearer of the vision.

Philosopher Thomas Metzinger argues that, because OBEs create new self-models consistently across cultures and time that are experienced as separate from the body, it may be the experiential basis for the concept of the soul. For many people, the OBE is interpreted as a religious or spiritual experience that can have long-term effects on the individual's fear of death as well as their beliefs about what happens after death. These extraordinary experiences can be integrated in counseling. For this reason, psychologists consider the OBE a visionary human experience, whether it is a neurological illusion, a portal beyond the veil, or both.

Ryan Hurd

See also: Astral Plane; Doppelgänger; Hypnagogic State; Lucid Dreams; Mystical Experience; Near-Death Experience (NDE); Remote Viewing; Sleep Paralysis; Spiritualism; Survival after Death; Swedenborg, Emanuel; Theosophy

Further Reading

Alexander, Eben. 2013. *Proof of Heaven: A Neurosurgeon's Journey into the Afterlife*. New York: Simon and Schuster.

Hurd, Ryan, and Kelly Bulkeley, eds. 2014. *Lucid Dreaming: New Perspectives on Consciousness in Sleep*. Santa Barbara, CA: Praeger.

Monroe, Robert. (1971) 1992. *Journeys out of the Body*. New York: Broadway Books.

Nelson, Kevin. 2011. *Spiritual Doorway in the Brain*. New York: Dutton.

Taylor, Greg. 2013. *Stop Worrying! There Probably Is an Afterlife*. Brisbane, AU: Daily Grail Press.

P

PARANORMAL

The term "paranormal" is derived from the Latin *para*, meaning "besides/beyond," used as a prefix to the word "normal." Thus "paranormal" is used to refer to phenomena that are besides or beyond what is considered normal. If the term is taken literally, then anything not reflective of the norm could be considered paranormal; for example, immense riches, winning a Nobel Prize, or giving birth to octuplets. Originally, however, the term was introduced by psychical researchers around 1915 with a more specific meaning in mind: its purpose was to replace the earlier term "supernormal." This latter word was originally used by psychical researchers to describe the large group of debatable phenomena that were the focus of their scientific investigations. These mainly consisted of experiences that potentially demonstrated evidence pertaining to the survival of bodily death and evidence of the existence of psychic abilities or, as it later came to be called, "psi." Therefore, the phenomena to which "supernormal" was applied were near-death experiences, deathbed visions, apparitions, ghosts, poltergeist activity, clairvoyance, telepathy, and psychokinesis.

The term "paranormal" was introduced as an alternative to "supernormal" because the prefix "super" implies that the phenomena described by the term are in some way above or superior to that of ordinary occurrences. Thus it was believed the term required alteration as it was loaded with bias. Alternatively, the prefix "para" conveys more clearly that the phenomena in question shared a commonality with those under the scrutiny of ordinary scientific endeavors, existing alongside but not far removed from them.

A second problem with the term "supernormal" was highlighted in the fact that some confusion occurred due to its apparent similarity with the term "supernatural." This misunderstanding was particularly profound, as many of the phenomena that psychical research was investigating had historically been explained in terms of the supernatural. What is meant by the term "supernatural," and why did psychical research wish to avoid association with it? Initially popularized by theologians in the Middle Ages, "supernatural" was used to refer to events described in the Bible, such as miracles—for example, the transformation of water into wine, Moses's parting of the Red Sea, the ten plagues of Egypt—that were considered reflections of the power of an omnipotent and transcendent God. Thus, when this word is applied to a phenomenon, it (the phenomenon) becomes laden with assumptions that some form of divine, occult, or magical force is responsible for its occurrence, a force that either breaks the rules of nature or operates outside of them.

The word "paranormal" literally means "that which lies beyond the normal." It was introduced by psychical researchers around 1915 to replace the word "supernormal." Although today it is an umbrella term that is used to describe virtually all anomalous and mystical things, from UFOlogy and the occult to cryptozoology and strange natural phenomena, in its original usage it applied to a more limited set of phenomena, specifically:

- Near-death experiences

- Deathbed visions

- Apparitions

- Ghosts

- Poltergeist activity

- Clairvoyance

- Telepathy

- Psychokinesis

This notion that the phenomena under investigation by psychical researchers were in some way nonadherent to the rules of nature was considered unlikely. Moreover, it implied that no objective method for investigating and understanding these phenomena would be possible. Therefore, it would nullify the purpose of any scientific inquiry into them at all, because they operate outside the boundaries of nature and thus scientific scrutiny. Ultimately, "supernormal" was considered too much at risk of being accidentally associated with supernatural, whereas the term "paranormal" implied that the phenomena, although they might lie beyond the scope of current scientific understanding, still conformed to natural laws. This would allow psychical researchers to demonstrate, through the use of the scientific method, that if real, the phenomena they had devoted themselves to investigating were as much a part of the natural world as any other.

The use and meaning of the term "paranormal" has changed over time, predominantly due to the popular media's adoption and expansion of the term to incorporate all mysterious phenomena. Many people now classify as paranormal such things as UFOlogy (the study of unidentified flying objects), alien abduction reports, the occult, magic, witchcraft, cryptozoology (the study of strange creatures such as Bigfoot and the Loch Ness Monster), anomalous natural phenomena (e.g., crop circles and the Bermuda Triangle), and folklore creatures (e.g., zombies and vampires). In this way, "paranormal" has become a much wider umbrella term to characterize all anomalous and mystical things. All of these mysterious phenomena would lie outside the remit of the term "paranormal" in its original conceptualization, but if the word is taken literally, in its etymological sense of "that which lies beyond the normal," then all of these things fit quite comfortably inside it, along with anything else that is not considered normal.

David Saunders

See also: Apparitions; Extrasensory Perception (ESP); Haunting; Psychical Research; Society for Psychical Research; Survival after Death; UFO; Witchcraft; Zombies

Further Reading

Inglis, Brian. 1978. *Natural and Supernatural: History of the Paranormal.* London: Hodder & Stoughton Ltd.

Inglis, Brian. 1984. *Science and Parascience: A History of the Paranormal 1914–1939.* London: Hodder and Staughton Ltd.

PARANORMAL DREAMS

Paranormal dreams are extraordinary dreams that cannot be satisfactorily explained by the conventional scientific worldview. Most researchers do not use the phrase "paranormal," however, as they believe these events are natural and will eventually be accepted and understood by mainstream science. Many researchers use the term "anomalous" more commonly than ESP (extrasensory perception). In this vein, anomalous dreams may be similar to other unexplained topics that were originally branded as fringe science, such as multiple personality disorder, hypnosis, and lucid dreaming and are merely awaiting the right political climate, fresh technological innovation, and a new generation of passionate scientists. The term "psi" is also preferred by many researchers to refer to "interactions between organisms and their environment (including other organisms) in which information exchange or influence has occurred that cannot be explained through mainstream science's understanding of sensory-motor channels. They are regarded as anomalous because they appear to occur beyond the constraints of time, space and energy" (Krippner et al. 2002, 93).

A paranormal dream typology includes most of the classically defined types of psi cognition that occur during sleep and are remembered as dreams, including telepathy, clairvoyance, precognition, and post-cognition. They can be seen as a subcategory of anomalous dream experiences that, unlike most ordinary dreams, are highly memorable, vivid, and intuitively known upon awakening as having extraordinary portent. Long-term effects of anomalous dreams include their potentially transformative influence on the individual's belief structures and subsequent life decisions. Other examples are spiritual, lucid, and healing dreams.

There are several kinds of evidence used in support of paranormal dreams. Historically, the most common is anecdotal evidence as well as medical expert testimonials, both of which are first-person narrative accounts. More formal kinds of descriptive analyses such as phenomenology and anthropological fieldwork (including ethnography and folklore) describe people's experiences and seek to understand the most common ways that people interpret these events from psycho-social and cultural points of views. Clinical laboratory data is the most direct scientific evidence, relying on electrical brain activity of in-lab dreamers and meta-analyses of older studies. Unfortunately, this is also the rarest type of evidence due to taboo and lack of funding in the scientific research world, and the results of the studies—although promising—should be considered preliminary.

Telepathic Dreams

Dreams that appear to include information that the dreamer received from another living human are known as telepathic dreams. The most common theme in telepathic dreams is death, such as dreaming that someone has died. Although the evidence is usually anecdotal, these narratives are also extremely common across cultures. Indeed, telepathic dreams are commonly reported by anthropologists themselves while doing field research within cultural groups that acknowledge these kinds of dreams.

The best clinical evidence comes from research in the 1960s and 1970s by Montague Ullman and Stanley Krippner at the Maimonides Medical Center in Brooklyn, New York. In 11 formal experiments, the team's results were reviewed by independent judges and were deemed statistically significant about two thirds of the time. Attempts at replicating this research in other laboratories have been sparse and inconsistent, and their results have been mixed. It's fair to say that scientists have not conclusively demonstrated telepathic communication in dreams, but research interest is gaining traction in several university settings due to these pioneering studies.

Clairvoyant Dreams

Clairvoyance is the alleged ability to receive new information about distant places and events without applying the known human senses or logical inference. Phenomenologically, clairvoyance is often associated with dream-like states of consciousness in which the seeker travels beyond the body and comes back with new knowledge. Known in antiquity and in many indigenous cultures as "soul travel," today in New Ages circles it is called "astral travel," and in the parapsychological research community, "remote viewing." Other clairvoyant dreams resemble telepathic and precognitive dreams; indeed it may be impossible to distinguish between them.

Ethnographic accounts of clairvoyance are common, in which, for example, informants claim to soul travel at night to discover imminent threats to their village or region. Clinical parapsychological research into clairvoyance has revealed positive results of matched targets during dreams, much greater than would be expected by chance alone, but these studies all have limitations and procedural differences. By and large, these studies have not convinced the scientific community. Still, several decades of funded studies by the U.S. government, which were

Types of Paranormal Dreams

Telepathic: A dream that appears to include information received from another living person.

Clairvoyant: A dream that appears to include information about distant places or events.

Precognitive: A dream that appears to include prophetic information about the future that later proves accurate.

Visitation: A dream that features an appearance by, and communication from, a deceased person or a supernatural/mystical being.

Past-life: A dream in which a person recalls or experiences events from a previous life.

declassified under Executive Order Nr. 1995–4-17, have documented successes in clairvoyance including the locating of a downed Soviet airplane by remote viewers. However, in 1995, after 20 years of research the U.S. government declared that there is no benefit to remote viewing or psi-ops in general, and no new studies have been declassified since (if they exist).

Precognitive Dreams

The precognitive dream is the most recognized type of extraordinary dream. Here is the prophetic dream, which seers, theologians, and diviners have been puzzling over for millennia—often putting their lives on the line as they distinguish a true dream from a false call as they stand before kings and between armies. The largest modern collection of precognitive dreams was collected by Louisa Rhine, wife of J. B. Rhine, and is now housed at Duke University Library. These letters include thousands of accounts of precognition, three out of four of which occurred during dreams. Beyond the anecdotal level, many trusted testimonials exist as well as some suggestive clinical trials, including the Maimonides trials.

Visitation Dreams

Dreams reliably connect people to the departed. These encounters can also come during waking life as well as in hypnagogic hallucinations. Visitation dreams can be seen as transpersonal encounters because they can be profound, impactful, remembered for a lifetime, and capable of forever shifting the individual's core beliefs about life and the universe. Visitation dreams are often reported to have clairvoyant or telepathic content that surprises the dreamer upon awakening. Many religious traditions, of course, revere stories of powerful visitation dreams from esteemed spiritual leaders and ancestors. Visitations can include spiritual messages or advice that are often beyond the individual's comprehension until reflected upon for some time. Are the figures in visitation dreams "really" them? Like many aspects of paranormal dreaming, there is no clear answer, but regardless, visitation dreams are often noted as being helpful for overcoming grief and letting go of the past.

Past-Life Dreams

Dreaming of past-life experiences is another commonly reported kind of paranormal experience. Although not as common as precognitive dreams, these dreams are similarly marked by a high degree of recall and life impact due to an internal sense that the experience is more than a normal dream. Some parapsychological researchers refer to these "memories" as "postcognition." Ethnographically, these dreams are common in societies that support belief in reincarnation. Often the first dream of an "arriving" old soul occurs in pregnant women. However, most research into past life dreams has involved collecting case studies of young people who dream about people, places, and things that they could not have otherwise known about by accepted means. Therapists who identify and work with past-life dreams argue that although it is impossible to know if their clients really are remembering past lives, the narratives created through the work are unusually empowering and result in good healing outcomes.

Critical Thinking and New Theories

The crucial role of critical thinking cannot be overstated. Even parapsychologists are skeptical and quick to point out fraudulent research. Many anecdotal accounts no doubt can be explained on the basis of coincidence, faulty memory, or information that was already available to the dreamer (so-called "unconscious processing"). Under all these conditions, it is easy and may even be advantageous for some dreamers to confabulate the significance of a dream, whether purposefully or unconsciously. No doubt some of the most famous prophetic dreams from history are fabrications and popular myths. Also, most dream researchers agree that, in general, dream content showcases past, present, and future possibilities. This creative drive is often misunderstood by those unfamiliar with powerful dreams and eager to showcase a paranormal ability to their peers.

With these reservations in mind, there are still several interesting theories about the prevalence of anomalous dreams. Recent analyses on the Maimonides data have correlated the best dream telepathy data with nights characterized by low sunspot activity or calm nights with no electrical storms in the vicinity. Therefore, geomagnetic activity may be a natural predictor of some anomalous events. A similar trend has been discovered by researcher Jorge Conesa Sevilla in regard to sleep paralysis, another anomalous sleep event that is correlated with telepathy, uncanny visitations, and mutual dreaming. Other researchers have been exploring the possibility that paranormal dreams are not so much a skill but rather a quantum effect involving non-locality or entanglement as possible mechanisms for this "spooky action." Chaos theory and Bohm's holographic model of reality may also prove to be fruitful theories for explaining why the brain may be susceptible to anomalous interactions. It is still too early to tell, but these paradigms certainly lead to more testable questions than theories of classical physics, which has largely become a dead end in consciousness studies in general.

Ryan Hurd

See also: Clairvoyance; Lucid Dreams; Precognition; Reincarnation; Sleep Paralysis; Telepathy; Unconscious Mind

Further Reading

Graff, Dale. (1998) 2003.*Tracks in the Psychic Wilderness: An Exploration of ESP, Remote Viewing, Precognitive Dreaming and Synchronicity.* London: Vega.

Krippner, Stanley, Fariba Bogzaran, and Andre Percia de Carvalho. 2002. *Extraordinary Dreams and How to Work with Them.* SUNY Studies in Dreams Series. Albany, NY: SUNY.

Laughlin, Charles. 2011. *Communing with the Gods: Consciousness, Culture and the Dreaming Brain.* Brisbane, AU: Daily Grail.

Men Who Stare at Goats, film. 2010. Beverly Hills, CA: Distributed by Anchor Bay Entertainment.

Sevilla, Jorge Conesa. 2004. *Wrestling with Ghosts.* Bloomington, IN: Xlibris.

Ullman, Montague, Stanley Krippner, and Alan Vaughan. (1974) 2003. *Dream Telepathy: Experiments in Nocturnal Extrasensory Perception.* 3rd ed. Charlottesville, VA: Hampton Roads Publishing Company.

Van de Castle, Robert. 1994. *Our Dreaming Mind.* New York: Ballantine.

PARANORMAL IN LITERATURE

The paranormal has been a consistent feature in world literature for as long as written records have existed. It was not until the Enlightenment in Europe that paranormal literature began to be dominated by its eerie and transgressive representatives. Before this time, paranormal forces were often as likely to be benign, neutral, or helpful as they were to be threatening and frightful.

Death for ancient Egyptians who had undergone the proper funerary rituals was an extension of life. The general ancient Egyptian approach to death meant their ghost stories often lacked the spooky quality of modern Western accounts. The living could communicate with the dead though many means. They could even write letters to them. In the *Teaching of Amenemhet* the dead king is depicted as merely returning to give his son and successor important advice about how to rule. One fragment of a ghost story from the Ramesside period in New Kingdom Egypt (c. 1279 BCE–c. 1213 BCE) depicts a series of instructions for how to properly honor the dead.

In contrast, ancient Mesopotamian accounts describe the underworld as a gloomy, gray place that is cut off from the land of the living. This is particularly the case in *The Epic of Gilgamesh*, which is generally believed to have originated in the 18th century BCE, though the most complete versions come from the seventh century BCE. In the epic, when the wild man Enkidu is cursed to die, he laments that he is going to a house without light, where he will have only dirt to drink and clay to eat. The second part of the epic deals with Gilgamesh's attempt to achieve immortality. While the paranormal in these tales tends to feature a bitter quality seldom seen in the ancient Egyptian accounts, they are nevertheless presented as also being part of life as such, and not exceptions to the natural order.

Paranormal forces and figures played many major roles in the literature of ancient Greece and Rome. The *Iliad* and *Odyssey*, attributed to the blind poet Homer, both date to around the eighth century BCE and were the basis of ancient Greek education. They also feature a host of paranormal creatures, sorcerers, and spirits. Likewise, many Greek tragedies by Aeschylus (c. 525 BCE–c. 456 BCE), Sophocles (c. 497 BCE–c. 406 BCE), and Euripides (c. 480 BCE–c. 406 BCE), while not always containing paranormal themes, often employ them. This continued to be the case in much Roman literature, such as Virgil's (70 BCE–19 BCE) *Aeneid* and Ovid's (c. 43 BCE–c. 17 CE) *Metamorphosi*.

The literature of the Abrahamic traditions feature many supernatural aspects. Yahweh tended to reveal himself in actions that were contrary to the normal processes of nature, such as pillars of flame, burning bushes that were not consumed, and bronze serpents that could harm or heal. One particularly noteworthy case of the supernatural in the Abrahamic tradition is the story of the Witch of Endor in the First Book of Samuel 28:3–25. King Saul asks the Witch of Endor to summon the spirit of the prophet Samuel, who reprimands the King for disturbing his rest and prophesizes his downfall. Also representative of paranormal literature in the Abrahamic tradition are the stories collected together under the title *One Thousand and One Nights*. The chronology of the text is uncertain, but it is generally believed to date from around the ninth century CE. The influence of *One Thousand and One Nights* on Middle Eastern and world literature is hard to overestimate. Scholars have noted that many of the stories in the collection possess features found in contemporary genres, such as horror, mystery, science fiction, and fantasy, and feature demons, *jinni*, ghosts, spirits, the first recorded use of the term "ghoul," and magical artifacts, among other supernatural tropes.

Japan and China have a long history of paranormal literature. Chinese ghost stories flourished during the Tang Dynasty (618 CE–907 CE), while the most prominent collection in Japanese was *Tales of Days Gone By*, collected during the late Heian period (894 CE–1185 CE). *Tales of Days Gone By* is an anthology of folktales from India, China, and Japan. The stories in the collection tend to be instructional but entertaining, often using stories of ghosts, Oni, and Tengu to teach the principles of Buddhism. *The Tale of Genji*, which is considered to be the world's first novel, appeared in the 11th century and also prominently features supernatural tales. During the Edo Period (1603 CE–1867 CE) and beyond, *kaidan*, a form of ghost story also drawing from Japanese and Chinese folklore, became increasingly popular. Unlike many Western narratives, the element of surprise in traditional Asian

What's So Paranormal about Paranormal Literature?

What we call "paranormal literature" today is a function of changes in sociocultural attitudes stemming from the Western Enlightenment. The modern use of the term usually connotes literature that deals with the uncanny, the frightening, and the horrific, but in wider historical perspective the literature of the paranormal is just as likely to deal with pleasant, benign, neutral, and other nonthreatening forces and themes. Nor did most of those who wrote it consider it to be paranormal in the way that we use the term today.

literature very rarely revolved around the mere presence of a ghost or supernatural force but was instead achieved through some twist or uncertainty surrounding the meaning of the force or what the ghosts were there to accomplish. Contemporary Asian literature is likewise replete with supernatural literature, and it now employs many of the characteristics of Western literature. However, it still maintains its own distinct form. One notable example of the difference between contemporary European and Asian paranormal literature is the large number of female ghosts that feature in the latter since the Japanese writer Koji Suzuki (1957–) first published *Ring* in 1991.

India also has a very old history of supernatural literature. The *Bytal Puchisi; or the Twenty-five Tales of Bytal* contains a collection of stories from the 11th century CE. The framing story surrounding the *Bytal Puchisi* features King Vikram's promise to a sorcerer that he will capture a Vetala, a kind of vampiric spirit capable of possessing the bodies of the dead. Every time the King captures the Vetala, it asks him a riddle in the form of a story in the collection. When the King answers the riddle correctly, the creature returns to hang upside down on its tree, and the King must try to capture it again. Another prominent collection of paranormal stories in Indian literature can be found in the Bengali language collection of stories called *Grandmother's Tales*, collected in the early 20th century by Dakshinaranjan Mitra Majumder (1877–1956). Rabindranath Tagore (1861–1941), the famous poet, polymath, and Bengali cultural icon, also authored several short stories that features ghosts, such as "Konkal," "Monihara," "Living or Dead?" and "Hungry Stones." In these stories, he often played with the question of whether or not something supernatural had occurred.

In the Western tradition medieval literature follows many of the same patterns as paranormal literature elsewhere. In particular there is also a tendency to treat the paranormal as a normal part of life. This trend is common in romantic literature. For instance, the romance writer Chrétien de Troyes (c. 1100) in his work *Yvain the Knight of the Lion* features a magical anvil that can be used to cause storms. Laudine, Yvain's wife, uses the anvil to express her displeasure, and while the anvil is considered rare, the characters in the story do not consider it to be exceptional.

The collection of works by Marie de France (c. 1100), *The Lais of Marie de France*, features a story titled "Bisclavret" in which a baron admits to his wife that he is a werewolf. Much of the drama of the story then revolves around the baron seeking to return to his human form after his wife rejects him for being a Bisclavret, takes a lover, and conspires with him to trap the baron in his animal form. However, when the king realizes what has happened, he helps return the baron to his human form. Similar motifs surrounding the acceptance of the supernatural can be found in many of the Arthurian legends, as well as in the writings of the poet Geoffrey Chaucer (c. 1343–1400).

The early modern period began to display an increasingly ironic approach to paranormal literature. Despite this, playwrights such as William Shakespeare (1564–1616) and Christopher Marlowe (1564–1593) made extensive use of paranormal themes, from the witches and Banquo's ghost in *Macbeth*, to the ghost of Caesar in *Julius Caesar*, to the spirits and magic of *The Tempest* and the playfulness of the spirits in a *Midsummer's Night's Dream*, to Marlow's *Dr. Faustus* with its devils and spirits.

It was during the Western Enlightenment and the periods that followed it that paranormal literature came to take on its current and more exclusive connection to horror, the uncanny, and fright. This was particularly the case with gothic literature, which is generally held to have begun in 1763 with the publication of Horace Walpole's (1717–1797) *The Castle of Otranto*. English gothic fiction had parallels throughout Europe. Even Johann Wolfgang von Goethe (1749–1832), who sometimes mocked what he saw as the morbid fascinations of the gothic romances of his age, greatly contributed to this body of literature with his *Faust*. However, not all gothic literature was paranormal, and not all paranormal literature was gothic. Ann Radcliffe (1764–1823) almost exclusively presented her readers with mysteries that appeared at the start to be supernatural, but which were by the end of the story explained as being brought about by completely natural events. Edgar Allan Poe (1809–1849), considered a master of gothic literature, also wrote very few works that could be described as paranormal.

The 20th and 21st centuries have seen an explosion of uncanny and horrific paranormal literature as well as its increased globalization. In some cases these works have been influenced by one or more aspects of real-world paranormal research; a notable example is Shirley Jackson's celebrated 1959 novel *The Haunting of Hill House*, whose fictional depiction of scientific research on a haunted house was modeled directly on the controversial 1898 book *The Haunting of B—House*, about the psychical research investigation of a Scottish haunting. However, it is important to note that this rising trend of the horrific in paranormal literature, while increasingly widespread, has many current exceptions in world literature. For instance, magical realism has become a major feature of Latin American literature. Gabriel García Márquez's (1927–2014) *One Hundred Years of Solitude* is considered to be a foundational work of this genre, as is the work of Jorge Luis

Borges (1899–1986). As a genre, one of the defining features of magical realism is the fact that the supernatural is dealt with as a part of everyday life and as part of otherwise realistic settings.

Enlightenment models of paranormal literature are also beginning to change. While the American writer Howard Phillips Lovecraft (1890–1937) attempted a broad overview of many of the classics of supernatural fiction in his now famous essay "Supernatural Horror in Literature," his own fiction considerably complicates the role of the supernatural in literature. In many of his writings what is "supernatural" is presented as not being *other than* nature but *beyond* the nature that human beings can comprehend. This form diverges considerably from both the normalization of the supernatural and what could be called its paranormalization, possibly pointing a way to a synthesis of the two traditions.

Paranormal literature is as old and diverse as any human literary product. However, the vast majority of what we call "paranormal" in paranormal literature was not seen as such by those who wrote it. If anything, the preponderance of the uncanny and frightening in contemporary Western paranormal literature says far more about the ways that modern society tends to view the paranormal as something transgressive and subversive than it does about the paranormal itself.

B. D. Mitchell

See also: Art, Creativity, and the Paranormal; Paranormal in Movies; Paranormal on Television; Religion and the Paranormal

Further Reading

Bond, Ruskin, ed. 1993. *Penguin Book of Indian Ghost Stories*. Westminster, UK: Penguin Books.

Davison, Jane P. 2012. *Early Modern Supernatural: The Dark Side of European Culture, 1400–1700*. Westport, CT: Praeger.

De Wolf, Charles, trans. 2003. *Tales of Days Gone By*. Tokyo: ALIS.

Dziemianowicz, Stefan R., and S. T. Joshi, eds. 2005. *Supernatural Literature of the World: An Encyclopedia*. Westport, CT: Greenwood.

Enright, D. J. 1994. *The Oxford Book of the Supernatural*. Oxford: Oxford University Press.

Felton, D. 1998. *Haunted Greece and Rome: Ghost Stories from Classical Antiquity*. Austin, TX: University of Texas Press.

Friesen, Ryan Curtis. 2010. *Supernatural Fiction in Early Modern Drama and Culture*. Eastbourne, UK: Sussex Academic Press.

Joynes, Andrew. 2003. *Medieval Ghost Stories: An Anthology of Miracles, Marvels and Prodigies*. Woodbridge, UK: Boydell Press.

Lovecraft, H. P. (1927) 2005. "Supernatural Horror in Literature." In *At the Mountains of Madness*, by H.P. Lovecraft, 103–182. New York: The Modern Library.

Manguel, Alberto. 1984. *Blackwater: The Book of Fantastic Literature*. New York: Clarkson Potter.

Manguel, Alberto. 1990. *Blackwater 2: More Tales of the Fantastic*. New York: Three Rivers Press.

Smajic, Srdjan. 2010. *Ghost-Seers, Detectives, and Spiritualists: Theories of Vision in Victorian Literature and Science*. Cambridge, UK: Cambridge University Press.

Tagore, Rabindranath. 1916. *The Hungry Stones and Other Stories*. New York: The Macmillan Company.

Traill, Nancy H. 1996. *Possible Worlds of the Fantastic: The Rise of the Paranormal in Literature*. Toronto, CA: University of Toronto Press.

PARANORMAL IN MOVIES

Since their earliest days, a tension has existed in the movies between an impulse to capture, preserve, and represent reality, and an impulse to use cinema's resources to present fantastical and otherworldly images. Even cinema's most realist tendencies shelter paranormal affinities, as it is a medium that bestows an immortality on its subject that is also a brand of living death. It is no surprise that, throughout the 20th century, the movies would become perhaps the prime means for depicting the paranormal. A large number of now ironclad conventions, such as the idea that vampires are destroyed by sunlight or that zombies are a shambling, leaderless horde, trace back to movies. While it is impossible to know how much cinematic convention has affected the public conception of the paranormal, anecdotal evidence, like the rise of public interest in Satanism and possession after hits like *Rosemary's Baby* in 1968, *The Exorcist* in 1973, and *The Omen* in 1976, suggests that the influence is considerable.

Depictions of the paranormal are as old as cinema itself. Beginning in the late 1890s, Georges Méliès and other trick filmmakers embraced cinema's potential for transpositions, substitutions, stop motion, and other formal tricks to import the whimsical merriment of the fairytale theater into the new medium. The superimposition, with its heritage in spirit photography and other 19th century trick photography, emerged as a privileged signifier of both the supernatural and hallucinations/dreams on screen and would remain so for decades, even if it would be eventually restricted to comedies. Even D. W. Griffith, better known for more realistic cinematic fare, directed the Poe-inspired *The Avenging Conscience* (1914), which made extensive use of superimposition effects to represent the psyche of its haunted protagonist. German Expressionism produced such paranormal-themed classics as *The Cabinet of Dr. Caligari* (1920), *The Golem* (1920), *Nosferatu* (1922), *Warning Shadows* (1923), *The Hands of Orlac* (1924), and *Faust* (1926), and even the science fiction allegory *Metropolis* (1927) featured a villain who is as much an alchemist as a scientist. The silent Swedish cinema made ghost films its signature, producing such classics as *The Phantom Carriage* (1921) and *Sir Arne's Treasure* (1919). Meanwhile, avant-garde/experimental filmmakers embraced supernatural themes as opening new worlds of cinematic possibility. Key examples include Hans Richter's *Ghosts Before Breakfast* (1928) and versions of *The Fall of the House of Usher* by Jean Epstein and James Sibley Watson (both 1928). In 1924, the great Hungarian-Jewish film scholar Béla Balázs wrote that it "is certain . . . that no written or oral literature is able to express the ghostly, the demonic, and the supernatural as well as the cinematic" (Balázs 59).

To some, more than just serving as a vehicle for depicting the paranormal, cinema was paranormal in itself. It was even claimed that the set of the pro-spiritualist film *Bishop of the Ozarks* (1926) hosted real ghosts who appeared to augment the film's special effects. However, cinema was also received from early on as an anti-spiritualist medium. Many 19th century magicians worked to debunk the claims of spiritualism by replicating their feats, and trick filmmakers continued this cause either implicitly or explicitly all through the silent era, from *A Visit to the Spiritualist* (1899), *Is Spiritualism a Fraud?* (1906), and *A Ghost Story; or, How a Spiritualist Séance Was Disturbed* (1908) to *Fraudulent Spiritualism Exposed* (1926). Harry Houdini, famous as a debunker of spiritualism, produced and starred in several films from 1919 to 1923; curiously, his reincarnation-themed *The Man from Beyond* (1922) approvingly waves a copy of Arthur Conan Doyle's *The Never Revelation* (1918) onscreen. If spiritualists hoped that cinema might someday produce convincing evidence of contact with the afterlife, it was more often used against them.

The Great Depression in the United States saw the advent of the Golden Age of Horror, beginning with highly successful and much-imitated adaptations of *Dracula* and *Frankenstein* in 1931. Throughout the 1930s and 1940s, Hollywood studios made innumerable monster and mad scientist movies, many of them borrowing the prestige of existing literary and theatrical properties to attract an audience and avoid censorship. It is this period that established many of the conventions and iconographies of the vampire, werewolf, zombie, mummy, and so on that would have to be either adhered to, modified, or consciously rejected by later filmmakers. Ghosts and similar themes proved rarer in this period, though examples such as *Supernatural* (1933) continued the tradition of mediums and spiritualists being depicted as frauds at best and villains at worst. In *Supernatural*, the medium uses an elaborate bag of tricks to deceive his clients and remorselessly poisons anyone who catches on to him. However, despite depicting spiritualism as fraudulent, the film affirms the reality of the supernatural, showing a dead murderess coming back to possess the living and continue her vile crimes.

Another, gentler tradition of the cinematic paranormal emerges in the 1930s, sometimes referred to by the retrospective labels "film blanc" or "afterlife fantasy." It presents the afterlife as benign and bureaucratic, and the encounter with paranormal forces as comedic, romantic, or both. Key examples include *The Ghost Goes West* (1935), *Topper* (1937), *Here Comes Mr. Jordan* (1941), *A Guy Named Joe* (1943), *A Matter of Life and Death* (1946), *It's a Wonderful Life* (1946), *The Ghost and Mrs. Muir* (1947), and *Portrait of Jennie* (1948). The fact that this anodyne genre thrived during World War II and its aftermath is often attributed to a mass cultural need for positive depictions of the afterlife. Consequently, horrific ghost films are a rarity in those years, though the creepy masterpieces *Dead of Night* (1945) and *The Uninvited* (1944) prove the exceptions. The film blanc was revived with

A Haunted Medium

The potential for movies to offer depictions of the supernatural and paranormal was exploited from the medium's earliest beginnings in the late 19th century. But more than that, some early filmmakers considered cinema itself to be an intrinsically paranormal medium that could potentially offer evidence of the reality of ghosts and an afterlife. This attitude continues as a subcurrent in world cinema to this day, with some filmmakers not only exploring supernatural and paranormal themes but actively seeking to exploit cinema's inherent "ghostliness."

Heaven Can Wait (1978), a highly successful remake of *Here Comes Mr. Jordan*, leading to such examples as *Ghost* (1990), *Truly Madly Deeply* (1991), *What Dreams May Come* (1998), *Just Like Heaven* (2005), and *Ghost Town* (2008). It is also possible to interpret the surprise blockbuster *The Sixth Sense* (1999) as more consistent with the film blanc than the horror film.

A parallel tradition of paranormal comedies dates back to the silent American film *The Cat and the Canary* (1927). It conventionally features an old dark house full of secret passages and panels, and often a scheming bad guy has been faking supernatural events for reasons of greed. These films' mixture of laughs and chills made for a natural province for comedians like Bob Hope (*The Ghost Breakers*, 1940), Abbott and Costello (*Hold That Ghost*, 1941), Dean Martin and Jerry Lewis (*Scared Stiff*, 1953), and Don Knotts (*The Ghost and Mr. Chicken*, 1966). *Ghostbusters* (1984) updated these comedies with hip dialogue, popular comedians, and a huge special effects budget.

Ghostbusters also points to a trend in the paranormal films of the latter half of the 20th century: the depiction of characters as professional experts in the paranormal. *Horror of Dracula* (1958) was the first adaptation of *Dracula* to present Van Helsing (Peter Cushing) as a vocational vampire hunter. Subsequently, cinema has regularly presented professional paranormal experts of one kind of another, from Father Merrin (Max von Sydow) in *The Exorcist* to Tangina Barrons (Zelda Rubinstein) in *Poltergeist* (1982) to the fictionalized presentation of real-life paranormal investigators Ed and Lorraine Warren in *The Conjuring* (2013). Psychical investigation becomes a key subject in films like The Legend of Hell House (1973), *The Entity* (1981), *Haunted* (1995), and *The Quiet Ones* (2014), often within narratives foregrounding tensions between empirical and religious approaches to the paranormal.

Films have been made largely about individual practices in paranormal investigation, including spirit photography (*Shutter*, 2004) and E.V.P. (*White-Noise*, 2005), and the *Paranormal Activity* series (2007–) crosses the classic haunted house story with contemporary amateur ghost hunting techniques. The year 1997 saw two films about the Cottingley Fairy Hoax of 1917, a children's film (*Fairy Tale: A True Story*) and a drama (*Photographing Fairies*). Ectoplasm has had a curious history on screen: while The Legend of Hell House is a rare film to depict ectoplasm extrusions in a manner largely consistent with spiritualist traditions, *Ghostbusters* repurposed the term to describe the sticky goo left by the abject specters. Séance scenes are legion in the cinema: *Dr. Mabuse, the Gambler* (1922), *The Uninvited* (1944), *Night of the Demon* (1957), *13 Ghosts* (1960), *Séance on a Wet Afternoon* (1965), *The Changeling* (1980), *Ghost, The Others* (2001), and *Drag Me To Hell* (2009) represent a few of the most memorable. These scenes often touch on the likenesses between moviegoing and the séance; both involve people assembling in the dark to receive messages from another place and time. Clairvoyance and other psychic powers appear in a diverse slate of films, from horror (*Don't Look Now*, 1973; *The Shout*, 1979) to dramas (*Premonition*, 2007) to comedies (*What Women Want*, 2000) to science fiction (*X-Men*, 1999; *Minority Report*, 2002).

The paranormal has also thrived in films worldwide, often adapting earlier literary, dramatic and folkloric traditions (like magic realism in Latin America). In various Asian cinematic traditions, ghosts and monsters have found a place on cinema, often mixing traditional elements with modern representational strategies. In Japan, films like *Kwaidan* (1964), *Onibaba* (1964), and *Kuroneko* (1968) adapted *Nōh* and *Kabuki* traditions to present beautiful and startling images. Decades later, with the explosion of J-Horror and its remakes, the *onryō*, the white-faced female ghost of Japanese folklore, has become a figure of international visibility, mostly through the popularity of Hideo Nakata's *Ringu* films (1998–2005) and Takashi Shimizu's *Ju-on* cycle (2000–2006). For a time, Hong Kong cinema favored romantic films like *A Chinese Ghost Story* (1987) and *Rouge* (1988), although it has produced notable horrific examples such as *The Eye* (2002) and *A Wicked Ghost* (1999). The People's Republic of China censored superstitious themes for decades, with *The Lonely Ghost in the Dark Mansion* (1989) constituting a major break; *Painted Skin* (2008) was a recent success, based on a classic supernatural tale by Pu Songling but downplaying its horrific elements and transforming the tale into more of a fantastic romance. The New Korean Cinema also embraced paranormal themes (e.g., in *A Tale of Two Sisters*, 2003). Movies about traditional Filipino monsters like *mananaggal* and *aswang* have been produced since the silent era, and Thai cinema has recently produced interesting paranormal films such as *Shutter* and *Ghost of Ma Nak* (2005). The increasing globalization of the film market triggered a wave of Hollywood remakes of Asian horror films (principally Japanese, although occasionally Korean, Hong Kong, and Thai), a cycle spanning roughly from *The Ring* (2002) to *One Missed Call* (2008). Meanwhile, several supernatural-themed Asian films became art house hits, notably Tsai Ming-Liang's Goodbye, Dragon Inn (2003) from Taiwan—the story of a haunted movie theatre—and Apichatpong Weerasethakul's *Uncle Boonmee Who Can Recall His Past Lives* (2006) from Thailand. The latter film makes brilliant use of superimposition techniques to conjure the history of cinema and its ghosts.

Nor did avant-garde/experimental filmmakers abandon their interest in the paranormal. Kenneth Anger, influenced by Aleister Crowley, described his films as magical ritual, casting their spell onto the audience: *Invocation of My Demon Brother* (1969) and *Lucifer Rising* (1980) are key examples. Filmmakers such as Martin Arnold, Peter Tcherkassky, the Quay Brothers, Bill Morrison, Ernie Gehr, and Zoe Beloff have variously used cinematic methods to explore supernatural themes and cinema's own ghostliness. Canadian director Guy Maddin has explored paranormal themes throughout his works, notably in *My Winnipeg* (2007) and *Keyhole* (2011); his most recent project, *Spitismes/Séances* (2012–), devotes itself to reimagining lost and unrealized films by famous directors of the silent era. This full circle approach evokes cinema's paranormal roots, embracing its status as a haunted, and haunting, medium.

Murray Leeder

See also: Ectoplasm; Ghosts; Paranormal in Literature; Psychical Research; Spirit Photography; Spiritualism; Survival after Death

Further Reading

Balázs, Béa. 2010. *Béla Balázs: Early Film Theory: Visible Man and The Spirit of Film*. New York: Beghahn Books.

Fowkes, Katherine A. 1998. *Giving Up the Ghost: Spirits, Ghosts, and Angels in Mainstream Comedy Films*. Detroit: Wayne State University Press.

Lim, Bliss Cua. 2009. *Translating Time: Cinema, the Fantastic, and Temporal Critique*. Durham, NC: Duke University Press.

Meehan, Paul. 2009. *Cinema of the Psychic Realm*. Jefferson, NC: McFarland.

Ruffles, Tom. 2004. *Ghost Images: Cinema of the Afterlife*. Jefferson, NC: McFarland.

Solomon, Matthew. 2010. *Disappearing Tricks: Silent Film, Houdini, and the New Magic of the Twentieth Century*. Urbana, IL: University of Illinois Press.

PARANORMAL ON TELEVISION

Regular television broadcasting went on the air in Britain and Europe in the mid-1930s, with commercial American broadcasting officially commencing in 1941. The form truly took off after World War II. Television quickly became a vibrant medium through which speculative imagination and real experiences alike could be represented. Today, the paranormal is among the most popular subjects appearing on television worldwide, from high-budget dramas to hunting down the uncanny on "reality television." Active hauntings, UFO sightings, near-death experiences, and supernatural hoaxes have been covered on the nightly news, current affairs magazine programs such as *60 Minutes* and the tabloid-styled *Inside Edition*, and talk shows with hosts like David Frost, Oprah Winfrey, and Larry King. Since the turn of the 21st century, the blending of television programming and the high-speed Internet brought on a deluge of dubious paranormal footage on

YouTube, amateur and professionally made web series—for example *The Hunted*, *Marble Hornets*, and *Divine: The Series*— and on-demand, subscription-based video-streaming services like Netflix. More than ever, people are watching paranormal programming that is often coupled with the allure of taboo extreme violence and sexuality that previously had been censored under public broadcast standards. Computer graphics technologies have further enhanced the depiction of supernatural manifestations in ways that are increasingly (hyper-)realistic. As with movies, television has blurred the line between actuality and the imagined.

Two television programs marked a major shift toward the serial format that is so popular today. One was the American situation comedy *Topper* (1953–1955), based on the novels by Thorne Smith about a couple who co-reside with ghosts of avalanche victims (including an alcoholic St. Bernard rescue dog). The other was the hugely popular British six-part series *The Quartermass Experiment* (1953). Written by Nigel Kneale, the series was about the first manned space flight crashing in London. Its sole surviving astronaut is possessed by an alien life form that absorbs the consciousness of his two fellow crewmembers. It was so popular that various sequels, remakes, and feature films have spun from *Quartermass*, most recently in 2005. Kneale went on to write shows about telepathic yetis (*The Creature*, 1955); hauntings (*The Stone Tape*, 1972); monstrous animals and shape-shifting (*Beasts*, 1976); and an acclaimed adaptation of Susan Hill's ghostly novel *The Woman in Black* (1989).

In the 1950s, many dramatic programs were presented with each episode a one-off story. This inspired the anthology formats of many early programs with paranormal themes: *Tales of Tomorrow* (1951–1953), *Science-Fiction Theater* (1955–1957), Rod Serling's *The Twilight Zone* (1959–1964), Algernon Blackwood's *Tales of Mystery* (1961–1963), *The Outer Limits* (1963–1965), and *Mystery and Imagination* (1966–1970). In each episode of *The Twilight Zone*, relatable characters found themselves in situations in which they crossed from their familiar reality to magical-surrealist situations, scenarios that were often allegorical to the issues that concerned Americans at the time such as civil rights, technological anxieties, social conformity, and Cold War fears. Inexplicable phenomena depicted in the show included time travel, clairvoyance, premonitions, magic, curses, doppelgängers, mass hysteria, alternate realities, and immortality. Other television series are undeniably inspired by *The Twilight Zone*, including its own movie and TV offshoots (1983, 1985–1989, 2002), Serling's follow-up *Night Gallery* (1970–1973), the misadventures of tourists visiting *Fantasy Island* (1977–1984), Steven Spielberg's *Amazing Stories* (1985–1987), and the popular children's programs *Are You Afraid of the Dark?* (1990–2000), *Eerie, Indiana* (1991–1992), and R. L. Stein's *Goosebumps* (1995–1998). Paranormal themes have been historically popular in programming for young people, from the first televised appearances of Casper the Friendly Ghost in the 1950s to Scooby Doo exposing supernatural hoaxes (1969 onwards) and the Saturday morning cartoon adaptations of popular films like *The Real Ghostbusters* (1986–1991), *Beetlejuice* (1989–1991), and *Avatar: The Last*

Airbender (2005–2008) and its spin-off *The Legend of Korra* (2012–). Live-action family fare has carried these themes as well: *My Favorite Martian* (1963–1966), *The Addams Family* (1964–1966), *The Munsters* (1964–1966), *I Dream of Jeannie* (1965–1970), *The Ghost and Mrs. Mui* (1968–1970), *Rentaghost* (1976–1984), *Dramarama* (1983–1989), *Down to Earth* (1984–1987), *Alf* (1986–1990), and the Australian series *Round the Twist* (1989–2001).

Early on, nonfiction television programs informed audiences about alleged paranormal events. NBC aired the first Fortean-type television documentary series *Ripley's Believe It Or Not!* (1949–1950, remade in 1982–1986). From 1959 to 1961, John Newland was "our guide to the supernatural" in the ABC docudrama series *One Step Beyond* that depicted accounts of premonitions, telepathy, hauntings, miraculous events, and synchronicities. The format set the tone for other popular non-fiction programs that retold events, including Newland's sequel *The Next Step Beyond* (1978–1979), BBC's *Leap in the Dark* (1973–1980), *In Search Of . . .* (1976–1982, hosted by *Star Trek's* Leonard Nimoy), science-fiction author Arthur C. Clarke's *Mysterious World* (1980), *World of Strange Powers* (1985), *Mysterious Universe* (1994), and the highly popular American show *Unsolved Mysteries* (1987–2010). The British series *Ghosthunters* (1996–1997) interviewed experienced psychical researchers on their studies of hauntings. Other notable programs included the UFO show *Sightings* (1992–1997), the Australian series *The Extraordinary* (1993–1996), the British programs *Strange But True?* (1993–1997) and *Fortean TV* (1997–98), the American-produced *The Unexplained* (1996–2000), and the first season of *Scariest Places on Earth* (2000–2004), hosted by *The Exorcist's* Linda Blair, which eventually reformatted as an early reality television series in which groups of people spent nights in allegedly haunted locales, initially popularized by MTV's *Fear* (2000–2002).

At the turn of the millennium, the "reality television" format emerged from a logistical quest to make cheaper, less labor-intensive programming. Ghost hunting shows combined witness interviews and site-based explorations using technological gadgets through which questionable evidence was presented; episodes were usually punctuated by interstitial promises that revealing moments were forthcoming—although they weren't really delivered. This format was popularized through *Most Haunted* (2002–) in Britain, which featured television host Yvette Fielding, celebrity psychic Derek Acorah, and parapsychologist Ciarán O'Keeffe. In the book *Will Storr vs. The Supernatural* (2006), the staged aspects observed on a *Most Haunted* location shoot are emphasized. In the United States, *Ghost Hunters* and its byproducts (2004–) are based on the investigations of the Atlantic Paranormal Society (TAPS) led by Rhode Island plumbers Jason Hawes and Grant Wilson, who originally investigated paranormal claims in their off-time. In many ways, this format emerged from the success of the low-budget movie *The Blair Witch Project* (1999) and the BBC mockumentary *Ghostwatch* (1992), which was inspired by the 1977–78 Enfield poltergeist case. Thousands of *Ghostwatch* viewers phoned the broadcaster concerned with the events being depicted. By approaching the show as an on-the-spot live news broadcast during which a haunting intensified, the lines between reality and fiction were effectively blurred, and the British Broadcasting Standards Council warned the BBC that they had not done enough to emphasize that the program was not real. Reality television producers have since taken advantage of this ambiguous approach.

Media scholar Annette Hill likened audiences for reality shows to "armchair ghost hunters" who would watch the shows and then interact with other viewers via social media and even collect paranormal evidence around their own home and communities. There is an incredibly long list of reality shows around the paranormal, including *A Haunting* (2005–14), *Destination Truth* (2007–12), *Paranormal State* (2007–11), and *Ghost Adventures* (2008–). People who claim to have psychic abilities have hosted a variety of TV shows, including John Edward, James van Praagh, the Canadian *Rescue Mediums*, Theresa Caputo's *Long Island Medium*, and Britain's "Psychic Sally" Morgan. Celebrity psychics have particularly incensed skeptics who argue that they use cold reading techniques or are given background information on those to whom they provide readings. Magicians have sought to debunk the paranormal on television, including James Randi, who guested multiple times on Johnny Carson's *The Tonight Show* in the 1970s and '80s to expose alleged faith healers and to confront Israeli mentalist Uri Geller. American magic duo Penn & Teller and British psychological illusionist Derren Brown have actively challenged paranormal claims on television.

The X-Files (1993–2002) transformed paranormal dramatic programming into a blockbuster, merchandisable format that competed with mainstream Hollywood films. The series depicted two FBI agents—Fox Mulder (David Duchovny), a believer pursuing his alien-abducted sister, and the skeptical Dana Scully (Gillian Anderson)—investigating UFOs, ghosts, possessions, psi abilities, and human mutations. At the forefront, the show pursued a theme of "The Truth Is Out There" (emphasized in its opening credits) as the agents sought to get a step ahead of conspiratorial cover-ups; the slogan on a UFO poster in Mulder's office with the phrase "I Want to Believe" divulged the tension between elusive phenomena and faith. At its fifth season peak, *The X-Files* attracted over 27 million American viewers. It spawned spin-off television series *Millennium* (1996–1999) and *The Lone Gunmen* (2001), as well as two movies (1998, 2008), elaborately packaged DVD sets, comics, games, books, and fan conventions. Preceding *The X-Files*, there were television programs in which investigations intersected with the paranormal, notably the British series *Randall and Hopkirk (Deceased)*, aired in the United States as *My Partner the Ghost* (1969–1970); *Kolchak: The Night Stalker* (1972–1975, remade in 2005); *Sapphire and Steel* (1979–1982); and the Canadian comedic drama *Seeing Things* (1981–1987). Paranormal elements also emerged in dramas such as *Beauty and the Beast* (1987–1990); *Friday the 13th: The Serie*, also known as *Friday's Curse* (1987–1990); David Lynch's *Twin Peaks* (1990–1991); and *Northern Exposure* (1990–1995), which helped pave the way for *The X-Files'* cultish paranormal brand. Since *The X-Files*, among the most successful series have been

Sliders (1995–2000); *Medium* (2005–2011), inspired by the real-life medium Allison Dubois; the similarly themed *Ghost Whisperer* (2005–2010); and the British series *Sea of Souls* (2004–2007), *Afterlife* (2005–2006), and *The Fades* (2011). On the more fantastical side, HBO's *The Game of Thrones* (2011–) features supernatural elements. Among the longest-running shows has been *Supernatural* (2005–), about two brothers who hunt down bizarre beings, which has an intensely loyal fan following. Perhaps the most mainstream of these paranormal cross-over dramas was J. J. Abrams' *Lost* (2004–2010), about a plane that crashes on a mysterious island where its survivors uncover mystical phenomena, time shifts, and spirits of the dead. Abrams went on to become an A-list Hollywood director, successfully rebooting the *Star Trek* film franchise and being entrusted with bringing the *Star Wars* saga back to the big screen. He also co-created the popular TV series *Fringe* (2008–2013), inspired by *The X-Files* and *The Twilight Zone*.

While American shows maintain audience dominance globally, the immense popularity of paranormal themes on television has resulted in well-regarded series emerging around the world in many languages. Among the most talked about has been *The Returned* (*Les revenants*, France, 2012–) about deceased individuals returning to life (fortunately not in decayed zombie form). The Danish film director Lars von Trier's television mini-series *The Kingdom* (*Riget*, 1994, 1997), about bizarre events and spirit encounters in Copenhagen's largest hospital, inspired an American version written by Stephen King, *The Kingdom Hospital* (2004). The online streaming media website Netflix has popularized numerous Korean television series with supernatural themes, including *My Girlfriend Is a Gumiho* (*Nae Yeojachinguneun Gumiho*, 2010–) and *Vampire Prosecutor* (2011–). Japanese anime series also draw heavily on paranormal themes, among the most innovative being Bleach (2004–2012), Mushi-shi (2005–2006), *Death Note* (2006–2007), and *Attack on Titan* (2013–). Live television programs in Japan include *Dark Tales of Japan* (*Nihon no Kowaiya*, 2004), the *Garo* fantasy series (2006–), and the situation comedy *Ghost Friends* (2009). In India there has been *Zee Horror Show* (1993–98), *X-Zone* (1998–2002), and *Ssshhh . . . Koi Hai* (2001–2010). Other international series include *13 Demon Street* (Sweden, 1959–1960); *Historias para no dormir* (Spain, 1964–1968); *Hora Marcada* (Mexico, 1986–1990), which had episodes written by film director Guillermo del Toro; *Brivido Giallo* (Italy, 1986); *The Fairies of Liaozhai* (China, 2006–2007), based on the stories of Pu Songling; and many from the Philippines, including *Wag Kukurap* (2004–2006), the *Pedro Penduko* series (2006–2007), *E.S.P.*, (2008), and *Illumina* (2010).

Paranormality has also emerged in science-fiction programming such as *Doctor Who* (1963–) and the *Star Trek* (beginning with the original series from 1966 to 1969). Superheroes such as Spider-Man, Wonder Woman, The Incredible Hulk, X-Men, and Superman later inspired shows about groups of average people acquiring extraordinary powers, including *The 4400* (2004–2007), *Heroes* (2006–2010), and the British comedy *Misfits* (2009–). Joss Whedon's 1992 movie *Buffy the Vampire Slayer* spawned the very popular TV series of the same name (1997–2003), opening a legacy of vampire-themed television programs such as *Buffy's* spin-off *Angel* (1999–2004); the British series *Being Human* (2008–2013), which featured a vampire, werewolf, and ghost as roommates; Alan Ball's Southern gothic *True Blood* (2008–2014); and *The Vampire Diaries* (2009–). These were notably preceded by the vampire prime-time soap opera *Dark Shadows* (1966–1971) as well as the cult series *Forever Knight* (1992–1996).

Perhaps zombies have taken over our TV (and increasingly our portable device) screens after their long success in the movies. Based on the graphic novels, *The Walking Dead* (2010–) is about the struggle to survive a zombie apocalypse in rural Georgia. Meanwhile, the anthology format has been making a comeback through the British satirist Charlie Brooker's *Black Mirror* (2011–), each episode featuring a speculative tale about how advanced technology enacts eerie hyper-realities, and *American Horror Story* (2011–), in which an ensemble cast returns to a new storyline each season. Such programs have undeniably raised the bar for the quality of dramatic programming with paranormal themes, signaling the strength of the genre on television and beyond.

Christopher Laursen

See also: Art, Creativity, and the Paranormal; Paranormal in Literature; Paranormal in Movies; Randi, James; Zombies

Further Reading

Beard, Drew, ed. 2013. "Horror and Television." Special issue, *Horror Studies* 4, no. 2.

Blanco, María del Pilar, and Esther Peeren, ed. 2010. *Popular Ghosts: The Haunted Spaces of Everyday Culture*, especially essays in Part Three: "Chasing Ghosts in(to) the Twenty-First Century." New York/London: Continuum Books.

Edwards, Emily D. 2005. *Metaphysical Media: The Occult Experience in Popular Culture.* Carbondale, IL: Southern Illinois University Press.

Hill, Annette. 2011. *Paranormal Media: Audiences, Spirits, and Magic in Popular Culture.* London/New York: Routledge.

Sayed, Deonna Kelli. 2011. *Paranormal Obsession: America's Fascination with Ghosts & Hauntings, Spooks & Spirits.* Woodbury, MN: Llewellyn Publications.

Sconce, Jeffrey. 2000. *Haunted Media: Electronic Presence from Telegraphy to Television.* Durham, NC: Duke University Press.

Wheatley, Helen. 2010. *Gothic Television.* Manchester, UK: Manchester University Press.

PARAPSYCHOLOGICAL ASSOCIATION

The Parapsychological Association (PA) is the international professional organization of scientists and scholars engaged in the study of psi (or psychic) experiences, such as telepathy, clairvoyance, remote viewing, psychokinesis, psychic healing, and precognition. Such experiences seem to challenge contemporary conceptions of human nature and of the physical world. They appear to involve the transfer of information and the influence of physical systems independently of time and space, via mechanisms we cannot currently explain. The primary objective of the Parapsychological Association is to achieve a scientific understanding of these experiences.

In view of this, PA members develop and refine methodologies for studying psi and its apparent physical, biological, or psychological underpinnings. They assess hypotheses and theories through experiments, conceptual models, and field investigations and seek to integrate their findings with other scientific domains. PA members also explore the meaning and impact of psychic experiences in human society and assess the possibility of practical applications and technologies.

While covering a wide range of perspectives, the PA, as a whole, is committed to promoting scholarship and scientific inquiry into currently unexplained aspects of human experience; disseminating responsible information to the wider public and to the scientific community; and integrating this information with knowledge from other disciplines.

The PA was first established in 1957, when it was proposed by the man now known as the father of modern parapsychology, Dr. Joseph Banks Rhine, in Durham, North Carolina. The first president of the organization was Dr. R. A. McConnell, then of the Biophysics Department, University of Pittsburgh, and the first vice-president was Dr. Gertrude R. Schmeidler of the Department of Psychology, City College of New York. Miss Rhea White was named secretary treasurer. Four others were elected to the council, bringing the total to seven: Miss (later Dr.) Margaret Anderson, Dr. Remi Cadoret, Dr. Karlis Osis, and Mr. (later Dr.) W. G. Roll.

The Parapsychological Association has been an affiliated organization of the American Association for the Advancement of Science (AAAS) since 1969. Physicist John Archibald Wheeler tried and failed to convince the AAAS to expel the PA in 1979, and the PA remains an affiliated organization.

By 1958 the PA had 103 members. As of the year 2002, there were approximately 300 PA members from all over the world. The PA has held an annual convention every year since 1957 where members and other researchers present their research findings. The convention has been held most often in the United States, but also in Europe and once in Brazil in 2011. Convention papers are double peer reviewed and were published in whole in the convention proceedings until 2008, after which only the abstracts are published. The PA also publishes a magazine three times a year, Mindfield: Bulletin of the Parapsychological Association, which is available to members, as is the Journal of Parapsychology, which is published by the Rhine Research Center and has been running continually since 1937.

David Luke

See also: American Society for Psychical Research; Koestler Parapsychology Unit; Parapsychology; Psi; Rhine Research Center; Society for Psychical Research

Further Reading
Parapsychological Association. 2014. http://www.parapsych.org.

PARAPSYCHOLOGY

The word *parapsychologie* was coined in 1889 by a German philosopher named Max Dessoir. In the 1930s Dessoir's neologism was adopted by Joseph Banks Rhine in order to distinguish this new experimental field from the practices of its predecessor, psychical research. There is considerable overlap between parapsychology and anomalistic psychology; however, the former is distinguished by its greater emphasis on controlled tests of alleged psychic capabilities.

According to the Parapsychological Association, parapsychology is "the scientific and scholarly study of three kinds of unusual events (ESP, mind-matter interaction, and survival), which are associated with human experience." This definition highlights an important feature of parapsychology: its scientific methodology. J. B. Rhine is widely regarded as the founding father of parapsychology. His laboratory at Duke University, North Carolina, developed research methods that were subsequently adopted by researchers worldwide.

Three principal methodological features set Rhine's research apart from most of its predecessors: using simple and easily controlled test procedures with restricted choice stimuli that allowed for scoring of the test as an unambiguous "hit" or a "miss"; statistical evaluation of the outcome; and working with ordinary participants, often student volunteers. Some elaboration is needed on the last point. Though he did not seek out "psychic superstars"—the 1930s equivalent of the Spiritualist mediums D. D. Home or Mrs. Piper, for instance—Rhine did begin his program of research by focusing on a small number of successful card-guessers from around the campus. Their purported ability could only be detected statistically, in the form of greater than chance scoring on hundreds of card-guessing trials. In this sense it was a far more modest psychic manifestation than was previously being claimed for famous mediums. The eventual decline in the performance of these high scorers meant Rhine later switched his strategy to testing unselected subjects, the research paradigm widely used by psychologists, and by most modern-day parapsychologists.

The usually implicit assumption adopted by most parapsychologists is that psi is postulated to be an ability that is normally distributed in the population much like any other psychological capability such as intelligence or mathematical skill. While a select few may manifest alleged psychic abilities to a high degree and have frequent seemingly psychic experiences, most individuals only occasionally have what they consider to be a psychic experience and do not feel that they have controllable psychic abilities. For most people, therefore, it is assumed that their alleged psychic abilities are quite weak. Nevertheless, by testing a sample of the general population and combining their results, parapsychologists feel that they may be able to detect evidence regarding the psi hypothesis.

Parapsychologists generally distinguish between two types of alleged psychic ability: psychokinesis (PK) and extrasensory perception (ESP). PK refers to the apparently anomalous influence of mind over matter, and can be further sub-divided into micro-PK (very small-scale effects that can only be detected statistically) and macro-PK (large scale effects such as bending metal or levitating tables, that can be seen with the naked eye). ESP refers to the apparently anomalous acquisition of information, either from another person's mind (telepathy), from the environment (clairvoyance) or regarding a future event (precognition). The umbrella term "psi" is used as a neutral term to designate this apparently anomalous effect, recognizing that the finer divisions of anomalous effects into PK, ESP, and ESP's subtypes are not well established theoretically. However, parapsychologists make clear distinctions when they design experiments to test PK as compared to ESP.

Despite claims by some skeptical commentators that parapsychology has shown no progress despite over a century of investigation, in fact there has been a clear evolution of the methodology for testing hypothesized ESP and PK phenomena. The Rhinean era focused on dice-rolling to test PK: the participant was required to influence the roll of dice. Methods of testing were gradually refined to eliminate sources of error—for instance, using a mechanical device to tumble the dice to help ensure a random throw, and filming the outcome to prevent human error biasing the recording of results. Statistics were used to determine whether the designated number appeared more often than chance. As technology developed, parapsychologists switched to testing micro-PK using random number generators (RNGs) that provide a source of randomness normally based on an unpredictable process such as electronic noise or decay of a radioactive particle. The output of these RNGs is in effect a string of 1s and 0s, and over time an approximately equal number of each should be produced if the device is operating randomly. The participant's goal in RNG-PK studies is to bias the outcome of the RNG towards a predetermined direction, for example a statistically significant excess of 1s over 0s. The binary RNG output can be linked to a more engaging (psychologically speaking) computer screen display, such as a flickering candle flame whose movements are influenced by the RNG, so that the participant has feedback on the RNG behavior and can visualize a change in the desired direction. RNG-PK data is collected and analyzed by computer, and "influence" periods are statistically compared with control periods or periods with opposite aims.

From the 1970s, a new variety of PK study began to develop alongside the RNG studies. These investigated the possibility of Direct Mental Interaction with Living Systems (DMILS). This work has tested whether one person can influence another person's psychophysiology (usually their skin resistance, known as EDA, which is an indicator of autonomic nervous system activity)—for instance, by remotely staring at them. This work assumes that unconscious measures of ostensible psi influence may be more sensitive detectors than conscious measures such as partic-

Far from being a pseudoscience, parapsychology is a rigorous scientific investigation of paranormal phenomena, complete with controlled experimental methods, publication in peer-reviewed journals, representation in universities, a professional association with a code of ethics and standards, and development of methods over time. It is related to anomalistic psychology but distinguished from it by a greater emphasis on controlled tests of alleged psychic capabilities.

ipants' guesses. As usual in parapsychology, careful experimental controls must be implemented to prevent the possibility of artifact.

In the Rhinean era, ESP was mostly tested using cards depicting five different simple geometric symbols: a circle, star, cross, square, and wavy lines. Called "Zener cards" these were commissioned by Rhine because he felt they would be easier to discriminate through extrasensorial abilities than standard playing cards. In telepathy tests, a sender would look at one card at a time, and the receiver would try to guess what card the sender was seeing. In clairvoyance tests, the experimenter might place each card face down, so that the participant would guess without anyone knowing the identity of each card. And in precognition tests the participant would guess a sequence of symbols, and then the cards were shuffled and laid out and it could be seen how many times the participant's guess matched the future target sequence. As there are five different symbols, the chance expectation of a hit is 20 percent. In all of these tests, careful randomization of the card sequence was crucial. In fact Rhine helped to develop ways to evaluate statistically the outcome of card-guessing studies. Historians have since argued that parapsychology led the way in developing an understanding of the importance of randomization in experimental design. Parapsychologists have often pioneered methodological developments, perhaps because of the challenges they face in testing claims of anomalous communication or influence.

Rhine observed a gradual decline in the outcome of his card-guessing studies and attributed this to a change in the psychological conditions of the experiment, as interest and motivation typically decreased over time. Conversely, skeptics have argued that effects declined because earlier studies contained methodological flaws that were later eliminated. In the 1960s, perhaps influenced by the cultural context at that time, parapsychologists began to move away from using card guessing to test ESP. They developed new procedures that attempted to be more naturalistic, such as using art prints as targets. This is known as free-response research because the participant does not know what the target is, and they must simply generate a verbal description or "mentation" that will later be blind-judged against the actual target and decoy targets. Some of the most famous and successful work of this period was dream-ESP research conducted by Stanley Krippner and Montague Ullman at the Maimonides Sleep Laboratory. However, dream research was time consuming and expensive, and researchers eventually developed a simpler way of testing for ESP in an altered state of consciousness, called the ganzfeld technique.

The ganzfeld technique is today one of the most important free-response ESP research paradigms. It involves placing the receiver in a condition of mild sensory deprivation, which is thought to make it easier to notice weak extrasensory impressions. The receiver relaxes and reports any thoughts or feelings that they are having (the mentation) while at the same time, in a different room, a sender views a randomly selected target (originally art prints, more recently short video or digitized movie clips). Later, the receiver or an independent judge blind rates the mentation against the target and three decoy clips, so the chance likelihood of a hit is 25 percent. It is notable that several meta-analyses of the ganzfeld database have been published in high profile psychology journals, and often these studies report a hit rate of around 33 percent. Many parapsychologists have therefore argued that this database represents replicable evidence of psi. However, mainstream scientists still seem to be reluctant to accept this claim, and researchers such as Daryl Bem are now developing alternative ESP testing methods that may encourage mainstream researchers to test the psi hypothesis themselves.

Parapsychologists are not completely uniform in their practices. While the majority use laboratory methods and unselected participants, some prefer to study gifted subjects either in the field or in the lab, and others collect and document descriptions of people's spontaneous alleged psychic experiences. This latter approach was exemplified by the work of Louisa E. Rhine, J. B. Rhine's wife and research partner. Unlike the earlier psychical researchers who went to great lengths in attempting to establish the authenticity and veridicality of spontaneous cases, Louisa Rhine's case collection accepted accounts at face value and sought no further documentary evidence. She assumed that, over a large accumulation of cases, inaccuracies would tend to cancel one another out to leave meaningful trends. Similarities between patterns observed in her collection compared to highly documented collections vindicate her approach. Furthermore, Louisa Rhine saw the purpose of her case collections as helping to identify patterns concerning real-world psi that could then be explored more systematically under controlled laboratory conditions. So Louisa Rhine's work, like much case collection research, provides a valuable complement and input to laboratory-based parapsychology.

In terms of number of researchers, parapsychology is quite a small field. Although Rhine eventually withdrew his laboratory from Duke University, it still exists in the form of the Rhine Research Center in North Carolina. The University of Virginia's Division of Perceptual Studies is another well-established U.S. research lab, founded in 1967 by the leading reincarnation researcher Ian Stevenson. And in California the Institute of Noetic Sciences, co-founded by former astronaut Edgar Mitchell in 1973, is still active in parapsychological research. In Europe, parapsychology is represented by a number of university-based research centers, such as the Koestler Parapsychology Unit and the Centre for the Study of Anomalous

Psychological Processes in the UK, and in Germany the IGPP. In Paris, the Institut Métapsychique International was founded in 1919 and is still active.

What can be concluded from this short review of parapsychology? Some critics have unjustly identified parapsychology as a pseudoscience. Parapsychology bears numerous hallmarks of science: controlled experimental methods, publication in peer-reviewed journals (specialist and mainstream), representation in universities, a professional association with a code of ethics and standards, and development of methods over time. However, it is fair to say that parapsychologists are still searching for a research paradigm that reliably demonstrates psi effects, and there is not yet a widely accepted theory of psi. Parapsychology's small size makes it difficult to establish systematic research programs. These factors mean that parapsychologists still face many challenges. But parapsychology persists due to the ubiquity of spontaneous paranormal experiences and the potentially revolutionary ramifications of the psi hypothesis.

Caroline Watt

See also: Anomalistic Psychology; Extrasensory Perception (ESP); Ganzfeld Technique, The; Paranormal Dreams; Pseudoscience; Psi; Psychical Research; Psychokinesis (PK), Rhine Research Center

Further Reading

Irwin, Harvey J., and Caroline Watt. 2007. *An Introduction to Parapsychology*. 5th ed. Jefferson, NC: McFarland.

Koestler Parapsychology Unit online parapsychology course: http://www.koestler-parapsychology.psy.ed.ac.uk/teachingDistanceLearning.html

PAST-LIFE READINGS

Past-life readings by psychics, mediums, and other sensitives have become very popular in Western culture, but the practice of determining the past-life identities of others is by no means new. In fact, if we may take contemporary tribal societies to be representative of bygone lifeways, it may be very old indeed. But how can we believe what psychic practitioners say about their clients' previous lives? Is there any objective reason to trust them?

Many tribal societies around the world have reincarnation beliefs, and for them it is important to know who a child was previously so that he or she may be given the same name as in the previous incarnation and properly reincorporated into the social order. Sometimes the spirit of the deceased person announces itself in a dream, and sometimes there are birthmarks or other physical signs, or perhaps telltale behaviors, that help to identify it as the return of a specific ancestor. When none of these signs are present, however, a psychic practitioner may be called in for a consultation.

In many African societies diviners try to determine the child's rightful name at birth or soon after. A series of names are called out until the baby stops crying or gives some other indication that it is the right one. Mistakes may be made, however, in which case a child may fail to thrive, and another sort of consultation is required. In one documented instance among the Nigerian Igbo, a child born with a hairless, circular mark on her head fell ill, and her parents consulted an oracle, fearing that she had been wrongly named. The oracle told them that their daughter was the reincarnation of her father's mother, who had had a similar lesion on her head from carrying heavy loads there all of her life. The child was renamed, recovered, and when she grew older, said a few things that suggested she had inherited her grandmother's memories.

In a case reported from a Canadian first nations people, a boy, Jeffery, was taken to a medicine man for identification soon after birth. The man held Jeffery in his arms and identified him as the come-back of his mother's brother Will. Will had died six years earlier after a horse he was harnessing had kicked him in the stomach and head. Jeffery gave no hint of remembering anything about Will's life until he was five years old, when his grandparents took him for the first time to the camp where Will had died. While there he began to say his name was not Jeffery, but Will, and to recount incidents in which Will had been involved. He began to dream about Will and continued dreaming about him into adulthood.

Western sensitives also sometimes supply information about previous lives that corresponds in some way to their clients' experiences or relate details that can be confirmed. In all of these cases, however, the psychic practitioners provide information only about the most recent past identity of the client. It is unclear when the practice of reporting lengthy series of lives, typical of modern past-life readings, was introduced, although it was most likely in the 1920s by Edgar Cayce.

Cayce was an American psychic who gave readings in a self-induced trance. He began his career with medical readings, for which he became renowned. Then in 1923 he gave a reading for a man named Arthur Lammers that concluded with a reference to a previous life. Lammers, who was widely read on esoteric matters, immediately realized the significance and encouraged Cayce to give readings focusing on past lives. These life readings quickly developed into a new specialty, and between 1923 and his death in 1945 Cayce gave 2,500 of them.

In the life readings, Cayce described a series of four or five previous existences that he said bore on the present life. A typical series began in Atlantis, moved to Egypt, and from there to Medieval Europe and colonial America. Cayce identified the akashic records as his primary source of information and evoked karma to explain the impact one life had on another. All the major features of this pattern—past lives reaching back to Egypt, Atlantis or beyond; centuries-long intervals between lives; the akashic records as the source of information; karma as the linkage between lives—have become staples of past-readings, but significantly, all are derived from Theosophy. Cayce in his normal state knew nothing about Theosophy, but Lammers was well acquainted with it. J. Gordon Melton suggests that

Lammers introduced these concepts to the entranced Cayce, whose subconscious incorporated them into his readings.

There have been attempts to check out the things that Cayce said in trance, and some have proved accurate, although others have not and most cannot be evaluated one way or another. Much of his information, especially regarding the earlier lives, contains glaring inconsistencies with the historical record. The most evidential and all of the verified lives are the most recent lives in the series that Cayce reported. Interestingly, Cayce said that in addition to the Akashic records, he sometimes got information directly from minds of his clients. That is what tribal practitioners assume they are doing as well, and it would make sense, if past-life memories are registered in people's subconscious mind rather than in a celestial repository such as the akashic records. In that case, however, the akashic records would be superfluous and perhaps no more than a figment of the Theosophical imagination.

James G. Matlock

See also: Akashic Records; Cayce, Edgar; Past-Life Regression; Reincarnation; Theosophy

Further Reading

Matlock, James G. 1993. *A Cross-Cultural Study of Reincarnation Ideologies and their Social Correlates.* Unpublished MA thesis, Hunter College, City University of New York. http://jamesgmatlock.net/wp-content/uploads/2013/12/Reincarnation-Ideologies-and-Social-Correlates.pdf.

Matlock, James G. 2014. "Lecture 12: Third-Party Testimonials of Past Lives." *Signs of Reincarnation.* Online seminar course offered through The Alvarado Zingrone Institute for Research and Education. http://theazire.org/moodle.

Melton, J. Gordon. 1994. "Edgar Cayce and Reincarnation: Past life readings as Religious Symbology." *Syzygy: Journal of Alternative Religion and Culture* 3, 1–2.

Muller, Karl E. 1970. *Reincarnation—Based on Facts.* London: Psychic Press.

PAST-LIFE REGRESSION

In age regression under hypnosis, a hypnotist guides a client back through the years of his or her life. In past-life regression, the hypnotist does not stop at birth but suggests that the client go back further still, until other images come to mind. This way of exploring what appear to be past lives has become very popular. Many stories have been recounted in books, and many sessions have been videotaped and posted on YouTube. A type of hypnotherapy called past-life therapy seeks to help patients resolve a variety of emotional complaints through reliving past traumas. Regressions are often dramatic and can be very convincing to those who experience and observe them, but is the technique what it purports to be? Can hypnosis really help to free up our memory and reveal who we were before?

The first person to conduct age regression under hypnosis was French physiologist Charles Richet in 1883, but he took his subject back only to age six. A few years later his countryman Albert de Rochas discovered that he could regress people beyond birth and into what seemed to be earlier lives. Rochas thought that he had found an experimental way of studying reincarnation, then a topic of much interest in France owing to the Spiritism of Allan Kardec. Rochas reported his experiments in his 1911 book *Les Vies Successives*. All of his subjects reported previous lives in France, which made it easy for Rochas to check what they said. Unfortunately, although a few details proved to be correct, many others were anachronistic or widely improbable, and he could not confirm the existence of any of the deceased persons whose names were given.

Experiments with past-life regression continued, although the results were usually not much better. Then in 1932 a book called *Soul of Nyria* appeared. This was based on regressions conducted in London beginning in 1899. It told the story of a Roman slave girl between 77 and 95 CE. With some effort the author was able to verify numerous names and other facts given in the regressions, but again, Nyria herself did not appear in the historical record. We find the same thing in an even more famous book, *The Search for Bridey Murphy*, which became an international bestseller immediately upon its release in 1956. Bridey Murphy mentioned, among other things, the names of shop owners in Belfast during the period when she claimed to have lived, and she knew the names of places that did not appear on maps. But no one named Bridey or Brian Murphy (her supposed husband) could be traced.

The sensation created by *The Search for Bridey Murphy* would not last. A tabloid newspaper published what it claimed was proof that it was all an unconscious fabrication by the regressed woman, Virginia Tighe (called Ruth Simmons in the book). The charges were discredited as soon as they were made, but it was already too late. The public lost interest in Bridey as quickly as it had embraced her. Many people continue to believe that the case was debunked, while others today have never heard of it. It has had an important legacy, however, in that it inspired additional past-life regressions and over the next two decades led to the establishment of past-life therapy. *The Search for Bridey Murphy* also initiated a critical push to explain the apparent memories that arise in past-life regression as due to suggestions by the hypnotist or cryptomnesia (source amnesia), or in some other way.

There is no question that much of the criticism is valid. Experiments have shown that memory is not necessarily enhanced under hypnosis and that hypnotists can shape what their clients experience through their questions. Cryptomnesia has been documented in a variety of contexts, including hypnosis, and some regression accounts have been traced to historical novels. A favorite technique used by researchers is to re-hypnotize subjects following a regression and ask them where they got their information. In one study, subjects said that it was from stories they had heard, books they had read, or things that had happened to them in their present lives, but did not mention previous existences.

On the other hand, there are cases like *Soul of Nyria* and *The Search for Bridey Murphy*, in which verified information from unexplained sources appears, so it would be wrong to dismiss past-life regression altogether as a means of accessing past lives. In a few cases, the previous person has been identified. Interestingly, in some of these cases the subjects had spontaneous memories of the same previous life. These cases suggest that age regression may occasionally tap into the same stream of consciousness as spontaneous memories, but a particularly deep trance seems to be required for this to occur. However, there have not yet been studies that allow us to be sure that depth of a trance is what makes some regressions more evidentiary than others.

The evidence suggests that we have unconscious blocks against remembering exactly who we were or what happened to us in previous lives. Given this, it is unlikely that most past-life therapy actually allows patients to relive past lives, although the therapy might nevertheless succeed if the patients were unconsciously reworking remembered events in ways that allowed them to be therapeutically efficacious.

Some materialistic researchers view consciousness as a product of brain states. For them, past-life memories, whether spontaneous or hypnotically induced, are false memories on par with unsubstantiated claims of satanic ritual abuse and abductions by aliens in UFOs. This position is as wrong as generalizing from spontaneous past-life memories to the images that arise under hypnosis. There is better evidence for reincarnation from spontaneous memories, but we should not generalize from them to age regression. Spontaneous and hypnotically induced past-life memories are different and should be kept conceptually and theoretically separate.

James G. Matlock

See also: Haraldsson, Erlendur; Reincarnation; Spiritism; Stevenson, Ian

Further Reading

Matlock, James G. 2014. "Lecture 11: Fantasy and Fact in Age-Regressions to 'Previous Lives.'" *Signs of Reincarnation*. Online seminar course offered through The Alvarado Zingrone Institute for Research and Education. http://theazire.org/moodle.

Mills, Antonia, and Jim B. Tucker. 2013. "Past-life Experiences." In *Varieties of Anomalous Experience: Examining the Scientific Evidence*, edited by Etzel Cardeña, Stephen J. Lynn, and Stanley Krippner, 303–332. 2nd ed. Washington, DC: American Psychological Association.

POLTERGEIST

The poltergeist is a physical phenomenon in which objects—from stones to large pieces of furniture—are moved as if by an invisible force. Objects have been frequently reported as flying through the air at slower-than-normal speeds and being warm to the touch when they are picked up. Sometimes objects mysteriously disappear, reappearing later in an unexpected place. Other typical manifestations associated with the poltergeist include strange noises, such as knocking, rapping, and tapping, ranging in volume from faint to explosive. Spontaneous fires and appearances of liquids have been described in many cases. Any combination of such manifestations may occur.

Historian P. G. Maxwell-Stuart traced the earliest written reference back to 480 CE, when Constance de Lyon wrote of an *infestatione terribili* (harassment by repeated attacks) of lithobolia (stone throwing) reportedly encountered by the French Bishop of Auxerre, St. Germain. In 1979, British psychical researchers Alan Gauld and Tony Cornell noted some earlier instances going as far back as the first century that may be suggestive of the poltergeist. The word *poltergeist*—from the German *poltern*, meaning "to make a loud noise or uproar," and *geist*, meaning ghost—did not appear in common usage until the 16th century in Germany. It first appeared in 1521 in the Reformation leader Martin Luther's written account of a bag of hazelnuts jumping about, his bed rattling, and a rumbling sound heard when he stayed at Wartburg Castle. Introduced to the English language in British writer Catherine Crowe's *The Night-Side of Nature* (1848), the term was mostly utilized in psychical research studies until the British press picked up on it while covering ghost hunter Harry Price's poltergeist investigations in the 1920s.

Historically, the poltergeist has been thought to be a mischievous spirit, a ghost, an elemental, or some other kind of disincarnate entity. Such interpretations remain popular in many world cultures, where poltergeist-type manifestations may be associated with ghostly phenomena such as *djinn* in the Islamic world, *duppies* in the Caribbean, or *bererong* in Bali, Indonesia. By the mid-19th century in Europe and North America, older interpretations holding that the devil, witchcraft, or even vampires were responsible had become uncommon.

Natural causes have been sought for the manifestations. British psychical researcher G. W. Lambert posited geophysical causes such as earth tremors. Electromagnetic or geomagnetic forces have been explored by cognitive neuroscientist Michael Persinger, parapsychologist William G. Roll, and Canadian experimenter John Hutchinson, who built a "poltergeist machine" using equipment such as Tesla coils and radio frequency transmitters. Electrical malfunctions, plumbing problems, meteorological conditions, whimsical wildlife, eerie infrasound, and earthly vibrations have all been found to be responsible for anomalous noises, object movements, and perceptual anomalies claimed to be hauntings or poltergeists. Otherwise, the mechanisms of the phenomenon remain elusive.

Critics of psychical phenomena such as British psychical researcher Frank Podmore and American magicians Milbourne Christopher and James Randi suspected that people, especially "unhappy adolescents," were purposefully or unconsciously deceiving others through sleight-of-hand hoaxes. Indeed, trickery has been exposed in a number of cases, and it is historically common that the events center on an adolescent individual. Yet in the majority of cases, observers

Reports of poltergeist-type phenomena have been traced as far back as the 1st century CE, but the word *poltergeist* itself, meaning "noisy ghost," did not appear until the 16th century, when Martin Luther used it in a written account of a series of anomalous occurrences. The famous association of poltergeist incidents with the turbulent psychic energy supposedly emanating from pubescent children, especially girls, was an even later development, not appearing until 1931 in the writings of American psychical researcher Hereward Carrington.

have remained stumped as to the causation when natural causes and deception were not evident.

In 1931, American psychical researcher Hereward Carrington suggested that there could be a relationship between sexual energies emerging around puberty and an unleashing of psychical forces. The explanation did not fit with all cases; Nandor Fodor, Manfred Cassirer, John and Anne Spencer, and others have assessed cases in which adolescents were not present at all. Yet the idea that the poltergeist could be an externalized energy or some type of thought-form emanating from living people was popularized through the convergence of psychical research with psychology and psychoanalysis in the mid-20th century. In a particularly interesting case, the "Philip Experiment" of the 1970s saw British mathematician and psychical research A. R. G. Owen advising a group of eight people in Toronto, Canada, led by his wife Iris, in focusing their psychic energies on collectively imagining a ghost (the Philip of the experiment's name) so vividly that it would manifest as an semi-independent thought form with the power to simulate spirit communications and poltergeist phenomena. The point was to prove experimentally that ghosts and poltergeists are not really independent, living entities but products of human psychic force.

A turning point was the coining of the term "recurrent spontaneous psychokinesis" (RSPK) by Duke University parapsychologists William G. Roll and J. Gaither Pratt in their investigation of a prototypical poltergeist in the suburbs of Seaford, Long Island, New York, in 1958. The events began with a ceramic doll and model ship discovered broken in the bedroom of 12-year-old James Herrmann, Jr. Popping sounds were heard around the house; subsequently bottles were found with caps unscrewed and their contents spilled. Then James and his mother saw a bottle of bleach jump out of a cardboard box and break on the floor when neither of them was near it. Over a five-week period, other objects would fly from their spots, including ceramic figurines, a dresser, a glass bowl, a record player, lamps, a globe, and more. The strange events at Seaford were witnessed by friends, neighbors, police, reporters, and parapsychologists. It attracted international media attention, even becoming the subject of a CBS television docudrama that year. Hundreds of people wrote letters to the Herrmanns suggesting what could be causing the trouble. Roll and

Pratt noted that the manifestations centered on young James, and that the objects that moved seemed to have psychological meaning to him. They wondered if James had somehow been expressing an unconscious force, psychokinesis (PK). A similar hypothesis animated the work of German parapsychologist Hans Bender, whose investigation of a reported poltergeist disturbance in the late 1960s in Rosenheim, Bavaria, attracted much attention. Bender attributed the anomalous phenomena taking place in a Bavarian attorney's office to the involuntary action of psychokinetic energy emanating from an unhappy 19-year-old female secretary.

The German psychologist and physicist Walter von Lucadou is continuing Bender's work on RSPK through his Model of Pragmatic Information (MPI). He shows how there is a common trajectory in the intensity of poltergeist events with the types of people who intervene. Events begin as a surprise around a "focus person," such as James Herrmann, Jr., but then attention is displaced from the focus as observers believe discarnate entities are at work. As critical observers arrive to assess what is going on, the manifestations decline and ultimately are suppressed by authorities as doubts and claims of deception are put forward, for example, by the media. This approach provides a holistic view of the poltergeist phenomena. Other researchers have focused recently on specific aspects of the poltergeist. In 2010, British psychical researcher Barrie Colvin demonstrated that poltergeist noises have a significantly different acoustic signature than human-made replications of the sounds.

In numerous cases, observers have reported being able to engage in "conversations" with the noise-maker—for example, through a question-and-answer system: one knock for yes, two for no. More complicated means of communication with the apparently intelligent rapping force were devised in some cases. In Battersea, England, in 1956, a poltergeist seemed to give messages by counting knocks through the letters of the alphabet. Eventually, handwritten and then typed notes were provided by the alleged spirit. In the case of British psychic and healer Matthew Manning, when he and his family reportedly experienced ongoing poltergeist disturbances during his boyhood, he eventually found that he could subdue the phenomena by using automatic writing to transcribe perceived messages associated with the paranormal force.

Some poltergeist cases have included a voice. Among the most famous of these was that of a talking mongoose that called itself Gef on the Isle of Man in the 1930s. In the late 1970s, a gruff male voice claiming to be the spirit of a man who had died in a house in Enfield, England, spoke at length through an 11-year-old girl, even when her mouth was filled with water. In 2006 in South Shields, England, a voice spoke through toy figures, phrases were written on magnetic doodle pads, and threatening text messages were received on a mobile phone.

The family in the South Shields case also claimed to have been physically assaulted by the poltergeist—a rare occurrence in the history of the phenomenon. In 1926, physical violence was also associated with a Romanian girl, Eleonore Zugun, who suffered from visible marks and scratches on her skin that she alleged were made by the devil. In 1974 in Culver City, California, a woman said she was sexually assaulted by a poltergeist-like force, inspiring the novel and film *The Entity*. In the controversial Bell Witch legend from Tennessee (1817–1821), the patriarch of the household was reportedly murdered by the diabolic force. Although stories and movies often depict the force as violent, people seldom report being injured or even struck by objects in poltergeist cases.

Spontaneous fires, another common manifestation around poltergeist cases, are typical to the phenomenon. Such fires are sometimes referred to in relation to psychokinesis as *pyrokinesis*, a concept that inspired Stephen King's popular 1980 novel *Firestarter*. Such spontaneous fire cases have been investigated by the Australian poltergeist researcher Paul Cropper in Malaysia (2010–2011) and Turkey (2012–2013), and have been known to burn homes to the ground, as was reported in a Canadian case known as the Baldoon mystery (1829–1830).

Today, the poltergeist remains a phenomenon described worldwide, although most cases are probably unreported. Causation and the mechanism of the phenomenon remain uncertain, particularly given how dedicated studies into it are deterred by the fact that such cases spontaneously appear in random places around the globe.

Christopher Laursen

See also: Demonology; Discarnate Entity; Enfield Poltergeist; Ghosts; Haunting; Krippner, Stanley; Psi; Psychokinesis (PK); Randi, James; Vampires and Poltergeists; Witches and Poltergeists

Further Reading
Gauld, Alan, and A. D. Cornell. 1979. *Poltergeists*. London: Routledge Kegan & Paul.
Hitchings, Shirley, and James Clark. 2013. *The Poltergeist Prince of London: The Remarkable True Story of the Battersea Poltergeist*. Stroud, UK: History Press.
Holder, Geoff. 2012. *What Is a Poltergeist?* Newton Abbot, UK: F&W Media.
Rogo, D. Scott. 2005. *On the Track of the Poltergeist*. San Antonio, TX: Anomalist Books.
Roll, William G. 2004. *The Poltergeist*. New York: Paraview.

POSSESSION

Possession is a large and complex category of experience related to a range of other anomalous phenomena such as mediumship, trance, shamanism, channeling, automatic writing, and glossolalia. Possession has been well documented since ancient times, and a transcultural study conducted in 1976 demonstrated the near universality of both trance and possession in cultures around the world. Possession, at its most basic level, involves the incorporation of some spirit, energy, force, or discarnate entity, whether malevolent or benevolent, into a body or object, which then acts as a vessel for the entering entity.

Possession can be categorized into two types. Negative possession involves possession by dangerous and destructive forces, usually interpreted as demonic beings, ghosts, or other types of malevolent entities that cause physical or mental afflictions to the host and must be exorcised. The causes for possession by these forces vary across cultures, but if untreated it is believed the possessing agent can cause madness, disease, and even death.

Although negative forms of possession tend to be highlighted in contemporary Western cultures, many cultures are equally familiar with, and have even built institutions around, positive forms of possession. Here the entering entity is thought to be a benevolent being, and the overall effects on the host are beneficial. Positive forms of possession are either induced through various rituals and techniques or may occur spontaneously. Possessing entities include a variety of beings and range from gods or goddesses, local spirits, and extra-terrestrial or extra-dimensional beings to ascended masters and even other people (e.g., sorcerers). In some cases, positive possession may be accompanied by the acquisition of supernatural powers such as divine vision, supernatural knowledge, or clairvoyance, which are used for purposes of divination, prognostication, prophecy, healing, and exorcising harmful spirits. Various forms of oracular possession and channeling fall into this category. Oracular possession results in the possessed person becoming a medium for the entering entity to speak through in order to foretell the future, give knowledge about the past, or offer consultation and healing for those in need. In a variant form, the possessing entity can enter objects such as mirrors, swords, or other reflective objects, which may be used by specialists for divination or prognostication.

Institutions of oracles and mediums are well attested and documented in a number of ancient cultures across the globe, many of which continue to thrive today. Perhaps the most well known throughout Western history was the institution of the Pythia, commonly known as the Oracle of Delphi, which was officially established in the eighth century BCE at the Temple of Apollo in what is now modern day Greece. The oracles of this time were said to be possessed by the god Apollo, and it was he who would communicate through the priestesses. The office of the Oracle of Delphi lasted until 395 CE, when such practices were deemed pagan by the growing Christian influences in Europe and forcibly stopped.

One of the most famous oracular institutions today is the position of the Nechung Oracle, who is considered the official state oracle of Tibet and is regularly consulted by the Dalai Lama. This position has historically been filled by men, although the Tibetan government also has three other state-sanctioned oracles, one of whom is a woman possessed by a high-ranking goddess. The Nechung Oracle, however, is considered the most prestigious of the four and is possessed by a Tibetan Buddhist protector deity known as Pehar or Dorje Drakden.

Neighboring Nepal is home to the ancient institution of the kumārī (literally "young girl"), in which prepubescent Newari girls are chosen by religious officiates for specific physical and mental characteristics and, after a variety of rituals, are worshipped as the instantiation of the goddess Taleju. A young girl holds this

Possession, defined as the use of an object or body by a spirit, energy, force, or discarnate entity that has entered it, can be categorized into two general types:

Negative possession is possession by dangerous and destructive forces (demons, ghosts, etc.) that cause distress and must be exorcised.

Positive possession is possession by benevolent beings (gods or goddesses, local spirits, ascended masters, extraterrestrials, etc.) that produce a beneficial effect upon the host and others around him or her.

Both types of possession may result in the apparent acquisition of paranormal powers by the host.

office until she menstruates, upon which the goddess is said to vacate her body. One of the functions of the Royal Kumārī during her time in office is to become ritually possessed by the goddess in order to act as an oracle for the Newari priests.

In the Western hemisphere, there are also a number of well-known and contemporary examples of spirit possession-oriented traditions in Brazil. The most widely known of these are the Spiritists, an international religious group whose doctrine was first codified in 19th-century France by Hippolyte Léon Denizard Rivail (better known by his pen name Allan Kardec), and later popularized in Brazil by the famous medium Chico Xavier in the 1960s. Much of Spiritism's popularity in Brazil can be attributed to a number of homegrown Afro-Brazilian possession-centered traditions such as Candomblé, which originated from Caribbean and West African traditions such as Vodoun. In Candomblé, practitioners believe that every human has their own personal deity that controls his or her destiny and acts as a protector and guide. Candomblistas become possessed by their tutelary deity and often function as mediums or healers for their larger community.

In North America possession-like states are said to manifest among practitioners of various New Age traditions in the forms of channeling and mediumship, which are rooted in the Theosophical Society and other Western esoteric traditions. Workshops on contacting and channeling spirit guides and guardian angels are commonly held, and a large number of American Spiritualists train to communicate with spirits of the dead. Channeling is similar to other forms of deity possession around the world in that channelers may enter a mild trance, allowing the entering entity to control their body and speak through them, an event usually marked by a sharp change in voice and expressive behavior. Some popular channelers of this variety in recent history are JZ Knight, who channels the spirit of Ramtha, a thirty-thousand-year-old Lemurian warrior, and Jane Roberts, who channeled Seth, a discarnate entity said to be from an adjacent plane of existence.

In a number of cultures oracles and mediums can be found in every town and village, and they fulfill vital functions for those societies, though their form and function vary greatly. In some cases there occurs "full possession" by an entity, in which the host's consciousness is said to be displaced, resulting in the host remembering nothing while in possession. In other cases, people maintain full consciousness of the event and can slip in and out of possession at will. Sometimes possession may include uncontrollable physical symptoms, such as trembling and shaking, leaping, speaking in tongues, shortness of breath, and/or feelings of electrical energy coursing the body, while in others there are few noticeable symptoms, and the medium is seemingly self-composed. Sometimes trance is involved, sometimes not, and some mediums may be possessed by multiple entities at the same time, while others are possessed only by one particular entity. Most possessions are temporary, while others may last indefinitely. Group possession has also been reported in a number of places.

Despite its global nature, there is little agreement regarding what possession is, how it works, and its function. There are few generalizations that can be made about possession as a cross-cultural phenomenon. One characteristic seems to be that possession is linked with certain groups or types; there is a preponderance of possession among women and children, persons belonging to marginalized groups, and among those who have experienced various forms of trauma. Additionally, the capacity to act as an oracle or a medium is often presented as a trait passed down through one's lineage. All of these seem to point to a dynamic exchange of cultural and biological processes involved in the phenomenon of possession. Because of this, scholars who study possession have begun using a variety of analytical tools and interdisciplinary methods from fields such as anthropology, sociology, religious studies, psychology, psychiatry, cognitive science, and neuroscience. The integration of these approaches has led to a greater understanding of possession.

In the Western world possession is generally understood to be a manifestation of mental illness, and recently possession as a category was formally incorporated in the 5th edition of the Diagnostic and Statistical Manual of Mental Disorders (DSM) as a part of its theoretical construction on Dissociative Identity Disorders. However, the DSM adds an important new caveat: possession may be considered non-pathological if it is "a normal part of a broadly accepted cultural or religious practice." This marks an important change in the field of psychiatry by recognizing, and bringing to the forefront, the fact that non-pathological forms of possession exist and may be an accepted and sought after cultural practice. Given its global nature and long history, possession is increasingly being recognized as an important dimension of human behavior and experience, and recent evidence shows that in many places the phenomenon of possession is in fact increasing.

Vikas Malhotra

See also: Automatic Writing; Channeling; Clairvoyance; Discarnate Entity; Divination; Exorcism; Mediumship; Myers, Frederic W. H.; New Age; Prophecy; Shamanism; Siddhis; Spiritism; Unconscious Mind

Further Reading

Bourguignon, Erika. 1976. *Possession*. San Francisco: Chandler & Sharp Publishers.
Schmidt, Bettina E., and Lucy Huskinson. 2010. *Spirit Possession and Trance: New Interdisciplinary Perspectives*. London: Continuum.
Smith, Frederick M. 2006. *The Self Possessed: Deity and Spirit Possession in South Asian Literature and Civilization*. New York: Columbia University Press.

PRECOGNITION

"Precognition" is a term that refers to a form of extrasensory perception (ESP)—or, more specifically, clairvoyance—of an event or state not yet experienced. The term was introduced to psychology in 1894 by Frederic Myers, co-founder of the Society for Psychical Research (SPR), to describe information obtained about the future in ways that could not be explained through presently available means, such as the normal senses, deductive reasoning, or currently held knowledge. It derives from the Latin *praecognitio*, meaning "to have foreknowledge," but is also commonly referred to as "second sight" or "future sight." The precognitive experience involves a clear presentation of visions that provide details about something yet to happen. The ways in which precognitive information is obtained are varied and range from waking visions to channeling, mediumship, divination, daydreams, trance, and meditative states. Despite this variety, the most frequently reported medium by which precognition is experienced is dreams. It is also the most frequently reported form of all extrasensory experiences; reviews published from 1960 to 2002 show that proportions ranging from 34 percent to 75 percent of all self-reported psychic experiences are classified as precognitive. Precognition is also closely associated with and commonly mistaken for two other phenomena: premonitions and prophecies. A premonition differs from precognition in that it is a forewarning, emotionally based, with no specific visions or knowledge of the coming event. A prophecy also refers to foreknowledge of an event, but this knowledge is seen as being in some way divinely inspired.

Historically, precognition was an ability held in high regard by many ancient civilizations. The Egyptians, Chinese, Greeks, and Romans all used various forms of wise men and soothsayers, individuals believed to possess precognitive insight. One of the most famous ancient accounts is the warning issued to Julius Caesar by the soothsayer Spurinna before his assassination, which later inspired Shakespeare to write the famous line "beware the ides of March" into his play of Caesar's assassination and its ensuing political turmoil.

Precognition is a type of clairvoyance in which a person gains information or knowledge about something that has not yet happened. The most frequently reported of all extrasensory experiences, it can occur independently or in conjunction with channeling, mediumship, divination, daydreams, trance, and meditative states.

Although Myers was the first to use the term "precognition" within psychical research, the first to publish a systematic investigation specifically focused on precognition was British aeronautics engineer J. W. Dunne in 1927. Dunne became intrigued by the precognitive content of some of his own dreams and thus kept a comprehensive record of them, attempting to identify links between his dream content and occurrences within the world. This technique involved careful cataloguing and analysis of spontaneous cases and was thus a very time-consuming endeavor that nonetheless produced some very interesting evidence for the existence of dream precognition.

During the 1930s the founder of parapsychology, J. B. Rhine, aimed to take the spontaneous phenomena of ESP experiences and operationalize them for laboratory testing. This would offer greater ease in studying the potential existence of precognition over spontaneous cases, while providing control to the researcher for ruling out alternative explanations for the phenomena such as chance coincidence or the use of unconsciously acquired information through the senses. In a typical example of Rhine's methodology, he would ask participants to guess the order of a deck of 25 cards, each of which bore one of five geometric shapes (Zener cards). Individuals made these guesses prior to the deck's being shuffled. The cards were then shuffled one, two, or ten days after the guesses had been made. Rhine's research findings demonstrated positive scoring for precognitive experiments significantly above chance levels. Debate about the accuracy of Rhine's findings was ongoing within the scientific community. Initially his statistical analysis was criticized, but this was rebutted by then president of the institute for mathematical statistics, Burton Camp, who supported the validity of Rhine's statistical method. One skeptic, Martin Gardner, argued that Rhine's work had been undertaken with care and competence, and overall could not be easily dismissed.

Since that time hundreds of laboratory-based precognition experiments have been published. The vast majority utilized methods similar to Rhine's forced-choice design, whereby participants are challenged to guess on each trial which of a range of potential targets would be randomly selected in the future. These targets ranged from Zener cards to die faces, colored light bulbs, and images on an automated computer display. A meta-analysis undertaken in 1989 of precognition experiments conducted from 1935 to 1987 included 309 experiments from 42 different researchers working with over 50,000 participants across two million research trials. The results demonstrated a small but highly significant effect, with performance levels higher than what would be expected by chance alone.

In 2011 the highly respected psychologist Daryl Bem published a series of nine precognition experiments in a top-tier psychology journal, eight of which demonstrated significantly positive effects. Across these experiments Bem used a variety of techniques; however, his general strategy involved a sequence-reversal technique for classical experiments of well-established psychological phenomena. Thus the "cause," such as learning a list of words to recall, occurred after the "effect" of recalling the list of words. Bem claimed his research provided convincing evidence for precognition and thus challenged mainstream scientific notions of the unidirectional nature of time. These findings led to considerable controversy and debate within the psychological community, with many skeptics raising alarms about the quality of the peer review process and criticizing the highly influential journal for considering the paper for publication. Bem himself requested that other researchers conduct independent replications of his research, and many answered the call. A review of seven failed replication attempts published in the following year claimed there was no evidence to support the existence of precognition from Bem's research methodology. A more recent and comprehensive review, including 90 experiments from 33 laboratories in 14 different countries, published in 2014, again demonstrated a small but significant effect similar to the effect size originally presented by Bem.

The debate for the scientific existence of precognition is still ongoing, with many parapsychologists believing that the weight of the evidence, from independently replicated, carefully controlled studies, is as strong as the evidence for many other phenomena that are currently widely accepted within mainstream psychology. They argue that this provides good evidence that precognition is a real phenomenon—a position with which skeptics continue to disagree.

David Saunders

See also: Clairvoyance; Extrasensory Perception (ESP); Myers, Frederic W. H.; Paranormal Dreams; Parapsychology; Prophecy; Rhine Research Center

Further Reading

Barden, Dennis. 1991. *Ahead of Time: The Mystery of Precognition*. London: Robert Hale Ltd.
Irwin, Harvey, and Caroline Watt. 2007. *An Introduction to Parapsychology*. 5th ed. Jefferson, NC: McFarland.

PRINCETON ENGINEERING ANOMALIES RESEARCH

The Princeton Engineering Anomalies Research, or PEAR, laboratory was established in 1979 in Princeton University's School of Engineering and Applied Science. Professor Robert G. Jahn, the program's founder, was dean of the engineering school at the time and a prominent aerospace scientist who has been honored with many prestigious academic awards.

The program was stimulated by an undergraduate project that explored the potential of the human mind to influence the output of a random number generator. The positive results of this student study and the potential implications of such anomalous phenomena for a wide range of engineering systems prompted Jahn to create a well-staffed and technically sophisticated research program dedicated to the study of anomalies in human/machine interactions, despite the reluctance of the university administration. Brenda Dunne, a developmental psychologist from the University of Chicago who also had a strong background in the humanities, joined him in Princeton in 1979 to serve as PEAR's laboratory manager. Since she had earlier conducted a large number of experiments in remote viewing, this topic was included as the second research portion of the program. A third component involved the development of a variety of conceptual models capable of accommodating the observed anomalies within a scientific framework.

The exploration of the role of consciousness in the establishment of physical reality was the main goal of the PEAR research program. To address this in the human/machine studies, a variety of physical random devices were developed, ranging from a microelectronic random event generator about the size of a microwave oven, to a large random mechanical cascade that became known as "Murphy": a 10-foot-by-8-foot device that loudly scattered 9,000 ¾ polystyrene marbles through a maze of 330 pegs into a series of collecting bins. Other experiments included a linear pendulum, a water jet fountain, and a Native American drum driven by a random process. A particularly popular experiment involved a toy frog who "drove" a randomly operated robot. The primary variable in all these experiments was the human operator's pre-stated intentions to shift the output distribution of the random binary events in positive or negative directions. Over the years these experiments collectively comprised well over a billion trials, with typically small effects that statistically proved highly significant across large databases.

PEAR's remote viewing studies explored a number of reliable analytical techniques for quantifying the information produced by human percipients in their attempts to describe remote geographical locations. Over 650 individual trials were generated, the composite results of which had a likelihood of occurring by chance of a few parts in a billion.

Some of the many insights gleaned from the work are objectively specifiable, such as the scale and structural character of the anomalous effects; their relative insensitivity to objective physical correlates, including distance and time; the oscillating sequential patterns of performance they display; the major discrepancies between male and female achievements; and their irregular replicability at all levels of experience. But many others relate to subjective issues, such as the responsiveness of the effects to conscious and unconscious intention and to individual and collective resonance; the relevance of ambience and attitude in their generation; and the importance of intrinsic uncertainty as a source of the anomalies. This blend of empirical features predicates radical excursions of their dedicated theoretical models, and hence of the more general scientific paradigms, to accommodate consciousness and its subjective information processing capacities as a proactive factor in the establishment of objective reality, with all of the complications that entails. Pragmatic applications now can be foreseen in many sectors of public endeavor.

All told, the PEAR laboratory produced the largest extant body of rigorous scientific evidence testifying to the reality of phenomena known in parapsychology as "psychokinesis" or "ESP." Over the years it has come to be recognized world-wide as one of the most highly respected institutions studying consciousness-related anomalies.

Jahn and Dunne closed the PEAR laboratory in 2007 and established in its place the International Consciousness Research Laboratories, or ICRL, a modest not-for-profit organization located in the Princeton community. Among its other activities, ICRL operates The ICRL Press, a niche publishing company that produces a series of outstanding books offering diverse perspectives on the nature of consciousness and reality.

Brenda J. Dunne

See also: Consciousness; Extrasensory Perception (ESP); Koestler Parapsychology Unit; Parapsychology; Psychokinesis (PK); Remote Viewing; Rhine Research Center; Stanford Research Institute

Further Reading

ICRL: International Consciousness Research Laboratories (official Website). http://icrl.org.

Jahn, Robert G., and Brenda J. Dunne. 2011. *Consciousness and the Source of Reality: The PEAR Odyssey.* Princeton, NJ: ICRL Press.

Jahn, Robert G., and Brenda J. Dunne. (1989) 2009. *Margins of Reality: The Role of Consciousness in the Physical World.* Princeton, NJ: ICRL Press.

Jahn, Robert G., and Brenda J. Dunne. 2005. "The PEAR Proposition." *Journal of Scientific Exploration* 19 (2), 195–246. http://www.scientificexploration.org/journal/jse_19_2_jahn.pdf.

Jahn, Robert G., and Brenda J. Dunne. 2011. *Quirks of the Quantum Mind.* Princeton, NJ: ICRL Press.

The PEAR Proposition: A Quarter Century of Princeton Engineering Anomalies Research. 2006. DVD/CD (3-discs). Directed by Aaron Michels. StripMind Media/ICRL.

Princeton Engineering Anomalies Research (official Website). 2010. http://www.princeton.edu/~pear.

PROPHECY

Prophecy (from the Greek *prophemi* meaning "to say beforehand, foretell") can be defined as the ability to foretell future events or conditions through an innate supernatural or paranormal ability to speak from a viewpoint of divine authority. Prophecy is therefore similar to mediumship or channeling in its purported ability to receive emanations from a divine being or higher intelligence, and convey these revelations to others. Prophets are found in all the world's major religions, and R. J. Stewart describes prophecy as "a spiritual and psychic event that has influenced the development of humankind upon the planet, and which forms, as a secondary ramification of the prophetic event itself, one of the foundations for cultures and religions through history" (Stewart, 1990, 7). Similarly, Jean-Pierre Vernant defines prophetic divination as an "irruption of divine immutability and omniscience into the inconstant flux of human existence" (Vernant, 1991, 315).

In the West there are two traditions in which prophecy plays a major role: ancient paganism (as practiced in the Graeco-Roman world, and as theorized in Greek philosophy) and Judeo-Christianity. In both cases, prophecy is clearly distinguished from sorcery, magic, and forms of inductive divination (divination using specific technical apparatus), being reliant on direct communication from a divine source that supersedes human will or inference. However, it is impossible to distinguish Christian prophecy from natural forms of pagan divination where information is gained through dreams, visions, or inspirations, because the spiritual authority may be identified in a variety of different ways (e.g., God, angels, saints, daimones, heroes, or deceased ancestors). From a psychological point of view, prophecy can be defined as a type of intuitive knowing that bypasses the usual sensory channels and rational intellect. From the perspective of Platonic and esoteric philosophy, such intuitive knowing is *ontologically prior* to rational deduction or sense-perception as it is conveyed directly from the Divine Mind to the highest part of the human soul, known as the intuitive intellect, and is then subject to rational interpretation and analysis.

Pagan Prophecy

In the Greek tradition, three contexts for prophecy can be distinguished: prophecy in archaic literature, oracular prophecy in classical Greece, and the Platonic philosophical tradition which theorizes on the nature of prophetic utterance.

Archaic Literature

Archaic Greek poetry is placed at the early stage of a long tradition of prophecy in the ancient world, and yet has distinct features. In the works of Homer and Hesiod (seventh—eighth c. BCE), oracles were not used for divination and had no bearing on prophecy. The distinction between inspired seer and rational prophet and the Judeo-Christian image of prophet as spiritual leader had not yet developed, and the archaic Greek seer was closer in spirit to a poet or healer than priest. Indeed the gods themselves could assume a prophetic role as they played an active role in the world and took on various disguises, often taunting humans with ambiguous messages and forcing them back on their own devices.

Oracles

The most famous prophets of the ancient world were the priestesses and priests of the oracle sanctuaries, such as Delphi, Dodona, Claros, and Didyma. Of note is the succession of female prophetesses known as the Sybils, of whom 10 were identified by the Roman period, each associated with a specific location. At Delphi, for example, the priestess (here called the Pythia) was seen to receive oracles from the god Apollo, becoming possessed and in a state of "enthusiasm," ," which means, etymologically, to be filled with a god. How did this happen? There are four theories: (a) that the Pythia sat over a chasm that emitted an intoxicating substance, enabling her to enter an altered state of consciousness and receive the god; (b) that a daimon (that is a lesser spirit in the train of Apollo, not Apollo himself), interacted with the priestess; (c) that the earth itself sent out streams of energies, opening up the Pythia's soul to receive impressions of the future; and (d) that Apollo manifested as a light that illuminated the soul of the Pythia but did not fully possess her. Plutarch (46–120 CE) discusses (b) and (c), suggesting that the gift of the gods is conveyed by the earth's exhalations. Iamblichus (c. 245–325 CE) tells us that the gods consist of light and specifies exact rituals in his work *De Mysteriis* for the invocation of daimonic and divine intelligence. Modern scholarship has revealed that gases did indeed rise up through fissures in the bedrock and in nearby springs—in particular ethylene, which may have triggered the Pythia's trance state but cannot necessarily be held responsible for the prophecies she uttered. Although in an ecstatic condition, she spoke in a controlled manner, and her message was subject to debate and interrogation in order to arrive at its correct interpretation.

Platonic Philosophy

Plato (c. 429/23–348 BCE) clearly distinguishes divination by inspired prophets, possessed by a kind of madness or frenzy (*mantike*), from deductive diviners who inquire into the future through rational means such as the interpretation of bird-omens (see *Phaedrus* , §244). This follows from his precise epistemology, whereby altered states of consciousness may be the result of divine possession and are to be clearly differentiated from the exercising of the human rational faculty. Following Plato, the Roman philosopher Cicero (106–43 BCE) also distinguishes between natural and inductive forms of divination in his *De Divinatione*, and this paradigm would deeply inform the Christian insistence on the distance between divine revelation bestowed by grace and the limits of human reason. In his Cave Allegory (*Republic* , Book 7), Plato suggests that the true prophet is the person who has escaped from the cave of ordinary reality, seen the archetypal Ideas underlying creation, and has returned to rescue mankind from their illusions.

Christian Prophecy

For Christians, prophecy is said to be one of the nine gifts of the Spirit described in I Corinthians 12:7–10, and indeed Paul encouraged everyone to prophesy (I Corinthians 14:27–28). In the Hebrew Bible, the *nabi* or prophets were believed to have supernatural powers and were accorded special status as servants of God. Prophecy here has the dual sense of prediction and proclamation; that is, the prophets were both foretellers of the future and preachers of the faith. In this sense, preachers such as St. Francis of Assisi, John Wesley, and Martin Luther King would also be seen as prophets. Israelite prophecy was of immense significance, and in the Greek translation of the Old Testament we find five books of the prophets: Isaiah, Jeremiah, Ezekiel, Daniel, and the Book of the twelve minor prophets. These prophets, dating from the eighth century BCE, claim divine authority and often clash with the temporal powers. They have an inner compulsion to prophesy, often in a state of ecstasy, trance, or inspiration, and sometimes in large groups (e.g., Numbers 11: 16–30; 1 Kings 22). Little is known of ancient Israelite divinatory or oracular practice, but insofar as they "consulted the Lord," prophets can be seen as diviners. We have the example of Deborah, an Israelite prophetess (Judges, 4:14) who prophesied the defeat of Sisera and the Canaanites. In Deuteronomy 18: 9–22 we read of the prohibition of pagan practices, although in essence the gifts of the Hebrew prophets are indistinguishable from those of the pagan practitioners. In Deuteronomy 22 we learn that true and false prophecy are to be distinguished according to their accuracy. An essential feature of ancient prophecy is the apocalyptic vision, which draws on creation myth, mythic cycles of time, and eschatology; examples might be the ancient war between the Titans and the Olympians, or the dramatic imagery of the Book of Revelation.

Some Later Prophets

From the later medieval period, prophecy took two main directions: the apocalyptic or millenarianist prophecies (which often contained political propaganda and agendas) and spiritual or mystical revelations. One of the most well-known European prophets was Nostradamus (1503–1566), who worked in the tradition of astrological prognostication. He has been credited with predicting many world events, and his book *Les Propheties* of 1555 has rarely been out of print. In the mid-19th century, Helena Blavatsky (1831–1891), founder of the Theosophical Society, published *The Secret Doctrine* (1855), in which Eastern wisdom and modern science are reconciled by spiritually advanced beings known as mahatmas, whose wisdom Blavatsky claimed to channel. More recently, the American "sleeping prophet" Edgar Cayce (1877–1945) became renowned for his psychic readings while in a trance state, including several that prophesied major physical changes to our planet. There are many examples of New Age prophetic texts—for example, the Seth material, channelled to the American writer Jane Roberts (1929–1984), and the best-selling "Law of Attraction" books (2004–2009) claimed by spiritual teacher Esther Hicks to be the utterances of spirit entities called Abraham. An example from the literary genre would be *The Celestine Prophecy* by James Redfield (1993), a story of spiritual initiation that sold over twenty million copies by 2005.

Angela Voss

See also: Angels, Apparitions; Astral Plane; Astrology; Automatic Writing; Cayce, Edgar; Channeling; Clairvoyance; Consciousness; Demonology; Discarnate Entity; Divination; Hallucinations; Hypnagogic State; Imaginal; Meditation; Mediumship; Mystical Experience; New Age; Paranormal Dreams; Precognition; Possession; Scrying; Spiritualism; Theosophy; Unconscious Mind

Further Reading

Iles Johnston, Sarah. 2008. *Ancient Greek Divination*. Chichester, UK: Wiley-Blackwell.
Sawyer, John F. A. 1987. *Prophecy and the Biblical Prophets*. New York: Oxford University Press.
Stewart, R. J. 1990. *The Elements of Prophecy*. Shaftesbury, Dorset, UK: Element Books.
Vernant, Jean-Pierre. 1991. *Mortals and Immortals*. Princeton, NJ: Princeton University Press.

PSEUDOSCIENCE

"Pseudoscience" is a term used to refer to a set of beliefs to indicate they are not based on the scientific method, although they may be purported to be. It has been widely used by skeptics of parapsychology and the paranormal as a derogatory term intended to imply that people who believe in a particular phenomenon are either intentionally misleading others to believe there is scientific evidence supporting the phenomenon or misguided in their understanding of the scientific method. Examples of phenomena that have been labeled pseudoscientific are astrology, UFOlogy, cryptozoology, telepathy, channeling, psychic surgery, intelligent design, hypnosis, chiropractic, homeopathy, and acupuncture, although there are many more. "Anomalistics" is a more neutral term used by some writers to describe the study of anomalous claims or experiences.

The term "pseudoscience" originated in 1796 when James Petit Andrew used it to refer to alchemy, which he called a "fantastical pseudo-science," in a historical account of Great Britain. Since that time it has been used primarily to describe beliefs or practices that originated since the early 19th century and the Industrial Revolution. Pseudoscience is narrower in scope than outright fraud, which encompasses a variety of incompetent or deceitful scientific practices.

A primary issue in identifying pseudoscience is called the demarcation problem, which is the problem of determining what is and is not science. Karl Popper proposed the criterion of falsifiability to resolve the demarcation problem. This principle of falsifiability says that a statement must be able to be contradicted by conceivable observations in order to be a scientific statement. "All dogs have four legs" would therefore be a falsifiable statement, given one three-legged dogs, whereas "Bigfoot lives in the Pacific Northwest" is not, since not finding evidence of Bigfoot does not prove Bigfoot does not exist. However, many writers have found Popper's falsifiability test neither necessary nor sufficient for resolving the demarcation problem.

Another set of criteria for distinguishing science from pseudoscience has been proposed by Paul Thagard. He suggested a discipline is pseudoscientific if it fails to make progress over time and the community of practitioners shows little interest in solving problems related to the theory. Thus, astrology, the practice of which has remained essentially the same for thousands of years, is a pseudoscience by this standard.

The Uses of Pseudoscience

The term "pseudoscience" was originally applied to alchemy in 1796. Since then it has been applied to many different things, including:

- Astrology
- UFOlogy
- Cryptozoology
- Telepathy
- Channeling
- Psychic surgery
- Intelligent design
- Hypnosis
- Chiropractic
- Homeopathy
- Acupuncture

As a label used to deny the valid scientific status of things that are claimed to be true science by their proponents, it remains controversial and is sometimes used as an ideological weapon.

However, Thomas Kuhn suggested that science progresses through paradigm shifts, which are sudden openings to new ideas and approaches. Thus, some people see areas labeled as pseudoscientific as precursors to more general shifts in scientific paradigms. For example, people who believe acupuncture stimulates meridians of energy may believe Western medicine will eventually identify the mechanism of action and incorporate this understanding into accepted medical techniques. Others, who reject acupuncture as pseudoscientific due to inconsistent or inconclusive results from empirical tests, may disagree since they see no possibility of the principles of acupuncture ever being incorporated into the dominant scientific paradigm. Kuhn also suggested that science can never be fully objective, as ultimate conclusions are always influenced by subjective worldview. Thus, what does and does not constitute legitimate scientific inquiry will always be somewhat subjectively determined.

In general, the process of science relies on accepted data, methods, and theories, which differ for investigations in different disciplines. Several authors have noted that calling an area of inquiry a pseudoscience implies it should be investigated scientifically, but many of the topics considered pseudoscientific are primarily psychological or quasi-religious. For example, Michael Shermer, a skeptic and debunker of pseudoscientific claims, emphasizes the distinction between science, which is progressive, and disciplines such as art and religion, which are not progressive and rely on individual subjectivity to a greater degree than the natural sciences. Henry Bauer, however, recognizes the social sciences as requiring different theories and methods than the natural sciences but considers them scientific disciplines nonetheless.

Current experts do not agree on a definition of science or pseudoscience, but many recognize the difficulty of defining pseudoscience in contrast to science, which is a culturally based practice partially determined by the object of study. Thus, definitions of pseudoscience range widely among authorities depending on their personal criteria for an acceptable scientific method, and the only consistently clear quality of pseudoscience is that the term is derogatory.

Jennifer Lyke

See also: Alchemy; Astrology; Committee for Skeptical Inquiry; Mesmerism; Parapsychology

Further Reading

Bauer, Henry H. 2001. *Science or Pseudoscience: Magnetic Healing, Psychic Phenomena, and Other Heterodoxies*. Urbana, IL: University of Illinois Press.

Gordin, Michael D. 2012. *The Pseudoscience Wars: Immanuel Velikovsky and the Birth of the Modern Fringe*. Chicago: The University of Chicago Press.

Shermer, Michael. 1997. *Why People Believe Weird Things: Pseudoscience, Superstition, and Other Confusions of Our Time*. New York: W. H. Freeman and Company.

PSI

"Psi" is a term used in parapsychology to describe paranormal events. The term usually refers to two types of phenomena, Extra-Sensorial Perceptions (ESP) and Psychokinesis (PK). The term comes from the Greek letter *psi*.

It was first proposed in 1942 by the Austrian physiologist Bertold Wiesner and the British psychologist Robert Thouless to serve as a neutral word for addressing paranormal phenomena. At the turn of the 20th century, paranormal research was often linked to proving the survival of the soul, something that made many researchers uncomfortable. It is in this historical context that the word "psi" was originally used in parapsychological laboratory tests on ESP and PK to refer only to scientific findings emerging out of small statistical deviations from the expected normal scores. Implicit in this approach was the notion that psi is a natural human ability, rather than being a supernatural phenomenon.

The limitation to laboratory research, however, did not remain for long. Beginning in the 1940s, Louisa Rhine, wife of parapsychologist J. B. Rhine, accumulated and analyzed several thousand accounts of ESP through letters sent to her by experiencers. She was a strong advocate for including research that had been conducted outside the laboratory in the total field of parapsychological research. These types of experiences were eventually labeled "spontaneous psi" to distinguish them from the induced psi of laboratory experiments.

Parapsychologists began conducting research on poltergeist disturbances in the 1950s. Contrary to previous approaches to the subject, they viewed this phenomenon as a form of PK and implicitly rejected the notion that poltergeist events involved supernatural entities. In the 1970s, the parapsychologist Scott Rogo extended the same line of thought by strongly advancing the idea that other phenomena such as ghosts and UFOs might be psi-related. This form of psi was eventually labeled "macro psi" to distinguish it from the "micro psi" of laboratory statistical findings.

Most parapsychologists think psi is something emerging from deep unconscious mental processes. Still, its exact nature remains a contentious issue. It was described in the early days as a force or a form of energy and as meaningful and unconsciously intended coincidences (synchronicities). Some more recent theories, such as the ones proposed by Russell Targ and Jane Katra in *Miracles of Mind* and James Carpenter in *First Sight*, propose that psi is an expression of human will and creativity at a different level of reality. Other theories, such as Dean Radin's in *Entangled Minds*, propose that psi could be a form of quantum entanglement. The notion of psi has been helpful and will likely continue to generate useful parapsychological research.

Eric Ouellet

See also: Drugs and the Paranormal; Extrasensory Perception (ESP); Ganzfeld Technique, The; Parapsychology; Poltergeist; Psychokinesis (PK); Synchronicity; Telepathy

Further Reading

Carpenter, James C. 2012. *First Sight: ESP and Parapsychology in Everyday Life*. Lanham, MD: Rowman & Littlefield.

Radin, Dean. 2006. *Entangled Minds: Extrasensory Experiences in a Quantum Reality*. New York: Paraview.

Rhine, Louisa. (1981) 2011. *The Invisible Picture: A Study of Psychic Experiences*. Jefferson, NC: McFarland.

Rogo, Scott. 1977. *The Haunted Universe*. New York: Signet.

Schoch, Robert M., and Logan Yonavjak. 2008. *The Parapsychology Revolution: A Concise Anthology of Paranormal and Psychical Research*. New York: Tarcher/Penguin.

Targ, Russell, and Jane Katra. 1999. *Miracles of Mind*. San Francisco: New World.

Wiesner, B. P., and R. H. Thouless. 1942. "The Present Position of the Experimental Research into Telepathy and Related Phenomena." *Proceedings of the Society for Psychical Research* 47: 1.

PSYCHIC ARCHAEOLOGY

Psychology archaeology is the use of psychic or paranormal methods such as clairvoyance, remote viewing, dowsing, psychometry, and others to aid in archaeological work. Perhaps its most famous case, and also the case that is often cited as representing the founding of the field, was the use of automatic writing by respected British architect and archaeologist Frederick Bligh Bond when he was appointed by the Church of England in 1908 to direct the excavations at Glastonbury Abbey. Bligh and a friend used automatic writing to communicate with spirits that, as they claimed, told them about the abbey's past. He later recounted these things in his 1918 book *The Gate of Remembrance*.

The field took another public leap forward some four decades later. Until 1959, the discussion of the paranormal in anything other than purely dismissive grounds had not occurred and had not even been allowed within the auspices of the American Anthropological Association. It was at one of the AAA's meetings in 1959 that Clarence Wolsey Weiant presented a controversial paper on "The Present Status of Parapsychology and Its Implications for Anthropology." The room was filled to the rafters for what probably would have been an academic lynching had not the infamous anthropologist Margaret Mead offered her support for Weiant's thesis, though some remained openly hostile.

Weiant himself had had his own paranormal experience and had located some extraordinary finds on an archaeological dig in Mexico in 1938 by employing the apparently clairvoyant skills of an indigenous workman, Emilio Tegoma. The dig had been the first joint National Geographic-Smithsonian Archaeological Expedition to Tres Zapotes, which became the location for the discovery of Cebezo Colosol, a giant 10-ton stone Olmec head, as well as the important Stela C, which had established the site as a meeting point for Aztec, Mayan, and Olmec cultures.

In Weiant's words (from a paper he presented in 1959 at the annual meeting of the AAA in Mexico City), "After we had spent some days in fruitless digging in the immediate vicinity of the Cabeza Colosal and had used a plough to tear up the small plaza situated between the giant head and the nearest mound, I was approached by Emilio Tegoma, one of our workmen, reputed to be the oldest man in Tres Zapotes. He assured me that he possessed the power to see things at a distance and things hidden. If we would listen to him, he would lead us to a place where we would find what we were looking for. He led us to what is referred to in our reports as the zone of the burials. Within 20 minutes after ground was broken here, the first beautiful and unbroken figurine of a Maya priest came out of the ground" (Weiant 1960, 4).

It is easy to see why Weiant kept this quiet for so long, considering that Bond was eventually sacked from his job as archaeologist for publishing *The Gate of Remembrance*, which revealed his supposed use of mediums not only in the successful excavation of Glastonbury Abbey but also in the discovery of Edgar Chapel some years earlier. Nevertheless, similar successful psychic archaeology experiments have been reported by others over the years and were particularly fashionable during the late 1970s, such as work of Prof. Norman Emerson, considered father of Canadian archaeology, who was chairman at the University of Toronto and a founder and past-president of the Canadian Archaeological Association. Emerson believed that a man called George McMullen was able to locate archaeological sites and accurately reconstruct the history of artifacts. Other researchers of that era include anthropology professor David E. Jones and Stephan Schwartz, one of the founding members of the AAA division, the Society for the Anthropology of Consciousness.

Despite some very promising findings, very little research has been conducted into psychic archaeology since the 1970s, probably because of intellectual taboo and perceived career jeopardy. More recently, scriptwriter Philippa Langley fought a five-year battle to commission an excavation of a council office car park in Leicester, England, following a strong intuitive experience that led to the discovery in 2012 of the lost buried body of English king Richard III. Ms. Langley pinpointed the exact spot were the body was ultimately found, in what the chief archaeologist had said was "a long shot."

David Luke

See also: Clairvoyance; Extrasensory Perception (ESP); Mediumship; Remote Viewing

Further Reading

Jones, David E. 1979. *Visions of Time: Experiments in Psychic Archeology*. Wheaton, IL: Quest Books.

Schwartz, Stephan A. 1983. *The Alexandria Project: An Extraordinary True Adventure in Psychic Archaeology*. New York: Dell Publishing.

Schwartz, Stephan A. 1978. *The Secret Vaults of Time: Psychic Archaeology and the Quest for Man's Beginnings*. New York: Grosset & Dunlap.

Weiant, Clarence W. 1960. "Parapsychology and Anthropology." *MANAS* 13 (15): 1–6. http://www.manasjournal.org/pdf_library/VolumeXIII_1960/XIII-15.pdf.

PSYCHICAL RESEARCH

Although the term "psychical research" is still used, the field's heyday was from the founding of the first Society for Psychical Research, in London in 1882, to the coining of "parapsychology," a term associated with the work of American psychologist J. B. Rhine in the 1930s. For these 50 years, psychical research was consistently intertwined with developments in experimental and dynamic psychology. Figures interested in psychical research included such central figures as Sigmund Freud, William James, Pierre Janet, and Carl Jung. Although its method and findings were always contested and controversial, there was constant interaction and dialogue with mainstream psychology. *Para*-psychology, in contrast, announced in its name that it had become marginal to the mainsteam, and this is where it has remained ever since.

"Psychical research" was a neutral name deliberately chosen in an attempt to transform the committed theological *beliefs* of Spiritualism into a skeptical empirical *science* without the predisposing hypothesis of spirit survival. Advocates claimed to be unbiased investigators seeking reiterable experimental methods to document evidence of phenomena hitherto deemed "supernatural." In the 1870s, when the Spiritualist movement innovated with dark séances and full bodily materialization of spirits, London's men of science established a new cultural authority by ridiculing the credulity of Spiritualists. In this context, the writer and jurist Edward Cox founded the Psychological Society of Great Britain in 1875 on the model of a secular scientific society from which theological questions would ostensibly be excluded. Although a Spiritualist, Cox adopted the rhetoric of sober scientific inquiry and published an annual *Proceedings* in which he outlined a new scientific terminology. Rather than oppose science, Cox sought to imitate and incorporate it. Cox had coined the term "psychic force" as a term to explain an invisible, as-yet-unexplainable energy directed by mediums during séances, and it was Cox who began to displace the loaded term "medium" with "psychic." Cox composed a massive two-volume synthesis of evidence, *The Mechanism of Man* (1876 and 1879), in which "supernatural" phenomena of mesmerism, Spiritualism, and a range of abnormal psychological states were swept into a grand scientific synthesis. Cox chose the term "psychical" with care: Victorians with a classical education would have heard in the Greek *psyche* the meaning "soul" or "spirit," letting Cox subtly bridge between religion and the new psychology. Cox died in 1879 but laid the foundations for the emergence of the Society for Psychical Research (SPR) in 1882.

The SPR was the brain child of the professor of physics William Barrett. Barrett had worked as assistant to the leading public advocate of secular science, the physicist John Tyndall. During the 1870s he was one of a number of leading men of science who attended séances and became convinced that the phenomena on display were reiterable empirical proof of an ultramundane world of spirit. Through Alfred Russel Wallace, the co-founder of the theory of evolution and a passionate Spiritualist, Barrett even presented his paper "On Some Phenomena Associated with Abnormal Conditions of Mind" to the British Association of the Advancement of Science in 1876. The paper's title was deliberately sober: scandalously, however, it detailed experiments in mesmerism where "community of sensation" was found in the uncanny rapport between mesmerist and mesmerized. That Wallace had let this be presented inside the bastion of science caused outrage.

In 1882, Barrett convened a meeting at the British National Association of Spiritualists to found the new society. The first president was the utterly respectable establishment figure Henry Sidgwick, professor of philosophy at Cambridge, the man whose principled agnosticism had forced Cambridge to abandon the requirement that all Fellows had to swear their affirmation of the Christian Articles of Faith. His public skepticism and his links to the political establishment were central to establishing the SPR. His wife, Eleanor Sidgwick, was also a leading public advocate of the SPR and brought her brother, the future Tory Prime Minister Arthur Balfour, into the orbit of the society. Sidgwick's former students, Frederic Myers and Edmund Gurney, both agonized young men who had experienced repeated crises of orthodox faith, were to become early psychological theorists for the SPR, producing thousands of pages of documentary evidence and innovative theory in books and articles and through the SPR's voluminous *Proceedings*. Both Myers and Gurney were amateur gentleman scholars, yet became serious and respected pioneers of the dynamic psychology of hypnotism, hallucination, subconscious states, and other aspects of abnormal psychology.

Spiritualists were initially strongly represented in the early SPR, but dislike of the neutral scientific stance led to a schism in 1884 and decades of abrasive relations between the SPR and Spiritualism. Arguably, this is exactly what the SPR wanted: it established their scientific credentials. In an investigation and denunciation of the Theosophical Society in 1885, the SPR dismissed the Theosophical Society, which represented the occult synthesis of all religions then in vogue in London, as being founded on open and outrageous fraud. This also consolidated their skeptical credentials.

The "Objects of the Society," outlined in the opening pages of their official *Proceedings*, declared that the SPR proposed "an organized and systematic attempt to investigate that large group of debatable phenomena designated by such terms as mesmeric, psychical, and Spiritualistic." They initially established six research committees: on hypnotism; on odylism and related claims that psychic sensitives could "see" invisible rays; on apparitions at death; on Spiritualist phenomena (which would shortly include a "haunted house" committee); a literary committee to build a library on the history of the supernatural; and most important, a committee to explore the "nature and extent of any influence which may be exerted by one mind upon another, apart from any generally recognised mode of perception." Frederic Myers, classicist and poet, proved himself rather adept at coining terms for this new science: haunted houses became "phantasmogenetic centers"; ghosts were "phantasms of the living," projections of psychic energy at moments of crisis rather than survivals of the dead; and psychic communication at a distance became "telepathy" (coined by Myers from the Greek "distant" "feeling" in December 1882). The magnum opus of psychical research was Myers's *The Subliminal Consciousness*, a huge compendium and synthesis of work that tied fugitive instances of telepathy ultimately into a vision of the universe tied together by animating principles of cosmic and divine love.

Many prominent and respected scientists, scholars, and other establishment figures were among those interested or involved in psychical research during its heyday from the 1880s to the 1930s. These included:

- Some of the founders of modern psychology, including Sigmund Freud, William James, Pierre Janet, Carl Jung, and Frederic Myers.

- Many scientists, including Alfred Russell Wallace, co-founder of the theory of evolution; Jean-Martin Charcot, Europe's leading neurologist; physiologist and Nobel laureate Charlet Richet; and many physicists, including William Barrett, Oliver Lodge, Lord Rayleigh, and J. J. Thompson, the last of whom discovered the realm of subatomic particles and non-radioactive isotopes.

- Renowned Cambridge philosophy professor Henry Sidgwick and his wife Eleanor, herself a major force in British higher education.

- Pioneering investigative journalist William Stead.

Barrett went on to help found the American branch of the SPR in 1885, a group that was dominated by the influential Harvard Professor William James (brother of novelist Henry James, who once read one of his brother's papers at a London meeting of the SPR). James prompted many of his fellow psychologists to investigate the claims of psychical research, including C. S. Peirce. Psychical research also found advocates in France, Russia, Italy, Germany, Switzerland, and Austria; it became a methodology with international reach remarkably quickly.

The methods for accumulating documentary evidence—questionnaires, the testimony of respected gentlemen and women—were frequently dismissed (quite rightly) as outmoded and unscientific. But it is also striking that the early experiments to prove the existence of telepathy innovated with "double-blind" tests in thousands of thought-reading tests that introduced methods still in use in mainstream psychology today. In the last decades of the 19th century, it was actually very difficult to separate the new dynamic psychology and psychical research. The leading neurologist in Europe, Jean-Martin Charcot, was a scourge of Catholic orthodoxy and Spiritualist heterodoxy alike, which he regarded as a mark of biological degeneracy, yet he also confirmed the objective existence of hypnotic trance states, and his staff experimented with transferring symptoms between patients in rapport with magnets. His colleague in Paris, Charles Richet, the physiologist who won the Nobel Prize for medical work in 1913, was also an ardent psychical researcher of Spiritualist mediums, publishing work on the "sixth sense" and a substantial summary of his investigations, *Thirty Years of Psychical Research*. Pierre Janet, the celebrated psychologist responsible for ideas of subconscious "dissociation," was involved in an experiment with Myers to see if it was possible to hypnotize at a distance—across the English Channel. Carl Jung's doctoral thesis focused on the psychology of mediumship, and Sigmund Freud did privately believe in psychical communications at a distance, including telepathy. His fellow psychoanalyst, Sandor Ferenczi, firmly believed that his patients could read his mind telepathically. The psychoanalytic concept of transference was routinely connected to occult communications and telepathy into the 1920s.

Early psychical research in Britain was also propped on advanced physics, then undergoing a revolution in the detection of forms of "invisible" energy. One of the earliest pioneers of wireless telegraphy, the physicist Oliver Lodge, was involved in psychical research and considered that his experiments in telepathy were equivalent to detecting Hertzian wave frequencies (first measured in the late 1880s). Lodge later became a leading Spiritualist. The Cambridge physicist Lord Rayleigh was also close to the Sidgwick circle, and this resulted in a long Cambridge connection between advanced physics and psychical research. The Cambridge physicist J. J. Thomson first detected and measured the action of electrons and thus discovered the realm of subatomic particles (in 1897) and nonradioactive isotopes (in 1913). In his memoirs, Thomson included a chapter called "Psychical Research," in which he affirmed that the study of short-range thought transference was of "the highest importance," although his own experiments with Rayleigh and Lodge were inconclusive. In an era of paradigm shift in physics and a coincident technological revolution, in which miraculous new communication devices like wireless telegraphy based on material supports undetectable to the ordinary human senses, telepathy seemed to many an entirely plausible phenomenon, on the cusp of being scientifically proven. It has remained in this promissory state for 130 years.

Although many respectable establishment figures and scientists were involved in psychical research, most scientific naturalists dismissed the field, and it remained marginal, a circumstance abetted by the occasional success of fake psychics and mediums in fooling respected establishment figures, as when no less an eminent scientific figure than William Crookes endorsed the veracity of Florence Cook's mediumistic abilities, after which she was roundly exposed as a fraud. Psychical research was also often publicly attacked by leading advocates of Spiritualism, which experienced a major revival during the Great War and remained a mass movement into the 1930s. In the 1880s and 1890s, the journalist and editor William Stead enthusiastically supported psychical research in his newspapers, even though he was a scourge of the establishment elite. His 1892 Christmas special for *The Review of Reviews*, called *Real Ghost Stories*, was effectively a popular anthology of psychical research case studies and sold over 100,000 copies. As Stead embraced Spiritualism, however, he became more critical and impatient of psychical research's skeptical stance. Sir Arthur Conan Doyle also attacked the SPR's "mingled record of usefulness and obstruction" in his *History of Spiritualism* (1926).

Critical and historical studies of psychical research have changed over time. Psychical research was for a long time ignored as an eccentric or embarrassing element in the careers of Victorian and Edwardian figures. Historians then began to explain the eccentricity of psychical research as a compromise formation resulting from the process of secularization. As the authority of science grew, many intellectuals experienced a crisis of orthodox Christian faith. Psychical research was ostensibly scientific yet refused a purely materialistic explanation of life, leaving instead a space for spirit. In the 1980s, social historians of science used "marginal sciences" like psychical research to explore how scientific concepts go through complex systems of legitimation, and by the 1990s there was an interest in understanding how phases of revolutionary paradigm shift in physics and psychology provided the perfect conditions for the flowering of this interstitial scientific project. This more nuanced historical understanding offers ways of grasping the remarkable influence of psychical research for 50 years, rather than simply excising it as an errant discourse in the history of science.

Roger Luckhurst

See also: American Society for Psychical Research; Haunting; James, William; Mesmerism; Myers, Frederic W. H.; Parapsychology; Society for Psychical Research; Spiritualism; Telepathy; Theosophy

Further Reading

Cerullo, John. 1982. *The Secularization of the Soul: Psychical Research in Modern Britain.* Philadelphia: Institute for the Study of Human Issues.

Gauld, Alan. 1968. *The Founders of Psychical Research.* London: RKP.

Luckhurst, Roger. 2002. *The Invention of Telepathy.* Oxford, UK: Oxford University Press.

Oppenheim, Janet. 1985. *The Other World: Spiritualism and Psychical Research in England 1850–1914.* Cambridge, UK: Cambridge University Press.

PSYCHOKINESIS (PK)

Psychokinesis (PK) describes the ability of a person or people to affect the physical world intentionally or unconsciously by some form of mental energy or psychic force. It is also known as "mind over matter." Moving objects from one position to another is perhaps the best known PK effect, but the purported talent may also involve levitation, creating sounds such as raps, contorting objects (for example, by bending metal), igniting fires at a distance, making an object disappear from one place and reappear in another, or even changing the weather. In other words, PK is a physical effect that operates outside of known natural laws.

In parapsychological studies, there are four major types of ongoing research into PK: macro-PK, where there is visible movement or change in inanimate objects; micro-PK, in which effects on the physical environment are less tangible but still measurable via statistical analysis of data, including on microscopic and sub-atomic levels; retro-PK, in which quantum-level effects occur before the experimental subject intends to affect subatomic matter; and bio-PK, which involves living organisms and people and may be suggestive of skills such as energy healing.

In essence, PK experiments all center on material effects that seem to relate to an individual's intention to get a specific result in the tests. PK subjects attempt to affect objects from a distance, often sitting in a concentrated, relaxed, or even altered state of consciousness. PK may occur by subtle contact, such as a group of people putting their finger tips on a table top, after which the whole table moves, or gently laying one's hands on a person to try and heal what ails them. The greatest difficulty in PK and psi experiments has been to achieve repeatability, therefore enabling testable results that would be accepted by most scientists. In his book *The Conscious Universe*, American psi researcher Dean Radin argues that results from experiments are small, but statistically significant enough to show that psychokinesis exists.

The word "psychokinesis" was derived from "telekinesis," coined by the Russian psychical researcher Alexander D. Aksakof in 1890. That same year, Frederic W. H. Myers, co-founder of Britain's Society for Psychical Research, noted that such manifestations appeared to have no visible cause and may occur either spontaneously and unexpectedly or willfully in the presence of a medium or individual with telekinetic talents. Among the most famous psychokinetic mediums were D. D. Home and Eusapia Pallidino. In 1914, the American writer, publisher, and psychical researcher Henry Holt suggested that the word "psychokinesis" would better suggest the potential mental mode of the force. By the 1940s, psychokinesis became widely adopted by parapsychologists, although telekinesis has remained a popular synonym.

Spontaneous macro-PK effects have been reported in everyday life. Here are three examples. (1) San Marino, 1992: an 85-year-old woman visiting the grave of her son who had died of leukemia 21 years earlier felt a pain in her left hand; her gold wedding ring had squashed into an ovoid shape. Examining the ring, the physicist Ferdinando Bersani of the University of Bologna could find no physical or mechanical explanation for the ring's unexpected deformation. (2) Around the world, people have reported street lamps and building lights commonly flickering off when they walk by—seemingly more often than chance would suggest. British paranormal researcher Hilary Evans wrote a book on this phenomenon, *The SLI Effect* (1995)—with SLI standing for "street light interference"—after receiving hundreds of letters from such individuals. (3) In Columbus, Ohio, starting in March 1984, lights and electrical appliances turned on and off, an unplugged stereo played music, objects from plastic lemons to candlesticks went flying, there were explosive sounds, and famously, a telephone receiver flew over 14-year-old Tina Resch's lap, photographed and published on the front page of the Columbus *Dispatch*. Multiple people witnessed many of these incidents, which took place anywhere Tina was present, including under observation in a research laboratory. American poltergeist researcher William G. Roll argued that the case was an example of recurrent spontaneous psychokinesis (RSPK).

Macro-PK experiments have sought to intentionally recreate spontaneous phenomena. In Victorian times, it was popular for groups of people to sit around a table at home and try to make it move on its own, proposing it to be a form of spirit contact. In the 1960s and 1970s, the British clinical psychologist Kenneth J. Batcheldor felt that PK, not spirit communication, arose from such group dynamics. Inhibition, disbelief, and fear among those in the group seemed to prevent table movements, so he encouraged a light-hearted gathering with conversation and singing. Sometimes a little purposeful cheating put sitters in the right frame of mind, and the table would then move or levitate apparently on its own volition, a sign of PK in action. Batcheldor's experiments were furthered by George and Iris Owen of the New Horizon Research Foundation in Toronto during the 1970s. Their experimental group created a fictitious persona, a 17th-century English aristocrat named "Philip," and made up a story about his unrequited, tragic love affair. They tried to communicate with the invented character's "spirit." Eventually, knocks came from the table that enabled interviews with "Philip" in which details of his fictional past were verified, whereas questions that contradicted the group's story were answered in the negative. The table they sat at began to move and levitate, at times dramatically. It seemed that they had created a ghost via their imagination, further evidence of human PK in relation to ghosts and poltergeists.

Micro-PK has been sought by analyzing a large number of trials—for example, in J. B. Rhine's dice-tossing experiments in the 1930s and 1940s or Dean Radin's meta-analyses of the statistically significant results of electronic random event or number generators (REGs/RNGs). Such generators were developed by the physicist Helmut Schmidt (binary numbers, like flipping a coin, produced by quantum-activated radioactive decay), Princeton Engineering Anomalies Research (intentionally willing balls rolling through a vertical board of pegs arranged in a quincunx geometric pattern to fall outside of the usual bell-curve pattern), and Richard S. Broughton (electronic die generated randomly by a computer program). If the probability for any these experiments was about 50/50, Radin found a 51 percent "hit rate" in a variety of experiments, suggesting odds against chance of more than a billion to one—statistically significant data in favor of a PK effect.

Another type of PK may affect living systems: plants, animals, and people. This concept of bio-PK relates to non-PK-related extraordinary human talents in controlling physiology, such as in the case of Buddhist monks who can dramatically alter their pulse or breathing, as well as psychosomatic effects where medical patients show recoveries from illnesses through suggestion, as in the use of hypnosis of the taking of placebo drugs such as sugar pills rather than pharmaceuticals. It has been posited that a person may heal him- or herself or other individuals using bio-PK. Parapsychological experiments have mostly been conducted on animals and plants. In the 1960s, Canadian biochemist Bernard Grad and the Hungarian energy healer Oskar Estabany conducted a series of experiments in which Estabany attempted to heal mice with surgically inflicted skin wounds; in another,

Research into psychokinesis (PK) is generally conducted along four lines:

- **Macro-PK** involves visible movement or change in inanimate objects.

- **Micro-PK** involves less tangible but still measurable physical effects, including on microscopic and sub-atomic levels.

- **Retro-PK** involves quantum-level effects that occur before the experimental subject intends to affect subatomic matter.

- **Bio-PK** involves living organisms and people, and may be related to skills such as energy healing.

he tried to assist barley seedlings grown under adverse conditions, such as being watered with a saline solution. In both experiments, Grad found that Estabany's targets became healthier than the controls.

Critics of such studies have suggested that researchers may be more prone to reporting successful results than when there are no significant results at all. Another issue arises around the experimenter effect in which the researcher subliminally or unconsciously may affect the results in a favorable way. The success of PK experiments has also been impacted by the tendency of the subject to believe in the alleged mental power or not (known as the sheep-goat effect). If tasks have been repetitive, such as dice-throwing, subjects tend to get bored, and thus the positive results decline over time. Spontaneity and group environments have brought about more dramatic results in macro-PK studies, but experimental control in these situations was lessened. Where controls are tightest, such as around micro-PK experiments, the results have been less noticeable. This may raise doubts about the existence of PK, but it also suggests limitations in accepted scientific procedures versus spontaneous occurrences in the real world, as philosopher Stephen E. Braude has written in his 1986 book *The Limits of Influence: Psychokinesis and the Philosophy of Science*.

Even before the words "telekinesis" or "psychokinesis" were coined, the idea mysterious forces or powers of intention affecting the physical environment had a historical basis that reached back to the foundations of magic, spiritual interactions, beliefs in demonism, and practices of witchcraft and sorcery. Notable examples include the story of Moses parting the Red Sea, Muhammad's fantastical flights, shamanic magic to control the weather, bodily harm inflicted by curses and spells, the laying on of hands to heal illness, and physics-defying miraculous abilities of mystics in many different religions.

The subject has a pop cultural side as well: from *X-Men* to *Avatar: The Last Airbender* and from *Carrie* to Harry Potter, such PK possibilities are depicted in movies, fiction, and comic books. PK also relates strongly to the illusions of stage and close-up magicians, including levitation, disappearing objects, passing through solid walls, and abilities to withstand pain and injury. Notably, magicians have been among the strongest critics of alleged PK abilities. In 1910 the British magician William Marriott duplicated a photograph of Polish medium Stanisła-wa Tomczyk levitating a glass by using a human hair to make it appear that his glass was suspended in mid-air. Likewise, in 1984 American secular humanist and founder of the Committee for Skeptical Inquiry (CFI) Paul Kurtz recreated the famous photo of the flying telephone receiver from the Tina Resch poltergeist case in the *Skeptical Inquirer*. It is worth considering the relationship here between magic, imagination, and purportedly real PK events.

Among the best known 20th-century PK subjects was a Russian housewife, Nina Kulagina, who participated in experiments with international researchers in the 1960s and 1970s. Famous films show Kulagina apparently influencing the movement of compass needles and a variety of small objects. The PK tests impacted her physiologically, causing a heightened pulse rate, intensified occipital lobe activity, and minor weight loss. Few PK claims have gained more attention that the metal-bending abilities of the Israeli mentalist Uri Geller, who inspired children around the world to duplicate his televised talents. Such claims have at times been energetically countered, for example in American magician James Randi's pursuits to debunk Geller's alleged PK abilities and to accuse Tina Resch of deceptive behavior. Critics have also questioned the validity of eyewitness accounts, which may be biased, for example, towards a religious or supernatural interpretation. However, psychologists Erlendur Haraldsson and Richard Wiseman have cautioned, "There is need to distinguish carefully between allegation and proof of trickery" (Haraldsson and Wiseman, 1995). Scientists such as the physicist Max Planck and many historians and philosophers of science have noted that scientific knowledge is dynamic and subject to change given improvements in experimental methodologies and measurement technologies, thus validating controversial PK effects for further scientific inquiry.

In Pamela Rae Heath's historical and phenomenological analyses *The PK Zone* and *Mind-Matter Interactions*, she writes that such experiments into PK have brought about more questions than answers and that attempts to develop PK skills have lacked success. She argues that there is enough proof that PK exists and that studies should focus more on the process involved in PK. Widespread reports of apparent psychokinesis around the world and throughout history suggest that it could be a universal human ability. In everyday life, PK may express itself most readily when a person pushes their body to the limit, as, for example, Esalen Institute co-founder Michael Murphy has shown with extraordinary feats in which athletes and martial artists enter a supernormal "zone" of performance, which may have some relationship to PK. Might specific individuals be more adept at producing such "wild talents," as Charles Fort named extraordinary human abilities? Research into the PK "zone" continues.

Christopher Laursen

See also: Apparitions; Geller, Uri; Healing, Psychic and Spiritual; Mediumship; Parapsychology; Poltergeist; Princeton Engineering Anomalies Research; Psi; Rhine Research Center

Further Reading

Braude, Stephen E. 2007. *The Gold Leaf Lady and Other Parapsychological Investigations.* Chicago: University of Chicago Press.

Haraldsson, Erlendur, and Richard Wiseman. 1995. "Reactions to and an Assessment of a Videotape on Sathya Sai Baba." *Journal of the Society for Psychical Research* 60 (839), 203–213.

Heath, Pamela Rae. 2011. *Mind-Matter Interaction: A Review of Historical Reports, Theory and Research.* Jefferson, NC: McFarland.

R

RANDI, JAMES

James Randi is a Canadian-American professional magician and skeptical investigator of paranormal and pseudoscientific claims. He is a founding member of the Committee for Skeptical Inquiry (CSI) and founder of the James Randi Educational Foundation (JREF). He has sought to promote science and reason, unmask supernatural fakery, and correct media credulity about paranormal and similar phenomena.

Randall James Hamilton Zwinge was born on August 7, 1928, in Toronto, Canada. After dropping out of high school, he read magic books and practiced illusions, eventually joining a touring carnival and becoming an escape artist. By the 1950s he was known as The Amazing Randi and traveled North America performing magic shows and appearing on TV. In the 1960s, frustrated with growing public and media acceptance of the paranormal, he began teaching people about how magicians' techniques could be used by those claiming paranormal powers to deceive the gullible.

This mission crystallized in the 1970s when he encountered Uri Geller, an Israeli psychic and media sensation who claimed to bend metal mentally and to read minds. Scientists at the Stanford Research Institute endorsed his paranormal abilities in leading scientific journals. Randi recognized that Geller's talents corresponded with simple magic tricks, which he showed in his book *The Magic of Uri Geller* (1975). For Randi, the Geller spectacle demonstrated how easily scientists can be fooled and how frequently the media will endorse paranormal claims uncritically, leading Randi to help found the Committee to Scientifically Investigate Claims of the Paranormal (CSICOP), now called CSI, in 1976. Geller repeatedly sued Randi for libel, but Randi won these cases, and Geller was ordered to pay Randi's legal costs.

From 1979–1981, Randi engineered the Project Alpha hoax, whereby he planted two fake psychics in a research lab connected to a major university in order to present parapsychology as a junk science. For three years, Randi's assistants used ordinary magic techniques to bend spoons or practice telekinesis while he wrote to the lab encouraging them to heighten the scientific rigor of their experiments. Instead of improving their methodology, the researchers marveled at the pair's abilities. Randi revealed the hoax in 1981, causing lasting damage to the lab.

In the 1980s, Randi began debunking Christian faith healing, a multimillion dollar ministry that purported to cure people through faith alone. Randi confronted these preachers because they failed to cure diseases, inspired false hope, and defrauded the vulnerable. In large stadiums, evangelists like Peter Popoff would call out names of strangers in the audience, identify their illnesses, and then miraculously "cure" them by laying on hands and ordering the disease gone. In his book *The Faith Healers* (1987) and on Johnny Carson's *Tonight Show*, Randi exposed how Popoff's wife read prayer notes written by the faithful into a radio transmitter that Popoff was able to hear through a receiver hidden in his ear. In Randi's follow-up work with those allegedly healed by Popoff, most remained disabled or diseased. For this research, Randi won a John D. and Catherine T. MacArthur Foundation grant.

Randi has since retired as a magician in order to devote himself full time to paranormal investigations. While avowing that he remains open to the possibility of paranormal phenomena, he nevertheless insists that it is more rational to suspect trickery than supernatural powers at play. Like Harry Houdini, Randi uses his illusionist know-how to challenge paranormal claimants. In 1964, he offered to pay $1,000 to anyone who could prove supernatural or paranormal abilities under mutually agreed upon scientific test conditions. This award has since been revised upwards, eventually to one million dollars in 1996, when he founded JREF, and remains unclaimed. JREF promotes critical thinking and scientific skepticism, educates the public and media about not accepting paranormal claims without scientific proof, and defends those who expose paranormal and pseudoscientific frauds.

Currently, Randi serves as chair of JREF and as a fellow of CSI. In 2012, he earned lifetime achievement awards from the American Humanist Association and the Academy of Magical Arts.

Dusty Hoesly

See also: Committee for Skeptical Inquiry; Geller, Uri; Healing, Psychic and Spiritual; Stanford Research Institute

Further Reading

Randi, James. 1987. *The Faith Healers*. Buffalo, NY: Prometheus Books.
Randi, James. 1982. *Flim-Flam: Psychics, ESP, Unicorns, and other Delusions*. Buffalo, NY: Prometheus Books.
Randi, James. 1975. *The Magic of Uri Geller*. New York: Ballantine Books.

REINCARNATION

Reincarnation, also known as *metempsychosis* from the Greek word for the transmigration of souls, refers to rebirth in a new human or animal form following the death of the physical body. The idea is ancient and almost universal. It is found within all the major world religions and in small-scale societies the world over. Reincarnation implies that the soul is separable from the material body and can gather experience and sometimes memories that can be carried from one life to another. Closely related to this idea is the belief or conviction that consciousness is nonlocal, originating outside the brain and matter. The soul, spirit, or conscious self may also be thought of as partible, existing on more than one plane of existence and perhaps in more than one physical body simultaneously. Reincarnation is invariably linked to moral concerns about the consequences of one's thoughts and actions. A person's past and present lives are thought to have an effect on, and possibly determine the nature of, any future incarnations.

Beliefs concerning reincarnation are highly developed within Eastern religions and cultures. In Hinduism and Jainism it is closely related to the notion of *karma*, a Sanskrit word meaning "deed" or "action." A person's actions in this life have inevitable consequences in future lives. At its simplest there is the idea of a scale from simple forms of life to humans, and it is possible to move up or down this scale in subsequent incarnations according to merit accumulated or lost. For Buddhists the emphasis is on detachment from the wheel of rebirth altogether so that reincarnation is unnecessary. Bodhisattvas are beings who have achieved this enlightened state of mind. Within Mahayana Buddhism a Bodhisattva will reincarnate out of compassion for fellow human beings to help them achieve enlightenment. The Gelug School of Tibetan Buddhism recognizes a line of succession in their religious leaders, the Dalai Lamas, through reincarnation. The successor has to pass a series of tests, which include recognizing items belonging to his predecessor. The current, 14th Dalai Lama (b.1935), has stated that he will decide in due course whether to reincarnate, or whether he will be the last in the line of succession. This is a politically sensitive issue for Tibetans as the Chinese Government does not recognize succession based on reincarnation.

In the Orphic religion of Classical Greece the aim of life was the release of the soul from the wheel of rebirth through the triumph of the Dionysian or divine element over the Titan or evil part of human nature, associated with the physical world.

The Semitic or Abrahamic religions, Judaism, Christianity, and Islam, also have traditions relating to reincarnation, most developed in the more mystical branches and teachings. There are many Biblical references to the soul existing before and after birth (e.g., Jeremiah 1:4; Romans 9:11–13) and important figures reincarnating as religious teachers, such as Elijah returning as John the Baptist (Malachi 4:5, Matthew 11:13–14). In John's Gospel (9:1), Jesus is asked whether a man was born blind because of his own sins or those of his parents, suggesting a *karmic* cause and effect similar to that found within Hinduism. Early Kabbalists, a mystical Jewish sect that originated in 12th century Spain, used the Hebrew word *gilgul* ("returning in a circle") or transmigration. By following religious teachings the soul could work out its sins and join figures like Moses who were exempt from transmigration. Within Islam, teachings on reincarnation are preserved today by Sufi mystical sects, but they may have been more common within the early years of Islam. The Orthodox teachings of Judaism, Christianity, and Islam have come to emphasis a single life followed by divine Judgment, with little or no chance to make amends once one reaches the end of life. Within Christianity the Fifth Ecumenical Council

Reincarnation is both an age-old religious belief and a matter of serious research in the modern world. Contrary to the mainstream Western cultural narrative that entirely relegates reincarnation to the status of an unscientific folk belief or credulous superstition, the subject has been given serious attention by a small but vocal number of scientists and scholars who have expressed at least a preliminary opinion that the evidence may support reincarnation's reality. These include Ian Stevenson, professor of psychology in the University of Virginia's Division of Perceptual Studies; Jim Tucker, professor of psychiatry and neurobehavioral sciences at the University of Virginia School of Medicine; Antonia Mills, professor in First Nations studies at the University of Northern British Columbia; and the legendary anthropologist Edith Turner.

in 553 CE, convened by the Emperor Justinius, was intent on refuting the Platonist ideas of Origen, one of the Church Fathers, who preached and wrote in favor of reincarnation. Reincarnation has not formed part of official Christian teachings since the sixth century CE.

In small-scale societies notions of reincarnation are common and may well be very ancient. The Victorian anthropologist Edward Tylor (1832–1917) speculated that both the notion of transmigration of souls and the survival of the individual soul after death date from the beginning of human evolution. These ideas would have been based on observation and experience. People would have noted resemblances between a newborn child and deceased ancestor, both physical and in terms of mannerisms. A woman might dream of a particular ancestor while pregnant, or a child might have memories of a previous life and recognize objects belonging to a forebear. Following the French sociologist Marcel Mauss (1872–1950) and his interest in the category of the person, many scholars have noted a distinction between the *individual*, represented by the flesh and blood human being, and a *person*, who is enmeshed in a web of social relationships. Following this logic, a person is not a single individual but a representative of a thread of connections into the past and future, often signified by bearing the same name. Children are therefore often named after the forebear with whom they are identified, sometimes according to lineage or other predicted naming rules. In a matrilineal society, for instance, reincarnation is likely to follow female lines. In bilateral kinship systems, with descent traced along both male and female lines, reincarnations are also likely to follow this pattern. Psychiatrist Ian Stevenson (1918–2007) spent 20 years from 1961 to 1981 studying cases suggestive of reincarnation among the Tlingit of Alaska. His observations confirmed Tylor's speculations that the announcing dreams of pregnant women, or other persons, often foretold the reincarnation of a particular deceased person and the importance of birthmarks and birth defects in identifying a reincarnated ancestor.

Strangers in kinship-based societies may be incorporated into kinship groups by being recognized as a reincarnation of a deceased member of that group. This does not necessarily imply a simple identity between the two individuals, as there is often the notion that the soul or spirit can separate its energy or different features, some of which may reincarnate and others of which may remain on other planes of existence. This idea of separable energy is also found in recent Western writings, such as those of hypnotherapist and author, Michael Newton, who focused in particular on the period between incarnations or "life-between-lives." Small-scale societies that depend on hunting, such as the Inuit and many Native American peoples, place great emphasis on the power of animals to reincarnate. One of the roles of a shaman in these cultures is to enable the dead animal's soul to successfully transfer to another body in order to ensure the continuation of the species on which their lives depend.

Ideas of reincarnation are also found within the Western esoteric traditions of Theosophy, Anthroposophy, Spiritualism, Spiritism, and in much of the literature on hypnotic past-life regression and pre-birth planning. The emphasis here is less on ascent and descent according to one's actions and more on the gathering of experience and balancing of energy. If one is female in many lives, one may wish to experience life as a man. If one has explored poverty and destitution, one may then choose to learn lessons about how to live with wealth and power. The element of divine judgment, characteristic of Abrahamic religions and the fatalistic or deterministic element that can be present in Eastern religions is replaced with what is described as a natural law of consequences. The individual is responsible for his or her actions. After death everyone undergoes a life review in which they come to understand the implications of their life choices and to experience the effects of everything they have done to others. There is an inexorable movement upwards over the course of many lives in which the soul gathers experiences and learns from them. The destination of the soul is toward ever-greater unity with the unconditionally loving source of energy that permeates the universe. The journey is individual but closely aligned with that of others, in particular with a close circle of other individuals, often referred to as a "soul-group."

In English-speaking Western countries reincarnation was popularized through the writings of American mystic, healer, psychic, and medium Edgar Cayce (1877–1945), and the 1956 publication of *The Search for Bridey Murphy*, in which a Colorado housewife, Virginia Tighe, claimed to recall, under hypnosis, a previous life as an Irish girl, Bridey Murphy. The latter case seems to owe more to the unconscious assimilation of information gathered in Mrs. Tighe's life, and as with many such cases, provides evidence more for the extraordinarily retentive capacity of the human brain than for reincarnation. There are many other accounts in which individuals appear to be able to recall verifiable details about previous lives. Some of the most impressive involve children, many of whom claim to have died violent or sudden deaths in a previous life. Young children are less likely to have acquired the information about a specific individual through normal means. An alternative explanation to reincarnation is that they could arguably be tapping into some form of collective memory. Ian Stevenson worked as a psychologist at the University of Virginia's Division of Perceptual Studies in the United States, pioneering the study of children who claim to remember past lives. He remained publically cautious about asserting that his thousands of cases from India, Lebanon, the United States, and elsewhere in the world provided proof of reincarnation but thought that many were highly suggestive of it. When memories of a past life are accompanied by birthmarks corresponding to wounds or injuries suffered in a previous life and where there is a physical resemblance between individuals, the data points more toward some form of individual reincarnation than to collective memory.

The therapeutic use of past-life regression therapy involves adults rather than children. Typically a Western psychologist or doctor using hypnotherapy in clinical practice asks a client or patient to go to the cause of a particular problem. This may be in childhood, but in some cases clients recall an incident in a previous life. This act of recall can be therapeutically effective. While the aim of such treatment is seldom verification of reincarnation, evidential information concerning the previous life or lives is sometimes available. In the majority of cases of hypnotic regression there is no way of knowing where the balance lies between imagination, some possible psi phenomenon or collective memory, and recall of an actual past life. In the latter case the remembered life could be of someone associated with the person recalling it (a member of the same soul group, or someone admired and identified with). Given the levels of uncertainty generally involved in identifying individuals in previous lives and the complexity and cultural variations in the understanding of what it is that composes a soul or person in the first place, it is unsurprising that many researchers remain unconvinced. Despite this skepticism, belief in reincarnation remains widespread, fueled by some apparently strong and intriguing cases, such as that of James Leininger, who from the age of two began to remember what appeared to be the life of a World War II fighter pilot named James Huston.

Edith Turner, an anthropologist who studied reincarnation in Alaska and Central Africa, notes that there are both universals and variations. Ordinary reincarnation involves the cyclical process of birth, death, and rebirth and includes the special case of violent death in which the soul may return to the body in a state of shock, perhaps not even properly aware of the transition that has taken place. A related but not identical process is one in which an adult may have a secondary spirit or personality merge with them, perhaps as part of a conversion or initiation process to become a healer, as among the Ndembu in Africa. The Ndembu also recognize succession to an ancestor's personality, sometimes termed "instantiation." The desirability of returning to earth varies among cultures and religions, with the highest objective in Hinduism and Buddhism being not to return at all. Both some Western channeled writings and the Shia Muslim tradition of the hidden 12th Imam recognize the possibility of returning as a fully formed adult, suddenly appearing to fulfil a certain task, bypassing the need to incarnate in a fetus and go through the normal process of birth and growth. Another form of this is the "walk-in" in which a reincarnating soul is able, with the agreement of the outgoing soul, to take over an existing body, perhaps at a moment of crisis, such as following a near-fatal accident. The universal patterns in reincarnation concepts as set out by Antonia Mills, who has studied the reincarnation beliefs of various indigenous peoples of North America, include young children apparently talking from the vantage point of a person they claim to have been in an earlier life; behavioral skills, memories, phobias, and physical characteristics associated with a previous personality; and the fading of past-life memories between about the ages of seven and nine years old. This combination of universal patterns with cultural variations suggests, as Ian Stevenson pointed out, that paranormal experiences probably influence culture just as much as culture influences paranormal experiences.

Fiona Bowie

See also: Cayce, Edgar; Haraldsson, Erlendur; Paranormal Dreams; Past-Life Readings; Past-Life Regression; Religion and the Paranormal; Spiritism; Spiritualism; Stevenson, Ian; Theosophy

Further Reading
Cayce, Edgar. 1923. *Reincarnation & Karma*. Virginia Beach, VA: ARE Press.
Fiore, Edith. 2005. *You Have Been Here Before: A Psychologist Looks at Past Lives*. Merrimack, NH: Advanced Studies Consultants.
Guirdham, Arthur. 1990. *The Cathars & Reincarnation*. Saffron Waldon, Essex, UK: C. W. Daniel.
Karlén, Barbro. 2000. *And the Wolves Howled: Fragments of Two Lifetimes*. London: Clairview.
Leininger, Bruce, Andrea Leninger, and Ken Gross. 2009. *Soul Survivor*. London: Hay House.
Mills, Antonia, and Richard Slobodin, eds. 1994. *Amerindian Rebirth: Reincarnation Belief among North American Indians and Inui*. Toronto, Buffalo, London: University of Toronto Press.
Newton, Michael. 2007. *Journey of Souls*. Woodbury, MN: Llewellyn Publications.
Semkiw, Walter. 2011. *Born Again: Reincarnation Cases Involving Evidence of Past Lives with Xenoglossy Cases Researched by Ian Stevenson*. Seattle, WA: Amazon Digital Editions.
Stevenson, Ian. 2001. *Children Who Remember Past Lives*. Revised edition. Jefferson, NC, London: McFarland & Co.
Stevenson, Ian. 1974. *Twenty Cases Suggestive of Reincarnation*. Charlottesville, NC: University of Virginia Press.
Tucker, Jim B. 2006. *Life Before Life: A Scientific Investigation of Children's Memories of Previous Lives*. London: Piatkus.
Tucker, Jim B. 2013. *Return to Life: Extraordinary Cases of Children Who Remember Past Lives*. New York: St Martin's Press.
Weiss, Brian. 1988. *Many Lives, Many Masters*. London: Piatkus.
Wilson, Ian. 1981. *Mind Out of Time? Reincarnation Investigated*. London: Victor Gollancz.

RELIGION AND THE PARANORMAL

Most religions claim that there is more to reality beyond what is recognized by scientific paradigms. In this sense, religion overlaps with the paranormal. However, while both religion and the paranormal are at odds with mainstream science, there is no universally recognized distinction between religious ideas and paranormal ones. Furthermore, the conceptual category of "paranormal" phenomena resulted from the historical tension between religious and scientific authorities. As such the paranormal is often defined only in relation to the categories of religion and science.

Paranormal ideas often conflict with religious claims, particularly regarding the interpretations of miracles and other anomalous events. However, some theologians and religious leaders have advocated cooperation with paranormal researchers. Social scientists are currently studying the relationship between traditional religious beliefs and paranormal beliefs. It is still not entirely known how religious affiliation and belief affects interest in the paranormal.

The Definitional Problem of Religion and the Paranormal

In popular discourse, religion and the paranormal are usually regarded as related but separate categories of belief and experience. For example, many large bookstores have a "religion" section with books on the world's religious traditions and another section labeled "metaphysical" or "New Age" with books on psychic phenomena and similar topics. This popular form of classification is imprecise and leaves no clear distinction between religion and the paranormal. For example, books pertaining to the supernatural, such as miracles or angels, could arguably go in either section. For sociologists and other researchers, there is no consensus as to how these two should be defined. Therefore, any comparison of these topics must begin with an operational definition of the paranormal.

Some scholars, such as psychologist Harvey Irwin and sociologist Erich Goode, define the paranormal as any belief that defies scientific paradigms or does not meet scientific standards of evidence. This approach categorizes even the most widely held religious beliefs, such as life after death or the existence of God, as paranormal. For Irwin and Goode, religious belief is largely a subcategory of paranormal belief. In fact, Goode's research explicitly examines biblical Creationism as a paranormal belief. The advantage of this definition is that it provides an objective standard of whether or not an idea is paranormal. The disadvantage is that by leaving no significant distinction between religion and the paranormal it renders any comparison between these types of beliefs impossible.

Other sociologists approach paranormal beliefs and experiences as a special subset of religious beliefs and experiences. Significantly, these sociologists rely on data from national surveys of religious belief. From this data set, certain beliefs are designated as "paranormal." For example, in 1975 Jesuit priest and sociologist Andrew Greeley wrote an analysis of the paranormal using data from the NORC-Luce Foundation Basic Belief Study. Greeley classified those questions relating to psychic or mystical experiences and contact with the dead as "paranormal" and used the data as the basis for his study. More recently, sociologists Christopher D. Bader, F. Carson Mencken, and Joseph D. Baker have produced research analyzing the 2005 Baylor Religion Survey. These scholars employ an operational definition of the paranormal as those ideas and beliefs that have been "dually rejected" by both mainstream religion and mainstream science. Nine beliefs from the Baylor religion survey—psychic abilities, fortune telling, communication with the dead, haunted houses, ghosts, Atlantis, UFOs, and monsters such as Bigfoot—were designated as "paranormal." Bader et al. concede that their operational definition remains messy at the edges. For instance, beliefs in Marian apparitions or demonic possession were designated as religious rather than paranormal, even though many mainstream churches do not encourage their congregations to believe in these phenomena. The advantage of defining the paranormal as a special subset of religious beliefs and experiences is that it allows sociologists to compare data about people who hold paranormal beliefs with data about people who hold traditional religious beliefs.

Also relevant is the work of religious studies scholar Jeffrey Kripal, who defines the paranormal as "the sacred in transit from the religious and scientific registers into a parascientific or 'science mysticism' register" (2010: 9). Like Bader et al., Kripal identifies the paranormal as a category of beliefs and experiences that is simultaneously related to and distinct from the two spheres of religion and science. Kripal argues that the field of religious studies has largely ignored accounts of paranormal experiences, precisely because they cannot be explained. He suggests that formulating a theory of paranormal phenomena is an important new frontier for the study of religion.

Historical Approaches to Religion and the Paranormal

A historical perspective is useful for understanding the ways that the categories of religion, science, and the paranormal have developed together. The category of the paranormal ultimately emerged from the tension between religious and scientific authority that arose in the wake of the scientific revolution. Many beliefs that were rejected by scientists were also rejected by religious authorities, who wanted to show that their religious views were rational. However, this body of rejected beliefs and inexplicable phenomena became a useful tool for anyone seeking to critique the cultural authority of both scientific and religious institutions. In this way, the idea of the paranormal developed as an entity distinct from either religion or science.

In the 17th century, both religious and scientific authorities were interested in "wonders"—unusual phenomena such as comets or abnormal animals. Scientific authorities hoped that wonders would allow them to better understand the natural world while religious authorities ascribed religious significance to such phenomena. Attitudes toward unusual phenomena changed by end of the century as scientific rationalism gained greater cultural authority. As scientific books were published that demystified comets and other natural phenomena, educated religious authorities became dismissive of those who ascribed supernatural significance to such events, framing such attitudes as "superstition" rather than "religion."

However, religious leaders also used wonders as weapons against skeptics. The Puritan Cotton Mather collected accounts of the supernatural in such books as *Wonders of the Invisible World* (1693) and *Things for a Distress'd People to Think Upon* (1696). Mather believed that stories of miracles were a powerful weapon against rationalist critiques of religion. Between these two responses by religious authorities, wonders were acquiring a new set of relationships in regard to both religion and science. Certain types of wonders were becoming dually rejected by both the scientific and religious establishments, but they were also becoming a form of evidence with which the authority of these establishments could be challenged.

This category of dually rejected ideas was given more significance in 1919 when Charles Fort published *The Book of the Damned*. Fort collected "damned facts" that could not be accounted for by either religious dogma or scientific paradigms. By drawing attention to such phenomena, Fort sought to challenge what he called "the two Dominants" of science and religion. He claimed that humankind was blinded to the true nature of reality because its thinking has always been conditioned, first by the "Spiritual Dominant" of religion, then by the "Materialist Dominant" of science. The ideas and phenomena that interested Fort came to define what is commonly thought of as "the paranormal" in popular discourse.

Religious and Paranormal Perspectives of Anomalous Phenomena

Sometimes anomalous events will be interpreted solely in religious terms, but often such events will have both religious and paranormal interpretations. This dividing line can be seen in, for instance, the phenomenon of Marian apparitions. In 1858 Bernadette Soubirous saw a Marian apparition in a grotto at Lourdes, France, leading to her canonization as a Catholic saint and mass pilgrimages to the site. This event has been encompassed solely in a religious interpretive context. By contrast, in 1917, 30,000 to 100,000 people in Fatima, Portugal, reported seeing the so-called "Miracle of the Sun," in which the sun appeared to dance in the sky. The miracle marked the climax of a series of Marian apparitions. The Catholic Church declared the apparition of Fatima "worthy of belief," meaning that Catholics are free to believe the event was a miracle. Conversely, paranormal authors, such as Jacques Vallée, have suggested that the miracle of the sun was not a divine miracle but a UFO or similar paranormal phenomenon. In fact, John Keel suggested that there was a single unified phenomenon behind all reports of religious miracles as well as UFO sightings and other paranormal events.

Some religious authorities find paranormal interpretations of miracles offensive. Several conservative Protestant leaders have claimed that paranormal ideas are a satanic ploy and represent a greater threat to Christianity than atheism. Other religious perspectives of the paranormal are more neutral. Jesuit theologian Karl Rahner called for further study of the relationship between parapsychological and mystical phenomena. He argued that seemingly miraculous abilities, such as clairvoyance, may have a paranormal explanation and are therefore not evidence of holiness or divine intervention. On the other hand, he suggested that paranormal abilities may be a normal means through which God communicates with humankind. As such, he argued that possible religious visions and miracles should be evaluated by their fruits and whether they transform lives for the better, not by whether they defy scientific explanation. Catholic theologian Lisa Schwebel has also written on miracles and the paranormal. Her concern is not that religious miracles will be misinterpreted as paranormal phenomena, but rather that all paranormal phenomena may be misinterpreted as miracles. Schwebel also compares the Catholic Church to a paranormal investigator, noting that it has been evaluating claims of the supernatural for 2,000 years.

Correlations between Religious and Paranormal Beliefs

Sociologists are interested in how religious beliefs and paranormal beliefs intersect. There are two main hypotheses regarding this problem. The first is that there is an inverse relationship between the two and that religious people are unlikely to hold paranormal beliefs. This approach assumes either that paranormal beliefs are a substitute for traditional religious beliefs or that religious people are discouraged from believing in paranormal phenomena by religious leaders. For example, many conservative religious leaders discourage their followers from consulting astrologers and psychics or engaging in other activities commonly regarded as paranormal. The second hypothesis is that people who hold religious beliefs will also be likely to hold paranormal beliefs. Tom W. Rice dubbed this the "small step" hypothesis because it assumes that believing in ghosts or UFOs is a "small step" from believing in angels and the devil.

Bader et al. present a model that combines these hypotheses. Their data indicate that people who hold traditional religious beliefs, such as belief in God, are also more likely to hold paranormal belief. However, they also found that members of certain denominations, such as evangelical Christians, were less likely to hold paranormal beliefs. They also found that people who believed the Bible is literally true or who attended church regularly were less likely to hold paranormal beliefs. They found that the person most likely to hold a paranormal belief is someone who holds traditional religious beliefs but is not active in a religious organization. Bader et al. propose that religious beliefs do predispose people to believe in the paranormal, but that religious leaders actively discourage interest in the paranormal.

Beginning in the 1980s, a number of studies were done on the correlation of religious beliefs and paranormal beliefs using survey data. Some found evidence for an inverse relationship, others for a direct relationship, and still others found no relationship at all. One problem with such studies is that the data are limited by the definitional problem outlined above. Additionally, most studies produce different results depending on what type of paranormal belief is being examined. For example, Bader et al. found that 71 percent of Catholics held at least one paranormal belief. However, while 47 percent of Catholics believe in hauntings, only 14 percent believed in psychic abilities. Such findings suggest that there are different social correlates for different types of beliefs and that analysis of "the paranormal" as a unified set of beliefs will not be particularly useful. Further research using more carefully designed studies is needed in order for social scientists to understand the relationship between traditional religion and the paranormal.

Joseph Laycock

See also: Fort, Charles; Keel, John A.; Miracles; Mystical Experience; New Age; Reincarnation; Shamanism; Spiritism; Spiritualism; Survival after Death; Theosophy; Vallée, Jacques

Further Reading

Bader, Christopher D., F. Carson Mencken, and Joseph D. Baker. 2010. *Paranormal America: Ghost Encounters, UFO Sightings, Bigfoot Hunts, and Other Curiosities in Religion and Culture.* New York: New York University Press.

Good, Erich. 2011. *The Paranormal: Who Believes, Why They Believe, and Why It Matters.* New York: Prometheus Books.

Irwin, H. J. 2009. *Psychology of Paranormal Belief: A Researcher's Handbook.* Chicago: University of Hertfordshire.

Kripal, Jeffrey J. 2010. Authors of the Impossible: The Paranormal and the Sacred. Chicago: University of Chicago Press.

Rice, Tom W. 2003. "Believe It or Not: Religious and Other Paranormal Beliefs in the United States." *Journal for the Scientific Study of Religion* 42 (1): 95–106.

Schwebel, Lisa J. 2004. *Apparitions, Healings, and Weeping Madonnas: Christianity and the Paranormal.* New York: Paulist Press.

REMOTE VIEWING

Remote viewing describes a repertoire of protocols in which individuals are asked to provide objectively verifiable information about a person, place, or object from which they are separated by time, space, or both. Under rigorous controls and double or triple blindness by design, the only way to accomplish the task is to open to an aspect of consciousness that is not physiologically based in, nor limited by, space or time: nonlocal consciousness.

Beginning in the early 1970s several new laboratories were founded in the United States, all sharing an interest in developing new protocols in consciousness research. The mechanistic number-guessing, dice-calling, Zener card-naming protocols that dominated the earlier era of parapsychology produced what came to be called the Decline Effect: the longer people did a repetitive protocol like Zener card naming, the worse the results. The Zener protocol came in several variants, but basically a researcher sat at a table across which a visual barrier had been placed, while a viewer sat on the other side of the table. The viewer could not see what the researcher was doing. The task was to describe or name the card the researcher held up. In his very his first monograph in 1934, J. B. Rhine reported that "When procedures . . . were used that required the subject to make his calls more slowly and deliberately, a decline effect (i.e., above chance scoring declining to chance as the run proceeded) was the most common tendency."

Reviewing those studies, researchers came to the conclusion that this decline was occurring because the protocols became boring, and this was damaging to performance. A more naturalistic experience seemed the direction to go, and remote viewing evolved because nonlocal perception lent itself to a more conversational approach.

The basic format for a remote viewing session is that one individual is the researcher/monitor, while another is the viewer. A third person, or sometimes a team of people, act as evaluators/judges. In the session, monitor and viewer sit together in a quiet place, or use video communications, and conversationally the monitor asks the viewer a series of non-cueing questions: "Could you make me a drawing of a prominent shape at this location? Do you have a sense of color at this location, and what can you say about it?" The questions are designed to get sense impressions as if the viewer was at the location, or holding the object in their hand. All the senses report. This information is recorded and is then given to the judge to be matched against a set of targets sufficiently large to yield a statistically significant result. The sessions are double or triple blind. Neither the monitor nor the viewer knows the answers. In fact, in the most frequently used protocol, the target is selected by a random number generator and a computer algorithm after the session data are collected. At the time the session takes place, there is no correct answer to the questions because the target has not yet been selected. This only happens when the judge receives the session data. In the latest protocols a computer carries out the judging task automatically.

Remote viewing began with a small community—no more than a dozen scientists—dedicated to understanding how this mysterious aspect of the mind involved with nonlocal perception works. Two distinct but related protocols emerged: remote viewing and the ganzfeld technique. Although there have been a number of single studies carried out, three laboratories emerged as the leaders: one initially part of Stanford Research Institute, subsequently (SRI), then part of Science Applications International Corporation (SAIC); and most recently Laboratories for Fundamental Research (LFR); the Princeton Engineering Anomalies Research (PEAR) lab; and The Mobius Society. The labs arose roughly concurrently, led the way, and maintained continuous, systematic, decades-long research programs on both nonlocal perception and nonlocal perturbation (consciousness directly affecting space time, whether a mechanism, a physical substance, or another living organism).

Each of the labs tended to specialize. The SRI lab, founded by two laser physicists, Harold Puthoff and Russell Targ, and joined shortly thereafter by nuclear physicist Edwin May, operated with funding from the military intelligence world and combined basic research with applied research using remote viewing as an

Few areas of serious parapsychological research have developed as wide a public following as the field of remote viewing—a development aided by the United States government's decision in 1995 to declassify information related to its Stargate Project, which conducted research into the practical applications of remote viewing. At the same time, few areas have been as controversial. Early research into remote viewing was carried out in the 1970s and 1980s under the auspices of respected establishment institutions such as Princeton University and Stanford Research Institute and was sponsored by national governments including not just the United States but the Soviet Union and China. There was a strong skeptical backlash, however, and today the results of that early research, as well as the reality of remote viewing itself, are subject to conflicting narratives.

intelligence resource to describe sites of interest to the military and intelligence communities during the height of the Cold War. In what became a 24-year-long research program, a unique two-tiered research effort took place. The researchers would do basic research on nonlocal phenomena that they could publish, while at the same time, under a variety of Code names—SCANANTE, PHOENIX, STUNT PILOT, SUN STREAK CENTER LANE, GRILL FLAME, and the best-known, STAR GATE—they would conduct a classified Top Secret applications-oriented remote viewing spying program with a shifting cast of personalities.

The SRI lab developed many of the basic remote viewing protocols. These included the Outbound Protocol, where someone hides at a randomly selected location, and the Coordinate Protocol, in which the viewer is asked to describe what is to be found at a certain longitude and latitude, which itself may be encoded so that the viewer is given only a direction such as, "Please go the location defined by 12345678 and describe what you perceive there." They also, with the help of psychologist Charles Tart and mathematician-statistician Jessica Utts, developed many of the analytical techniques. Prominent viewers involved with SRI are Ingo Swann, Hella Hammid, Pat Price, and Joseph McMoneagle.

The PEAR Lab was founded by plasma physicist Robert Jahn, Professor of Aerospace Science and Dean of Engineering at Princeton University. The principal researchers in addition to Jahn were psychologists Brenda Dunne and Roger Nelson and theoretical physicist York Dobyns. PEAR pioneered the use of computer analysis and descriptors in an attempt to computerize accuracy assessment, removing as far as possible subjective human judgment. The PEAR laboratory did not cultivate the identification and cultivation of "star" viewers, as was the case at both SRI and Mobius, but took an "everyman" approach

Mobius' work was interdisciplinary by design and more anthropological in orientation. Stephan Schwartz, later joined by Rand De Mattei along with a rotating team of specialists in other disciplines, focused on understanding variables that could affect performance, exploring personality issues, and exploring the nature of the remote viewing session and the role of observer effects. In addition to laboratory sessions, assessed statistically, Mobius developed and used in many settings a consensus protocol to accomplish application tasks. Remote viewing was particularly efficacious in archaeology with its challenges: Where to look? What will be there? Remote viewers would locate archaeological sites in both terrestrial and marine environments that were known to exist, although their location was not. They would then be asked to describe in detail what would be found at that location. Mobius also developed the Associated Remote Viewing (ARV) Protocol, which was used both to demonstrate that nonlocal perception was not electromagnetic in nature and as a predictive investment strategy. Principal Mobius viewers were Ingo Swann, Hella Hammid, George McMullen, Michael Crichton, Alan Vaughan, Judith Orloff, Ben Moses, and Andre Vaillancourt.

The result of all this work has been several hundred studies. For a number of years they were subjected to vigorous attacks by deniers. These tapered off, however, when it was repeatedly shown that the critics' arguments were without substance. Today, independent assessments and meta-analyses have shown that remote viewing overall has produced a six sigma effect—odds of better than one in a billion that the results are due to chance.

It is not easy to assess the SRI/SAIC applied work because critical details are still classified. However, an indication of the military assessment can be seen in the Legion of Merit—the military's second highest noncombat award—given to Warrant Officer Joseph McMoneagle for actionable intelligence he provided as a remote viewer. The Mobius work was unclassified, and the remote viewing session data was always compared with standard remote sensing electronic technology surveys of the selected sites using a wide range of instruments, satellite imagery, side-scan sonar, proton-precession magnetometers, ground penetrating radar, and ground coring. In every instance what the electronic surveys could not locate, remote viewing could. The projects were filmed and witnessed by teams of archaeologists and other scientists. They resulted in the discovery of previously unknown wrecks in Western U.S. Bahamian, Jamaican, and Egyptian waters, as well as Cleopatra's Palace, Mark Antony's Timonium, and the Lighthouse of Pharos, one of the seven wonders of the ancient world

As that research has been carried out, something completely unexpected by the researchers has occurred: remote viewing has gone from being an obscure laboratory protocol to an avocational movement, with discussion lists on Yahoo! and Google running to the thousands worldwide. There are journals, courses, and classes, and nearly a million hits come up on the Internet search term "remote viewing." What was once a controversial science protocol has become a hobby and passion for thousands.

Stephan A. Schwartz

See also: Clairvoyance; Extrasensory Perception (ESP); Ganzfeld Technique, The; Princeton Engineering Anomalies Research; Psychic Archaeology; Stanford Research Institute; Vasiliev, Leonid Leonidovich

Further Reading

Jahn, Robert G., and Brenda J. Dunne. 1987. *Margins of Reality: The Role of Consciousness in the Physical World*. New York: Harcourt, Brace, Jovanovich.

McMoneagle, Joseph. 2002. *The Stargate Chronicles: Memoirs of a Psychic Spy*. Charlottesville, VA: Hampton Roads Publishing Company.

Schwartz, Stephan A. 2007. *Opening to the Infinite*. Langley, WA: Nemoseen Media.

Schwartz, Stephan A. 1978. *The Secret Vaults of Time: Psychic Archaeology and the Quest for Man's Beginnings*. New York: Grosset & Dunlap.

Schwartz, Stephan. 2014. "Through Time and Space: The Evidence for Remote Viewing." In *The Evidence for Psi: Essays on the Reality of Paranormal Phenomena*, edited by Damien Broderick, and Ben Goertzel. Jefferson, NC: McFarland.

Targ, Russell. 2012. *The Reality of ESP: A Physicist's Proof of Psychic Abilities*. Wheaton, IL: Quest Books.

Targ, Russell, and Harold E. Puthoff. (1977) 2005. *Mind Reach: Scientists Look at Psychic Abilities*. Charlottesville, VA: Hampton Roads Publishing Company.

RHINE RESEARCH CENTER

The Rhine Research Center (a.k.a. the Rhine) in Durham, North Carolina, is the oldest operational parapsychology laboratory in the United States. Founded by J. B. Rhine, who is often considered the father of modern parapsychology, the Rhine defined the field of parapsychology as the study of extrasensory perception (telepathy, clairvoyance, and precognition) and psychokinesis. Extrasensory perception (ESP) and psychokinesis are now grouped together as a phenomenon called psi (pronounced like the word "sigh"), and the field has expanded to include more traditional-survival issues such as near-death experiences, out-of-body experiences, spirit communications, apparitions and haunting activities, and past-life memories. The Rhine Research Center traces its roots to Duke University, but now it is an independent nonprofit research center that incorporates research, education, and community outreach to provide an environment for the exploration of human consciousness through the study of exceptional human experiences and unusual or unexplained phenomena.

History

J. B. Rhine began his experiments on ESP at Duke in 1930, with special cards designed by Duke psychologist Karl Zener. He published his book *Extra-Sensory Perception* in 1934, and in 1935 established a Parapsychology Laboratory within Duke's Department of Psychology. The researchers at this lab used strict scientific methods and state-of-the-art statistical analysis techniques to study ESP. The formal scientific approach that was introduced at the parapsychology lab provided

The Rhine Center: A Brief Timeline

The history of parapsychology and the history of the Rhine Research Center are inextricably linked. Originally founded as the Parapsychology Lab at Duke University, the Rhine Center is currently the oldest operational parapsychology lab in the United States.

1935   The Parapsychology Laboratory at Duke is founded by J. B. Rhine to study ESP using strict scientific methods and state-of-the-art statistical analysis techniques.

1937   The Duke Lab publishes the first issue of the *Journal of Parapsychology*.

1964   J. B. Rhine reaches retirement age and leaves Duke.

1965   Rhine moves the lab away from Duke and creates the nonprofit Foundation for Research on the Nature of Man, which includes the Institute for Parapsychology.

1995   The foundation is renamed the Rhine Research Center.

a solid foundation for researchers around the world to study ESP using standard tools to implement the scientific method.

The Zener cards used at the Parapsychology Laboratory included five simple symbols (circle, cross, square, star, and wavy lines), and they quickly became identified as the symbols of scientific parapsychological research. By using five standard symbols on the cards, the experiments that used Zener cards could be easily evaluated using simple statistical methods. Zener cards were used in many different studies to test telepathy, clairvoyance, and precognition. The first manufactured cards were issued in 1937, permitting the lab's work to be replicated in other places.

Beginning in 1934, Parapsychology Laboratory also tested for psychokinesis (mind-matter interaction). Participants were asked to try to affect the outcome of dice rolls and cause a specific number to appear. Using only their thoughts, the participants would observe hundreds of dice rolls to try to influence the dice so that the target numbers would appear more often than predicted by chance.

In 1937, the Duke Laboratory published the first issue of the *Journal of Parapsychology*, a peer reviewed academic journal, which provided a forum for researchers to share information about this new field in an academic and professional forum. The results of the laboratory experiments were published in this journal and in a number of books by scientists including J. B. Rhine and J. Gaither Pratt. The experiments appeared to demonstrate ESP and psychokinesis as real phenomena worthy of further scientific study.

Early studies at the laboratory were criticized for methodological flaws and the possibility that the participants could have cheated in the experiments. Though many people in the scientific community rejected the results of the studies based on the methodological problems, the public continued to accept that ESP was real and that it had been demonstrated in a laboratory environment. The criticisms were addressed in 1940 in the important book, *Extra-Sensory Perception after Sixty Years*, by Pratt, Rhine, and others.

In subsequent years, the research methods were improved based on suggestions from critics. The results from the experiments continued to indicate that psi was occurring, but today people who are skeptical that psi exists still reject the results from the Parapsychology Laboratory because of the flaws in the early experiments. In 1945 the Parapsychology Laboratory moved out of the Psychology Department and was established as the Parapsychology Laboratory at Duke University.

Parapsychological research at Duke continued through 1964 when Rhine reached retirement age and left the university. In 1962 he founded a nonprofit organization called the Foundation for Research on the Nature of Man, and in 1965 reopened the Parapsychology Laboratory there as the Institute for Parapsychology. In 1995 the foundation was renamed the Rhine Research Center. The Rhine today continues to follow its original mission to explore the nature of human consciousness using innovative scientific methods and formal research techniques.

Skepticism

Research in the field of parapsychology is controversial and often considered to be pseudoscience by skeptics of psi phenomena. The research performed at the Rhine is widely considered the most credible and reliable research in the field, but many skeptics believe the results of the experiments were exaggerated or the result of bias. Parapsychologists stand behind the work performed at the Rhine as sound scientific research.

Today

The Rhine Research Center today is a nonprofit research center that promotes research and education in parapsychology while fostering an environment for a community of scientists and people who have psi experiences. The Rhine is still located in Durham, NC, but it is no longer affiliated with Duke University.

Current research at the Rhine explores all aspects of human consciousness, including psi phenomena, human energy fields, physical indications of psi activity, psychological factors that affect performance on laboratory tests, and the subjective nature of psi experiences.

The Rhine presents educational talks by noted parapsychologists and lecturers throughout the year, and many of these lectures are simulcast live through the Rhine website (www.rhine.org). Workshops related to psi and other paranormal topics are also regularly presented at the Rhine.

The Rhine Education Center provides online courses in the field of parapsychology covering scientific studies that have been completed on topics such as premonitions and precognition, dreams, and mediumship. Courses are presented in an academic manner with certificate programs available.

The modern Rhine is focused on creating a community that will accommodate researchers and people who have psi experiences. Discussion groups, training sessions, educational opportunities, and an extensive website provide balance to an active research organization that seeks to uncover the nature of human consciousness and explore unexplained experiences.

John G. Kruth

See also: Extrasensory Perception (ESP); Koestler Parapsychology Unit; Near-Death Experience (NDE); Out-of-Body Experience (OBE); Parapsychology; Princeton Engineering Anomalies Research; Pseudoscience; Psi; Psychokinesis (PK); Stanford Research Institute; Survival after Death

Further Reading

Horn, Stacy. 2009. *Unbelievable: Investigations into Ghosts, Poltergeists, Telepathy, and Other Unseen Phenomena, from the Duke Parapsychology Laboratory*. New York: Ecco.

Matlock, J. G. 1991. "Records of the Parapsychology Laboratory: An Inventory of the Collection in the Duke University Library." *Journal of Parapsychology* 55: 301–314.

Mauskopf, Seymour. 1980. *The Elusive Science: Origins of Experimental Psychical Research*. Baltimore: Johns Hopkins University Press.

RITUAL MAGIC

Ritual magic, sometimes called ceremonial magic, is a broad category of varied practices dating back to antiquity, by which an individual or individuals attempt to obtain a specific outcome or secret knowledge. It is a subset of the larger category of magic, which denotes particular ideas, practices, and world views purportedly originating in ancient Persia. Remaining constant from the ancient world to the modern is the fact that magic, and its subsequent rituals and ceremonies, are generally deemed illegitimate and against the established order and thus have generally been socially or governmentally prohibited.

Antiquity

The earliest forms of magic ritual date back to ancient Greece and Rome. Both societies used the terms *magia* (Latin), *magike*, or *magoi* (Greek) as a cognate for *magus* as found in ancient Persian. The Greeks and Romans believed that the earliest form of magic ritual was derived from the Persian religious reformer Zoroaster, famed as the founder of Zoroastrianism. This origin allowed the societies to question and contest the legitimacy of magic ritual activities while they continued to be practiced in both societies. The earliest kinds of ritual magic include binding spells, divination, object animation, and medical care. Binding spells consisted of writing the desires of the individual into a permanent form, such a metal sheet of lead, or onto a sheet of parchment or papyrus, and then hiding the talisman so that its power cannot be undone by being destroyed. Binding spells that have been found include those associated with harming one's enemies, winning court cases, overcoming difficult situations, winning athletic contests, and gaining business success—for example, against a rival craftsman or competitor. Some binding spells included dolls or effigies made of wood or wax and depicting an individual with the hope to influence or harm them.

Divination spells attempted to tell the future in a variety of ways. Sometimes they use astrological events, and other times they used augury, which is the prediction of the future by analyzing various omens. The animation of an object is a type of magical ritual in which spirits, gods, or some other kind of spiritual entity is invited to reside within an inanimate object. This object could be a statue, as explained in the second century CE text, *The Asclepius*, or mummified animal bodies, as described in magical Greek papyri. Animated objects were believed to give the owner supernatural powers. Finally, ritual magic associated with medical care included the saying of spells to staunch bleeding, lower fevers, or cure disease. Rituals included the making and wearing of talismans, the invocation of deities and spirits, and the ritual exorcism of harmful entities believed to have inhabited the diseased person.

The social legitimacy of these magic rituals varied depending on where, when, and how the rituals were practiced. By the third and fourth centuries, the influence of Christianity began to characterize earlier magical practices as forms of paganism, and they were prohibited. The early Christian fathers, such as Augustine, categorized magic rituals as different from orthodox religion and claimed that ritual magicians made pacts with demons. In contrast, groups of Neoplatonists, from the second to fourth century, practiced a variety of ritual magic that they claimed allowed them to reach higher states of consciousness and interact with the source of being. These Neoplatonists were not Christian, but they practiced religious ideas loosely derived from the Greeks, specifically adopting the ideas of Plato. Despite the activity of the Neoplatonists, as Christianity began to spread across Europe, the distinction between heretical magic and orthodox religion began to create a category in which ritual magic was prohibited.

Middle Ages

The early Middle Ages saw a significant change in the overall attitude regarding ritual magic. The Catholic Church made concerted efforts to spread itself over the whole of Europe, and anywhere it became established, magic rituals, often associated with paganism or barbaric religion, were condemned and the practitioners persecuted. Nevertheless, the same period also saw the early emergence of new kinds of ritual magic practices based on Christianity itself. For instance, the term "hocus pocus" was a corruption of the Christian Mass in which the priest holds up the Eucharist saying in Latin, "hoc est corpus," or "this is [my] body." In other cases, various symbols, such as the cross and verses from the Bible, were used as talismans. So were Christian relics. These practices were generally permitted by local and regional clergy, all while being prohibited by higher ecclesiastical authorities. It is important to note that at the same time and completely separate from Christianity, Judaism had its own forms of ritual magic, derived from both canonical and noncanonical texts. These magical practices were discovered by Christians and incorporated into Christian ritual magic.

During the late Middle Ages new ritual magic literature emerged in the form of the so-called *Ars notoria*, or the *Art of Magic*, a text associated with King Solomon that purports to detail how he conscripted demons to build the Holy Temple in Jerusalem, and the *Sworn Book of Honorius*, which also claims to instruct the reader on demonic invocation. These texts, sometimes called grimoires, became instruction manuals on ritual magic and were condemned by the Christian church.

Renaissance Period

By the 14th century, Europe slowly emerged out of the dark ages and experienced a renaissance, initially beginning in the south of Europe and then moving north. Among of the most important literary sources discovered during this period were Arabic translations of Plato and other Arabic mathematic and astrological texts. One important text was Al-Kindi's *De Radiis Stellicis*, or *On the Stellar Rays*, which asserts that planets and stars have direct correspondences and natural relationships with objects. The idea that nature has secret or occult properties that can be studied and manipulated produced the category of natural magic. This opened up a debate by the European intelligentsia, such as Marsilio Ficino and Cornelius Agrippa, about what was natural magi, and thus permitted, and what was demonic, and thus prohibited. As part of this debate Agrippa published *Three Books on Occult Philosophy*. Even Thomas Aquinas entered this debate, stating in his *Summa Contra Gentiles* that natural things such as stones and herbs having occult affinities are permitted, but not written words, as these make pacts with the devil. In 1486 Heinrich Kramer, a German Catholic clergyman, produced *The Malleus Maleficarum*, a treatise on the persecution of witches. This became a standard manual on how to discover those who practice ritual magic, invoke demons, and make pacts with the devil.

Early Modern and Modern Period

In the early modern period, the influences of the Renaissance flowered into the Enlightenment. Rationality and experimentation became emphasized, and ritual magic itself became transformed by this cultural transformation. While it remained based on Judeo-Christian cosmology, a scientific approach and system emerged. Individuals such as John Dee, the court astrologer for Elizabeth I in England, used ritual magic to systematically communicate with angels and gain answers to questions about the end of the world as described in the *Book of Revelation*. More and more ritual manuals were composed, frequently modifying prior ritual practices.

By the 19th century, ritual magic had become a practice that was investigated and practiced by many throughout Europe, especially in France and England. In France, individuals including Eliphas Levi and Gérard Encausse (the latter known by the pseudonym Papus) produced numerous new texts on ritual magic. In England a small group of high-degree Freemasons took an interest in ritual magic and first produced new fringe Masonic groups and then, a bit later, a new magical society named the Hermetic Order of the Golden Dawn. Founded in 1887, the Golden Dawn went on to become one of the most influential ritual magic orders, with many famous individuals numbering among its members, including the poet William Butler Yeats and the notorious "wickedest man in the world," Aleister Crowley. The latter in particular became a prolific writer on ritual magic, producing one of the field's most influential manuals, *Magick in Theory and Practice* (1929). Crowley was also the leader of the largest secret society devoted to ritual magic, the *Ordo Templi Orientis*, which still exists today.

By the late 1930s interest in ritual magic had diminished, but it was revived by a new generation in the 1950s and 1960s during what some have called a "magical revival." Since then ritual magic has become integrated into a number of occult and esoteric traditions, as well as into new religions such as Wicca and Neopaganism. By the mid-20th century, ritual magic was no longer a secret or forbidden act, and today most of the magical texts of antiquity, the Middle Ages, and the Renaissance are readily available in translation, while numerous grimoires are published and republished in print and digital form on the Internet for collectors and practitioners alike. Ritual magic is also on display in many novels, television shows, comic books, and video games and has becomes a central storytelling element on silver screens across America and elsewhere. Nevertheless, the entire subject, and especially the practice of ritual magic itself, still occupies a position of illegitimacy in mainstream societal opinion.

John L. Crow

See also: Demonology; New Age; Occultism; Spiritualism; Theosophy; Witchcraft

Further Reading

Crowley, Aleister. 1929. *Magick in Theory and Practice.* http://www.sacred-texts.com/oto/aba/aba.htm.

Davies, Owen. 2009. *Grimoires: A History of Magic Books.* Oxford, UK: Oxford University Press.

Davies, Owen. 2003. *Popular Magic: Cunning-folk in English History.* London: Hambledon Continuum.

Flint, Valerie I. J. 1992. *The Rise of Magic in Early Medieval Europe.* Oxford, UK: Clarendon Press.

Leventhat, Herbert. 1976. *In The Shadow of the Enlightenment: Occultism and Renaissance Science in Eighteenth-Century America.* New York: New York University Press.

Wilson, Leigh. 2013. *Modernism and Magic: Experiments with Spiritualism, Theosophy and the Occult.* Edinburgh, UK: Edinburgh University Press.

Yeats, Frances A. 1964. *Giordano Bruno and the Hermetic Tradition.* Chicago: University of Chicago Press.

Yeats, Francis A. 1972. *The Rosicrucian Enlightenment.* London: Routledge and Kegan Paul.

SCIENCE OF MYSTICISM

Mathematician and mystic Michael Whiteman (1906–2007) developed "scientific mysticism," aimed at bringing mysticism into the field of science as "open-minded, rigorously tested, rationally coherent, and illuminating" (Whiteman 1986, vii). He defined mysticism as "the study of everything nonphysical, including the other worlds and their archetypal governance, as well as our spiritual bodies, the facts and their relationship being known by the self-evidence of direct observation and not by reasoning or speculation" (Whiteman 1961, 1). Mysticism is seen here as an empirical science, sharing territory with psychical research, yet Whiteman drew a distinction between "psychical" and "mystical." The former includes the study of purportedly nonphysical events; the latter extends to states that have a sense of higher significance and ultimates, openness to guidance, transformed being, and orientation to the perceived source of the Right and Good.

Whiteman's methods rested on observation, conceptual analysis, and insight, in tune with the philosopher Edmund Husserl's phenomenology. This aims at gaining face-to-face self-evidence and detailed precision, shedding the usual cloak of ideas. Science in Whiteman's usage is not an exercise in theorizing, and mysticism is not some vague mystification. A key to his scientific mysticism is the idea of potentiality and actualization. The idea had been worked over by Werner Heisenberg in his *Physics and Philosophy* (1959). Heisenberg saw that a physical "happening" comes about through an occasion of observation, and this "happening" is open to physical description. But what governs the happening is not open to physical observation; at best it can be given mathematical expression. So behind a physical event one has to recognize what Heisenberg called "an objective tendency or possibility, a 'potentia' in the sense of Aristotelian philosophy" (Heisenberg 1959, 56). The governing potentia, the "reason" for something to happen, is abstract in a physical sense.

Thus, structures of potentiality underlie the observed material world, and these become actualized as things to an observer according to his/her state and abilities. As the state of the observer is itself a part of the potentiality governing any appearances, the process of actualization will be different for different people. An observer who is freed in some way from the physical state will actualize for himself or herself things that are beyond the reach of ordinary physical sensing. So, in Whiteman's words, "The difference between one 'world' and another then depends upon the state of life in which the observer happens to be settled" (Whiteman 2006, 3). This is the beginning of mystical perception.

According to Whiteman's system, psychical phenomena are explicable as resonance between individual and universal potentiality fields, not observable (or actualized) in physical space and time. Potentiality-actualization relationships should not be seen as static; potentiality-fields continually change or develop, although not in physical time. In a way they could be seen as spatial fields, and mystical or psychical perception comes about by an individual's being able to integrate his own potentiality fields with those affecting events in the physical past, present, and future. The individual may even intervene in the physical actualization of future events by altering the potentiality-fields, so allowing prevention of a precognized event from happening. Potentiality-fields are accessible in states of physical detachment and so allow limited alteration and the exercise of free will. Such understanding of free will is required by mysticism.

Also required by mysticism is an understanding of other-world experience and states. As noted, potentiality-fields have the capacity to deliver different spaces or worlds of physical and nonphysical actuality, depending on the state of the observer. Direct experience of other worlds occurs mainly in out-of-body experience, in which consciousness enters a nonphysical spatial field (referred to by some as the "astral plane"; also see the concept of the "imaginal"). This may be very similar to a physical scene, and may even be mistaken for one. Whiteman noted that such nonphysical experience may range in reality-impression and intensity from being weak to seeming even more real and meaningful than in physical life. At its most powerful, termed by him mystical, "Everything in such states, spatial characteristics included, is known as if in archetypal unchanging form, and is therefore startlingly more real (rationally objective, ever-present) than the derivative and shifting forms of the physical world" (Whiteman 1986, 143).

Highest development leads to "perfectly acceptable forms of transcendent unified beauty," where "the surroundings, correspondingly, are distinguished by the quality of the light, and gain in *intelligible* character, perfection of beauty, depth of glowing heart quality, unitive freedom and sense of blending with other minds, as the highest condition, which is that of Mystical Form Liberation, is approached" (Whiteman 1961, 153). In these descriptions, Whiteman states, "'I' and 'me' do not stand for the familiar consciousness of self in the physical personality, or in fact for anything that can be known in an ordinary physical state of mind. To understand what is meant, the characteristics of the merged ordinary *self* must be ruled out" (Whiteman 1961, 158).

Achievement of higher states received Whiteman's close attention. We cannot achieve these states, he believed, without psychological and spiritual faculties of attention, judgement, purposiveness, and self-discipline, based on "foundational skills" named Recollection and Obedience. Recollection involves removal of automaticity and attainment of pure consciousness; Obedience is not a state of subservience but orientation to the transcendent "Source of the Right and Good" (Whiteman 2006, 177). The foundational skills were structured into a four-part system known since ancient times and appearing in modern contexts in learning theory, Freud, and Jung. Described as the four creative functions, these are "purposive *drive*, deciding on *means*, putting into *practice*, and a virtually secret *maturing* of one's skills in consequence" (Whiteman 2006, 314). He placed great importance on this cycle having its opposites or "counterfeits" of self-will, self-satisfaction, automaticity, and complacency, which may lead to a corresponding cycle of "stresses" of death-feeling, shame, pain, and fear. Correction involves "inner contests" between helpful and harmful impulses. These were recognized as essential for spiritual growth, although fraught with turmoil.

As evident from this compact summary, Whiteman's scientific mysticism stands as an important contribution to the field of paranormal studies because of its penetrating exploration of the overlapping realms of psychical research and mysticism, and of the import of both for our understanding of our world and ourselves.

John Poynton

See also: Astral Plane; Imaginal; Mystical Experience; Out-of-Body Experience (OBE); Religion and the Paranormal; Whiteman, Michael

Further Reading

Heisenberg, Werner. 1959. *Physics and Philosophy: The Revolution in Modern Science*. London: George Allen & Unwin.

Whiteman, J. H. M. 1986. *An Introduction to Scientific Mysticism*, vol. 1 of *Old and New Evidence on the Meaning of Life*. Gerrards Cross, UK: Colin Smythe.

Whiteman, J. H. M. 1961. *The Mystical Life*. London: Faber.

Whiteman, J. H. M. 2006. *Universal Theology and Life in the Other Worlds*, vol. 3 of *Old and New Evidence on the Meaning of Life*. Gerrards Cross, UK: Colin Smythe.

SCRYING

Scrying has been variously defined as "the faculty of seeing visions in a smooth surface or clear deep, or both" (Besterman 1995, 2), "an occult method for obtaining oracular visions in water, glass or crystal" (Tyson 1997, xvi), and "the deliberate act of perceiving events that lie beyond the range of the physical senses by using the agents of the unconscious mind" (Tyson 1997, 3). As such, scrying is a form of clairvoyance or cryptesthesia (the subconscious perception of occurrences not ordinarily perceptible to the senses). It can also be considered as a form of divination, in that messages and insights will often arise from the vision. Visions may be of an objective reality, person, or place with self-evident meanings, or they may be symbolic, requiring interpretation. They may be actively sought through ritual intention (inductive divination) or spontaneously observed with no expectation or preparation (natural divination).

Scrying has been practiced at all times and in all cultures. Its many variants include catoptromancy (mirror), crystallomancy (crystal), cyclicomancy (cup of water or wine), gastromancy (marks on belly), hydromancy (water, river, lake), lecanomancy (water in basin or other receptacle), lithomancy (stone), onycho-

Types of Scrying

In scrying a person seeks special knowledge by gazing into a smooth or clear surface or object. It is subdivided into different types based on the type of item used:

Cataptromancy   uses mirrors.

Crystallomancy   uses crystals.

Cyclicomancy   uses a cup of water or wine.

Gastromancy   uses marks on the belly.

Hydromancy   use water in rivers or lakes.

Lecanomancy   uses water in a basin or other receptacle.

Lithomancy   uses stone.

Onychomancy   uses fingernails.

Pegomancy   uses spring water.

mancy (fingernails), and pegomancy (spring water). In ancient Greece, Pausanias (110–180 CE) tells us of a tradition of catoptromancy at the sanctuary of Demeter at Patras, where rituals for the prognosis of illness involved lowering a mirror into a spring. After various ritual activities, the images in the mirror would reveal whether the person inquired about was alive or dead. More recently, famous scryers include Nostradamus (1503–1566) and Dr. John Dee (1527–1608/9), the latter of whom used a black obsidian "shew-stone" in which his medium Edward Kelley saw visions of angels. Today scrying is usually associated with crystal ball gazing and has gained considerable popularity as a New Age meditation or guidance technique.

What is paranormal about scrying? In the act of gazing into a shining surface, a state of relaxed consciousness may come about in which hidden dimensions of reality are revealed to the diviner. These may be interpreted as messages from gods or spirits or assume significance as omens; but equally they may be attributed to an unconscious dimension of the human mind. The psychical researcher Frederic Myers (1843–1901) was the first to propose the theory of the "subliminal self," an unmanifested part of human consciousness responsible for precognitive or telepathic events. He concluded that crystal gazing was "an empirical method of developing internal vision; of externalizing pictures which are associated with changes in the sensorial tracts of the brain, due partly to internal stimuli, and partly to stimuli which may come from minds external to the scryer's own" (Myers, 1919, 150). In fact it is impossible to clearly differentiate between unconscious mind and external entities, and scrying is probably best understood as a method of accessing, through the imagination, an intermediary world of "sensory metaphor" (Tyson, 1997, 144) whose sources are open to both naturalistic and supernatural explanations but can be reduced to neither.

Angela Voss

See also: Clairvoyance; Divination; Extrasensory Perception (ESP); Myers, Frederic W. H.; Occultism; Unconscious Mind

Further Reading

Besterman, Theodore. 1995. *Crystal Gazing: A Study in the History, Distribution, Theory and Practice of Scrying.* Whitefish, MT: Kessinger Publishing.

Myers, F. W. H. 1919. *Human Personality and Its Survival of Bodily Death.* London: Longmans.

Tyson, Donald. 1997. *Scrying for Beginners: Tapping into the Supersensory Powers of Your Subconscious.* St. Paul, MN: Llewellyn Publishing.

SÉANCE

Many cultures have historically employed rituals and rites in order to communicate with the dead. Textual evidence of necromancy has been recorded in ancient Babylon, Egypt, Greece, Rome, China, India, and Japan, and is also common in the shamanistic and indigenous practices of many cultures that rely on oral traditions. However the séance is a particularly modern, Western form of communication with the dead that often combines elements of entertainment, religious or spiritual practice, and scientific investigation. The term "séance" itself comes directly from the common French word *séance*, which means "a sitting" and does not necessarily have the occult connotations of its English counterpart.

The séance as a practice is closely associated with 19th-century Spiritualism, a syncretic spiritual movement that unites Christian mysticism with revelations from the spirit world about the progressive development of human moral and intellectual qualities in mortal life and beyond. The birth of Spiritualism is generally believed to have taken place in New York State in 1848 when two sisters from Ontario, Kate Fox (1837–1892) and Margaret Fox (1833–1893), began to receive communications from spirits in the form of coded rapping on a table.

There are many different kinds of séance, with most of them being led by a spiritual medium, an individual who is so constituted that she can serve as a channel through which spiritual presences manifest themselves. The most well-known type of séance is when the medium sits around a table holding hands with those present in order to create a rapport with the spirit world. While in such a rapport, mediums often claim that the spirits talk, write, or even paint, using the medium herself as a host for their physical activity. They can also cause other dramatic effects, such as playing musical instruments or materializing ghostly or tangible forms such as flowers or other objects. Following the late 19th century search for the ways in which matter and space store memory, the French physiologist Charles Richet (1850–1935) coined the term "ectoplasm" by analogy with organic "protoplasm" to describe the physical manifestations of mediums in their trance states. Increasingly after this, mediums began manifesting organic looking "ectoplasmic" forms in their séances. Another well-known kind of séance is that in which sitters collectively use a Ouija board to spell out answers posed to spirits. Less well known are such methods as slate writing, in which a piece of chalk is placed tight against a downturned slate upon which spirits can record messages, or spirit photography, in which a medium's presence is said to allow a spirit to manifest itself upon photographic plates or in digital form.

Alfred Russel Wallace (1823–1913), the co-discoverer of natural selection, observed in the 19th century that mediums are influenced by the combined psychological state of all those present at a sitting. He used this to explain why many mediums have historically claimed that séances are disrupted by such things as light and by the negative thoughts of those present. For opponents of Spiritualism, however, these claims tend to be seen as convenient justification that make it easier for mediums to mask their deceptions or to explain away why skeptics are so often disappointed by what they witness during séances.

Many different groups have either outright condemned or else expressed caution about séances as a practice. Orthodox followers of the Abrahamic religions tend to view the entities contacted as evil spirits or demons, while even more unorthodox groups, such as the Theosophists, express concerns about the reliability of such communication. According to Helena Blavatsky (1831–1891), the beings communicated with during séances are astral shells, the aspect of humans that cannot transcend to higher realms upon death. Either this, or they are elemental beings that can inhabit the ethetic body of the medium, but that are no wiser than the humans they inhabit. Max Dessoir (1867–1947) warned that such practices, while not inherently harmful, could endanger the sanity of unskilled mediums and investigators and were best left to professional psychical researchers.

Skeptical critiques of séances have revolved around questions of deception or delusion, as in Ronald Pearsall's widely read 1973 book *Table-Tappers: The Victorians and the Occult*, which is devoted to chronicling the credulity of believers and the trickery of hoaxers during the high age of Victorian Spiritualism. In a separate but still related vein, stage magicians such as John Nevil Maskelyne (1839–1917) have been particularly known for performing séances for the purpose of public entertainment, showing how such effects as spirit photography, slate writing, and materialization can be done without any supernatural agency. Since séances are often considered to be fraudulent, legal attempts have often been made to prosecute the mediums who perform them.

A notable case of the criminalization of séances in the 19th century was the Slade Trial, in which the zoologist Edwin Ray Lankester (1847–1929), a student of the biologist Thomas Henry Huxley (1825–1895), charged the famed medium Henry Slade under the terms of the Vagrancy Act. The Vagrancy Act was enacted under King George IV in 1824. Though it has gone through further amendments since then, it is still in force in the United Kingdom today. As an act to police public morals, the Vagrancy Act originally covered a wide range of offenses such as being idle, squatting, begging, and distributing pornography, as well as homelessness and exhibitionism. It also condemned to three months hard labor "every Person pretending or professing to tell Fortunes, or using any subtle Craft, Means, or Device, by Palmistry or otherwise, to deceive and impose on any of His Majesty's Subjects." This clause was seen to include the subtle "craft, means, or device" of the séance, and the act was often employed to prosecute mediums throughout the British Empire.

When not denying séances as deceptions, opponents often describe them as being brought about the delusions of those involved. An early proponent of this theory was the physiologist William Benjamin Carpenter (1813–1885), who sought to demonstrate that expectant attention was enough to explain séances that could not be explained by deception alone. Expectant attention is the capacity of people to experience what they expect to experience. Carpenter held that spiritualists were doomed to see what they wanted to see during their séances exactly because of the strength of their beliefs. Citing the example of the Ouija board, Carpenter argued that the collective, unconscious, muscular actions of those present led the sitters to spell out the kinds of messages that they were expecting to see. Wallace critiqued Carpenter, claiming that arguments about expectant attention could be directed towards opponents of Spiritualism themselves, whose own presuppositions led them to not see the very things that spiritualists were trying to demonstrate. In this way arguments about expectant attention remain notoriously difficult to prove in any conclusive way, especially to those deeply embroiled in the debates surrounding them.

Frederic Myers (1843–1901) presented an alternative account of the delusions experienced during séances. While Myers admitted the possibility of communicating with the dead, he maintained that the majority of cases of mediumistic possession were brought about by the actions of the medium's subliminal self. The subliminal self was an early precursor to contemporary accounts of the unconscious. Myers employed a range of analogies to explain how the subliminal self could be both other than, and yet a part of an individual's personality. He compared it to the visible and invisible wavelengths of light, to the relationship between colonies, or to a kingdom "insensibly dissolving into a republic." Through his researches into séances and allied phenomena, Myers contributed greatly to the modern understanding of the psyche.

B. D. Mitchell

See also: American Society for Psychical Research; Automatic Writing; Channeling; Ectoplasm; Fox Sisters, The; Gooch, Stan; Jung, Carl; Mediumship; Myers, Frederic W. H.; Ouija Board; Society for Psychical Research; Spiritualism; Theosophy; Unconscious Mind

Further Reading

Hazelgrove, Jenny. 2000. *Spiritualism and British Society between the Wars.* Manchester, UK: Manchester University Press.

Hess, David J. 1993. *Science in the New Age: The Paranormal, Its Defenders & Debunkers.* Madison, WI: University of Wisconsin Press.

Kontou, Tatiana, and Sarah Willburn, eds. 2012. *The Ashgate Research Companion to Nineteenth-Century Spiritualism and the Occult.* Farnham, Surrey, UK; Burlington, VT: Ashgate.

Oppenheim, Janet. *The Other World: Spiritualism and Psychical Research in England, 1850–1914.* Cambridge, UK: Cambridge University Press, 1985.

Owen, Alex. 1989. *The Darkened Room: Women, Power, and Spiritualism in Late Nineteenth Century England.* London: Virago Press.

Owen, Alex. 2004. *The Place of Enchantment: British Occultism and the Culture of the Modern.* Chicago: University of Chicago Press.

SHAMANISM

The word "shaman" is widely regarded as having entered English, via Russian, from the language of the Evenki people in Siberia. Among the Evenki, the word *samán* indicates one who has served an apprenticeship to the spirits and to an existing shaman, so as to become a communicator and traveler between the human and spirit worlds; *samán* is often translated as "knower," indicating the heightened awareness attributed to recognized practitioners. From its origins in Asiatic Russia, the figure of the shaman has been identified in a wide variety of cultural settings, with overlapping but rarely identical characteristics. The relevance of shamanism to the paranormal lies in the fact of the preternatural knowledge and powers that shamans are commonly said to possess, and in the broad outlines of what might be called the shamanic worldview, which overlaps in a number of significant ways with Spiritualism, Spiritism, Theosophy, the New Age, and other religious and metaphysical traditions and belief systems that involve some form of spirit mediumship.

The modern scholarly tendency is to speak of shamanisms in the plural, showing due sensitivity to cultural context; shamanism in the singular is more properly thought of as an academic model or category, having an analytical purpose, rather than as any particular tradition. The figure of the shaman has been especially significant within English-speaking North American scholarship in comprehending many native North American spiritual traditions. In Western society in recent decades, a variety of practices, including healing modalities and techniques of spirit communication perceived as shamanic in nature, have been appropriated to form new popular, hybrid versions of shamanism (sometimes referred to as neoshamanism).

In Russian anthropology, there are references to shamans dating from the 18th century. The most extended study of the Evenki was undertaken by Sergei Shirokogoroff during the period 1913–1918, with his most significant work published in

1935. Shirokogoroff presented a detailed account of shamans as experts who interacted with human and animal spirits, both by incarnating them (controlled possession) so as to allow others to speak to them and by traveling (or journeying) to the
spirit world(s). The purpose of these interactions could be varied: to gain useful
information, to enlist the support of spirits in dealing with worldly problems, to
diagnose when illness had a spirit origin, to assist in childbirth so as to bring new
spirits into the world safely, and to act as psychopomp (a conductor of the souls of
the deceased to their proper place) where needed. Although important, Shiroko-
roff's work was not immediately influential in Russia—he published outside Russia
in English—nor in the West, where his work ran counter to the then current trend
of seeking psychological explanations for shamanic practices.

In North America, attempts to comprehend native spirit practitioners or healers
used terms such as shaman, medicine man, spirit medium, sorcerer, and witch
doctor; indeed, such terms were often used interchangeably, even into the 1920s
and 1930s. Many scholars felt that there might be an underlying commonality
between different traditions, but Mircea Eliade at Chicago was the first to attempt
a cross-cultural synthesis. Eliade drew upon examples from around the world but
made particular use of Shirokogoroff's work on the Evenki.

The shamanic model Eliade developed presented the shaman as a master of
ecstasy, meaning a practitioner who used altered states of consciousness to access
additional realities, for purposes that had communal value. Although significant in
the development of shamanic models, Eliade's work has since been criticized on a
number of grounds. Eliade emphasized the active, journeying aspect of shamanic practices, masking the significance of possessory elements; he suggested that
present-day traditions involving communication with the spirits of the dead and
animals were a deteriorated version of an older shamanism that had emphasized
travelling to meet a "high god," which some suspected might be a hidden Christian agenda supported by the masking of possessory practices. In addition, Eliade's
examples and analysis of shamanism used examples of particular practices drawn
from a wide variety of contexts, whereas more recent scholarship is inclined to emphasize the importance of social setting and the particularity of different traditions
in reaching a useful understanding of them.

Ioan Lewis is one scholar who raised many of these concerns and who suggested
that, as users of consciousness, it is possible to identify shamanic traditions that
use a wide range of practices, both possessory (passive) and journeying (active).
Western culture has a history of treating possession as uncontrolled and dangerous,
which has perhaps led some scholars to overlook, or be reluctant to recognize, its
place in cultures that regard it as useful when undertaken by trained practitioners.

There is a scholarly trend toward detailing the cultural setting of particular shamanisms, and there are now few parts of the world where traditions with shamanic
characteristics have not been identified. Shamanic models are now used in relation to indigenous traditions in Central and South America as well as Africa and
Southeast Asia. In relation to Africa, British scholarship has a long history of using

possession as the preferred analytical model, leading to an implicit assumption that shamanic traditions were not possessory in nature. The boundaries between models such as shamanism, mediumship, and possession have become increasingly blurred; shamanism is now such a widely used term that it has become necessary to explain why we might describe a particular tradition or practice as shamanic.

One indication that researchers have always been, in some degree, aware that possession might be relevant is that there has long been discussion as to whether shamans are in control of the spirits they interact with or whether the spirits control the shaman. Eliade emphasized the importance of the shaman's being in control of the spirits, but many scholars prefer to think in terms of more complex relationships involving various forms of cooperation. Some scholars have pointed out that in order to cooperate productively, the most important form of control is self-control, which is a common feature of shamanic training.

In terms of commonality between traditions, the trend is away from seeking similar practices or demonstrations in favor of understanding the ways in which new shamans are chosen and trained. Shamans are often said to be chosen by the spirits and are described as undergoing some form of personal crisis prompted by the spirits as a way of telling the potential shaman that he or she has been identified as a possible future practitioner. The ability to recognize this stage properly can be the first of a number of tests to be undergone. In most cultures, the position of shaman could transmit within families but need not do so.

The next stage is to commence training under the guidance of an existing practitioner, who teaches the apprentice how to interact with the spirits by sharing accumulated experience and wisdom, both personal and communal. A significant part of what is transmitted is knowledge of what will be accepted as useful and valid by the apprentice's own society or future clientele, as this is crucial to achieving communal recognition as a practitioner. Beyond this, the apprentice must use what is taught so as to learn how to interact with his or her own particular spirits (which can include the spirits of past shamans); in shamanic traditions, it is commonly taught that this knowledge can only be gained from the spirits themselves.

In some traditions, consciousness-altering substances are employed to give access to the spirits, but this is not a common feature across shamanic traditions. Among the Evenki, for example, Shirokogoroff noted only the use of alcohol and tobacco among shamans, and even then no more widely than in Evenki society generally. The duration of traditional shamanic apprenticeships is usually measured in years, rather than months, as it is fundamentally a process of personal development. In many cultures, shamans are expected to continue to develop throughout their careers, so as to enhance the range of their skills for the benefit of the community.

Although shamans can take on leadership roles in some societies, they are not necessarily good or spiritually enlightened figures; they are trained practitioners whose personal motivation can vary as widely as it does with other individuals.

Anthropological literature offers many examples of shamans who use their skills for personal gain or advantage; indeed, one of the functions of more highly regarded shamans can be to oppose "bad" shamans by limiting their influence. In Evenki culture, most clans only had one shaman at any given time; where clans came into conflict, or one clan feared antagonism from another, they would naturally expect their own shaman to use his or her abilities to the full in protecting the clan he or she belonged to.

Shamans are usually also storytellers, entrusted with remembering and teaching the history of the clan or community. In many shamanic societies, the body of lore maintained by the shamans includes creation accounts, and possibly ancient accounts of where the people came from originally. As healers, shamans often maintain extensive herbal lore, reflecting that fact that although shamans are ultimately spirit practitioners, the problems they are expected to deal with are often very immediate and practical.

In Western society in recent decades, shamanism has attracted much popular interest, with individuals learning a variety of shamanic techniques and subsequently passing on their knowledge through workshops and seminars. At the farthest margin of such activities lies the cultural movement sometimes known as "neoshamanism," representing the splicing together of New Age and neopagan ideas and practices with those drawn liberally from one or more traditional shamanisms. In this context, the latter can be and sometimes are distinguished as "core shamanism." Such activities can attract criticism on the basis that practices are taken out of context. However, to the extent that new traditions develop that are based on some form of apprenticeship to an existing practitioner, it may be possible to claim a degree of authenticity, particularly where a shaman serves a wider community of non-practitioners.

David Gordon Wilson

See also: Discarnate Entity; Drugs and the Paranormal; Healing, Psychic and Spiritual; Krippner, Stanley; Mediumship; Possession; Reincarnation; Religion and the Paranormal; Spiritualism; Witchcraft

Further Reading

Eliade, Mircea. (1951, 1964) 1989. *Shamanism: Archaic Techniques of Ecstasy.* Translated by Willard R. Trask. London: Arkana.

Jakobsen, Merete Demant. 1999. *Shamanism: Traditional and Contemporary Approaches to the Mastery of Spirits and Healing.* New York: Berghahn.

Lewis, I. M. (1971, 1989) 2003. *Ecstatic Religion: A Study of Shamanism and Spirit Possession.* London: Routledge.

Shirokogoroff, S. M. (1935) 1999. *The Psychomental Complex of the Tungus.* Berlin: Reinhold Schletzer Verlag.

Stutley, Margaret. 2003. *Shamanism: An Introduction.* London: Routledge.

Vitebsky, Piers. (1995) 2001. *The Shaman: Voyages of the Soul, Trance, Ecstasy and Healing from Siberia to the Amazon*. London: Duncan Baird.

Wilson, David Gordon. 2013. *Redefining Shamanisms: Spiritualist Mediums and Other Traditional Shamans as Apprenticeship Outcomes*. London & New York: Bloomsbury.

SHEEP-GOAT EFFECT

The sheep-goat effect refers to a phenomenon in parapsychology whereby believers in ESP, called "sheep," consistently perform better on ESP related tasks than nonbelievers, called "goats."

This phenomenon was first demonstrated in 1942 by Gertrude Schmeidler, a professor of psychology at the City University of New York. Schmeidler asked her students about their belief in psi and then categorized them depending on whether they generally believed in the reality of psi (sheep) or doubted its existence (goats). She then gave the students a classic ESP test in which they attempted to guess a sequence of cards. The sheep scored significantly above chance in their performance, while the goats scored significantly below it. This effect has been found repeatedly by many different investigators, and a meta-analysis by Tony Lawrence in 1992, which summarized the results of 73 experiments by 37 investigators, confirmed that believers in psi tend to perform better than nonbelievers on psi-related tests. In addition, the sheep-goat effect also appears to apply to the investigators themselves. That is, investigators who are believers in psi are more likely to find results in their experiments that confirm the reality of psi, while investigators who are nonbelievers tend to find results that disconfirm the reality of psi.

The psychological phenomena of selective attention and confirmation bias are well known and often used to explain differences in the frequencies with which believers and nonbelievers report experiences they believe are paranormal. People tend to pay more attention to stimuli that confirm their beliefs and attitudes than those that contradict them, so believers are more likely to interpret their experiences as paranormal than nonbelievers, who are prone to seek normal explanations for their experiences. In addition, several researchers have found differences in how sheep and goats estimate probability and have used these findings to explain differences between belief in psi among the two groups. However, the sheep-goat effect has been demonstrated in experiments conducted under controlled conditions and relates to the participant's performance on psi-related tasks, not just their interpretation of their experiences.

A related phenomenon is called "psi missing," which refers to cases in which individuals perform significantly worse on psi-related tasks than they would be expected to by chance. Many theorists view psi missing as just as important as psi hitting for demonstrating psychic ability since both are equally unlikely compared to random chance. Consistent with the sheep-goat phenomena, goats are more likely than sheep to exhibit psi missing, which some researchers have suggested supports the hypothesis that goats' negative expectations about their psi abilities unconsciously block their ability to receive psi information.

Although investigators have demonstrated the sheep-goat effect repeatedly with a wide variety of experimental protocols, there is currently no accepted explanation for the phenomenon. For example, Mario Varvoglis, president of the Parapsychological Association in 2001 and 2002, suggests that it is the beliefs themselves of sheep and goats that influence the occurrences around them. In other words, goats' reductionist mindset inhibits the likelihood that psi phenomena will manifest in the first place. This is one of many factors that may contribute to the sheep-goat effect.

Jennifer Lyke

See also: Art, Creativity, and the Paranormal; Parapsychology; Psi

Further Reading
Irwin, Harvey J., and Caroline Watt. 2007. *An Introduction to Parapsychology.* 5th ed. Jefferson, NC: McFarland.

SIDDHIS

Siddhi is a Sanskrit term derived from the verbal root *sidh*, "to be accomplished, to succeed." This is the term that scholars most widely use to refer to the attainment of supernatural powers in South Asian religious traditions. These powers are typically gained through practices such as yoga, meditation, mantra recitation, the consumption of mind-altering substances, possession, and the performance of various rituals. The term siddhi began to denote the attainment of supernatural powers with the emergence of Hindu and Buddhist tantric traditions in the seventh to eighth centuries CE.

The earliest appearance of siddhi-like powers in South Asian literature is found in the Vedas (c. 1500 BCE), the foundational texts of the Hindu tradition. These powers are most evident in the hymns to the Vedic deity *Soma*, who is portrayed as both a divine being and as a psychoactive substance that, when consumed, brings one riches, produces visions of the gods, allows one to travel through space, and grants the ability to see for long distances.

In the Buddhist tradition, enlightened beings are understood to possess many supernatural powers (*ṛddhi*), including the ability to create entire universes. Buddhist meditators are said to attain the "supernatural cognitions" (*abhiññā*), a term that most often denotes the profound expansion of sensory perception. Other supernatural powers listed in early Buddhist texts include invisibility, passing through solid objects, the ability to travel through the ground, walking on water, clairvoyance, and flight.

The third chapter of Patañjali's *Yogasūtra* (c. second century BCE), the "Vibhūti-pada" or "Chapter on Powers," contains a lengthy description of the supernatural powers one attains through the practice of yoga. A standard list of eight primary siddhis has developed out of this tradition: (1) miniaturization, (2) weightlessness, (3) expansion, (4) attainment, (5) replication, (6) control of the elements, (7) sovereignty, and (8) the end of desire. The yogic traditions of India were overwhelmingly concerned with the attainment of supernatural powers and the employment of these powers toward both worldly ends and the final goal of immortality and the attainment of omniscience.

Both Hindu and Buddhist tantric traditions are particularly oriented toward the attainment of siddhis. Although the traditional lists of supernatural powers that a tantric yogī attains are by no means uniform, one often finds a somewhat standardized grouping of eight primary siddhis in tantric texts. One such group of eight found in the Buddhist *Cakrasaṃvara-Tantra* (c. eighth century CE) includes (1) the ability to travel in the underworld, (2) resurrecting the dead, (3) the sword (to defeat any enemy), (4) subjugation, (5) the pill (that grants invisibility), (6) the ability to find buried treasure, (7) the foot-ointment (for traveling at fast speeds), and (8) alchemy. Tantric texts are a vast repository for the South Asian cultural lore of magic, sorcery, and supernatural powers. Many of the ritual technologies that appear in these traditions such as the use of complex diagrams (*yantras*, or *maṇḍalas*), the visualization of various deities, the recitation of spells (*mantras*), sexual yoga practices, and the manipulation of the subtle energies of the body, to name a few, are intended to confer siddhis or supernatural powers on the practitioner.

The Buddhist, Yogic, and Tantric traditions all distinguish between the attainment of supernatural powers that are directed toward worldly gain and those that are directed toward the attainment of liberation from the world. The previous group, which by far dominates the literature, is often referred to as the "worldly" siddhis, while the supernatural power that confers liberation is referred to as the "ultimate" or "trans-mundane" siddhi. Some traditions emphasize the worldly siddhis over the ultimate, while others emphasize the ultimate siddhi and criticize those who seek the worldly siddhis. Still others suggest that the worldly siddhis inevitably result from the progress that the practitioner has made toward attaining the "ultimate" siddhi.

Adam Krug

See also: Alchemy; Drugs and the Paranormal; Meditation; Possession; Religion and the Paranormal; Ritual Magic

Further Reading

Jacobson, Knut A., ed. 2012. *Yoga Powers: Extraordinary Capacities Attained through Meditation and Concentration.* Leiden, NL: Brill.

White, David G. 1996. *The Alchemical Body: Siddha Traditions in Medieval India.* Chicago: University of Chicago Press.

SLEEP PARALYSIS

In modern scientific research "sleep paralysis" (SP), defined as a brief inability to perform voluntary movements while falling asleep or awakening while consciously aware, is a "parasomnia," a sort of glitch in the brain's sleep apparatus. Sometimes SP is accompanied by frightening hallucinations. But in folk traditions around the world this event is a supernatural assault, perpetrated by witches, vampires, ghosts, or demons, not hallucinations. The connection between these categories came to light in David Hufford's research, first published in 1974. Since then the scientific and the folk traditions have gradually illuminated each other, but the process has raised as many mysteries as it has solved.

"The Old Hag" and Modern Sleep Paralysis Research

In 1971 Hufford was studying traditional beliefs in Newfoundland, an isolated island in the North Atlantic with a strong set of old traditions. There he encountered "the Old Hag." When you "have the Old Hag," Newfoundlanders say, you awake unable to move. The "Hag," an evil, terrifying *something*, can be heard coming, footsteps approaching. It enters your room, comes to your bed, and presses you, crushing the breath out of you. The conventional scientific explanation for such beliefs is that tradition gives rise to experiential stories, and these cause experiences that seem to support the tradition: a self-fulfilling prophecy. For example, a person might dream of the Hag after hearing a traditional account and consider it real because of traditional beliefs.

Hufford had personal reasons to doubt this cultural process model of supernatural belief. In 1963, as a college sophomore, he went to bed exhausted after his final exams, looking forward to a long and uninterrupted night's sleep. After two hours he was awakened by the sound of his door opening, and footsteps approached his bed. He could see nothing in the inky darkness, and when he tried to turn on his bedside light, he discovered that he could not move. The footsteps came to his bed, and the mattress went down as someone climbed onto the bed, knelt on his chest, and strangled him. He thought he was dying, but worse was his overwhelming impression of *evil*. His reaction was revulsion; whatever was on his chest was not only destructive, it was disgusting. He finally managed to move— first his hand, then his whole body—and when he leaped out of bed and turned on the light, he found the room was empty. He told no one about the experience for eight years.

The convergence of Hufford's terrifying experience and Newfoundland's Old Hag contradicted the conventional cultural process model and led him to develop a novel method, "the experience-centered approach" (Hufford 1982), for studying supernatural belief traditions. From that came some very unconventional findings about the "Old Hag" and other spirit traditions that make empirical claims. The method begins with the possibility that a tradition claiming experiences, no matter how impossible the experiences sound, may in fact have an experiential base. Second, the typical cultural source explanations are rigorously tested. Firsthand

Sleep Paralysis, Religion, and the Paranormal

Sleep paralysis has played a crucial role in helping to form and inform notions of the paranormal, and it may also have played an important role in the evolution of religion and culture at large. Dr. David Hufford and others have speculated that the visions and entities encountered in many sleep paralysis episodes may be implicated in the very origin of human religiosity on the deepest historical and psychological levels. Additionally, the fact that these experiences are cross-cultural but do not appear to be transmitted by culture itself, arising instead as a spontaneous and primary human experience, is at odds with many conventional attempts to account for paranormal phenomena in materially reductive terms. Sleep paralysis stands as a singularly significant phenomenon of its own in the realm of paranormal studies.

accounts related to the tradition are sought and not only stories in oral circulation. If firsthand accounts are found, their relationship to cultural models—for example, books, folktales, movies—is assessed. If people unfamiliar with the relevant traditions report traditional-appearing experiences, the cultural source explanation does not hold.

Hufford's personal experience occurred long before he had ever heard of anything like the Old Hag, and the details of his experience provided a match too perfect and complex to be coincidental. Therefore, his "hagging" could not be an imaginary cultural product. Further research soon confirmed this.

In the United States Hufford found many who had experienced the same thing, including hearing footsteps, experiencing the sense of being pressed, sensing a terrifying evil, and so on, but who had never heard of such an experience before. Strikingly, even the most sophisticated among them insisted that their experiences were *real*. Simultaneously Hufford searched the historical and anthropological literature for similar accounts. He quickly found many, and more continued to turn up in succeeding years. Witches, for example, were believed to sit on their victims in their beds ("witch riding"), rendering them immobile. Several accounts indistinguishable from Newfoundland hag attacks appear in Cotton Mather's narrative of the Salem witch trials (1692). In Sweden the attacker is framed as a malevolent spirit, the *Mara*; in early English it is the *mare*, from the Anglo-Saxon root *merran*, "to crush," origin of *nightmare*, the crusher who comes in the night and the French *cauchemar*, "the crusher that comes to the bed." In Southeast Asia it is the *da chor*, *dab coj*, *poj ntxoog*, or *dab tsog*, and in China the sitting ghost or *bei Guai chaak* (being pressed by a ghost). In Japan it is *kanashibari* (literally "metal bound"), a sorcerous practice of *ninja*. These terms and many more from around the world refer to the same paralysis event accompanied by the "awful presence," soft shuffling footsteps, the "shadow man," and spiritual rituals to prevent them.

Causes, Diagnoses, and Prevalence

Modern sleep researchers have shown that SP is produced by the intrusion into wakefulness of the atonia (loss of muscle tone) characteristic of rapid eye movement (REM), the sleep stage during which most dreams occur. The scientific literature describes SP content in vague and ambiguous terms (e.g., "frightening hallucination") rendering invisible the complex, robust experiential pattern so evident in folk tradition, a pattern not accounted for by SP research: if this is a dream, why are the dreams so similar the world over? Assuming that the scientific and folk viewpoints are mutually exclusive creates serious problems. Full, subjectively accurate accounts of SP are reported but are often not recognized as SP, being mistaken instead for psychotic illness or seizures. Hufford's *The Terror That Comes in the Night* documents such diagnostic errors. Over the past 20 years the high prevalence of idiopathic sleep paralysis has become much better known in the scientific literature, but not its robust and compelling subjective pattern, so sleep paralysis remains a likely source of misdiagnosis. Because of this ignorance SP has also been mistaken for narcolepsy, repressed memories of sexual abuse, alien abduction, and Sudden Unexplained Nocturnal Death, among others.

The risk of psychiatric misdiagnosis and the resulting suppression of disclosure largely accounts for the invisibility of SP in modern society. When Hufford began his research, SP was considered relatively rare, but his initial findings, now reliably upheld, indicates that about 18 percent of the general population has had this experience, complete with the threatening presence. The experience-centered approach to the study of such extraordinary spiritual experiences reveals similar cultural dynamics for other events such as near-death experiences and after-death contacts.

Sleep Paralysis and the Paranormal

Current knowledge about SP is contrary to conventional theories of the paranormal. Theories based on a reductive, physicalist worldview are crafted to discredit observations supportive of those ideas once called *supernatural* that today constitute the *paranormal*. If the cultural source explanations do not account for this widespread experience—and they do not—then there are no alternative conventional explanations available for the cross-cultural distribution of these experiences with their recognizable complex, robust phenomenological pattern. This pattern is characteristic of accurate reports of real events.

SP experiences also contain direct reference to the paranormal. For example, SP attacks are common in hauntings. Even more striking, in some traditions certain people can *cause* others to experience SP complete with the terrifying threatening presence. One such account has been published by a well-known and respected anthropologist who was challenged by a West African sorcerer using SP; see *In Sorcery's Shadow: A Memoir of Apprenticeship among the Songhay of Niger* by Paul Stoller and Cheryl Okes. More common is the connection between sleep paralysis and out-of-body experiences (OBE). In some traditions people actually overcome the terror to induce SP as a kind of gateway to OBE.

In SP/"Hag" events science and supernatural folk tradition converge, illuminating, not contradicting, each other and further deepening the mysteries of human experience.

David J. Hufford

See also: Abduction Experience; Anomalistic Psychology; Discarnate Entity; Hallucinations; Haunting; Hypnagogic State; Lucid Dreams; Out-of-Body Experience (OBE); Paranormal; Paranormal Dreams

Further Reading

Adler, Shelly R. 1991. "Sudden Unexpected Nocturnal Death Syndrome among Hmong Immigrants: Examining the Role of the Nightmare." *Journal of American Folklore* 104: 57–71.

Emmons, Charles F. 1982. *Chinese Ghosts and ESP: A Study of Paranormal Beliefs and Experiences*. Metuchen, NJ: Scarecrow Press.

Hufford, David J. 1995. "Awakening Paralyzed in the Presence of a 'Strange Visitor.'" In *Alien Discussions: Proceedings of the Abduction Study Conference*, edited by Andrea Pritchard, David E. Pritchard, John E. Mack, Pam Kasey, and Claud Yapp, 348–353. Cambridge, MA: North Cambridge Press.

Hufford, David J. 1995. "Beings without Bodies: An Experience-Centered Theory of the Belief in Spirits." In *Out of the Ordinary: Folklore and the Supernatural*, edited by Barbara Walker, 11–45. Logan, UT: University of Utah Press.

Hufford, David J. 2001. "An Experience-Centered Approach to Hauntings." In *Hauntings and Poltergeists: Multidisciplinary Perspectives*, edited by James Houran and Rense Lange, 18–40. Jefferson, NC: McFarland.

Hufford, David J. 1976. "A New Approach to 'The Old Hag': The Nightmare Tradition Reexamined." In *American Folk Medicine*, edited by Wayland D. Hand, 73–85. Los Angeles: University of California Press.

Hufford, David J. 2014. "Sleep Paralysis, Lucid Dreams, and the Non-Physical." In *Lucid Dreaming: New Perspectives on Consciousness in Sleep*, edited by Ryan Hurd and Kelly Bulkeley, 255–276. Practical and Applied Psychology. Santa Barbara, CA: Praeger.

Hufford, David J. 1982. *The Terror That Comes in the Night: An Experience-Centered Study of Supernatural Assault Traditions*. Philadelphia: University of Pennsylvania Press.

Mather, Cotton. 1692. *On Witchcraft: Being the Wonders of the Invisible World*. Boston. Reprint as *Cotton Mather on Witchcraft*. 1988. New York: Bell Publishing Co.

Munger, Ronald G. 1986. "Sleep Disturbances and Sudden Death of Hmong Refugees: A Report of Fieldwork Conducted in the Ban Vinai Refugee Camp." In *The Hmong in Transition*, edited by Glen L. Hendricks, Bruce T. Downing, and Amos S. Deinard, 379–398. Staten Island, NY: New York Center for Migration Studies.

Stoller, Paul and Cheryl Okes. 1987. *In Sorcery's Shadow: A Memoir of Apprenticeship among the Songhay of Niger*. Chicago: University of Chicago Press.

Tillhagen, Carl-Herman. 1969. "The Conception of the Nightmare in Sweden." In *Humaniora: Essays in Literature, Folklore and Bibliography Honoring Archer Taylor*, edited by Wayland D. Hand and Gustave O. Arlt, 317–329. New York: Augustin.

Tobin, Joseph Jay, and Joan Friedman. 1983. "Spirits, Shamans, and Nightmare Death: Survivor Stress in a Hmong Refugee." *American Journal of Orthopsychiatry* 53: 439–448.

SOCIETY FOR PSYCHICAL RESEARCH

The objective of the Society for Psychical Research is, and has been since its inception, to investigate scientifically the phenomena described as "psychic" or "paranormal." The SPR aims to learn more about such phenomena by supporting research, both in academia and by private individuals; by disseminating and sharing information; and by encouraging debate. One of the main principles of the Society is that it has no corporate opinion, and membership does not imply adherence to any particular explanation of the phenomena investigated.

The Society was founded in 1882 and is the oldest organization of its kind. It could be said that its early activities defined the subject of psychical research. The period during which the Society came into existence saw great intellectual tensions arising between the latest findings of science and the traditional views of Western religion. Darwin's theory of evolution was interpreted as a challenge to humankind's importance in a materialistic universe and to the religious worldview. At the same time, extraordinary paranormal claims were spreading with the growth of a new religion, that of Spiritualism, which claimed that spirits of the deceased could be communicated with through the channel of a "medium," a person with special psychic sensitivity.

The founders of the Society responded to this challenge with a determined effort to examine these fundamental questions in the spirit of scientific inquiry, with the objectivity and the methodological tools that made science so successful in other areas. At the center of their initial activities was the collection and investigation of data, and this work was divided among a number of committees (governed by a council), which investigated such topics as telepathy (a term coined by Frederic Myers, one of the SPR's founding members), mesmerism (hypnotism) and clairvoyance, and physical phenomena, as well as apparitions and haunted houses. Methodologies were developed for carrying out investigations and for experimental research, and standards of evidence were established for case studies. The founders also helped to establish psychical research as a branch of learning by starting a book collection, which in time became an extensive psychical research library, and by producing a scholarly journal for reporting and discussing psychical research worldwide.

The SPR's first president was Henry Sidgwick, professor of moral philosophy at Cambridge University, one of the many prominent intellectuals whose efforts contributed to the Society's achievements at that time. Other founding members included Frederic Myers and Edmund Gurney, both classical scholars and men of wide-ranging interests, while among the early members were also such figures as the physicists William Barrett, Lord Rayleigh, and Sir Oliver Lodge; Arthur Balfour, philosopher and later Prime Minister; and Eleanor Sidgwick, wife of Henry Sidgwick, herself a mathematician and later principal of Newnham College at Cambridge University. The famous psychologists William McDougall and William James were also early members of the SPR and served as its presidents, while among European scientists interested in the Society's activities we find such names as the physicists Marie Curie and Heinrich Hertz, and the psychologists Alfred Binet, Pierre Janet, and Theodore Flournoy.

What has been described as the "heroic age" of the SPR produced a number of landmark publications. The first of these originated from the committee to which the public sent reports of spontaneous cases of psychic phenomena. The work of Edmund Gurney, Frederic Myers, and Frank Podmore, *Phantasms of the Living*, published in 1886, presented, within a theoretical framework, more than 700 carefully analyzed cases of reported telepathic communications from people who were dying or were in life-threatening situations (known as crisis apparitions), and this still remains an often quoted resource. This was followed by another ground-breaking project, the Census of Hallucinations (published in 1894), the first large-scale survey that set out to establish the probability of reports of crisis apparitions being due to chance coincidence. The year 1903 saw the posthumous publication of Frederic Myers's *Human Personality and Its Survival of Bodily Death*, which constituted a vast synthesis of his thinking and presented his theory of subliminal self, now a classic of psychical research literature.

Alongside accounts of spontaneous phenomena, much of the early work of the Society involved investigating mediumistic claims, often leading to the exposure of fake claimants. Members of the Society originated the "fake séance" technique for educating the public (including SPR members), aimed at demonstrating how phenomena could be faked. Although the great majority of claimants turned out to be deceitful or deluded, a number of mediums were identified whose probity was not in question, and these were studied in great detail. First and foremost among them was the American mental medium Leonora Piper, studied in great detail by many prominent psychical researchers, including William James. The work done with her had significant influence on the development of mediumship investigation on both sides of the Atlantic.

The study of mediumship also provided much information on aspects of human personality and altered states of consciousness. Alongside research into these and following the general trend in psychology toward a more biological approach, experimental methods kept undergoing refinements and improvements. Much important pioneering work on free-response and quantitative experiments was done in the 1920s and 1930s by researchers such as George Tyrrell, best known for his theory of apparitions, who explored a variety of methods for inducing altered states of consciousness and techniques to differentiate between telepathy and clairvoyance and made attempts to automate the randomization of targets. In the 1930s in the United States J. B. Rhine initiated a new approach to investigating psychic abilities, that of using large numbers of ordinary people as subjects and simple, standard procedures to test them, and the Society became involved in collaborative studies aimed at replicating his results (both J. B. Rhine and his wife Louisa served as presidents of the SPR). There was collaboration between the SPR in Britain and the American Society for Psychical Research, as well as a close relationship with various European organizations formed to investigate the phenomena.

The "Heroic Years" of the SPR: A Brief Chronology

1882 The Society for Psychical Research is founded in London at a meeting of the British National Association of Spiritualists.

1884 The first issue of the *Journal of the Society for Psychical Research* is published. A schism erupts between the SPR and Spiritualism.

1885 The SPR investigates the Theosophical Society and dismisses it as being based on fraud. The SPR's chief founder, William Barrett, helps to found an American branch.

1886 The SPR publishes its first major work, the landmark book *Phantasms of the Living* by Edmund Gurney, Frederic Myers, and Frank Podmore.

1894 The SPR publishes another pioneering work, the *Census of Hallucinations*.

1903 The SPR publishes Frederic Myers' *Human Personality and Its Survival of Bodily Death*.

As knowledge about aspects of psychical research and related areas expanded, so did the role of the SPR, from a mainly investigative to an educational body. Its history and the involvement of many significant intellectual figures in its activities means that it has become an important historical research resource in its own right. It continues to maintain a psychical research library and an archive of original documents, now housed both at its offices in London and at Cambridge University Library. The Society publishes (continuously since 1884) a peer-reviewed quarterly *Journal* that carries papers relating to investigations and experiments past and present, as well as theoretical studies and papers on areas relevant to psychical research, such as psychology, philosophy, physics, medicine, evolutionary biology, and social sciences. A quarterly magazine, the *Paranormal Review*, carries a mixture of articles, letters, and accounts of current cases as well as events organized by the Society. All of the Society's periodicals, as well as the classics of psychical research, are available to members online. Regular events organized by the Society include study days devoted to a particular topic and an annual conference, and both are open to members of the public.

The Society's most essential function continues to be the promotion of scientific research. Since parapsychology (a term often used as equivalent to "psychical research") became an academic subject, with postgraduate courses offered at a number of universities in the UK, much of the work supported by the Society is in the form of projects carried out as part of university research and financed by the Society's grants, administered by two funds. The Research Fund considers applications both from academics and from knowledgeable individuals and supports projects concerning exchanges between minds, or between minds and the environment; these have included experiments in dowsing, investigations of mental healing, working with mediumship groups, and surveys of psychic experiences. The Survival Research Fund supports scientific research into the question of whether some aspect of consciousness or personality survives the death of the body; this may include projects aimed at generating new evidence, analyzing existing evidence, or generating relevant theoretical frameworks. Reports of anomalous phenomena from the public, which have continued throughout the Society's existence, continue to be evaluated and investigated where appropriate. It could thus be claimed that while the subject of psychical research has expanded and grown alongside other branches of learning, taking from them and contributing to them, the essential aim of the SPR, of investigating scientifically psychic or paranormal phenomena, in order to throw light on the fundamental question of humankind's place in the universe, remains the same.

Zofia Weaver

See also: American Society for Psychical Research; Apparitions; Haunting; James, William; Mediumship; Myers, Frederic W. H.; Paranormal; Parapsychology; Precognition; Psychical Research; Séance; Spiritualism; Survival after Death; Telepathy

Further Reading

Beloff, John. 1993. *Parapsychology: A Concise History*. London: The Athlone Press.
Broughton, Richard. 1992. *Parapsychology: The Controversial Science*. London: Rider.
Gauld, Alan. 1968. *The Founders of Psychical Research*. London: Routledge & Kegan Paul.
Society for Psychical Research (official Website). 2009. http://www.spr.ac.uk.

SPIRIT PHOTOGRAPHY

Spirit photography is the attempt to photograph ghosts and other disembodied spirits and entities. It is particularly associated with the rise of the Spiritualist movement in America, where it represented a striking confluence of religion, science, and technological innovation at a very specific moment in Western cultural history.

Shadows haunted 19th-century America. Since the colonial period, physical and imaginative landscapes had been a "world of wonders" in which providential designs and nefarious forces vied for the souls of persons both free and in bondage. The philosophical and scientific revolutions of the 18th century curbed a good deal of inherited enthusiasms, but Americans in 1835 were often just as sure of the existence of unseen forces as their 17th-century ancestors had been. Optical marvels and the urgency of scientific discovery in the early decades of the 19th century played on these fears and fantasies for profit, and, in 1839, photography became the latest in a series of new techniques that wed scientific empiricism to imaginative wonder. The products of photographic techniques were known as "shadows" in the parlance of the period and were approached simultaneously as "receipts" of physical nature—direct imprints of empirical truth—and also as conduits of unseen social and spiritual natures. Studio photography was born into this spiritual landscape and quickly became a vehicle for conveying the spirits of the departed. The entire industry of studio portraiture in the mid-to late 19th century, from full-plate daguerreotypes to photograph albums to treasured lockets, can be understood as a kind of popular necromancy, a communion of shadows.

Both modern Spiritualism and commercial photography entered American cultural imaginations in the 1840s. Long exposure times required in the earliest techniques led to an early fascination with seemingly spectral figures in landscape and architectural photographs, but spirit photography proper did not enter the trade in shadows until modern Spiritualism emerged on the American scene in 1848 and did not become a national sensation until the 1860s when new techniques made studio photography far more accessible and popular than it had ever before been. Over the course of the 1850s, American newspapers were increasingly filled with stories of séances and spirit communications, from the humble parlor to the lavish public hall. The spread of Spiritualism was, not surprisingly, met with skepticism. In an 1856 treatise on stereographs, the famous British scientist David Brewster— who had invented the kaleidoscope earlier in his career—included instructions for photographers to "give a spiritual appearance to one or more of his figures" in a chapter on "amusement." A decade later the American entertainment giant Phineas Taylor Barnum included a chapter on "Spirit Photography" in his famous catalogue of "humbugs." But whereas skeptics like Brewster and Barnum profited from revealing spirit pictures as amusement or humbug, thousands of Americans found something reassuring in the possibility of proving the soul's existence after death.

The emergence of spirit photography was at the intersection of 19th-century American religion and scientific curiosity. The telegraph, the steam-powered locomotive, and newspapers collapsed time and space, bringing people into nearly instantaneous communication. Spirit photography's success traded just as much on rising confidence in empirical method as it did on belief in spirits or affiliation with the religious movement of Spiritualism. Far from being a radical departure from mainstream culture, moreover, spirit pictures shared quite a bit with memorial photography in general, which became an industry in itself during the mid-19th-century's decades of high infant mortality, war, unregulated industry, population concentration, and medicinal hackery. Given this convergence of circumstances—religious reform, scientific advancement, technological progress, demographic upheaval—there is little historical utility in debating whether spirit photographs were real or fake, proof or deception. The better question to ask is: why were 19th-century Americans so invested in convincing each other of the truth or falsehood of spirits, and why was photography so instrumental in this debate?

Modern spiritualism and photography share not only a coincidence of generation in the 1840s but also a common promise: they each promised access to what
the unassisted faculties of sight precluded. Spiritualists contended that conventional measures of presence—namely, sight—were challenged by other forms of
evidence at the same time that photographic technologies magnified microorgan-
isms and captured the surface of the moon, among other things—begging the
question, if all of these tiny organisms and celestial bodies existed all along, and we
simply lacked the ability to perceive or scrutinize them, what is so different about
spirits? The notion that photography provided "evidences of a future existence," as
the spirit photographer William Mumler put it in his 1875 memoir, was a powerful
idea and not one so easily sequestered to the margins of 19th-century American society. In fact, even at the end of the century, Spiritualism's defenders were still making strong associations between the empirical conceit of photography and, as one
such defender put it, the "most momentous [question] ever asked, viz. 'If a man die
shall he live again?'" For this particular commentator, spirit photographs answered
this question triumphantly, concluding that "every true scientist and philosopher
and every Christian ought to rejoice that science and art have now so wonderfully
combined to demonstrate objectively the fundamental claim of all religions, that
man has a substantial existence after so-called death" (Clarke 1894, 859).

This was no rhetorical flourish. The majority of spirits who appeared in studio
portraits from the 1860s through the end of the century were deceased family
members—mothers, wives, fathers, husbands, children—although Alvin Adams,
the famous courier, was delighted when none other than Daniel Webster appeared
on his plate. Familiar spirits were far more common, however, and often appeared
in poses cradling the sitter. When one Mrs. Hubbard came to Mumler for a like-
ness, she "mentally requested that her little boy would show himself as he used to
while saying his prayers." When the negative was developed, the image revealed
"the boy's form . . . standing in front of her, and resting his head on her breast."
Dr. William Edwards, of Washington, D.C., reported having "obtained likenesses
of nearly all the members of his family who have passed to the spirit-life, which
he fully and unmistakably recognized." For countless Americans, spirit pictures
provided "satisfactory evidences of immortality" (Mumler 2008, 74, 88, 89, 124).

It is worth lingering briefly on the question of evidence. Well before the invention of photography, American audiences had delighted in the visual trickery
of optical marvels such as magic lanterns, thaumatropes, and kaleidoscopes. The
popularity of spirit photographs did not indicate gullibility. On the contrary, they
evoked the slipperiness between what cameras recorded and what beholders perceived. The notion that photographs provided religious evidence was voiced in
an address to the Auxiliary Congress of Photographers at the World's Columbian
Exposition when the Methodist minister Amos William Patten spoke about "The
Camera and the Pulpit." In his paper, Patten spoke of the camera as a "servant of
God" made "to render vivid and clear spiritual truth." In all, he recognized five
uses of the camera in American churches, each of them instructional and each

of them built upon a presumption of direct correspondence between empirical referent and the resulting photographic image (Stead 1893, 429). In other words, confidence was based on the idea that the camera doesn't lie. Photographs were religious evidence.

This confidence was less apparent when William Mumler was tried for defrauding the public in 1869. On the one hand, the empirical conceit of photography lent the authority of evidence to Mumler's defense. But the trial quickly turned from a narrow focus on ghost pictures to an interrogation of spiritualism broadly, at which point the Bible itself was entered as a catalog of spectral events. To substantiate their case in an idiom common to many Americans, Mumler's defense entered a litany of scriptural references to spirits and into court as evidence, asking "would there be anything remarkable if photography had been introduced and had taken the image" of these appearances? In response, Elbridge T. Gerry, the prosecutor in Mumler's case, proceeded to exegete the references as evidence of the contrary, that is, to argue that spectral events in the Bible were fundamentally different from the claims made through Mumler's photographs. The point here is that even if both Spiritualism and photography each promised access to what the unassisted senses could not perceive, there was still a great deal of disagreement about what that access disclosed.

A comprehensive treatment of spirit photography would follow the threads of technology and religion into ectoplasmic phenomena, Polaroid apparitions, and other 20th-century developments. And yet all forms of spirit photography play on the central premise of evidence of things unseen. The camera, like the telegraph, provided a scientific vehicle of communion with departed spirits and, for many, produced a physical relic that limned the continuity of life after death. Rather than approaching spirit pictures as fringe religion or intentional deception, it is far more constructive to approach them as an intersection of technology and religion that provides insight on the development and experience of 19th-century American religion.

Rachel McBride Lindsey

See also: Kirlian Photography; Séance; Spiritualism; Thoughtography

Further Reading

Braude, Ann. 2001. *Radical Spirits: Spiritualism and Women's Rights in Nineteenth-Century America*. 2nd ed. Bloomington, IN: Indiana University Press.

Carroll, Bret E. 1997. *Spiritualism in Antebellum America* Bloomington, IN: Indiana University Press.

Chéroux, Clément, Andreas Fischer, Pierre Apraxine, Denis Canguilhem, and Sophie Schmit, with contributions by Crista Cloutier, and Stephen E. Braude. 2005. *The Perfect Medium: Photography and the Occult*. New Haven, CT and London: Yale University Press.

Clarke, Dean. 1893. "Spirit Photography." *The Californian Illustrated Magazine* 4 (November): 851–859.

Ferris, Alison, Tom Gunning, and Pamela Thurschwell. 2003. *The Disembodied Spirit.* Brunswick, ME: Bowdoin College Museum of Art.

Gettings, Fred. 1978. *Ghosts in Photographs: The Extraordinary Story of Spirit Photography.* New York: Harmony Book.

Harvey, John. 2007. *Photography and Spirit.* London: Reaktion Books.

Jolly, Martyn. 2006. *Faces of the Living Dead: The Belief in Spirit Photography.* West New York, NJ: Mark Batty Publisher.

Kaplan, Louis. 2008. *The Strange Case of William Mumler, Spirit Photographer.* Minneapolis: University of Minnesota Press.

McGarry, Molly. 2008. *Ghosts of Futures Past: Spiritualism and the Cultural Politics of Nineteenth-Century America.* Berkeley, CA: University of California Press.

Mumler, William H. (1875) 2008. *The Personal Experiences of William H. Mumler in Spirit Photography.* Reprinted in *The Strange Case of William Mumler, Spirit Photography* by Louis Kaplan, 69–139. Minneapolis: University of Minnesota Press.

Stead, William T. 1893. "The Lantern and the Pulpit: An Encouraging Report from America." *Review of Reviews* 8 (July–December): 429.

SPIRITISM

Spiritism refers to the belief in discarnate spirits and the practice of communicating with these spirits for healing and spiritual evolution. Spiritism emerged out of the Spiritualist movement in mid-19th century France. Begun by physician and writer Hippolyte Leon Denizard Rivail (1804–1869), who took the pseudonym Allan Kardec, Spiritism is also known as Kardecism or Kardecismo in Brazil.

Born in Lyon, France, Rivail received degrees in science, letters, and medicine in Switzerland, where he worked with Johann Heinrich Pestalozzi (1746–1827) on educational models for teaching in France and Germany. By the early 1850s he had become interested in the theory of "animal magnetism" offered by Franz Anton Mesmer (1734–1815) and the spiritualist movement, popular in France and the United States, which involved the movement of material objects by spirit forces in response to questions.

In 1855, Rivail began to attend spiritualist séances, in which he communicated, through mediums (or magnetized somnambules), with a collection of entities that called themselves "the Spirit of Truth." Although not a medium himself, he was determined to discover the truths and purpose of human existence. Rivail accepted Spiritualist beliefs that individual souls live on after the death of the body and that these souls or spirits communicate with living persons, usually through intermediaries such as mediums or channelers, but Rivail's teaching was more philosophical and intellectual than Spiritualist teachings. In contrast to the informality of Spiritualist beliefs and practices, Rivail constructed a formal doctrine and philosophy to explain life after death, a soul's progress across lives to ultimate perfection, and communication across planes of existence, all with the purpose of spiritual teaching and physical healing. His doctrinal approach integrated beliefs in reincarnation and karma (which are not essential to Spiritualist beliefs) into requirements for a moral and ethical life in an effort to unite science and religion into a rational system. According to Rivail, science and religion will understand each other only when science resists its exclusively materialist worldview and recognizes the spiritual element that underlies all of creation and when religion recognizes the organic laws of the material world. Contradictions between religion and science will cease and a higher reason will emerge. Spiritism provides the link between the material world and the world of spirits and, with this link, lays a foundation for a new era, a "new age."

The Spirits' Book, published in 1857 under Rivail's pseudonym Allan Kardec, is the groundbreaking work that outlines the principles of spiritist doctrine: the immortality of the soul; the nature of spirits and their relationships with humankind; moral laws; the present life, the future life, and the destiny of humanity; the provenance of the teachings, which are received through mediums from highly evolved spirits; and the universal laws that govern bodily as well as spiritual existence. As the first of five texts authored by Kardec that constitute the "Spiritist Codification," *The Spirits' Book* was followed by *The Medium's Book*, *The Gospel According to Spiritism*, *Heaven and Hell*, and *The Genesis According to Spiritism*.

Kardec's philosophy of human existence relies upon the doctrine of reincarnation that posits multiple lives for each soul, so that ultimately each learns from past mistakes and achieves a more perfected being, cyclically, until it is prepared for a higher plane of existence. All souls are created equal and endowed with free will, but without the understanding of how to progress to higher levels. With multiple incarnations, they learn the universal moral lessons of compassion, love, and forgiveness. When these lessons are learned, their souls rise to ever-higher levels of existence.

According to Kardec, all incarnate humans are made up of three entities: a physical body, an immaterial soul, and a perispirit, which is a semi-material substance that unites body and soul. Among living persons, the perispirit constitutes the "vital fluid" that enlivens the body. Among the dead, the perispirit constitutes a connection between the soul and physical reality, so that a disembodied spirit can produce tangible phenomena. The perispirit acts through mediums to allow spirits to move objects in séances, produce automatic writing, and affect the energy fields of incarnate humans. Thus, disembodied spirits act through the intervention of well-trained mediums to teach and to heal embodied persons. Kardec felt that he was expanding the definition of human physiology to include previously deemed supernatural phenomena in an inclusive understanding of material manifestation, which is properly studied through the scientific method. Communication with spirits and mediumship are to be investigated through the positivist paradigm as objective documentations, not merely subjective impressions. In this way, he claimed to integrate science and religion.

Certain illnesses, according to Kardec, have spiritual causes. Especially epilepsy, schizophrenia, and multiple personality disorder can be treated psychically through the intervention of mediums, who offer insights from spirit guides.

Through communication by mediums with spirits, disease in this life can be discerned as a product of problems in the current life, or previous lives, of the patient. As part of his doctrine of reincarnation, Kardec stressed the existence of "subsystems" of karma that are brought with each soul into any incarnation, which may be stronger in determining the trajectory of a life than any forces of current life.

Despite opposition from the Roman Catholic Church in both Europe and Brazil, Kardecism enjoyed an early acceptance by educated and wealthy classes. In Europe since the days of Mesmer, influential and distinguished clients had sought and received healing through heterodox treatments, including animal magnetism and mediumistic teaching.

Spiritist groups remain stable in major cities throughout France, and Kardec's books have never gone out of print since the 19th century. In Brazil, where it was introduced in the early 1870s, Spiritism almost saturates the society, with more than 7,000 centers operating today. Although the organization of Spiritist centers varies by location, they all agree with Kardec's doctrine and offer the same services to all who attend: meditation, prayer services, energy healing through mediumship, psychic surgery, study of Spiritist doctrine, and charitable work. An atmosphere of democracy infuses all Spiritist centers, as no official clergy administers the centers, and all individuals are considered mediums in some stage of development. Importantly, all services are available and free to all. Spiritist centers welcome members of any religion and incorporate elements of African, shamanic, and Christian beliefs and practices, depending upon location. One does not have to give up membership in any religious group to participate in the services of a Spiritist center. In this way, Spiritist centers function as alternative health organizations, interfaith religious centers, and schools for study.

Constance A. Jones

See also: Mediumship; Mesmerism; Possession; Reincarnation; Religion and the Paranormal; Spiritualism; Survival after Death

Further Reading

Bragdon, Emma. 2004. *Kardec's Spiritism: A Home for Healing and Spiritual Evolution.* Woodstock, VT: Lightening Up Press.

Hanegraaff, Wouter J., ed. 2006. *Dictionary of Gnosis and Western Esotericism.* Leiden, NL: Brill.

Hess, David J. 1994. *Samba in the Night: Spiritism in Brazil.* New York: Columbia University Press.

Hess, David J. 1991. *Spiritists and Scientists: Ideology, Spiritism, and Brazilian Culture.* University Park, PA: Pennsylvania University Press.

Kardec, Allan. 2006. *Heaven and Hell.* 2nd ed. Translated by Darrel W. Kimble, and Marcia M. Saiz. Brazilia, BR: International Spiritist Council.

Kardec, Allan. 2009. *The Medium's Book.* 3rd ed. Translated by Darrell W. Kimble, and Marcia M. Saiz. Brazilia, BR: International Spiritist Council.

Kardec, Allan. 2006. *The Spirit's Book.* 3rd ed. Translated by Darrel W. Kimble, and Marcia M. Saiz. Brazilia, BR: International Spiritist Council.
Monroe, John Warne. 2008. *Laboratories of Faith: Mesmerism, Spiritism, and Occultism in Modern France.* Ithaca, NY: Cornell University Press.
Wyckoff, James. 1975. *Franz Anton Mesmer: Between God and Devil.* Englewood Cliffs, NJ: Prentice-Hall.

SPIRITUALISM

Spiritualism is the name given to a Western religious and philosophical tradition that uses mediumship to communicate with the souls or spirits of the dead. Spiritualism is best understood as a tradition or movement employing a range of particular practices, within which there are many organizations and many independent churches or other centers. Some Spiritualists regard Spiritualism as a science rather than a religion, leading to a complex relationship with traditional forms of Christianity, the Western scientific tradition, and psychical researchers.

The Spiritualist movement commonly traces its origins to 1840s America and the psychic phenomena (rappings and knockings) reported in 1848 in connection with the Fox sisters and their family home in Hydesville, New York. These were interpreted as spirit communications, which quickly became a major news phenomenon, and prompted others to explore the possibility of similar communications being achieved by other mediums. The public demonstrations and careers of the Fox sisters led the way for other professional mediums, and many small groups were set up by those wanting to explore the possibility of spirit communication in private.

Through the 1850s and 1860s, a growing number of professional mediums spread awareness of mediumship in America and visited Great Britain, as well as other European countries such as France, Germany, Italy, and Russia. Many early Spiritualists were enthusiastic about the possibility of a new revelation, enabling the verification or correction of traditional Christian teachings. Why Spiritualism became so popular so quickly is still a question that is debated, but it is likely that early Shaker groups from the 1830s and 1840s had already created familiarity with the idea that certain individuals could be impressed or possessed by the Holy Spirit in certain ways. The Spiritualist tradition of native North American spirit guides speaking through mediums is almost certainly derived from Shaker practices.

The purpose of most Spiritualist groups was to explore possible ways of communicating with the souls or spirits of deceased humans, both to seek guidance for the living, and as a way to demonstrate personal survival beyond death. The range of practices developed includes astral travel, clairvoyance, channeling (or trance mediumship), inspired or automatic writing (also painting or drawing of deceased persons by mediums they were unknown to), materialization of spirits using a substance called ectoplasm drawn from the body of the medium, transfiguration (where the image of a spirit is visibly superimposed on the body of the medium), psychom-

A Brief Timeline of Early Spiritualism

1848   The Hydesville knockings in New York give birth to modern Spiritualism when the young Fox sisters claim to have received communication from a spirit.

1849   The first public demonstration of mediumship is given by Margareta Fox in the Corinthian Hall in Rochester, New York.

1850s–1860s Professional mediums spread across America, Britain, and Europe. American newspapers are filled with stories of séances and spirit communications.

1863   Andrew Jackson Davis establishes the Lyceum movement in New York, with explicitly Spiritualist aims.

1873   The British National Association of Spiritualists is founded in London.

1893   The National Spiritualists' Association is founded in America.

1884–1885   The Society for Psychical Research subjects the mediumship of Leonora Piper to scientific scrutiny.

1918   Sir Arthur Conan Doyle publicly announces his belief in Spiritualism.

1923   The International Spiritualists' Federation is formed.

etry, and the use of trumpets or other devices to amplify spirit voices. Devices such as Ouija boards and planchettes (on which the hand of the medium rests, rather than writing directly) were also employed. The other significant feature of traditional Spiritualist practice is the giving of channeling of spiritual healing through a medium, a feature Spiritualism shares with a number of other Protestant traditions.

Spiritualist churches and other groups came to function not only as ways to explore these phenomena but also as ways to transmit accumulated knowledge to succeeding generations, with the development of various conventions surrounding a process of apprenticeship (known as development); in this way, Spiritualism matured from a new phenomenon into a continuing tradition. The apprenticeship of mediums is traditionally extended, in some cases lasting over decades rather than years, before proficiency as a medium is communally recognized. Further, mediums are often said to continue developing throughout their working careers as they become practiced at additional forms of mediumship.

The format of public demonstrations of mediumship was often adopted from nonconformist forms of Protestant Christianity; for example, many Methodist hymns can still be found in Spiritualist churches. Over time, many Spiritualist groups organized themselves into churches, some of which came together in regional or national organizations, such as the National Association of Spiritualist Churches in the United States. The two organizations of note in the history of British Spiritualism are The Greater World Christian Spiritualist Association and the Spiritualists' National Union, which has affiliated churches internationally and remains the world's largest Spiritualist organization.

Organizationally, Spiritualism is often described as weak, as it has never developed one, or even a few, bodies to which most Spiritualist groups belong. Many Spiritualist groups prefer to remain independent so as to avoid adherence to any particular theology or other set of teachings; the freedom to express spirit spontaneously has been highly valued both by Spiritualist groups and individual mediums. Against this, a degree of coherence was achieved by adopting, from 19th-century Methodism, the practice of having visiting speakers serving a circuit of churches; this led to a uniformity of approach, which was further reinforced by the Spiritualist apprenticeship.

In the United States, the disruption caused by the Civil War interrupted the processes that might have led to a more established tradition; many commentators have noted that although U.S. Spiritualism was hugely popular in its early years, this enthusiasm was not sustained. Similarly, in many European countries, Spiritualism often gives the impression of a pursuit that was fashionable during the 1860s and 1870s, but it did not go on to fulfil its early promise. The two countries where Spiritualism found particularly fertile soil are, from the 1860s, Great Britain and, from around 1900, Iceland. In both countries, Spiritualism appears to have tapped into stable but complex societies with religious and scientific traditions, which also contained older folklore involving ghosts and nature spirits; these combined to give Spiritualism an unexpected relevance in the modern era.

Although American Spiritualism did not become as well established as its British counterpart, it still managed to achieve a significant degree of popularity into the 1940s, and Spiritualist ideas exerted a significant influence in American literature and political thought. Spiritualists were often associated with radical social agendas, including anti-slavery campaigns, female emancipation, and Prohibition. Victoria Woodhull, for example, who became the first female candidate for president of the United States in 1872, was simultaneously a suffragette, a free love advocate, and a Spiritualist medium. Today Spiritualists often continue to be interested in a variety of other subjects, such as divination or fortune-telling, astrology, numerology, reincarnation, herbal lore, and unidentified flying objects, often making it difficult to distinguish between Spiritualism and New Age interests.

Spiritualism in Great Britain enjoyed particular periods of popularity in the aftermaths of the two World Wars, with memberships of Spiritualist churches reaching a 20th century peak in the 1950s; individual memberships of the Spiritualists' National Union peaked in the 1960s, even although the number of affiliated churches began to decline.

British Spiritualism (as compared with American Spiritualism) is often said to be more focused on the use of mediumship to communicate with known (deceased) individuals as a way of demonstrating personal survival. More empirical research is needed to sustain this claimed difference, but it enjoys a degree of anecdotal support and is mentioned in academic writing. This may indicate a more traditionally religious tone to British Spiritualism, although in recent years, many British Spiritualist groups have also moved away from traditional Christian language in favor of a dialogue that expresses expectations of overt rationality characteristic of Western scientific tradition.

The social space occupied by Spiritualism has always been contested, as the movement has always been susceptible to allegations of superstition, irrationality, and/or irreligiosity, according to the standpoint of the opponent. The lack of a common set of teachings can give the impression of confusion within the movement, which has also long been marked in both Britain and America by a division between those churches wishing to maintain a clearly Christian identity and those preferring a more secular one.

It has been suggested that Spiritualism is Western culture's traditional form of shamanism but that it now struggles because of the traditional Christian language in which it is expressed in addition to continuing opposition from other Christian churches.

On both sides of the Atlantic, the history of the movement in recent decades is largely a narrative of decline, though not entirely. In America, two long-standing Spiritualist communities continue to thrive at Lily Dale, New York, and at Cassadaga, Florida. In Britain, the Spiritualists' National Union maintains a residential teaching college at Stansted, near London and has recently established a number of regional teaching centers across the rest of the country. Since the 1960s, Christian Spiritualist churches in Britain have declined much more rapidly than others. Spiritualist churches continue in countries sharing Anglo-American culture such as Canada, South Africa, Australia, and New Zealand; a small number of churches continue to operate in Nigeria and India.

A limited amount of academic writing about Spiritualism was produced in the late 1960s and early 1970s and remains valuable; a renewed level of interest is evident from around 2000, although a comprehensive history of the movement is yet to be written. Geoffrey Nelson's work from 1969 remains the most comprehensive account of the Spiritualist movement as a whole.

David Gordon Wilson

See also: Automatic Writing; Channeling; Clairvoyance; Fox Sisters, The; Ghosts; Healing, Psychic and Spiritual; Lily Dale Assembly; Mediumship; New Age; Ouija Board; Out-of-Body Experience (OBE); Psychical Research; Religion and the Paranormal; Séance; Shamanism; Spirit Photography; Survival after Death; Theosophy

Further Reading

Bennet, Bridget. 2005. "Sacred Theatres: Shakers, Spiritualists, Theatricality, and the Indian in the 1830s and 1840s." *The Drama Review* 49 (3): 114–34.

Blum, Deborah. 2007. *The Ghost Hunters: The Victorians and the Hunt for Proof of Life after Death*. London: Arrow Books.

Braude, Ann. (1989) 2001. *Radical Spirits: Spiritualism and Women's Rights in Nineteenth-Century America*. 2nd ed. Bloomington, IN: Indiana University Press.

Gutierrez, Cathy. 2009. *Plato's Ghost: Spiritualism in the American Renaissance*. Oxford, UK: Oxford University Press.

Hazelgrove, Jenny. 2000. *Spiritualism and British Society between the Wars*. Manchester, UK: Manchester University Press.

Nelson, Geoffrey K. 1969. *Spiritualism and Society*. London: Routledge.

Owen, Alex. 1989. *The Darkened Room: Women, Power and Spiritualism in Late Victorian Britain*. Chicago: Chicago University Press.

Skultans, Vieda. 1974. *Intimacy and Ritual: A Study of Spiritualism, Mediums and Groups*. London: Routledge.

Wilson, David Gordon. 2013. *Redefining Shamanisms: Spiritualist Mediums and Other Traditional Shamans as Apprenticeship Outcomes*. London and New York: Bloomsbury.

STANFORD RESEARCH INSTITUTE

The Stanford Research Institute (SRI), now SRI International, is an independent California-based research institution that for nearly 20 years was the site of U.S. government experiments in remote viewing, or clairvoyance. The remote viewing program began 1972 under the leadership of physicists Harold Puthoff and Russell Targ, who in 1977 published a book, *Mind-Reach*, outlining the supposed positive results of their experiments. The remote viewing program, which moved to Science Applications International Corporation in 1991, was controversial within SRI International and was frequently under threat of loss of organizational support. The project was canceled and many of its documents made public in 1995.

The Stanford Research Institute was founded by Stanford University in 1946. In 1970, Stanford Research Institute separated from the university, becoming SRI International in 1977. SRI supports research in fields as varied as electron microscopy, solar energy, and computer science. Inventions at SRI have included the computer mouse, the Apple voice assistant Siri, and Technicolor. In 1969, SRI was the recipient of the first Internet message, transmitted from UCLA.

During the 1970s, SRI scientists Puthoff and Targ began receiving piecemeal funding from U.S. intelligence and defense agencies to investigate remote viewing. The Soviet Union had allegedly been pursuing research in psychic spying, leaving American intelligence organizations nervous that the Soviets could develop clairvoyant spy capabilities. Because of the stigmas associated with psychic research, the CIA sought a nonacademic site where such research could be carried out with a low profile. Following the suggestion of well-known psychic Ingo Swann—who later became one of the project's primary subjects—the CIA contacted Puthoff and Targ at SRI.

Funding under the CIA began in 1972, using the term "remote viewing" to avoid the lurid connotations of such words as clairvoyance or telepathy. The project tested numerous subjects to determine whether, using introspection, they could gather enough information about distant locations to generate identifiable descriptions. In 1975, the project was taken over by the Air Force, then the Army in 1977. Finally, the Defense Intelligence Agency (DIA) consolidated all remote viewing projects in the 1980s, eventually assigning the project its most famous code name, STAR GATE.

SRI projects used different methodologies to test subjects' supposed remote viewing capabilities. Many experiments used a variation on a protocol in which a target experimenter was given a randomly selected location in the San Francisco Bay Area, which he or she then drove to and observed. The remote viewing subject, in an isolated room, then attempted to intuit the target's location, recording impressions, images, and sketches. Later, transcripts of subjects' reports and their drawings would be given to third-party judges, who would attempt to match each report with its supposed target. In their book and in papers published in *Nature* and other journals, Puthoff and Targ claimed that the number of correct matches exceeded chance expectations, proving that remote viewing could statistically be successful.

Criticisms of the SRI program have been widespread. In a rejoinder to Targ and Puthoff's 1974 *Nature* article, other researchers pointed out that transcripts often included time-sensitive cues that could allow judges to match subjects' descriptions to the target locations based solely on the order in which the experiments were carried out. The skeptic James Randi accused Puthoff and Targ of deliberate fraud, scientific ineptitude, and bullying of laboratory assistants and subjects. In the 1990s, a CIA-commissioned study to evaluate the success of the remote-viewing program concluded that the project had no intelligence value and recommended its closure.

Puthoff, Targ, and other remote viewing researchers continue to argue that SRI experiments were successful. They claim that remote viewing is a legitimate, if often unreliable, human capacity that can be improved with effort. Puthoff, Targ, and many of their former subjects argue that remote viewers had better success with sensory aspects of their targets than with analytical or verbal descriptions, and that subjects can become desensitized by monotonous experiments. Skeptics cite such claims as evidence that remote viewing simply does not work. As of mid-2015, there is no mention of remote viewing research on SRI International's website.

Connor Wood

See also: Clairvoyance; Extrasensory Perception (ESP); Koestler Parapsychology Unit; Princeton Engineering Anomalies Research; Pseudoscience; Randi, James; Remote Viewing; Rhine Research Center

Further Reading

McMoneagle, Joseph. 2000. *Remote Viewing Secrets: A Handbook*. Charlottesville, VA: Hampton Roads Publishing Company.

Randi, James. 1982. *Flim-Flam: Psychics, ESP, Unicorns and Other Delusions*. Amherst, MA: Prometheus Books, 1982.

Ronson, Jon. 2004. *The Men Who Stare at Goats*. New York: Simon & Schuster.

Schnabel, Jim. 1997. *Remote Viewers: The Secret History of America's Psychic Spies*. New York: Dell.

SRI International. "About Us." Last modified 2014. http://www.sri.com/about.

Targ, Russell, and Harold Puthoff. 2005. *Mind-Reach: Scientists Look at Psychic Abilities*. Charlottesville, VA: Hampton Roads Publishing Company.

STEVENSON, IAN

Ian Stevenson (1918–2007) was an American psychiatrist and psychical researcher best known for his studies of children who remember previous lives, but he conducted investigations in many areas of parapsychology. He spent the latter part of his career at the University of Virginia Medical Center, where from 1964 until his retirement in 2001 he was Carlson Professor of Psychiatry. After retirement until the end of his life, he remained attached to UVA as Research Professor of Psychiatry.

Stevenson was born in Montreal, Quebec, on October 31, 1918, and died in Charlottesville, Virginia, on February 8, 2007. He studied history at the University of St. Andrews, Scotland, but decided to pursue medicine instead and enrolled at McGill University in Montreal. He received his MD degree from McGill in 1943 and held a succession of positions in the United States before being appointed chairman of the department of psychiatry at the University of Virginia in 1957, when he was 39.

By the time he reached UVA, Stevenson had made significant contributions in several areas. At the start of his medical career he did experiments on the oxidation of rat kidneys, an experience that turned him against reductionism. He moved into psychosomatic medicine, but when that field failed to develop into a regular specialty, he took up psychiatry. However, the field psychiatry was then (in the 1950s) dominated by psychoanalysis, which was not to his liking. He began to read extensively in parapsychology, finding in that field a more congenial approach to the human experience, and so he changed direction once again.

Stevenson's earliest parapsychological studies were on precognitive dreams and telepathic impressions, and it was almost by happenstance that he came to specialize in reincarnation. He began collecting accounts of people (mostly children) who claimed to recall having lived before and in 1960 published a paper reporting 44 cases in which the deceased person spoken about had been identified. His paper attracted wide attention and led to his receiving funds to investigate new cases in the field. This research resulted in his best-known book, *Twenty Cases Suggestive of Reincarnation*, first published in 1966, with an updated second edition in 1974.

Stevenson's most important financial backer was Chester Carlson, the multi-millionaire inventor of the xerographic process. Carlson's support made *Twenty Cases* possible, but it did not end with *Twenty Cases*. In 1964, Carlson endowed the chair for Stevenson at UVA, and when he died in 1968, he left the university a $1,000,000 bequest in furtherance of Stevenson's work. Stevenson did not disappoint him. Between 1975 and 1983, he produced another four volumes of case reports under the general heading, Cases of the Reincarnation Type. These cases came from India, Sri Lanka, Burma, Thailand, Lebanon, and Turkey, but Stevenson studied cases in Western countries also, leading in 2003 to *European Cases of the Reincarnation Type*. Stevenson was especially intrigued by cases with physical anomalies, the subject of what many regard as his most important work, the massive two-volume, 2,268-page *Reincarnation and Biology*, which appeared in 1997. He summarized his reincarnation research in *Children Who Remember Previous Lives* in 1987, reissued in a revised edition in 2001. His many journal papers include studies of mediums, apparitions, poltergeists, and other phenomena, in addition to the reincarnation cases.

Stevenson never claimed to have proved that reincarnation occurs, only that the evidence he had collected supported belief in it. Nonetheless, his research was highly controversial, in parapsychology as well as outside it. Stevenson had identified a type of spontaneous case that had received little attention before him, and there was great skepticism about it. Gradually, as other investigators began to report similar cases, attitudes began to change, and today reincarnation is an accepted area of study within parapsychology. It also has gained respect outside that field. Astronomer and science writer Carl Sagan, a long-time critic of paranormal claims, wrote in 1997 that he regarded reincarnation research as one of the three most promising areas of parapsychology, the others being in the experimental domain.

Stevenson died of pneumonia on February 8, 2007.

James G. Matlock

See also: Reincarnation; Survival after Death

Further Reading

Kelly, Emily Williams, ed. 2013. *Science, the Self, and Survival after Death: Selected Writings of Ian Stevenson*. Lanham, MD: Rowman and Littlefield.
Matlock, James G. 2011. "Ian Stevenson's *Twenty Cases Suggestive of Reincarnation*: An Historical Review and Assessment." *Journal of Scientific Exploration* 25: 789–820.

STRIEBER, WHITLEY

Whitley Strieber (born 1945) is best known for 1987's *Communion*, which was instrumental in bringing the "alien abduction" narrative into popular culture. Over his career, however, the extraterrestrial aspects of his work have become progressively less emphasized, replaced by a more paranormal and spiritual interpretation. Strieber is typical of a move away from the "nuts and bolts" explanation of the

UFO due to the increasingly evident realities of space travel and the impossibility of faster-than-light travel. Influenced by Jacques Vallée, Strieber has argued that abductions are identical with supernatural encounters in earlier eras, but interpreted in a way that better suits a modern scientific framework.

Strieber was already a successful horror novelist with several books to his credit when his first nonfiction work, *Communion* (1987), became a *New York Times* #1 best seller and perhaps the most successful nonfiction UFO book in publishing history. It recounts that late at night on December 26th, 1985, Strieber woke while being taken from his bedroom by a group of identical squat, blue beings. They took him to a brightly lit room where he encountered other beings, which were willowy, short, and large-eyed. The book's cover image portraying one of these beings likely influenced the popularity of the now-ubiquitous image of the "gray" alien.

According to *Communion*, probes were inserted into Strieber's brain and anus, and he awoke with a sense of unease. After becoming withdrawn and hypersensitive in the weeks that followed, he made contact with UFO artist, writer, and researcher Budd Hopkins, who suggested that they could recover more of Strieber's memories through hypnosis. With Hopkins' help, Strieber began to recall multiple abductions stretching back into his early childhood. Despite doubts being raised about the provenance of the tales, Strieber eventually received many thousands of letters from members of the public describing their own experiences with seemingly sinister extraterrestrials (selections of which were published as 1997's *The Communion Letters*). These accounts are frequently and puzzlingly idiosyncratic, a tendency known in UFOlogy as "high strangeness."

The latter third of *Communion* is a meditation as to the possible nature of what Strieber calls "the visitors." He suggests five possibilities: that they are extraterrestrials, time-travelers, fairies, the dead, or the human collective unconsciousness. This latter section shows Strieber's engagement with religious, philosophical, and mythological ideas and recalls many tropes and themes of mystical texts with its language of transformation and "higher consciousness" (Strieber 1987, 280). Although raised Catholic, Strieber had become disenfranchised, and he had a 15-year association with the Gurdjieff Institute, involvement with Wicca, and an ongoing interest in meditation and the Tarot.

In later works, Strieber became convinced that the visitors' ultimate aims were benevolent, appearances notwithstanding. *Breakthrough* (1995) contains an astonishing sequence describing a visitor that meditated with Strieber every evening for a period of months, although Strieber was apparently unable to photograph it. *The Secret School* (1996) elaborates upon Strieber's recovered childhood experiences with the visitors, recounting his nocturnal involvement in what he describes as a kind of school in 1954, aged nine. He now claims that the experience may be universal, but only rarely remembered. He also stresses a connection between the visitors and the dead and suggests that the Earth is a school in which humans are students, the visitors are teachers, and the dead are graduates. In this framing, the visitors are no longer constructed as extraterrestrial but as a misunderstood, hidden agency in the natural world. Strieber interprets all UFO, religious, and paranormal experiences as having a common source in the visitors.

Strieber also has an interest in conspiracy theories, again coming initially through UFOs, and the alleged governmental cover-up of a UFO crash near Roswell, New Mexico, in 1947. In 1999, Strieber and *Coast to Coast AM* host Art Bell collaborated on *The Coming Global Superstorm*, a work of "speculative nonfiction" that described rapid and dramatic climatic change and that later became the basis of the 2004 disaster movie *The Day After Tomorrow*. In 1999, Strieber took over *Coast to Coast AM*'s sister show, *Dreamland*, which had a greater emphasis on extraterrestrials and spirituality. The show is still broadcast weekly through Strieber's website, unknowncountry.com.

David G. Robertson

See also: Abduction Experience; Discarnate Entity; Meditation; Paranormal in Movies; Religion and the Paranormal; Tarot; UFO; Vallée, Jacques

Further Reading

Kripal, J. 2011. *Mutants and Mystics: Science Fiction, Superhero Comics, and the Paranormal.* Chicago: University of Chicago Press.
Robertson, David G. 2014. "Transformation: Whitley Strieber's Paranormal Gnosis." *Nova Religio* 18 (1): 58–78.
Strieber, W. 1987. *Communion.* New York: Morrow.

SURVIVAL AFTER DEATH

Human beings have buried their dead for at least 100,000 years, quite possibly much longer. It is assumed that burial, often with red ochre and grave goods, indicates belief in postmortem survival. The observation that the animating life force is very different from the physical vehicle of the corpse, together with dreams, apparitions, and intimations that the dead are not altogether departed, may have led very early on to the belief that death is not the end of life. If something survives death, the questions are what, and do we have any evidence? All religious traditions have an answer to this question, but so do metaphysicians and scientists.

Contemporary debates center on the origin and nature of consciousness and how this relates to matter, often characterized as a choice between consciousness seen as an emergent property of the brain and some form of dualism, with consciousness separate from the body it inhabits. The relationship between mind or consciousness and matter is far from settled. René Descartes (1596–1650) is credited with developing the Western mind/body dualism that had also occupied Classical Greek thinkers. William James (1842–1910), while not claiming to solve the problem of the relationship between mind and body, insisted that consciousness and its object should be seen as part of the same functional complex. James argued that metaphysical or religious experiences should not be ignored simply because they cannot be reduced to a material cause. Physicalism, the belief that everything we need to know can be understood by scientific means, is itself an unproven supposition. James can be seen as an exemplar of scientifically trained scholars who sought to leave open the possibility of a transcendental realm that can be studied empirically, in its effects if not directly.

Religious traditions differ in their focus, emphasizing either the individual and material aspect of human nature as in the Semitic religions (Judaism, Christianity, and Islam), or the Higher Self and immaterial nature of the soul (as in Hinduism and Buddhism). *The Egyptian Book of the Dead*, parts of which date back to around 2600 BCE, describes the newly deceased souls making a gradual separation from the physical body or *ka*, and its life force. A soul or *ba* is then judged and purified, and the heart weighed on a balance against a feather belonging to Ma'at, the goddess of justice, truth, and order. A good moral life lightens the heart, and only those whose hearts weigh less than a feather can proceed to an afterlife in the realm of the sun god. The idea of individual judgment and image of the scales features in the Semitic religions, sometimes after a period of sleep or waiting. They also have the notion that souls will be separated according to their deeds, damned if found wanting or going to a place of purgation where they can make spiritual progress before passing to a paradise or heaven in or near the presence of a supreme being. The holiest or worthiest souls might pass directly to this heavenly realm. The details and conditions that determine the destiny of the soul, and how it is constituted vary between these religions and within them. Christianity, for example, has at some times entertained the possibility of reincarnation and at other times condemned the idea.

For the Greeks the afterlife was a rather shadowy concept, although from Plato's dialogue "On the Soul" (*Phaedo*), in which Socrates discusses the nature of the afterlife before his execution, it is clear that the soul is immortal. The four proofs put forward are echoed by other scholars and religious thinkers down the centuries and can be summed up as the "cyclical argument," which states that as we alternate being awake and being asleep, so too do life and death alternate. The body decays, but the soul continues exist so as to return to life. The "recollection argument" asserts that we carry some knowledge with us at birth, implying a previous existence. The "affinity argument" posits that the soul is immortal and divine, and the body mortal and material. Someone whose life is dedicated to the pleasures of the body will carry those desires with them after death and find themselves in Hades, imprisoned by their desires, until dragged back to another corporeal incarnation. The punishment is one of cause and effect and not the intervention of a judgmental God. Those who were given over to the higher things of the mind will continue to live as a soul in the underworld (equivalent to the Semitic heaven). The "argument from the form of life" is based on the idea that everything that exists does so because there is an unchanging Form, whose nature it shares. Just as manifestations of beauty participate in the incorporeal, unchanging Form of Beauty, so the soul, which gives life to the body, participates in a Form of Life that is immortal and unchanging. The influence of the *Phaedo* can be seen in Western formulations of the body and soul, mind and matter, perfection and imperfection, mortality and immortality, that continue to occupy us today.

Hinduism and Buddhism have a rather different emphasis. The Indian Vedas teach that Brahman, the source of life, is manifest as *atman*, the divine spark in every human being. All life is a manifestation of the one entity. In Buddhism what we regard as the real world is in fact an illusion, *maya*, and the notion of an individual soul gives way to the idea of no-self, or *anatta*. We think of ourselves as individuals, but this is a false self, a bundle of dispositions and attitudes that we need to shed if we are to realize our true nature. Common to Indic religions is the notion of *karma*, the results of our thoughts and actions that we carry from one life to another, perhaps rising and falling on a scale of consciousness. Eventually a soul has experienced everything it needs and can shed the trappings of personality, breaking the cycle of transmigration from one body and form to another. The progress from life to the death of the body and journey of the soul back to another life or beyond is set out graphically in *The Tibetan Book of the Dead*. It focuses on the period of 49 days immediately following the death of the physical body, with the aim of preparing the soul for what is to come, thus easing its journey. This is broken into three stages. In the first stage of the *bardo* (the intermediate or transitional state) the soul gets used to its disembodied state and to the sense of transcendental presence and clear white light. In the second stage of the "luminous mind" the soul has to deal with its accumulated *karma*, its attachments, projections, expectations, beliefs, and fears. Many of these will appear as externalized beings, often terrifying if the soul is unprepared and unaware of their subjective nature. In the third stage the purified and enlightened soul is prepared to move on to a higher state or *nirvana* or to transition into a new incarnational form.

The European Enlightenment raised the specter of a material world explicable ultimately through reason and scientific investigation. At the same time, metaphysical teachings about alternative realities continued within the Western esoteric traditions, drawing heavily on Eastern ideas. The theosophical teacher Annie Besant (1847–1933) popularized the idea that human beings exist on different planes simultaneously. The material plane includes the physical world and the energetic or etheric. Around the physical body we possess an etheric double that transmits our life force, giving rise to phenomena such as phantom limbs. The etheric body normally dissipates shortly after death and can sometimes be seen as wraiths in churchyards as the energy disperses. The emotional, or astral, and the mental planes continue after death. Our emotions and thoughts have a material, if normally invisible, substance. Whatever we think, feel, and do in this life we will find manifest on these planes. After shedding our physical bodies we continue to exist and to work on these levels, communicating telepathically and mentally creating the world we inhabit. Ultimately these too are illusions, however solid and real they seem. Our spiritual or causal self (also referred to as our Higher Self or Buddha nature, depending on the source) coexists with these other selves, but at a certain point, almost certainly after many reincarnations, we undergo a "second death" and shed the astral body and its trappings. As communication with earth is much more limited at this point, most of what reaches us through channeled or other forms of communication comes from the astral planes. Each level is subdivided many times, and although there is a generally upward progression, individuals move at different paces and will be drawn to the vibratory level at which they feel most at ease. Annie Besant was scathing about mediumship, as the closer a spirit is to the earth plane and the less its knowledge, the easier it will find it to communicate. The majority of such communications therefore come from relatively low, ignorant spirits.

Rudolf Steiner (1861–1925), who broke away from the theosophical movement to found anthroposophy, presented a slightly different hierarchical scheme that distinguishes between the sentient soul that receives sense impressions and connects with our feelings and desires; the thinking soul, which is capable of experience and evaluation, making rational plans, and executing them; the intellectual soul, by means of which the thinker becomes convinced of the truth of his or her own thought processes; and the consciousness soul that strives for objective thinking in accord with the harmony of the world. This is the point of enlightenment at which an individual connects with something true and unchanging, eternal, and immortal. Although these processes can be seen as sequential we also inhabit these different souls, or they inhabit us, simultaneously.

Theosophy and anthroposophy promoted the idea of talented individuals with clairvoyant powers, linked to or associated with spiritually evolved teachers or "ascended masters" as a source of knowledge about the nature of this world and the immaterial planes. They remained close to the Hindu and Buddhist ideal of the guru or teacher, who may have quasi-divine attributes, to whom others attach themselves as disciples. A more democratizing version of these teachings comes in the form of Spiritualism (in North America and the UK) and Spiritism (in France and Brazil). Here it was assumed that direct and valid knowledge of the afterlife realms is accessible through various forms of mediumship. The French scientist Hippolyte Léon Denizard Rivail (1804–1869), who under the pen name Allan Kardec is regarded as the founder of Spiritism, gathered the results of numerous interviews with mediums concerning the nature of survival after death. Kardec makes a useful three-fold distinction in the ways in which we use the term "soul." It can be regarded as the principle of organic life with no existence of its own, ceasing with the life of the body. From this perspective the soul is an *effect*, not a cause. At the other end of the spectrum the soul can be seen as the principle of a universal agentive intelligence, of which each individual soul absorbs a portion. At death each soul loses its individuality, reuniting with the universal principal. The third, and commonest, idea of the soul, certainly in Western thinking, is that it is a distinct moral being, linked to but not identical with matter. Kardec points out that the conviction that the soul is distinct from the body and survives death is found as an instinctive belief in one form or another among all nations. According to this view the soul is a *cause* rather than an effect. Kardec suggests that the term "soul" in its generic form can be used to encompass all three aspects, which can be regarded as co-existing rather than exclusive: the vital principle of material life, the intelligence underlying all things, and an individual moral faculty.

Views of the soul and of survival after death display cultural and historical variations, but these can to some extent be seen as different emphases. Contemporary sources, from many thousands of accounts of post-mortem existence channeled through mediums, obtained by telepathic communication from the deceased, from inter-life hypnotic regression, from near-death and out of body experiences, or from electronic trans-communications, display consistencies with one another and with the various religious teachings outlined above. While these may not constitute absolute proof of survival after death, they suggest that there is an experiential component to these ideas.

In summary, a common core includes some or all of the following propositions: At least some part of us, some vital force that may have an individual moral component, survives the death of the body. It coexists with the material plane but at a higher frequency. It is normally invisible, like radio or gamma waves, but like these it can be picked up by a suitable receiver (a medium) or in dreams. The place to which the soul or separable component goes depends on its particular vibrational range, which in turn will depend on how spiritually evolved the individual is at death. Progress is possible in the afterlife realms, and help available if asked for. Material existence, whether envisaged as a realm of suffering or as a privileged opportunity, is like a school in which we garner experience. All souls eventually move upward toward a source of beauty and perfection, characterized by unconditional love. The life in the intermediate planes is one of work and service in a world constructed mentally and therefore not unlike the one we have left. Some people can get stuck in their own particular mental, often religious, constructions (which Robert Monroe termed "belief zones"). Our energy is separable, and while some part of us (our higher self or spirit) may remain in the spirit world, other parts, linked to a particular earth life, may continue to inhabit the lower realms, and even try to possess or become attached to the living, or to a particular place. More evolved spirits (some see these as angels; others see angels as a different class of being) try to help humans and spirits stuck at the lower levels of the astral plane. As the frequencies become finer so the beauty and light increases, souls become less individuated, and the sense of love and perfection is consolidated. At a certain point souls may choose or feel compelled to return to another earth life, until they have gathered enough experience to leave these planes for good. Some sources speak of incarnations on other material and immaterial planes. The law of the universe is one of cause and effect, rather than external judgment. Loving mercy exists because unconditional love is the mechanism by which souls are attracted to one another and to the source of existence. The higher realms and true nature of existence remain to some extent hidden from even the most enlightened souls, as there is a point beyond which we are unable to receive information while still in our earthly bodies.

For some people the notion of survival remains an unproven supposition, for others a matter of faith. Increasingly it is seen as a working hypothesis with sufficient evidence from a wide range of sources, including quantum physics and cosmology, to make its exploration a real possibility.

Fiona Bowie

See also: Angels; Apparitions; Astral Plane; Consciousness; Ghosts; Haunting; Imaginal; James, William; Myers, Frederic W. H.; Near-Death Experience (NDE); Reincarnation; Religion and the Paranormal; Spiritism; Spiritualism; Theosophy

Further Reading

Barker, Elsa. 1995. *Letters from the Afterlife: A Guide to the Other Side*. Hillsboro, OR: Beyond Words Publishing.

Besant, Annie. 1977. *The Ancient Wisdom*. Adyar, India: Theosophical Publishing House.

Borgia, Anthony. 2011. *Life in the World Unseen*. London: Two Worlds Publishing.

Bowie, Fiona. 2011. *Tales from the Afterlife*. Winchester, UK: O Books.

Cummins, Geraldine. 1967. *The Road to Immortality*. London: Psychic Press.

Findlay, Arthur. 1986. *On the Edge of the Etheric: Survival after Death Scientifically Explained*. London: Two Worlds Publishing.

Fontana, David. 2005. *Is There an Afterlife?* Winchester, UK: O Books.

Greaves, Helen. 1969. *Testimony of Light*. London: Random House.

Heath, Pamela Rae, and Jon Klimo. 2010. *Handbook to the Afterlife*. Berkeley, CA: North Atlantic Books.

Huxley, Aldous. 1990. *The Perennial Philosophy*. New York: HarperCollins.

Kagan, Annie. 2013. *The Afterlife of Billy Fingers*. Charlottesville, VA: Hampton Roads Publishing.

Kardec, Allan. 1996. *The Spirits' Book*. Translated by Anna Blackwell. Sao Paulo, Brazil: Lake - Livraria Allan Kardec Editora. www.allankardec.com/Allan_Kardec/Le_livre_des_esprits/lesp_us.pdf.

Kelly, Emily Williams, ed. 2013. *Science, the Self, and Survival after Death: Selected Writings of Ian Stevenson*. Lanham, MD: Rowman & Littlefield.

Moen, Bruce. 2005. *Afterlife Knowledge Guidebook*. Charlottesville, VA: Hampton Roads.

Monroe, Robert A. 2001. *Journeys Out of the Body*. New York: Broadway Books.

Newton, Michael. 2007. *Journey of Souls*. Woodbury, MN: Llewellyn Publications.

Ronpoche, Sogyal. 1992. *The Tibetan Book of Living and Dying*. Edited by Patrick Gaffney, and Andrew Harvey. San Francisco: HarperSanFrancisco.

Sandys, Cynthia, and Rosamond Lehmann. 1978. *The Awakening Letters: Varieties of Spiritual Experiences in the Life after Death*. Jersey, UK: Neville Spearman.

Sherwood, Jane. 1991. *Post-Mortem Journal*. Saffron Walden, Essex, UK: C. W. Daniel.

Shushan, Gregory. 2011. *Conceptions of the Afterlife in Early Civilizations*. London, New York: Bloomsbury.

Steiner, Rudolf. 2003. *Life Beyond Death: Selected Lectures*. Forest Row, UK: Rudolf Steiner Press.

Swedenborg, Emanuel. 1946. *Heaven and Its Wonders and Hell.* New York: Swedenborg Foundation. http://www.swedenborgdigitallibrary.org/contets/HH.html.

Zaleski, Carol, and Philip Zaleski, eds. 2000. *The Book of Heaven.* New York: Oxford University Press.

SWEDENBORG, EMANUEL

Emanuel Swedenborg (1688–1772) was a Swedish scientist, theologian, and mystic seer whose prolific writings on many subjects, including visionary accounts of life after death, have continued to be profoundly influential in the centuries since his death. A contemporary of Enlightenment thinkers like Sir Isaac Newton and Edmund Halley, Swedenborg spent the latter years of his life extending his scientific curiosity into the realms of the unseen, rigorously detailing an elaborate Christian cosmology revealed to him by spirits in a series of lengthy books, most famously the eight volumes of *Arcana Cœlestia* (1749–1756) and *Heaven and Hell* (1758). His teachings inspired the founding of several Christian denominations during the 19th century, some of which, including the Swedenborgian Church of North America and the General Church of the New Jerusalem, remain active in the present day.

Born Emanuel Swedberg on January 29, 1688, in Stockholm, Sweden, to a family that had achieved considerable wealth through the mining trade, his surname was changed to Swedenborg when his father, Jasper Swedberg (later the Bishop of Skara), was ennobled in 1719. After studying moral philosophy, mechanics, and mathematics at the University of Uppsala, Swedenborg traveled widely through Europe, including a four-year stay in London, then the center of the European scientific universe. In 1716, he was appointed by Charles XII to the Board of Mines, an office he held until his early retirement in 1747. A polymath with powerful facilities in a vast array of fields, Swedenborg completed pioneering scientific studies during this period and published treatises on a wide variety of subjects, including mineralogy, human anatomy, cosmology, and philosophy.

The course of Swedenborg's life changed radically however, when he was already well into his middle age. Beginning in 1743, Swedenborg had a series of mystical experiences both while sleeping and awake, during which he felt he was able to communicate with God, angels, and other spiritual entities. In April of 1745 he received divine instruction to commence on what would be his life's work: a reinterpretation of the scriptures of the Bible. In a series of works beginning with the *Arcana Cœlestia* ("Heavenly Secrets"), Swedenborg offered an exegesis of the Bible provided to him by angels and the dead who accompanied him through the astral worlds between heaven and earth. According to their instruction, Swedenborg gave a highly symbolic interpretation of the Bible, in which each verse is read for its spiritual content, rather than its literal meaning.

Swedenborg is perhaps most famous for his detailed, matter-of-fact accounts of life after death, offered in *Heaven and Hell* and other works. In the cosmology

I am well aware that many will say that no one can possibly speak with spirits and angels so long as he lives in the body; and many will say that it is all fancy, others that I relate such things in order to gain credence, and others will make other objections. But by all this I am not deterred, for I have seen, I have heard, I have felt.

Man was so created by the Lord as to be able while living in the body to speak with spirits and angels, as in fact was done in the most ancient times; for, being a spirit clothed with a body, he is one with them. But because in process of time men so immersed themselves in corporeal and worldly things as to care almost nothing for aught besides, the way was closed. Yet as soon as the corporeal things recede in which man is immersed, the way is again opened, and he is among spirits, and in a common life with them.

—Emanuel Swedenborg, *Arcana Coelestia* (1749–1756)

revealed by Swedenborg, in addition to the divine realm of heaven and the demonic world of hell, there is a world of spirits that serves as a kind of purgatory, and it is to this world that angels bring souls immediately after their earthly demise. Once they are in this world, which Swedenborg describes as being much like the terrestrial world, with features like parks and lecture halls, they initially partake in an existence not very dissimilar from that which they had known on earth. For this reason, some of the recent additions to this world do not always know that they are dead. Gradually, through association with like-minded spirits and the guidance of angels, these spirits are purified to the point where they can enter heaven, shedding their external selves, or they hold on to the fantasy of their materiality and thereby undergo the punishments of hell. These spirits, as well as the angels of heaven and the demonic spirits of hell, also interact with humans in their everyday lives, attracted to (and affecting) human beings who act with like-minded interests. Swedenborg also met and talked with spirits from the moon, Mars, Jupiter, and other planets from our solar system and beyond, leading him to believe that life existed throughout the universe.

The basis of Swedenborg's cosmology was his doctrine of correspondences, which holds that everything on earth is a reflection of the spiritual realm. The material world is itself inert, only alive insofar as it is animated by spirit. Swedenborg details the corresponding spiritual meanings of certain animals, plants, and minerals in *Doctrine of Holy Scripture* (1763) and *True Christian Religion* (1771). The human being in his cosmology integrates the spiritual and the material and is therefore a microcosm of the universe.

During his lifetime, stories of Swedenborg's clairvoyant powers spread widely. While visiting Gothenburg in July of 1759, Swedenborg exclaimed at a dinner party that a perilous fire had broken out in Stockholm, and that his own house was in danger. Later he expressed relief that his house had been spared. News of Sweden-borg's predictions swept through Gothenburg, resulting in Swedenborg relating his vision to the governor. Two days later, a messenger arrived with a dispatch from the Stockholm Board of Trade that contained a description of the fire corresponding precisely to Swedenborg's vision. Two other cases seemed to confirm Swedenborg's ability to communicate with the dead. In one, according to eyewitness accounts, Swedenborg provided secret information to the Queen of Sweden that had been known only to her and her dead brother. In another, Swedenborg aided a woman in finding an important document belonging to her recently deceased husband, hidden in a secret compartment in his desk.

In addition to inspiring the inauguration of the new church envisaged in his writings, Swedenborg's writings have been read by and influenced a diverse array of artists, writers, thinkers, and spiritual leaders, including Paul Gauguin, William Blake, W. B. Yeats, Ralph Waldo Emerson, August Strindberg, Joseph Smith, and Jorge Luis Borges.

Swedenborg died on March 29, 1772, in London, at the age of 84.

Robert Quillen Camp

See also: Astral Plane; Channeling; Clairvoyance; Mystical Experience; Religion and the Paranormal; Theosophy

Further Reading

Goodrick-Clarke, Nicholas. 2008. "Emanuel Swedenborg." In *The Western Esoteric Traditions*, by Nicholas Goodrick-Clarke, 155–173. Oxford, UK: Oxford University Press.
Jonsson, Inge. 1971. *Emanuel Swedenborg*. New York: Twayne Publishers.
Swedenborg, Emanuel. 2001. *Heaven and Hell*. West Chester, PA: Swedenborg Foundation.
Toksvig, Signe. 1948. *Emanuel Swedenborg: Scientist and Mystic*. New Haven, CT: Yale University Press.

SYNCHRONICITY

Synchronicity is a concept in Jungian psychology that refers to apparently mean-ingful coincidences. If a person experiences separate events with personal signif-icance but no connections through practical chains of cause and effect, he or she may claim to have experienced a synchronicity. For instance, a person might dream about eagles at night, see an eagle on the way to work, and then discover that she has been assigned a new marketing client whose mascot is an eagle. Synchronic-ity implies that there is some sort of connection between a person's inner, mental world and the external, physical universe. Because of this, the concept of synchro-nicity is incompatible with most materialist beliefs about the nature of reality and with neuroscientific accounts of consciousness. However, synchronicity plays a central role in Jungian psychology and is influential in Western popular culture.

The concept of synchronicity was put forth by the Swiss psychologist Carl Gustav Jung (1875–1961) and is intimately associated with Jung's works and legacy. After breaking from his former teacher and collaborator Sigmund Freud, Jung developed his controversial ideas about the nature of spirituality, including the role of meaningful coincidences and dreams in psychological development. He coined the word "synchronicity" in the mid-1930s and in 1952 published a long essay, "Synchronicity: An Acausal Connecting Principle," which is the source of most contemporary ideas about synchronicity.

One anecdote from this essay has become the most famous example of synchronicity. Jung had been psychoanalyzing a profoundly depressed patient for some time, without making any progress. According to Jung, the patient suffered from an excessively rational worldview, which left her feeling trapped in a mechanical reality without personal meaning. One day the patient recounted a unique dream about receiving a golden Egyptian scarab beetle as a gift. In Egyptian mythology, scarabs can symbolize rebirth. As the patient told Jung about the dream, a slight tapping noise came from the window. Jung opened the window and a rose-chafer beetle—belonging to the same Scarabaeidae family as the Egyptian scarab—flew into the room. This experience shook the patient's conviction in a rigidly ordered, meaningless universe and helped cure her depression.

While to an outside observer this story may appear to contain nothing more than a chance coincidence, to Jung the number of improbabilities in the account was too great to be rationally explainable. This illustrates one of the central features of a synchronicity: the coinciding events must exhibit significant improbability. For Jung, the sheer unlikelihood of especially meaningful coincidences meant that the normal laws of cause and effect were transcended. Thus, a synchronicity was an "acausal" connection between things. The patient's dream didn't cause the beetle to show up at the window, nor did the beetle itself somehow go back in time to cause her dream. Instead, both events were linked non-causally by their meaning.

Although meaning is conventionally considered to be purely subjective, in Jungian psychology, synchronicities are objective. In other words, they are not merely projections from our minds. Synchronicities occur when the normal flow of physical cause and effect is superseded by what Jung called the collective unconscious of the psyche. Jung argued that, in the collective unconscious, all people share certain symbols and patterns called archetypes. These archetypes are not subjective, because they exist beyond any individual mind. A synchronicity occurs when events coincide in the external world in a way that activates or expresses a universal archetype and interrupts normal causality. For instance, in the anecdote above, the archetype that was activated was a scarab beetle symbolizing rebirth.

Thus for Jung and his followers, synchronicities are events in which the psyche is made manifest in the physical world. This is especially likely to happen when an individual is on the cusp of a major life transition or when an emotionally arousing or traumatic event has occurred or is about to occur. According to Jung, the heightening of emotions diverts energy to the unconscious, which then can break through into physical reality as symbols and archetypes. Synchronicity experiences are therefore often catalysts for psychological growth and development, because they allow the unconscious to express itself and become integrated with the conscious mind. (This integration of conscious and unconscious psyches, called "individuation," is a central goal of Jungian psychoanalysis.)

Historical Antecedents

Jung was highly influenced by a number of thinkers in his concept of synchronicity. In the medieval era, the Muslim philosopher Avicenna and the Catholic theologian Albertus Magnus both argued that the soul possesses an inherent capacity to alter events in the physical world; according to Albertus Magnus, this capacity is enhanced or activated by passionate emotions or by strongly felt desire. In the early modern era, the German philosopher Gottfried Wilhelm Leibniz argued for a "pre-established harmony" between all things, which could manifest as meaningful connections between seemingly independent events. This line of thinking was taken up again in the 19th century by Arthur Schopenhauer, who claimed that every individual's life follows a pre-established fate or pattern, and that meaningful coincidences are evidence or signals of this destiny. Jung was also inspired by Paul Kammerer, an Austrian biologist who wrote about meaningful coincidences as a form of "seriality," or a universal tendency of related events to group together despite being physically independent of each other.

Critiques

Numerous skeptics have attacked the concept of synchronicity from both skeptical and religious perspectives. Secular skeptics typically reject the concept of synchronicity for its supposed mysticism and its flouting of scientific models of consciousness and physical reality. Since neuroscientific models describe consciousness as a product of the brain, any claim that events in the external physical world can be somehow related to our conscious experience is simply incompatible with neuroscience. Many skeptics thus call on cognitive error and perceptual biases to explain why people think they experience synchronicities. Robert Carroll, author of the *Skeptic's Dictionary*, has argued that synchronicities are actually examples of apophenia, or the tendency to erroneously see connections where none in fact exist. Such skeptics also challenge the supposed improbability of synchronicities, arguing that such experiences are actually the result of normal chance. Since each of us experiences countless different events and situations each day, they argue, it is statistically likely that at least some of those events will seem meaningfully related—just as a quarter flipped a million times will show a few surprising streaks of, say, fifteen heads in a row.

Many skeptics bemoan the social and psychological implications of the public acceptance of synchronicity. The cultural critic Wendy Kaminer has written that synchronicity is the "latest fashion in irrationality," claiming that talk about synchronicity is a sign of the decline of public critical thinking (Kaminer 1996, 103). The psychologist and writer M. D. Faber, meanwhile, argues that synchronicity is a self-serving tool of the psychotherapist and that synchronicities are best explained as projections of our infant experiences. When babies' inner worlds register a need—such as hunger—their objective, outer world seems to respond "magically" with a bottle or breast. By pointing out synchronicities and supporting belief in meaningful coincidences, Faber claims, therapists encourage patients to believe that the objective world responds to their needs just like a parent.

Ironically, religious critics often complain that talk of synchronicity detracts from religious faith, because it attempts to paint a scientific veneer on experiences that should properly be understood as religious. One Catholic writer, Victor Write, argues that the meaningful experiences Jung calls synchronicities would have simply been recognized as interactions with angels or with God during other eras. Even today, when Americans who claim to have interacted with angels are asked to describe those interactions, they typically relate experiences that are essentially meaningful coincidences. For religious critics, synchronicity is therefore merely an impersonal and irreligious term that atheistically suppresses the religious dimension of supernatural messages.

Influences

The concept of synchronicity has been widely influential in American popular culture and in New Age thinking. Countless New Age books have been published on synchronicity, and many Hollywood movies use meaningful coincidences as a plot device. (For instance, in the 2002 American movie *About Schmidt*, a character mourning his dead wife looks at the sky just in time to see a shooting star, which he takes to be a message from her.) Despite its pop cultural and New Age appeal, synchronicity remains a formal element within Jungian psychotherapy, where it serves as an indicator of psychological breakthrough, the expression of the unconscious, and adaptive individuation.

Connor Wood

See also: Jung, Carl; New Age; Psi

Further Reading

Carroll, Robert Todd. 2003. "Jung, Carl (1875–1961)." In *The Skeptic's Dictionary*, by Robert Todd Carroll, 186–187. Hoboken, NJ: John Wiley & Sons.
Carroll, Robert Todd. "Synchronicity." http://www.skepdic.com/jung.html.
Faber, M. D. 1998. *Synchronicity: C. G. Jung, Psychoanalysis, and Religion.* Westport, CT: Praeger.
Jung, C. G., and Wolfgang Pauli. 1955. *The Interpretation of Nature and the Psyche.* Translated by R. F. C. Hull. New York: Pantheon.
Koestler, Arthur. 1979. *The Roots of Coincidence.* New York: Picador.
Peat, F. David. 1987. *Synchronicity.* New York: Bantam.

T

TAROT

Tarot is central to the philosophies of the New Age. The numerous popular books about tarot report that ancient Egyptians encoded their secrets into these mysterious cards when they were threatened by brutal invaders. Yet others say that tarot were invented by the Gypsies, then thought to be Egyptians. However, neither of these theories is true.

The tarot deck consists of 56 numbered cards distributed across four suits called the Minor Arcana and the Major Arcana with 21 trump cards and one "wild" card. The suits of the Minor Arcana cards are unfamiliar to most modern people but are very familiar to those who play with regular cards in Italy. The tarot suits are variously represented but are generally Cups, Batons, Coins, and Swords. The Major Arcana cards are numbered and bear mysterious scenes that look magical in the 21st century. These cards are The Magician, The Popess, The Empress, The Emperor, The Pope, The Lovers, The Chariot, Justice, The Hermit, Wheel of Fortune, Strength, The Hanged Man, Death, Temperance, The Devil, The Tower, The Star, The Moon, The Sun, Judgment, The World, and The Fool.

Tarot cards were invented in northern Italy toward the beginning of the 15th century. The innovation was the addition of the trump cards to the regular playing card deck that was popular at that time. Duke Filippo Maria Visconti, the brutal ruler of Milan, is credited with their invention, and the oldest surviving decks come from this former city-state. Though the imagery on those original cards seems very mysterious today, the scenes depicted were commonly found in Italian art. It is thought that Duke Visconti used the cards' imagery to represent various aspects of political, cultural, and spiritual life. For example, The Emperor, The Empress, and The Pope all represented the political struggles between the Holy Roman Empire and the Papacy. The Popess is most likely to represent a famous relative of the Viscontis, Sister Maifreda da Pirovano, a member of a heretical sect called the Guglielmites.

Though tarot cards soon became common in Italy, they were used to play a game very similar to modern-day bridge. This game was called Tarocchi or Trionfi (or Triumphs). The game, and variations upon it, soon became popular across Europe. It was not until the last part of the 18th century that tarot was used for fortune-telling. This transformation occurred in France just before the French Revolution. This was an intriguing time in France, when there was a great interest in every aspect of the paranormal. Astrology was very popular, as were Kabbalah, ritual magic, Rosicrucianism, alchemy, and all forms of divination. It was in this charged milieu that a French Freemason, Antoine Court de Gébelin (1719–1784), saw tarot for the first time and declared it to be the work of ancient Egyptians. He said tarot was the remnants of the lost Book of Thoth, a mythical work supposedly penned by the ancient Egyptian god, Thoth. The symbolism, taken from its original context in Renaissance Italy, was very mysterious to Court de Gébelin. He wrote about the deck in his grand multi-volume work, *Le Monde Primitif*, published in 1781, and altered the tarot imagery to incorporate Egyptian motifs.

At that time in France, Egypt was seen as a magical land because of the mysterious monuments and hieroglyphs that were found there. These hieroglyphs had not yet been deciphered, and they were believed to carry all manner of magical meaning. Many French occultists would build on the esoteric interpretation of tarot, often producing their own rectified decks, incorporating additional symbolism. Etteilla, a major influence on the development of tarot, was the first to ascribe meanings to reversed cards, a practice that remains to this day. Magus Éliphas Lévi (1810–1875) amalgamated many forms of esotericism including Kabbalah, ritual magic, alchemy, Hermeticism, astrology, and animal magnetism into a coherent doctrine of which tarot was an integral part. Lévi did not believe that tarot should be used for fortune-telling, instead believing it contained all the wisdom of the universe.

From France, the interest in tarot spread to England, where its use was codified by a magical society, the Hermetic Order of the Golden Dawn. It was this group that first associated the tarot trumps with the twenty-two pathways of the Kabbalistic Tree of Life. Two Golden Dawn members were to have a significant influence on the development of tarot: A. E. Waite (1857–1942) and Aleister Crowley (1875–1947). The tarot deck envisioned by Waite and painted by Pamela Colman-Smith in 1909 is perhaps the most popular tarot deck in use today. The innovation in this deck was the illustration of the Minor Arcana cards, which now carried elaborate scenes and symbolism. Waite also published a popular guide to tarot reading, *A Pictorial Guide to the Tarot*, in 1910. Aleister Crowley, popularly known at that time as "the wickedest man alive," also conceived of a tarot deck, which he called *The Book of Thoth*. The deck was painted by Lady Frieda Harris as a series of paintings between 1938 and 1943. The deck is resplendent with elaborate symbolism and remains popular to this day.

As time has gone on, the tarot deck has been reinterpreted and recast along just about as many themes as could be conceived. There are tarot packs that incorporate feminist imagery, various types of religious imagery, psychological imagery, and all sorts of cultural references. These different tarot packs still generally retain a similar structure to those original Milanese packs but with the substitution of various Major Arcana cards, usually to align with the overall themes depicted in the cards. There are many ways to read cards, often depending on the purpose of the reading. Undoubtedly, tarot will continue to evolve, reflecting the thoughts, ideals, and values of the culture in which it is considered.

Helen Farley

See also: Alchemy; Astrology; Divination; New Age; Occultism; Ritual Magic

Further Reading

Dummett, Michael, and Sylvia Mann. 1980. *The Game of Tarot: From Ferrara to Salt Lake City*. London: Gerald Duckworth and Co. Ltd.

Farley, Helen. 2009. *A Cultural History of Tarot: From Entertainment to Esotericism*. London: I. B. Tauris.

Moakley, Gertrude. 1966. *The Tarot Cards Painted by Bonifacio Bembo for the Visconti-Sforza Family: An Iconographic and Historical Study*. New York: The New York Public Library.

TELEPATHIC HYPNOSIS

The word "telepathy" was originally coined by Frederic Myers, one of the founding members of the Society for Psychical Research, in London in 1882. Telepathy is defined as an extrasensory communication between minds of thoughts, ideas, and/or visions. Myers' articulation of the law of telepathy has had far-reaching significance in modern research into the nature of consciousness. By some accounts, the ability of one mind to communicate with another is confirmed by modern research into psi phenomena, distant healing practices, and spiritual mediumship.

The word "hypnosis," for its part, has been associated with such concepts as somnambulism, sleep-walking, dissociative disorders, magnetic sleep, mesmerism, trance, altered states of consciousness, shamanic journeying, mystical and religious experience, stage entertainment, and remote viewing.

For Myers, "telepathic-hypnosis" was a combination of the two concepts that embraced the limitless character and potential of the subliminal mind. It could, he said, be applied in two directions. An *agent* could induce a hypnotic state of mind (one receptive to suggestion) in a *percipient* via telepathy, or the *agent* could self-induce a trance-like state in order to effectively communicate with a person (or spirit) at a distance in much the same way that a Spiritualist trance medium communicates with the spirit world.

Observations of hypnosis at a distance were first recorded by the Marquis de Puységur, a disciple of Anton Franz Mesmer, in 1785. These led Puységar to agree with Mesmer that the influence of what they then perceived as "magnetic fluid" (a substance thought to pervade everything like electricity) was not impeded by physical obstacles. Researchers who investigated the phenomenon of telepathic influence in the 1880s included Frederic Myers, Pierre Janet, and Charles Richet. Telepathic hypnosis effects have also been reported by surgeons James Esdail in India and John Elliotson in England.

The Russian neurologist Leonid Vasiliev was inspired by the work of Myers and Janet and replicated their results successfully over long distances—for example, from Leningrad to Sevastopol—a distance of 1,700 kilometers. Vasiliev hypothesized that telepathic suggestions were carried by electromagnetic waves, but he failed to prove it. His research was stopped by Stalin's government because it suggested that there was something paranormal involved. However, Vasiliev's experiments inspired the work of J. B. Rhine and others into psi phenomena, where the search continues for an explanation that fits the mechanistic scientific paradigm. In contrast to this, some psychiatrists use telepathic hypnosis to help those patients who are deemed to be possessed by discarnate spirits. This method, which was pioneered by Dr. Carl Wickland, has become known as Spirit Release Therapy. Modern research has yet to test it under controlled conditions.

Terence Palmer

See also: Extrasensory Perception (ESP); Myers, Frederic W. H.; Possession; Society for Psychical Research; Telepathy; Vasiliev, Leonid Leonidovich

Further Reading

Gurney, Edmund, Frederic W. H. Myers, and Frank Podmore. 1886. *Phantasms of the Living.* London: Society for Psychical Research.

Myers, Frederic. 1903. *Human Personality and Its Survival of Bodily Death.* Edited by Susy Smith. New York: Longmans, Green & Co.

Vasiliev, Leonid. 1963. *Experiments in Mental Suggestion.* Charlottesville, VA: Hampton Roads Publishing.

Wickland, Carl A. 1924. *Thirty Years among the Dead.* Mokelumne Hill, CA: Amherst University Press.

TELEPATHY

The idea that it may be possible to transfer thought directly from one person to another is older than the coining of the term "telepathy" itself. In the 1780s it had been considered by figures such as the Marquis de Puységur (1751–1825) and Anton Mesmer (1734–1815). In 1876, the psychical researcher and physicist William Fletcher Barrett (1844–1925) presented a controversial lecture at a meeting of the British Association for the Advancement of Science titled "On Some Phenomena Associated with Abnormal Conditions of Mind," in which he discussed the possibility. Barrett, along with Frederic Myers (1843–1901) and others, went on to found the London-based Society for Psychical Research (SPR). It was Myers who coined the term "telepathy" in 1882 to describe cases where impressions were received at a distance by one individual from another without the apparent mediation of any known sensory organs. He was in partly inspired to call this ability telepathy by analogy with wireless telegraphy, which was a prominent technological innovation at the time.

Working with the American thought-reader Washington Irving Bishop (1855–1889), the members of the SPR became convinced in the winter of 1882–1883 that they had acquired preliminary experimental proof of the existence of telepathy. Importantly, however, Bishop never claimed to possess any supernatural powers. He believed that he was particularly sensitive to unconscious bodily cues from those who were present during the tests. A similar view was also held by another prominent thought-reader of the time, Stuart Cumberland (1857–1922). The tendency of Bishop, Cumberland, and the SPR to explain telepathy in naturalistic terms tended to be at odds with the spiritual hypothesis offered for the same phenomena by Spiritualists and Theosophists. Even today telepathy stands at the crossroads of "fringe" research and more mainstream technological, psychological, and physiological investigations.

In 1893 the soldier Hans Berger (1873–1941) had a serious accident when he fell from his horse while on duty with his regiment. Far from the scene of the accident, Berger's sister claimed to have had a terrible premonition of her brother's fate and urged her father to send a telegram to see if he was all right. The telegram arrived well before any news of the accident could have reached his family, and after he recovered, the experience inspired Berger to take up medicine and psychiatry in order to explore how such a thing was possible. Later on in his career as a psychiatrist, Burger eventually succeeded in producing electrical recordings from electrodes connected to a patient's scalp. His techniques for achieving recordings of the electrical activity of the brain would later became known as electroencephalography, or EEG, and played a major role in the development of neuroscience in the 20th century. However, Berger largely pursued the technology in order to explore the possibility of telepathy.

In the 1930s the psychical researcher Joseph Banks Rhine (1895–1980) founded a parapsychology lab at Duke University for the purposes of studying such cases of abnormal psychology as telepathy, precognition, and remote viewing. Many consider Rhine to be the premier proponent of parapsychology as a branch of experimental psychology in the 20th century. Along with Karl Zener (1903–1964), he pioneered the use of Zener cards for the evaluation of telepathic abilities.

Zener cards feature five distinctive symbols of differing colors and shapes. The "receiver" in such experiments was expected to visualize what symbol was on the card drawn by the "sender," the person performing the tests. Statistically, guessing at random the receiver should be correct approximately 20 percent of the time, and so for telepathy to be present it was determined that they had to have a success rate far in excess of 20 percent. However, Zener cards came under increased scrutiny as a method for testing for telepathic or precognitive abilities after critics raised concerns about Rhine's experimental setup, and the cards eventually fell out of favor among parapsychologists.

In the 1930s while experimenting with individuals subjected to various states of sensory deprivation, the German psychologist Wolfgang Metzger (1899–1979) discovered the ganzfeld effect. This occurs when subjects in a state of sensory deprivation begin to hallucinate. Researchers hypothesize that the effect is produced when the brain amplifies the effects of "neural noise," which are then translated into sensory perceptions as hallucinations. In the 1970s the parapsychologist Charles Honorton (1946–1992) began pursuing ganzfeld experiments at the Maimonides Medical Center to test subjects in a condition of sensory deprivation for the presences

Mental Telegraphy?

When Frederic Myers coined the word "telepathy" in 1882 as the name for what happens when a person apparently receives thoughts or impressions from someone else at a distance by direct mental transmission, he may have been influenced by one of the most prominent technological innovations at the time: telegraphy. Nor was he the only one; the borrowing of technological terminology to describe paranormal phenomena was and still is common. Mark Twain, for instance, famously referred to instances of extrasensory perception as "mental telegraphy"—four years before Myers coined what would become the more commonly known term.

of psi or telepathic ability, and many contemporary researchers interested in telepathy continue to employ version of the experiment in their own studies.

Opponents of telepathy claim that the evidence put forward for it has either been not statistically relevant upon deeper analysis, or has failed to be consistently and independently replicated. Critics tend to point to a combination of fraud and/ or self-deception as sufficient to explain the persistence of telepathic claims in the face of these critiques and claim that there is currently no known mechanism that could explain how telepathy functions at a distance. However, proponents of cosmological theories surrounding the "holographic universe" and researchers interested in the consequences of quantum nonlocality contest that there are potential mechanisms.

This is one reason why proponents of telepathy research have grown increasingly interested in the prospect of quantum biology. In 2012, researchers at Oxford University and National University of Singapore announced that special molecules in the eyes of European robins could actually maintain a state of quantum entanglement for longer periods of time than those achievable in a laboratory setting using current techniques. The robins appear to use this ability to help them navigate based on the Earth's magnetic field. This is noteworthy because most researchers have generally held that quantum mechanical effects could not directly influence objects at scales that would be biologically relevant. The fact that it appears to be possible for biological systems to take advantage of these effects means that there may be viable mechanisms that could help support the idea of spontaneous cases of organic telepathy.

Telepathy has made innumerable appearances in popular culture. The most prominent early incorporation was in Bram Stoker's *Dracula*, published in 1897, in which the vampire's natural telepathy is juxtaposed with the technologically mediated telepathy of wireless telegraphy employed by his human adversaries. Since then, the genres of science fiction, fantasy, and horror have been replete with references to telepathic communication, from the way that H. P. Lovecraft described the elder god Cthulhu speaking to his cultists through dreams, to the Vulcans and the Betazoids of the science fiction series *Star Trek* and the telepathic community in John Wyndham's *The Chrysalids*.

Recently, futurists have become increasingly interested in the prospect of technological telepathy, observing that with the further refinement of nanotechnology, intercranial implants, and existing nueroimaging technologies it will soon be possible to send and receive information directly from one human mind to another. Supporters of such technologies point to the success researchers have had in communicating with otherwise nonresponsive coma patients. In 2011, a group of scientists at the University of California, Berkley, led by Jack Gallant, announced that they could scan the brains of experimental subjects and digitally recreate images of what the subject was thinking. In 2013, researchers at Duke University Medical Center in Durham, North Carolina reported that they had successfully wired together the sensory areas of the brains of two rats, with the result that one rat responded to the experiences to which the other rat was exposed. Generally, proponents of technological telepathy do not support claims for organic or spontaneous telepathy. However, the two communities are closely interconnected at the level of popular culture. This persistent popular interest and its reciprocal relationship with technological development has been a consistent part of the history of telepathy since Myers's coinage of the term.

B. D. Mitchell

See also: Anomalistic Psychology; Committee for Skeptical Inquiry; Consciousness; Ganzfeld Technique, The; Hallucinations; James, William; Jung, Carl; Myers, Frederic H. W.; Parapsychological Association; Parapsychology; Precognition; Pseudoscience; Psi; Psychical Research; Rhine Research Center; Society for Psychical Research; Telepathic Hypnosis; Thoughtography

Further Reading

Andriopoulos, Stefan. 2013. *Ghostly Apparitions: German Idealism, the Gothic Novel, and Optical Media*. Brooklyn, NY: Zone Books.

Luckhurst, Roger. 2002. *The Invention of Telepathy*. Oxford, UK: Oxford University Press.

Mayer, Elizabeth Lloyd. 2007. *Extraordinary Knowing: Science, Skepticism, and the Inexplicable Powers of the Human Mind*. New York: Bantam Books.

Otis, Laura. 2011. *Networking: Communicating with Bodies and Machines in the Nineteenth Century*. Ann Arbor, MI: University of Michigan Press.

Schoch, Robert M., and Logan Yonavjak. 2008. *The Parapsychology Revolution: A Concise Anthology of Paranormal and Psychical Research*. New York: Tarcher.

Sconce, Jeffrey. 2000. *Haunted Media: Electronic Presence from Telegraphy to Television*. Durham, NC: Duke University Press Books.

Talbot, Michael. 1992. *The Holographic Universe*. New York: Harper Collins Publishers.

Wolffram, Heather. 2009. *The Stepchildren of Science: Psychical Research and Parapsychology in Germany, C. 1870–1939*. Amsterdam: Rodopi.

THEOSOPHY

As far back as late antiquity, the word "theosophy" was synonymous with "theology," which meant "the study of the divine" or "monotheistic-based philosophy." During the first several centuries of the Common Era, the meanings assigned to theosophy seldom strayed too far from those of theology. However, century after century, when theosophical works were persistently associated with heterodox religious traditions, and as the content within theological texts remained within the parameters set by orthodoxy, the distinctions between these two terms increased. Once the accumulation of centuries approached a second millennium, the differences were significant, and in some cases, they were irreconcilable.

Between the 15th through 18th centuries, theosophical texts emerged with increasing frequency from each of the Abrahamic traditions, and by the end of the 18th century, they were also frequently linked with fringe religio-philosophical traditions that were more esoteric in nature and/or shunned by each tradition's orthodoxy. This loose conglomerate of doctrines and praxis was held together by a relationship primarily defined by a shared unorthodoxy, until eventually, an entirely new internationally recognized body of literature emerged, complete with a relatively consistent collection of doctrine and praxis, which paradoxically only increased the number of variant meanings already assigned to the term "theosophy."

During the late 19th-century, proponents of a doctrine known as Theosophy (capitalized) emerged as self-proclaimed heirs of theosophy (lower-case), but this easier-to-define and-quantify spiritual movement was significantly distinct from a vast majority of the previous satellite theosophical lineages orbiting more orthodox religious communities. Founded in 1875 by Helena Blavatsky (1831–1891), Henry Steel Olcott (1832–1907), and William Quan Judge (1851–1896), the Theosophical Society's new vision of Theosophy appealed to Westerners of a post-Darwinian age, to those who were wary of radical materialist assertions. Seeking a viable spiritual path as an alternative to what they perceived to be an increasingly out-of-touch Christian orthodoxy, the Theosophical Society offered its initiates a method of investigating the laws of the physical and metaphysical universe. It also provided them an opportunity to study and practice powerful esoteric teachings that were purportedly devoid of the more extreme biases of scientism, materialism, and orthodox fundamentalism.

Henry Steele Olcott was one of the first well-known Westerners to formally convert to Buddhism, and William Quan Judge developed the Society's organizational infrastructure in America, but it was the heroine among them whose tireless enthusiasm and unmatched charisma catapulted the group to international fame. The enigmatic Helena Blavatsky was born in 1831 to Ukrainian parents with alleged ties to both German and Russian aristocracy, but Helena's vision, which became the basis of Theosophy, was only possible after the title of "Madame" was bequeathed upon her. Although this was quite unorthodox for a woman of her standing, Madame Blavatsky abandoned her husband for a life of adventure across Europe, Asia, the Americas, and the Middle East. During her travels, she was exposed to the Hinduism and Buddhism that inspired some of Theosophy's core doctrines and practices. With an ambition that nearly matched her charisma, she quickly transitioned from being a promising spiritual medium familiar with Eastern religions, to becoming the face of Theosophy, to becoming one of the most recognizable personalities of her time.

The Theosophical Society's teachings were loosely based on preceding Western theosophical traditions, but they favored Blavatsky's own adaptation of the Buddhist and Hindu esoteric traditions. Blavatsky's appropriation of Eastern esotericism also appealed to Occultists fascinated with, and open to, studying the "mysteries" of the Orient. Her major work, *The Secret Doctrine* (1888), immediately resonated with the more adventurous spiritual seekers of the era, and Blavatsky's teachings neither required faith in a Christian God nor excluded the faithful from practicing. Blavatsky claimed that she was a spiritual medium who channeled the wisdom of adepts, just as proponents of Spiritualism, one of the more popular Occult movements of the time, had previously claimed. According to Blavatsky, it was highly realized spiritual beings, known as Mahatmas, who possessed her, and it was *they* and not *she* who outlined the core doctrines and praxis of Theosophy. Through the practice of automatic writing (also popular at the time), these Mahatmas purportedly provided the quintessential message found in the teachings of all other religious, philosophical, and scientific pursuits.

Unless Blavatsky's word is taken at face value, it seems most likely that she wrote her major works and became well read in Eastern literature after colonial scholars and missionaries developed the level of cultural and linguistic expertise that enabled them to publish reasonable translations of Buddhist and Hindu teachings. From the beginning, Theosophists favored Oriental practices and perpetuated the exotic vision of the East that emerged once ethnographies, diaries, and travel novels of colonial administrators, missionaries, and explorers became increasingly public. Although the Theosophical Society would later become more accommodating to some of the Christianity-based theosophical lineages of previous centuries, Blavatsky's comparative and ecumenical approach to studying religion, along with her Mahatma's vision of a perennial religion that was based on a shared foundation of a single universal truth, included more than a few anti-Christian polemics.

Blavatsky and the Theosophical Society also capitalized on other *en vogue* occult trends of the time, and from the beginning, the Theosophical Society was modeled after the elitist Freemasonry, while also utilizing the passwords, the signs, and the ritualism that were popular within other Occult organizations. As a result, membership was required to gain access to the more profound teachings and practices of Theosophy, which promised its adherents a formidable degree of spiritual realization if they joined this modern-day esoteric cabal, the self-proclaimed heir to a secret lineage that had previously remained the exclusive domain of only the most advanced adepts.

Madame Blavatsky and the Theosophical Society frequently encountered significant opposition from Western scholars, particularly those well versed in the languages, cultures, and religions of Asia. One of the most famous among them, Max Müller (1823–1900), published a lengthy essay arguing that Blavatsky's teachings were Buddhism misunderstood, distorted, and grossly caricatured. Müller's critiques were potentially threatening; if he was correct, and Blavatsky had misunderstood the basic principles of Buddhism, she could not have possibly understood the complexities of advanced Eastern esoterica. The reports of Frederic Myers (1843–1901), the founder of the Society for Psychical Research (SPR), were even more threatening; Myers concluded his in-depth study of Blavatsky and the Theosophical Society by writing, in a report published in the SPR's *Proceedings* in December 1885, that she was "one of the most accomplished, ingenious and interesting imposters in history." The implications are quite explicit: Blavatsky's Mahatmas did not exist, and even if they were real persons and enlightened beings, she was nothing more than a phony medium who lacked the ability to channel them. If the results of Myers's fairly even-handed research are regarded as being conclusive, the core doctrinal works of the Theosophical must be regarded as little more than fraudulent forgeries, particularly because Blavatsky did not read Pali, Sanskrit, or Tibetan. In response, the Theosophical Society insisted that her lack of linguistic expertise was of little consequence because she had channeled the teachings of nearly omniscient beings, and thus translating their philosophy into English was of little more than a minor inconvenience. Predictably, members of the Theosophical Society also offered "evidence" in the form of letters and reports of other mediums from across the globe, who claimed to have also encountered, and even channeled, Blavatsky's Mahatmas.

Despite the legitimacy of the aforementioned criticisms, as well as those that came later, which accused the Theosophical Society of supporting and fostering an oppressive brand of colonialism tied to British Imperialism, those who have argued that Blavatsky was little more than an opportunist capitalizing on the "exotic" allure of the East have also oversimplified (often in the most cynical of ways) the complexities of her spiritual interests and accomplishments. Rather than label her a conniving and malicious fraud or, conversely, arguing that she was an enlightened saint, it seems more likely that the popularity of the enigmatic Blavatsky's Theosophy was neither the result of enlightened activity nor purely the result of guileless business acumen and good timing. Rather, it would be more accurate to argue that Blavatsky's Theosophy was the result of decades of travel and study and the product of a spiritual seeker with a keen eye for recognizing common threads within esoteric traditions. It was the compilation of a woman who also had a unique talent for integrating a diverse array of traditions into a somewhat cohesive system.

The Theosophical Society is no longer nearly as influential as it once was, but the organization has maintained a presence in England, Scotland, Wales, the United States, Australia, Canada, France, Germany, Italy, Greece, and even Sri Lanka and South India. Moreover, Blavatsky is often considered a central figure in the development of the New Age movement. Perhaps the Society's most enduring legacy remains the modern-day belief that Theosophy (capitalized) is in actuality the theosophy (lower-cased) primarily affiliated with fringe heterodox traditions, which for most of recorded history were based on monotheistic Abrahamic teachings.

Joel Gruber

See also: Akashic Records; Automatic Writing; Cayce, Edgar; Channeling; Haunting; Mediumship; Myers, Frederic W. H.; New Age; Occultism; Society for Psychical Research

Further Reading

Goodrick-Clarke, Nicholas. 2008. *The Western Esoteric Traditions: A Historical Introduction.* Oxford, UK: Oxford University Press.
Lachman, Gary. 2012. *Madame Blavatsky: The Mother of Modern Spirituality.* New York: Tarcher.

THOUGHTOGRAPHY

"Thoughtography" refers to the alleged ability to transport or project images from one's mind onto photographic material. The term was first introduced in 1910 in Japan by Tomokichi Fukurai, a professor of psychology at the Imperial University in Tokyo. Fukurai was conducting studies on clairvoyance when he discovered his subjects, female mediums, were capable of telepathically imprinting images onto photographic plates, a phenomena he later renamed "nensha." For three years he conducted a number of nensha experiments with female mediums after inducing them into periods of deep concentration. Fukurai published his results in the book *Clairvoyance and Thoughtography* (1913). His university colleagues immediately disparaged the work for its lack of scientific methodology. Fukurai was forced to resign his position later that year. Part of his story and concept of nensha were the basis of the popular horror novel and movie series *Ringu* (1991) in Japan and *The Ring* (1998) in the United States.

One of the earliest documented telepathic photography trials was conducted in Romania in 1893 by the writer Bogdan Petriceicu Hasdeu and Dr. Constantin Istrati. The goal of their experiment was to have Istrati's image appear on a photograph by the power of projection. Hasdeau, in the city of Bucharest, set up two loaded cameras at the foot of his bed, opened their shutters, and went to sleep. Istrati, in the city of Campina, went to bed with the intention of appearing on his friend's equipment. The next morning, Hasdeu developed the exposed plates and found a shape that he identified as Istrati's profile. Both deemed their experiment a success.

Simultaneously, researchers in France took the pursuit of mind photography much further. Dr. Hippolyte Baraduc, a physician at La Salpêtrière Hospital in Paris, erected a complete theoretical structure surrounding the photography of thoughts, feelings, and the soul. His extensive theories and experimentations were published in *The Human Soul, Its Movements, Its Luminosity and the Iconography of the Fluidic Invisible* (1896). French independent researcher Louis Darget used a range of procedures to photographically document what he termed the "radiation of thought" over a 30-year period. One technique he designed utilized equipment inspired by the X-ray, called the "portable radiographer." The device allowed a photographic plate to be fixed onto a person's forehead in order to catch the imprint of his or her mind. Darget used the portable radiographer in a variety of experiments. One involved his attempt to photograph the thoughts of a "very angry person" over a period of 10 minutes. Another trial sought to intercept the dreams of his wife while she slept. He also attempted to capture images of planets and satellites from a woman while she gazed at a celestial atlas. Darget's experiments produced figurative patterns that were viewed by critics as accidents caused by the chemical processes of photography. Others, including Darget, read direct meaning into the results or considered them to be, at the very least, powerfully synchronistic.

The most famous and best-documented example of thoughtography is the case of Ted Serios, a Chicago bellhop with an alcohol addiction. Serios claimed he used psychokinetic mind power to produce images on Polaroid instant film. From 1964–1967, he was studied by the psychiatrist Dr. Jule Eisenbud, who conducted thousands of sessions with Serios in which the latter apparently produced figurative imagery under a wide variety of controlled conditions. Serios often used what he referred to as a "gizmo," a small cylinder held up to the lens of the Polaroid camera. He explained the gizmo as a tool to direct his energy and to prevent too much light from affecting the projection. Critics claimed it was a prop used to import imagery onto the film. Supporters pointed out that the gizmo was always inspected before, during, and after the photographs were made, and that nothing suspicious was ever discovered. Serios also created some images without the gizmo, and some while other people held the camera. Thirty-six of his images were created from a physical distance between one and 66 feet away from the camera. Sometimes an electrically shielded Faraday cage additionally separated him. Eisenbud published his endorsement of Serios's abilities in *The World of Ted Serios: "Thoughtographic" Studies of an Extraordinary Mind* (1967). Later that year, the magazine *Popular Photography* claimed to have exposed Serios as a fraud. Soon afterward Serios produced his last thoughtograph, an image of curtains, on June 15, 1967. *The Jule Eisenbud Collection on Ted Serios and Thoughtographic Photography* is currently held in its entirety at the University of Maryland, Baltimore County.

Shannon Taggart

See also: Art, Creativity, and the Paranormal; Kirlian Photography; Spirit Photography; Telepathy

Further Reading

Eisenbud, Jules. (1967) 1989. *The World of Ted Serios: Thoughtographic Studies of an Extraordinary Mind.* 2nd ed. Jefferson, NC: McFarland.

Eisendrath, David. 1967. "An Amazing Weekend with Ted Serios: Part II." *Popular Photography* (October): 85–87, 131–33, 136.

Jaszi, Peter. 1967. "Ted Serios: Mind over Molecules?" Review of *The World of Ted Serios* by Jules Eisenbud. The *Harvard Crimson*, October 13. http://www.thecrimson.com/article/1967/10/13/ted-serios-mind-over-molecules-pbtbhe.

Reynolds, Charles. 1967. "An Amazing Weekend with Ted Serios. Part I." *Popular Photography* (October): 81–84, 136–40, 158.

TRANSPERSONAL PSYCHOLOGY

Transpersonal psychologist Mike Daniels defines the word "transpersonal" as meaning "beyond (or through) the personal. It refers to experiences, processes and events in which our normal limiting sense of self is transcended and in which there is a feeling of connection to a larger, more meaningful reality" (Daniels 2005, 11). Transpersonal psychology, for its part, is defined by Lajoie and Shapiro as being "concerned with the study of humanity's highest potential, and with the recognition, understanding, and realization of unitive, spiritual, and transcendent states of consciousness" (Lajoie and Shapiro 1992, 91). At its core transpersonal psychology is concerned with human transformation and the psychology of exceptional human experience, be that paranormal experience or mystical experience or states of deep empathy, ecstasy, love, and compassion. As a psychology it is scientific but emphasizes understanding and interpretation of the human condition and our highest potential, and it is normative rather than merely descriptive in that it not only studies transformation but actively engages it.

In the early 1950s there were essentially two forces within psychology: psychoanalysis and behaviorism. Dissatisfied with the largely pathological view of humanity put forth by psychoanalysis and the mechanistic view of humanity put forward by behaviorism, the psychologist Abraham Maslow initiated the field of humanistic psychology and shortly after joined together with Anthony Sutich to form the Association for Humanistic Psychology in 1961.

However, within a number of years Maslow and Sutich became dissatisfied with the lack of a spiritual dimension within the movement they had founded. Cultural changes also had a profound influence during the 1960s, and transpersonal psychology became forged at the confluence between psychedelic and Eastern traditions emerging within psychology and psychotherapy. Ultimately, at a meeting in 1967 in California between Sutich and Maslow and Stanislav Grof, James Fadiman, Miles Vich, and Sonya Margulies, a fourth force was formed within psychology, which aimed to honor the entire spectrum of human experience and included spiritual experiences and altered states of consciousness. Adopting the term first used by the father of American psychology, William James, transpersonal psychology was reintroduced and the Association for Transpersonal Psychology was shortly after formed.

Within a few years Robert Frager founded the Institute of Transpersonal Psychology in Palo Alto, California, as a graduate training center. Then in 1978 the founders of Esalen Institute, Michael Murphy and Richard Price, founded the International Transpersonal Association along with Stanislav Grof, who became the founding president. Between 1984 and 1986 three attempts were made from within the Humanistic Psychology Division of the American Psychological Association (APA) to get transpersonal psychology recognized as a division of the APA, though none were successful. The same situation is not evident elsewhere, however, and in 1996 psychologists David Fontana, Ingrid Slack, and Martin Treacy formed the Transpersonal Psychology Section as an official part of the British Psychological Society.

A similar development to that occurring within psychology occurred under the umbrella of anthropology, and the Association for Transpersonal Anthropology (ATA) was formed as a corporation in 1980. The ATA fractured shortly after, additionally forming the Society for the Anthropology of Consciousness, which was itself accepted as a formal section of the American Anthropological Association in 1990.

David Luke

See also: James, William; Mystical Experience; Unconscious Mind

Further Reading

Daniels, Mike. 2005. *Shadow, Self, Spirit: Essays in Transpersonal Psychology.* Exeter, UK: Imprint Academic.
Lajoie, Denise, and S. I. Shapiro. 1992. "Definitions of Transpersonal Psychology: The First Twenty-five Years." *Journal of Transpersonal Psychology* 24: 79–98.

U

UFO

UFO, or unidentified flying object, is a term coined by the Air Force in the early 1950s as a catch-all phrase for the various anomalous aerial objects witnessed by the public beginning in the late 1940s. Many consider the modern UFO phenomenon to have begun on June 24, 1947, when pilot Kenneth Arnold witnessed nine unknown objects flying in formation near Mount Rainier, Washington. Arnold reported that these objects were flat and crescent-shaped, and he characterized their movement as appearing "like a saucer if you skip it across the water." The associated press misquoted Arnold as having seen "flying saucers," but this description was soon used by others to identify the anomalous aerial objects witnessed by hundreds of people by summer's end.

On July 7th, 1947, just weeks after Arnold's sighting, a flying circular object appeared in the restricted air space of Muroc Air Force Base (now Edwards Air Force Base) near Lancaster, California. The next day, on July 8th, the Roswell Army Air Field in New Mexico issued a press release that they had recently recovered a crashed "flying disc" at a ranch just outside of town. The military changed their story hours later, claiming that, in actuality, the disc was nothing more than a weather balloon. The events at Roswell were eventually forgotten until, several decades later, Charles Berlitz and William Moore coauthored the book *The Roswell Incident* (1980), which introduced the notion that alien bodies were uncovered at the crash site. Since that time, Roswell has remained one of the most well-known UFO cases.

As interest in flying saucers grew in the late 1940s, so did speculation as to what they were: some thought these objects were foreign technology, while others thought they might be some sort of unknown biological entity. Little thought was given to the idea that flying saucers might be spacecraft piloted by extraterrestrial beings until United States Marine Corps pilot Donald Keyhoe published his book *Flying Saucers are Real* (1950), in which he argued that there was a vast cover-up to hide the fact that alien beings were visiting the earth.

Beginning in 1952 with George Adamski, a spate of individuals who eventually came to be called "contactees" started to publicly claim that they were in contact with "space brothers," peaceful extraterrestrial beings who often traveled to earth in flying saucers. Many of these contactees published their stories, and the sum of these books, together with the writings of Keyhoe, eventually led to the dominant idea that flying saucers, together with other kinds of UFOs, were craft piloted by alien beings. Within the field of UFO studies or UFOlogy, this remains a popular interpretation of UFOs.

From UFO to Flying Saucer

Unidentified flying or aerial objects have been observed throughout recorded history, but the "flying saucer" has only been around since 1947, when pilot Kenneth Arnold saw nine unknown objects flying in formation near Mount Ranier and reported that their motion was like saucers skipping on water. This comparison effectively captured the public imagination and reshaped an age-old phenomenon that had formerly been associated with religious beliefs into a mechanical object believed by many to represent advanced extraterrestrial technology. Alternative interpretations continue to abound, however, with many speculating that UFOs are really an other-dimensional, spiritual, or imaginal phenomenon, while many others maintain an attitude of unmitigated skepticism about the whole subject.

While the stories told by contactees often included spiritual and religious overtones and resulted in the formation of various UFO-related new religions, the military and others remained more interested in the scientific and technological aspects of unidentified flying objects. The Air Force officially investigated the UFO phenomenon from 1948 until 1969, although the majority of these later investigations did not seriously consider the extraterrestrial hypothesis. Due in part to the military's disavowal of UFOs as alien craft, civilian groups interested in UFO investigations began to appear, beginning with Keyhoe's own National Investigations Committee on Aerial Phenomena (NICAP) in 1956. Several civilian-operated UFO investigation groups remain active to this day, including the Mutual UFO Network or MUFON, which was founded in 1969.

One of the strongest advocates for scientific study into the UFO phenomenon was the astronomer J. Allen Hynek (1910–1986), who once served as a scientific advisor for the Air Force. While working for the military, Hynek actively debunked the majority of UFO reports, as he considered most cases to be the results of erroneous judgment or hoaxing. But over time Hynek concluded that many UFOs and related phenomena constitute a genuine mystery, and he, along with others, eventually came to consider UFOs as objects operating within currently unknown scientific principles that were controlled by some form of inter-dimensional intelligence.

Over time, various influential writers have speculated upon the nature of UFOs. Psychologist Carl Jung hypothesized that UFOs are external manifestations of a psychological reality. Fortean writer John Keel believed that UFOs are modern manifestations of otherworldly beings that were once commonly referred to as demons. Many contemporary UFO enthusiasts focus on the more bizarre aspects of UFO reports and argue that several UFO encounters have themes similar to those found in occult, psychical, and paranormal literature. Psychedelic experiences have also been compared to UFO reports: Terrence McKenna theorized that many UFO motifs are themselves psychedelic in nature and may be somehow related to certain psychoactive substances produced naturally in the human body, such as DMT (dimethyltryptamine). The idea that UFOs exist within an imaginal realm, some kind of "third-space" where the psychical and physical meet in ways that defy conventional logic, has been incorporated by many contemporary metaphysical ideas and alternative spiritualities, although there remain large numbers of UFO enthusiasts who still view the phenomenon as spacecraft controlled by advanced extraterrestrial beings.

Even though the vast majority of contemporary UFO reports arise from the misidentification of conventional aircraft or naturally occurring phenomena, some of these reports appear to defy explanation according to mainstream canons of rationality, and thus the subject remains a popular topic upon which to theorize. Adding to the modern UFO phenomenon are those stories of individuals reporting alien contact or abduction experiences.

UFO studies are often considered to be pseudoscientific, even though the militaries and universities of several nations participated in multiple scientific studies into the nature of UFOs from the 1940s until the late 1960s. This has not, however, stopped individuals around the world from devoting their time and effort to attempts at discovering what this phenomenon really is.

Michael Kinsella

See also: Abduction Experience; Drugs and the Paranormal; Fort, Charles; Fortean Phenomena; Imaginal; Jung, Carl; Keel, John A.; Strieber, Whitley; Vallée, Jacques

Further Reading

Hynek, J. Allen. (1972) 1989. *The UFO Experience: A Scientific Inquiry.* Cambridge, MA: De Capo Press.

Jung, Carl. 1978. *Flying Saucers: A Modern Myth of Things Seen in the Skies.* Princeton, NJ: Princeton University Press.

Kean, Leslie. 2010. *UFOs: Generals, Pilots, and Government Officials Go on the Record.* New York: Three Rivers Press.

UNCONSCIOUS MIND

The term "unconscious mind" broadly indicates those mental processes that take place beyond conscious awareness but that are nonetheless theorized to have an effect on internal phenomena (such as thoughts and emotions) and external events. Processes of the unconscious mind are thus expressed indirectly: though unseen, they are inferred to be the underlying causes of consciously observable effects. Researchers theorize that the unconscious mind is responsible for a wide range of mundane phenomena—such as habitual or automatic actions, slips of the tongue, phobias, and intuitive thinking—as well as many ostensibly paranormal phenomena—such as channeling and mediumship, clairvoyance, psychokinetic phenomena, telepathic communication, UFO sightings, and possession states.

The history of the term "unconscious" begins with the German Idealist philosopher Friedrich Schelling (1775–1854). Drawing on the writings of mystics, alchemists, and occultists such as Jakob Böhme and Paracelsus, Schelling envisioned all of reality as a unified mind—the mind of God, the "Absolute I"—that possesses conscious and unconscious aspects. Here, the unconscious signifies an utterly unknowable aspect of reality that is, in an absolute sense, paranormal. Schelling's version of the unconscious was eventually eclipsed by Freud's psychoanalytic version. Nevertheless, elements of Schelling's unconscious continue to characterize contemporary thinking about the relation between the unconscious and the paranormal.

Freud's psychoanalytic theories located the unconscious solely within the individual. For Freud, the unconscious was the source of a person's primal drives and conscience. These two unconscious forces, which we can never control or become consciously aware of, are frequently at odds with each other. They are, moreover, at odds with the conscious aims of the ego. Consequently, the ego works to keep these forces out of the conscious mind by repressing them. In Freud's view, these repressed unconscious forces do not disappear. They instead exert a latent influence on the individual. A primary task of the psychoanalyst is thus to discern these latent influences in dreams, slips of the tongue, and neurotic behaviors.

As a rule, Freud discouraged any association of psychoanalysis with research into the paranormal, citing fears that it would jeopardize the respectability of his still-young science. Publicly, he explained away paranormal occurrences as projections of the unconscious mind arising from primitive, animistic beliefs. However, there is some reason to believe that Freud's private attitude toward the paranormal was more positive. In 1911 he became a member of the Society for Psychical Research, and later in his life he confided to the psychical researcher Hereward Carrington that if he had the chance to live his life again, he would devote himself to the study of the paranormal. His sole public foray into the paranormal research concerned telepathy, or "thought transference," which took place via the unconscious mind. Despite the objections this investigation raised among his peers, Freud remained convinced of the existence and psychoanalytic significance of telepathy, citing instances that arose in the course of patient analysis and in experiments carried out with his daughter, Anna Freud.

Significantly, Freud's version of the unconscious drew from the work of theorists who were more sympathetic to the existence of paranormal phenomena. One important influence was Georg Groddeck (1866–1934), a German physician, self-proclaimed "wild analyst," and forefather of psychosomatic medicine. For Groddeck, the unconscious—which he called the "It"—was the main factor in all of life. Illnesses, accidents, prophetic thoughts, and so on were all considered by Groddeck to be symbolic communications from the unconscious. By interpreting

The action of the unconscious mind is theorized by many to be partly or wholly responsible for a broad range of paranormal phenomena, including:

- Channeling and mediumship, including automatic writing
- Clairvoyance
- Precognition
- Prophetic and other paranormal dreams
- Psychokinesis
- Telepathy
- UFO sightings
- Possession states

these symbols, thereby gaining direct access to the unconscious mind, Groddeck hoped to unlock what he considered to be its extraordinary capacity to heal otherwise incurable conditions. Even though Freud openly admitted to borrowing his "id" concept from Groddeck's "It," Groddeck and those in the psychoanalytic community like him (e.g., Ferenczi, Rank) remained fringe elements in the early history of the unconscious.

A positive association between the unconscious and the paranormal was developed by Freud's former student, Carl Jung (1875–1961). His most enduring contribution was the notion of the "collective unconscious," which he claimed contained the inherited symbolic structures, or archetypes, of the history of human consciousness. The collective unconscious was thus a deeper and more powerful layer of the unconscious than the individual unconscious posited by Freud.

In order to arrive at his theory of the collective unconscious, Jung performed extensive research into the symbols of humankind as they are portrayed in religion, folktales, and other narratives that touch upon the meaning of the paranormal. Jung claimed that the archetypes of the collective unconscious were ultimately responsible for a vast array of paranormal phenomena, including poltergeists, possession states, UFO sightings, and prophetic dreams. For instance, Jung held that UFO sightings were modern reconfigurations of myths narrating man's encounters with the archetypal forces of the collective unconscious. They are thus the living part of the ongoing mythic narrative of the psychic life of the unconscious mind.

Since Jung, two basic perspectives on the unconscious mind and its relation to the paranormal have emerged. First, there are the believers, who hold that paranormal phenomena are real and have some as-yet undecided relationship to the unconscious mind. Believers often emphasize the utter unknowability and immeasurability of the unconscious mind and sometimes employ it as a catchall explanatory term. Second, there are the skeptics, who view the unconscious as an aspect of the individual mind glimpsed in the relationship between mentality and physiology. They insist upon measurability and experimental repeatability and resist ascribing unconscious causes to phenomena that cannot be scientifically studied. Of course, these two perspectives are in actuality two poles on a spectrum of attitudes. In practice, such attitudes are mediated by the type of phenomena under consideration and the target audience of the research.

For instance, skeptical psychiatrists consider possession states to be caused by a maladjusted relationship between the conscious and unconscious aspects of an individual's mind. Normally, the unconscious works (more or less) cooperatively with the conscious mind. But in possessed individuals, the unconscious is thought to break away from the conscious mind and manifest as a secondary personality. In severe cases of prolonged possession states, the unconscious mind is thought to revolt against the conscious mind, suppressing it in the manner of a hostile takeover.

In the case of the Ouija board and table turning phenomena, studies note the influence of subtle, unconscious hand movements, resulting in what is called the "ideomotor effect." This same effect has been interpreted by paranormal enthusiasts as the true significance of the psychokinetic abilities of the unconscious.

Several investigations into channeling and mediumship conclude that, if these are not outright performances, they are either expressions of the individual's unconscious or manifestations arising from the archetypal reservoir of the collective unconscious. Scientists and analysts have even adopted the medium's practice of automatic writing as a means of exploring the unconscious. Those who are more sympathetic to the authenticity of channeling, however, warn that the unconscious mind is a potential impediment to genuine channeling. The true channel, they argue, makes contact with realms beyond even the unconscious mind. Surprisingly, this sentiment reflects the attitude of the usually skeptical Freud, who, near the end of his life, qualified mysticism as a kind of self-perception beyond even the ego and the id.

The unconscious is frequently invoked with regard to clairvoyance and prophetic dreams. Early on, Carl Jung held that the unconscious mind is essentially unfixed in time and space, and that the archetypes of the collective unconscious allow one to simultaneously reach into the past while discerning the contours of the future. Since then, several contemporary studies have demonstrated a relationship between the unconscious mind and precognition. In one representative study, subjects who were shown a series of photographs displayed emotional arousal prior to being shown emotionally charged photographs, perhaps indicating that the unconscious mind anticipated the content of pictures prior to their appearance.

In a related and ongoing study, Princeton's Global Consciousness Project has been measuring the effect of globally significant emotionally affective events (like the death of Nelson Mandela) on random number generators since 1998. The Project has reported highly statistically significant results, suggesting that human consciousness is affectively connected across the globe and that it systemically affects physical reality.

While these modern experiments offer some validation, in most cases the scientific standards of documented evidence and experimental replicability continue to elude research into the role of the unconscious in relation to the paranormal. Believers in the paranormal remain unswayed in any case, for the paranormal, like the unconscious, is precisely that which is incapable of being directly investigated and understood. One thing is clear: the investigation of the paranormal directly entails an investigation into the unknown terrain of the unconscious mind.

Matthew Robertson

See also: Art, Creativity, and the Paranormal; Automatic Writing; Channeling; Exorcism; Gooch, Stan; James, William; Jung, Carl; Mediumship; Myers, Frederic W. H.; Ouija Board; Paranormal Dreams; Possession; Psi; Scrying; Synchronicity; UFO

Further Reading

Carpenter, James C. 2012. *First Sight: ESP and Parapsychology in Everyday Life.* Lanham, MD: Rowman & Littlefield.

Ellenberger, Henri F. (1970) 2008. *The Discovery of the Unconscious: The History and Evolution of Dynamic Psychiatry.* New York: Basic Books.

Fuller, Robert C. 1986. *Americans and the Unconscious.* Cambridge, UK: Oxford University Press.

Jung, Carl Gustav. (1934) 1981. *The Archetypes and the Collective Unconscious.* Vol. 9. Princeton, NJ: Princeton University Press.

Totton, Nick, ed. 2003. *Psychoanalysis and the Paranormal: Lands of Darkness.* London: Karnac Books.

V

VALLÉE, JACQUES

Dr. Jacques Vallée (b. 1939) is a well-known researcher in the field of Unidentified Flying Objects (UFOs), who has written many books on the topic. He was among the first to propose the idea that UFOs might be paranormal events instead of spaceships coming from another planet. In 1969, he published a significant book entitled *Passport to Magonia*, where he compared accounts provided by witnesses of UFO occupants with tales of supernatural beings (like fairies and elves) described in the mythological literature. He found many similarities between them.

Vallée was born in France in 1939 near Paris. He studied mathematics at the Sorbonne University and Astrophysics at the University of Lille, in northern France. In 1962, he moved to the United States to work at the University of Texas in Austin. He also enrolled for doctoral studies in computer science at Northwestern University (Chicago), where he graduated with a PhD in 1967. He worked on a number of scientific projects with NASA, and he was one of the pioneers of the Internet through his work on DARPAnet. He published his first book on UFOs in 1965. He is also a science fiction novelist.

He was profoundly marked by the wave of UFOs seen in the sky of France in 1954 and also by the negative attitudes of scientists and government officials toward the topic. At first Vallée seriously considered that UFOs could be machines used by extraterrestrial visitors, an interpretation of the UFO phenomenon usually referred to as the Extra-Terrestrial Hypothesis (ETH). But he also noted that witnesses of UFO events oftentimes described very strange paranormal phenomena such as levitation of objects or people, telepathic communications, premonitions, and a feeling that time was flowing at a different speed than normal.

The more he researched the phenomenon, the more he found that the paranormal aspect is a common feature of the UFO experience rather than the exception. He eventually concluded that the ETH is weak and inconsistent and that UFO researchers should put their efforts in exploring other approaches. He proposed that UFOs might be entities or multi-dimensional occurrences from another reality beyond the physical universe of conventional science.

Another important aspect of Vallée's UFO research is its focus on the impact the UFO phenomenon has on people and societies. In 1979 he published a book entitled *Messengers of Deception: UFO Contacts and Cults*, in which he took a critical look at UFO-related cults and how they have changed the lives of people for the worse. Notably, he raised concerns about a UFO group organized by a man named Marshall Applewhite, who created a cult named Heaven's Gate and led this group to commit collective suicide in March 1997. Vallée also proposed that UFOs might act as a sort of control system for societies to help them evolve over time.

His ideas have not always been well-received by the community of UFO researchers, among whom the ETH remains the most popular explanation for the UFO phenomenon. Adherence to the ETH is so widespread and intense among UFOlogists that it sometimes amounts to more of a belief system than a research hypothesis, and it is in this sense that Vallée, with his criticisms of this position, has considered himself "a heretic among the heretics" (Vallée n.d.).

Vallée currently remains somewhat active in the UFO research community, giving speeches and interviews. He has also written a number of prefaces for UFO books by other authors. He remains active in the scientific community as well, supporting and financing new technological leading-edge ventures.

Eric Ouellet

See also: Abduction Experience; Fortean Phenomena; Religion and the Paranormal; UFO

Further Reading

Vallée, Jacques. 1965. *Anatomy of a Phenomenon*. New York: Ace Books.

Vallée, Jacques. 1988. *Dimensions*. London: Sphere Books.

Vallée, Jacques. 1990. "Five Arguments Against the Extraterrestrial Origin of Unidentified Flying Objects." *Journal of Scientific Exploration* 4 (1): 105–117.

Vallée, Jacques. n.d. "Heretic Among Heretics: Jacques Vallée Interview." *UFO Evidence*. Accessed June 16, 2014. http://www.ufoevidence.org/documents/doc839.htm. Originally published at www.conspire.com.

Vallée, Jacques. 1975. *The Invisible College*. New York: Dutton.

Vallée, Jacques. 1979. *Messengers of Deception*. Berkeley: And/Or Press.

Vallée, Jacques. 1969. *Passport to Magonia*. Chicago: Regnery.

Vallée, Jacques, and Chris Aubeck. 2009. *Wonders in the Sky*. New York: Tarcher/Penguin.

VAMPIRES AND POLTERGEISTS

The figure of the vampire and the phenomenon of the poltergeist are generally regarded as separate in modern technological societies, but in history and human experience they have often been deeply intertwined. This relationship forms an especially interesting subdomain in the field of paranormal studies.

Reading about the folkloric vampires of Greece, Romania, or Bulgaria, one often has a sense of hazy unreality or incredulity. Classic vampire incidents only rarely feature claims of blood drinking, and the vampire is credited with numerous bizarre habits, such as banging on roofs, beating people, or hurling around household furniture and dung—even urinating on terrified villagers from a convenient rooftop.

Surprisingly, however, all this can be explained in relatively objective terms. The key is fear. While vampires were not real, fear of them was. This fear was so great that it could kill people. Usually, such deaths occurred as a result of vivid nocturnal hallucinations, sparked by a very real form of sleep disorder, now known as Sleep Paralysis (SP) Nightmares. Accounts from modern sufferers confirm that this experience is utterly terrifying; that its hallucinations of an attacking figure feel overwhelmingly real; and that—even for die-hard atheists—it has a strong aura of supernatural menace.

In some SP Nightmares, the psychosomatic force of fear is so great that victims who feel they have been choked or bitten can actually sustain bruise or bite marks on their bodies. As with certain witch cases, the furthest extreme of this terror was voodoo death—a radical physiological shutdown caused by a mixture of general supernatural belief and particular terror, centered on a seemingly supernatural event. In Serbia in 1731, during the protracted aftermath of the Arnold Paole vampire case, the haiduk Jowiza reported that "his stepdaughter . . . Stanacka, lay down to sleep fifteen days ago, fresh and healthy, but at midnight she started up out of her sleep with a terrible cry, fearful and trembling, and complained that she had been throttled by the son of a haidul . . . [named] Milloe, who had died nine weeks earlier." Stanacka "experienced a great pain in the chest and became worse hour by hour, until finally she died on the third day" (Barber 1988, 16). Stanacka had almost certainly suffered an SP Nightmare (complete with the well-attested breathlessness, or strangling). Her demise, too, neatly fits voodoo death, which typically occurs in one to three days.

Bizarrely, almost everything about the vampire is real—except the vampire itself. This supposed revenant was often a very practical scapegoat for people seeking to explain (and combat) outbreaks of ordinary death or disease. The chosen corpse would tend to be that of someone who had died, usually recently, and perhaps in some unnatural way. So: we have real deaths or sickness; real nightmares; and fear so real it could kill its victims, or catalyze hysteria great enough to supply the energy for poltergeist outbreaks. Where more familiar poltergeist cases (e.g., the Enfield case in London, 1977–1978, or Tina Resch in Ohio, 1984) clearly feature one central agent, usually teenaged and suffering emotional trauma, vampire poltergeist events almost certainly involve multiple agents in many cases. The human energy sustaining the bizarre events, moreover, is not emotional tension, but sheer supernatural terror.

At the same time, this circular economy of fear and superstition carried its own solution. Belief in the vampire gave it life. And so, sufficiently strong belief in the vampire's destruction could also kill it. After the anti-vampire ritual (staking, burning, dismemberment) there was relief and calm. Without the energy of terror, poltergeist events ceased.

This hypothesis is borne out by an independent eyewitness, the French botanist Pitton de Tournefort. In December 1700, de Tournefort was at once bemused and

Vampires and Poltergeists

Most people think of vampires and poltergeists as inhabiting two distinctly different areas in the total realm of paranormal studies, but in fact they overlap in many striking ways. In accounts coming from all of the typical vampire territories—Greece, Bulgaria, Romania, Poland, Germany, and the Ukraine—vampires appear to have behaved like poltergeists. From troublesome rappings and bangings to showers of strange objects and furniture being thrown around, vampires were associated with what would automatically be labeled poltergeist activity today.

astonished at the vampire hysteria he saw on the Greek island of Mykonos. He reports repeated poltergeist events, night after night, in all houses except that of the French consul, with whom he was lodging. He also implies that all these problems stopped when the alleged revenant was burnt on a neighboring island. Fear gave this vampire a kind of poltergeist-life, and relief took it away. Meanwhile, Tournefort and friends, having no fear of the vampire, suffered no poltergeist incidents.

Vampires seem to have behaved like poltergeists in all of the typical vampire territories: Greece, Bulgaria, Romania, Poland, Germany, and the Ukraine. Around 1600, after a man named Cuntius was killed by a horse, a carnival of poltergeist activity exploded in Pentsch, Silesia. From February to August there were inexplicable hammerings, smells, beatings, and invisible horses galloping in courtyards. All this was documented by the local parson; again almost certainly involved multiple agents; and ceased only when Cuntius was ruthlessly burned in August.

In that case, as with Mykonos, the more violent poltergeist habits are easy to spot. The same was true of a vampire attack in Belgrade in 1923. A baffled Montague Summers, reporting on the stones and bricks hurled at just one house, and the furniture tumbled about inside, commented, "It was stated that the troublesome apparition was a vampire, although its activities certainly seemed to be those of a poltergeist" (Summers 2001, 175–177). But other cases are less clear-cut. With these, one needs to know quite a lot about poltergeists to gauge what was actually happening.

On the Greek island of Kythnos, sometime around 1890, a man called Andilaveris died, presently returning to terrorize villagers by "smashing the plates and the glasses, by clattering the pots and the pans, howling horribly all the while like a mad werewolf." Having a varied repertoire of tricks, Andilaveris would also, "on certain days . . . take it into his head to climb up onto the roof of the church, and from that height he would drench those that passed underneath with floods of urine." Even after defiant villagers had taken away the temporarily sleeping vampire, to bury it on another island, he suddenly "awoke from his weekly slumber, and attacked the good priest with vollies of mud and ordure" (Summers 2001, 268–9).

At first glance, this looks like the most extravagant nonsense. In fact, there is actually a very good chance that these villagers really *were* pelted or showered with excrement and fluid. The key to these seemingly impossible events is the poltergeist's ability to *apport* substances and liquids. Sometimes these may have been to hand (as when excrement was close to the surface of a rudimentary privy). But on many well-documented occasions they simply appeared from nowhere. Compare an example from Cuddapah, in India, in 1935. Here, as well as being beset with peltings of stones, spontaneous burning of clothing, movements of objects, and sprinkling with water, one luckless family found that, "when the inmates were at meals, within closed doors, human excreta fell near their plates" (Carrington and Fodor 1952, 78). Meanwhile, in the Essex home of PC Caroline Mitchell in 2010, several people, including fellow officer Paul Brassey, saw that yellow "liquid was not coming from the ceiling, but a couple of inches below it . . . literally . . . from thin air" (Mitchell 2013, 237–8).

Imagine being in vampire country when liquid (even if it was only water) was falling from around the church, out of an otherwise clear sky. Explanation? The vampire . . . was urinating on you. Here we find that the supposedly superstitious people of Vampire Country could hardly be blamed for excessive credulity. When confronted by apported liquid, then a vampire urinating on you is at least as rational an explanation as most others. The same held for the dung, which started flying from around the vampire corpse just at the very moment when people were expecting some sort of last resistance, and therefore generating an extra supply of energizing fear.

At the level of cultural history, the vampire-poltergeist shows that the supernatural is often a case of people choosing their local demon. Witches or ghosts would be the preference elsewhere (and supposed encounters with ghosts certainly caused voodoo death in Britain, right through the 19th century). But the vampire-poltergeist offers a unique variation on this kind of cultural gestalt, in that vampire victims do not just see what they expect to; they can also make real poltergeist events occur.

Moreover, while poltergeist data can explain some seemingly bizarre vampire incidents, the vampire can also throw light on the poltergeist. Outside of strongly supernatural cultures, poltergeist incidents typically involve one clear agent, with a second person sometimes "catching" the energy or power after an extended period, as Janet's sister, Rose, appeared to do in Enfield in 1978. In Vampire Country, by contrast, there repeatedly seem to be several agents in a given case. This not only says something about the contagious possibilities of poltergeist energy under certain belief systems, it also suggests that some degree of paranormal ability exists in many or all people, albeit usually deeply buried or inaccessible.

Richard Sugg

See also: Enfield Poltergeist; Poltergeist; Sleep Paralysis; Witches and Poltergeists

Further Reading

Adler, Shelley. 2011. *Sleep Paralysis: Night-mares, Nocebos, and the Mind-Body Connection.* Piscataway, NJ: Rutgers University Press.

Barber, Paul. 1988. *Vampires, Burial, and Death: Folklore and Reality.* New Haven, CT: Yale University Press.

Calmet, Augustin. 1759. *Dissertations upon the Apparitions of Angels, Dæmons, and Ghosts.* London: M. Cooper. Reprinted as *The Phantom World.* 1850. London: Richard Bentley. http://www.gutenberg.org/ebooks/29412.

Carrington, Hereward, and Nandor Fodor. 1952. *Haunted People: The Story of the Poltergeist Down the Centuries.* New York: Dutton.

Mitchell, Caroline. 2013. *Paranormal Intruder: The True Story of a Family in Fear.* Charleston, SC: Createspace.

Playfair, Guy. 2011. *This House is Haunted: The Amazing Inside Story of the Enfield Poltergeist.* Guildford, UK: White Crow Books.

Roll, William G., and Valerie Storey. 2004. *Unleashed: Of Poltergeists and Murder: The Curious Story of Tina Resch.* New York: Paraview Pocket Books.

Sugg, Richard. Forthcoming. *The Real Vampires.*

Summers, Montague. 2001. *The Vampire in Lore and Legend.* Mineola, NY: Dover. Reprint of *The Vampire in Europe*, 1929.

VASILIEV, LEONID LEONIDOVICH

Leonid Vasiliev (1891–1966) was professor of neurology at the University of Leningrad, where he conducted experiments in mental suggestion at a distance (telepathic hypnosis) and is acknowledged as a significant pioneer in parapsychological research.

Born in Russia in 1891, Leonid Leonidovich Vasiliev graduated from Petersburg University in 1914. He was head of the physiology department, Bekhterev Brain Institute, Leningrad, from 1921 to 1938 and was a professor of physiology at Leningrad University from 1943 until his death in 1966. Vasiliev pioneered parapsychology in the Soviet Union and helped to establish the first parapsychology laboratory at Leningrad (now St. Petersburg). His work was a precursor to that of J. B. Rhine in the United States and inspired the United States Department of Defense's Remote Viewing project at the Stanford Research Institute. Vasiliev was himself inspired by the work of Frederic Myers, one of the founders of the British Society for Psychical Research, and the French psychiatrist Pierre Janet, both of whom experimented with the phenomenon of telepathic hypnosis.

Vasiliev's work with telepathic hypnosis was conducted in Russia during the 1920s and 1930s. One of his methods of testing the efficacy of the hypnotic suggestions delivered to the percipient was based on the findings of the physiologist V. V. Pravditch-Neminsky in 1925 that brain activity can be measured by the use of an electroencephalogram or EEG. Right up to the present day it is acknowledged that brain waves operate at different frequencies according to the level of mental activity.

Vasiliev noted that natural obstacles such as hills and the curvature of the earth's surface did not affect the phenomenon or impede the progress of the mental suggestion. He further commented on what he believed to be the unusual nature of the factor that transmits the "telepatheme" (his name for the theoretical mental energy) from the sender's brain to the percipient's. He noted that, like the usual radio waves, it operated at long distances, but unlike radio waves it was not impeded by metal screening with iron or lead-lined rooms.

The successes of Vasiliev's and others' experiments, and their collective failure to arrive at a theory to explain them, led to more and more researchers studying the various aspects of these complex and unexplained phenomena as they became convinced of the real existence of what Vasiliev came to call "mental suggestion."

Vasiliev's experiments produced results that were rigorously subjected to tests of statistical significance, and that appeared to show that telepathically induced hypnosis over long distances was a scientific reality. These results further reinforced the experiments conducted by others in Athens, New York, and elsewhere, and there was general agreement among the researchers that although the results were conclusive, they were difficult for mainstream science to acknowledge because they could not be accommodated within the prevailing scientific paradigm. The theory that thoughts are carried by electromagnetic waves (see below) was never proven.

Vasiliev's spectacular success gave parapsychology some recognition in the highly politicized atmosphere of Stalinist Russia. He first developed the politically acceptable hypothesis of a material basis for telepathy whereby mental suggestions are carried by electromagnetic waves. But his experiments to establish this theory proved quite the opposite and supported the hypothesis that thoughts are transmitted from person to person beyond the constraints of time and space. Financial support was withdrawn, and Vasiliev's work was not published until 1963, after Stalin's death. Not long before his death in 1966, Vasiliev expressed regret that the telepathic hypnosis method was no longer being used in research in other countries, but he noted that its development was a great achievement for Soviet research.

Vasiliev's work remains an important landmark in parapsychology, both on its own and when read against the general global backdrop of new developments in the field during the mid-20th century. In 1947 Thouless and Weisner introduced the term "psi" to identify the mysterious connection or unidentified energy form that links people in telepathy and other psychic phenomena. Debates took place during the 1950s when the term "parapsychologist" emerged to describe those who took on the task of researching psi, including J. B. Rhine, who established the Rhine Institute. Amidst all this, extensions of Vasiliev's research branched into several other areas, including distance healing, remote viewing, and distant mental influence on living systems (DMILS).

Terence Palmer

See also: Myers, Frederic W. H.; Psi; Remote Viewing; Rhine Research Institute; Stanford Research Institute; Telepathic Hypnosis

Further Reading

Vasiliev, Leonid. (1963) 2002. *Experiments in Mental Suggestion.* Revised edition. Charlottesville, VA: Hampton Roads Publishing.

W

WHITEMAN, MICHAEL

Michael Whiteman (1906–2007) was emeritus associate professor of applied mathematics, University of Cape Town, South Africa. A prolific writer on the paranormal and mysticism, he died while still active at the age of 100 in 2007. His work was unique in combining physics, psychical research, Eastern and Western mysticism, ancient and modern philosophy, depth psychology, and music. He treated the subjects with utmost rigor yet from the level of personal knowledge, being himself directly acquainted with psychical and mystical experience.

Joseph Hilary Michael Whiteman was born in London, November 1906. At Cambridge he obtained a first class in the mathematics tripos in 1929, and became scholastic head at Staffords School in London's Harrow Weald. There he met his musician wife, and the couple emigrated to South Africa in 1937, settling in Cape Town. He first taught at the Diocesan College (Bishops) before taking up a lecturing appointment in the department of pure mathematics at the University of Cape Town. His involvement with music led to his being appointed a lecturer in music at Rhodes University in Grahamstown, South Africa, yet in 1946 he returned to the University of Cape Town to lecture in the department of applied mathematics. He retired in 1972 as an emeritus associate professor and remained in Cape Town until his sudden death.

Often at variance with conventional academic views, he developed what he termed "scientific mysticism," aimed at providing an "open-minded, rigorously tested, rationally coherent and illuminating" treatment of nonphysical states and happenings. Building on concepts of potentiality and actualization derived from quantum theory and classical sources and on concepts from relativity, he maintained that the rational structure of space, time, and physical laws cannot be comprised in a material world but belongs to a realm of universal reason or general logic. He saw a cramping error in standard science, which takes objects of observation in the physical state as primary causes, whereas the causes of what is observed physically, or at any other level of manifestation, cannot themselves be observed at that level. He held the intelligible constitution of nature to be multilayered and thought psychical phenomena were explicable only in those terms.

At a deeper level this reached the matter of spirituality and religion. To prepare himself for their study, Whiteman became fluent in classical Greek, Biblical Hebrew, Vedic, Sanskrit, and Pali. He made a close study of thinking from Minoan, Vedic, and early Hebrew times up to the apostolic period of early Christianity, after which he saw religious thinking corrupted by dogma and theorizing. To him theology simply meant "the application of the phenomenological method to our awareness of the Divine." So, "the word 'God' *(Theos)* must be taken to stand for the Archetypal Reason in all." From such a radical approach came ideas that fly against conventional religious thinking, yet that are compatible with scientific exploration. He was critical of most standard translations and interpretations of Eastern and Western scriptures, since the authors, he thought, showed little or no direct mystical or psychic experience. He believed this was essential if the deeper meaning of the texts was to be understood. His writings carried out this exploration, informed by his own psychic and mystical experience.

Primacy was given in Whiteman's life and work to direct experience. Mysticism, in Whiteman's, understanding, is "the study of everything non-physical, including the other worlds and their archetypal governance, as well as our spiritual bodies, the facts and their relationship being known by the self-evidence of direct observation and not by reasoning or speculation." Direct evidence was emphasized in the subtitle of his first book of 1961, *The Mystical Life* (Faber & Faber), whose subtitle is *An Outline of Its Nature and Teachings from the Evidence of Direct Experience.* The word "evidence" also appears in the title of his three-volume series, *Old and New Evidence on the Meaning of Life*, 1986, 2000 and 2006 (Colin Smythe). His methods rested on observation, conceptual analysis, and insight regarding what he termed "the inner constitution of nature." This is a phrase from the subtitle of his book, *The Philosophy of Space and Time* (George Allen & Unwin, 1967), which was also subtitled *A Phenomenological Study.* Phenomenology was understood in Husserl's sense to be the rare gaining of "face-to-face self-evidence and detailed precision," shedding the usual "cloak of ideas." This formed the basis for what he termed "scientific mysticism."

The sixth book he wrote is titled *Aphorisms on Spiritual Method: The "Yoga Sutras of Patanjali" in the Light of Mystical Experience* (Colin Smythe, 1993). This is a unique presentation of the Sanskrit text with interlinear and idiomatic English translations and commentaries. Based on his wide knowledge of classical Indian languages, he recognized that the Sutras incorporated an abundance of Buddhist technical terms, a fact underplayed in standard translations made within the Hindu tradition. The nonmystical, physical interpretation of passages in the Sutras, as generally encountered in English translations, were rigorously criticized in his radically authentic treatment.

Number systems, he pointed out, conform to groups and cycles recognized in ancient thinking, physics, and psychology. In physics the four dimensions of space-time correspond with four-fold psychological and ancient systems: aspiration, assessment, action, fulfillment, depicted as the four stations of the sun: east, north, west, south. A sixteen-fold system was noted in quantum field theory and the sixteen *kalās* of the Upanishads.

He was an honorary life member of the Society for Psychical Research and contributed several papers to their *Journal.* He also published in the *Journal of the American Society for Psychical Research* and contributed chapters to several books on parapsychology. His death in February 2007 was recorded in extended obitu-aries in the local media, the *Journal of the Scientific and Medical Network*, and the *Journal of the Society for Psychical Research* among others. A biography and guide to his work was published in the *Proceedings of the Society for Psychical Research*, vol. 59 (222), 2011, by Professor John Poynton, who is preparing a book on his scientific mysticism.

John Poynton

See also: American Society for Psychical Research; Mystical Experience; Parapsychology; Religion and the Paranormal; Society for Psychical Research

Further Reading

Poynton, John C. 1994. "Making Sense of Psi: Whiteman's Multilevel Ontology." *JSPR* 59: 401–412.

Poynton, John C. 2007. "Michael Whiteman at One Hundred." *JSPR* 71: 43–44.

Whiteman, J. H. M. 1961. *The Mystical Life: An Outline of Its Nature and Teachings from the Evidence of Direct Experience.* London: Faber & Faber.

Whiteman Mystical Experience. 2009, September 25. Accessed October 18, 2014. http://www.whiteman.co.za.

WILSON, COLIN

The prolific English writer and philosopher Colin Wilson (1931–2013) is best known for his first book, *The Outsider* (1956), published when he was 25. A study in "alienation and extreme mental states," *The Outsider* earned Wilson the sobriquet of England's own "home grown existentialist." Seen as part of the postwar "Angry Young Men" literary movement, *The Outsider* became a bestseller, although Wilson himself admitted that he had little in common with the other "angries." Wilson's success soon turned to notoriety as the press, tired of the "angries," turned on him; his subsequent books were either vilified or ignored. Wilson's status as persona non grata in the English literary world continued off and on throughout his long career, although in recent times important figures such as the novelist Philip Pull-man, author of the *His Dark Materials* trilogy, have spoken out in favor of his work.

Colin Henry Wilson was born to a working class family in Leicester, England. In his teens his early interest in science turned to literature. After graduating from school he did not attend university but instead took a variety of menial jobs while teaching himself how to write. After a period of wandering in England and France in his early twenties, Wilson settled in London, where he became friends with other writers in the burgeoning postwar Soho bohemian scene. After a failed first marriage Wilson slept rough on London's Hampstead Heath while writing by day in the Reading Room of the British Museum. It was during this period that he worked on his first novel, *Ritual in the Dark* (1960)—an existential study of a serial killer—and *The Outsider.*

By the late 1950s, Wilson had left London and settled in Cornwall with his second wife. There he wrote the books of his Outsider cycle, aimed at forming a new existentialism based on the philosophy of Edmund Husserl, that would transcend the dead-end existentialism had reached in the work of Heidegger, Sartre, and Camus. Central to Wilson's new existentialism was Husserl's notion of "intentionality."

In the late 1960s, Wilson was asked by an American publisher to write a book about the occult. Wilson was interested in the subject but did not take it seriously, and he only accepted the commission because he needed the money. Ironically, the book he ended up producing, titled simply *The Occult* (1971), reestablished his reputation and sold almost as well as *The Outsider*. Initially skeptical of occult ideas and phenomena, Wilson came to believe while researching and writing the book that there is as much evidence for the reality of occult and paranormal phenomena as there is for particle physics. The central theme of *The Occult* is what Wilson calls "Faculty X," the little-understood human ability to grasp "the reality of other times and places." A more intense form of ordinary consciousness, the idea of Faculty X is an outgrowth of Wilson's earlier insights into Husserl's intentionality, and it informs all of his subsequent writing.

The Occult was followed by two sequels: *Mysteries* (1978) and *Beyond the Occult* (1987). In *Mysteries* Wilson developed his notion of the "ladder of selves," an insight that came to him following a series of panic attacks that were a result of overwork. Wilson uses the metaphor of a "ladder of consciousness" to account for a variety of paranormal, mystical, and occult states. In *Beyond the Occult*—which he considered his most important nonfiction book—he brought together the existential insights of his early philosophical work with his 20-year study of the paranormal, arguing that everyday consciousness is a kind of "confidence trickster," and that more powerful and intense levels of consciousness are available to us. These other levels are responsible for mystical insights and paranormal phenomena.

In *Poltergeist* (1981) Wilson came to the controversial conclusion that spirits actually exist and are responsible for poltergeist activity, as opposed to the more widely accepted view that such disturbances are a product of the unconscious mind. His *The Psychic Detectives* (1984) focuses on the use of the paranormal in crime detection, while in *Afterlife* (1987) Wilson weighed the evidence for "life after death." In later years he explored the possibility of prehistoric civilizations (*From Atlantis to the Sphinx*, 1996) and the meaning of UFO phenomena (*Alien Dawn*, 1998). An incorrigible workaholic, in his long career Wilson produced some 181 titles, including occult-themed science fiction novels—*The Mind Parasites* (1967), *The Philosopher's Stone* (1969), and *The Space Vampires* (1976)—as well as biographies of central occult figures such as Aleister Crowley, C. G. Jung, Rudolf Steiner, Rasputin, G. I. Gurdjieff, and P. D. Ouspensky.

After a long illness following a stroke, Wilson died on December 5, 2013, at the age of 82.

Gary Lachman

See also: Occultism; Paranormal; Paranormal in Literature; Poltergeist; Psi

Further Reading
Wilson, Colin. (1988) 2008. *Beyond the Occult: Twenty Years' Research into the Paranormal.* London: Watkins.
Wilson, Colin. (1978) 1999. *Mysteries.* London: Watkins.
Wilson, Colin. (1971) 1999. *The Occult.* London: Watkins.
Wilson, Colin. (1956) 1989. *The Outsider.* New York: Tarcher/Penguin.

WITCHCRAFT

Witchcraft is the practice of magic, usually malevolent, by witches, as well as a general term for malicious and anti-social magical practice. Both witchcraft itself and the lore about it are very old in human history, but in a more modern vein the word has become associated with Wicca, the neopagan religion that was founded by Gerald Gardner and his New Forest Coven in 1938. Witchcraft and Wicca are not exactly identical, as witchcraft represents a loose body of cultural beliefs and practices with no codified, coherent core across different times and cultures, whereas Wicca is an actual religion with a core belief system that happens to draw on elements of witchcraft. Both have resonances with the paranormal, but this is especially true of the wider realm of historic witchcraft, which swirls with beliefs, accusations, and numerous stories of people who are able to cast spells, conjure spirits and devils, manipulate the elements, access supernatural knowledge, and exercise other paranormal powers.

In earlier eras when there was little popular medical understanding or aid available to most people, disease, infant mortality, poor mental health and other illness, as well as bad weather, the failure of crops, the loss of livestock, or any other inexplicable misfortune could and would be blamed on witchcraft. The Hermetic philosophers, with their desires to understand God and the universe, were above and apart from witches, whose concerns are earthly and often domestic. Unlike the cunning men or cunning women (professional practitioners of folk magic) with their talismans and spell-books, the witches' power was often intrinsic to themselves. As well as knowledge of herbal lore and the occult, witches may have second sight, the destructive evil eye, or a tongue that can curse under its own power. Witches can bring bad luck, cause children or adults to be hysterically possessed, and change into the form of an animal (often a dog, wolf, or hare). In England witches kept supernatural pets known as "familiars," which they fed with their own blood.

The witch has always stood outside of society. In Greek myth for instance, Hecate, the goddess of witchcraft, was brazen and lawless, and her daughter Circe was exiled to a deserted island with a group of women followers. The infamous witches of Thessalia, for their part, lived in their own community with the power to raise the dead and draw down the moon, and Thessalian soil was said to grow plants that would "constrain the gods." In the Hebrew religious tradition, when the biblical King Saul wants to speak with the ghost of the prophet Samuel, he must travel incognito, outside of the reach of his own law, to the witch of Endor, for he himself has already driven necromancers and sorcerers from his kingdom.

In medieval Europe, witches, folk-magic practitioners, midwives, and herbal lore experts were mostly tolerated by the church, and the existence of actual witches was often in doubt. Charlemagne and King Coleman of Hungary were among the 8th to 12th century figures—many others of whom were bishops—who refuted the existence and power of witches and forbade their persecution. The 10th century *canon Episcopi* law stated that any person who believed in night-flying or metamorphosis, and so sought to punish those whom they imagined to be involved in these activities, "is beyond doubt an infidel and a pagan."

This tolerance was not to last, however. The famed European witch hunts began officially in December 1484 when Pope Innocent VIII issued his papal bull *Summis Desiderantes Affectibus*, condemning the spread of witchcraft and authorizing its persecution. Witchcraft had become a criminal heresy. In 1486 the *Malleus Maleficarum* (English: *Hammer of the Witches*) was published; it described, in a question and answer style, what witches did and how they should be dealt with. Kramer, the author, wrote the guide after being expelled from Innsbruck for attempting his own witch trial. The *Malleus Maleficarum* gave details of the witches' Sabbath, where witches would gather at night to conspire and give themselves sexually to the devil in return for power. The devil, for his part, would mark the witch as his own after their encounter.

As witch trials progressed from the 15th to the 18th centuries, the methods of dealing with the accused perpetuated these fantasies. Supposed witches were tortured and fed leading questions and preconceived narratives from their inquisitors, and their answers to these interrogations confirmed both the diabolic horrors in the *Malleus Maleficarum* and the greater suspicions of church and community.

Those who confessed to witchcraft often recanted once away from their tormentors. There is some evidence that those accused of witchcraft who truly did think they had magical abilities considered these to come from different, nondiabolical sources. Some English witches stated that they worked with fairies; cunning men claimed they had the spirits of holy men, Moses or Elias, working with them.

The witch-panic soon migrated across Western Europe, and Catholic and Protestant countries alike embraced the hunt. Witch accusations each had their idiosyncrasies, but the general pattern had an individual, usually a woman, being accused of witchcraft. Specialist witch-hunters would check for the "devil's mark," which played a major role in witch detection. This consisted of a special mark that was believed to be located on the body of the accused and that would not bleed when pricked. In England, which had a different witch narrative, the mark was the place where a witch's familiar would feed on her blood. Witch dipping, or swimming, hinged on the idea that water would not accept a witch, and so a guilty witch

A Partial Timeline of Witch Persecution

1484   The European witch hunts begin in December when Pope Innocent III formally condemns witchcraft and authorizes its persecution.

1486   The *Malleus Maleficarum*, the most famous witch hunter's manual, is published.

1593   In England the entire Samuels family is hanged for bewitching Lady Cromwell.

1612   14 of the 20 "Pendle Witches" are executed.

1692–1693 Twenty people are executed in the famous Salem witch trials.

2014   In July, *The Washington Post* reports that more than 2,000 people were killed for accusations of witchcraft in India between 2000 and 2012. In October, 23 people are arrested in Tanzania for killing seven alleged witches

would float, whereas an innocent woman would sink and possibly drown. These folk methods would lead to a criminal trial by either secular or church authorities where the witch would be accused of the heresy of witchcraft and the crimes committed through its practice. Witches and their influence were deterred by placing magical objects on the threshold of the home, such as a buried "witch bottle" containing urine, fingernail clippings, hair, and iron objects. St. John's Wort, knives, or horseshoes were placed under the doormat or over the door frame, and in England horseshoes are still placed over doors "for good luck." A more physical deterrent was to approach the witch who was causing the trouble and to scratch them in an attempt to draw their blood.

Notable witch cases from the time of the great witch hunts include, for example, the Witches of Warboys case in England, in which Lady Cromwell, the grandmother of Oliver Cromwell, was bewitched by a local family, the Samuels, and subsequently died. All three members of the Samuel family were hanged in 1593. In 1612 16 women and 4 men were accused of witchcraft in the Lancaster Assizes. The Pendle Witches, as they were known, had a number of accusations leveled against them, from folk magic to using a murdered baby's corpse for food and its fat as an ointment for shape-shifting. Fourteen were executed, one died in prison, four were acquitted, and one was found guilty of merely bewitching a horse. In 1594 Gonstanza, a 60-year-old midwife from Tuscany, was accused of witchcraft following the death of a number of infants. She quickly agreed and shared her fantasy of a devil lover who took her to feasts at his palace, although she said she declined the orgies. After refusing to confirm her confession in her second interrogation, she was ultimately acquitted. Less fortunate was the Scottish witch Isobel Gowdie, who confessed, without torture, to transforming into a hare and being entertained by the Queen of the Fairies in her "home under the hill." Gowdie was convicted in 1662, although no record of her execution exists. The witch craze successfully migrated to America, the most famous case being at Salem, where 20 people were executed for witchcraft, with at least five others dying in prison. They were by no means the only case in New England, and at least 12 people were executed before the trials began.

Due to the broad span of time and locations, the actual death toll of the witch craze is difficult to estimate. Numbers have ranged from nine million in Europe, sliding down to one hundred thousand, sixty thousand, and forty thousand, to a recent estimate by Professor Ronald Hutton of forty thousand.

Periods of social upheaval are dangerous for outsiders: the witch hunts began in the aftermath of the Hundred Years War and during the great changes of the Renaissance and then the Reformation. England's most notorious witch-hunter, Matthew Hopkins, worked during the civil war, and the Salem trials were part and parcel of an air of social and political uncertainty accompanied by a projection of Puritan Christian values onto and into everyday life. In the European witch trials, witches were often associated with other outsiders: the anti-witch tract *Errores Gazariorum* was entitled "Errors of the Cathars," mixing the two heresies, and in medieval Hungary first-time witchcraft convictions were made to stand in public all day in a "Jews' hat." During the witch craze the persecution of Spanish Muslims and European Jews often coincided with that of witches, such as Navarre in 1610.

The decline in the witch trials came due to another cultural change: the advent of the Enlightenment, accompanied by a growing skepticism about witchcraft. Those harassing witches were themselves prosecuted from 1735 onward under England's Witchcraft Act. And although great progress has been made in the last two centuries, fear of witch conspiracies can still emerge in the Western world. As late as 1944 Helen Duncan, a Scottish grandmother, became the last person imprisoned under the Witchcraft Act. In 1994 anthropologist Jean La Fontaine aroused controversy with her report denying the existence of contemporary satanic child abuse. Her report methodically disproved fears of "human sacrifice, cannibalism, bestiality, dismemberment of foetuses, witchcraft, and devil-worship"; the *Independent* newspaper ran with the headline "GOVERNMENT INQUIRY DECIDES SATANIC ABUSE DOES NOT EXIST." Public reaction was heated and polarized (Kitzinger). (La Fontaine later published a book about her research, 1998's *Speak of the Devil: Tales of Satanic Abuse in Contemporary England*.)

When the torso of an African boy was discovered floating in the Thames River in London, the world of folk magic was brought to the world's attention. The boy, named Adam by investigators, was thought to have been brought to Europe from Nigeria and fed a magical potion before being murdered and dismembered. Despite some claiming to have known and cared for Adam, his identity has not been confirmed at the time of this writing. Attempts to understand and investigate this and other crimes, such as the murder of alleged witch Masego Kgomo in South Africa in 2009, have been undertaken with a desire to punish the crime and not the communities related to the criminals. Clearly, the topic of witchcraft remains unresolved in the modern public mind.

Scott Wood

See also: Demonology; Occultism; Paranormal in Literature; Ritual Magic; Shamanism; Sleep Paralysis

Further Reading

Kitzinger, Celia. 1995. "Satanic Disabuser." *Times Higher Education*, August 28. Accessed October 16, 2014. http://www.timeshighereducation.co.uk/94959.article.

Ogden, Daniel. 2009 *Magic, Witchcraft, and Ghosts in the Greek and Roman Worlds*. Oxford, UK: Oxford University Press.

Rosen, Barbara. 1991. *Witchcraft in England 1558–1618*. Amherst, MA: University of Massachusetts Press.

Russell, Jeffrey B., and Brooks Alexander. 2007. *A History of Witchcraft: Sorcerers, Heretics, and Pagans*. New York: Thames & Hudson.

Trever-Roper, H. R. 1969. *The European Witch-Craze of the 16th and 17th Centuries*. London: Penguin

WITCHES AND POLTERGEISTS

In the 21st century, poltergeist phenomena are often frightening and mind-bending for the most hard-headed rationalist. They are, simply, beyond belief. They defy the laws of physics. People and objects are levitated. Noises are produced by no detectable agency. Inexplicable fires break out. Substances and objects ("apports") appear from nowhere or disappear into thin air. The best working hypothesis for such events is that they are somehow produced by a human agent—a person usually around the age of puberty or in their teens. This agent will typically be suffering some kind of emotional trauma or frustration, and this tension is itself almost always dependent on the presence of others—a family or a surrogate family. Using a slightly loose shorthand, we can then say that the energy required for the phenomena is a negative emotional energy, and one which, lacking normal means of expression, is unconsciously released in the form of poltergeist phenomena.

In certain witch cases, pre-existing fear of a supposed witch has provided a negative energy that was also able to spark poltergeist events. We already know that such fear can actually scare people to death. In October 2014 the Royal Shakespeare Company staged *The Witch of Edmonton*. This now neglected play, first produced in 1621, was based on the real life case of Elizabeth Sawyer, who was tried and executed in April that year after various supposedly occult happenings in Edmonton, Middlesex. One central charge was that Sawyer had "witched to death" her neighbor, Agnes Ratcliffe. What actually happened was this: after Sawyer and

Ratcliffe argued, Ratcliffe feared that she had been cursed by Sawyer. She fell sick, foaming at the mouth, and within four days she was dead. Both these symptoms and the timespan (reported in the pamphlet on which the play was based) are typical of cases of tribal voodoo death. Simply, Ratcliffe died of her fear of Elizabeth Sawyer.

Clearly, then, in witch cases levels of terror have been high enough to supply the energy required for poltergeist activity. How have such cases themselves played out? Most common is a version of the above scenario, where someone has an argument with a woman suspected of being a witch. This "victim," primed by pre-existing fears and the particular event of the quarrel, then develops hysterical symptoms. Often limited just to fits and psychosomatic injury, in certain instances these symptoms also include poltergeist events.

On March 24, 1661, Florence Newton was committed to prison in Cork, Ireland, on the charge of bewitching a young girl, Mary Longdon. The two had argued, and in following weeks Longdon's fear of Newton produced a startling amount of poltergeist activity: small stones fell from nowhere around Longdon, following her as she moved; she was levitated; and at least once she was put inside a linen chest, underneath the linen, without disturbing it. Along with apports, levitation, and dematerialization, Longdon was beset by a variant of apport phenomena, much of it extremely common in witch cases. She vomited up enormous quantities of wool, pins, needles, nails, straw, and moss, and repeatedly had pins stuck into her. Sometimes these pierced her skin, but sometimes were found under it, without having broken the surface.

Many aspects of the early modern witch hunts have been rightly derided as extremes of human folly and ignorance. Of the approximately fifty thousand people who died as witches, many were blamed for freak weather or the frequent infant mortalities now known as cot-deaths or Sudden Infant Death Syndrome. These witches were straightforward social scapegoats, singled out for natural problems that people could not understand. Yet when it comes to poltergeist-witch cases, we can actually begin to see why certain features of witchcraft were almost impossible to explain in anything but supernatural terms. Put another way, while witch crazes have often been seen as a classic example of persecuting people for things they simply could not have done, the poltergeist forces us to realize that seemingly impossible things did *actually happen* in such incidents. They were misunderstood, but they were not fictions or delusions. They had objective reality. We may not now want to call them "supernatural," but "paranormal" they surely were.

Equally real was the human misery poltergeists inflicted in this context. Failure to understand poltergeist events has almost certainly caused the bullying or sacking of supposedly hoaxing agents. In Newton's case it probably caused her death. Although final records have been lost, it is reliably believed that she was executed in 1661. If so, the Longdon poltergeist had an especially odd status, given how extremely rare official witch trials actually were in Ireland.

Over in England, at Brightling, Sussex, a similar case occurred sometime before 1691. The minister Richard Baxter (d. 1691) tells of how an old lady came one Monday to the young servant girl of Joseph Cruttenden and told her that various misfortunes, including fire, were to fall on the master's house. That night Cruttenden and his wife were showered with dust and dirt as they lay in bed. The next day the house burned down. The home of a man who gave them shelter also caught fire, and when they moved next into a hut, the belongings they had saved were hurled around. As in so many poltergeist cases, objects that struck people caused them no injury. Here all evidence points to the servant girl as agent, sparked into terror by the old lady, and then carrying the phenomena with her from one place to another. But Baxter (and doubtless many of his readers) held the cause to be the witchcraft of the anonymous old woman. In a strange sense she probably was partly responsible, yet nothing would have happened if no one had been sufficiently afraid of her.

This directly causative version of poltergeist-witchcraft is the most startling. But other variants could be equally dangerous to alleged culprits. When aggravated poltergeist events burst out around young John Stiles in Newbury, Massachusetts from 1679–1680, his grandmother, Elizabeth Morse, was suspected of bewitching him by some, and perhaps narrowly escaped hanging as a result.

In England, witch accusations or trials were no longer legally possible after the Witchcraft Act of 1736. Yet while educated rational Englishfolk now found themselves "in denial" about their superstitious ancestors, popular witch beliefs ran on and on. If this context of popular superstition could make life difficult enough for anyone perceived as strange, matters were again doubly aggravated by poltergeist phenomena. During the long-running poltergeist stone-throwing around Carelew Street, Cornwall in May 1821, a mob of children at one stage pursued an old woman with the aim of stripping her and drawing blood from her—a classic popular technique designed not to punish a witch, but to rob her of her power. In 1896, explosive and repeated hammerings at a house in Edithweston, Rutland, caused the owners to consider demolishing the property and prompted older villagers to pin the blame on the young servant girl, aged around 14, and supposedly "in league with the Devil" (*Leeds Mercury*, December 29, 1896). Given that young girls often were the genuine (though unwitting) agents of such phenomena, it is again possible to see how such accusations could prove especially difficult for people who were followed around by poltergeist events. In 1983 Carole Compton, a Scottish nanny working on the Italian island of Elba, endured a spectacular trial after unexplained fires endangered the life of her three-year-old charge. She was accused of casting the evil eye on the child, and the word "witch" was repeatedly hurled at or associated with her. In reality, the unexplained fires and falling objects around the 20-year-old woman were almost certainly poltergeist phenomena.

One last link between witch and poltergeist is especially surprising. George Pickingale (d. 1909), the male witch of Canewdon in Essex, was genuinely feared by all of those around him. He appears not to have suffered from this fear but to have actively exploited it: he compelled people to fetch his water for him and was credited with the ability to stop farm machinery by the power of his eyes. Accordingly, farmers bribed him to keep away from it. Remarkably, their belief may have been true. Certain psychics and poltergeist agents have apparently been able to voluntarily produce paranormal events by staring at objects. Nina Kulagina could move things by looking at them, and more recently, in the 1980s an Italian boy, Benedetto Supini, could make things burst into flames—at will, and again apparently through the power of his gaze. Although usually unconscious and unintentional, interference with telephones and other electronic machinery is extremely common in poltergeist cases of recent decades.

Richard Sugg

See also: Fortean Phenomena; Occultism; Poltergeist; Psychokinesis (PK); Vampires and Poltergeists; Witchcraft

Further Reading

Baxter, Richard. 1691. *The Certainty of the World of Spirits.* London: T. Parkhurst and J. Salisbury. https://archive.org/details/certaintyofworld00baxt.

Compton, Carole, and Gerald Cole. 1990. *Superstition: The True Story of the Nanny They Called a Witch.* London: Ebury Press.

Glanvill, Joseph. 1681. *Saducismus Triumphatus, or, Full and Plain Evidence Concerning Witches and Apparitions.* London: A. L. https://archive.org/details/saducismustriump00glan.

Goodcole, Henry. 1621. *The Wonderful Discovery of Elizabeth Sawyer, a Witch, Late of Edmonton.* London: William Butler. http://myweb.dal.ca/dv392553/nonsword/goodcole.htm.

Leeds Mercury, December 29, 1896.

Maple, Eric. 1960. "The Witches of Canewdon." *Folklore* 74 (1): 241–250.

Mather, Increase. (1684) 1890. *An Essay for the Recording of Illustrious Providences.* London: Reeves and Turner. https://archive.org/details/remarkableprovi01mathgoog.

Z

ZOMBIES

The zombie is a being that is neither fully alive nor fully dead. Dwelling between states of existence, the zombie is a liminal figure: it both *is* and *is not*. On one hand, it behaves in ways that are recognizably human. On the other hand, it does so while lacking the type of soul or consciousness that arguably makes one human. The zombie is a grotesque, unsettling, contradictory, and impossible thing. For this reason, many scholars use and interpret the concept of the zombie as one that is capable of expressing the various ways that human beings can experience being alive and dead at the same time.

Scholars tend to distinguish between the "zombi" of Vodou religion and the "zombie" of American popular culture, even though the American zombie was adapted from Haitian Vodou religion. (The spelling "Voodoo" is widely considered pejorative, since it has historically been used to portray Haitian and other Caribbean religious traditions in inaccurate and racist ways.) Vodou developed among enslaved Africans in 18th-century Haiti. It is a diverse and syncretic religion that combines elements of Roman Catholicism, a variety of West African religions, and the spiritual traditions indigenous to the so-called "New World." Today it is also practiced elsewhere in the West Indies, parts of the American South, and in the Haitian diaspora. Although the exact origin of the word "zombie" remains uncertain, scholars have suggested different West African languages (*zumbi*: fetish; *ndzumbi*: corpse; *zan bii*: night bogey), and Louisiana Creole (*jumbie*: curse/ghost), which is itself influenced by terms from Spanish (*sombra*: ghost/shade) or French (*sans vie*: without life; *les ombres*: shadows). The zombie is most widely known as a resurrected corpse. However, as some of these terms suggest, within Vodou the zombi can refer to either a disembodied soul that is captured and manipulated by another person or the soulless body that has been resurrected in order to do another's bidding.

Wade Davis is an ethnobotanist who did fieldwork in Haiti in the early 1980s and argued that the zombies of Vodou religion were based not merely on belief but on the actual transformation of living bodies into zombies. That is to say, Vodou priests were feeding zombi powders to individuals in order to render them catatonic, or zombie-like. The person would then be buried and dug up as though resurrected from the dead. The powders consisted largely of tetrodotoxin, the same substance found in poisonous puffer fish. These individuals were zombified as a punishment, Davis argued, because they committed a social or moral transgression serious enough to threaten the stability of the local community. After being fed the powder, the individual's eyes would glaze over, he would speak in a nasal voice if at all, and he would temporarily lose his will and memory. He was also fed a saltless porridge, since anything more substantive would revive him from his zombified state. Through this process, the Vodou priest effectively imprisoned the wrongdoer inside his own body. Such practices were serious enough to be prohibited by Article 246 of the Haitian Penal Code. Davis's work remains controversial because some scholars question the methods he used to gather data, and other scholars dismiss the idea of taking the existence of actual zombies seriously. In any case, most zombie scholars analyze how zombies are represented, rather than the question of whether zombies exist in reality or not.

In the American imagination, zombies have undergone several transformations. The first published reference to a zombie in the United States appeared in 1838 in a short story entitled "The Unknown Painter." In it, a young slave in 17th-century Spain works for an artist who notices that his paintings are being altered overnight. The slave claims the changes are being made by an "African zombi," an explanation the artist dismisses as the boy's superstition. Other zombie narratives appear in novels and newspapers after this time. In them, the zombie is depicted as a benign protector spirit, a Vodou god, and even as the name (Jean Zombi) of a leader of pre-19th-century Haitian slave revolts. The 1929 publication of *The Magic Island* by William Seabrook, however, dispensed with the idea of the zombie as a helpful spirit and introduced the zombie as a dangerous resurrected corpse. The book is Seabrook's account of his travels in Haiti, in which his informants describe the digging up and reanimation of dead bodies through magical means. In 1968, George Romero's film *Night of the Living Dead* established the kind of infectious, flesh-eating zombie that is most popular today. Recently, there has been a surge in zombie narratives whose focuses range from post-zombie apocalypse human society (*The Walking Dead* and *World War Z*) to the meaning of human relationships (*Warm Bodies*).

A notion of the living dead is not limited to Haiti or America. In the Jewish tradition, for example, the *golem* is a man ritually created out of clay who can obey his creator's commands but is not endowed with a soul. Similarly, Tibetan texts speak of the *rolang*, or the "raised corpse." In one Tibetan memoir, a lama (Buddhist teacher) is on his way to a religious retreat when his traveling companion dies on their journey. The lama decides to turn the companion into a *rolang* and have him carry their luggage. There is also an account of the Sixth Dalai Lama using spiritual means to subdue a pair of *rolang* who burst out of a temple, slapping nearby villagers and turning them into *rolang* also. In both cases, it is the accomplished Buddhist master who is able to control the *rolang*.

Mayumi Kodani

See also: Consciousness; Paranormal in Movies; Possession; Survival after Death

Further Reading

Curran, Bob. 2009. *Zombies: A Field Guide to the Walking Dead.* Franklin Lakes, NJ: New Page Books.

Kordas, Ann. 2011. "New South, New Immigrants, New Women, New Zombies: The Historical Development of the Zombie in American Popular Culture." In *Race, Oppression, and the Zombie*, edited by Christopher M. Moreman and Cory James Rushton, 15–30. London: McFarland and Co.

Bibliography

General Books on the Paranormal

Bader, Christopher D., F. Carson Mencken, and Joseph O. Baker. 2010. *Paranormal America: Ghost Encounters, UFO Sightings, Bigfoot Hunts, and Other Curiosities in Religion and Culture.* New York and London: New York University Press.

Caterine, Darryl. 2011. *Haunted Ground: Journeys through a Paranormal America.* Santa Barbara, CA: ABC-CLIO/Praeger Press.

George, Leonard. 1995. *Alternative Realities: The Paranormal, the Mystic and the Transcendent in Human Experience.* New York: Checkmark Books.

Gooch, Stan. 1978. *The Paranormal.* London: Fontana.

Good, Erich. 2011. *The Paranormal: Who Believes, Why They Believe, and Why It Matters.* New York: Prometheus Books.

Guiley, Rosemay Ellen. 1994. *Harper's Encyclopedia of Mystical and Paranormal Experience.* San Francisco: Harper.

Inglis, Brian. 1978. *Natural and Supernatural: History of the Paranormal.* London: Hodder & Stoughton Ltd.

Inglis, Brian. 1984. *Science and Parascience: A History of the Paranormal 1914–1939.* London: Hodder and Staughton Ltd.

Rickard, Bob, and John Michell. 2007. *The Rough Guide to Unexplained Phenomena.* 2nd ed. London: Rough Guides.

Parapsychology and Psychical Research

Beloff, John. 1993. *Parapsychology: A Concise History.* London: The Athlone Press.

Blum, Deborah. 2006. *Ghost Hunters: William James and the Search for Scientific Proof of Life after Death.* New York: Penguin Press.

Carpenter, James C. 2012. *First Sight: ESP and Parapsychology in Everyday Life.* Lanham, MD: Rowman & Littlefield Publishing Group.

Cerullo, John. 1982. *The Secularization of the Soul: Psychical Research in Modern Britain.* Philadelphia: Institute for the Study of Human Issues.

Gauld, Alan. 1968. *The Founders of Psychical Research.* New York: Schocken Books.

Horn, Stacy. 2009. *Unbelievable: Investigations into Ghosts, Poltergeists, Telepathy, and Other Unseen Phenomena, from the Duke Parapsychology Laboratory.* New York: Ecco.

Irwin, Harvey J., and Caroline Watt. 2007. *An Introduction to Parapsychology.* 5th edition. Jefferson, NC: McFarland.

Jahn, Robert G., and Brenda J. Dunne. 2011. *Consciousness and the Source of Reality: The PEAR Odyssey.* Princeton, NJ: ICRL Press.

Mauskopf, Seymour. 1980. *The Elusive Science: Origins of Experimental Psychical Research.* Baltimore: Johns Hopkins University Press.

Ostrander, Sheila, and Lynn Shroeder. 1977. *Psychic Discoveries behind the Iron Curtain.* London: Abacus.

Ramakrishna, Rao. 2001. *Basic Research in Parapsychology.* 2nd ed. Jefferson, NC: McFarland & Co.

Schoch, Robert M., and Logan Yonavjak, eds. 2008. *The Parapsychology Revolution: A Concise Anthology of Paranormal and Psychical Research.* New York: Tarcher/Penguin.

Wolffram, Heather. 2009. *The Stepchildren of Science: Psychical Research and Parapsychology in Germany, C. 1870–1939.* Amsterdam: Rodopi.

Psi, Healing, and Other Paranormal Powers

Barden, Dennis. 1991. *Ahead of Time: The Mystery of Precognition.* London: Robert Hale Ltd.

Braude, Stephen E. 2007. *The Gold Leaf Lady and Other Parapsychological Investigations.* Chicago: University of Chicago Press.

Braude, Stephen E. 1997. *The Limits of Influence: Psychokinesis and the Philosophy of Science.* New York: University Press of America.

Carpenter, James C. 2012. *First Sight: ESP and Parapsychology in Everyday Life.* Lanham, MD: Rowman & Littlefield Publishing Group.

Duffin, Jacalyn. 2009. *Medical Miracles: Doctors, Saints, and Healing in the Modern World.* New York: Oxford University Press.

Graff, Dale. 2003. *Tracks in the Psychic Wilderness: An Exploration of ESP, Remote Viewing, Precognitive Dreaming and Synchronicity.* London: Vega.

Heath, Pamela Rae. 2011. *Mind-Matter Interaction: A Review of Historical Reports, Theory and Research.* Jefferson, NC: McFarland.

Jacobson, Knut A., ed. 2012. *Yoga Powers: Extraordinary Capacities Attained through Meditation and Concentration.* Leiden, NL: Brill.

Jones, David E. 1979. *Visions of Time: Experiments in Psychic Archeology.* Wheaton, IL: Quest Books.

Luckhurst, Roger. 2002. *The Invention of Telepathy.* Oxford, UK: Oxford University Press.

McMoneagle, Joseph. 2000. *Remote Viewing Secrets: A Handbook.* Charlottesville, VA: Hampton Roads Publishing Company.

McMoneagle, Joseph. 2002. *The Stargate Chronicles: Memoirs of a Psychic Spy.* Charlottesville, VA: Hampton Roads Publishing Company.

Radin, Dean. 2006. *Entangled Minds: Extrasensory Experiences in a Quantum Reality.* New York: Paraview.

Rhine, Louisa. 2011. *The Invisible Picture: A Study of Psychic Experiences.* Jefferson, NC: McFarland.

Ronson, Jon. 2004. *The Men Who Stare at Goats.* New York: Simon & Schuster.

Schnabel, Jim. 1997. *Remote Viewers: The Secret History of America's Psychic Spies.* New York: Dell.

Schwartz, Stephan A. 2007. *Opening to the Infinite.* Langley, WA: Nemoseen Media.

Schwartz, Stephan A. 1978. *The Secret Vaults of Time: Psychic Archaeology and the Quest for Man's Beginnings.* New York: Grosset & Dunlap.

Stewart, R. J. 1990. *The Elements of Prophecy.* Shaftesbury, Dorset, UK: Element Books.

Targ, Russell. 2012. *The Reality of ESP: A Physicist's Proof of Psychic Abilities.* Wheaton, IL: Quest Books.

Targ, Russell, and Harold E. Puthoff. (1977) 2005. *Mind Reach: Scientists Look at Psychic Abilities.* Charlottesville, VA: Hampton Roads Publishing Company.

Ullman, Montague, Stanley Krippner, and Alan Vaughan. 2003. *Dream Telepathy: Experiments in Nocturnal Extrasensory Perception*. 3rd ed. Charlottesville, VA: Hampton Roads Publishing Company.

Vasiliev, Leonid. 2002. *Experiments in Mental Suggestion*. Revised edition. Charlottesville, VA: Hampton Roads Publishing.

Young, Alan. 1981. *Spiritual Healing: Miracle or Mirage?* Marina del Rey, CA: DeVorss & Co.

Spiritualism, Mediumship, Séances, and Channeling

Braude, Ann. 2001. *Radical Spirits: Spiritualism and Women's Rights in Nineteenth-Century America*. 2nd ed. Bloomington, IN & Indianapolis: Indiana University Press.

Gauld, Alan. 1982. *Mediumship and Survival: A Century of Investigations*. London: Palladin.

Gutierrez, Cathy. 2009. *Plato's Ghost: Spiritualism in the American Renaissance*. Oxford, UK: Oxford University Press.

Hazelgrove, Jenny. 2000. *Spiritualism and British Society between the Wars*. Manchester, UK: Manchester University Press.

Hunter, Jack, and David Luke, eds. 2014. *Talking with the Spirits: Ethnographies from between the Worlds*. Brisbane, AU: Daily Grail Publishing.

Klimo, Jon. 1987. *Channeling: Investigations on Receiving Information from Paranormal Sources*. Los Angeles: Jeremy P. Tarcher.

Kontou, Tatiana, ed. 2011. *Women and the Victorian Occult*. London and New York: Routledge.

Kontou, Tatiana, and Sarah Willburn, eds. 2012. *The Ashgate Research Companion to Nineteenth-Century Spiritualism and the Occult*. Farnham, Surrey; Burlington, VT: Ashgate.

McGarry, Molly. 2008. *Ghosts of Futures Past: Spiritualism and the Cultural Politics of Nineteenth-Century America*. Berkeley, CA: University of California Press.

Nelson, Geoffrey K. 1969. *Spiritualism and Society*. London: Routledge & Kegan Paul.

Oppenheim, Janet. 1985. *The Other World: Spiritualism and Psychical Research in England, 1850–1914*. Cambridge, UK: Cambridge University Press.

Owen, Alex. 1989. *The Darkened Room: Women, Power, and Spiritualism in Late Nineteenth Century England*. London: Virago Press.

Washington, Peter. 1995. *Madame Blavatsky's Baboon: A History of the Mystics, Mediums, and Misfits Who Brought Spiritualism to America*. New York: Schocken Books.

Wicker, Christine. 2003. *Lily Dale: The True Story of the Town that Talks to the Dead*. New York: HarperCollins.

Wilson, David Gordon. 2013. *Redefining Shamanisms: Spiritualist Mediums and Other Traditional Shamans as Apprenticeship Outcomes*. London & New York: Bloomsbury.

Ghosts, Poltergeists, Apparitions, and Hauntings

Auerbach, Loyd. 1986. *ESP, Hauntings and Poltergeists: A Parapsychologist's Handbook*. New York: Warner Books.

Carrington, Hereward, and Nandor Fodor. 1952. *Haunted People: The Story of the Poltergeist Down the Centuries*. New York: Dutton.

Davies, Owen. 2007. *The Haunted: A Social History of Ghosts*. Basingstoke, UK and New York: Macmillan.

Finucane, R. C. 1996. *Ghosts: Appearances of the Dead and Cultural Transformation*. Amherst, NY: Prometheus Press.

Fontana, David. 2005. *Is There an Afterlife?* Winchester, UK: O Books.

Gauld, Alan, and A. D. Cornell. 1979. *Poltergeists.* London: Routledge Kegan & Paul.

Green, Celia, and Charles McCreery. (1975) 1989. *Apparitions.* London: Hamish Hamilton.

Gurney, Edmund, Frederic W. H. Myers, and Frank Podmore. (1886) 2011. *Phantasms of the Living.* 2 vols. Cambridge Library Collection: Spiritualism and Esoteric Knowledge. Cambridge, UK: Cambridge University Press.

Haraldsson, Erlendur. 2012. *The Departed among the Living: An Investigative Study of Afterlife Encounters.* Guildford, UK: White Crow Books.

MacKenzie, Andrew. 1982. *Hauntings and Apparitions.* London: Heinemann.

Playfair, Guy Lyon. 2011. *This House Is Haunted: The Amazing Inside Story of the Enfield Poltergeist* (originally subtitled *The True Story of a Poltergeist*). 3rd ed. Guildford, UK: White Crow Books.

Rogo, D. Scott. 2005. *On the Track of the Poltergeist.* San Antonio: Anomalist Books.

Roll, William G. 2004. *The Poltergeist.* New York: Paraview.

Tyrrell, George. N. M. (1943) 1973. *Apparitions.* London: The Society for Psychical Research.

Science, Skepticism, and the Paranormal

Bauer, Henry H. 2001. *Science or Pseudoscience: Magnetic Healing, Psychic Phenomena, and Other Heterodoxies.* Urbana, IL: University of Illinois Press.

Braude, Stephen E. 1997. *The Limits of Influence: Psychokinesis and the Philosophy of Science.* New York: University Press of America.

Broughton, Richard. 1992. *Parapsychology: The Controversial Science.* London: Rider.

Cardeña, Etzel, Stephen J. Lynn, and Stanley Krippner, eds. 2013. *Varieties of Anomalous Experience: Examining the Scientific Evidence.* 2nd ed. Washington, DC: American Psychological Association.

Frazier, Kendrick, ed. 1986. *Science Confronts the Paranormal.* Amherst, NY: Prometheus Books.

Gordin, Michael D. 2012. *The Pseudoscience Wars: Immanuel Velikovsky and the Birth of the Modern Fringe.* Chicago: The University of Chicago Press.

Hess, David J. 1993. *Science in the New Age: The Paranormal, Its Defenders & Debunkers.* Madison, WI: University of Wisconsin Press.

Krippner, Stanley, and Harris L. Friedman. 2010. *Debating Psychic Experience: Human Potential or Human Illusion?* Santa Barbara, CA: Praeger.

Kurtz, Paul, ed. 2001. *Skeptical Odysseys: Personal Accounts by the World's Leading Paranormal Inquirers.* Amherst, NY: Prometheus Books.

Mayer, Elizabeth Lloyd. 2007. *Extraordinary Knowing: Science, Skepticism, and the Inexplicable Powers of the Human Mind.* New York: Bantam Books.

Randi, James. 1982. *Flim-Flam: Psychics, ESP, Unicorns, and Other Delusions.* Buffalo, NY: Prometheus Books.

Sagan, Carl. 1996. *The Demon-Haunted World: Science as a Candle in the Dark.* New York: Ballantine Books.

Shermer, Michael. 1997. *Why People Believe Weird Things: Pseudoscience, Superstition, and Other Confusions of Our Time.* New York: W. H. Freeman and Company.

Strange Phenomena

Fort, Charles. 1974. *The Complete Books of Charles Fort.* Mineola, NY: Dover Publications.

Hansen, George. 2001. *The Trickster and the Paranormal.* Bloomington, IN: Xlibris Press.

Hynek, J. Allen. (1972) 1989. *The UFO Experience: A Scientific Inquiry.* Cambridge, UK: De Capo Press.

Jung, Carl. 1978. *Flying Saucers: A Modern Myth of Things Seen in the Skies.* Princeton, NJ: Princeton University Press.

Kean, Leslie. 2010. *UFOs: Generals, Pilots, and Government Officials Go on the Record.* New York: Three Rivers Press.

Keel, John A. 2013. *The Mothman Prophecies.* New York: Tor.

Lecouteux, Claude. 2003. *Witches, Werewolves and Fairies: Shapeshifters and Astral Doubles in the Middle Ages.* Rochester, VT: Inner Traditions.

Rogo, Scott. 1977. *The Haunted Universe.* New York: Signet.

Vallée, Jacques. 1975. *The Invisible College.* New York: Dutton.

Vallée, Jacques. 1969. *Passport to Magonia.* Chicago: Regnery.

Religion, Mysticism, and the Paranormal

Albanese, Catherine. 2007. *A Republic of Mind and Spirit: A Cultural History of American Metaphysical Religion.* New Haven, CT: Yale University Press.

Bader, Christopher D., F. Carson Mencken, and Joseph O. Baker. 2010. *Paranormal America: Ghost Encounters, UFO Sightings, Bigfoot Hunts, and Other Curiosities in Religion and Culture.* New York and London: New York University Press.

Brown, Michael F. 1997. *The Channeling Zone: American Spirituality in an Anxious Age.* Cambridge, MA: Harvard University Press.

Eliade, Mircea. (1951, 1964) 1989. *Shamanism: Archaic Techniques of Ecstasy.* Translated by Willard R. Trask. London: Arkana.

Fox, Mark. 2003. *Religion, Spirituality and the Near-Death Experience.* New York: Routledge.

Hanegraaff, Wouter. 1996. *New Age Religion and Western Culture: Esotericism in the Mirror of Secular Thought.* New York: Suny Press.

Heath, Pamela Rae, and Jon Klimo. 2010. *Handbook to the Afterlife.* Berkeley, CA: North Atlantic Books.

James, William. (1902) 1982. *The Varieties of Religious Experience.* New York: Penguin Paperbacks.

Kripal, Jeffrey J. 2010. *Authors of the Impossible: The Paranormal and the Sacred.* Chicago: University of Chicago Press.

Lewis, I. M. 2003. *Ecstatic Religion: A Study of Shamanism and Spirit Possession.* London: Routledge.

Lewis, James R., and J. Gordon Melton, eds. 1992. *Perspectives on the New Age.* New York: Suny Press.

Palmer, Terence. 2013. *The Science of Spirit Possession.* Saarbrucken, DE: Lambert Academic Publishing.

Schmidt, Bettina E., and Lucy Huskinson. 2010. *Spirit Possession and Trance: New Interdisciplinary Perspectives.* London: Continuum.

Schwebel, Lisa J. 2004. *Apparitions, Healings, and Weeping Madonnas: Christianity and the Paranormal.* New York: Paulist Press.

Twelftree, Graham H., ed. 2011. *The Cambridge Companion to Miracles.* Cambridge, UK: Cambridge University Press.

Psychology, Neurology, and the Paranormal

Alexander, Eben. 2013. *Proof of Heaven: A Neurosurgeon's Journey into the Afterlife.* New York: Simon and Schuster.

Crabtree, Adam. 1993. *From Mesmer to Freud: Magnetic Sleep and the Roots of Psychological Healing.* New Haven, CT: Yale University Press.

Daniels, Mike. 2005. *Shadow, Self, Spirit: Essays in Transpersonal Psychology.* Exeter, UK: Imprint Academic.

Darnton, Robert. 2009. *Mesmerism and the End of the Enlightenment in France.* Cambridge, MA: Harvard University Press.

Fiore, Edith. 2005. *You Have Been Here Before: A Psychologist Looks at Past Lives.* Merrimack, NH: Advanced Studies Consultants.

French, Christopher C., and Anna Stone. 2014. *Anomalistic Psychology: Exploring Paranormal Belief and Experience.* Basingstoke, UK: Palgrave Macmillan.

Gauld, Alan. 1992. *A History of Hypnotism.* Cambridge, UK: Cambridge University Press.

Gooch, Stan. 2007. *The Origins of Psychic Phenomena: Poltergeists, Incubi, Succubi, and the Unconscious Mind.* Rochester, VT: Inner Traditions. Retitled edition of *Creature from Inner Space.* 1984. London: Rider and Company.

Holt, Nicola, Christine Simmonds-Moore, David Luke, and Christopher C. French. 2012. *Anomalistic Psychology.* Basingstoke, UK: Palgrave Macmillan.

Hurd, Ryan, and Kelly Bulkeley, eds. 2014. *Lucid Dreaming: New Perspectives on Consciousness in Sleep.* Santa Barbara, CA: Praeger.

Irwin, H. J. 2009. *Psychology of Paranormal Belief: A Researcher's Handbook.* Chicago: University of Hertfordshire.

Jung, Carl. 1997. *Jung on Synchronicity and the Paranormal.* Edited by Roderick Main. London: Routledge.

Kelly, Edward F., Emily Williams Kelly, Adam Crabtree, Alan Gauld, Michael Grosso, and Bruce Greyson. 2007. *Irreducible Mind: Toward a Psychology for the 21st Century.* New York: Rowman & Littlefield.

Krippner, Stanley, Fariba Bogzaran, and Andre Percia de Carvalho. 2002. *Extraordinary Dreams and How to Work with Them.* SUNY Studies in Dreams Series. Albany, NY: SUNY.

Krippner, Stanley, and Harris L. Friedman, eds. 2010. *Mysterious Minds: The Neurobiology of Psychics, Mediums and Other Extraordinary People.* Oxford, UK: Praeger.

LaBerge, Stephen, and Howard Rheingold. 1990. *Exploring the World of Lucid Dreaming.* New York: Ballantine Books.

Laughlin, Charles. 2011. *Communing with the Gods: Consciousness, Culture and the Dreaming Brain.* Brisbane, AU: Daily Grail.

Mavromatis, Andreas. 1987. *Hypnagogia: The Unique State of Consciousness between Wakefulness and Sleep.* New York: Routledge.

Myers, Frederic W. H. (1903) 2011. *Human Personality and Its Survival of Bodily Death.* 2 vols. Cambridge Library Collection: Spiritualism and Esoteric Knowledge. Cambridge, UK: Cambridge University Press.

Nelson, Kevin. 2011. *Spiritual Doorway in the Brain.* New York: Dutton.

Sacks, Oliver. 2012. *Hallucinations.* London: Pan Macmillan.

Stevenson, Ian. 2001. *Children Who Remember Past Lives.* Revised edition. Jefferson, NC, London: McFarland & Co.

Stevenson, Ian. 1974. *Twenty Cases Suggestive of Reincarnation.* Charlottesville, VA: University of Virginia Press.

Tart, Charles, ed. 1972. *Altered States of Consciousness*. 2nd ed. Garden City, NY: Anchor.

Tart, Charles T. 1975. *States of Consciousness*. New York: E.P. Dutton.

Totton, Nick, ed. 2003. *Psychoanalysis and the Paranormal: Lands of Darkness*. London: Karnac Books.

Van de Castle, Robert. 1994. *Our Dreaming Mind*. New York: Ballantine.

Waterfield, Robin. 2002. *Hidden Depths: The Story of Hypnosis*. London: Pan Books.

Winter, Alison. 1998. *Mesmerized: Powers of Mind in Victorian Britain*. Chicago: University of Chicago Press.

Magic, Divination, and Occultism

Albertus, Frater. 1987. *The Alchemist's Handbook*. Revised expanded edition. York Beach, ME: Weiser Books.

Besterman, Theodore. 1995. *Crystal Gazing: A Study in the History, Distribution, Theory and Practice of Scrying*. Whitefish, MT: Kessinger Publishing.

Cottnoir, Brian. 2006. *The Weiser Concise Guide to Alchemy*. York Beach, ME: Weiser Books.

Davies, Owen. 2009. *Grimoires: A History of Magic Books*. Oxford, UK: Oxford University Press.

Farley, Helen. 2009. *A Cultural History of Tarot: From Entertainment to Esotericism*. London: I. B. Tauris.

Hauck, Dennis William. 2008. *The Complete Idiot's Guide to Alchemy*. New York: Alpha Books.

Lachman, Gary. 2005. *A Dark Muse: A History of the Occult*. New York: Thunder's Mouth Press.

Leventhat, Herbert. 1976. *In The Shadow of the Enlightenment: Occultism and Renaissance Science in Eighteenth-Century America*. New York: New York University Press.

Loewe, Michael, and Carmen Blacker, eds. 1981. *Divination and Oracles*. London: Allen & Unwin.

Newman, William R., and Anthony Grafton, eds. 2006. *Secrets of Nature: Astrology and Alchemy in Early Modern Europe*. Transformations: Studies in the History of Science and Technology. Cambridge, MA: The MIT Press.

Owen, Alex. 2004. *The Place of Enchantment: British Occultism and the Culture of the Modern*. Chicago: University of Chicago Press.

Rosenthal, B. G. 1997. *The Occult in Russian and Soviet Culture*. Ithaca, NY: Cornell University Press.

Russell, Jeffrey B., and Brooks Alexander. 2007. *A History of Witchcraft: Sorcerers, Heretics, and Pagans*. New York: Thames & Hudson.

Silberer, Herbert. 1971. *Hidden Symbolism of Alchemy and the Occult Arts*. New York: Dover.

Wilson, Colin. (1988) 2008. *Beyond the Occult: Twenty Years' Research into the Paranormal*. London: Watkins.

Wilson, Colin. (1971) 1999. *The Occult*. London: Watkins.

Yeats, Francis A. 1972. *The Rosicrucian Enlightenment*. London: Routledge and Kegan Paul.

Extraordinary Experiences

Adler, Shelly. 2011. *Sleep Paralysis: Night-Mares, Nocebos, and the Mind-Body Connection*. New Brunswick, NJ: Rutgers University Press.

Bourguignon, Erika. 1976. *Possession*. San Francisco: Chandler and Sharp.

Clancy, Susan. 2007. *Abducted: How People Come to Believe They Were Kidnapped by Aliens*. Cambridge, MA: Harvard University Press.

Denning, Melita, and Osborne Phillips. 1979. *The Llewellyn Practical Guide to Astral Projection: The Out-of-Body Experience*. Woodbury, MN: Llewellyn Publishing.

Evans, Hilary. 1987. *Gods, Spirits, Cosmic Guardians: A Comparative Study of the Encounter Experience*. Wellingborough, UK: The Aquarian Press.

Fox, Mark. 2003. *Religion, Spirituality and the Near-Death Experience*. New York: Routledge.

Holden, Janice Miner, Bruce Greyson, and Debbie James, eds. 2009. *The Handbook of Near-Death Experiences: Thirty Years of Investigation*. Santa Barbara, CA: ABC-CLIO, LLC.

Hopkins, Budd. 1988. *Missing Time*. New York: Ballantine Books.

Hufford, David J. 1982. *The Terror That Comes in the Night: An Experience-Centered Study of Supernatural Assault Traditions*. Philadelphia: University of Pennsylvania.

Mack, John. 1999. *Passport to the Cosmos: Human Transformation and Alien Encounters*. New York: Crown Publishing.

Monroe, Robert. 1992. *Journeys out of the Body*. New York: Broadway Books.

Moody, Raymond A. 1975. *Life after Life*. Atlanta: Mockingbird Books.

Strassman, Rick. 2001. *DMT: The Spirit Molecule: A Doctor's Revolutionary Research into the Biology of Near-Death and Mystical Experiences*. Rochester, VT: Park Street Press.

Strieber, W. 1987. *Communion*. New York: Morrow.

Voss, Angela, and William Rowlandson, eds. 2013. *Daimonic Imagination: Uncanny Intelligence*. Newcastle Upon Tyne, UK: Cambridge Scholars Press.

Paranormal Art, Literature, and Media

Chéroux, Clément, Andreas Fischer, Pierre Apraxine, Denis Canguilhem, and Sophie Schmit, with contributions by Crista Cloutier, and Stephen E. Braude. 2005. *The Perfect Medium: Photography and the Occult*. New Haven, CT and London: Yale University Press.

Davison, Jane P. 2012. *Early Modern Supernatural: The Dark Side of European Culture, 1400–1700*. Westport, CT: Praeger.

Eisenbud, Jules. 1989. *The World of Ted Serios: Thoughtographic Studies of an Extraordinary Mind*. 2nd ed. Jefferson, NC: McFarland.

Enright, D. J. 1994. *The Oxford Book of the Supernatural*. Oxford, UK: Oxford University Press.

Iovine, John. 1993. *Kirlian Photography: A Hands-on Guide*. New York: McGraw Hill.

Kaplan, Louis. 2008. *The Strange Case of William Mumler, Spirit Photographer*. Minneapolis: University of Minnesota Press.

Kripal, Jeffrey J. 2013. *Mutants and Mystics: Science Fiction, Superhero Comics, and the Paranormal*. Chicago: University of Chicago Press.

Meehan, Paul. 2009. *Cinema of the Psychic Realm*. Jefferson, NC: McFarland.

Nadis, Fred. 2013. *The Man from Mars: Ray Palmer's Amazing Pulp Journey*. New York: Tarcher/Penguin.

Ruffles, Tom. 2004. *Ghost Images: Cinema of the Afterlife*. Jefferson, NC: McFarland.

Sconce, Jeffery. 2000. *Haunted Media: Electronic Presence from Telegraphy to Television*. London: Duke University Press.

Smajic, Srdjan. 2010. *Ghost-Seers, Detectives, and Spiritualists: Theories of Vision in Victorian Literature and Science*. Cambridge, UK: Cambridge University Press.

Traill, Nancy H. 1996. *Possible Worlds of the Fantastic: The Rise of the Paranormal in Literature*. Toronto: University of Toronto Press.

Warner, Marina. 2006. *Phantasmagoria: Spirit Visions, Metaphors, and Media into the Twenty-first Century*. Oxford, UK: Oxford University Press.

Biographies

Geller, Uri. 1975. *My Story*. New York: Praeger. http://www.uri-geller.com/books/my-story/ms.htm.

Hamilton, Trevor. 2009. *Immortal Longings: F.W.H. Myers and the Victorian Search for Life after Death*. Exeter, UK: Imprint Academic.

Lachman, Gary. 2010. *Jung the Mystic: The Esoteric Dimensions of Carl Jung's Life and Teachings*. New York: Tarcher/Penguin.

Lachman, Gary. 2012. *Madame Blavatsky: The Mother of Modern Spirituality*. New York: Tarcher.

Lamont, Peter. 2006. *The First Psychic: The Peculiar Mystery of a Notorious Victorian Wizard*. Boston: Abacus.

Steinmeyer, Jim. 2008. *Charles Fort: The Man Who Invented the Supernatural*. London: William Heinemann.

Stuart, Nancy Rubin. 2005. *The Reluctant Spiritualist: The Life of Maggie Fox*. Boston: Houghton Mifflin Harcourt.

Sugrue, Thomas. 1945. *There Is a River: The Story of Edgar Cayce*. New York: H. Holt and Company.

Toksvig, Signe. 1948. *Emanuel Swedenborg: Scientist and Mystic*. New Haven, CT: Yale University Press.

Weisberg, Barbara. 2005. *Talking to the Dead: Kate and Maggie Fox and the Rise of Spiritualism*. New York: HarperOne.

Wyckoff, James. 1975. *Franz Anton Mesmer: Between God and Devil*. Englewood Cliffs, NJ: Prentice-Hall.

Organizations and Institutions

American Society for Psychical Research. 2009. http://www.aspr.com.

The Committee for Skeptical Inquiry. http://www.csicop.org/.

GHost. http://www.ghosthostings.co.uk.

Institute of Noetic Sciences. 2014. http://www.noetic.org.

Koestler Parapsychology Unit. 2014. http://www.koestler-parapsychology.psy.ed.ac.uk.

Lily Dale Assembly. 2014. https://encrypted.google.com/search?hl=en&q=lily%20dale%20assembly.

Parapsychological Association. 2014. http://www.parapsych.org.

Princeton Engineering Anomalies Research. 2010. http://www.princeton.edu/~pear.

Rhine Research Center. 2013. http://www.rhine.org.

Society for Psychical Research. 2009. http://www.spr.ac.uk.

About the Editor and Contributors

The Editor

Matt Cardin is an author, editor, independent scholar, and college English instructor living in Central Texas. He has a master's degree in religious studies and writes frequently about the intersection of religion, horror, psychology, creativity, consciousness, and dystopian and apocalyptic cultural trends. He has published three books of fiction and nonfiction. In addition to editing *Ghosts, Spirits, and Psychics*, he has edited *Mummies around the World: An Encyclopedia of Mummies in History, Religion, and Popular Culture* (ABC-CLIO, 2014) and *Born to Fear: Interviews with Thomas Ligotti* (Subterranean Press, 2014). He has also contributed to ABC-CLIO's *Encyclopedia of the Vampire*, *Icons of Horror and the Supernatural*, *Spirit Possession around the World*, *Pop Culture Universe*, and *World Religions: Belief, Culture, and Controversy.*

The Contributors

Fiona Bowie is a social anthropologist specializing in the anthropology of religion. She is the author of the bestselling textbook *The Anthropology of Religion* (2000) and founder of the Afterlife Research Centre (ARC), a forum for ethnographic and anthropological research into the afterlife, mediumship, the paranormal, and religious experience.

Robert Quillen Camp is a PhD student at the University of California, Santa Barbara, whose research interests include the phenomenology of performance and the intersection of religious belief and theatrical experiment, especially as seen in the mystical drama of William Butler Yeats, Maurice Maeterlinck, and August Strindberg. He also researches contemporary sound-based performance, collaborative creation, and the intersection of theater and conceptual visual art.

Darryl V. Caterine is a historian of religions whose research focuses on the intersections of religion, culture, and politics in the United States and parts of Latin America. He is the author of *Haunted Ground: Journeys through a Paranormal America* (2011), an exploration of America's longstanding fascination with spirits, UFOs, and parapsychological phenomena.

Callum E. Cooper is a PhD candidate within the Centre for the Study of Anomalous Psychological Processes (CSAPP) at the University of Northampton. His research and lectures cover topics such as the psychology of death and bereavement, parapsychology and anomalous experiences, and Egyptology. He is the author of *Telephone Calls from the Dead* (2012) and a 2009 recipient of the Eileen J. Garrett Scholarship from the Parapsychology Foundation.

John L. Crow is a PhD graduate student in the Department of Religious Studies at Florida State University. His training is in both American religious history and Western esotericism, and his research interests include Theosophy, modern Spiritualism, the intersection of science and religion, notions of the body in a religious context, and the development of Eastern religions within the Western world.

Philip Deslippe is a doctoral student in the Department of Religious Studies at the University of California, Santa Barbara, focusing on Asian and metaphysical traditions in modern America. He has published articles in *Ameriasia*, *Contemporary Buddhism*, and *Sikh Formations*, and he wrote the introduction to the definitive edition of *The Kybalion*.

Brenda J. Dunne is president and treasurer of International Consciousness Research Laboratories. Formerly, she was laboratory manager of the Princeton Engineering Anomalies Research (PEAR) laboratory from its inception in 1979 until its closing in 2007. With Robert Jahn, she is coauthor of three major textbooks on consciousness-related anomalies.

Helen Farley is a Senior Research Fellow with the School of History, Philosophy, Religion and Classics at the University of Queensland and an Associate Professor (Digital Futures) at the Australian Digital Futures Institute at the University of Southern Queensland. She has taught and researched in world religions, meditative and esoteric traditions, religion and popular culture, and religion in virtual worlds.

Christopher C. French is head of the Anomalistic Psychology Research Unit, Goldsmiths, University of London. He frequently appears on radio and television casting a skeptical eye over paranormal claims. He writes for the *Guardian* and *The Skeptic* magazine. His most recent book is *Anomalistic Psychology: Exploring Paranormal Belief and Experience*.

Joel Gruber is a PhD candidate in religious studies at the University of California, Santa Barbara. His research interests include Tibetan Buddhism, Tantra, comparative religion, and Buddhism in America.

Dusty Hoesly is a PhD candidate at the University of California, Santa Barbara, in the Department of Religious Studies. His research focuses on the sociology of religion in the United States; the history and sociology of secularism, globalization, and religion; new religious movements; and religion in the American West.

Nicola Holt is lecturer in psychology at the University of the West of England, Bristol, and Honorary Research Fellow at the Anomalous Experiences Research Unit at the University of York, UK. She is coauthor (with Christine Simmonds-Moore, David Luke, and Christopher French) of the textbook *Anomalistic Psychology* (Palgrave McMillan, 2012).

David J. Hufford is University Professor Emeritus of Humanities and Psychiatry at Penn State, Senior Fellow in the Brain, Mind, and Healing Division of the Samueli Institute, and adjunct professor of Religious Studies at the University of Pennsylvania. His influential book *The Terror That Comes in the Night* (1982) examines the experiential basis for belief in the supernatural.

Jack Hunter is a PhD candidate in the Department of Archaeology and Anthropology at the University of Bristol. In 2010 he established *Paranthropology: Journal of Anthropological Approaches to the Paranormal* to promote an interdisciplinary dialogue on issues relating to paranormal beliefs, experiences, and phenomena. He is the author of *Why People Believe in Spirits, Gods and Magic* (David & Charles, 2012) and the coeditor, with Dr. David Luke, of *Talking with the Spirits: Ethnographies from Between the Worlds* (Daily Grail, 2014).

Ryan Hurd is the founder of the blog *Dream Studies Portal* and writes books and essays about culture, consciousness, and dreams. He has an MA in Consciousness Studies from John F. Kennedy University in Pleasant Hill, California, and a BA in Anthropology from the University of Georgia in Athens.

Constance A. Jones is professor in the Transformative Inquiry Department at the California Institute of Integral Studies, San Francisco, California. She is author of *The Legacy of G.I. Gurdjieff* (Elli-Di-Ci Press, 2005) and *Encyclopedia of Hinduism* (Facts-on-File, 2007) and is associate editor of *Melton's Encyclopedia of American Religions*, Eighth Edition (Gale, 2009), by J. Gordon Melton.

Michael Kinsella is a PhD candidate in the Department of Religious Studies, University of California, Santa Barbara. He specializes in anomalous experiences and paranormal beliefs. He is currently conducting ethnographic and experimental studies on the afterlife movement. He is the author of *Legend-Tripping Online: Supernatural Folklore and the Search for Ong's Hat* (2011).

Mayumi Kodani is a PhD student at University of California, Santa Barbara where she works on Buddhist scholasticism in pre-modern Tibet. She is also interested in theories of the grotesque and wrote her MA thesis on Tibetan "zombies," entitled "The Improperly Dead: Tibetan Rolang as Buddhist Grotesquerie."

Kevin Kovelant received his master of arts in consciousness studies from John F. Kennedy University in 2008. He has presented at a number of conferences on the subject of visitation dreams from the dead. He lives in Monterey, California, with his wife and son. He also enjoys horror fiction.

Adam Krug is a PhD candidate in religious studies at the University of California, Santa Barbara, in Buddhist Studies and South Asian Religious Traditions. His research interests include Buddhist traditions in India, Nepal, Tibet, and Mongolia.

John G. Kruth is executive director of the Rhine Research Center and founder of the Rhine Education Center for Professional Education in Parapsychology. He has used his extensive technology background to help make the Rhine more accessible to a worldwide audience.

Gary Lachman is the author of more than a dozen books on the meeting ground between consciousness, culture, and the Western esoteric tradition, including *Aleister Crowley: Magick, Rock and Roll and the Wickedest Man in the World*; *Madame Blavatsky: The Mother of Modern Spirituality*; *The Secret History of Consciousness*; and *Jung the Mystic*. In a previous life he was a founding member of the rock group Blondie and in 2006 was inducted into the Rock and Roll Hall of Fame. He can be reached at http://www.garylachman.co.uk.

Christopher Laursen is a PhD candidate in history at the University of British Columbia. His research focuses on the socio-cultural intersection of religion, science, and society through how people have encountered, experienced, and attempted to explain extraordinary things, with a special focus on shifting explanations of the poltergeist phenomenon in the 20th century. He curates and edits the digital press and journal *Extraordinarium*.

Joseph Laycock is an assistant professor of religious studies at Texas State University. His publications include *Vampires Today: The Truth about Modern Vampirism* (Praeger, 2009), *The Seer of Bayside: Veronica Lueken and the Struggle for Catholicism* (2014), and *Dangerous Games: What the Moral Panic Over Role-Playing Games Says About Religion, Play, and Imagined Worlds* (2015).

Murray Leeder teaches in the film studies program at the University. of Calgary and specializes in cinematic ghosts and horror film. His is the author of *Halloween* (Auteur, 2014) and editor of *Cinematic Ghosts: Haunting and Spectrality from Silent Cinema to the Digital Era* (Bloomsbury, 2015).

Rachel McBride Lindsey is a historian of religion in America who has teaching and research interests in visual and material culture, religion in popular culture, race, and gender. She received her PhD from Princeton University in 2012. Her current book project is entitled *A Communion of Shadows: Vernacular Photography in Nineteenth-Century American Religion*.

Roger Luckhurst is professor of modern literature at Birkbeck College, University of London. Books include *The Invention of Telepathy* (2002), *The Mummy's Curse* (2012), and *The Shining* (2013).

David Luke is senior lecturer in psychology at the University of Greenwich, where he teaches an undergraduate course on the Psychology of Exceptional Human Experience. His research focuses on transpersonal experiences, anomalous phenomena, and altered states of consciousness, especially via psychedelics, an area where he has published more than one hundred academic papers.

Jennifer Lyke is a counseling psychologist and associate professor of psychology at Richard Stockton College in New Jersey. She teaches courses in consciousness and anomalous experiences and sees clients in private practice.

Vikas Malhotra is a doctoral candidate in the Department of Religious Studies at the University of California, Santa Barbara, specializing in South Asian Religions. His doctoral research focuses on positive forms of possession and mediumship in Hindu and Buddhist Tantric traditions using integrated perspectives and methods from various disciplines within the humanities and sciences.

James G. Matlock has worked at the American Society for Psychical Research in New York City and the Rhine Research Center in Durham, North Carolina. His chief research interests are the history of parapsychology, anthropology of religion, and reincarnation. He has a PhD in anthropology from the University of Southern Illinois at Carbondale.

David Metcalfe is a researcher, writer, and multimedia artist focusing on the interstices of art, culture, and consciousness. His essays have appeared in *Exploring the Edge Realms of Consciousness* (North Atlantic Books/Evolver Editions, 2012), *The Immanence of Myth* (Weaponized, 2011), and elsewhere. He is a contributing editor for Reality Sandwich, The Daily Grail, and *The Revealer*, the online journal of NYU's Center for Religion and Media.

B. D. Mitchell is currently an assistant professor in the history of science and technology program at the University of King's College as well as a PhD candidate in science and technology studies at York University. His thesis explores the influence of physiological research on the thought of Friedrich Nietzsche.

Rico G. Monge is assistant professor of comparative theology at the University of San Diego. As a comparative theologian, Monge specializes in Christian and Islamic mystical and ascetic traditions, as well as the mystical element in continental philosophical thought.

Alan Murdie is a lawyer based in Great Britain. He is chairman of the Spontaneous Cases Committee of the Society for Psychical Research and chairman of the Ghost Club (founded 1862). He has written and broadcast extensively on ghosts and poltergeist phenomena, and he writes a monthly column on ghosts for *Fortean Times* magazine.

Eric Ouellet is associate professor in the Department of Defence Studies with the Royal Military College of Canada. He focuses his research on the social dimension of psi effects, with a special focus on the UFO phenomenon. He maintains the blog *Parasociology* and has a PhD in sociology from York University.

Terence Palmer has been a practitioner and researcher of hypnosis since 1994 and a spirit release practitioner since 2001. His doctoral thesis on the experimental methods of the 19th-century researcher F. W. H. Myers has been published under the title *The Science of Spirit Possession* (2014, 2nd edition).

Anna Pokazanyeva is a PhD candidate in religious studies at the University of California, Santa Barbara, with specializations in American metaphysical and South Asian yogic traditions. Her dissertation is titled "Here Comes The Yogiman: Tales of Enlightenment and (Super)power with Particular Reference to the Life and Work of Paramahansa Yogananda."

John Poynton is emeritus professor of biology at the University of KwaZulu-Natal, and currently a scientific associate at the Natural History Museum, London. He is a past president of the Society for Psychical Research and currently their honorary secretary. He has published in African zoology, philosophy of science, and psychical research.

David G. Robertson holds a PhD in religious studies from the University of Edinburgh and publishes widely on conspiracy theories and alternative religions. He is co-founding editor at www.religiousstudiesproject.com and a committee member of the British Association for the Study of Religions. His website is davidgrobertson.wordpress.com.

Matthew Robertson's research investigates religious ideology in the early medical practices of South Asia and Greece and its influence on early modern medicine and psychotherapy. His ongoing work examines the impact of some of the earliest European thinkers of the unconscious: Paracelsus, Jakob Böhme, Friedrich Schelling, and Georg Groddeck.

Serena M. Roney-Dougal did a PhD thesis in parapsychology at Surrey University and is the author of *Where Science and Magic Meet* and *The Faery Faith*. She has studied scientific, magical, and spiritual realities for over 40 years and has taught in America, Japan, Britain, Europe, and India.

David Saunders is a PhD student in psychology at the University of Northampton and a member of the university's Centre for the Study of Anomalous Psychological Processes. His research interests include dreams and lucid dreaming, the psi and survival hypotheses, and physiological monitoring of altered states of consciousness.

Stephan A. Schwartz is a Research Associate of the Cognitive Sciences Laboratory of the Laboratories for Fundamental Research, editor of the daily web publication Schwartzreport. net, columnist for the journal *Explore*, and the author of several books on remote viewing and consciousness. One of the founders of modern remote viewing research, he has written for the *Huffington Post*, *Smithsonian*, *American Heritage*, the *Washington Post*, the *New York Times*, and others.

Simon Sherwood is a senior lecturer in psychology at the University of Greenwich and specializes in teaching and research relating to parapsychology and the psychology of anomalous experiences. He collects cases of Black Dog apparitions (www.blackshuck.info), has investigated numerous allegedly haunted locations, and has written a book, *Haunted Northamptonshire*.

Albert C. Silva is a PhD candidate in religious studies at the University of California, Santa Barbara. His research interests include American religious history, philosophy of religion/science, religious experience, metaphysical religions, and religion and healing.

Christine Simmonds-Moore is an assistant professor of psychology at the University of West Georgia. She has a PhD in psychology from the University of Northampton and serves on the board of the Parapsychological Association, where she is also the vice president. She is a coauthor (with Nicola J. Holt, David Luke, and Christopher C. French) of a textbook on anomalistic psychology and is the editor of *Exceptional Experience and Health: Essays on Mind, Body and Human Potential* (McFarland, 2012).

Sarah Sparkes is an artist, curator, and lecturer. She runs the visual arts and research project *GHost* and was a research fellow at UOL (2009–2012). She has lectured widely and has published chapters on Ghosts and the *GHost* project, including in *The Ashgate Research Companion to Paranormal Cultures*.

Richard Sugg is the author of five books, including *Mummies, Cannibals and Vampires: The History of Corpse Medicine from the Renaissance to the Victorians* (Routledge, 2011). He lectures in Renaissance literature at Durham University. He is currently completing *The Real Vampires* and beginning research into the history of the poltergeist.

Shannon Taggart is a photographer, researcher, and programmer-in-residence at the Morbid Anatomy Museum in Brooklyn, New York. Her photographs have been exhibited and featured internationally in such publications as *Time*, the *New York Times Magazine*, and *Newsweek*. She is currently working on a book about mediumship and Spiritualism. For more, visit shannontaggart.com.

Angela Voss is a cofounder of the MA program Myth, Cosmology, and the Sacred at Canterbury Christ Church University. For 10 years she pioneered and taught an MA program in Cosmology and Divination at the University of Kent, Canterbury. She earned a PhD in Renaissance music and astrology from the City University, London, and is coeditor (with William Rowlandson) of *Daimonic Imagination: Uncanny Intelligence* (Cambridge Scholars Publishing, 2013).

Caroline Watt is a founding member of the University of Edinburgh's Koestler Parapsychology Unit. She has authored numerous articles on her research, and is coauthor, with Harvey Irwin, of the leading textbook *An Introduction to Parapsychology*. She designed and runs a popular online Introduction to Parapsychology course, and is a past president and international liaison for the Parapsychological Association.

Zofia Weaver is a past editor of the Society for Psychical Research *Journal* and *Proceedings*. Together with Mary Rose Barrington and the late Professor Ian Stevenson, she coauthored a comprehensive study of the Polish clairvoyant Stefan Ossowiecki. Her latest research project is an in-depth study of the Polish medium Franek Kluski.

David Gordon Wilson is the author of *Redefining Shamanisms: Spiritualist Mediums and Other Traditional Shamans as Apprenticeship Outcomes* (Bloomsbury, 2013). His PhD at the University of Edinburgh focused on spiritualist mediumship as a contemporary form of shamanism. He is a practicing spiritualist medium and healer, and is currently the president of the Scottish Association of Spiritual Healers.

Simon Wilson has a long-standing interest in esotericism and the imagination. He has lectured and published on a wide range of subjects, including the Grail, John Dee, and UFO myths, and he writes regularly for *Fortean Times*. He is currently a sessional lecturer and PhD supervisor at Canterbury Christ Church University, England.

Connor Wood is a doctoral candidate at Boston University. His work focuses on the evolutionary study of religion. He has contributed to *Science and the World's Religions* (Praeger, 2012) and *Spirit Possession around the World* (ABC-CLIO, 2015). He writes a popular science blog, *Science on Religion*, at Patheos.com.

Scott Wood runs the South East London Folklore Society and founded the London Fortean Society. He regularly gives guided walks on the themes of ghosts, folklore, and London's forgotten history. He writes an occasional column on "Fortean London" for the website Londonist, and he wrote the afterword on contemporary folklore for Antony Clayton's book *The Folklore of London*.

Index

Bold page ranges indicate a main entry.